Beginning ASP.NET
with VB.NET 20

Beginning ASP.NET 1.1 with VB.NET 2003

Chris Ullman
John Kauffman
Chris Hart
Dave Sussman

WILEY
Wiley Publishing, Inc.

Beginning ASP.NET 1.1 with VB.NET 2003

Published by
Wiley Publishing, Inc.
10475 Crosspoint Boulevard
Indianapolis, IN 46256
www.wiley.com

Copyright © 2004 by Wiley Publishing, Inc., Indianapolis, Indiana

Published simultaneously in Canada

Library of Congress Card Number: 2003114198

ISBN: 0-7645-5707-6

Manufactured in the United States of America

10 9 8 7 6 5 4 3 2 1

1B/RW/RS/QU

For general information on our other products and services or to obtain technical support, please contact our Customer Care Department within the U.S. at (800) 762-2974, outside the U.S. at (317) 572-3993 or fax (317) 572-4002.

Wiley also publishes its books in a variety of electronic formats. Some content that appears in print may not be available in electronic books.

About the Authors

Chris Ullman

Chris Ullman is a freelance web developer and technical author who has spent many years stewing in ASP/ASP.NET, like a teabag left too long in the pot. Coming from a Computer Science background, he started initially as a UNIX/Linux guru, who gravitated towards MS technologies during the summer of ASP (1997). He cut his teeth on Wrox Press ASP guides, and since then he has written over 20 books, most notably as lead author for Wrox's bestselling Beginning ASP/ASP.NET series, and has contributed chapters to books on PHP, ColdFusion, JavaScript, Web Services, C#, XML and other Internet-related technologies too esoteric to mention, now swallowed up in the quicksands of the dot.com boom.

Quitting Wrox as a full-time employee in August 2001, he branched out into VB6 programming and ASP development maintaining a multitude of sites from http://www.cuasp.co.co.uk, his "work" site, to http://www.atomicwise.com, a selection of his writings on music and art. He now divides his time between being a human punchbag for his 26-month-old son Nye, composing electronic sounds on bits of dilapidated old keyboards for his music project Open E, and tutoring his cats in the art of peaceful co-existence, and not violently mugging each other on the stairs.

Chris Ullman contributed Chapters 1, 14, 15, 16, 17, and Appendix E to this book.

John Kauffman

John Kauffman was born in Philadelphia, the son of a chemist and a nurse. He received his degrees from The Pennsylvania State University, the colleges of Science and Agriculture. His early research was for Hershey foods in the genetics of the chocolate tree and the molecular biology of chocolate production. Subsequently he moved to the Rockefeller University, where he cloned and sequenced DNA regions which control the day and night cycles of plants.

Since 1997 John has written ten books, six of which have been on the Amazon Computer Best Seller List. His specialty is programming web front-ends for enterprise-level databases.

In his spare time, John is an avid sailor and youth sailing coach. He represented the USA in the sailing world championship of 1985 and assisted the Olympic teams of Belgium and China in 1996. He also enjoys jazz music and drumming and manages to read the *New Yorker* from cover-to-cover each week.

My portions of this book are dedicated to the instructors of two drum and bugle corps. These men taught me about precision, accuracy, and discipline: Ken Green and John Flowers of the Belvederes 1976 and Dennis DeLucia and Bobby Hoffman of the Bayonne Bridgemen 1978.

John Kauffman contributed Chapters 2, 3, 4, 5, 6, and Appendix B to this book.

Chris Hart

Chris Hart is a full-time .NET Developer and part-time author who lives in Birmingham (UK) with her husband James. While she's most at home in the world of the web, she's recently been working with the .NET Compact Framework. In her spare time, Chris spends much of her time playing with beta technologies, then attempting to write about them.

Chris has contributed many chapters to a variety of books, including *Beginning ASP.NET* (Wrox Press), *Beginning Dynamic Websites with ASP.NET Web Matrix* (Wrox Press), and most recently, *A Programmer's Guide to SQL* (Apress).

When she gets away from computers, Chris enjoys travel, especially when it involves driving along narrow winding roads to get to out-of-the-way parts of Scotland. She dreams of building her own house somewhere where she can keep a cat.

Chris Hart contributed Chapters 10, 11, 12, 13, and Appendices C and D to this book.

Dave Sussman

Dave Sussman is a writer, trainer, and consultant living in the wilds of the Oxfordshire countryside. He's been working with ASP.NET since before it was first released and still isn't bored with it. You can contact him at davids@ipona.com.

Dave Sussman contributed Chapters 7, 8, and 9 to this book.

Credits

Authors
Chris Ullman
John Kauffman
Chris Hart
David Sussman

Senior Acquisitions Editor
Jim Minatel

Vice President & Executive Group Publisher
Richard Swadley

Vice President and Executive Publisher
Bob Ipsen

Vice President and Publisher
Joseph B. Wikert

Executive Editorial Director
Mary Bednarek

Project Coordinator
Mary Richards

Project Manager
Ami Frank Sullivan

Senior Production Manager
Fred Bernardi

Editorial Manager
Mary Beth Wakefield

Book Producer
Peer Technical Services Pvt. Ltd.

Contents

Contents

Contents

Contents

Contents

Contents

Contents

Introduction

ASP.NET is a radical update of Microsoft's *Active Server Pages* (*ASP*). ASP.NET is a powerful server based technology designed to create dynamic and interactive HTML pages on demand for your World Wide Web site or corporate intranet. It is designed to improve upon nearly every feature of classic ASP, from reducing the amount of code you need to write to giving you more power and flexibility.

ASP.NET also constitutes a key element in Microsoft's .NET Framework, providing Web-based access to the immensely powerful .NET development environment. It allows us to create Web applications in a new, flexible way by placing commonly used code into reusable controls of various kinds that can be fired by events initiated by our site's users.

ASP.NET branches out into many other technologies, such as Web Services, ADO.NET, custom controls, and security. We will briefly touch upon its relationship with these fields throughout the book to provide a solid, comprehensive understanding of how ASP.NET can benefit your work in a practical way.

ASP.NET 1.1 itself is a fairly light update to the complete wholesale changes that occurred in ASP.NET 1.0. This book by and large covers features that are available in both 1.0 and 1.1, but it does cover the pertinent new features of 1.1 that will be of interest to the novice user. So if you are already running ASP.NET 1.0, you will be expected to upgrade to 1.1.

By the end of this book you will be familiar with the anatomy of ASP.NET 1.1 and be able to create powerful, secure, and robust Web sites that can collect and work with information in a multitude of ways to the benefit of both yourself and your users.

Who Is this Book For?

The purpose of this book is to teach you from scratch how to use ASP.NET to be able to write Web pages and Web applications whose content can be programmatically tailored each time an individual client browser calls them up. This not only saves you a lot of effort in presenting and updating your Web pages, but also offers tremendous scope for adding sophisticated functionality to your site. As ASP.NET is not a programming language in its own right, but rather a technology (as we shall explain in the book), we will be teaching some basic programming principles in *Chapters 2 to 7* in Visual Basic.NET, our chosen language for implementing ASP.NET.

This book is therefore ideal for somebody who knows some basic HTML but has never programmed before, or somebody who is familiar with the basics of old style ASP, but hasn't investigated ASP.NET in any detail. If you are an experienced programmer looking for a quick crash course on ASP.NET, or somebody who's worked extensively with ASP, we suggest that you refer to *Professional ASP.NET 1.1 Special Edition, Wiley, ISBN: 0-7645-5890-0* instead, as you'll most likely find that the early chapters here just reiterate things you already know. If you are not familiar with HTML, then we suggest that you master the basics of building Web pages before moving on to learning ASP.NET.

What Does this Book Cover?

This book teaches everything the novice user will need to know, from installing ASP.NET and the relevant information for creating pages and putting together the concepts to create a whole application using ASP.NET 1.1.

Although ASP.NET 1.1. isn't a huge update from version 1.0, this book has been considerably overhauled since edition 1.0. Some of the old chapters have been removed and new ones introduced. We've removed three chapters because we wanted to simplify the experience of learning ASP.NET. We've created a brand new case study – an amateur sports league Web site – which is then used throughout the later chapters in the book.

If you compare the previous edition, you will find this one to be more cohesive, aimed towards the complete novice *and* the developer with some ASP experience, and written with the benefit of hindsight from experienced developers who have have been employed in creating ASP.NET applications. We trust that you will find it a great improvement over the last, just as every new edition should be.

In the course of this book you will learn:

❑ What is ASP.NET

❑ How to install ASP.NET and get it up and running

❑ The structure of ASP.NET and how it sits on the .NET Framework

❑ How to use ASP.NET to produce dynamic, flexible, interactive Web pages

❑ Basic programming principles, such as variables, controls structures, procedural programming, and objects

❑ How to use ASP.NET to interface with different data sources, from databases to XML documents

- ❑ What ready-made controls ASP.NET offers for common situations
- ❑ How to create your own controls
- ❑ How to debug your ASP.NET pages
- ❑ How to deal with unexpected events and inputs
- ❑ How to create your own Web application
- ❑ How to integrate your applications with Web Services, and create your own Web Services
- ❑ Some simple security features and how to create a login for an application

How this Book Is Structured

Here is a quick breakdown of what you will find in this book:

- ❑ **Chapter 1 – Getting Started with ASP.NET**: In the first chapter we introduce ASP.NET and look at some of the reasons that you'd want to use server-side code for creating Web pages and the technologies that are available to do so. This done we spend the bulk of the chapter explaining the ASP.NET installation process in detail, how to install a Web server to run ASP.NET on (we will be using the Web server that accompanies Web Matrix), along with the ancillary installation of MDAC. We finish up with a simple ASP.NET example page to check that our installation is working correctly.

- ❑ **Chapter 2 – Anatomy of an ASP.NET Page**: Having completed the installation in the previous chapter, we consider the structure of an ASP.NET page and the way that it functions in relation to the .NET Framework. We use examples to demonstrate how the ASP.NET module parses the page.

- ❑ **Chapter 3 – Server Controls and Variables**: Having acquainted ourselves with the basics of ASP.NET controls this chapter considers the use of variables for holding data in Visual Basic .NET. We look at how variables are implemented, what they can contain, and how they can be placed into your ASP.NET pages.

- ❑ **Chapter 4 – Control Structures and Procedural Programming**: This chapter takes a whirlwind tour of the key building blocks of VB.NET in the context of an ASP.NET page. We learn how to make our ASP.NET pages more responsive through the use of VB.NET branching and looping structures that enable us to control the order in which our program's statements execute.

- ❑ **Chapter 5 – Jumping Structures, Subroutines, and Functions**: We cover how the modularization and reusable ASP.NET code works in this chapter. We look at subroutines and functions and how they are used together with Web controls. We learn how to pass parameters within ASP.NET pages and the different ways in which ASP.NET can handle them.

- ❑ **Chapter 6 – Event-Driven Programming and Postback**: We talk about how ASP.NET revolves around an event-driven model, and how things occur in strict order and ways in which the ASP.NET page can react to user intervention. We also look at the concept of postback and how it is used to send information back from the user to the Web server, to preserve the "state" of a page.

❑ **Chapter 7 – Objects**: This chapter deals with the thorny subject of objects. ASP.NET pages derive a great deal of their flexibility and power from the object-oriented way they are structured. This chapter introduces concepts such as properties, methods, constructors, collections, andoverloading using plentiful examples relating to real-world objects to aid your understanding. We also discuss the concepts that make objects very powerful, such as inheritance and encapsulation, and how they greatly reduce the amount of code you need to use.

❑ **Chapter 8 – Reading from Databases**: At this point in the book we're familiar with the basic anatomy of ASP.NET pages and objects, so we branch out to look at ADO.NET in the context of ASP.NET. Most specifically we look at the use of the Connection and Command objects for opening data sources and retrieving information into DataSets.

❑ **Chapter 9 – Advanced Data Handling**: Having mastered the basics of reading data in the previous chapter we take things much further; looking in detail at the way we can manipulate the information in DataTables and DataSets, and store the results back to the data source from which they came.

❑ **Chapter 10 – ASP.NET Server Controls**: This chapter explains how ASP.NET server controls derive their properties and methods from the various classes and objects that make up the .NET Framework. It explains the syntax required to make their functionality available, together with a look at the benefits that these controls can give. We also start to create the Wrox United application case study that is used throughout the rest of the book.

❑ **Chapter 11 – Users and Applications**: This chapter deals mainly with the process of tracking users across pages. We look at the objects that ASP.NET uses to enable this. We also tie this into our case study by creating the facility for adding valid email addresses and passwords to a site via an admin interface, and then we play the part of one of those users logging in and viewing pages.

❑ **Chapter 12 – Reusable Code for ASP.NET**: Here we consider the great benefits that can be achieved by encapsulating our code to make it more maintainable. Firstly we cover the idea of user controls designed to store sections of your ASP.NET code that are repeated on multiple pages of your site before going on to consider the idea of code behind, where the `<script>` block of our ASP.NET code is placed in its own file in order to separate the page's logic from its presentation.

❑ **Chapter 13 – .NET Assemblies and Custom Controls**: We continue the ideas of the previous chapter here. We cover how to compile a .NET assembly and use it from within our ASP.NET page, as well as how to encapsulate our business logic into a component that can be reused on other projects.

❑ **Chapter 14 – Debugging and Error Handling**: No matter how careful you are, things can always go wrong within your code. This chapter explains the steps you can take to minimize these occurrences and how to recover when things go wrong.

❑ **Chapter 15 – Configuration and Optimization**: We start by explaining how ASP.NET applications can be managed from a series of XML configuration files, and then our discussion takes a more general turn as we consider the many ways that you can streamline and speed-up your ASP.NET applications.

❑ **Chapter 16 – Web Services**: You learn how to expose functionality from your Web site to others as a Web Service. We then discuss how this functionality can be discovered by other users of the Web, and the form that the data exchange takes.

❑ **Chapter 17 – ASP.NET Security**: We conclude the book with a quick overview of some of the simple precautions that you can take using forms authentication and authorization to safeguard your ASP.NET pages and ensure that they're only accessed by authorized users in the way that you want them to be accessed.

What Do You Need to Use this Book?

The only prerequisite for this book is to have a machine with the .NET Framework installed upon it. This means that you'll need to be running Windows 2000 Professional or Server, Windows XP (either Professional or Home edition) or Windows 2003 Server.

The .NET Framework itself is available as a free download from http://www.asp.net/ and http://www.gotdotnet.com. This download is known as the .NET Framework Redistributable and its approximate size is 20Mb. It includes everything you need to run any .NET application.

Also available is another complementary free download, which might be useful to you throughout the book, although not essential. This is the .NET Framework SDK (Software Development Kit) and it contains samples and tutorials that you can refer to in order to learn more about .NET, as well as some useful tools, some of which we make use of in the book. However it doesn't include the .NET Framework. The SDK is of size 130Mb approximately.

This book is designed with Web Matrix in mind, so we strongly suggest that you download this as well. Web Matrix is a free download also available from http://www.asp.net. It will provide you with a Web server capable of running ASP.NET if you haven't already got one. However while this book has been designed with Web Matrix in mind, you will find that all of the examples can be created, run, and understood using *any* simple text editor such as Notepad, although the instructions will be geared to the point of view of someone who is running Web Matrix.

Windows XP Home Edition does not support IIS, so if you use this version of Windows, you will have to download Web Matrix.

You do not need Visual Studio .NET in order to use this book.

Conventions

To help you get the most from the text and keep track of what's happening, we've used a number of conventions throughout the book.

> **Boxes like this one hold important, not-to-be forgotten information that is directly relevant to the surrounding text.**

While this background style is used for asides to the current discussion.

As for styles in the text:

- ❑ When we introduce them, we *italicize* important words
- ❑ We show filenames and code within the text like so: `persistence.properties`
- ❑ We present code in two different ways:

```
In code examples, the Code Foreground style shows new, important, pertinent code.
The Code Background style shows code that's less important in the present
context, or has been shown before.
```

Source Code

As you work through the examples in this book, you may choose either to type in all the code manually or to use the source code files that accompany the book. All of the source code used in this book is available for download at http://www.wrox.com. Once at the site, simply locate the book's title (either by using the Search box or by using one of the title lists) and click the Download Code link on the book's detail page to obtain all the source code for the book. Because many books have similar titles, you may find it easiest to search by ISBN, which for this book is 0764557076. Once you download the code, just decompress it with your favorite compression tool. Alternately, you can go to the main Wrox code download page at http://www.wrox.com/dynamic/books/download.aspx to see the code available for this book and all other Wrox books.

Errata

We make every effort to ensure that there are no errors in the text or in the code. However, no one is perfect, and mistakes do occur. If you find an error in one of our books, like a spelling mistake or faulty piece of code, we would be very grateful for your feedback. By sending in errata you may save another reader hours of frustration, and you will be helping us provide even higher quality information.

To find the errata page for this book, go to http://www.wrox.com and locate the title using the Search box or one of the title lists. Then, on the book details page, click the View Errata link. On this page, you can view all errata that has been submitted for this book and posted by Wrox editors. A complete book list including links to each book's errata is also available at www.wrox.com/misc-pages/booklist.shtml.

If you don't spot your error on the View Errata page, go to www.wrox.com/contact/techsupport.shtml and complete the form there to send us the error you have found. We'll check the information and, if appropriate, post a message to the book's errata page and fix the problem in subsequent editions of the book.

p2p.wrox.com

For author and peer discussion, join the P2P forums at p2p.wrox.com. The forums are a Web-based system for you to post messages relating to Wrox books and related technologies and interact with other readers and technology users. The forums offer a subscription feature to email you topics of interest of your choosing when new posts are made to the forums. Wrox authors, editors other industry experts, and your fellow readers are present on these forums.

At http://p2p.wrox.com you will find a number of different forums that will help you not only as you read this book, but also as you develop your own applications.

> *You can read messages in the forums without joining P2P, but in order to post your own messages, you must join the forum.*

To join the forums:

1. Go to p2p.wrox.com and click the Register link.
2. Read the terms of use and click Agree.
3. Complete the required information to join as well as any optional information you wish to provide and click Submit.
4. You will receive an email with information describing how to verify your account and complete the joining process.

Once you have joined, you can post new messages and respond to messages other users post. You can read messages at any time on the Web. If you would like to have new messages from a particular forum emailed to you, click the Subscribe to this Forum icon by the forum name in the forum listing.

For more information about how to use the Wrox P2P be sure to read the P2P FAQs; they answer questions about how the forum software works as well as many common questions specific to P2P and Wrox books. To read the FAQs, click the FAQ link on any P2P page.

Getting Started with ASP.NET

ASP.NET is a powerful and flexible technology for creating dynamic Web pages. It's a convergence of two major Microsoft technologies, *Active Server Pages* (*ASP*) and the .NET Framework. ASP (or *classic* ASP as it's often referred to), is a relative old-timer on the Web computing circuit and has provided a sturdy, powerful, and effective way of building dynamic Web pages for seven years or so now. The .NET Framework, on the other hand, is a whole suite of technologies designed by Microsoft with the aim of revolutionizing the way in which all programming development takes place and the way companies carry out business. ASP.NET is a way of creating dynamic Web pages while making use of the innovations present in the .NET Framework.

The first important thing to know about ASP.NET is that you don't need any ASP skills to learn it. All you need is a little HTML knowledge for building Web pages. In fact, knowing ASP could be a disadvantage in some ways because you may have to unlearn some of the principles you followed earlier. ASP.NET allows you to build dynamic Web pages and tailors the HTML output to the browser you're using. It also comes with a great set of reusable, predefined, and ready to use controls for your ASP.NET projects. These reduce the amount of code you have to write, so you can be more productive while programming.

So, what can you do with ASP.NET? It may be easier to list what you can't, as that is arguably shorter! One of the most eye-catching things about ASP.NET is the way you can use any programming language based on the .NET Framework, such as VB .NET, JScript.NET, or C# to create your Web applications. Within these applications, ASP.NET allows you to customize pages for a particular user, and makes it simpler to keep track of a particular user's details as they move around.

ASP.NET makes storing information to a database or self-describing XML document faster and easier. You can alter the layout of the page using a free Web page editor – Web Matrix – designed to be used with ASP.NET, rather than having to position everything manually within code, and even alter the contents of files on your machine, if you have the correct permissions.

In addition, you can use bits and pieces of other applications without downloading the whole application. For example, you can access a zip code verifier that is part of another Web site's features, without having to download the whole application or even giving your users the impression that they've left your site (*Chapter 16* will cover Web Services as well as accessing specific features of your application via the Web). With ASP.NET, the applications that you create are only limited by your imagination.

This chapter will cover the installation process of ASP.NET, Web Matrix, and the .NET Framework. Let's start with a quick introduction to the world of Web servers, dynamic Web pages, and a little bit about what ASP.NET is. This will help accomplish the main aim of this chapter – to get you running a fully functional Web server, with a fully functional ASP.NET installation. We will create a short ASP.NET test page to check that both the Web server and ASP.NET are working as intended. We'll also look at some of the most common pitfalls encountered.

The topics discussed in this chapter are:

- ❑ Static Web pages
- ❑ Dynamic Web pages
- ❑ What is ASP.NET?
- ❑ Installing the .NET Framework
- ❑ Installing Web Matrix
- ❑ Testing and troubleshooting your installation

What Is a Static Web Page?

If you surf the Web, you'll see many *static* Web pages. Essentially, this type of Web page consists of some HTML code typed directly into a text or Web page editor and saved as a `.htm` or `.html` file. Thus, the author of the page has already determined the exact content of the page, in HTML, at some time before any user visits the page.

Static Web pages are often easy to spot; sometimes you can pick them out by just looking at the content of the page. The content (text, images, hyperlinks, and so on) and appearance of static Web pages is *always* the same – regardless of *who* visits the page, or *how* and *when* they arrive at the page, or any other factors.

For example, you can create a page called `Welcome.htm` for your Web site, by writing some simple HTML like this:

```
<html>
<head><title>A Welcome Message</title></head>
<body>
  <h1>Welcome</h1>
  Welcome to our humble website. Please feel free to view our
  <a HREF="contents.htm">list of contents</a>.
  <br><br>
  If you have any difficulties, you can
  <a href="mailto:webmaster@wrox.com">send email to the webmaster</a>.
</body>
</html>
```

Whenever a client comes to your site and views this page, it will look like the screenshot depicted in Figure 1-1:

Figure 1-1

The content of the page was determined *before* the request to view the page was made – in fact, it was determined at the time the Webmaster saved the `.htm` file to disk.

How Are Static Web Pages Served?

Let's think for a moment about how a static, pure HTML page finds its way to a client browser (the process is depicted in Figure 1-2):

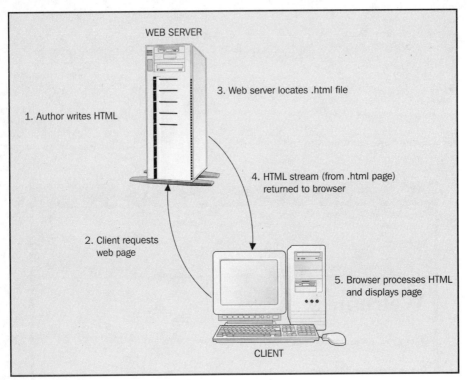

Figure 1-2

1. A Web author writes a page using only HTML and saves it within an .htm file on the Web server.

2. Sometime later, a user types a *page request* (URL) into a browser, and the request passes from the browser to the Web server.

3. The Web server locates the .htm page and converts it to an HTML stream.

4. The Web server sends the HTML stream back across the network to the browser.

5. The browser processes the HTML and displays the page.

Static, pure-HTML files like Welcome.htm make perfectly serviceable Web pages. You can even spruce up the presentation and usability of such pages by adding more HTML to alter fonts and colors. However, there are limitations with what you can achieve with pure-HTML pages because their content is completely determined before the page is requested. There's no facility for user interaction or dynamic responses (even simple objects like forms and buttons require more than just HTML to make them work).

Limitations of Static Web Pages

Static Web pages limit you in several ways. For example, suppose you want to enhance your Welcome page so that it displays the current time or a special personalized message for each user. These are simple alterations, but they are impossible to achieve using HTML alone. If you're not convinced, try writing HTML for a Web page that displays the current time as shown in Figure 1-3:

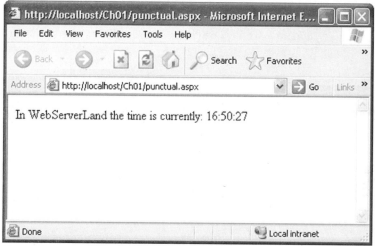

Figure 1-3

As you type in the HTML, you'll soon realize the problem – you know that the user will request the page sometime, but you don't know *what time* they will do it! Hardcoding the time into your HTML will result in a page that always shows the same time (that will almost always be wrong). In other words, you're trying to write pure HTML for a Web page that displays the time, but you can't be sure of the *exact* time that the Web page should display until the time the page is requested. This can't be done using HTML alone.

HTML offers no features for personalizing your Web pages; the same Web page is served to every user. There's also no security with HTML; the code is there for everybody to view, and there's nothing to stop you from copying somebody else's HTML code and using it in your own Web page. Static pages can be very fast, as quick as copying a small file over a network, but they cannot provide any *dynamic* features.

Since you can't create this page by saving hard-coded HTML into a file *before* the page is requested, what you need is a way to generate the HTML *after* the page is requested. There are two ways of doing this; we'll look at both of them in this chapter. However, before going any further let's make sure everybody is up to speed on the terminology we've introduced here.

What Is a Web Server?

Web servers are software that manage Web pages and make them available to client browsers – via a local network or over the Internet. In the case of the Internet, the Web server and browser are usually on two different machines, possibly many miles apart. However, in a local situation you can set up a machine that runs the Web server software, and then use a browser on the same machine to look at its Web pages.

It makes no difference whether you access a remote Web server (that is, a Web server on a machine different from your browser application) or a local one (Web server and browser on the same machine), since the Web server's function (to make Web pages available to all) remains unchanged. It may be that you are the only person with access to your own machine nevertheless the principles remain the same.

While there are many Web servers available (the common ones being Apache, *Internet Information Services* (IIS), and Iplanet's Enterprise server) we're only going to talk about two in this book, *IIS* and *Web Matrix*, both of which are supplied by Microsoft. Only these Web servers run ASP.NET.

IIS

IIS Web server comes bundled with Windows 2000, Windows XP Professional, and Windows 2003 Server. IIS version 5.0 comes with Windows 2000, IIS version 5.1 with Windows XP Professional, and IIS version 6.0 with Windows 2003. However, there is little to distinguish between the different versions of IIS, so we shall treat them as the same product.

Web Matrix

Web Matrix is a free Web page editor tailored specifically towards ASP.NET pages. It came late to the party, as ASP.NET had already been out for a little while before Microsoft decided to release a free Web page editor to accompany it. Actually, Web Matrix wasn't exactly a new product – more an inspired resurrection of an old but not quite forgotten product for editing Web pages, namely Visual Interdev. While Web Matrix is quite different from Visual Interdev, there are enough similarities for people familiar to Interdev to recognize them.

However, to be able to test Web pages you also need something to run them on, so supplied together with Web Matrix is an integrated Web server. This is ideal as several Windows systems aren't capable of running IIS, and until Web Matrix released, it wasn't possible to run ASP.NET on operating systems such as Windows XP Home Edition. We have used Web Matrix for testing Web pages throughout the book, and have occasionally made use of its automatic Web page creation facilities as well – although most of the time we have created the code in the old-fashioned way, by hand.

You will learn about installing Web Matrix shortly (see *Appendix B*); however, first let's take a look at the Web server's role in helping create dynamic Web pages.

How Are Dynamic Web Pages Served?

To fully understand the nature of dynamic Web pages, let's first understand what you can and can't do with a static Web page.

Providing Dynamic Web Page Content

In this book, you're only going to create dynamic Web pages on the server-side, because that's where ASP.NET resides. However, it will aid your understanding of the process to look at how content is served on the client-side because the underlying principles are similar and will give you a fuller overview of how Web page content is sent to the browser.

Client-Side Dynamic Web Pages

In the client-side model, modules (or plug-ins) attached to the browser do all the work of creating dynamic pages. The HTML code is typically sent to the browser along with a separate file containing a set of instructions, which is referenced from within the HTML page. However, it is also quite common to find these instructions intermingled with HTML code. The browser then uses them to generate pure HTML for the page when the user requests the page – in other words, the page is generated *dynamically* on request. This produces an HTML page, which is sent back from the plug-in to the browser.

So in this model, the set of five steps that we looked at in the static pages section now becomes a set of six, as depicted in Figure 1-4:

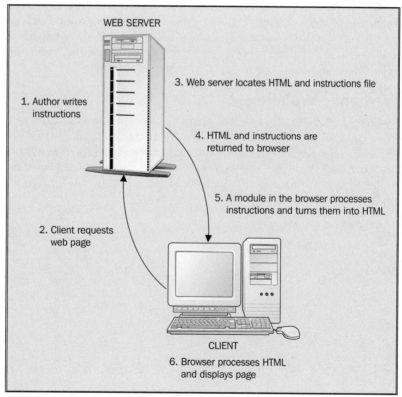

WEB SERVER

1. Author writes instructions

2. Client requests web page

3. Web server locates HTML and instructions file

4. HTML and instructions are returned to browser

5. A module in the browser processes instructions and turns them into HTML

CLIENT

6. Browser processes HTML and displays page

Figure 1-4

1. A Web author writes a set of instructions for creating HTML and saves it within a .htm file. The author also writes a set of instructions in a different language. This might be contained within the .htm file, or within a separate file.

2. Sometime later, a user types a page request into the browser, and the request is passed from the browser to the Web server.

3. The Web server locates the .htm page, and may have to locate a second file that contains the instructions.

4. The Web server sends both the newly created HTML stream and instructions back across the network to the browser.

5. A module within the browser processes the instructions and returns it as HTML within the .htm page – only one page is returned, even if two were requested.

6. The HTML is then processed by the browser, which displays the page.

Client-side technologies have fallen out of favor in recent times as they take a long time to download, especially if you have to download several pages in a row that use them. A second drawback is that since each browser interprets client-side scripting code differently, you have no way of guaranteeing that all browsers will interpret and execute the code in the same way. Another drawback is the problem associated with writing client-side code that uses server-side resources such as databases, because it is interpreted at client-side. In addition, client-side scripting code isn't secure and can be easily viewed with the View | Source option on any browser, which is also undesirable.

Server-Side Dynamic Web Pages

With the server-side model, the HTML source is sent to the Web server with an extra set of instructions (that can be intermingled or sent separately). This set of instructions is again used to generate HTML for the page at the time the user requests the page. Once again, the page is generated dynamically upon request. The set of five steps once more becomes one with six steps, as depicted in Figure 1-5:

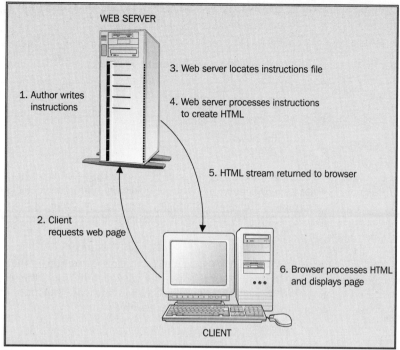

WEB SERVER

3. Web server locates instructions file

1. Author writes
   instructions

4. Web server processes instructions
   to create HTML

5. HTML stream returned to browser

2. Client
   requests web page

6. Browser processes HTML
   and displays page

CLIENT

Figure 1-5

1. A Web author writes a set of instructions for creating HTML and saves these instructions within a file.

2. A user types a page request into the browser, and the request is passed from the browser to the Web server.

3. The Web server locates the file of instructions.

4. The Web server follows the instructions in order to create a stream of HTML.

5. The Web server sends the newly created HTML stream back across the network to the browser.

6. The browser processes the HTML and displays the page.

This time, there is a subtle twist regarding where the instructions are processed. The entire processing takes place on the server *before* the page is sent back to the browser. One of the key advantages this has over the client-side model is that only the HTML is actually sent to the browser. This means that the page's original code is hidden away on the server, and you can safely assume that most browsers should be able to at least have a go at displaying it.

> *ASP.NET does its processing on the server-side.*

While neither client-side nor server-side technologies add much complexity to the normal process for serving a static Web page (Step 5 on the client, or Step 4 on the server), this single step is crucial. Here, the HTML that defines the Web page is not generated until after the Web page has been requested.

For example, you can use either technique to write a set of instructions for creating a page that displays the current time:

```
<html>
<head><title>The Punctual Web Server</title></head>
<body>
  <h1>Welcome</h1>
  In Webserverland, the time is exactly
  <INSTRUCTION: write HTML to display the current time>
</body>
</html>
```

In this case, you can compose most of the page using pure HTML. It's just that you can't hard-code the current time. Instead, you write a special code (that would replace the highlighted line here) that instructs the Web server to generate that bit of HTML during Step 5 on the client, or Step 4 on the server, at the time the page is requested. Let's return to this example later in the chapter, and see how to write the highlighted instruction using ASP.NET.

Server-side technologies are installed on the Web server and so the pages are run on the server. With client-side technologies, the Web page is run on the browser. Consequently, before the server-script can be sent back to the browser, the Web server must first translate it into HTML. The browser doesn't understand server-side code and therefore will never get to see any.

What Is ASP.NET?

The original definition of ASP.NET, right at the start of the chapter, portrayed ASP.NET as a powerful and flexible technology for creating dynamic Web pages, and this still holds true. However, as you now know, it isn't the only way to deliver dynamic Web pages, so let's refine our definition a little so it reads as follows:

> **ASP.NET is a powerful and flexible server-side technology for creating dynamic Web pages.**

Secondly, ASP.NET is only one of a set of technologies that comprise the *.NET Framework*. For now, you can think of this as a giant toolkit for creating all sorts of applications, and in particular, for creating applications on the Web. When you install ASP.NET, you will also install the .NET Framework at the same time. You will use bits and pieces of the .NET Framework throughout this book. In fact, you can also use the old versions of ASP with the .NET Framework, so why are we not using that instead?

How Does ASP.NET Differ from ASP?

ASP is restricted to using scripting languages, mainly JavaScript or VBScript (although it can be any scripting language supported by the Windows system). Scripting languages are like cut-down or junior versions of full programming languages in that they aren't as powerful and don't support all the features of full programming languages. In addition, when you add ASP code to your pages, you do it in the same way as you would do client-side script, and this leads to problems such as messy coding and restricted functionality.

ASP.NET has no such problems. It allows you to use a far greater selection of full programming languages and fully utilize the rich potential of the .NET Framework. It helps you create faster, more reliable, dynamic Web pages with any of the programming languages supported by the .NET Framework. Typical languages supported natively are VB.NET, C#, and JScript.NET (a new version of Jscript). On top of this, it is expected that third-party developers will create versions of Perl, Python, and many others to work in ASP.NET.

Secondly, ASP.NET comes with a far greater set of controls that you can place on a page without any extra ASP.NET coding. With classic ASP, programmers tended to rely on six objects, (for example Request and Response) to do everything, along with a couple of extra components that came with ASP. With ASP.NET, things are more *jargon-free*. If you want to put a button on your page, you put an ASP.NET *button control* on your page, and if you want a text box, you place an ASP.NET *text box control*. ASP.NET comes with a rich set of controls that can be applied to many common development scenarios.

A third and final reason is the separation of your ASP.NET from your HTML. It's a commonly cited reason, if not always a well-explained one. Designers and developers play two very different roles in Web development. For instance, a developer could program a lottery number generator, but probably couldn't design a logo for a company. It makes sense to keep these two disciplines separate.

However, in ASP they aren't separate. The ASP code is sprinkled liberally between the HTML lines, like nuts over an ice cream sundae. That might be fine, unless you happen to be allergic to nuts. Now stretching this allegory a bit, it's quite common for designers to need to tinker with the actual HTML code on a Web site, but how can they alter it with confidence, if it's totally interspersed with the ASP code? In ASP.NET, you can keep the ASP code and HTML in separate files, making both the developer and the designer's life much simpler.

Using VB.NET

ASP.NET has been described as a technology and *not* a language, and this is an important distinction! ASP.NET pages can be made from one of many languages. However, you are not expected to know many different languages, nor are we going to teach them to you. This book uses just one language, VB.NET, to demonstrate ASP.NET. We've chosen VB.NET as it's arguably the simplest for beginners, and it can do just about anything that the other .NET languages can. Lastly and most importantly, VB.NET comes free with ASP.NET – so when you install ASP.NET you get VB.NET as well!

At this stage you may be thinking, "Hang on, I've got to figure out VB.NET, then I've got to get a handle on ASP.NET – that sounds like an awful lot to learn." Don't worry; you won't be learning two languages. ASP.NET, as we said right from the beginning, is not a language – it is a technology. This technology is accessible via a programming language. What we're going to be doing is teaching you ASP.NET features as we teach you VB.NET. In other words, you will be creating your Web pages using VB.NET and using ASP.NET to drive it. However, before you rush out and get a VB.NET book instead, remember that this book will approach the language from the angle of creating dynamic Web pages only.

> **ASP.NET is a server-side technology that lets you use fully-fledged programming languages to create your Web pages.**

I'm Still Confused about ASP, ASP.NET, and VB.NET

It's really important to get these terms separate and distinct in your mind, so before we move on to actually installing and running ASP.NET, let's go back and redefine them just to make sure:

❑   **ASP**: A server-side technology for creating dynamic Web pages that only lets you use scripting languages

❑   **ASP.NET**: A server-side technology for creating dynamic Web pages that lets you use any full-fledged programming language supported by .NET

❑   **VB.NET**: This book's chosen programming language for writing code in ASP.NET

Now it's time to get it all installed!

The Installation Process

You're going to spend a fair amount of time on the installation process of ASP.NET, because it isn't as straightforward as with ASP. Remember, if you don't get it right, you won't be able to continue to the *Chapter 2* of this book!

The installation process is done in three stages:

❑   Installation of the prerequisites for .NET

❑   Installation of the .NET Framework 1.1

❑   Installation of Web Matrix (and the Web server)

Before starting the installation process let's talk about the operating system you have, because this affects some aspects of the process.

Which Operating System Do You Have?

While writing this book, we installed Web Matrix and used the server that comes with it to test code. However, Windows 2000 and Windows XP Professional already come with a Web server – IIS. You can use IIS to run ASP.NET pages on just as easily as Web Matrix's Web Server, and you will get exactly the same results. However, we recommend that you use Web Matrix to test the examples in this book.

If you have Windows XP Home edition, you have no choice but to install Web Matrix, because it does not come with a Web server. If you have an older operating system such as Windows ME or Windows 98 then you cannot use ASP.NET or Web Matrix and will have to upgrade. Despite initial claims from Microsoft about backwards compatibility of the .NET Framework with systems as far back as Windows 95 made in the early days of the .NET Framework's beta program, only the following list of supported operating systems can run ASP.NET and the .NET Framework:

Supports all of the .NET Framework except Microsoft ASP.NET	Supports the entire .NET Framework	Supports Web Matrix
Windows 98	Windows 2000 (all versions – no Service Packs required)	Windows 2000
Windows 98 SE	Windows XP Professional	Windows 2003
Windows ME	Windows 2003	Windows XP Professional and Home Edition
Windows NT 4.0 (all versions – Service Pack 6a required)		
Windows XP Home Edition		

While Window XP Home edition doesn't natively support ASP.NET, it does support Web Matrix. However, Windows 98/Windows ME do not support Web Matrix, and while in theory they could both run it, we have not tested this. We will *not* be covering the use of Web Matrix with these latter two systems in this book.

If you have an operating system that comes with IIS and wish to use that instead of Web Matrix, then you need to install IIS before you install the ASP.NET. However, most will probably find it easier to install Web Matrix and use it even if you have IIS already installed. To use Web Matrix correctly you need to install it after you have installed ASP.NET. The next section assumes that you have chosen to install Web Matrix and will detail the installation process. You will start by installing the prerequisites for ASP.NET followed by the .NET Redistributable.

> **If you wish to install IIS as well as Web Matrix, then you will need to jump to Appendix E found at the end of this book, where there are complete instructions for the installation and testing of IIS. If you have either the Windows 2000 Server or Windows 2003 Server operating system, then the good news is that IIS is automatically installed as part of the operating system.**

Prerequisites for Installing ASP.NET

Anybody who is familiar with ASP might be used to ASP being installed automatically with the Web server, and thereby doing it all in one step. This is true – classic ASP is still installed with the Web server; however, ASP.NET is only available as a separate download. This means you will have to download ASP.NET from Microsoft's Web site or from CD (if you have one) even if you already have IIS installed.

Before ASP.NET or the .NET Framework is used you will need to install the *Microsoft Data Access Components* (*MDAC*) version 2.7 or later. This is a set of components to enable you to use ASP.NET to communicate with databases and display the contents of your database on a Web page. Without these components installed, you won't be able to run any of the database examples in this book. This will affect examples as early as *Chapter 2*, so please don't skip this stage!

MDAC is a small download (roughly 5 to 6 MB) available free from Microsoft's site at http://www.microsoft.com/data. The most recent version at the time of writing is 2.8, although version 2.7 is also adequate for this book.

The MDAC installation is quite straightforward. Version 2.7 also comes as part of the Windows Component Update of the .NET Framework and the Windows XP Service Pack, so if you've installed these you won't need to install it again.

However, in case you haven't installed either of these, we'll run through it quickly just to make sure that everything is clear.

Try It Out   Installing MDAC 2.8

1. MDAC 2.8 comes as a single file `MDAC_typ.exe` that you will need to download. Run this file to begin the installation process.

2. After agreeing to the terms of the license, it will scan your hard drive for space. If there's enough space, you will get to a dialog from which you can begin the installation by clicking Finish as shown in Figure 1-6:

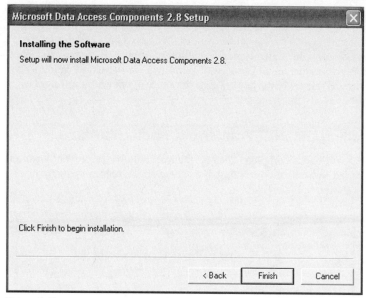

Figure 1-6

3. The installation process will continue without requiring further intervention, although you may have reboot the system afterwards. Once MDAC is installed, you are ready to install ASP.NET.

Installing ASP.NET and the .NET Framework

Before you install ASP.NET, you need to know a couple of important things. The first is that there have been two full release versions of the .NET Framework – 1.0 and 1.1. ASP.NET is an integral part of the .NET Framework, and so ASP.NET 1.1 accompanies the .NET 1.1 Framework. If you have previously installed .NET 1.0, then installing .NET 1.1 won't automatically erase or upgrade your 1.0 installation.

The new Framework installs alongside the old version and you can run both. You need to be aware of this because unless you have previously created applications in 1.0, it's likely that you only need the most current version (1.1) and therefore you should probably remove the previous installation using Add/Remove Programs in the Windows Control Panel. This will avoid any hiccups that may arise when running both installations together.

The second point is that while there used to be two different types of .NET installation files available from Microsoft's http://www.asp.net site, there is now only one type. In version 1.0, there was a .NET redistributable file and a .NET Framework SDK. Both files contained ASP.NET, VB .NET, and the .NET Framework. With version 1.1, only the *.NET Framework Redistributable* contains ASP.NET, and the SDK is entirely devoted to samples, examples, and documentation. As the SDK is a hefty 108 MB, don't download it unless you really want to (although one example in *Chapter 16* requires a tool present in the SDK). The .NET Framework Redistributable download contains everything you need to run ASP.NET and the .NET Framework. There is no accompanying extra documentation or samples in the redistributable, but this book will take you through all the necessary areas.

Also, don't worry about replacing an existing classic ASP installation, since ASP.NET will be installed alongside ASP and they will both continue to work fine without any new settings.

The next section walks you through a typical installation of the .NET Framework Redistributable. The installation process is the same on all versions of Windows, so we're only going to detail the installation process on Windows XP Home edition. Although the wizard looks a bit different on other versions of Windows, it asks for exactly the same things.

Try It Out   Installing the .NET Framework Redistributable

1. After the download is complete, click on the installation file (currently called `dotnetfx.exe`). You are asked to confirm your intent and after a short interval, you are taken to the setup wizard as shown in Figure 1-7:

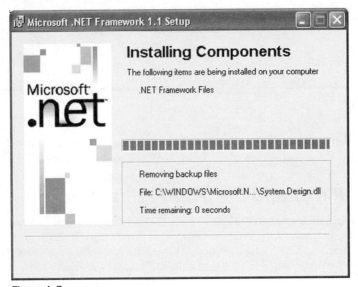

Figure 1-7

2. Check I agree to accept the License agreement and click on Install. ASP.NET will now install without further intervention.

3. You will be notified when the installation is completed. You can now move on to the tips followed by the installation of Web Matrix.

Troubleshooting Hints and Tips

The installation process is straightforward, and works without errors on a majority of machines. However, sometimes the particular configuration of your machine will prevent it from installing. Unfortunately, this book can't cover all eventualities, but if the installation doesn't work on yours, you should check that you have enough hard disk space, as this is the most common cause of such problems. Also, ensure that the installation process isn't curtailed half way, as no installer is foolproof at removing all the different bits and pieces of the aborted install and this can cause problems when you try to reinstall. Additionally, check the list of newsgroups and resources later in this chapter; however, as far as I've seen, the .NET Framework rarely causes problems during installation.

> **If you download the SDK as well, you must load the redistributable *first*, otherwise you will only be allowed to load the accompanying documentation and not the samples and example code.**

Installing Web Matrix

You should have MDAC and .NET Framework installed on your machine so far. This leaves the last part of the equation, Web Matrix.

Web Matrix is an application development tool that you can use to create both ASP.NET and ASP pages. In previous editions of this book, we shied away from using *what you see is what you get (WYSIWYG)* development tools as they have a nasty tendency to add extra lines of code to your own code. For example, FrontPage, a WYSIWYG tool, allows you to create pages easily by dragging and dropping objects onto your Web page. However, it hides the HTML code away behind the interface, so you never get to understand any HTML code. Having a tool create ASP.NET code for you isn't the best way to go about learning ASP.NET – it would be trying to learn French and then getting a translator to speak all your lines for you!

This viewpoint hasn't changed, but there are some mitigating circumstances, as already pointed out. The first is that without Web Matrix there is no way of running your ASP.NET pages on Windows XP Home Edition. The second is that there are circumstances under which, automatically generated code can make your life a lot simpler, and it won't ultimately hinder your understanding of the way in which ASP.NET works.

Therefore, we are using Web Matrix within this book primarily for its Web serving capabilities and not its Web page creation abilities, although we will be using some of its wizards in certain appropriate situations.

You can download the latest version of Web Matrix from http://www.asp.net.

Try It Out   Installing Web Matrix

1. Go to the http://www.asp.net site and download Web Matrix. Save the file to your local drive as shown in Figure 1-8:

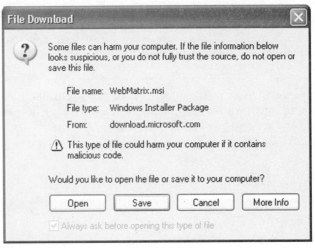

Figure 1-8

2. Once the download is complete, go to Windows Explorer and run the `Web Matrix.msi` file. The wizard should start up as shown in Figure 1-9. If it doesn't, verify that you have downloaded the whole package, roughly 1339KB:

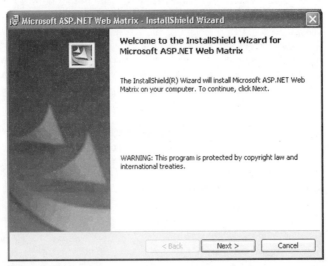

Figure 1-9

3. Click on Next and accept the terms of your license agreement. In the next dialog, shown in Figure 1-10, add your user name and organization details and choose whether the installation should be just for yourself or all users of the computer:

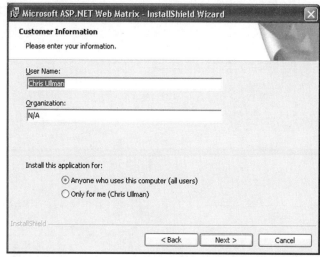

Figure 1-10

4. Click on Next and leave the options for ASP.NET Web Matrix (shown in Figure 1-11) exactly as you find them, checking that you have enough free space on your hard drive:

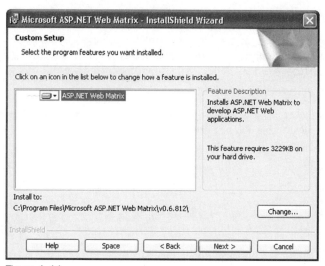

Figure 1-11

5. Click on Next and then click on Install in the final dialog to start the installation as shown in Figure 1-12:

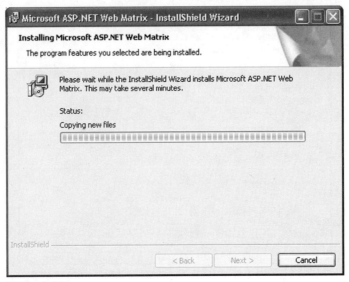

Figure 1-12

6. When Web Matrix has finished installing, you will be shown a final dialog confirming this.

Configuring Web Matrix for .NET Framework 1.1

Before you can run Web Matrix, you need to configure it to use the 1.1 version of the Framework. If you have the 1.0 version of the Framework, it will automatically use that instead.

Try It Out   Configuring Web Matrix

1. Open the `WebMatrix.exe.config` file that is located in your installation directory using Notepad. Typically, this will be found in `C:\Program Files\Microsoft ASP.NET WebMatrix\v0.6.812`

2. Scroll down the file and add the following snippet immediately before the `<runtime>` section on line 18:

```
<startup>
   <supportedRuntime version="v1.1.4322" />
</startup>
```

3. After modification, the file should look like this:

```
<?xml version="1.0" encoding="utf-8" ?>
<configuration>
    ...
   </configSections>
```

```
    <startup>
        <supportedRuntime version="v1.1.4322" />
    </startup>
        <runtime>
        ...
</configuration>
```

4. Save the file and run Web Matrix. Select the About ASP.NET Web Matrix... item from the Help menu. The .NET Framework version should now be 1.1.x.

Running Web Matrix and Setting Up the Web Server

The next thing to do is to test the Web server to verify that it is working correctly and serving pages as it should. To do this, start Web Matrix and create a new folder, `BegASPNET11`, where you can store files that you use throughout this book.

Try It Out   Starting the Web Server

1. Go to `Program Files\Microsoft ASP.NET Web Matrix` and run Web Matrix. The screen that appears is shown in Figure 1-13:

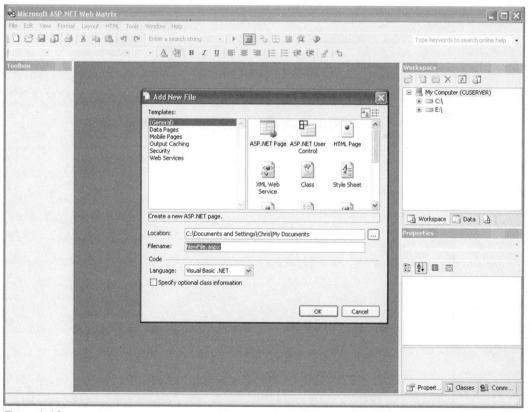

Figure 1-13

2. Change the Location to C:\BegASPNET11\, and the Filename to test.aspx, and make sure that the Language reads Visual Basic.NET, as shown in Figure 1-14:

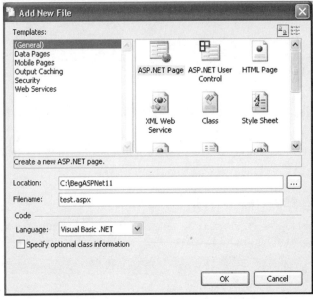

Figure 1-14

3. You are greeted with a blank page with four tabs at the foot of the page as shown in Figure 1-15:

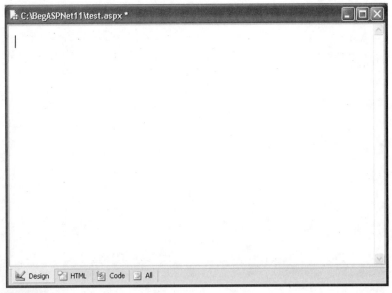

Figure 1-15

4. Without adding any code to the dialog, click on the arrow icon (shown in Figure 1-16) which appears centrally in the toolbar above this dialog:

Figure 1-16

5. The dialog in Figure 1-17 will appear and enable you to start up the Web server:

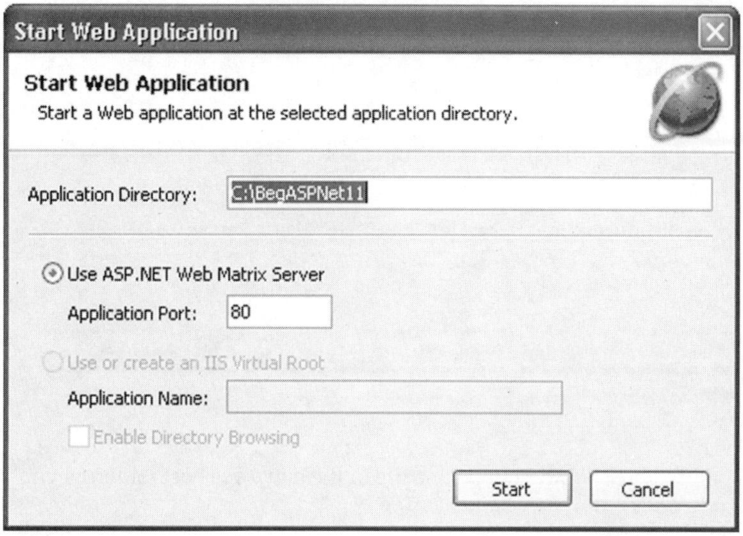

Start Web Application

Start Web Application
Start a Web application at the selected application directory.

Application Directory: C:\BegASPNet11

⦿ Use ASP.NET Web Matrix Server

Application Port: 80

○ Use or create an IIS Virtual Root

Application Name:

☐ Enable Directory Browsing

[Start] [Cancel]

Figure 1-17

> **If you have already installed IIS or another Web Server that uses application port 80, the application port may well be 8080 in this dialog and not 80. Don't change this; using 8080 is perfectly acceptable.**

6. Click on Start and the browser will appear with a blank page, reading http://localhost/test.aspx. More importantly, a globe with a ring like the planet Saturn (incidentally, Web Matrix was code-named Project Saturn) as shown in Figure 1-18, will appear in your taskbar:

Figure 1-18

7. This indicates that the Web server is working. Right-click on it and select Open in Web browser (Figure 1-19):

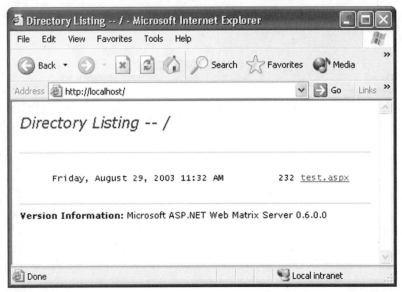

Figure 1-19

8. At this point, there should only be one file in the http://localhost folder, as you've only just created it!

> **If you have IIS installed, you will see http://localhost:8080 when this screen comes up. This means both Web Matrix and IIS are running simultaneously – IIS is accessible via http://localhost, and Web Matrix via http://localhost:8080. From now on, you will need to add :8080 to localhost if you intend to use Web Matrix as your Web server.**

How It Works

You created a physical folder called BegASPNET11 and a *blank* file (it isn't literally blank as Web Matrix has auto-generated some HTML in it) called test.aspx, that you placed inside your folder, and the browser was able to view this file. When you created the physical folder using Web Matrix, it automatically created a Web directory that can be accessed by a browser.

Normally when you create a new folder, it isn't automatically accessible to all and sundry on the Web. If this did happen, just about everyone would be able to see the contents of your hard drive, which would be very insecure. To allow access to files on the Web, you must place them in a specifically allotted area. Luckily, Web Matrix has done this task automatically for you!

There is something important to note about using browsers to access files as well. When you access files via the Web, you use the http:// prefix to indicate that you are looking for something on the Web. *HTTP* stands for *HyperText Transfer Protocol*, the protocol by which Web pages are transferred over the Internet.

The role of HTTP is discussed in the next chapter in greater depth. For now, just remember that when you use the http:// prefix you are also going to a Web server, whether on your own machine or on the Web. As ASP.NET is attached to the Web server, you must go via the Web server if you wish to use ASP.NET. For instance, you could type in C:\BegASPNET11\test.aspx into the address bar of the browser, and the browser will act like Windows Explorer, but this wouldn't let ASP.NET run your file, as you haven't gone via the Web server. When running any ASP.NET file, you must always go the http:// route.

Notice from Figure 1-19 on the previous page that the machine is called localhost. When you run the example on your own machine, it will also be called localhost. It is the term used to refer to your own PC. It tells the browser not to go onto the Web to search for a particular page.

This raises another question: what happens if you have two computers on the network and you wish to view ASP.NET files on one machine from the other? Simply typing in http://localhost will just go to the machine on which you're working. The answer is that each machine has a unique name. If you go to Control Panel and select the System option, you'll find a dialog with several tabs. Choose the Computer Name tab to view a list of identifiers for your computer as shown in Figure 1-20:

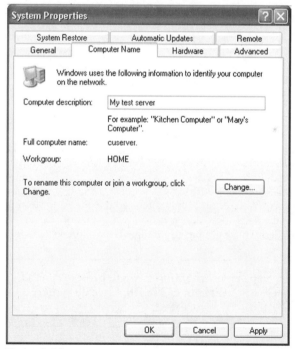

Figure 1-20

The full computer name is of particular interest, because you can use this to uniquely identify your computer on your network. My machine is named cuserver, so instead of typing in http://localhost on my machine, I could have also typed http://cuserver for the same results. You can always use your machine name instead of localhost. This name is called an alias.

To recap, you created a folder called BegASPNET11. You can access this via the Web server, using http://localhost, and can see the contents of this folder via the browser. On your own machine, you can also use your machine name to view the folder. Thus, the folder has two aliases on the Web server.

However, if you try to view your Web server via another machine, you receive an HTTP Error 403. If I logged on to another machine on my network and tried to view http://cuserver, I would receive an error as shown in Figure 1-21:

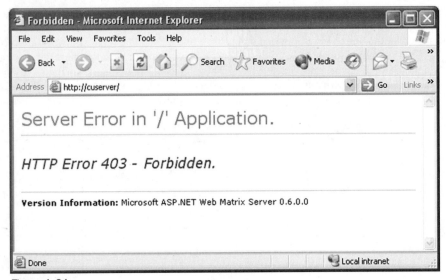

Figure 1-21

This is because Web Matrix's Web server is only intended to be used for testing purposes, and does not allow other machines on the network to access it. You can use it only to view ASP.NET files on the machine where it is installed. This has a big advantage in that it makes the server secure.

> **If you want to use a Web server that allows you to browse ASP.NET files from other machines on your network, you should use IIS. Check *Appendix E* for more details on how to do this.**

Troubleshooting Web Matrix's Web Server

Unfortunately, there is no guarantee that everything will install properly, but there is another tool at your disposal. Within the Web Matrix files is a `WebServer.exe` file. You shouldn't need to run this file separately as it runs automatically when you start `Web Matrix.exe`. For example, there may be a problem when the port number that Web Matrix is trying to use (default is 80) has already been taken by another application. In such a case, you can run this EXE from the command prompt to try some other configurations.

If you run the `WebServer.exe` file from Explorer, you will get the dialog shown in Figure 1-22:

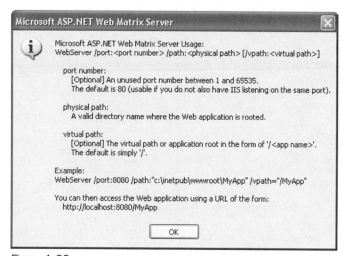

Figure 1-22

If you already have IIS installed, you will probably find that you can't use the default port 80, and may need to change to another port. It should do this automatically, but to do this you can go to the command prompt and type in the following command from the folder in which Web Matrix was installed.

```
WebServer /port:8080 /path:"C:\BegASPNET11"
```

You should get a popup from a planet icon confirming that you have started this instance of a Web server. If not, then it should display an error message that instructs you on what has been done incorrectly, and how it needs to be amended.

ASP.NET Test Example

Ok, you've now reached the crux of the chapter, getting your first ASP.NET page up and working!

Do you remember the punctual Web server code discussed earlier in the chapter, in which we wanted to write a Web page that displays the current time? Let's return to that example now. It's quite a simple bit of code, but should be more than enough to check that ASP.NET is working OK.

Try It Out   Your First ASP.NET Web Page

1.   Go to Web Matrix and close `test.aspx` if it is still open. Then select New Files from the File menu and in the dialog change the Location and Filename details as shown in Figure 1-23:

Figure 1-23

2.   We've created another folder for this chapter's code, called `Ch01`. For each chapter, we will put the code in a corresponding folder's `/Web` directory. Click on OK.

3.   Next, select the Code tab and type in the following code, replacing the Insert code here:

```
Sub Page_Load()
    time.text=Hour(Now) & ":" & Minute(Now) & ":" & Second(Now)
End Sub
```

4.   Now select the HTML tab and add the following between the `<form>` tags:

```
    In WebServerLand the time is currently:
<asp:label id="time" runat="server" />
```

5. Click on the arrow button to view the page from within Web Matrix. An instance of Internet Explorer appears as shown in Figure 1-24:

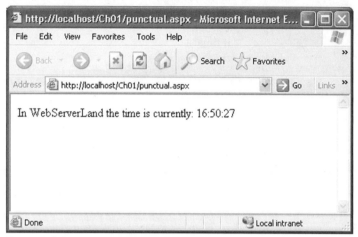

In WebServerLand the time is currently: 16:50:27

Figure 1-24

6. To view the page outside of Web Matrix, you need to start a browser and specify the *Uniform Resource Locator (URL)* of the ASP.NET page into the browser's **Address** box, as you do when browsing on the Internet. If you're using a single machine for both Web server and browser, specifying http://localhost/Ch01/punctual.aspx should be enough.

7. Notice that there is now a folder in the URL, because you added a folder in Web Matrix. Moreover, if you look on the computer's hard drive, you can see the corresponding folder.

8. Click on the browser's **Refresh** button, and the displayed time will change as shown in Figure 1-25. In effect, the browser is showing a new and different instance of the same page:

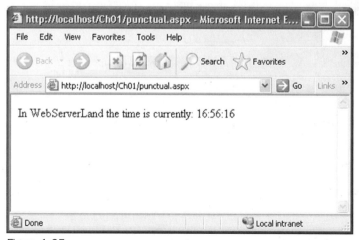

In WebServerLand the time is currently: 16:56:16

Figure 1-25

9. Now on your browser select View | Source or something similar (depending on which browser you're using) to see the HTML source that was sent from the Web server to the browser. The result is shown in Figure 1-26. Notice that there is no ASP.NET code, and nothing before the first `<html>` tag. This is because the ASP.NET code is processed on the Web server. The Web server will then generate pure HTML from the ASP.NET code. This HTML source is then sent back to the browser:

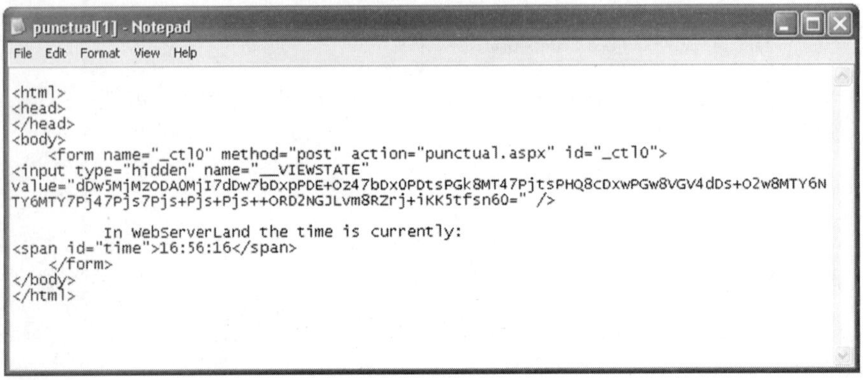

```
punctual[1] - Notepad
File   Edit   Format   View   Help

<html>
<head>
</head>
<body>
        <form name="_ctl0" method="post" action="punctual.aspx" id="_ctl0">
<input type="hidden" name="__VIEWSTATE"
value="dDw5MjMzODAOMjI7dDw7bDxpPDE+Oz47bDxOPDtsPGk8MT47PjtsPHQ8CDxwPGw8VGV4dDs+O2w8MTY6N
TY6MTY7Pj47Pjs7Pjs+Pjs++ORD2NGJLvm8RZrj+iKK5tfsn60=" />

            In WebServerLand the time is currently:
<span id="time">16:56:16</span>
        </form>
</body>
</html>
```

Figure 1-26

Here, you can see the HTML that was sent to the browser when the page was refreshed at 16:56:16.

10. As mentioned before, you can expect this to work in any browser, because ASP.NET is processed on the Web server and not on the browser. If you have another browser available, give it a go!

How It Works

Easy, wasn't it? Even if you didn't get it to work first time, don't rush off to e-mail technical support just yet – have a look at the next section – *ASP.NET Troubleshooting*. Let's look at the ASP.NET code that makes this application tick.

There is only one block of ASP.NET code in the whole program, ignoring the server control placed under the HTML tab. It is as follows:

```
Sub Page_Load()
    time.text=Hour(Now) & ":" & Minute(Now) & ":" & Second(Now)
End Sub
```

If you ignore the `Sub Page_Load()` and `End Sub` lines that are standard to many ASP.NET programs and which are discussed in *Chapter 3*, you're left with only one line:

```
time.text=Hour(Now) & ":" & Minute(Now) & ":" & Second(Now)
```

The line of code tells the Web server to run the VB.NET `Now()` function on the Web server. The VB.NET `Now()` function returns the current time at the Web server. It returns the values of the `Now()` function divided into hour, minute, and second values. The result of this function is returned as part of the `<asp: label>` control. This control is discussed in *Chapter 3*.

If the Web server and browser are on different machines, then the time returned by the Web server might not be the same as the time kept by the machine you're using to browse. For example, if this page is hosted on a machine in Los Angeles, then you can expect the page to show the local time in Los Angeles – even if you're browsing to the page from a machine in Cairo.

This example isn't wildly interactive or dynamic, but it illustrates that you can ask the Web server to do something for you, and the server can return the answer within the context of an HTML page. You can use this technique with things like HTML forms and other tools to build a more informative and responsive interface with the user.

ASP.NET Troubleshooting

If you had difficulty in executing the preceding example, perhaps you fell into one of the simple traps that commonly snare new ASP.NET programmers, but these could be easily rectified. This section will look at few common errors and reasons due to which your script might not run. If you had problems, this section may help you identify them.

Program Not Found, or the Result of the ASP.NET Isn't Being Displayed, or the Browser Tries to Download the File

You'll have this problem if you try to view the page as a local file on your hard drive like this:

C:\BegASPNET1.1\Ch01\punctual.aspx

You'll also face this problem if you click on the file in Windows Explorer. If you have Microsoft FrontPage or Visual Studio.NET installed, then it will start up and attempt to help you to edit the code. Otherwise, your browser may display a warning message, or (most likely) it will ask you which application you wish to use to open up the ASPX file as depicted in Figure 1-27.

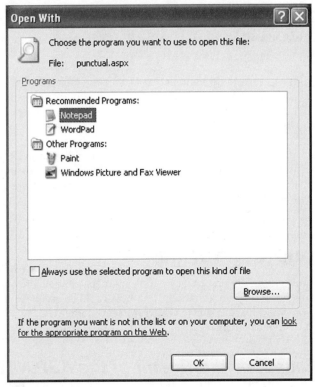

Figure 1-27

Older browsers may try to download the file.

This is because you're trying to access the page in a way that doesn't cause the ASP.NET page to be requested from the Web server. Because of this, the ASP.NET code isn't processed and that's why you don't get the expected results.

To call the Web page through the Web server and have the ASP.NET code processed, you need to reference the Web server in the URL. Depending on whether you're browsing to the server across a local network or across the Internet, the URL should look something like http://localhost/Ch01/punctual.aspx or http://www.distantserver.com/Ch01/punctual.aspx.

Page Cannot Be Displayed: HTTP Error 403

If you get a HTTP Error 403 message as shown in Figure 1-28, it's probably because you don't have permission to execute the ASP.NET code contained within the page. Notice the Forbidden error message at the end of the error page:

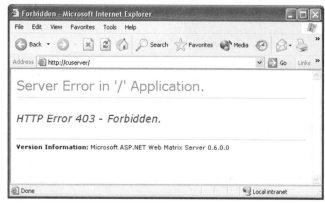

Figure 1-28

Recall that it isn't possible to view ASP.NET pages from a place other than the computer on which you have installed Web Matrix!

Page Cannot Be Found: HTTP Error 404

If you get this error message as shown in Figure 1-29, it means that the browser has managed to connect to the Web server successfully, but the Web server can't locate the page you asked for. This could be because you mistyped the URL at the browser prompt.

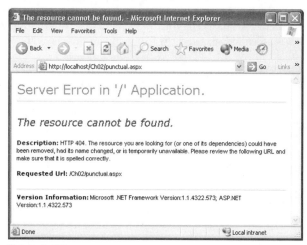

Figure 1-29

If you see Figure 1-29, you might have made the following errors:

❑   A simple typing error in the URL, such as http://localhost/BegASPNET/ch01/punctually.aspx

❑   A wrong directory name, like http://localhost/BegASPNET/punctual.aspx instead of http://localhost/ch01/punctual.aspx or http://localhost/ch01/punctual.aspx like we have above

❑   Including a directory separator (/) after the file name, like this http://localhost/ch01/punctual.aspx/

❑   Using the directory path in the URL, rather than using the alias, such as http://chrisu//ch01/punctual.aspx

❑   Saving the page as .html or .htm, rather than as an .aspx, like http://localhost/ch01/punctual.htm

Web Page Unavailable While Offline

Very occasionally, you'll come across a message box as shown in Figure 1-30:

Figure 1-30

This happens because you've tried to request a page and you haven't currently got an active connection to the Internet. This is a misperception by the browser, unless your Web server isn't the same machine as the one on which you're working. It is trying to get onto the Internet to get your page when there is no connection, and it's failing to realize that the page you've requested is present on your local machine. One way of retrieving the page is to hit the Connect button in the dialog; that's not the most satisfactory solution, since you might incur call charges if you are using dialup. Alternatively, you need to adjust the settings on your browser. In IE5 and IE6, select the File menu and uncheck the Work Offline option.

This could also happen if you're working on a network and using a proxy server to access the Internet. In this case, you need to bypass the proxy server or disable it for this page, as described earlier in the chapter. Alternatively, if you're using a modem and you don't need to connect, you can correct this misperception by changing the way that IE looks for pages. To do this, select the Tools | Connections option and select Never dial a connection.

I Just Get a Blank Page

If you see an empty page in your browser, it probably means that you saved your punctual.aspx page without entering any code into it or that you didn't remember to refresh the browser.

The Page Displays the Message But Not the Time

If the Web page displays the message In WebServerLand, the time is currently but doesn't display the time then you might have mistyped the code. For example, you might have mistyped the name of the control:

```
time.text=Hour(Now) & ":" & Minute(Now) & ":" & Second(Now)
```

and:

```
<asp:label id="hour" runat="server" />
```

The name of the `hour` control must match the first word in the line of ASP.NET code; otherwise the control won't be able to identify it.

I Get an Error Statement Citing a Server Error

If you get a message stating that the page cannot be displayed, citing a server error as shown in Figure 1-31:

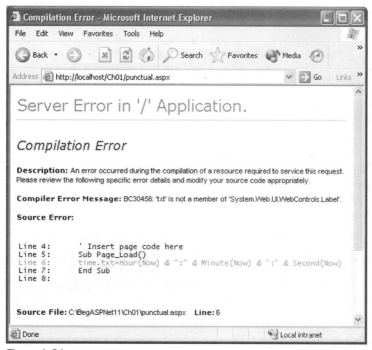

Figure 1-31

It means that there's an error in the ASP.NET code itself. Usually, there's additional information provided with the message. For example, you'd get this error message if you omitted the closing `</script>` tag on your code. To verify that this isn't the case, use the sample `punctual.aspx` page from the Wrox site at http://www.wrox.com.

I Have a Different Problem

If your problem isn't covered in the preceding sections, it's worth testing some of the sample ASP.NET pages that are supplied with the QuickStart tutorials at http://www.asp.net. They should help you to check that ASP.NET has actually installed properly. You can always uninstall and reinstall if necessary, although before you do this, rebooting your server might solve the problem.

You can get support from http://p2p.wrox.com, which is the Web site dedicated to support issues in this book. Alternatively, there are many Web sites dedicated to ASP and ASP.NET. In fact, you will find very few sites that focus on just one of the two technologies. Here are just a few resources:

- ❏   http://www.asp.net
- ❏   http://www.asptoday.com
- ❏   http://www.asp101.com
- ❏   http://www.15seconds.com
- ❏   http://www.4guysfromrolla.com

There are many solutions, discussions, and tips on these pages, plus references to other related pages. Moreover, you can try the newsgroups available on www.asp.net, such as Free For All.

By now, you should have successfully downloaded, set up, and installed both Web Matrix and ASP.NET, and got your first ASP.NET application up and running. If you've done all that, you can pat yourself on the back, make a cup of tea, and get ready to learn some of the principles behind ASP.NET in the next chapter.

Summary

This chapter started with a brief introduction to ASP.NET and dynamic Web pages in general and looked at some of the reasons you'd want to use a server-side technology for creating Web pages. You looked at some of the history behind dynamic Web pages, in the form of an overview of the other technologies. The next chapter will expand on this brief introduction to ASP.NET.

The bulk of the chapter was taken up by descriptions of the various installation processes. You will need a Web server (preferably Web Matrix), MDAC 2.7 or higher, and the .NET Framework Redistributable to be able to progress further with this book, so please don't be tempted to skip parts that might not have worked. We've listed plenty of resources that will help you get everything up and running.

The next chapter will explain in detail what ASP.NET does, what the .NET Framework is, and how the two work together.

Anatomy of an ASP.NET Page

In this chapter, we'll start by talking about some of the overall theory around .NET and ASP.NET. Then in the second half, we will get down to some coding. We won't cover all of the theory and won't explain every line of the examples, but at the end you will have some theoretical background and some working pages. These will provide the bookends for the details of ASP.NET that are presented in the remaining chapters.

We will cover the following:

❑   A description of the .NET Framework, and its purpose

❑   How ASP.NET fits into the .NET Framework

❑   The role of the Common Language Runtime

❑   Core concepts of ASP.NET

❑   Some examples of ASP.NET and the .NET Framework in action

What Is .NET?

I recently attended one of Microsoft's .NET road shows, and between talks, one of the speakers was giving out free software to anyone in the audience who could answer one of several simple questions. He challenged the audience by asking them to define what they thought .NET was. Tellingly, in a room full of experienced developers, not a single hand was raised. He moved on quickly, and instead chose to ask what a 'delegate' in the C# language was, and was greeted with a much larger response, even though describing a delegate is potentially a much more difficult task.

.NET is a catchall term that embraces Microsoft's core strategy, plans, and vision for the near future. At the heart of this strategy is the *.NET Framework*, which provides the core technology that underpins it all. ASP.NET is just one of several components that are present in the Framework.

.NET is designed to help solve several fundamental problems faced by programmers:

❑ It takes care of a great deal of the hard work involved in building large, reliable applications.

❑ It allows programmers to unify two kinds of architectures – applications that run locally on a machine and applications that are accessed over the Web.

❑ It reduces the overheads traditionally associated with programming frameworks – you don't need to write complex code in a high-powered language to get impressive performance out of .NET programs.

❑ It allows programmers in different languages to work together on a single application.

❑ It has been built from the start to accommodate various end-user tools, including desktops, PDAs, and cell phones.

To summarize, .NET provides an easier, and thus faster and cheaper way, to get efficient programs into the hands of users.

Since the aim of this book is to get you writing ASP.NET Web applications, we're not going to go into every detail of the Framework. In many cases, all you really need to know is what its elements can do, and what they need from you in order to do it. Other elements provide us with important functions, and these will merit further discussion. In this way, you'll gain not only a working knowledge of ASP.NET, but also a sense for how it fits in with the .NET Framework as a whole.

We can break down our discussion of the entire .NET Framework into several core concepts:

❑ **MS Intermediate Language (MSIL)**: All the code we write is compiled for us into a more abstract, trimmed-down form before it is executed. A programmer can use any .NET language to write the code, including VB, C#, Jscript, and about 20 others. The result is then compiled to MSIL, the Common Language of .NET. This level of .NET operates without our interaction so we have not covered it in this book.

❑ **The Common Language Runtime (CLR)**: This is a complex system responsible for executing the MSIL code on the computer. It takes care of all the nitty-gritty tasks involved in talking to Windows and IIS. This level is also behind-the-scene for this book.

❑ **The .NET Framework Class Libraries**: These are code libraries containing a mass of tremendously useful functionality, which we can very easily bolt onto our own applications to make complex tasks much more straightforward. We will explore these functions throughout this book.

❑ **The .NET Languages**: These are simply programming languages that conform to certain specific structural requirements (as defined by the Common Language Specification, or CLS), and can therefore, be compiled to MSIL. You can develop in any of the languages, such as C# or VB .NET, without any restrictions and make applications constructed out of more then one of these languages. Several chapters of this book will discuss the application of VB to ASP.NET and we will use VB in all code examples.

- ❑ **ASP.NET**: This module of code extends the Internet Information Server (IIS) so that it can implement the .NET Framework for Web pages. The chapters of this book cover almost all of the ASP.NET features.

- ❑ **Web Services**: Although not strictly part of .NET, Web services are definitely enabled by .NET. They are programs that can be accessed via the Web, and can be anything from news headlines, weather forecasts, and stock tickers to virus protection and operating system updates. *Chapter 16* discusses Web services in detail.

Before we go into detail, let's look at some fundamental code concepts and terminology.

From Your Code to Machine Code

As you probably know, computers understand everything in terms of binary bits – sequences of ones and zeros that represent instructions and data – hence the enthusiastic use of the word 'digital' to describe anything even vaguely related to computers. We refer to these binary instructions as *machine code*. Obviously, for most humans, it's impractical to remember the particular sequence of ones and zeros that prints "Good Morning" (let alone one that defines a sophisticated Web application). To overcome the problem, we use high level programming languages that permit us to write code using English-like words.

Once we've written some code in a human-friendly language, we need to convert it into machine code. This process is called *compilation*. The compiler software translates the human-readable instructions into machine-readable instructions. Part of this compilation process involves coding information regarding the local environment into the compiled code, so that the machine code can make the most efficient use of all the computer resources available to it.

For many years, there's been a simple choice between two types of compilation, which differ in when the compilation takes place:

- ❑ **Pre-compiled code**: The code is compiled when we get done writing it, well before we need to use it. This makes for very fast execution, as the compiler has the opportunity to spend time considering the full set of code and the machine upon which it will run. However, because pre-compiled code is for a specific machine, we're now tied to using it on that machine, or we need to set up another machine with the same system and resources that the code requires.

- ❑ **Interpreted code**: This code is compiled at the time of its execution (when the user requests the page). This is slower because we do a compilation for each request and the system doesn't have the chance to fully optimize the code we've written. However, the advantage is that the interpretation can adapt to the machine hosting the code.

So, developers are left with a dilemma when selecting a language. They can either select slower interpreted code that is adopted to the machine, or the programmer can go with the faster pre-compiled code that does not take advantage of the specific machine's benefits.

Introducing Two Intermediate Languages

.NET solves the problem by using a two-step process for compilation. When we write a program to run on the .NET Framework – generally using VB.NET or C# – we compile our human-readable code as we finish writing it. However, .NET's compilers are designed such that this only takes us halfway to the usual binary code that presents such problems of portability. .NET compiles our code into a special format, the MSIL. Some optimization can be done as part of this process, since the MSIL's structure doesn't have to be as easily human-readable as our original code. However, no machine-specific optimization is done. Thus, MSIL has the benefits of general optimization and of portability to any .NET server.

When we execute this MSIL (when the user requests an ASP.NET page), we pass our code from MSIL to the Common Language Runtime (CLR), another cornerstone of the .NET Framework. The CLR uses another compiler – the *JIT (Just-In-Time) compiler* to compile to true machine code and make any last minute machine-pecific optimizations to the program, so that it can run as quickly as possible on the machine it inhabits.

> **MSIL and the CLR together give us the best of both worlds: the structural optimization of pre-compiled code along with the portability of interpreted code.**

Most importantly, MSIL itself is not at all machine-specific, so we can execute it on any machine that has the CLR installed. In essence, once we've written and compiled some .NET code, we can copy it to any machine with the CLR installed, and execute it there. While the CLR is currently only compatible with Windows (9x, NT, 2000, and XP versions), moves are already afoot to build versions for other operating systems. You can find more about one of those efforts by searching the Web for information on the Mono Project.

MSIL can be generated from any human-readable language that conforms to CLS. The big three are VB.NET, C#, and JScript.NET, but another couple dozen languages are now supported by MSIL compilers. We can therefore use all compliant languages *interchangeably* within our applications – once a set of files have been compiled to MSIL, they're all effectively written in the same language! This flexibility allows different teams to work on the same Web site in different languages.

Objects, Objects Everywhere

In order to grasp how .NET works, you need to have a notion of what we mean when we talk about *objects*. Just about everything you come across within the .NET Framework is implemented as a software object – we can, in fact, describe .NET as an *object-oriented environment*. So what does that mean? Simply put, an object is a set of code (or data) that we develop or buy once and then can easily reuse. An object is self-contained and offers a set of functions to the rest of your code. Writing code in objects and using pre-written objects has some important benefits:

- ❑ We avoid rewriting code for multiple uses.

- ❑ Objects allow us to buy functionality that may be beyond our ability or resources to develop.

❑ .NET objects are standardized, which means other programmers can easily discover and use an object's functionality.

❑ Objects can be written in any .NET-compliant language.

Thus, objects are a way to organize code so that programming is more efficient.

An object is a self-contained unit of functionality – almost like a miniature program that holds data (or code) to achieve specific tasks. Once an object is written, other code can access and manipulate the object in simple, well-defined ways. The model object is called a *class definition*. We can create as many copies of the object as we need from this model. We only need to create one class definition (model object) for each particular task.

For example, consider a publishing company – there are many different jobs defined within the company, such as Manager, Editor, Proof Reader, and Layout Person. Once we've established the basic jobs that an Editor does, (edit chapters, review chapters, send chapters to authors for rewrites), we probably don't need to know all the details of how they do those jobs. You could simply say "Jim, please edit Chapter 2" and leave the Editor to get on with it. You might also phrase it differently, though and ask, "Jim, is the chapter edited yet?" and expect the Editor to give you a true or false response about the current state of the chapter.

This is essentially how objects make our lives as programmers easier – in this instance, there's an `Editor` class, from which template we've built an `Editor` type object called `Jim`. We can instruct the object to `Edit`, `Review`, or `Return To Author`, and we can ask it about its state, that is, whether its `EditComplete` value is set to `True` or `False`. We can create multiple copies of the `Editor` object as needed. For example, if we had three editors on books we could create three copies of the `Editor` object and name them `Jim`, `Jane`, and `Joe`. Each could handle their own project.

We can create as many objects as we need, we don't need to know *how* the `Jim` object edits, we can use a standard way of asking the `Editor` object to do its work or report to us and the `Editor` object can be written in any language that is .NET-compliant.

As said earlier, objects can be written or bought. Some come with the .NET Framework, for example, Microsoft includes a group of objects called ADO.NET that can create a connection to a database and read values from tables. It would take many weeks for a programmer to write and troubleshoot similar code. Instead, we get it with ASP.NET and all we have to do is understand how to use it. As an exercise at the end of this chapter, we will be reading values from a database and writing them onto our ASP.NET Web pages.

The advantages of this type of programming are fairly obvious. First, we don't need to worry about how each object does its job, so we are free to focus on the big picture of our application. Second, we can rapidly create applications by building or buying objects and hooking them together in simple, well-defined ways. Once you understand how to use (and later, to write) objects, you will be able to produce more stable code in less time.

The .NET Base Classes

One feature of the .NET Framework that saves us from hideous amounts of tedious coding is the *base class library*. This contains an enormous amount of code written by Microsoft, that you can include in any of your programs. In order to take advantage of this code, you only have to know how to work with objects – there is no need to understand the inner workings of the code.

The base Framework classes cover a multitude of different functions. For instance, you'd expect to be able to display text, but what if you want to perform more specialized graphical operations such as drawing a circle or a rectangle? Or, add an animated image to an ASP.NET page? These functions are all provided in a number of base classes that are grouped together under a *namespace* called `System.Drawing`.

> **Namespaces are used by .NET to group together classes in functionally similar groups. Namespaces are not unique just to .NET but are found in many languages as well.**

In terms of our earlier business analogy, this is equivalent to a departmental grouping. For example, all the jobs directly involved with producing book content (Editor, Author Agent, and Project Manager) are grouped within the Editorial namespace. Likewise, jobs involving the layout and printing of the physical book (Cover Designer, Illustrator) would be classified within the Production namespace.

To be able to use the classes contained within a namespace, you need to *import* the namespace first. We can import these classes into our ASP.NET pages by simply adding a *directive* to the very top of the file (before any HTML and before the language tag). For example, if we want to make use of all the classes defined in the `System.Drawing` namespace, we just say:

```
<%@ Import Namespace=System.Drawing %>
```

This literally *directs* the Framework to apply a specific setting to the page as a whole; in this case, make the classes in `System.Drawing` available to code in our page.

> *There are whole varieties of .NET classes, from classes that look after generating graphics to classes that help to simplify data access. We'll see some examples that rely on our importing namespaces towards the end of the chapter. After you've run them, try removing them and seeing what error messages are produced!*

It is then possible to use the classes in `System.Drawing`, although you will need to reference this namespace in front of each class name to uniquely indicate which class it is you want to use. So why does .NET do this? Why can't you have access to all the classes you need, all of the time? The reason is to keep your application small. The more you include in an application, the more bloated it will become, and the more difficult it will be to understand, maintain, and use. So it makes sense to only include the bits you need to use. ASP.NET includes on every page the most commonly used classes by default. This concept of including classes has been a standard feature in many programming languages for a long time.

The Class Browser

You might be wondering how to get a list of these predefined .NET classes. One great tool that makes all of this more transparent is the .NET Framework *Class Browser*. This ASP.NET application lists the Framework classes defined on the IIS serving the page as shown in Figure 2-1. The class browser is available as part of the QuickStart tutorials that are provided along with the *.NET Framework SDK*. If you have these installed, you'll be able to run it locally from:

http://localhost/quickstart/aspplus/samples/classbrowser/vb/classbrowser.aspx

> *In case of a "Type not found" Compiler Error Message, execute the setup procedure for QuickStarts from the* starthere.htm *(in the SDK's "v1.1" dir). This automatically installs the required classes.*

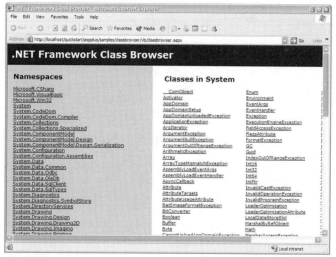

Figure 2-1

If you've only installed the *.NET Framework Redistributable,* then you won't have the class browser installed. It is possible, however, to access the class browser online at:

http://www.gotdotnet.com/quickstart/aspplus/samples/classbrowser/vb/classbrowser.aspx

This will list the `System` classes available on that site's Web server (the standard set of base classes under the `System` namespace). You won't be able to browse any additional namespaces, such as custom namespaces or add-ins that you've installed on your server, or configure the browser application. Nevertheless, it should cover most of your needs. It really is a very handy tool for students, beginning programmers, and experienced developers alike. You'll find the class browser useful in later chapters, as much of the book will be concerned with exploring .NET's various classes.

> *A form of the class browser is built into Web Matrix, as covered in Appendix B.*

So, we have our three sections of .NET Framework: MSIL, the CLR, and the .NET Language Base classes. But where and how does ASP.NET fit into this model?

How ASP.NET Works

For most purposes, simply think of ASP.NET pages as normal HTML pages that have sections marked up for special consideration. When .NET is installed, the local IIS Web server is automatically configured to look out for files with the extension ASPX and to use the ASP.NET module (a file called aspnet_isapi.dll) to handle them.

Technically speaking, this module parses the contents of the ASPX file – it breaks them down into separate commands in order to establish the overall structure of our code. Having done this, it arranges the commands within a predefined class definition – not necessarily together and not necessarily in the order in which we wrote them. That class is then used to define a special ASP.NET Page object. One of the tasks this object performs is to generate a stream of HTML that can be sent back to IIS, and from there, back to the client. Simply put, when a user asks the IIS server to provide a page, the IIS server builds the page based on the text, HTML, and (most importantly to us) code on that page.

> *We'll take a more detailed look at various aspects of this process as we progress through the book – in particular, Chapter 7 will explore the* Page *object, and discuss some of the things it can do for us.*

For now though, we're more concerned with the immediate business of getting a page up and running. The first step is to learn to create pages that identify themselves to the Web server as ASP.NET pages.

Saving Your ASP.NET Files with an ASPX Suffix

In the last chapter, we defined an ASPX .NET page simply by saving some appropriate code in a file with a .aspx extension. This extension identifies the page as one to be processed by the ASP.NET module. Without it, IIS will just send the page to the user without actually executing the code.

Although it's possible to use <script> tags in an .htm file, nothing you put between them would be interpreted as ASP.NET code. Instead, it will be sent to the browser for client-side execution, which is unlikely to work because the browser will only be expecting HTML and client-side script.

Students and beginners frequently have a problem with the extension when using Notepad. They get .txt added to the extension so it looks like MyFile.aspx.txt. You can avoid this by setting the file type as All Files in the save dialog box of Notepad. You can also change the file extension in Windows explorer after saving the file. This is not a problem when using Web Matrix because it is aware of proper extensions.

Inserting ASP.NET Code into Our Web Pages

If we place any kind of server-side code (not just ASP.NET code) within our Web page source files, we need to label it so that the server can identify it as server-side code and arrange for it to be handled correctly. There are three ways of placing ASP.NET code in your HTML:

❏   inline code blocks

❏   script tags

❏   server controls

Inline code blocks (the `<% %>` delimiters) will seem familiar to the users of classic ASP. However, these are not the preferred technique in ASP.NET. The latter two techniques offer more robust performance and code that is easier to maintain.

The <script> Tags

The best way to identify ASP.NET code within the HTML and text of your pages is by using `<script>` tags, with the `runat` attribute set to `server`. The default when using the `<script>` tag is for the script to be executed on the browser (client-side), so if you're writing a server-side script, remember to specify `runat = "server"` with the double quotes.

As we discussed, ASP.NET itself is not a language, but a technology for creating dynamic pages. The technology allows us to use various programming languages within our pages. The default language for coding in ASP.NET is VB .NET. However, to be explicit, it is best to include a `Page` directive at the top of the page as follows:

```
<%@ Page language="VB" %>
```

To indicate a section of code, we can then do the following (note the double quotes around `VB`):

```
<script language="VB" runat="server">
... Visual Basic.NET statements go here ...
</script>
```

Since the `<%@ Page language>` tag already specified VB .NET as our language of choice, the `language` attribute in the above example isn't essential, and can be omitted. However, it serves to clarify which language we're using, which makes it easier to maintain the code. The sub can go anywhere in the ASPX page, but in this book we put code at the top of the page. The lines of code can go anywhere in the ASPX page a long as they are within `<script>` tags; in this book we put code at the top of the page because that is how it is done by ASP.NET Web Matrix.

To define a page in a different language, C# for example, you can do the following:

```
<%@ Page language="C#" %>
<script language="C#" runat="server">
... C# declarations go here ...
</script>
```

In both these snippets, all code enclosed within the `<script>` element must be in the language specified. While you can have an application (multiple pages) with parts coded in more than one language, it isn't physically possible to mix languages in one page.

Although we put code into a page, it isn't necessarily executed. Each block of code goes within a *declaration*, generally called a *Sub Procedure*. A Sub is executed when some other code triggers it. It may be triggered once, many times or not at all. We'll cover that idea in detail over the next few chapters.

A logical question arises: "What if we want some sort of trigger to run the code automatically as soon as a page is built for the first time?" In other words, what if we want some code to run regardless of what events may occur? When the page is created, the ASP.NET module will execute any code that is written within one specific sub named `Page_Load()`, as demonstrated in the following structure:

```
<script language="VB" runat="server">
  sub Page_Load(source As Object, e As EventArgs)
... Location for Visual Basic.NET code to be run when the page is started
  end sub
</script>
```

We won't go into detail explaining this format, suffice to say that when the page is loaded, the declarative block that we've labeled sub Page_Load() is triggered automatically. Any code we want to run when the page starts up should be located here.

Try It Out Inserting Server-Side (ASP.NET) Code

In this example, we're only concerned with how we insert code, not with how the ASP.NET code works, so the code is trivial. This example demonstrates how Web pages are affected by the placement of ASP.NET code.

1. Let's start with a test of just HTML – no code for ASP to execute. Open Web Matrix and create a new ASPX page named messageHTML.aspx in your test directory. If you've followed the steps from *Chapter 1*, this will be C:\BegASPNET11\Ch02\. Go to All view, remove all existing code, and type in the following code:

```
<html>
<head>
    <title>Inserting ASP.NET code Example</title></head>
<body>
    Line1: First HTML Line<br />
    Line2: Second HTML Line<br />
    Line3: Third HTML Line<br />
</body>
</html>
```

2. Open your browser, and call up http://localhost/BegASPNET11/Ch02/messageHTML.aspx as shown in Figure 2-2:

Figure 2-2

3. Now go back to Web Matrix and place the following code at the top of the page in All view:

```
<script language="VB" runat="server">
Sub Page_Load()
  Response.Write ("First ASP.NET Line<br />")
  Response.Write ("Second ASP.NET Line<br />")
  Response.Write ("Third ASP.NET Line<br />")
End Sub
</script>
<html>
```

```
  <head>
    <title>Inserting ASP.NET code Example</TITLE>
  </head>
  <body>
    Line1: First HTML Line<br />
    Line2: Second HTML Line<br />
    Line3: Third HTML Line<br />
  </body>
</html>
```

The `<script language="VB" runat="server">` *line is automatically generated by Web Matrix for every ASPX page, so we never have to put it in manually. Even if you delete it, it will automatically reappear! However, if you are using a text editor for you pages, you need to insert this line at the top of all your ASPX pages.*

4. View this example in your browser by typing in the URL: http://localhost/BegASPNET11/Ch02/messageASPXtop.aspx. You should get a result similar to that shown in Figure 2-3. However, this time we can see the results from the ASP.NET code we just added above the HTML:

Figure 2-3

5. Return to your editor and save as `messageASPXbottom.aspx`. Now copy the code between the `<script>` tags (including the `<script>` and `</script>` tags), and paste it at the end of the body section as follows:

```
<html>
  <head>
    <title>Inserting ASP.NET code Example</title>
  </head>
  <body>
    Line1: First HTML Line<br />
    Line2: Second HTML Line<br />
    Line3: Third HTML Line<br />
<script language="VB" runat="server">
Sub Page_Load()
 Response.Write ("First ASP.NET Line<br />")
 Response.Write ("Second ASP.NET Line<br />")
 Response.Write ("Third ASP.NET Line<br />")
End Sub
</script>
  </body>
</html>
```

6. Call up `messageASPXbottom.aspx` in your browser. Notice that the browser still displays the ASP.NET code first, as shown in Figure 2-4:

Figure 2-4

How It Works

The first thing to note is that although this is ASP.NET code, we're not actually creating a dynamic Web page that can display different pages to different users. All we're doing is demonstrating the order in which ASP.NET code and HTML are executed. The next point is that all three examples use the `.aspx` suffix despite the fact the first page, `messageHTML.aspx`, only contained HTML code. So, as far as the Web server is concerned, all three pages are ASP.NET pages and will be checked for script to be executed. This demonstrates that HTML is treated in the same way in both pure HTML pages and ASP.NET pages.

The code in the first page, `messageHTML.aspx`, just displays some HTML lines and some plain text. When the code is parsed in your browser, the lines are displayed in order, as you would expect.

```
<html>
  <head>
    <title>Inserting ASP.NET code Example</TITLE>
  </head>
  <body>
    Line1: First HTML Line<br />
    Line2: Second HTML Line<br />
    Line3: Third HTML Line<br />
  </body>
</html>
```

In the second Web page, `messageASPXtop.aspx`, we have a combination of some pure HTML, some plain text, and a little server-side script. By using `runat="server"`, we specified that the following script should be processed on the server, before the page is sent to the browser:

```
<script language="VB" runat="server">
Sub Page_Load()
 Response.Write ("First ASP.NET Line<br/>")
 Response.Write ("Second ASP.NET Line<br/>")
 Response.Write ("Third ASP.NET Line<br/>")
End Sub
</script>
```

The ASP.NET code is placed within a subroutine called `Page_Load()`. Whenever ASP.NET loads up a page, it executes any code contained within the `Page_Load()` subroutine first. So if you place code that writes to the page inside this subroutine, that text will always precede any text from the HTML part of the file even if you had put the code after the HTML lines (as in `messageASPXBottom.aspx`. The ASP.NET code uses a `Response.Write` statement to display three ASP.NET lines. We'll talk more about `Response.Write` in *Chapter 3*.

Take a moment here to understand another important ASP.NET concept. Open `messageHTML.aspx` in your browser and look at the source (in Internet Explorer, go to View | Source). You will see a page that starts with the following line:

```
First ASP.NET Line<br />Second ASP.NET Line<br />Third ASP.NET Line<br />
<html>
...
```

The ASP.NET module on the server interprets the code `Response.Write` and performs that writing to the page on the server. IIS only sends plain HTML to the browser. Thus, no special plug-ins or interpreters are needed on the browser. Since no browser modifications are needed, any browser can display the results of ASP.NET code.

Finally, we moved the ASP.NET code to follow the HTML lines. The browser still displays the ASP.NET code first. The Web server first scans the file to see if there is a `<script runat="server">` tag. In case some script exists, ASP.NET arranges for the `<script>` tag to be processed first. Because the ASP.NET code is in the `Page_Load()` subroutine, which always runs as soon as the page is loaded (created), the ASP.NET output always appears first, even if the `<script>` tag is not at the top of the code page. In other words, the server takes no notice of the position of the `<script>` tag relative to other elements of the page.

There's an important lesson to be learned here – if you place ASP.NET code in the `Page_Load()` subroutine within the `<script>` tag, it will always be processed before the HTML code. Later we will learn how to execute other Sub procedures.

Inline Code Blocks (the <% %> Delimiters)

We now know how to output text to a browser using ASP.NET. Unfortunately, anything we output from ASP.NET in the `Page_Load()` sub procedure will always write to the page before the rest of the HTML. This is pretty awkward if we want to insert ASP.NET output anywhere lower on the page. We will now look at a couple of ways we can interweave ASP.NET output with HTML.

It's possible to incorporate code into our pages much more directly. If we specify a *render code block* (also known as an *inline code block*), any code it contains is executed as part of the page rendering process. This is the process by which we get our `Page` object to send back HTML for the browser to display. If you try coding the following block, save it as `messageASPXmiddle.aspx`. We can write render code blocks as follows:

```
<html>
<head>
</head>
<body>
<%
Response.Write ("Hello!<br>")
%>
<html>
  <body>
    Line1: First HTML Line<br />
    <% Response.Write ("First ASP.NET Line<br />") %>
    Line2: Second HTML Line<br />
    <% Response.Write ("Second ASP.NET Line<br />") %>
    Line3: Third HTML Line<br />
    <% Response.Write ("Third ASP.NET Line<br />") %>
  </body>
</html>
<%
Response.Write ("Goodbye!")
%>
</body>
</html>
```

This gives the result shown in Figure 2-5:

Figure 2-5

We can thus write code that executes wherever you put it, whether it's inside the HTML <head> tags, inside the <body> tag, or even at the end of the page. Also note in the following line that that we are able to write both text like "Hello!" and HTML tags like <br> in an ASP.NET Write:

```
Response.Write ("Hello!<br>")
```

Server Controls

Although using the <% %> inline code delimiters saves on keystrokes, it ultimately produces rather intractable code. This was one of the problems of classic ASP; the pages became a jumble of text, HTML tags, and scripting statements, and it was very difficult to follow the objectives and troubleshoot. Therefore, you are encouraged to use alternatives wherever possible, and *Chapter 3* looks at one very powerful way of doing this, using *server controls*.

Separating the ASP.NET code from the HTML and text not only makes the code easier to read, but also much easier to strip out either part and reuse it in another page. As we'll see later on in the book, we can separate code and HTML blocks even further, into separate files. For now, we'll keep them in one file for clarity. We recommend (and will actively practice throughout the book) placing the ASP.NET code in a declarative code block near the top of the file, just before the line of first `<html>`, as follows (this is done automatically when you use the Web Matrix editor):

```
<script language="VB" runat="server">
... ASP.NET code here ...
</script>
<html>
... HTML code here ...
</html>
```

Try It Out Interweaving ASP.NET Output with HTML

You may still be wondering: "how do we intersperse static content with dynamic content if the code and the HTML are separated like this?" Let's take a quick look at how to get around this problem; you'll soon realize that this doesn't restrict us nearly as much as you might think.

1. Enter the following code into a new page and save it as `messageServerControl.aspx`:

```
<script language="VB" runat="server">
Sub Page_Load()
  Message.Text="The ASP.NET line"
End Sub
</script>
<html>
<head>
<title>Inserting ASP.NET code Example</title>
</head>
<body>
First HTML Line<br/>
<asp:label id="Message" runat="server"/> <br />
Second HTML Line<br/>
    <form runat="server">
        <!-- Insert content here -->
    </form>
</body>
</html>
```

2. Point your browser to `messageServerControl.aspx` to see Figure 2-6:

Figure 2-6

How It Works

You might have noticed that we now completely avoid the use of <% . . . %> delimiters to create *inline code blocks*. First, we have a difference in the HTML code. Notice that we have added a special <asp:label> tag, which creates an HTML tag with the name message:

```
<html>
<head>
<title>Inserting ASP.NET code Example</title>
</head>
<body>
First HTML Line<br/>
<asp:label id="Message" runat="server"/> <br />
Second HTML Line<br/>
</body>
</html>
```

This named object is now available for manipulation by our ASP.NET code. Instead of having the Response.Write statements that send text to the browser as we did in the previous example, we have code that sets a property (or attribute) of the label, namely the string of text that the label will display:

```
<script language="VB" runat="server">
Sub Page_Load()
   Message.Text="The ASP.NET line"
End Sub
</script>
```

First, the HTML (below) has a special tag known as a *server control* created by the <asp:label...>. That control has a runat="server" attribute, which instructs that the code be executed by the ASP.NET module in IIS (not to execute on the browser):

```
<asp:label id="Message" runat="server"/> <br />
```

Second, we have a Sub Procedure named Page_Load() that changes the text of the label from nothing to "The ASP.NET line." This leaves us with much cleaner code that is easier to write and easier to maintain.

ASP.NET in Action

This has been a very theoretical chapter until now. Let's now see a couple of examples. Since we've still not looked at much ASP.NET code, the commands in these examples won't make a lot of sense at this stage. However, you will get an overview of the basic tasks that our code is performing, and later in the book you can build up a more detailed picture of the syntax as your understanding grows. We'll do two exercises, of which both read data and display the information on your ASP.NET page. The first reads from an Access .mdb, and the second from an XML file.

Binding to a Database

For most people, the key reason for using ASP.NET is the ability to connect a Web page to a database, and then, read and update data from the browser. ASP.NET does this task more easily than classic ASP. In classic ASP, *binding* a page to data took many lines of code. ASP.NET provides a set of server controls that significantly cuts the amount and complexity of coding.

Try It Out Binding to a Database

1. In this exercise we'll use one of the example databases provided with the .NET Framework, the grocertogo database (MS Access format), to build a quick Web page that allows us to browse the contents of the Products table. There's a copy of grocertogo in the code download from www.wrox.com, but you'll have to alter the path name to point to where you've saved it on your system. If you don't have the grocertogo database, modify the lines beginning with "strConnect += "Data Source=" to point to any database you have on your system.

2. Find or get the database. Find it with a search of your drives for GrocerToGo.mdb. Alternatively, you can download it from www.wrox.com. If you want to become familiar with the database, you can open it in Access, but that is not necessary for this exercise. Copy the .mdb into the C:\BegASPNET11 folder. As we will use it for more then one chapter, do not store it in the Ch02 subfolder.

3. Open Web Matrix, create datacontrolMDB.aspx, and type in the following:

```
<%@ Import Namespace="System.Data" %>
<%@ Import Namespace="System.Data.OleDb" %>
<script language="vb" runat="server" debug="true">
Sub Page_Load(Sender As Object, E as EventArgs)
   Dim objConnection As OleDbConnection
   Dim objCommand As OleDbDataAdapter
   Dim strConnect As String
   Dim strCommand As String
   Dim DataSet1 As New DataSet
   strConnect =  "Provider=Microsoft.Jet.OLEDB.4.0;"
   strConnect += "Data Source=C:\BegASPNET11\grocertogo.mdb;"
   strConnect += "Persist Security Info=False"
   strCommand = "SELECT ProductName, UnitPrice FROM Products"
   objConnection = New OleDbConnection(strConnect)
   objCommand = New OleDbDataAdapter(strCommand, objConnection)
   objCommand.Fill(DataSet1, "products")
   DataGrid1.DataSource=DataSet1.Tables("Products").DefaultView
   DataGrid1.DataBind()
End Sub
</script>
<html>
<head>
<title>Data Grid Control example</title>
</head>
<body>
<asp:DataGrid id="DataGrid1" runat="server"  />
</body>
</html>
```

4. Open `datacontrolMDB.aspx` in your browser as shown in Figure 2-7:

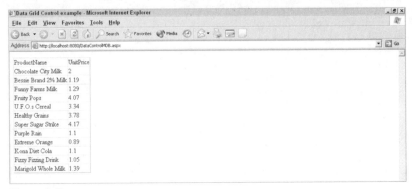

Figure 2-7

How It Works

The ASP.NET code looks quite daunting, but is easily understandable when we examine the different sections. First, look at the `<body>` tag:

```
<body>
<asp:DataGrid id="DataGrid1" runat="server"  />
</body>
```

We have a tag here that creates a DataGrid named `DataGrid1` in the page. This will be an object that we can manipulate in our code, but when the page is requested by a user and built by the ASP.NET module in IIS, the DataGrid object will create in its place the `<table>`, `<th>`, `<tr>`, and `<td>` HTML tags so that a table appears in the browser.

Now let's go back up in the code and examine the `Page_Load` procedure. We're not going to enter into a detailed discussion about all of these lines (see that in *Chapters 8* and *9*). However, we can break it into several parts. We start by importing the namespaces (collections of objects) that we will need for working with the data. Second, we establish our language:

```
<%@ Import Namespace="System.Data" %>
<%@ Import Namespace="System.Data.OleDb" %>
<script language="vb" runat="server" debug="true">
```

Then we enter our sub procedure and create some variables to hold information we will need:

```
Sub Page_Load(Sender As Object, E as EventArgs)
   Dim objConnection As OleDbConnection
   Dim objCommand As OleDbDataAdapter
   Dim strConnect As String
   Dim strCommand As String
  Dim DataSet1 As New DataSet
```

Next, we create a string of text in a variable called `strConnect`, which will inform the connection what kind of database we are using (the Microsoft Jet provider in the case of Access), where to find the file, and how to handle one of the security settings:

```
strConnect =  "Provider=Microsoft.Jet.OLEDB.4.0;"
strConnect += "Data Source=C:\BegASPNET11\grocertogo.mdb;"
strConnect += "Persist Security Info=False"
```

Next, ASP.NET needs a description of exactly what data we want from the database. This is written as a SQL statement. You don't need to know SQL at this point because the general syntax is obvious. We want to read (SELECT) values from two fields (`ProductName` and `UnitPrice`) located in the `Products` table:

```
strCommand = "SELECT ProductName, UnitPrice FROM Products"
```

The next three lines take the information above and use it to create two objects, (`Connection` and `Command`) and fill our `DataSet1` object with data read from `GrocerToGo`:

```
objConnection = New OleDbConnection(strConnect)
objCommand = New OleDbDataAdapter(strCommand, objConnection)
objCommand.Fill(DataSet1, "products")
```

Lastly, we use two lines to instruct the DataGrid (from the HTML section) to use `DataSet1` as the source of its values as follows:

```
DataGrid1.DataSource=DataSet1.Tables("Products").DefaultView
DataGrid1.DataBind()
End Sub
```

As always, with ASP.NET, this code is interpreted on the server by the ASP.NET module of IIS to create a page of pure HTML that is sent to the browser. If you open `datacontrol.aspx` in your browser and then view the source, you will see only standard HTML table tags but none of the ASP.NET code.

Binding to a Simple XML File

ASP.NET is not limited to connecting with relational databases. We'll now look at how we can use the data controls to connect to a short XML document. This book does not go into the theory of XML. In case you are not familiar with the standard, XML is a format to holding data, normally in a text file. The file is self-describing in that each piece of data has a label that identifies its classification in the scheme of records and fields. XML is becoming the standard for data exchange. To learn more about XML, refer to *Beginning XML 2nd Edition (ISBN 0-7645-4394-6) by Wrox Press*.

Let's create a short XML document and then an ASPX page that demonstrates the technique to create a DataGrid control and bind it to the contents of an XML document. Overall, the procedure is even easier than connecting to a database.

Try It Out Binding to a Simple XML Document

1. Open up your Web page editor; create a document named `artists.xml` in your
`C:\BegASPNET11\Ch02` folder and type in the following XML document. Alternatively, you can
download the file from www.wrox.com:

```xml
<?xml version="1.0" encoding="utf-8" ?>
<artists>
  <artist>
    <name>Vincent Van Gogh</name>
    <nationality>Dutch</nationality>
    <movement>Post Impressionism </movement>
    <birthdate>30th March 1853</birthdate>
  </artist>
  <artist>
    <name>Paul Klee </name>
    <nationality>Swiss </nationality>
    <movement>Abstract Expressionism </movement>
    <birthdate>18th December 1879</birthdate>
  </artist>
  <artist>
    <name>Max Ernst </name>
    <nationality>German </nationality>
    <movement>Surrealism </movement>
    <birthdate>2nd April 1891</birthdate>
  </artist>
</artists>
```

2. Keeping your Web page editor open, create a second file named `datacontrolXML.aspx`
containing the following lines:

```vb
<%@ Page language="VB" runat="server" %>
<%@ Import namespace="System.Data" %>
<%@ Import namespace="System.XML" %>
<script language="vb" runat="server">
  Sub Page_Load()
    Dim xmlFilename As String
    xmlFilename= "C:\BegASPNET11\ch02\artists.xml"
    Dim newDataSet As New DataSet
    newDataSet.ReadXML(xmlFilename)
    DataGrid1.DataSource = newDataSet
    DataGrid1.DataBind()
  End Sub
</script>
<html>
  <head>
    <title>Data Grid Control example</title>
  </head>
  <body>
    <asp:DataGrid id="DataGrid1" runat="server"  />
  </body>
</html>
```

3. View `datacontrolXML.aspx` in your browser; the result should look like Figure 2-8:

Figure 2-8

How It Works

Our XML file is pretty much like a database table. We've kept it simple, so that you can see what is happening. The first line notifies users that the file is XML. An overall pair of tags, `<artists>`, encapsulates all of the data:

```
<?xml version="1.0" encoding="utf-8" ?>
<artists>
...
</artists>
```

There are three artists. Each artist's individual entry is held with a single set of item tags structured as follows:

```
<artist>
  <name>Vincent Van Gogh</name>
  <nationality>Dutch</nationality>
  <movement>Post Impressionism </movement>
  <birthdate>30th March 1853</birthdate>
</artist>
```

Within each artist, we can see four elements (which are like fields or columns in other data systems), one each for `name`, `nationality`, `movement`, and `birthdate`. Notice that each value of data is inside a pair of tags and that the same set of tag names is used within each artist. Even without knowledge of XML, it is easy to see how the file is organized.

Now let's look at the `datacontrolXML.aspx` ASP.NET page. At the top of the page, we must establish the language and import the namespaces that hold objects we will need to work with XML data:

```
<%@ Page language="VB" runat="server" %>
<%@ Import namespace="System.Data" %>
<%@ Import namespace="System.XML" %>
```

Next, jump down to the `<body>`, where we use the `DataGrid` control to format and display the information as an HTML table. Again, the code is very neat and simple. It is crucial to include the attribute `runat="server"` in order for ASP.NET to work. Furthermore, every control must have a name (ID); in this case `DataGrid1`.

```
<body>
  <asp:DataGrid id="DataGrid1" runat="server"  />
</body>
```

Last, we will examine the ASP.NET code. Because it is in the `Page_Load()` Sub Procedure, it is automatically executed when the page is created. The first few lines record the name of the file into a variable:

```vb
<script language="vb" runat="server">
  Sub Page_Load()
    Dim xmlFilename As String
    xmlFilename= "C:\BegASPNET11\ch02\artists.xml"
```

Then we make a DataSet and read into it the contents of the XML file:

```vb
    Dim newDataSet As New DataSet
    newDataSet.ReadXML(xmlFilename)
```

Last, we identify that DataSet as the source of information for the DataGrid:

```vb
    DataGrid1.DataSource = newDataSet
    DataGrid1.DataBind()
  End Sub
</script>
```

As you can see, reading from an XML file is even simpler than the code we used for connecting to a database. However, at this point do not be concerned about the details of each line of code. We will discuss the exact meaning of each statement in *Chapters 8* and *9*.

Summary

This chapter has been quite theoretical, but balanced with some simple applications, ranging from a simple display of text up to two types of data connections. You should now understand several basic points about .NET and ASP.NET.

The .NET Framework is a guideline and standard for the tools that Microsoft produces for programmers. It is flexible across languages, suitable for both desktop and Webbased applications.

.NET is based on objects, a programming convention which puts related code together in a structure that represents an entity in the real world. The model from which objects are copied is called the class and a group of related classes is called a namespace.

ASP.NET is a module that adds on to the Microsoft Internet Information Server (IIS). ASP.NET checks pages for code and executes that code to create an HTML page. The resulting pages are pure HTML and thus require no addins for the browser hence can be viewed on any browser.

After writing an ASP page, it is partially compiled to MSIL (Microsoft Intermediate Language) and stored on the server. When requested, the page is run through the CLR (Common Language Runtime) for a final compilation. This two-stage compilation gives both performance advantages and optimization for different servers.

When we write an ASP.NET page we must include several key parts such as:

- ❑ The `.aspx` filename extension.

- ❑ A directive to import namespaces and a directive designating the language.

- ❑ HTML and text.

- ❑ ASP.NET controls such as `<asp:label>` which are named with an ID and `runat="server"`.

- ❑ The scripts.

Although scripts can be designated in line by `<% %>`, it is better to designate them by `<script>` tags. Within the script, we create Sub Procedures. The one we have studied so far is named `Page_Load`; it automatically executes when a page is requested. Any `Write` commands from `Page_Load` will appear on the page above HTML and text.

Once created and named, an object can be manipulated. For example, we used script to change the text that was displayed by an `<asp:label>`. We also observed how easy it is to create and manipulate objects that Microsoft provides for working with data such as the connection, command, and DataGrid objects. However, before exposing objects to this type of manipulation, we must designate both the script and the control as `runat="server"`.

We can now move on to discuss in detail the various components of the pages we tested. We will start with how to hold and display information (*Chapter 3*), then how to control which lines of code are executed (*Chapters 4 to 6*).

Exercises

1. Describe what the .Net Framework provides for programmers.

2. Which encompasses more code, a Class or a Namespace?

3. The ASP.NET module of code adds on to which part of Windows?

4. What special modifications to the browser are required on the client-side in order to view an ASP.NET page?

5. Why does an ASP.NET page get compiled twice?

6. Why does the first display of an ASP.NET page take several seconds but subsequent views appear in only milliseconds?

7. What two attributes should always be included in all ASP.NET Web controls?

Server Controls and Variables

One of the most common tasks for any Web developer is collecting and storing of information from the user. It could simply be a name and e-mail address, but whatever the information you want to gather, the processing cannot be performed within the confines of HTML on the browser alone. You need to send the information to the Web server for processing or storage.

Information is transmitted via Web pages by a *form*. HTML forms contain controls such as textboxes, checkboxes, and dropdown lists, all of which aid the passage of information from the user to the server. Moreover, ASP.NET adds its own extra controls for dealing with forms. With these, ASP.NET introduces some new concepts to the control of forms, such as remembering what text you've typed into a textbox, or what selection you made in a list box between page refreshes, which must be carried out on the server.

During the manipulation of user data, variables are used to persist data from one command to another. VB .NET is a *strongly typed* language, which means each variable has a data type associated with it, such as String, Integer, or Date. This chapter will look at each of the main data types available in VB .NET and why you must assign each variable a particular data type and what types of errors you might encounter if you don't.

We will cover:

- ❑ Forms
- ❑ Client-server model of the Web
- ❑ ASP.NET server controls (or Web controls)
- ❑ Theory and practice of variables
- ❑ Data types
- ❑ Arrays and collections

Forms

The main focus of the chapter is forms and, implicitly, the transfer of data from the browser to the server. Before delving into the inner workings of the form, let's see a few situations in which forms would be required in the business world. If you take a look at a few commercial Web sites, you'll find that most forms are for the same kinds of situations. For example:

❑ To take information from a user for the purpose of registration, the purchase of a product, or joining an e-mail list, forum, or a newsgroup

❑ To take note of a user's preferences so that we can customize other pages in the site to include just the relevant information

❑ To act as frontend for a forum or newsgroup, where a user can enter and edit their text online

❑ To capture business transactions and display reports and related information in e-commerce applications

This chapter will first discuss how to use ASP.NET to create powerful forms with very little programming, and then the holding of data in variables. Let's start with a quick overview of forms, and the effects that ASP.NET has on them.

Web Pages, HTML Forms, and Web Forms

With the introduction of any new technology comes new terminology and jargon. ASP.NET is no different in this respect. With ASP.NET, even the terms you use to describe a simple Web page have been updated to describe more accurately the processes that are going on within them. To avoid confusion, let's start by defining a few familiar concepts and their ASP.NET equivalents.

A *Web page* is a bundle of ASCII characters including HTML code and text to be marked up and beginning and ending with <html> and </html> tags. The Web page is placed on a machine known as a *Web server*, and the Web server sends that page to any requestors (users). HTML pages are typically saved with the suffix .html or .htm.

An *HTML form* is a Web page that contains one or more *form controls* (grouped together inside an HTML <form> element) that allow the user to enter information on the Web page and send that information back to the Web server. Commonly used form controls include buttons, textboxes, checkboxes, and dropdown lists. The user fills in details and generally presses a submit button to send data back to the Web server.

Although you don't need anything more than HTML to send form data to the server, the server needs some sort of extra technology (in this case, ASP.NET) to actually work with the information it receives.

ASP.NET introduces a new concept, the *Web form*. Behind the scenes, a Web form is much easier and faster to program than HTML forms. Technically, the term Web form refers to the grouping of two distinct blocks of code:

❑ **HTML template** containing page layout information and ASP.NET server controls. This is responsible for the presentation of the Web form on the browser.

❑ **ASP.NET code** that holds a script containing the Web form's processing logic. This is responsible for generating dynamic content to be displayed within the Web form. This content is typically exposed via server controls defined in the HTML presentation block.

When you start using ASP.NET to create Web forms, you can use a new breed of ASP.NET server controls within your HTML. Not only do they duplicate the functionality of many HTML elements (including the form controls), but also they provide additional features. A server control has the appearance of an HTML-like element, but actually it only marks a point in the page at which the server needs to generate a corresponding true HTML element. We will be discussing in depth how to use ASP.NET server controls.

> **Although a Web form may also be an HTML form (that is, there's nothing to stop you using <form> elements inside an ASPX), remember that these two entities are quite distinct. An HTML form can only use standard HTML tags while a Web form can use the more powerful ASP.NET server controls.**

It is possible for Web forms to use normal HTML form controls, but ASP.NET also comes with its own set of Web form controls that are run on the server. We will be using these in preference most of the time, because they offer other advantages such as being able to remember the state of the different controls, such as what text has been typed into a textbox. These ASP.NET controls are run within specially modified HTML `<form runat="server">` tags, and are *ASP.NET forms*.

Let's review the four terms just introduced:

❑ *Web page* is any page that contains HTML (they can also contain script or other languages not covered by this book, but in this book a web page will refer to pages containing only HTML).

❑ *HTML form* is an HTML element that contains HTML form controls.

❑ *Web form* is any page that combines ASP.NET code with an HTML template.

❑ *ASP.NET form* is a form that contains ASP.NET server controls inside a web form.

Let's start by considering the whole process of data transmission on the Web to understand the role of forms in this context.

Response and Request in Non-ASP.NET Pages

Chapter 1 discussed the installation of ASP.NET and the concept of a Web server, which makes your Web pages available to users. Another job of the Web server is to provide an area (typically in a directory or folder structure) in which to organize and store your web pages or whole Web site.

When a user views a Web page, they will automatically be making contact with a Web server. The process of submitting the URL is called making a *request* to the server. The server receives the URL and locates the corresponding page on the disk drive. In the case of a simple page (HTML and text only), the Web server sends the page back to the user in a *response*. The browser then takes the code it has received from the Web server and compiles a viewable page from it. The browser is referred to as a *client* in this interaction, and the whole interaction as a *client erver relationship*. If the Web server cannot find the requested page, it issues a response that features an appropriate error message, and dispatches the error to the browser.

The term client server describes the workings of the Web by outlining the distribution of tasks. The server (the web server) stores pages, interprets scripts, and distributes data (that is compiled into Web pages), and the client (browser) accesses the server to get at the data.

The Internet is a network of interconnected nodes. It is designed to carry *information* from one place to another. When the user tells the browser to fetch a web page, a message is sent from the browser to the Web server. This message is sent using HTTP. The World Wide Web uses HTTP for transfer of information from one machine to another. When you see a URL prefixed with http://, you know that the Internet protocol being used is HTTP. It is the default protocol used by Web browsers. The process is illustrated in Figure 3-1:

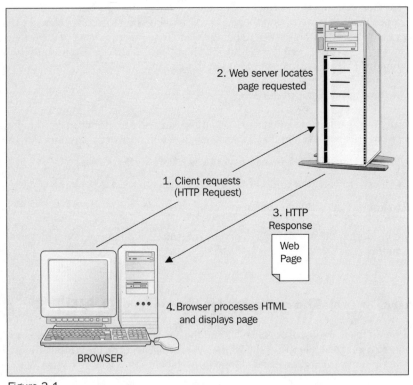

Figure 3-1

1. The client browser requests a Web page by typing a URL into the browser and clicking GO.

2. The Web server hosting that URL locates on its hard drive the HTML page that was requested. The page is read into a stream of characters.

3. The server sends the stream to the browser.

4. The browser interprets (converts) the HTML code and text into a displayed web page.

HTTP is known as a *stateless* protocol. This is because it doesn't know whether the request that has been made is part of an ongoing correspondence or just a single message; just the same way your postman won't know whether a letter is the first from your friend or fifteenth. HTTP is stateless because it was only intended for the simple task of retrieving pages for display.

The Internet would be very slow and might even collapse if permanent connections (states) needed to be maintained between browsers and servers, as people moved from one page to another. Statelessness makes the Internet faster, but the downside is that HTTP by itself can't distinguish between different users. A Web server based on pure HTML will treat all requests with the same status, that of *unknown user*. Obviously the modern needs of the Internet require that you can identify users and track their moves through the various pages needed for accomplishing a task on a Web site. As seen later in the book, ASP.NET creates a state that can be used by programmers.

Where ASP.NET Fits in with the .NET Framework

ASP.NET adds a step. After the server receives the request it reads the page from the hard drive. But rather then containing just text and HTML tags, an ASP.NET page also contains script that is interpreted to build features into the page. The process is illustrated in Figure 3-2 and explained below:

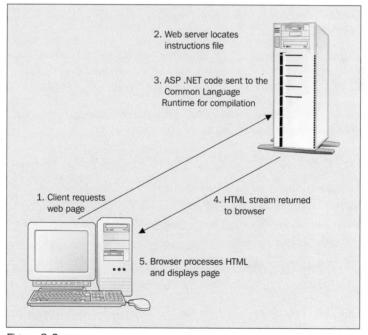

2. Web server locates instructions file

3. ASP .NET code sent to the Common Language Runtime for compilation

1. Client requests web page

4. HTML stream returned to browser

5. Browser processes HTML and displays page

Figure 3-2

1. Client requests a Web page by typing an URL into the browser and clicking GO.

2. Web server locates on its hard drive the page that was requested.

3. If the name of the Web page has an `.aspx` extension, the server processes the page – it runs the script code. If the ASP.NET code hasn't been compiled before, it is compiled now. The code is executed to create a pure HTML stream.

4. The HTML stream is returned to the browser.

5. The browser interprets (converts) the HTML code and text into a displayed Web page.

The addition of ASP.NET means the HTML is created *dynamically*. This has many advantages. You can return information to the user on the basis of their responses in a form, or you can customize Web pages for a particular browser; you can even personalize information for each user. All of this is possible because the code you write is converted into an HTML page when it is requested.

Now that you have a basic understanding of how the ASP.NET compares to plain HTML pages, it's time to start studying forms. Mastery of forms allows us to obtain information from the users. The subsequent chapters will discuss manipulation of this information and saving it to databases.

The <form> Tag in ASP.NET

ASP.NET has a set of form controls that are similar to HTML form controls. The main difference is that ASP.NET controls are actually constructed dynamically on the server at the time of request, and then sent out. The ASP.NET version requires only a few characters of coding, as follows:

```
<form ID="MyForm" runat="server">
... ASP.NET form...
</form>
```

It takes only one attribute (`runat="server"`) to tell the Web server that it should *process* the form itself, rather than just sending it out to the browser. If you have worked with HTML forms you may wonder about which METHOD is used. All ASP.NET forms are sent by the POST method.

The `<form>` tag allows you to process form controls (such as check boxes and dropdown lists) on the server. ASP.NET introduces its own customized versions of these controls.

There are several advantages to using ASP.NET form controls:

❑ .NET will automatically create and handle state for us. This allows us to know if the person requesting the form is the same person that just requested another page.

❑ ASP.NET offers some very sophisticated controls including calendars and grids for the display of data.

❑ The content of the controls can be generated from databases or business logic.

❑ The information entered by users into controls can be validated to avoid data entry mistakes.

Using ASP.NET Server Controls

This section demonstrates how some of the ASP.NET server controls work, and compare the way they are used to the way their equivalent HTML form control passed information. It also shows the separation of the presentation code (HTML) from the code that provides the content (ASP.NET). These controls are also called as Web controls, a term that we'll be mostly using throughout this book (though occasionally you might find us referring to it as ASP.NET Web controls).

All Web controls have two required attributes. The first is `runat="server"`, which instructs ASP.NET to handle the control at the server and thus implement all of the ASP.NET features for the control, including the creation of state. The second is the `ID="MyControlName"` that manipulates the control in code.

Before going into the details, let's take a look at the most commonly used ASP.NET server controls. We've included a comparison to the HTML form tags that you have used in the past.

ASP.NET Web Control	Similar HTML Form Tag	Purpose
`<asp:label>`	`<Span>`, `<Div>`, simple text	Display text
`<asp:listbox>`	`<Select>`	Offer the user a list of items from which to select.
`<asp:dropdownlist>`	`<Select>`	Offer the user a list of items from which to select in a compact format
`<asp:textbox >`	`<Input Type="Text">`	Accept typed input from user
`<asp:radiobutton>` and `<asp:radiobuttonlist>`	`<Input Type="Radio">`	Allow user to make one selection from a list of options.
`<asp:checkbox>` and `<asp:checkboxlist>`	`<Input Type="Checkbox">`	Allow user to turn a feature on or off
`<asp:button >`	`<Input Type="submit">`	Send the user's input to the server

The <asp:label> Control

Let's start with a small but very useful control: the `<asp:label>` control. This control provides an effective way of displaying text on your Web page in ASP.NET, similar to the HTML `<span>` tag. By having a control for text, you can manipulate its contents and visibility from your ASP.NET code.

The <asp:label> Control Attributes

The `<asp:label>` control is just like any normal HTML form control in that it has a collection of attributes you can set: The `runat="server"` and `ID` attributes are used in every ASP.NET control. Other attributes are optional, including:

- ❏ `Text`: Sets the text that you want the label to display.
- ❏ `Visible`: Sets whether the label control is currently visible on the page (true or false).
- ❏ `BackColor`: Sets the background color of the label.
- ❏ `ForeColor`: Sets the foreground color of the label.
- ❏ `Height`: Sets the height in pixels of the label.
- ❏ `Width`: Sets the width of the label control.

Recall that the class browser shown in *Chapter 2* will display all the properties of any control.

<asp:label> Control Examples

The basic syntax of `<asp:label>` is simple:

```
<asp:label id="lblMyLabel" runat="server">Sale Ends May 2nd</asp:label>
```

The `<asp:>` prefix indicates that this control is part of the set of built-in ASP.NET controls. It is possible to create custom controls that have prefixes of the developer's choice. We will look at this in *Chapter 13*.

Placed in the context of a Web page, the `<asp:label>` control looks like the following (please refer to the file `ch03\DemoLabel01.aspx` in the code download):

```
<html>
  <head>
    <title>ASP.NET Controls Demo</title>
  </head>
  <body>
  Demo of the asp:label control<br />
    <form id="frmDemo" runat="server">
      <asp:label id="lblGreeting1" runat="server">Text of asp:label</asp:label>
    </form>
  </body>
</html>
```

The `id` attribute is used to uniquely identify the `<asp:label>` control so you can refer to it in your ASP.NET code. The `runat="server"` attribute tells the server to process the control and generate HTML code to be sent to the client. The text between the opening and closing labels provides the characters to show up in the label.

Alternatively, you can specify the text in an attribute. This way, everything can be contained within the opening tag, in which case you need to close the tag in the following way:

```
<asp:label id="lblGreeting3" runat="server" text="Internal Greeting" />
```

Here, the closing tag is omitted, and instead a closing / is supplied within the tag itself to indicate that the tag is closed. Throughout the book we will use this latter notation in preference to having a closing tag. Let's look at an example to set the color of a text message to red as follows (download file `ch03\DemoLabel02.aspx`):

```
<asp:label id="lblGreeting2" forecolor="red"  text="Red Text" runat="server" />
```

Let's now look at an example of how you can use the `<asp:label>` control to display some text for a tourism company. In this example, it's assumed that values of the user's name and desired destination have already been passed to the server, and all you need to do is output a message displaying confirmation that you have received the user's details.

Try It Out **Using the `<asp:label>` Control**

1. Open ASP.NET Web Matrix and create a new item (folder) named `ch03`. Within that folder, create a new item of the type ASP.NET page named `TIO-Label.aspx`. Enter code as needed to create the following page. Some lines are pre-typed for you by Web ASP.NET Web Matrix. (You can learn basic techniques for working with ASP.NET Web Matrix in *Appendix B*.)

```
<html>
<head>
    <title>Label Control page</title>
</head>
<body>
    <h1>Feiertag Holidays
    </h1>
    <form runat="server">
        <asp:label id="Message1" runat="server" text="Chris"></asp:label>,
        you have selected to receive information about
        <asp:label id="Message2" runat="server" text="Oslo"></asp:label>.
        The information package will be sent to you.
    </form>
</body>
</html>
```

2. View it from your browser; the page should be displayed as shown in Figure 3-3:

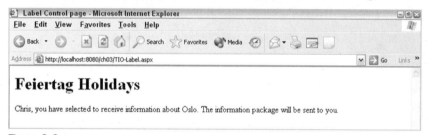

Figure 3-3

How It Works

The text of your `<asp:label>` that appears on the page is the same as that obtained as a result of typing it in a standard HTML `<span>` tag. More interestingly, take a look at the source code to notice two items by selecting View | Source from your browser. First, the ASP.DLL has processed your `<asp:label>` controls into `<span>` tags. Second, ASP.NET has added to your form an extra tag of `name` =`"_VIEWSTATE"` with a value of a long string of characters. The `VIEWSTATE` tag will be discussed shortly.

Modifying ASP.NET Controls

Although this exercise works, it still does not give us the ability to modify the text in code. Recall from Chapter 2 where we used code in a Page_Load() event that affected controls. You can do the same here, as follows (you might want to save as TIO Label2.aspx). First delete the Text attribute (shown as bold in the following code listing) at the end of both <asp:label> controls:

```
<asp:label id="Message1" runat="server" text="Chris"></asp:label>
  , you have selected to receive information about
<asp:label id="Message2" runat="server" text="Oslo"></asp:label>
    . The information package will be sent to you.
```

Now add the following ASP.NET script block before your HTML code:

```
<script language="vb" runat="server">
  Sub Page_Load()
    Message1.Text = "Vervain"
    Message2.Text = "Madrid"
  End Sub
</script>
<html>
```

If you run the example again, you'll see that the output has changed as shown in Figure 3-4:

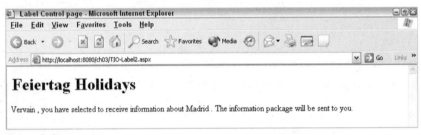

Figure 3-4

Ignore the `Sub Page_Load()` and `End Sub` statements (the `page_load()` section is executed whenever the page is requested or refreshed; we will discuss this in more detail in *Chapter 6*). It's the code they contain that's important for now. The following line refers to the identity of your first `<asp:label>` control, while text refers to its `Text` attribute (also called as property). So we're saying "change the `Method1 <asp:label>`'s `Text` attribute to "Vervain".

```
Message1.Text = "Vervain"
```

This example allowed you to change the contents of the `<asp:label>` control by modifying code. The future chapters will discuss how to modify the values in much more sophisticated ways, including changing the text to be values read from a database. All of the ASP.NET control attributes (properties) can be changed in code in the same way. For example:

```
Message1.Text = "Vervain"
Message1.backcolor = Drawing.color.red
Message1.font.italic=true
Message1.font.size = FontUnit.large
```

The <asp:dropdownlist> Control

Before moving onto the <asp:dropdownlist> control, let's pause to look at its HTML form control equivalent. Dropdown listboxes are a series of <option> tags within a pair of <select> tags:

```
<select name="lstCities">
  <option>Madrid</option>
  <option>Oslo</option>
  <option>Lisbon</option>
</select>
```

The <asp:dropdownlist>control will produce the same output when coded in the following way:

```
<asp:dropdownlist id="lstCities" runat="server">
  <asp:listitem>Madrid</asp:listitem >
  <asp:listitem >Oslo</asp:listitem >
  <asp:listitem >Lisbon</asp:listitem >
</asp:dropdownlist >
```

The three important differences between the ASP.NET control and the HTML form control are as follows:

- ❑ The <asp:dropdownlist> tag directly replaces the <select> tag

- ❑ The <asp:listitem> tag replaces the <option> tag

- ❑ The id attribute replaces the name attribute

Visually, the <asp:dropdownlist> control is identical to the HTML dropdown list control; it's what goes on behind the scene that is different. The best way to explain this is to look at an example. Let's create a form that asks the user to select the particular holiday destination they wish to know more about.

Try It Out Using the <asp:dropdownlist> Control

1. Continuing to use ASP.NET Web Matrix, in your ch03 folder, create a new item of the type ASP.NET page named TIO-DropDownList.aspx, and type in the following. As always, with ASP.NET Web Matrix, some lines are pre-typed for you.

```
<script runat="server" language="vb">
  Sub Page_Load()
    if Page.IsPostback then
      lblMessage.Text = "You have selected " + list1.SelectedItem.Value
    end if
  End Sub
</script>

<html>
<head><title>Drop Down List Example</title></head>
<body>
  <asp:label id="lblMessage" runat="server"/><br/>
```

```
<form runat="server">
  Which city interests you?<br />
  <asp:dropdownlist id="list1" runat="server">
    <asp:listitem>Madrid</asp:listitem>
    <asp:listitem>Oslo</asp:listitem>
    <asp:listitem>Lisbon</asp:listitem>
  </asp:dropdownlist>
  <input type="Submit">
  </form>
</body>
</html>
```

2. Take a look in your browser; the page should be displayed as shown in Figure 3-5

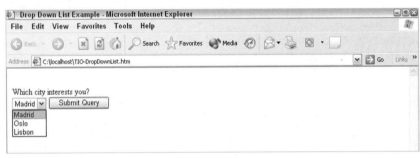

Figure 3-5

3. Select Oslo and click on Submit Query.

4. Now click on View | Source. You should see something like the following; don't worry if your version isn't exactly the same – the code has been tailored to your personal browser:

```
<html>
<head><title>Drop Down List Example</title></head>
<body>
  <span id="lblMessage">You have selected Oslo</span><br/>
  <form name="_ctl0" method="post" action="TIO-DropDownList.aspx" id="_ctl0">
<input type="hidden" name="__VIEWSTATE"
value="dDwtMTMyNTU5Mzc0Njt0PDtsPGk8MT47PjtsPHQ8cDxwPGw8VGV4dDs+O2w8WW91IGhhdmUgc2Vs
       ZWN0ZWQgT3Nsbzs+Pjs+Ozs+Oz4+Oz4qihTIIzJYjhyzz+oJsyJ1gevEaQ==" />

    Which city interests you?<br />
    <select name="list1" id="list1">
  <option value="Madrid">Madrid</option>
  <option selected="selected" value="Oslo">Oslo</option>
  <option value="Lisbon">Lisbon</option>

</select>
  <input type="Submit">
  </form>
</body>
</html>
```

How It Works

As you can see, everything that has been sent to the browser is HTML code and text; there are no proprietary tags or script to run on the browser. Also note that this is a one page solution, in contrast to the old two page approach with HTML forms. This form page submits to itself. To explain how it works, we're going to reference the source code that we can view in our browser, and compare it to our original ASPX code.

Let's start from the `<form>` section of the script. The `<form runat="server">` attribute tells ASP.NET to execute the form on the server. If you compare this line to what has been returned to the browser, you can see a large difference:

```
<form name="ctrl0" method="post" action="listpage.aspx" id="ctrl0">
```

ASP.NET has generated four new attributes. The `name` and `id` attributes serve a similar purpose, to uniquely identify the form. But it's the other two that are of interest. HTML forms require a page to receive the form data, and a method of transmission. We didn't specify either of these in our ASPX code, so ASP.NET specified them for us by default to be the same page. It also specifies the POST method by default.

The main item on the form is the `<asp:dropdownlist>` control:

```
Which city interests you?<br />
  <asp:dropdownlist id="list1" runat="server">
    <asp:listitem>Madrid</asp:listitem>
    <asp:listitem>Oslo</asp:listitem>
    <asp:listitem>Lisbon</asp:listitem>
  </asp:dropdownlist>
```

It's crucial to note how this is rendered. If you view the source code that's been sent back to the browser, you should see something like the following:

```
<input type="hidden" name="__VIEWSTATE"
value="dDwtMTMyNTU5MzcONjtOPDtsPGk8MT47PjtsPHQ8cDxwPGw8VGV4dDs+O2w8WW91IGhhdmUgc2V
       sZWNOZWQgT3Nsbzs+Pjs+Ozs+Oz4+Oz4qihTIIzJYjhyzz+oJsyJ1gevEaQ==" />
    Which city interests you?<br />
    <select name="list1" id="list1">
 <option value="Madrid">Madrid</option>
 <option selected="selected" value="Oslo">Oslo</option>
 <option value="Lisbon">Lisbon</option>
</select>
```

It's the first line that is of particular note. This is a hidden control called VIEWSTATE, whose value is an encoded representation of the overall state of the form as it was when last submitted. This is used by ASP.NET to keep track of all the server control settings from one page refresh to another. Without this record of the state of the controls, the dropdown listbox would revert to its default setting every time you submitted a value.

It may not be immediately obvious how useful this can be – consider a non ASP.NET registration form in which you have to enter a full set of personal details. If you forget to fill in a required field, and then submit the form, you may well be prompted with the same empty form again. ASP.NET solves this problem for us with the VIEWSTATE; all that data is automatically persisted through to the refreshed page, and you have barely raised a finger to code!

The string of characters contained in the value attribute is a condensed and encoded depiction of each control on the page as it was when the submit button was clicked. When this information is sent back to IIS on a subsequent submit, it is decoded and ASP.NET can work with the values.

The second half is just a <select> HTML form control; this is the HTML output of a <dropdownlist>. Note that it had one of the <option> tags altered to reflect the selection you made before submitting the form.

How ASP.NET Code Works

We've seen that the ASP.NET server control passes form values to the ASP.NET code. Now let's see how you can use a control's values in your code. Assume we have a label named lblMessage.

```
<script runat="server" language="vb">
  Sub Page_Load()
    If Page.IsPostBack Then
      lblMessage.Text = "You have selected " + DropList1.SelectedItem.Value
    End If
  End Sub
</script>
```

There are three lines of code here inside Page_Load(). The first line of code (if Page.IsPostBack Then) checks whether the page has been returned by the user before. This check involves using the Page object which keeps a record of whether this is the first time a form is shown or is the result of the form being re-shown after clicking the submit button.

If the form has been submitted, IsPostBack returns true, otherwise it returns false. The code inside If Then...End If will only be run if the form has been posted back by the user. So, if this is the first time the user has seen the form (Page.IsPostBack would equal FALSE) then ASP.NET will jump over the second line and end. The page would not show any text in the message control. But, if the user has submitted the page, then the following line will be run first:

```
lblMessage.Text = "You have selected " + DropList1.SelectedItem.Value
```

This line has two parts. The right side of the equals sign picks up the text that the user clicked in the dropdown listbox. Note that the SelectedItem.Value keeps a record of which item the user has selected. The left side identifies where to put that text, namely the <asp:label> control. On both sides we refer to the server control by its ID value.

The <asp:listbox> Control

The <asp:listbox> server control resembles the dropdown list control except that it doesn't drop down, and is capable of multiple selections. The <asp:listbox> has the following syntax:

```
<asp:listbox id="list1" runat="server" selection mode = "multiple">
  <asp:listitem>Madrid</asp:listitem >
  <asp:listitem >Oslo</asp:listitem >
  <asp:listitem >Lisbon</asp:listitem >
</asp:listbox>
```

The `selectionmode` attribute is used to determine whether you can select multiple or only single items from the listbox. By default it is set to single. Let's alter our previous example to use a listbox so as to allow multiple selections.

Try It Out Using the `<asp:listbox>` Control

1. Create a `TIO-ListBox.aspx` file in the `ch03` folder, and enter the following:

```
<script runat="server" language="vb">
  Sub Page_Load()
    If Page.IsPostBack Then Dim msg As String
      If list1.Items(0).Selected Then msg = msg & list1.Items(0).Text & "<br />";
        If list1.Items(1).Selected Then msg = msg & list1.Items(1).Text & "<br />"
        If list1.Items(2).Selected Then msg = msg & list1.Items(2).Text & "<br />"
      If msg <> ""  then
        Message.Text = "You have selected: <br />" & msg
        Else
        message.text = ""
      End if
    End If
  End Sub
</script>

<html>
  <head>
    <title>List Box Example</title>
  </head>
  <body>
    <asp:label id="Message" runat="server"/><br/>
    Which city do you wish to look at hotels for?<br/>
    <form runat="server">
      <asp:listbox id="list1"
        runat="server" selectionmode="multiple">
        <asp:listitem>Madrid</asp:listitem>
        <asp:listitem>Oslo</asp:listitem>
        <asp:listitem>Lisbon</asp:listitem>
      </asp:listbox><br/>
      <input type="Submit">
    </form>
  </body>
</html>
```

2. Run this page in your browser, and use the Ctrl or Shift key to select multiple choices, then click on Submit Query to see the page as depicted in Figure 3-6:

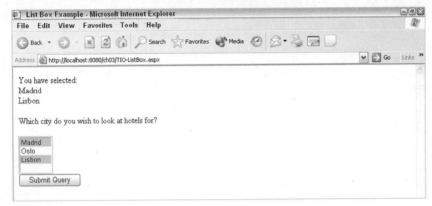

Figure 3-6

How It Works

The controls in this example have hardly really changed from the previous `listpage.aspx` example. All we've done is switched from `DropDown` to `ListBox` and set the `selectionmode` attribute to allow us to make multiple selections:

```
<asp:listbox id="list1" runat="server" selectionmode="multiple">
```

However, we've had to completely overhaul the ASP.NET code to accommodate the possibility of several cities selected. We will build the list to display in a variable named `msg` starting with the boilerplate:

```
Dim msg As String = "You have selected:<br />"
```

Then for each possible city choice we check whether it was selected, and if yes, we will add the city name to the `msg` variable. The trick here is to understand that the choices are numbered (indexed) in the list box and if they are selected then the selected property is switched to `TRUE`. Finally, we assign the value of the variable `msg` (a string of text and HTML) to the `Text` attribute of the `Message` label, so that it can be seen on the page. This is more complicated than handling the results of single selections, but produces the needed result.

The *<asp:textbox>* Control

This control is ASP.NET's version of the HTML `<textbox>` and `<textarea>` controls. In fact, text areas are simply text boxes that feature multiple lines, thus allowing you to input larger quantities of text. The textbox control is also able to supply the functionality of an HTML form password control. To enable these variations, the `<asp:textbox>` control needs some extra attributes:

❑   `textmode`: Specifies whether you want the control to have one line (don't set it), many lines (set it to multiline), or have a single line of masked content (set it to password).

❑   rows: Specifies the number of rows you want the textbox to have and will only work if textmode is set to multiple.

❑   columns: specifies the number of columns you want the textbox to have, and will only work if textmode is set to multiple.

If you wish to provide any default text that appears in the control, you can either place it between the opening and closing tags or set it in the text attribute:

```
<asp:textbox id="text1" runat="server">Default text here...</asp:textbox>
<asp:textbox id="text1" runat="server" text="Default text here..."/>
```

Let's look at an example that uses the textbox control to ask for the name and address of the user, and a password as well. Previously in HTML, this would require three different types of controls; here we shall only use the <asp:textbox> control.

Try It Out   Using the <asp:textbox> Control

1.   In the ch03 folder, create TIO-TextBox.aspx and type in the following:

```
<script runat="server" language="vb">
  Sub Page_Load()
  If Page.IsPostback
    lblName.Text = ""
    lblAddress.Text = ""
    lblPassword.Text = ""

    if txtName.Text <> "" then
      lblName.Text = "You have entered the following name: " +  txtName.Text
    end if

    if txtAddress.Text <> "" then
      lblAddress.Text = "You have entered the following address: " +
                        txtAddress.Text
    end if

    if txtPassword.Text <> "" then
      lblPassword.Text = "You have entered the following password: " +
                        txtPassword.Text
    end if
  End If
  End Sub
</script>

<html>
  <head>
    <title>Text Box Example</title>
  </head>
  <body>
    <asp:label id="lblName" runat="server" /><br />
    <asp:label id="lblAddress" runat="server" /><br />
    <asp:label id="lblPassword" runat="server" /><br />
    <form runat="server">
```

```
        Please enter your name:
        <asp:textbox id="txtName" runat="server" />
        <br /><br />
        Please enter your address:
        <asp:textbox id="txtAddress" runat="server" textmode="multiline" rows=5 />
        <br/><br />
        Please enter your password:
        <asp:textbox id="txtPassword" runat="server" textmode="password" />
        <br /><br />
        <input type="Submit">
    </form>
  </body>
</html>
```

2. Open `TIO-Textbox.aspx` in your browser, and type in some details, then click on Submit Query to see the results as shown in Figure 3-7:

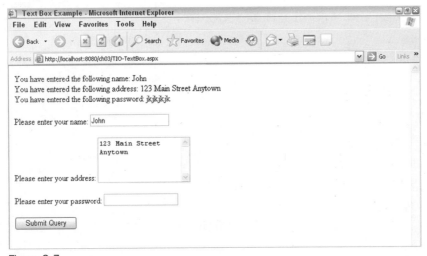

Figure 3-7

How It Works

Within the form, we have created three types of `textbox` control:

```
<asp:textbox id="txtName" runat="server" />
<asp:textbox id="txtAddress" runat="server" textmode="multiline" rows=5 />
<asp:textbox id="txtPassword" runat="server" textmode="password" />
```

The first is identified as `txtName`, and requires no other attributes other than `id` and `runat`. This is displayed as a single text field. The second control, `txtAddress`, is a multiline textbox (which will render as a text area), and requires that we set the `textmode` attribute to `multiline`, so that we can set the number of rows we wish this textbox to have. Here, we have set it to 5 for the address. Lastly, we create a third control, `txtPassword`, which is set to `password` with the `textmode` attribute. This, again, will display a single line text field, but any text typed into it is represented by a set of asterisks.

To display the results from three sets of controls, we have used three separate `<asp:label>` controls:

```
<asp:label id="lblName" runat="server" /><br />
<asp:label id="lblAddress" runat="server" /><br />
<asp:label id="lblPassword" runat="server" /><br />
```

Each one is identified with a different `id` attribute so that we can refer to them individually in other lines of our code. The job of assigning text values to these three label controls falls to the ASP.NET code contained within `<script>` tags at the top of the page.

```
Sub Page_Load()
If Page.IsPostback
  lblName.Text = ""
  lblAddress.Text = ""
  lblPassword.Text = ""
    if txtName.Text <> "" then
      lblName.Text = "You have entered the following name: " +  txtName.Text
    end if
End If
...
End Sub
```

First we make sure that blank values are assigned to each of the `<asp:label>` controls in the first three lines. This is because once the page has been posted back, it will display the old messages, unless we clear them.

Then we check if `txtName` is not empty (its text value is something other then `""`). If it is not empty, we take the contents and show them in `lblName` along with some boilerplate text. That is repeated for the other labels.

The *<asp:radiobuttonlist>* and *<asp:radiobutton>* Controls

The `<asp:radiobuttonlist>` control works the same as its HTML forms equivalent or the Windows interface. Choice of one button excludes selecting another button within the group. Note that the identifier for the whole group is set only in the `id` attribute of the `<asp:radiobuttonlist>` control, otherwise the syntax is simple:

```
<asp:radiobuttonlist id="radSample" runat="server">
  <asp:listitem id="option1" runat="server" value="Option A" />
  <asp:listitem id="option2" runat="server" value="Option B" />
  <asp:listitem id="option3" runat="server" value="Option C" />
</asp:radiobuttonlist>
```

You can programmatically find out which option was selected by the user by checking the `radSample.SelectedItem.Value` to see, for example, `"Option A"`.

The following example uses a group of radio buttons to decide which destination a user has selected on an HTML form, and relays that information back to the user.

Try It Out Using the <asp:RadioButtonList> Control

1. Create `TIO-RadioButtonList.aspx` within the ch03 folder and type in the following:

```
<script runat="server" language="vb">
  Sub Page_Load()
    if Page.IsPostBack then
     Message.Text = "You have selected " + radCity.SelectedItem.Value
    end if
  End Sub
</script>

<html>
  <head>
    <title>Radio Button List Example</title>
  </head>
  <body>
    <asp:label id="Message" runat="server" />
    <br /><br />
    Which city interests you? <br /><br />
    <form runat="server">
      <asp:radiobuttonlist id="radCity" runat="server">
        <asp:listitem id="optMadrid" runat="server" value="Madrid" />
        <asp:listitem id="optOslo" runat="server" value="Oslo" />
        <asp:listitem id="optLisbon" runat="server" value="Lisbon" />
      </asp:radiobuttonlist><br />
      <input type="Submit">
    </form>
  </body>
</html>
```

2. View it in your browser as shown in Figure 3-8, select a city, and click on Submit Query:

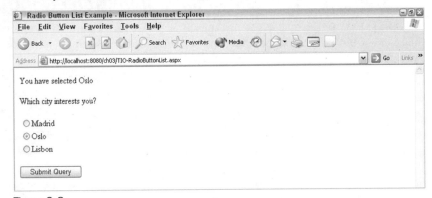

Figure 3-8

How It Works

The `TIORadioButtonList.aspx` page has a form with three radio buttons in a single group with the ID `radCity`. Note that we use a different ID and value for each option:

```
<form runat="server">
  <asp:radiobuttonlist id="radCity" runat="server">
    <asp:listitem id="optMadrid" runat="server" value="Madrid" />
    <asp:listitem id="optOslo" runat="server" value="Oslo" />
    <asp:listitem id="optLisbon" runat="server" value="Lisbon" />
  </asp:radiobuttonlist><br />
  <input type="Submit">
</form>
```

In the ASP.NET code at the top of the page delimited within the `Sub Page_Load()` and `End Sub` statements, we have used the familiar three lines to return to the user the information from the form. In a way similar to when we used the `<asp:listBox>`, we can get the selected option by reading the `SelectedItem.Value` property:

```
if Page.IsPostBack then
    Message.Text = "You have selected " + radCity.SelectedItem.Value
end if
```

If a radio button is selected, then the label named 'message' will have its text set to "You have selected" followed by the user's choice that is returned by `SelectedItem.Value`.

The <asp:checkbox> and <asp:checkboxlist> Controls

Checkboxes are similar to radio buttons in that they present multiple choices from a group of buttons. However, `<asp:checkbox>` is for where there is one option only ("Do you want to pay $5 more for quick shipping?") whereas with the `<asp:checkboxlist>` control, the user can select more then one options ("Which free catalogs can we send you: Sports, Clothing, Shoes?"). The other fundamental difference between a checkbox and a radio button is that, unlike in case of the radio button, once you have selected a checkbox you are able to deselect it by clicking on it again.

Most of the same principles that you followed in the `<asp:radiobuttonlist>` examples apply to checkboxes. The main difference is the syntax – radio buttons use `"options"` whereas check boxes use `"listitems"`.

A solo `<asp:checkbox>` has a single ID:

```
<asp:checkbox id="chkQuickShipping" runat="server" />
```

An array of checkboxes can be contained inside an `<asp:checkboxlist>` control. You need to set an `id` attribute for the `<asp:checkboxlist>` control itself, and create a `<asp:listitem>` control for each option inside the control:

```
<asp:checkboxlist id="chkCatalogs" runat="server">
  <asp:listitem id="itmSports" runat="server" value="Sports" />
  <asp:listitem id="itmClothes" runat="server" value="Clothes" />
  <asp:listitem id="itmShoes" runat="server" value="Shoes" />
</asp:checkboxlist>
```

The next example is a tweaked version of the previous one, where it uses our established holiday selection to allow the user to select more than one option for a particular destination.

Try It Out Using the <asp:checkbox> Control

1. Open up the TIO-RadioButtonList.aspx and save it in the ch03 folder as TIO-CheckBoxList.aspx. Amend the code as highlighted in gray:

```
<script runat="server" language="vb">
  Sub Page_Load()
    Dim msg As String = "You have selected the following items:<br />"
    If chkCities.Items(0).Selected Then msg += chkCities.Items(0).Text & "<br />"
    If chkCities.Items(1).Selected Then msg += chkCities.Items(1).Text & "<br />"
    If chkCities.Items(2).Selected Then msg += chkCities.Items(2).Text & "<br />"
    lblCities.Text = msg
  End Sub
</script>

<html>
<head>
  <title>Check Box List Example</title>
</head>
<body>
  <asp:label id="lblCities" runat="server" /><br /><br />
  Which city do you wish to look at hotels for?<br /><br />
  <form runat="server">
    <asp:checkboxlist id="chkCities" runat="server">
      <asp:listitem id="optMadrid" runat="server" value="Madrid" />
      <asp:listitem id="optOslo" runat="server" value="Oslo" />
      <asp:listitem id="optLisbon" runat="server" value="Lisbon" />
    </asp:checkboxlist><br /><br />
    <input type="Submit">
  </form>
</body>
</html>
```

2. Open `TIO-CheckBoxList.aspx` in your browser as shown in Figure 3-9, select several options, and click on **Submit Query**:

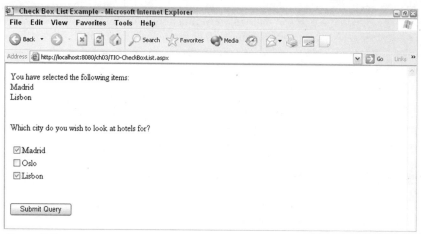

Figure 3-9

How It Works

Very little has changed with the page – all we've done is changed the HTML control to an `<asp:checkboxlist>` and changed its ID. Notice that within checkbox groups the choices are labeled as `"listitem"` rather than `"options"`.

Our ASP.NET code is the same as that we used for the `TIO ListBox` example except that here it refers to a checkbox rather than a listbox. The syntax has also been modified to join the city name onto the end of the value in `msg`. Note that we can use the syntax `msg +=` to get the same result as the syntax `msg = msg &`

```
Sub Page_Load()
  Dim msg As String = "You have selected the following items:<br />"
  If chkCities.Items(0).Selected Then msg += chkCities.Items(0).Text & "<br />"
  If chkCities.Items(1).Selected Then msg += chkCities.Items(1).Text & "<br />"
  If chkCities.Items(2).Selected Then msg += chkCities.Items(2).Text & "<br />"
  lblCities.Text = msg
End Sub
```

This covers a set of basic ASP.NET server controls. Note that all start with `<asp: >`, all contain the attribute `runat="server"`, and each has an ID. You have seen how to use them to gather information from the user and then utilize that information in your code. In a number of pages you have used variables; for example, `msg` in the radio button and checkbox pages. You have also used control structures such as `IF THEN`.

Before going on to chapters with other ASP.NET features, let's pause to look more closely at how to use variables in ASP.NET pages. Following that we will take a deeper look at the control structures in the logic being used.

Storing Information in VB.NET Variables

Variables are fundamental to programming – they let you store information in memory. Once the information is stored, you can perform mathematical functions, calculate new dates, manipulate text, count the length of sentences, and perform many other functions. This book discusses the techniques of using variables in VB .NET. The syntax would be different if you work in C# or another language, but the theory is very similar.

A *variable* is a space in memory that is allocated a name and given a data type by the programmer. These spaces in memory can be used to store pieces of information that will be used in the program. Think of variables as you might think of boxes. They're simply repositories for information that you wish to store. Different data types require different sizes and shapes of boxes – in different amounts of memory. Any variable is empty until you put information into it (although the memory space is reserved while the code runs.) You can then view the information inside the variable, get the information out, or replace the information with new data.

VB.NET is a *strongly typed* language, which means that every variable has a data type associated with it, such as String, Integer, or Date. Typing tells VB.NET how to deal with the data so that, for example, dates can be seen as proper dates and not a long division such as: 5/10/2003.

Variables have four parts; a name, a space in memory, a data type, and the value that they hold.

Declaring Variables

Good programming practice requires that you explicitly create, or *declare* variables before you use them. In VB .NET, the simplest type of variable declaration is made with the keyword `Dim`, which is short for 'dimension.' A `Dim` does three tasks. First, the name of the variable is established, second the data type is noted, and third a space is allocated in the memory. Until the variable is assigned a value, it contains *nothing* (bear in mind zero *is* a value, so it won't contain zero or even a blank space).

> You can check if a variable contains a value by using: IsNothing(myVariable), which returns True if the variable is empty and False if the variable has a value.

While naming a variable you have to remember the following three rules:

- ❑ All variable names must begin with a letter (not a number or symbol).
- ❑ They may not contain an embedded period/full-stop or a space.
- ❑ They cannot be the same as VB.NET reserved words (keywords) such as `If` and `End`.

In the following example, the first line declares a variable as a string type with the name `strCarType`; the second line assigns a string value to that variable:

```
Dim strCarType As String
strCarType = "Buick"
```

It's also possible to declare a variable and assign a value to it in one line:

```
Dim strCarType As String = "Buick"
```

If you have several variables of the same type you can set them up with one line of code:

```
Dim strCarType1, strCarType2, strCarType3 As String
strCarType1 = "Buick"
strCarType2 = "Cadillac"
strCarType3 = "Pontiac"
```

Now let's put our knowledge of variable declaration and assignment to use in an example. We'll take the code above and combine it with ASP.NET server controls.

Try It Out Using Variables

1.   Create a file ch03\TIO-Variable1.aspx and type in the following:

```
<script language="vb" runat="server">
Sub Page_Load()
  Dim CapitalCityOfUK As String
  Dim NumberOfStates As Integer
  Dim IndependenceDay As Date

  CapitalCityOfUK = "London"
  NumberOfStates = 50
  IndependenceDay = #7/4/1776#

  lblCapital.Text = CapitalCityOfUK
  lblNumStates.Text = NumberOfStates
  lblDateIndependence.Text = IndependenceDay
  End Sub
</script>

<html>
<head>
<title>Creating Variables Example</title>
</head>
<body>
  The contents of CapitalCityOfUk is:
  <asp:label id="lblCapital" runat="server" />
  <br>The contents of NumberOfStates is:
  <asp:label id="lblNumStates" runat="server" />
  <br>The contents of IndependenceDay is:
  <asp:label id="lblDateIndependence" runat="server" />
</body>
</html>
```

2. Open `TIO-Variable1.aspx` in your browser as shown in Figure 3-10:

Figure 3-10

3. Add to the code a line that uses a variable (`NumberofDaysInJuly`) that we have not declared:

```
CapitalCityOfUK = "London"
NumberOfStates = 50
IndependenceDay = #7/4/1863#
NumberOfDaysInJuly = 31
```

4. Save this file as `TIO-Variable2.aspx` and run the example. You will get an error screen, shown in Figure 3-11:

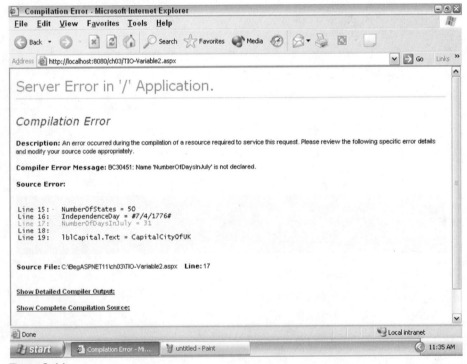

Figure 3-11

5. As you can see, variables cannot simply appear within your script or code – they must first be explicitly declared and then assigned. An error is generated because the variable `NumberOfDaysInJuly` that is used in the script, is not declared.

How It Works

The first section of code declares each of the variables we wish to use in the example. Note the difference in type (the designation after `As`) to match the data we will store:

```
Dim CapitalCityOfUK As String
Dim NumberOfStates As Integer
Dim IndependenceDay As Date
```

In the next section, having declared the variables, we can now assign values to each:

```
CapitalCityOfUK = "London"
NumberOfStates = 50
IndependenceDay = #7/4/1863#
```

Note that text must be within double quotes. Numbers do not get quotes, while dates are enclosed in # symbols. In the last section, we created three `<asp:label>` controls. We then set these label's `Text` values to the contents of our three variables:

```
lblCapital.Text = CapitalCityOfUK
lblNumStates.Text = NumberOfStates
lblDateIndependence.Text = IndependenceDay
```

Your web form duly displays the contents of your variables. You might be wondering what stops a control from displaying the literal text `CapitalCityOfUK`. The answer is the absence of quotation marks. Anything inside quotation marks is interpreted as literal text. Anything not contained in quotes is treated as a variable, numeric value, or object. We then amended the example to add another line:

```
NumberOfDaysInJuly = 31
```

This line looks perfectly okay, but it nevertheless caused an error – because we haven't declared the variable prior to using it.

You've seen how important data types are in your ASP.NET Web forms. Let's discuss what the possible data types are and when you should use them.

Simple Data Types

There are twelve different built in data types in VB .NET, and they can be divided into three groups: numeric, text, and a set of miscellaneous types. This chapter will look at eleven of these twelve data types; the `Object` data type will be discussed in *Chapter 7*.

Numeric

Numeric data types make up about half of VB.NET's built in data types, representing seven of the twelve data types.

Integer

Integers are whole numbers (numbers without a decimal component). Examples of integers are 3, 12, and 0. The integer data type can handle whole numbers up to about 2 billion (2,147,483,648), either plus or minus.

Byte

Bytes are integers within the range 0 to 255, negatives are not allowed. It's a useful type because a variable can be easily stored by the computer within a single byte – a computer's basic storage unit – and any processing or arithmetic done with them is therefore faster.

Short

The short data type is a form of integer, but as the name implies, can only accept a limited range of values. The range of values is -32,768 to +32,767.

Long

The long type is very similar to the integer type, but supports a much larger range. A long variable can contain a value up to 9,223,372,036,854,775,808 (that is 9 x 1019), either positive or negative.

Single

The single type holds single precision floating point numbers. By *floating* we mean that the values can have decimal places. The single type supports values within the range 3.402823E38 to 1.401298E 45 (for negative values), and 1.401298E45 to 3.402823E38 (for positive values).

Double

The double type holds double precision floating point numbers. The range of double is 1.79769313486232E308 to 4.94065645841247E324 (for negative values), and 4.94065645841247E324 to 1.79769313486232E308 (for positive values).

Decimal

The decimal type accepts numbers with about 28 digits. You can allocate them between the left and right side of the decimal place. With zero decimal places, it can support large positive or negative numbers with up to twentyeight following zeros. Alternatively, you can store a very accurate number with about twentyeight digits to the right of the decimal point.

Given the wide range represented by these seven types, here is a short guide to selecting the correct type for your needs. Your code will be most efficient if you use the smallest and simplest type that will do the job.

❑ If you must use decimal places and you need less than twenty eight digits, you can use `Decimal`. If you need decimal places and more digits then go to `Single`, and if you need even more then go to `Double`. Currency is generally stored as a `Decimal` type.

❑ If you don't need decimal places, then start with `Byte` (up to 256). Keep in mind that byte does not handle negative values. If you need to use larger numbers or negative values, then first use `short` type, then `integer`, and finally use `long` type.

If you have violated the limits of a Numeric type you will get an error that your value "is not representable in type x."

Text Data Types

Normally text data types store words or letters, but you can also use them to store symbols and numbers. However, you should not store numbers that you plan to use in arithmetic. For example, a `string` variable called `MyString` can hold values like `"2.0"` or `"July 4, 2004"`. However, you would not be able to directly find half of the number or the number of days since the date. Numbers normally go into one of the numeric data types.

An exception is a number that you absolutely will not perform math with, such as telephone numbers, social security numbers, and catalog numbers that may contain a mix of numbers and letters; these are usually better stored as strings.

There are just two data types for storing text. The `String` data type is almost always used. The other, `Char`, stores only one character of text and it is in a coded form.

String

The `string` type identifies its stored value as text, even if you supply it with a mixture of text and numerical data, numerical data alone, or even date information. A `string` type variable will grow or shrink to accommodate essentially any number of characters. However, it does not inherently contain any sense of formatting like line breaks:

```
Dim CarType As String
Dim CarEngineSize As String
Dim CarModel as String
Dim DatePurchased As String


CarType = "Buick"         ' this is normal
CarEngineSize = "2.0"     ' this works, but is not normal
CarModel = "123-Z-456"    ' OK because these numbers do not have math values
DatePurchased = " July 4, 1999" ' this works, but better to use date
type
```

As mentioned earlier, `string` values are encapsulated in double quotation marks, so they can be differentiated visually from numerical values, without having to reference their actual declarations.

> **Use double quotation marks to encapsulate strings, never use the single quotation marks (in VB.NET, they create a comment).**

The .NET Framework provides a number of special methods by which you can manipulate strings. These methods allow you to measure the length of a string, truncate a string at the beginning or end, return certain characters from a given string, or even convert a string into its numerical equivalent. String manipulation and conversion requires the use of the .NET String object and hence will be discussed in a future chapter.

Char

The char data type is a bit strange, because it stores text as a number! This means you place a single character in a variable, defined as a char, and it is stored as a number between 0 and 65535. The large values are to cover characters from non English languages. You store the value as follows – note the 'C' is used after the quotes to indicate that this is a char and not a string:

```
Dim Letter As Char
Letter = "Q"C    'This would be stored as 81
```

When you display the contents of a char variable, you see a text character, despite the fact that it is stored as a code number.

> For Western languages almost all characters (called ASCII) are represented from 0 to 255 - a total of 256 including 0. However, to support additional languages (like Chinese with a large number of characters) we need more space to store them. Therefore we use 256 squared = 655356 possible characters in a system called UNICODE.

Other Data Types

The next few data types don't really fit together, as they have nothing in common other than the fact that they are not numeric or text.

Date

The date data type is treated as separate from the numerical types by VB.NET. Dates must be defined in the mm/dd/yyyy format (for example, 12/15/1984) and delimited using the # symbol (VB.NET will tolerate the use of double quotation marks). The date type can store any value between January 1, year 0001, and December 31, year 9999. The date data type is also used to store time information as well. You can configure it to store time between 00:00:00 and 23:59:59 as follows:

```
Dim datMyDate As Date
datMyDate = #1/1/2005#
datMyDate = #4:25:05 PM#
datMyDate = #16:25:05#
datMyDate = #1/1/2005 16:25:05#
datMyDate = #16:25:05 PM#     'fails – use 24 hour time or AM/PM but not both
```

Boolean

Boolean variables can be set to one of two values: True or False. Alternatively, Boolean values can be a numeric value. Zero equals false, all other numbers equal true.

Boolean Value	Numeric Value	Text Value
True	−1 or +1 or any other number	"True"
False	0	"False"

```
Dim IsMember As Boolean 'my variable to indicate membership
IsMember = True 'this means true
IsMember = "True"        'this means true
IsMember = 1      'this means true
IsMember = -1     'this means true

IsMember = 0      'this means false
IsMember = False         'this means false
IsMember = "False"        'this means false
```

Note that `True` or `False` as a value should *not* be in quotes.

Naming Variables

As we've seen earlier, there are three basic rules on naming variables. First, all variable names must begin with a letter (not a number or symbol). Second, they must not contain an embedded period (or full stop) or a space. Last, they cannot be the same as VB.NET reserved words (keywords) such as If and End.

Some programmers use the following kinds of nondescript variable names:

```
Dim i as Integer
Dim varBoolean as Boolean
Dim Counter as integer
Dim Date as Date
```

This is a sloppy way of coding. Nondescript variable names are not particularly helpful and thus increase the cost of creating and maintaining an application. At the same time, excessively long variable names are unwieldy and easy to mistype. Good programming practice should is to find suitable names for the variables that are meaningful to those who subsequently read the code.

When your variable name has more than one word you can use two techniques. Some people like to separate the words with underscores like `Name_First`. Some prefer to use 'camel case', wherein letters are lower case except the first of each word, like `NameFirst`. Here are some additional naming tips:

❑ `DataStart` and `DateEnd` are better than `StartDate` and `EndDate`, as these two related variables will then come next to each other in an alphabetically sorted search.

❑ Variables like `Price`, `Name,` and `Number` are confusing because there are usually more than one of these. Better to use `NounAdjective` combination like `NameFirst` and `NameLast`.

❑ Variable names that coincide with data types aren't allowed, (for example, `Dim Integer as Integer`.

❑   Avoid confusing and non-intuitive abbreviations, such as FDOM for first day of month – the acronym FDOM could stand for anything.

❑   Never use the same variable name for two different variables in a website, no matter how sure you are that they will not conflict.

Naming Conventions

A very common mistake occurs in programming when a variable of one type is used as if it is of another type. For example, a line of code tries to subtract a string from a date and throws an error. The sensible answer is to use a naming convention that identifies the type of a variable. The most common convention, known as *Hungarian Notation*, is to use the first three letters of a variable's name to distinguish the type. The fourth letter of the variable is then typed in uppercase, to indicate that this is where the actual variable name starts.

Data Type	Prefix	Example
Boolean	bln	blnMember
Byte	byt	bytDaysInMonth
Char	chr	chrWang
Date	dat	datDatePurchased
Double	dbl	dblPi
Decimal	dec	decSalary
Integer	int	intDistanceToSun
Long	lng	lngDistanceToStar
Single	sng	sngNumberOfMolecules
Short	sho	shoNumberOfAtoms
String	str	strNameFirst

There are variations to this convention that are used by programmers.

Variable Scope

A few simple questions arise when we consider using variables. How widely available is a variable? If a variable is created, can it be used by other events and procedures on the page? Can it be seen by other pages, can other users visiting the same web site see it? This is the issue of *scope*; a sense of how widely a variable can be used. We will study three levels of variables: block, procedure, and global. It is important to create your variables with the least amount of scope to do the job. Then, when a variable is no longer needed it destructs and memory is freed up. So the more limited the scope of variables the faster your programs will run.

> You can't have two variables with the same name within the same scope. To be safe,
> avoid duplicating a variable name anywhere within a Web site.

Block Variables

The most limited type of scope is known as block level. A set of statements terminated by an `End If`,
`Else`, `Loop` or `Next` statement is considered a block (these structures are discussed in detail in the next
chapter). Variables created within a block level scope can be used only within that block. When the block
is finished (for example, after the last loop) the variable is destroyed. In the following example, the scope
of the variable `strBlockLevelVariable` is the block between `If` and `End If`, and
`strBlockLevelVariable` can no longer be referenced when execution passes out of the block, so
`lblMessage1.Text` would contain nothing.

```
If 1=1 Then
   Dim strBlockLevelVariable As String
   strBlockLevelVariable = "Very Short Lived!"
End If
lblMessage.Text = strBlockLevelVariable
```

However, if we try to use `strBlockLevelVariable` within the block where it was created, as follows,
then our `lblmessage` shows the message.

```
If 1=1 Then
   Dim strBlockLevelVariable As String
   strBlockLevelVariable = "Very Short Lived!"
   lblMessage.Text = strBlockLevelVariable
End If
```

The advantage of block variables is that they save resources for variables not needed outside the block.
The disadvantage is that if you aren't careful, you can accidentally declare a variable inside a block, and
then try to access it outside the block scope. For this reason, many programmers avoid block declaration
of variables.

Procedure-Level Variables

The next wider level of scope is the procedure variable. These variables are available to all of the code
within a procedure (for example, the `Page_Load()` that we have worked with). They can also be called
local variables because they are local to the subroutine that created them. Outside that subroutine, the
local variable has no value; this is because the lifetime of the variable ends when the subroutine ends.

Try It Out **Creating Procedure-Level and Block-Level Variables**

1.   In the `ch03` folder, create the `TIO-VariableScope1.aspx` file and enter the following code:

```
<%@ Page Language="vb" %>
<script runat="server">

    Sub Page_Load()
    Dim strMyProcVariable = "Procedure Variable"
    If ISPostBack Then
```

```
              Dim strMyBlockVariableUsedInside = "Block Variable Used In Block"

              lblMessageBlockInBlock.text = strMyBlockVariableUsedInside
              lblMessageProcedure.text = strMyProcVariable
        End If

        End Sub

</script>
<html>
<head>
    <title>Variable Scope</title>
</head>
<body>
    <form runat="server">
        <asp:Label id="lblMessageBlockInBLock" runat="server" text="DEFAULT _
                  BlockInBlock"></asp:Label>

        <br />

        <asp:Label id="lblMessageProcedure" runat="server" text="DEFAULT _
                  Procedure"></asp:Label>
        <br />
        <asp:Button runat="server" Text="Submit"/>
    </form>
</body>
</html>
```

2. Open it in your browser as shown in Figure 3-12:

Figure 3-12

3. Now add three lines that try to declare a block variable inside a block but use it outside the block:

```
<%@ Page Language="vb" %>
<script runat="server">

    Sub Page_Load()
    Dim strMyProcVariable = "Procedure Variable"
    If ISPostBack Then
        Dim strMyBlockVariableUsedInside = "Block Variable Used In Block"
        Dim strMyBlockVariableUsedOutside= "Block Variable Used After Block"
        lblMessageBlockInBlock.text = strMyBlockVariableUsedInside
        lblMessageProcedure.text = strMyProcVariable
    End If
```

```
        lblMessageBlockOutBlock = strMyBlockVariableUsedOutside
    End Sub

</script>
<html>
<head>
    <title>Variable Scope</title>
</head>
<body>
    <form runat="server">
        <asp:Label id="lblMessageBlockInBLock" runat="server" text="DEFAULT _
                    BlockInBlock"></asp:Label>
        <br />
        <asp:Label id="lblMessageBlockOutBlock" runat="server" text="DEFAULT _
                    BlockOutBlock"></asp:Label>
        <br />
        <asp:Label id="lblMessageProcedure" runat="server" text="DEFAULT _
                    Procedure"></asp:Label>
        <br />
        <asp:Button runat="server" Text="Submit"/>
    </form>
</body>
</html>
```

4. Save as `TIO-VariableScope2.aspx` and view the page in your browser and note the **strMyBlockVariable2** not declared error as shown in Figure 3-13:

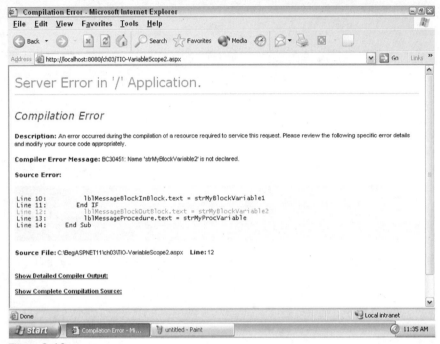

Figure 3-13

5. Move the offending line up into the block as follows, and the variable is now available to use:

```
Sub Page_Load()
Dim strMyProcVariable = "Procedure Variable"
If ISPostBack Then
    Dim strMyBlockVariableUsedInside = "Block Variable Used In Block"
    Dim strMyBlockVariableUsedOutside= "Block Variable Used After Block"
    lblMessageBlockInBlock.text = strMyBlockVariableUsedInside
    lblMessageProcedure.text = strMyProcVariable
    'NOW FIXED TO INSIDE BLOCK
    lblMessageBlockOutBlock = strMyBlockVariableUsedOutside
End If
End Sub
```

6. Open the page in your browser as shown in Figure 3-14:

Figure 3-14

How It Works

Let's start with the `<form>` section where we have two labels to show variables in different situations: a block variable used in a block and a procedure variable. Note that they have a default text, so if we do nothing we will see the DEFAULT message:

```
<form runat="server">
    <asp:Label id="lblMessageBlockInBLock" runat="server" text="DEFAULT _
                BlockInBlock"></asp:Label>
    <br />

    <asp:Label id="lblMessageProcedure" runat="server" text="DEFAULT _
                Procedure"></asp:Label>
    <br />
    <asp:Button runat="server" Text="Submit"/>
</form>
```

Now let's look at our `Page_Load()` procedure as follows. We start by declaring a variable in a procedure (but outside a block), so this will be a procedure scope (or local) variable. We will use it later at the end of the procedure and it works fine.

```
Sub Page_Load()
Dim strMyProcVariable = "Procedure Variable"
If ISPostBack Then
    Dim strMyBlockVariableUsedInside = "Block Variable Used In Block"

    lblMessageBlockInBlock.text = strMyBlockVariableUsedInside
    lblMessageProcedure.text = strMyProcVariable
End If

End Sub
```

Then we have a block that is used if `Postback=True`. So the first time the code is run, you will just see the default text from the label. But after clicking on Submit this will run and the contents of the two variables will be put into the labels.

In step three, we added three lines of code. First was a new label. Second was the declaration of a variable inside a block. The third was the assignment of the variable's contents to the new label. But we performed that assignment outside the block and thus created an error.

In step five we moved the assignment line inside the block, so now the variable is available and the code runs without problems.

Global Variables

If variables created in subroutines are local to the subroutine that created them, how do we go about ensuring that the value of a variable persists after a subroutine is done and is still available to other subroutines on the page? The answer comes in the form of a *global* variable that is simply declared **outside** any individual procedure (this is in `DemoVariableGlobal.aspx` in the download files):

```
<%@ Page Language="vb" %>
<script runat="server">
Dim strVariableGlobal = "Use me anyplace on the page"
```

```
Sub Page_Load()
...
End Sub
```

The lifetime of a global variable begins at the start of the ASP.NET page and ends at the end of the page, and spans any procedures created within the script. In ASP.NET you can create variables with a scope beyond the page, for example for a user's session or for all of the users at a Web site. These techniques are covered in *Chapter 11*.

Constants

There will be occasions when you want the value assigned to a variable to remain constant throughout the execution of the code, for example a sales tax. This value will rarely change, yet when calculating the total of a shopping basket, you'll probably need to refer to it several times. Even if the tax is changed, you would not need to change the value during the code execution – rather, you would change it manually during a design mode edit of the code. VB.NET allows you to store unchanging data in a *constant*. The main reason you'd assign a value to a constant is to prevent its alteration by a mistakenly written line of code.

In VB.NET,we create a constant with the Const keyword followed by the data type, generally outside of a procedure like a global variable. By convention, constants are named in uppercase:

```
Const ABSOLUTEZERO As Integer = -273
```

Suppose we then tried to assign another value to ABSOLUTEZERO, such as:

```
ABSOLUTEZERO = 0
```

This change would be rejected, and an error message produced. Constants remain in force for the duration of the script, just as global variables do. It isn't possible to amend their value once they have been set. Constants make code easier to read and maintain, as they require less updating. Also, if you choose a self explanatory name, they make your code easily understandable. They also give a performance increase over variables.

Conversion Functions

A common variable problem in ASP.NET programming arises when a value of one type could be used as another type, but VB.NET will not allow the crossover. For example, if you have a text box where a user enters a date like 1/1/2005, you will not be able to directly use that as a date in many VB.NET commands. Text boxes deliver the user's input as string typed data. To overcome the problem, VB.NET offers functions that convert data of one type into another type.

Conversion functions are simple to use. They are all named starting with a C followed by the type you want as output. So you have CInt(), CDate(), CStr(), and so on. Put the original value into the parenthesis and the function will return the converted value:

```
Dim MyDate as Date
MyDate = CDate(txtInput.text)
```

Arrays

Arrays are like a variable, but can store a series of related values. Each value has an identifying number called an *index*. You could use them to store the names of the Marx brothers, for instance:

```
Dim strMarx(5) As String
strMarx(0) = "Groucho"
strMarx(1) = "Harpo"
strMarx(2) = "Chico"
strMarx(3) = "Zeppo"
strMarx(4) = "Gummo"
strMarx(5) = "Karl"
```

The first thing to note is that arrays are zerobased, meaning the first member has an index of zero, not one. There are actually six Marx brothers here (even if one isn't related by family!), and they occupy the positions 0 to 5 in the array. It's not mandatory to store a value in each item of the array, or to store values sequentially:

```
Dim strHouse(5) As String

strHouse(1) = "Mr. Jones"
strHouse(4) = "Mr. Goldstein"
strHouse(3) = "Mrs. Soprano"
```

Arrays are particularly useful if you want to manipulate a whole set of data items as though they were one. The next chapter will discuss *looping*, using which we can make changes to all the values in an array with just a few lines of code.

Declaring Arrays

Arrays, like variables, have to be declared using the Dim keyword before they can be used. However, an array declaration needs an extra parameter at the end, which is used to specify the maximum index of the array. The array can then hold a number of values equal to the maximum index plus one (the plus one is for the value where the index equals zero). As with variables, you must declare which type of data (string, integer, date, and so on) goes into the array. All of the values must be of the same data type. For example, you could set up an array to have 50 entries, one for each of the states in the US, with the following statement:

```
Dim StatesInUS(49) As String
```

The index number 49 isn't a mistake because arrays count from zero upwards in VB .NET, rather than from one. So in this case the 50 states are indexed by the 50 different parameter values 0, 1, ... 49.

Try It Out Using Arrays

This simple page allows a user to submit a shipping company code and get back the actual name of the shipper. We will hold the shippers' names in an array where a shipper's code number is the same as its index number in the array.

1. Create a new page named `TIO-Array.aspx` in the `ch03` folder and enter the following lines:

```
<%@ Page Language="VB" %>
<script runat="server">

Sub Page_Load
  If IsPostBack
  Dim VendorShipping(3) as string
  VendorShipping(0) = "no shipping"
  VendorShipping(1) = "Canada Post"
  VendorShipping(2) = "UPS"
  VendorShipping(3) = "FedEx"

    lblShipper.text = "Shipper is " & VendorShipping(txtShipNum.text)
    lblShipper.visible = TRUE
  End If
End Sub
</script>

<html>
<head><title>Array Example</title></head>
<body>
    <form runat="server">
        Please enter your shipper code number from your invoice<br/>
        (should be between 0 and 3)
        <asp:TextBox id="txtShipNum" runat="server" width="30px"/><br />
        <asp:Button id="Button1" runat="server" Text="Submit"/><br />
        <asp:Label id="lblShipper" runat="server"/>
    </form>
</body>
</html>
```

2. View this page in the browser, then enter a number between 0 and 3, both inclusive, and submit it to see the results as seen in Figure 3-15:

Figure 3-15

3. Let's look at some errors:

- ❏ Try entering '5' and note the error message that an index was outside the bounds of the array.

- ❏ Note the results of submitting with no number at all.

- ❏ Modify your code so the #2 index is not filled, and then ask for it. You can do that by adding an apostrophe as follows:

```
VendorShipping(0) = "no shipping"
VendorShipping(1) = "Canada Post"
' VendorShipping(2) = "UPS"
VendorShipping(3) = "FedEx"
```

4. Re-activate the index #2 and save again so it works when you review this chapter.

How It Works

Let's start on the form where the three controls are seen. The first allows the user to enter their shipper code number and the second submits the form. The third control, a label, displays the answer:

```
<form runat="server">
    Please enter your shipper code number from your invoice<br/>
    (should be between 0 and 3)
    <asp:TextBox id="txtShipNum" runat="server" width="30px"/><br />
    <asp:Button id="Button1" runat="server" Text="Submit"/><br />
    <asp:Label id="lblShipper" runat="server"/>
</form>
```

Now, we use the `Page_Load()` procedure in the script, but we only run the code if the page is a *postback*. A postback page means the page is shown after the user clicks on a submit button (as opposed to the first time it is requested by the browser's URL Address input tool). Thus, the entire process of creating and filling the array only occurs with postback. Likewise, the `lblShipper` only appears on the page in a postback, not at the first request:

```
<%@ Page Language="VB" %>
<script runat="server">
Sub Page_Load
  If IsPostBack
  Dim VendorShipping(3) as string
  VendorShipping(0) = "no shipping"
  VendorShipping(1) = "Canada Post"
  VendorShipping(2) = "UPS"
  VendorShipping(3) = "FedEx"
  ...
  lblShipper.visible = TRUE
  End If
```

We assume that the user has entered a number. In the following line, we set the text of `lblShipper` to some boilerplate, plus a value from the `VendorShipping` array. The index will be whatever number was typed into the `txtShipNum`.

```
lblShipper.text = "Shipper is " & VendorShipping(txtShipNum.text)
```

We then looked at three kinds of errors. The first was the result of VB.NET trying to look up a code number (5) that was not in the array. This is common and requires that you validate user data before trusting it as an index value. Likewise, you can never assume that a given textbox will actually have data. The error from the missing index #2 was subtler. Like a variable, an array when created does not have data. If you request the value of an empty index you will get back nothing.

The `Array` class also provides us with an `IndexOf` method, which returns an integer representing the first occurrence of a value in a specified array, but only works on single dimension arrays. For example, to find out which element contains the first occurrence of the `FedEx` string, we use the expression:

```
IntShipperCode = Array.IndexOf(VendorShiping, "FedEx")
```

Multi-Dimensional Arrays

You can keep information of a two dimensional nature in a two dimensional array. For instance, you might want to store a set of related information separately, such as a first name, last name, and employee number. A normal (one dimensional) array would be unsuitable because all three pieces of information would have to be in one string. You can achieve far better results by adding another parameter to your array declaration:

```
Dim strClient(3,3) As String
```

This will set up a two dimensional array of up to 4 by 4, which can hold a total of 16 values. You can assign values to a multi dimensional array by referencing each element of the array through its two value index. For example, you could use such an array to store first and last names and phone numbers:

```
strClient(0,0) = "John"
strClient(0,1) = "Buck"
strClient(0,2) = "111-111-1111"
strClient(1,0) = "Jane"
strClient(1,1) = "Doe"
strClient(1,2) = "222-222-2222"
```

The first dimension stores the information that is related to one person, while the second dimension holds data of the same type for a different person. To get the last name of the first client, use `strClients(0,1)`, which is Buck.

You can also think of the data as stored in a table where the first index represents columns and the second index, rows. Therefore the value in `strClient(0,1)` means the first (0) column and the second (1) row which would be Buck)

	0	1
0	John	Jane
1	Buck	Doe
2	111-111-1111	222-222-2222

Benefits of Arrays

Arrays are a very popular way to group elements together and there are some good reasons for that:

❑ **Easy to use**: Arrays really are very easy to use, and are present in almost every programming language – if you have done any programming before you will almost certainly have come across them.

❑ **Fast to alter elements**: Arrays are just a consecutive list of items, so altering one of the items is extremely fast and pretty easy, as we can easily locate any element.

❑ **Fast to move through elements**: Because an array is stored contiguously in memory, it's quick and easy to cycle through the elements one by one from start to finish in a loop.

❑ **You specify the type of the elements**: When you create an array, *you* define the data type.

Limitations of Arrays

However, as we noted earlier, arrays also have some distinct limitations:

❑ **Fixed size**: Once you have created an array, it will not automatically resize if you try to add more items onto the end. Although you can use the ReDim statement to change the size of an array's dimension, it is slow for large dimensions, and the fact that you have to perform the operation explicitly is far from ideal.

❑ **Inserting elements is difficult**: If you wanted to add an element between two existing elements, it can be quite challenging. Firstly, you may have to increase the size of the array to make space. Also, you then have to move all the existing elements up one so you have a gap for your new element.

Data Collections

All in all, arrays are quite simple to understand and very easy to use. However, we often need more sophisticated ways to group items together. These advanced techniques in VB.NET are grouped as *collections* and include the ArrayList, the HashTable, and the SortedList. Collections are characterized by:

❑ A collection can contain an *unspecified* number of members.

❑ Elements of a collection need be *related* only by the fact that they exist in the collection.

❑ Elements of a collection do not have to share the same *data type*.

❑ An object's *position* in the collection can change whenever a change occurs in the collection as a whole. Therefore, the position of any specific object in the collection can vary.

ArrayList

The ArrayList is a special array that provides us with some functionality over and above that of the standard Array. Most importantly, you can dynamically resize it by simply adding and removing elements. Let's see how an ArrayList measures up.

Benefits of ArrayList

The benefits of ArrayList are as follows:

- ❑ **Supports automatic resizing**: When creating an `ArrayList`, you do not need to specify the array bounds (size) – as we add elements, the array automatically ensures there's enough space.

- ❑ **Inserts elements**: An `ArrayList` starts with a collection containing no elements. You can add them as you choose (and in any position you choose for) them.

- ❑ **Flexibility when removing elements**: An `ArrayList` can completely remove elements very easily.

- ❑ **Easy to use**: Using an `ArrayList` requires you to learn a few new commands, but they are intuitive.

Limitation of ArrayLists

There is one major limitation to an `ArrayList`. Given that the `ArrayList` control seems to offer so much more than arrays, you may be wondering why we bother using arrays at all – the reason is simply a matter of speed. The flexibility of an `ArrayList` comes at a cost, and since memory allocation is a very expensive business (in performance terms at least), the fixed structure of the simple array makes it a lot faster to work with.

Using ArrayLists

We create objects from the `ArrayList` by using a general type of syntax that will be covered in detail later. Since an ArrayList is an object, we create it as follows:

```
Dim myArrayList as new ArrayList()
```

Use whatever name you want instead of `myArrayList` but it must follow the same rules as naming variables (start with a letter, no spaces). We're using the `new` keyword since we are creating a new instance of the `ArrayList` object. As you can see, you don't need to specify how large it should be. Once you have an empty `ArrayList` object, you can use the `Add()` method to add elements to it:

```
myArrayList.Add("MyData1")
myArrayList.Add("MyData2")
```

Each new item in the `ArrayList` is added to the end of the list, so it has the largest index number. If we want to insert an item into the middle of the list (in the example below, this is location 2), we can use `Insert()` with a numeric first argument as follows:

```
myArrayList.Insert(2,"MyDataNew")
```

> `myArrayList.Add` puts the new member at the end. `myArraylist.Insert` lets you specify where in the list to put the new member.

You can also remove members of an `ArrayList` using either of the following two syntaxes. Notice they use slightly different keywords; if you are providing an index number use `RemoveAT`:

```
myArrayList.RemoveAt(2)
myArrayList.Remove("MyData2")
```

Try It Out Using an ArrayList

Let's create a page that creates an `ArrayList` of shippers and then shows them in a dropdown list box. This will introduce us to some data binding concepts covered later, but they are not difficult.

1. In your `ch03` folder, create `TIO-ArraylList.aspx` and enter the following:

```
<%@Page language="vb" %>

<script runat="server" language="vb">
Sub Page_Load()
    Dim ShippersArrayList as new ArrayList()
    ShippersArrayList.Add("none")
    ShippersArrayList.Add("Canada Post")
    ShippersArrayList.Add("UPS")
    ShippersArrayList.Insert(1,"FedEx")

    MyDropDownList.DataSource = ShippersArrayList
    MyDropDownList.DataBind()
End Sub
</script>

<html>
<head><title>ArrayList Example</title></head>
  <body>
    <form id="Form1" method="post" runat="server">
      <asp:dropdownlist id="MyDropDownList" runat="server" />
    </form>
  </body>
</html>
```

2. Call it up in your browser as shown in Figure 3-16:

Figure 3-16

How It Works

There are just two changes here from when we used a simple array. First, we are using an array list that requires us to use the special syntax for creating objects:

```
Dim ShippersArrayList as new ArrayList()
```

Note that we don't specify a length or a data type. This is because the elements will be assigned dynamically (as and when we need them) and can be of any type.

Next we use the object's `Add()` method to add three strings as elements, each added to the end:

```
ShippersArrayList.Add("none")
ShippersArrayList.Add("Canada Post")
ShippersArrayList.Add("UPS")
```

Next we test the `Insert` by adding one to the second position (index #1 since first position is index #0):

```
ShippersArrayList.Insert(1,"FedEx")
```

Finally, we specify `ShippersArrayList` as a data source for the dropdown list and bind the data:

```
MyDropDownList.DataSource = ShippersArrayList
MyDropDownList.DataBind()
...
  <asp:dropdownlist id="MyDropDownList" runat="server" />
```

Obviously an `ArrayList` is much more amenable to manipulation than a simple array, even if it is slower and more resource intensive. Read on for an option that moves us completely away from the use of index numbers.

Hashtables

In some respects, the `Hashtable` object is quite similar to `ArrayList`, except that we don't have to use a numerical index. Instead, we use a *key* that can be numeric, text, or date. Some people refer to Hash keys as an index, but it is best to leave the term index for arrays and arraylists. For example, we might want our index to be text of country codes (such as US and UK) rather than numbers.

Benefits of Hashtables

The benefits of Hashtables are as follows:

❑   **Non-numeric index allowed**: Because you can use text, numbers, or dates as your key, the Hashtable is more amenable to doing lookups from one piece of data to another.

❑   **Inserting elements**: When you use a Hashtable, you can add as many pairs of key/value elements as necessary. You do not have to specify the size ahead of time (as simple arrays require).

❑   **Removing elements**: You can remove items from Hashtable objects very easily.

❑   **Fast Lookup**: The Hashtable collection provides very fast lookup.

Limitations of Hashtables

The limitations of Hashtables are as follows:

❑   **Performance and speed**: Although the lookup speed is very quick, each time we add and remove items from a Hashtable, .NET has to do quite a bit of work in order to keep its lookup mechanism optimized. This work ultimately makes Hashtable objects slower to update but faster to use in a look-up than ArrayList objects.

❏ **Keys must be unique**: An array automatically keeps the index values unique. In a Hastable we must monitor the key uniqueness. If you expect to have duplicate keys (like more then one person as a salesman for a given company) then you should store the information in a relational database.

❏ **No useful sorting**: The items in a Hashtable are sorted internally to make it easy for the Hashtable to find objects very quickly. But it's not done by using the keys or the values, so for our purposes, the items may as well not be sorted at all.

Using a Hashtable

We create a Hashtable as an object using the same syntax as an ArrayList:

```
Dim myHashtable As New Hashtable()
```

Once it's created, we can then add the key/value pairs. Remember that the key is like an index for the entry and the value is the data we're storing. We store each element using the Add() method with either of the following syntaxes:

```
myHashtable.Add("UK", "United Kingdom")
myHashtable.Add("US", "United States")
' or
myHashtable("UK") = "United Kingdom"
myHashtable("US") = "United States"
```

Most programmers consider the second syntax easier to read. Hashtables with numbers or dates for the keys are written as follows:

```
hashShippers(1) = "Canada Post"
hashShippers(2) = "UPS"

hashConcerts(#1/1/2004#) = "The Keystone Band"
hashConcerts(#2/2/2004#) = "Bridgemen"
```

Note that you must use the # symbol around dates. If you used hashConcerts(1/1/2000), then VB.NET will consider the key to be numbers, do the math, and create a key value of 0.0005 which is 1 divided by 1 divided by 2000!

To read an element, just specify the key, and the value is returned. The following code puts the value United Kingdom into a variable named CountryName. Remember that the keys are *case sensitive*, so the second line below would put nothing into CountryName:

```
myHashtable("UK") = "United Kingdom"
CountryName = myHashtable("UK")    ' works fine
CountryName = myHashtable("uk")    ' blank result because incorrect case
```

Let's look at an example page that uses hashtables.

115

Try It Out Hashtable

Let's build a page that allows users to find out who is performing on a date of a concert series.

1. In the ch03 folder create TIO-HashTable.aspx and enter the following code:

```
<%@ Page Language="VB" %>
<script runat="server">

    Sub Page_Load
     lblShow.Visible = False
    If IsPostBack Then
      Dim datDateIn as Date
      Dim hashConcerts as new Hashtable
      hashConcerts(#1/3/2005#) = "Bridgemen"
      hashConcerts(#1/4/2005#) = "Vanguard"
      hashConcerts(#1/2/2005#) = "Blue Devils"
      hashConcerts(#1/1/2005#) = "Belevederes"

      datDateIn = cDate(txtDateIn.text)
      lblShow.text = "On this date enjoy the: "
      lblShow.text += hashConcerts(datDatein)
      lblSHow.Visible = True
    End If
    End Sub

</script>
<html>
<head>
    <title>HashTable Example</title>
</head>
<body>
    <form runat="server">
        <h3>2005 Drum and Bugle Corps Concert</h3>
        Please enter a date between 1/1/2005 and 1/4/2005
        <asp:TextBox id="txtDateIn" runat="server"></asp:TextBox>
        <br />
        <asp:Button id="Button1" runat="server" Text="Look up"></asp:Button>
        <br />
        <asp:Label id="lblSHow" runat="server"></asp:Label>
    </form>
</body>
</html>
```

2. Call up the page in your browser, and enter some dates as shown in Figure 3-17:

Figure 3-17

How It Works

In the form, we have a text box to receive a date and a label that displays the performer:

```
<form runat="server">
    <h3>2005 Drum and Bugle Corps Concert</h3>
    Please enter a date between 1/1/2005 and 1/4/2005
    <asp:TextBox id="txtDateIn" runat="server"></asp:TextBox>
    <br />
    <asp:Button id="Button1" runat="server" Text="Look up"></asp:Button>
    <br />
    <asp:Label id="lblSHow" runat="server"></asp:Label>
</form>
```

Up in the script we start by hiding the results label until we know a date has been requested. We then check if this is a postback. If it is not (that means the page is being displayed for the first time and does not have a date entered) then we do not want to do anything:

```
Sub Page_Load
 lblShow.Visible = False
If IsPostBack Then
...
  End If
  End Sub
```

However, if it is postback, it should have a date. We start with two declarations. The first will hold the incoming date and the second will create our Hashtable:

```
Dim datDateIn as Date
Dim hashConcerts as new Hashtable
```

Then we fill our hashtable using dates as the keys. Note that we must enclose the dates in # symbols. Also note that we can add items in any order because VB.NET will find them by their keys:

```
hashConcerts(#1/3/2005#) = "Bridgemen"
hashConcerts(#1/4/2005#) = "Vanguard"
hashConcerts(#1/2/2005#) = "Blue Devils"
hashConcerts(#1/1/2005#) = "Belevederes"
```

Now we have to take the text that comes from `txtDateIn` and convert it to a date using the `cDate` function:

```
datDateIn = cDate(txtDateIn.text)
```

We put some boilerplate into the label and then add on the value returned when we used our date formatted value to search the keys of the hashtable. Now we can show the label with the performer:

```
lblShow.text = "On this date enjoy the: "
lblShow.text += hashConcerts(datDatein)
lblShow.Visible = True
```

SortedList

A `SortedList` is another collection that stores keyvalue pairs, in which we can not only insert and remove items at will, but can also rely on the items being usefully ordered. In fact it's really just like a `Hashtable` object whose elements are automatically sorted according to their keys. Just like `ArrayList` and `Hashtable`, the `SortedList` class lives in the `System.Collections` namespace.

Since the items in a `SortedList` are always stored in a well defined order, we get the best aspects of a `Hashtable` object (the ability to use key-value pairs) along with the best aspects of an `ArrayList` (the ability to sort the items). Remember, however, that the items in a `SortedList` are sorted on the **key**, and not on the value. `SortedList`, thus, is most useful when we have to sort a list of keyvalue pairs for which the ordering of the key is what matters, rather than the order of the values. For example, we might use a sorted list to hold entries in a dictionary.

We create and use a `SortedList` collection in the same manner as a `HashTable`. Remember, we have to use the `new` keyword when creating the object. Adding items to a `Sortedlist` is exactly the same as with a `Hashtable`, the only difference being that each item is automatically inserted in the correct position in the list, according to the keybased sort order. A value can be read from the `SortedList` as follows (you can see this in action in download file `TestSortedList.aspx`):

```
Dim stlShippers as new SortedList
stlShippers("cp")="Canada Post"
stlShippers("fe")="Federal Express"
stlShippers("us")="United State Postal Service"

lblDisplay.text = "The full name of shipper = " & stlShippers(txtCodeIn.text)
```

The last dozen pages covered four ways to handle sets of related data. First, we used an array, which gave us indexed access to a group of data. Although fast, it is limited in capabilities. Then we used an `ArrayList`, which gives us more power to arrange the order of items, but still within a numeric index system. The `Hashtable` broke free of numeric indexing by using a key, which can be of numeric, text or date types. And last we used the `Sortedlist`, which added automatic maintenance of the keys order, but at a performance price.

Summary

The chapter started with a discussion of the difference in the way that an HTML page is handled on the server as opposed to the way that an ASPX goes through the additional interpretation step. The result is a page built for each request, thus enabling dynamic content on web sites.

The ASP.NET server controls were introduced and their server side capabilities were demonstrated. All of these controls require you to use their specific `<asp:...>` tag and to include the `runat="server"` attribute. In addition, make it a habit to always include the `ID="MyName"` attribute so you can refer to the control in code.

When using a control in code, refer to it in the syntax `ControlName.Property` where property is most commonly `text`. All controls have three basic properties: `runat`, `ID`, and `visible`. Most have additional properties such as `text`, `backcolor`, and `width`.

The most common mistakes with ASP.NET controls arise from radio buttons and list controls. Be careful to use `<asp:RadioButtonList>` if there is more than one option (as opposed to `<asp:RadioButton>`) so that you have one ID for the list and within there a different value for each option. When we need the user's choice we are interested in the `RadioButtonList.SelectedItem.Value`. ListBoxes can be of single or multiple selection modes.

We temporarily store information in variables that consist of four parts: a name, space in memory, a data type, and the value they contain. When you name a variable, you must start with a letter and cannot have spaces or periods (full stops). It is best to keep the names descriptive but short, in camel case and avoid using a variable name twice in an application.

Three types of Numeric data types can support decimals: (from smallest to largest) decimal, single, and double. Numeric types that support only integers (no decimals) include (again, smallest to largest) byte, short, integer, and long. Always select the smallest numeric type that will do the job; for currency use decimal.

Text information is stored in a string type variable. Strings are also used for numeric characters that are identifiers or codes and have no arithmetic value (for example telephone numbers). True False data is stored in a Boolean type variable. Both dates and times are stored in the Date variable. When assigning a text value, enclose it in quotes; dates are enclosed in the # symbol; numbers are naked. The conversion functions (such as `CStr`, `CDate`, `CInt`) allow you to change data so it can be used as a different type.

Scope establishes how long a variable will exist, or to put the idea another way, how much other code can use the variable. Block variables are declared within a block and only available to that block. Procedure (local) variables are limited to the procedure in which they are declared. Global variables, declared outside of any procedure, are available to the entire page. Always use the smallest scope possible.

We studied four ways to store related groups of information of the same data type. The simplest and fastest is the array, which tracks members by an index number. `ArrayLists` have more capabilities to sort, add, and remove members, but still use a numeric index. `HashTables` allow you to use non numeric identifiers called keys such as text or dates, but are slower then arrays. Finally, you can use `SortedLists` which are even slower, but hold the members in the order of the keys.

Exercises

1. Explain the difference between `<form>` and `<form runat="server">` and describe how each one is handled.

2. What is a variable, and how is it related to data types in VB.NET?

3. Use string, numeric, and date variables to create an ASPX file that displays your name, age, and date of birth.

4. Arrange the following into groups of Numeric, Textual, and Miscellaneous data types. Rank the Numerics according to the size number they can hold. Give an example of a value and use for each.

    `Integer, Char, Byte, Short, Boolean, String`

    `Long, Single, Double, Date, Decimal`

5. Create an array containing your five favorite singers. Concatenate the elements of your array into one string, and after the opening sentence "My 5 favorite singers , display them in a clear way using the `<asp:label>` control.

6. Describe a situation in which you would use each of the following and state why that choice is the best:

❑ arrays

❑ arraylists

❑ hashes

❑ sorted lists

Control Structures and Procedural Programming

In this chapter, we continue to explain techniques of VB.NET. In the last chapter, we focused on obtaining and holding information in variables or server controls. Now we work on manipulating that data using lines of code. Specifically, we want to know how to control the order of execution of those lines of code.

First, we will cover the basics of creating expressions. Then we will study two of the three groups of control structures: *branching* and *looping*. We will cover the third group, *jumping*, in the next chapter.

This chapter will cover:

❑　Assignments, arithmetic operators, and concatenations

❑　Comparison operators

❑　Overview of control structures

❑　Branching structures: If...Then and Select Case

❑　For...Next loops

❑　Do While and Do Until loops

❑　For Each and With... End With structures

Operators

We use *operators*. to manipulate values. An operator is a symbol that carries out a predefined operation on the operands and generates a result. If X=1+2, then X is a variable (or control property value), = and + are operators and 1 and 2 are operands. We have already seen many examples of basic data manipulation using operators in the last two chapters, but in this section we'll introduce the concepts more formally.

Assignment Operator

The familiar equals sign (=) *assigns* a value to a variable or control property. The variable *name* goes on the left; the variable *value* goes on the right. VB .NET doesn't enforce spaces on either side of the equals sign, but you may prefer to include some to make your code easier to read:

```
intMyVariable = 2
lblMyLabel.Text = "Sale Ends January 15."
```

You can also use the assignment operator to change values of variables using the following syntax:

```
intMyVariable = 2
intMyVariable = intMyVariable + 1
```

At the end of these two lines, intMyVariable equals three. Mathematicians will be scratching their heads, wondering how intMyVariable can be equal to intMyVariable plus 1; it's similar to saying 2 = 2 +1, which is impossible. In VB .NET, variable values are calculated on the right, and then stored on the left of the equals sign. Thus in this example intMyVariable + 1 is evaluated first, and *assigned* to intMyVariable at the end, replacing the old value in intMyVariable.

VB.NET also offers a shorter syntax to perform the above task, at the end of which intMyVariable equals three:

```
intMyVariable = 2
intMyVariable += 1
```

Arithmetic Operators

The arithmetic operators available in VB .NET are:

Addition	+	Exponentiation	^
Subtraction	–	Negation	–
Multiplication	*	Modulus	MOD
Division	/		

Here is a very simple example that assigns values to the variables `intNumber1` and `intNumber2` before adding them together, and assigns the result to a third variable, `intNumber3`:

```
Dim intNumber1 As Integer
Dim intNumber2 As Integer
Dim intNumber3 As Integer
intNumber1 = 14
intNumber2 = 12
intNumber3 = intNumber1 + intNumber2
```

Because of this, `intNumber3` will contain the value `26`.

You can also use brackets (parentheses) to influence the order in which a calculation is performed. For example, in the following code we divide the variable `intNumber2` by 6 and add the result to the variable `intNumber1`:

```
Dim intNumber1 As Integer
Dim intNumber2 As Integer
Dim intNumber3 As Integer
intNumber1 = 14
intNumber2 = 18
intNumber3 = intNumber1 + (intNumber2/6)
```

First, the computer evaluates the contents of the brackets, following normal mathematical procedure: `intNumber2` is divided by 6 and yields the result 3. This is added to the value of `intNumber1`, and the result of this is `17`, which is assigned to the variable `intNumber3`.

As a quick reminder, normal mathematical procedure is to start inside the innermost pair of parentheses and work from left to right performing exponentiation. Next, inside these parentheses, go left to right performing multiplication and division and then finally go left to right performing addition and subtraction. Then repeat the above steps again for the next innermost set of parentheses, until you've calculated the expression. All programming languages use these rules for performing arithmetic. Using parentheses is a good idea to make your code more readable, even when they may not be technically required for the evaluation to occur correctly.

Let's have a go at a quick example that performs a simple tax calculation. To do this you need to create three variables, one for earnings, one for the tax percentage, and one for the total. We're going to deduct the earnings by whatever percentage the tax rate is set to, and display the output in the familiar `<asp:label>` control.

Try It Out   Performing a Calculation on an ASP.NET Page

1.   Create a folder named `C:\BegASPNET11\ch04` and within this folder create `TIO-CalculateTax.aspx` as follows:

```
<%@ Page Language="vb" Debug="true"%>
<script runat="server">
Sub Page_Load()
  If IsPostBack
    lblTax.text = "Your tax bill would be $"
```

```
      lblTax.text += CStr(txtEarnings.text*txtTaxRate.text/100)
      lblTax.visible=True
   End IF
End Sub
</script>
<html>
<head><title>Calculate Tax Bill</title></head>
<body>
<h3>Tax rates</h3>
<form runat="server">
    Please enter your earnings: $
    <asp:TextBox runat="server" ID="txtEarnings" width="80px"/><br/>
    Please enter your tax rate, for example enter '7' for 7%
    <asp:TextBox runat="server" ID="txtTaxRate" width="30px"/><br/>
    <asp:Button runat="server" Text="Submit"/><br/>
    <asp:Label runat="server" ID="lblTax" visible=False/><br/>
</form></body></html>
```

2. View this in your browser. Note that the output label does not appear. When you enter some
values and click Submit, the calculation is made and the label appears as shown in Figure 4-1:

Figure 4-1

How It Works

The form has two `asp:textbox` controls to receive data. Interspersed with some explanatory text there
is a submit button and a label for output. Note that the label is set to be invisible:

```
<form runat="server">
    Please enter your earnings: $
    <asp:TextBox runat="server" ID="txtEarnings" width="80px"/><br/>
    Please enter your tax rate, for example enter '7' for 7%
    <asp:TextBox runat="server" ID="txtTaxRate" width="30px"/><br/>
    <asp:Button runat="server" Text="Submit"/><br/>
    <asp:Label runat="server" ID="lblTax" visible=False/><br/>
</form></body></html>
```

In the script, we execute the code during page load, but only if it is a postback. If not a postback, then it
is the first time the user has requested the page and thus the input textboxes would be empty:

```
<%@ Page Language="vb" Debug="true"%>
```

```
<script runat="server">
Sub Page_Load()
    If IsPostBack
```

In the next line, we put some boilerplate text into the `lblTax.text`:

```
lblTax.text = "Your tax bill would be $"
```

Then we do the calculation inside the parentheses. That result is then converted to a string because a label can have difficulty with non-string data types:

```
lblTax.text += CStr(txtEarnings.text*txtTaxRate.text/100)
```

Finally, we make the label visible:

```
        lblTax.visible=True
    End IF
End Sub
</script>
```

Some find the modulo operator difficult to understand. The symbol is a backslash \. Modulo will return the remainder of a division. For example, 10 mod 3 = 1 because 10 divided by 3 gives 3 with a remainder of 1. It is the value of the remainder that is returned by the modulo operator.

Modulo is useful when you want to identify every *nth* occurrence. For example, if you numbered your site visitors using `intUser` you could identify every 100th visitor with `intUser mod 100 = 0`. This expression would be true for every hundredth visitor. Each visitor would have their number divided by 100 and most would have some remainder. Only the visitors numbered 100, 200, 300, and so on would have an exactly divide 100 and leave no remainder (modulo = 0). We will present an example later in the chapter where it fits in nicely with the `Do...While` looping exercise.

String Concatenation

Programmers frequently need to append new text to old, as you did with the contents of `lblTax` when you appended the dollar amount to the end of the string to get "Your tax bill would be $". Programmers speak of "adding" strings, but that is only a manner of speaking, as tthere is no mathematical addition. The proper term is *concatenation*, which means to join or link strings together to make a larger string. In .NET there are two ways of concatenating.

Concatenation by Ampersand

To concatenate two strings you can use the ampersand operator (`&`). Some older forms of Visual Basic supported the + sign, but that should be avoided. You can concatenate the strings "`Spring`" and "`Sale`", as follows:

```
Dim strSaleNote As String
strSaleNote = "Spring" & "Sale"
```

Here, the result of the concatenation is the string `"SpringSale"`, which will be assigned to the variable `strSaleNote`, of type String. You should note that VB .NET doesn't automatically put in spaces. You can concatenate any number of strings within the same expression. You can also concatenate the contents of variables. However, it is best to covert them to string using `CStr()`. Here, you'll concatenate three strings, one of which is a space (also a string, since a space is a character):

```
Dim strSaleNote As String
Dim datSaleSpring as Date = #3/3/2005#
strSaleNote = "Spring" & " " & "Sale begins "
& Cstr(datSaleSpring)
```

VB.NET handles the text value of a control in the same way as a variable or literal string, as follows (You can see these samples in action in the download file `ch04/DemoConcatenation.aspx`):

```
txtSaleEnd.text = "Spring" & " " & "Sale begins " & Cstr(datSaleSpring)
...
<asp:TextBox runat="server" ID="txtSaleEnd"/>
```

What if you already have information in a variable and want to add to that? As with numeric addition, you can use the recipient's name on the right side of the equals sign as follows:

```
StrSaleNote = "Sale starts on 3/1/2005"
strSaleNote = strSaleNote & " and ends on " & txtSaleEnd.text
```

Concatenation by Assignment

In addition to the `&` operator, VB.NET supports a second method to concatenate strings, the `+=` operator:

```
StrSaleNote = "Sale starts on 3/1/2005 and ends on "
strSaleNote += txtSaleEnd.text
```

`strSaleNote` will then contain the string `"Sale starts on 3/1/2005 and ends on "` followed by the value the user entered into `txtSalesEnd`.

> String concatenations can be slow. If your program performs a great deal of these operations, it is recommended that you study and use the .NET **StringBuilder** class.

Numeric Comparison Operators

When you get to control structures in the second half of this chapter, you will have to create expressions that use comparison operators as follows:

Equality	=	Inequality	<>
Less than	<	Greater than	>
Less than or equal to	<=	Greater than or equal to	>=

You've already seen the equals sign (=) in its role as the assignment operator. You can also use it to test if something is true, for example:

```
DatDOB = #1/1/2005#
IntCode = 36
StrNameFirst = "John"
```

If you have used other programming languages, you might be accustomed to the double equality operator (==) that is used to test for equality. VB.NET doesn't use this operator.

These statements say, for example, "If the value in `DatDOB` is #1/1/2005#" then consider this expression to be `True`. Later you will build control structures that make decisions based on whether an expression is true or false. Remember that result of the comparison expression is a Boolean value, either `True` or `False`.

Other comparison operators work in the same way. If, for example, you want to compare two numbers to check whether one is greater than the other, you could do the following:

```
number1 > number2
```

This would test whether the first number was greater than the second and the expression would evaluate to either of the Boolean values `True` or `False`, depending on the contents of the variables.

For `Date` type data < means earlier and > means later (test and observe code from the download file `Demo-DateComparison.aspx`). For strings, things are a little trickier since the comparison is by ASCII code. In general, ASCII codes are lowest for number characters, then go up through the uppercase letters, then through the lowercase letters and finish with European diacritics. The symbols are sprinkled throughout the numbering system.

Download and try `Demo-StringComparison.aspx` from the book's Web site at www.wrox.com to test various combinations of letters, numbers and symbols as well as view a list of ASCII numbers as shown in Figure 4-2:

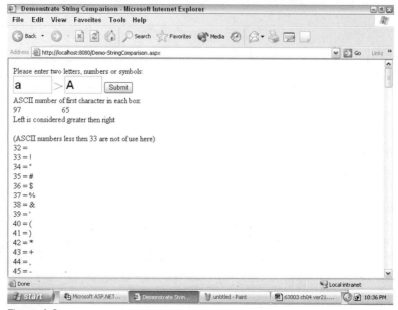

Figure 4-2

Logical Operators

There's also a set of three common logical operators you can use in your code:

❑ AND

❑ OR

❑ NOT

Logical operators are used in the same way as comparison operators and the whole expression evaluates to a Boolean value:

```
If intNumber1 = 1 AND intNumber2 = 2 Then
```

In the above line, if `intnumber1` is 1 and `intnumber2` is 2, then the whole phrase `intNumber1 = 1 AND intNumber2 = 2` will evaluate to `true` and the line will become "If true Then" and the code for true will be executed.

When using AND, *both* expressions have to be `True` for the whole expression to be true. When using OR, only *one* out of the two conditions has to be `True` for the expression to be true:

```
If intNumber1 = 1 OR intNumber2 = 2 Then
```

> The most common logical operator mistake is an incomplete syntax such as:
> `If intNumber1 = 1 OR 2` This line fails because VB.NET requires a complete expression on each side of the logical operator. The correct syntax is:
> `If intNumber1 = 1 OR intNumber1 = 2`

The third logical operator, NOT, simply implies the reverse of the condition. If number1 isn't equal to 1 then the expression is true. For example, you have been using a property of the page called IsPostBack. If the page is posted back then this property will be True. You can use NOT to give a False when the page is posted back, as follows:

```
NOT IsPostBack
```

When a statement contains more than one logical operator, VB .NET decides which operator to execute first according to a simple rule. Operators are executed in the following order known as the order of *operator precedence*:

- ❑ NOT
- ❑ AND
- ❑ OR

Consider the following code:

```
If number1 = 1 OR NOT number2 = 1 AND NOT number3 = 1 Then
```

What does this expression actually test? Well, first it checks that number2 is not equal to 1, and that number3 is not equal to 1. It then evaluates the AND operation and uses the result to evaluate the OR operation.

Beware of these kinds of logical 'traps' in the same way as you would with mathematical operators.

> To ensure that your code works in the way you intend, use parentheses wherever possible.

You can make the same expression more readable by adding parentheses:

```
If number1 = 1 OR (NOT number2 = 1 AND NOT number3 = 1) Then
```

There's another important operator you need to be aware of that can make writing complex logic a lot easier. It is the inequality operator, <>. This operator looks a little odd, but it means *not equal to*. In fact, you can use the inequality operator to compare strings and other types of values as well.

The preceding example can be rewritten using this operator:

```
If number1 = 1 OR (number2 <> 1 AND number3 <> 1) Then
```

Now, that's quite a lot easier to read. Let's now look at three practical examples.

Try It Out Performing a Calculation on an ASP.NET Page

We will create three pages, each demonstrating a logical operator to determine whether an input date is in the year 2005 or not.

1. In your ch04 folder create a file named TIO-LogicalAND.aspx as follows:

```
<%@ Page Language="VB" %>
<script runat="server">
  Sub Page_Load
    If IsPostBack
       lblout.text="Date outside year 2005"
       Dim datInput as Date
       datInput = CDate(txtIn.text)
       If (datInput>=#1/1/2005#) AND (datInput<=#12/31/2005#) Then
       lblOut.text = "Date inside year 2005."
    End If
    End If
End Sub
</script>
<html>
<head><title>Logical AND Example</title></head>
<body>
    <form runat="server">
        Please enter a date, first in 2005. <br />
        Next try a date not in 2005 <br />
        <asp:TextBox id="txtIn" runat="server"/><br />
        <asp:Button id="Button1" runat="server" Text="Submit"/><br />
        <asp:Label id="lblOut" runat="server"/><br />
    </form>
</body></html>
```

2. Now save the file as TIO-LogicalNOT.aspx and change the code to the following. Carefully check the two lines of lblOut.text and the >= and <= symbols:

```
Sub Page_Load
  If IsPostBack
     lblOut.text="Date inside year 2005"
     Dim datInput as Date
     datInput = CDate(txtIn.text)
     If NOT ( (datInput>=#1/1/2005#) AND (datInput<=#12/31/2005#) ) Then
     lblOut.text = "Date outside year 2005."
     End If
  End If
End Sub
```

3. Now save the file as TIO-LogicalOR.aspx and change the code to the following. Carefully check the two lines of lblOut.text and the >= and <= symbols:

```
Sub Page_Load
        If IsPostBack
          lblOut.text="Date inside year 2005"
            Dim datInput as Date
```

```
        datInput = CDate(txtIn.text)
        If (datInput<=#1/1/2005#) OR (datInput>=#12/31/2005#) Then
        lblOut.text = "Date outside Year 2005."
    End If
  End If
End Sub>
```

4. View and test all three pages in your browser. The `TIO-LogicalAND.aspx` page is shown in Figure 4-3:

Figure 4-3

How It Works

In the form, we simply pick up a user's date input, offer a submit button, and create a label for output. Up in the script we have the lines of interest. There are several points germane to all three pages:

❏   First, we reset the text of the output label with every page response so that there is no hangover of text from the last update of the page.

❏   Second, since all of the `lblOut.text` is inserted in script we do not have to worry about making the label invisible. When the `IsPostBack` is `false`, the script does not run and the label is empty and thus effectively invisible.

❏   Third, the `If` block either changes the `lblOut.text` or leaves it the same.

❏   Fourth, we are working with dates so in our expressions we put the dates within # marks and use the `Cdate()` function to convert the input to a proper date data type.

Now let's look at the code specific for `TIO-LogicalAND`:

```
  If IsPostBack
    lblOut.text="Date outside year 2005"
    Dim datInput as Date
    datInput = CDate(txtIn.text)
    If (datInput>=#1/1/2005#) AND (datInput<=#12/31/2005#) Then
    lblOut.text = "Date inside year 2005."
    End If
  End If
```

Here we start with a text of Date outside year 2005 and want to run code to change the text to inside 2005 if the expression is true. To be in the year 2005, a date must meet two criteria: it must be *after* (greater than or equal to) January 1, 2005 and it must be *before* (less then or equal to) December 31, 2005. In other words, both of these conditions must be true in order for a date to be in 2005 and thus we use the AND logical comparator.

In TIO-LogicalNOT we can reverse the situation with a single logical word and a reversal of the label text values. We change the default text to inside year 2005 and the text executed by the If block to outside year 2005. Then we merely add a NOT around the entire comparison we did on the AND page. For dates that are in the year 2005, the NOT reverses the True into False.

In TIO-LogicalOR we start with a text of Date inside year 2005 and want to run code to change the text to outside year 2005 if the expression is true. Our expression will test if the date is before 1/1/2005 and if the date is after 12/31/2005. If either *is* true then the date is not in 2005. Only one has to be true to know that the date is *not* in the year 2005, so we can use the OR operator.

As a last note on logical operators, the NOT works to change control properties that are true or false. For example, you may want certain actions to switch the visibility of a control between visible=true and visible=false. Within the action just include the MyControl.Visible = NOT(myControl.Visible) line as shown in DemoLogicalNotToggle.aspx.

Having looked at the types of operators you can use with control structures, it's time to look at the structures themselves in more detail.

An Overview of Control Structures

When programming VB .NET or just about any other computer language, we have three types of structures (groups of control statements) to control the order in which the lines of code are executed. These are branching structures, looping structures, and jumping structures. We'll look at each of these in detail.

- ❑ Branching structures decide which of two or more sections of code to run, for example, you can display either "Good Morning" or "Good Afternoon" depending on the time of day.

- ❑ Looping structures repeat consecutively a section of code as many times as needed – for example, you can write a line to a schedule page again and again, once for each upcoming event.

- ❑ Jumping structures move out of the code sequence and execute sections of code in another part of your script – for example, on a library receipt page we run the same few lines to calculate the due date for each item borrowed. This topic is covered in *Chapter 5*.

Overview of Branching Structures

Branching structures work by first performing some kind of test. Based on the test results, one set of code is executed and other sets of code are skipped. Consider a quick real life example. Imagine you're in a car and pull up to a set of traffic lights. If the lights are red, you'll have to stop the car and maybe switch it off, and wait until the lights change before going. If the lights are green, you can drive on through immediately. The course of action you take is determined by the result of the test condition (the color of the traffic light).

VB.NET offers two types of branching structures:

❑ `If...Then ... Else` is generally used to select one of two or more sets of lines of code depending on a condition. For example, in a Web page featuring news stories, you could choose whether to display the international or regional news headlines, depending on a user's preferences. `If...Then` is also the tool of choice for complicated comparisons, such as expressions using the terms AND, OR, and NOT.

❑ `Select Case` is generally used to select which lines to execute from many possibilities. For example, in a page featuring news stories, we could choose which of several icons to include in the page next to the story, depending on whether the story was about politics, business, sport, entertainment, or technology.

Overview of Looping Structures

Looping structures allow the same block of code to run a number of times immediately after each other. Instead of skipping code, which is what the branching technique does, we *repeat* code. Let's go back to our previous real life example. I frequently go to the airport in my car to pick up my brother. I don't like to pay the parking fee, so he comes out the door to the street for pick up. I go around the terminal road past the door and check if he is there. If yes, I stop and pick him up and we go home. But if he is not out yet I do another loop around the terminal and re-check the door. I continue to loop (both literally and procedurally) until he comes out the door.

In the holiday booking site example of *Chapter 3*, you could use looping to generate a page for each person who is going to be staying at a hotel. The construction of those lines (print the description, print the quantity, print the price, put in a line break) would be looped to produce one line for each item ordered:

❑ `For...Next` is used to repeat line(s) when, at the beginning of the repetitions, you know exactly how many repetitions you want, or you can use a test, such as the `sizeof()` function to determine the number of repetitions needed. For example, if you know there are five trucks needing a wash, you could repeat five times the set of steps involved in successfully washing a truck.

❑ `Do While` is used to repeat line(s) when you don't know at the time you write the code, how many repetitions you want. You build a test condition into the loop that is checked after each loop. The loop will repeat as long as this condition is `True`.

❑ `For...Each` is a convenient alternative to `For...Next` when you have a defined collection of items, but don't know how many, and want to repeat the loop for every item in the collection.

Overview of Jumping Structures

Jumping structures allow the programmer to pause the execution of the current code and jump to another named code block. For example, we may need directions during our car trip. Therefore, we have a procedure that is to pull over, dial our friend on the cell phone, write down the directions, and then proceed. It is good to have this type of code in a separate section for the following reasons:

❑ You may never need it.

❑ You might have to perform the code several times but probably not consecutively (thus it is not amenable to a loop).

❑ It makes sense when you maintain your code to have a discrete job such as this in its own section, not mixed into the main code.

For example, a Web page may have a block of code called `ShowOrder` that produces lines to show the customer the goods they ordered. Whenever you want VB.NET to show those lines you don't have to rewrite or copy all of that code. Instead, just have VB.NET jump out of the current code, execute `ShowOrder` and then come back and continue executing the original code. There are two types of jumping controls:

❑ **Subroutines** (or **procedures**) run the statements in the subroutine, and then return control to the line that called them. For example, a procedure could set a change in information to a database.

❑ **Functions** run the statements in the function, and then return control to the line that called them along with a result of the function, which must be used in some way. Functions are same as subroutines but they can return information. For example, a function could calculate the total of an order and then return that value to the main body of code to be used as the value in an `lblTotal.text`.

Branching, looping, and jumping form the backbone of just about every program or application you will come to write in ASP.NET. This chapter will cover branching and looping and the next chapter will cover jumping.

Many find it difficult to decide which type of structure to use. This is understandable for several reasons. First, there are many choices (plus some that we won't even discuss). Second, there is some overlap in their functionality. Third, in some cases the decision of which structure to use is entirely the programmer's discretion, so studying one set of code may not match the tactics of another code sample. In this chapter, we will spend a lot of time comparing the options and guiding you to making wise selections.

Uses of Control Structures

The following table lists several programming objectives and suggests which type of structure will help us achieve the desired results:

Situation	Solution	Why?
I want ASP.NET to show page A or page B.	Branching If Then	You want to perform only one of two possible events.
I need to show the user one of several meetings they should attend. The meeting displayed is based on which department they belong to.	Branching Select Case	You want to write to the page only **one** out of several possible meeting locations.
I want ASP.NET to list each member of a club. The data about each member is held in essentially the same manner, with a name, photo, address, and other contact information.	Looping Do While	You will be performing the same set of code (that retrieves a member's name) many times (once for each member, until all members are listed).
I want to present a known number of records of data in a table.	Looping For Next	You will perform the same code (make a row for a table) repeatedly until you have built all of the rows needed.
After placing an item that I describe in a catalog page, I want to put in a few lines of information about 'How to Order'. There will be several items across several pages that I need to do this for.	Jumping Subroutine (Procedure)	You want to pause the main code and perform several lines of *another* set of code that describes 'How to Order'. Then you want to resume execution of the main code. Since the 'How to Order' set of code will be performed at various times across the page, it is best to write it once and call that one piece of code as needed.
I need to calculate prices in several places on each page. The prices will be set according to input from a user form.	Jumping Function	You will pause building the page, jump out to execute code that calculates the price of an item, and then return to building the page and return the calculated amount. Since you will calculate many prices it is best to write the formula once and have it called when needed.

Let's recap what we've discussed so far. There are three kinds of statements to control the flow of your code's execution:

❑ Branching statements perform a test and then execute some lines of code, but not others.

❑ Looping statements execute a set of code repeatedly.

❑ Jumping statements pause the execution of the current code, jump over to another set of code, and then return to where they started sometimes bringing values back with them.

Let's look at branching statements in detail, and see what we can do with them.

Branching Structures in Detail

Branching controls perform some type of test called an *expression*. Based on the test results, a set of code is executed and other sets of code are skipped.

ASP.NET offers two techniques for branching. `If...Then` is used when there are only a few choices of outcome. Bear in mind that the more lines you use in `If...Then`, the more difficult your code will become to follow. It is better to use `Select Case` when there are several outcomes.

For example, if you are deciding on how to proceed having asked the user, "Do you want a confirmation by telephone?", the outcome is either "Yes" (`True`) or "No" (`False`), so you would perform the branch using `If...Then...Else`. But if you ask the user "Do you want confirmation by telephone, fax, FedEx, e-mail, voicemail, or telepathy?" given the number of outcomes, it is better to use `Select Case`.

The If...Then Structure

The basic `If...Then` statement has four parts:

❑ An *expression*: that is, a test that evaluates to either `True` or `False`

❑ An *if true* section of code

❑ An (optional) *if false* section of code

❑ An *ending* statement

The first part is the expression, which can be a combination of keywords, operators, variables, and constants. The expression must be Boolean, and evaluates to either `True` or `False`. If the test evaluates `True`, then only the lines of code in the *if true* section are executed. If the test evaluates `False`, then only the lines of code in the *if false* section are executed. After either the *true* or *false* section is executed, the execution jumps down to the ending statement and continues with the next line of code. There is never a situation where both the true *and* false sections are executed in a given case.

There are four ways of building `If...Then` statements. To select the proper syntax you must consider:

❑ Do I want to do anything if the test is `False`?

❑ Do I want to execute *more than one statement* if the test is `True`?

If...Then

The first and simplest syntax is useful if you only want to run one statement in the case of a True condition. Using this method, you will not be able to execute any statements if your expression evaluates to False. For example, if a user checks a box to inform you that they have a fax, you want them to enter the number. If they don't check the box then you want to take no action. In this case, you can use a simple one line syntax:

```
If faxConfirm = "Yes" Then Message.Text = "Please enter your fax number."
```

If...Then...End If

A more complex syntax is where you want to execute more than one statement in the case of True, but still nothing if the test is False. For example, if the user wants a fax confirmation, then ask for the fax number and jump over to the fax entry page.

In this case write the If...Then with two changes from the syntax outlined above: the statements must go on their own lines, not the same one as in the simple example previously shown. Since there is now more than one line for the If...Then code, you must use a closing line of End If:

```
If faxConfirm = "Yes" Then
   Message1.Text = "Please provide your fax number."
   Message2.Text = "Thank you for your business."
End If
```

If...Then...Else...End If

The third level is where you want to execute one or more statements in the case of True, and also one or more lines of code if the test is False. For example, if the user has requested a fax confirmation then ask for the fax number and jump over to the fax entry page. If they haven't requested a fax, then show a line that says that a fax will not be sent. In this situation, write the If...Then with a line containing the word Else to separate the code that will run in the True case from the code that will run in the False case:

```
If strFaxConfirm = "Yes" then
   Message.Text = "Please enter your fax number."
Else
   Message.Text = "No fax confirmation will be sent."
End If
```

Note that we still write End If, not End Else.

If...Then...ElseIf

The fourth level is quite complex but there are some situations where it cannot be avoided. It allows you to choose between several different pieces of code to execute according to multiple expressions. To do this, you need to separate each new expression with the keyword ElseIf. You still close the condition with End If. You can also include a generic Else clause that will be executed if none of the other cases were chosen.For example, you can structure a list of options for a customer to confirm an order:

```
If lstConfirm.SelectedItem.Value = "Fax" then
   Message.Text = "Please enter your fax number."
```

```
ElseIf lstConfirm.SelectedItem.Value = "Email" then
  Message.Text = "Please enter your email address"
ElseIf lstConfirm.SelectedItem.Value = "Voicemail" then
  Message.Text = "Please enter your voice mail number"
Else
  Message.Text = "No confirmation will be sent."
End If
```

Here we test the data to see if it meets Condition 1. If it doesn't, we test it to see if it meets Condition 2. If it doesn't meet that either, we test it to see if it meets Condition 3, and so on. When the data meets one of the criteria, or if the criteria isn't met, the appropriate branch is decided and we arrive at a suitable outcome.

> *There is an alternative structure (`Select Case`) that provides a simpler solution to this problem, and we'll be looking at this shortly. Generally, if you are only testing to see if a variable contains one of several specific values, you will use `Select Case` rather than `If...Then ... ElseIf`.*

The following table contains a summary of four kinds of `If...Then` control structures:

Situation	Syntax	Example

If expression is True
 	
do one statement
 	
Otherwise do nothing
	`If expression`
	`Then statement`
		`If age < 18 Then`
		
		`    Message.Text =`
		`"You must be 18 or`
		`older to order by`
		`credit card."`

If the expression is True
 	
do two or more statements
 	
If the expression is False do nothing
	`If expression`
	`Then`
	
	`True code line 1`
	`True code line 2`
	
	`...`
	
	`End If`
		`If age < 18 Then`
		
		`    discount = True`
		
		`    Message.Text =`
		`"You are eligible`
		`for the student`
		`rate of $49."`
		
		`End If`

Situation	Syntax	Example

If the expression is `True`
 	
 do one or more statements
 	
 If the expression is `False`
 	
 do a different set of one or more statements
	`If expression`
	`Then`
	
	`True code line 1`
	`True code line 2`
	
	`Else`
	
	`False code line 1`
	`False code line 2`
	
	`End If`
		`If age < 18 Then`
		
		  `discount = True`
		
		  `Message.Text =`
		`"You are eligible`
		`for the student`
		`rate of $49."`
		
		`Else`
		
		  `Message.Text =`
		`"The fee for this`
		`service is $59."`
		
		`End If`

If the first expression is `True` do one or more statements
 	
 Else if the second expression is `True`
 	
 do a different set of one or more statements
 	
 Else if the *n*th expression is `True`
 	
 Then do a different set of one or more statements
 	
 If all expressions are `False` do nothing
	`If expression`
	`Then`
	
	`True code line 1`
	`True code line 2`
	`ElseIf expression`
	`Then`
	
	`True code line 1`
	`True code line 2`
	
	`ElseIf`
	`expression Then`
	
	  `True code line 1`
	  `True code line 2`
	
	`End If`
		`If age < 18 Then`
		
		  `discount = True`
		
		  `Message.Text =`
		`"You are eligible`
		`for the student`
		`rate of $49."`
		
		`ElseIf age > 65`
		`Then`
		
		  `discount = True`
		
		  `Message.Text =`
		`"You are eligible`
		`for the senior rate`
		`of $49."`
		`ElseIf age > 18 And`
		`age < 65 Then`
		  `Message.Text =`
		`"The fee for this`
		`service is $59."`
		
		`End If`

> When using the one-line form of `If...Then`, you do not use `End If`.
> When using any multi-line form of `If...Then`, you must use `End If`.

Try It Out Using the If...Then Structure

It's time for a quick example that involves a number guessing game. The computer 'thinks' of a number between one and five and you have to guess what it is.

1. In the `ch04` folder, create a file named `TIO-IfThen.aspx` and type in the following:

```vb
<script language="vb" runat="server">
Sub Page_Load()
  Dim theNumber As Integer
  Dim theGuess As Integer
  theNumber = int(5 * rnd) + 1
  If Page.IsPostBack Then
    theGuess = Guess.SelectedItem.Value
    If theGuess > theNumber then
      Message.Text = "<BR><BR>Guess is too high<BR>Try again - it was " _
      & theNumber
    End If
    If theGuess < theNumber then
      Message.Text = "<BR><BR>Guess is too low<BR>Try again - it was " _
      & theNumber
    End If
    If theGuess = theNumber then
      Message.Text = "<BR><BR>Guess is correct!"
    End If
  End If
End Sub
</script>
<html>
<head><title>IF THEN example - solution 1<title></head>
<body>
<form runat="server">
  What number am I thinking of?
  <asp:dropdownlist id="Guess" runat="server">
    <asp:listitem>1</asp:listitem>
    <asp:listitem>2</asp:listitem>
    <asp:listitem>3</asp:listitem>
    <asp:listitem>4</asp:listitem>
    <asp:listitem>5</asp:listitem>
  </asp:dropdownlist><br><br>
  <input type="submit" value="Submit guess">
  <asp:label id="message" runat="server"/>
</form></body></html>
```

2. View `TIO-IfThen.aspx` in your browser to see Figure 4-4:

Figure 4-4

3. Choose a number and click on Submit guess. Carry on guessing until you get the correct answer.

How It Works

As it's such a simple example, it doesn't require too much code. We get the user to enter a guess into the Web form with the `<asp:dropdownlist>` control:

```
<asp:dropdownlist id="Guess" runat="server">
  <asp:listitem>1</asp:listitem>
...
  <asp:listitem>5</asp:listitem>
</asp:dropdownlist>
```

Using a dropdown list ensures that you get a valid response back from the user, as they can only choose from what you place in the list. You can then interrogate the drop-down list box via its name, `Guess`, directly through the code.

The actual VB.NET code is the most interesting. You start by defining two variables:

```
Sub Page_Load()
    Dim theNumber As Integer
    Dim theGuess As Integer
```

These two variables respectively contain the randomly generated number and the user's guess:

```
theNumber = int(5 * rnd) + 1
```

Next, we randomly generate a number. VB.NET has a function called `rnd()`, which will generate a decimal number less than 1 and greater than or equal to zero. To get a random number between 1 and 5, we have to multiply this value by 5, which will generate a number between 0 and 4.999... (not 5 itself). We use the `int()` function to cut off the decimal part so we have a whole number between 0 and 4, and then we add 1 to it, giving us what we need: a number from 1 to 5. Any range of random integers in VB.NET can be generated with the following equation:

RandomNumber = int((1 + *upperbound* – *lowerbound*) * rnd) + *lowerbound*

So we've generated our random number, we've got the guess from the user stored in the `Guess` variable; so all we need to do now is compare them, right?

Well, not quite! As this is a Web form with just one single page, you need to check whether the user has ever been there before. On their first arrival they won't have entered a number, and you don't want to test the random number against an empty variable.

The first time the page is run, it can't have been posted back, as the user hasn't guessed yet, so it will return `False` and run the code contained within. Each time the user submits a guess, there will be a value:

```
If Page.IsPostBack Then
    ...do code inside when True...
End If
```

So the first time the user accesses the page, `IsPostBack` will return `False`, and the page execution will jump to the end of the `If...Then` structure, marked by `End If`. After the related `End If`, is an `End Sub`, so the program ends until the page loads again:

```
    End If
End Sub
```

You may be wondering how ASP.NET knows that this is the correct `End If`, as there are several in the code. The answer is that they have been *nested* inside each other. Where there is an `If` statement inside the block of code belonging to another `If` statement, the inner `If` statement has to have a matching `End If` statement, before the outer block can be ended. This means that `If...Then` blocks can be treated as completely separate self-contained entities:

```
If Page.IsPostBack Then
    theGuess = "", so ignore all this code
End If
End Sub
```

There are three separate `If...Then` structures inside this code. You can see how useful it is to indent your code in these structures to keep track of which `End If` statement applies to which `If Then` structure:

```
if Page.IsPostBack <> "" Then
    theGuess = Guess.SelectedItem.Value

    if theGuess > theNumber then
        STRUCTURE 1
    End If
    if theGuess < theNumber then
        STRUCTURE 2
    End If
    if theGuess = theNumber then
        STRUCTURE 3
    End If
End If
```

These are all ignored the first time around because `IsPostBack` has returned `False`. Second time around, the `IsPostBack` is true (and we assume the user has submitted a guess) so the code inside will be run. It's worth to note that if the user has not selected a number then the page will process the default value of 1. Each structure is considered as a separate test in its own right. Before we do the test though, we set our `theGuess` variable to be equal to the contents of the `SelectedItem.value` of the dropdown list box, to save us a bit of typing each time we refer to the user's guess:

```
theGuess = Guess.SelectedItem.Value
```

The first test checks to see whether the guess is bigger than the number:

```
if theGuess > theNumber then
   Message.Text = "<BR><BR>Guess is too high<BR>Try again - it was " & theNumber
End If
```

If it is, then it sets the `<asp:label>` control to display a message informing the user that their guess was too high, along with the number that the user failed to guess.

The second test checks whether the guess is smaller than the number:

```
if theGuess < theNumber then
   Message.Text = "<BR><BR>Guess is too low<BR>Try again - it was " & theNumber
End If
```

In this case, we then display a message saying that the guess was too low, and display the number.

The last test checks to see whether the number is correct, and displays an appropriate message in the `<asp:label>` control:

```
if theGuess = theNumber then
   Message.Text = "<BR><BR>Guess is correct!"
End If
```

There are other ways to use `IF` to achieve the same goals, for example (`TIO-IfThenAlternate.aspx`):

```
Sub Page_Load()
    Dim theNumber As Integer
    Dim theGuess As Integer
    theNumber = int(5 * rnd) + 1

    If Page.IsPostBack Then
       theGuess = Guess.SelectedItem.Value
```

```
        If theGuess > theNumber then
          Message.Text = "<BR><BR>Guess is too high<BR>Try again - it was " _
          & theNumber
        ElseIf theGuess < theNumber then
          Message.Text = "<BR><BR>Guess is too low<BR>Try again - it was " _
          & theNumber
        Else
          Message.Text = "<BR><BR>Guess is correct!"
        End If
    End If
End Sub
```

This alternative logic uses the `ElseIf` clause for `If Then` to perform the second test and assumes that negatives from the first two tests will result in a correct guess.

Select Case Structure

One problem of `If...Then` is that it can start getting unwieldy after more than three possible outcomes. What happens if you want to show a different page to visitors from each of five departments? What happens if you want to do a calculation based on the user providing one of twelve salary grades? Or if you have different procedures for confirming an order by telephone, fax and e-mail? Your code is going to become difficult to maintain with more then a few nested `ElseIf`s. In addition, code with many layers of nesting runs slow.

`Select Case` is the alternative control structure for handling branching and it caters much more neatly for these situations by providing a better structure, better performance, and extra readability.

Anytime you need to make a choice among several answers (more than just True or False) use Select Case.

The syntax for `Select Case` has four parts:

❑   Statement of a value to be tested against (the *test value*)

❑   Statement of a *possible value* and what to do if that possible value matches the test value (this part is repeated for all possible values)

❑   An optional catchall `Case Else`, in case the variable matches a value you haven't anticipated

❑   An ending statement for the `Select Case` control structure, `End Case`

The following example carries out one of three actions depending on what is contained in the variable `confirmation`:

```
    Select Case confirmation
      Case "Fax"
        Message.Text = "<a href='FaxConfirmation.htm'>Fax</a>"
      Case "Telephone"
        Message.Text = "<a href='telephone.htm'>Telephone</a>"
      Case "Email"
        Message.Text ="<a href='Email.htm'>Email</a>"
    End Select
```

VB.NET knows from the first line that you want to compare answers to the contents of the variable `confirmation`. Next, it will begin testing the contents of the variable against the values shown in the `Case` lines. When VB.NET finds a match, it executes the following code up to the next `Case` line, and then jumps down to the first line after the `End Select` statement.

The previous `If...Then` example used a dropdown list to ensure that the user could only enter a valid answer. When checking user input using `Select Case` we often need to do the same thing, as string comparisons in VB.NET are case-sensitive. If you allow the user to enter text in response to a Yes/No question, be prepared to handle the fact that Yes, yes, and YES will all be handled differently. Additionally, prepare to handle unexpected inputs (like the user entering Yeah) as well. This can be done using the `Case Else` statement as shown here:

```
Select Case question
   Case "yes"
      Message.Text= "Details will be sent."
   Case "YES"
      Message.Text= "Details will be sent."
   Case "Yes"
      Message.Text= "Details will be sent."
   Case "no"
      Message.Text= "We will not contact you."
   Case "NO"
      Message.Text= "We will not contact you."
   Case "No"
      Message.Text= "We will not contact you."
   Case Else
      Message.Text "Your answer " & strQuestion & " is not recognized."
End Select
```

In this example, a user who decides to type Yeah will receive a custom error message.

You can further refine this code by having VB.NET test for more than one result on each `Case` line. As an example, for both yes and YES we would do the same thing, so we can handle them together:

```
Select Case question
   Case "yes","YES","Yes","Y"
      Message.Text= "Details will be sent."
   Case "no","NO","No","N"
      Message.Text= "We will not contact you."
   Case Else
      Message.Text= "Your answer " & strQuestion & " is not recognized."
End Select
```

This will work fine, but do you really want to spend all that time dreaming up possible cases? VB.NET offers a completely different way to solve the case problem. If you change all input text to *uppercase* before testing, you can reduce the number of tests needed. The `ToUpper()` method of the string object will convert a string to uppercase, as follows, before we test it:

```
Dim upperCaseQuestion as String
upperCaseQuestion = question.toUpper
Select Case upperCaseQuestion
   Case "YES","Y"
      Message.Text= "Details will be sent."
```

```
Case "NO","N"
  Message.Text= "We will make further contact by email."
Case Else
  Message.Text= "Your answer " & strQuestion & " is not recognized."
End Select
```

We've managed to cut down on the number of test statements. However, in some situations, such as the previous random number guessing example, it proved more beneficial to use a drop-down list control to limit the range of possible answers.

Let's look at an example that uses `Select Case` to make a more detailed set of selections. In *Chapter 3*, we used an example that showed how the user could select a holiday from a set of destinations. We're now going to go one better and provide a brief sales pitch depending on which destination the user selects. We will use `Select Case` to decide which pitch to use.

Try It Out Using Select Case

1. Create `TIO-SelectCase.aspx` in the `ch04` folder and type in the following:

```
<script language="vb" runat="server">
Sub Page_Load()
  If Page.IsPostBack Then
    Select Case(Destination.SelectedItem.Value)
      Case "Barcelona":
        Message.Text = "You selected Spain's lively Catalan city"
      Case "Oslo":
        Message.Text = "Experience the majesty of Norway's capital city"
      Case "Lisbon":
        Message.Text = "Portugal's famous seaport and cultural hub"
      Case else
        Message.Text = "you did not select a destination we travel to"
    End Select
  End If
End Sub
</script>
<html>
<head></head>
<body>
  <form runat="server">
  Select your choice of destination:
  <br><br>
  <asp:radiobuttonlist id="destination" runat="server">
    <asp:listitem>Barcelona</asp:listitem>
    <asp:listitem>Oslo</asp:listitem>
    <asp:listitem>Lisbon</asp:listitem>
  </asp:radiobuttonlist>
  <br><br>
  <input type="submit" value="Submit Choice">
  <br><br>
  <asp:label id="message" runat="server"/>
  </form>
</body>
</html>
```

2. View this in your browser, make a choice and click on Submit Choice as shown in Figure 4-5:

Figure 4-5

How It Works

There's a lot of code here, but it's actually simpler than the last example you looked at. The form has a radio button list control called `destination`, that allows the user to select a holiday destination:

```
<asp:radiobuttonlist id="destination" runat="server">
  <asp:listitem>Barcelona</asp:listitem>
  <asp:listitem>Oslo</asp:listitem>
  <asp:listitem>Lisbon</asp:listitem>
</asp:radiobuttonlist>
```

The `IsPostBack` test checks whether the page has been run before, as in the last example. If it hasn't, there will be nothing in either of these values, and you can skip to the end of the program and wait until the page is run again. If it has been posted back, then you take the contents of the radio button's `SelectedItem.Value` and test it for various values:

```
Select Case(Destination.SelectedItem.Value)
    Case "Barcelona":
      Message.Text = "You selected Spain's lively Catalan city"
    Case "Oslo":
      Message.Text = "Experience the majesty of Norway's capital city"
    Case "Lisbon":
      Message.Text = "Portugal's famous seaport and cultural hub"
```

As the page contains one question with three options, we deal with all of these possibilities within our `Select Case` structure. So if the user selects Oslo, then only the code in the `Case "Oslo"` section will run.

There is a `Case Else` at the end. This should never be generated unless you have made a mistake in matching up the cases you can handle with the options presented to the user:

```
Case else
    Message.Text = "you did not select a destination we travel to"
End Select
```

If they don't select anything, then no message at all is displayed, as this is caught by the `If...Then` structure. It's a simple example, but it demonstrates the potential power of case structures. Most importantly, it should be obvious how easy it is to add additional cases to a structure of this type, particularly compared to adding additional code to an `If...Then...ElseIf...Else` structure. There is one drawback of `Select Case` though – that it doesn't support comparison operators. You can only check for different cases of equality within the terms of the case. This means it might not always be appropriate in some situations (such as our age-range selector previously shown).

Looping Structures in Detail

ASP.NET has several types of looping structures:

- ❑   `Do...While`
- ❑   `Do...Until`
- ❑   `For...Next`
- ❑   `For...Each`

When you are deciding between `For..Next` and `Do...While`, consider whether you know in advance how many loops you want to do. If you *can* determine the number of loops at the point when your program is about to begin the loop (for example, the loop will always be performed exactly ten times, or you have the number of loops stored in a variable), then use `For...Next`. If you *do not* know ahead of time how many loops you want to do, and will have to decide after each loop whether to continue, then use one of the `Do` loops.

`For...Each` is used only in the case when you have a collection and need to loop through each member. In this sense, the term *collection* has a specific definition (not just any old group) such as the collection objects `ArrayList` and `HashTable` that were discussed in *Chapter 3*.

Technique	When Used
For...Next	The code knows before the first loop how many loops will be performed.
Do...While	The code does not know how many loops to perform and thus must decide at the end of each loop whether to perform another loop.
For...Each	Only used for collections. Performs one loop for each member of the collection.

The For...Next Structure

The `For...Next` structure has three parts. The first is a line that describes how many times to repeat the loop. Next come a set of lines with action statements that carry out the task you want repeated. Finally, a line indicates the end of the action statements and tells VB.NET to go back and repeat the action statements again:

```
For LoopCounter = StartValue To EndValue
    ...Loop Code here...
Next LoopCounter
```

Here is a simple example to get started. In the holiday example discussed earlier, some of the adventure holidays require participants to be over a certain age and so we need a signed age declaration form from each traveler. The trip organizer wants to get a Web page with a blank line for each person and then print that page to use as the sign-in sheet. If you imagine we needed a sheet for groups that always have five people you could use the following code:

```
For intCounter = 1 to 5
   Message1.Text += "Attendee Name _____<br />"
   Message1.Text += "Attendee Age _____<br /><hr /><br />"
Next intCounter
```

From the first line, VB.NET begins the process of running the loop five times. In order to keep count we provide a variable called intcounter. The lines that will be repeated five times are contained *between* (but not including) the For line and the Next line. In this case, two statements are needed to create lines for an attendee to write their name and their age as shown in Figure 4-6:

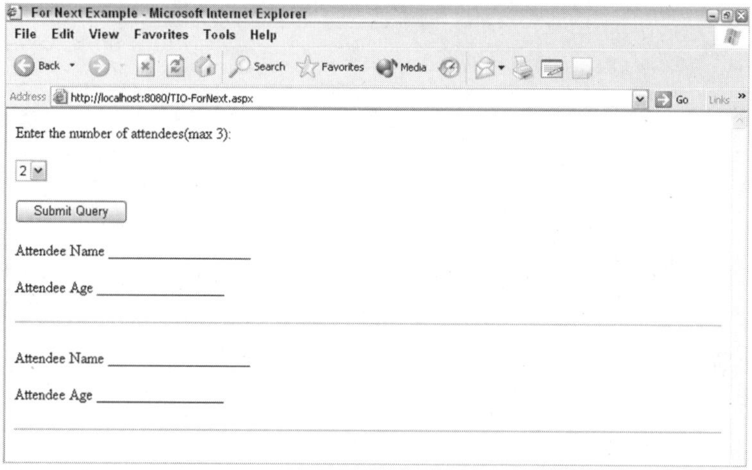

Figure 4-6

One quick point to note in the preceding code is that to get the `<asp:label ID="Message1">` control to display five sections for signatures you concatenated the next name to the contents of Message1.Text. This is because if you simply assigned the string to Message1.Text each time around the loop it would replace the previous contents and you would end up with just one line of text.

This example assumes that you would always have five attendees. What if that number varied? In that event, you could have a list box that asks for the number of attendees, for example, lstNumberAttendees, and then use that number to determine how many lines to print. You can use For...Next (instead of Do While) because when you start the loop you know how many loops to make. You may not know at design time, but will know when you run the code and get to the Next line.

A sample follows:

```
number = numberAttendees.SelectedItem.Value
For counter = 1 to number
  Message1.Text = Message1.Text & "Attendee Name _____" & _
    "<br /><br />Attendee Age _____<br /><br /><hr /><br />"
Next counter
```

Let's implement this code into a page that takes a number from the user and supplies the requisite amount of signature/age lines for a printout.

Try It Out   Using For...Next

1.   Within the folder ch04 create a file TIO-ForNext.aspx and type in the following:

```
<script language="vb" runat="server">
Sub Page_Load()
  Dim intLineLoopcounter As Integer
  If Page.IsPostBack then
    Message1.Text = ""
    For intLineLoopcounter = 1 to NumberAttendees.SelectedItem.value
      Message1.Text += "Attendee Name _____<br /><br />"
      Message1.Text += "Attendee Age _____<br /><br /><hr /><br />"
    Next intLineLoopcounter
  End If
End Sub
</script>
<html>
<head><title>For Next Example</title></head>
<body>
<form runat="server">
Enter the number of attendees (max 3):<br><br>
<asp:dropdownlist id="numberAttendees" runat="server">
  <asp:listitem>1</asp:listitem>
  <asp:listitem>2</asp:listitem>
  <asp:listitem>3</asp:listitem>
</asp:dropdownlist><br><br>
<input type="submit"><br><br>
<asp:label id="message1" runat="server"/>
</form>
</body>
</html>
```

2.   Open and view this page in your browser. Select a number and check that the sheet that appears looks like the Figure 4-7:

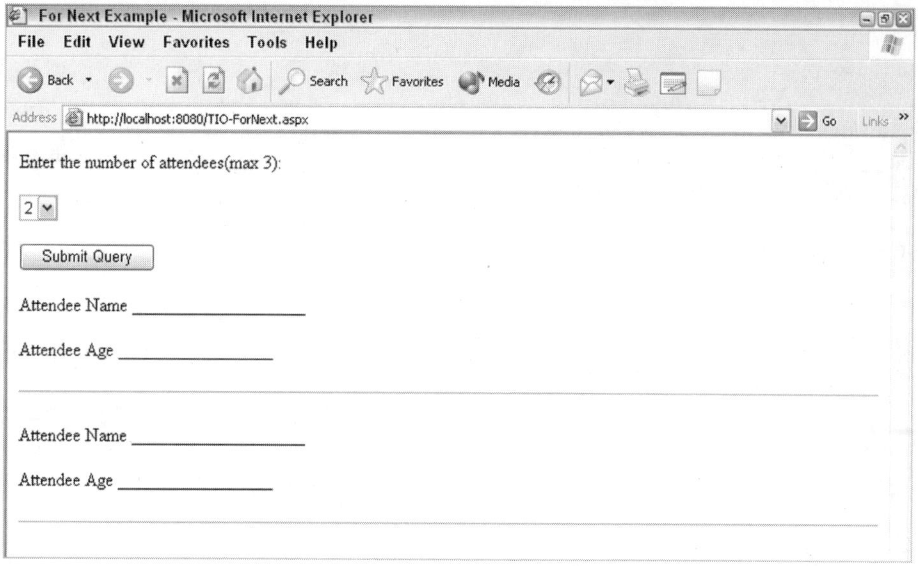

Figure 4-7

How It Works

The form should not be a problem for you by now – it is a simple `<asp.listbox>`. This control makes the selection available to our code as `numberAttendees.SelectedItem.Value`.

Moving into the code, you only need one variable, the counter for your `For...Next` looping. Next, blank the contents of the `<asp:label>` control to get a clean message after each refresh:

```
Message1.Text =""
```

Then you create a loop starting at one and stopping when it has reached the value that was picked by the user in the list box:

```
For intLineLoopcounter = 1 to NumberAttendees.SelectedItem.value
    Message1.Text += "Attendee Name _____<br /><br />"
    Message1.Text += "Attendee Age _____<br /><br /><hr /><br />"
Next intLineLoopcounter
```

Each time the loop is executed, VB automatically increases `intLineLoopCounter` by one. If that number is not greater than the value in `NumberAttendees.SelectedItem.value`, then the loop runs again. When the number of the counter equals the number held in the value, then the contents of the loop structure are executed a last time and VB then carries on past the `Next` statement and moves on to the statement after.

The value held in `intLineLoopCounter` (and automatically increased with each loop) is available to you just like any other variable. Recall from your study of HTML that `<br/>` puts in a line break and `<hr/>` adds a horizontal line. Try changing your `Message1.Text` as follows (`TIO-ForNextNumbered.aspx`):

```
Message1.Text += "Number " & intLineLoopCounter & ": "
Message1.Text += "Attendee Name _____<br /><br />"
Message1.Text += "Attendee Age _____<br /><br /><hr /><br />"
```

In the first line of the preceding code, VB.NET automatically handles converting the integer-type `intLineLoopCounter` into a string so it can be concatenated and added to the value for the text property of `Message1` as shown in Figure 4-8:

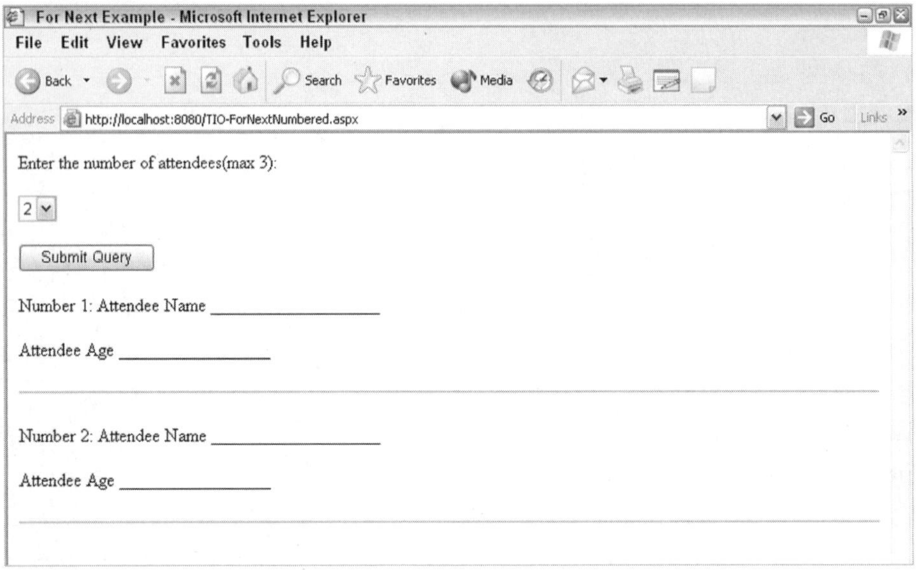

Figure 4-8

The Do While Structure

Use a Do While loop to repeat lines of code when you are not sure of how many iterations to perform. On each loop, it evaluates an expression and if the test resolves to True then it does another loop. Do While continues looping as long as the expression its true. If the expression resolves to False, then the loop is not executed again and execution jumps down to after the block. In some cases you might want to put the expression in a NOT so that the loop will continue as long as the expression is false. The differences in syntax between `For...Next` and `Do While` loops are shown in the following table:

For...Next Key Words	Do While Key Words
`For LoopCounter = StartValue To EndValue`	`Do While loopCounter [meets a specified condition]`

`...`
   `Lines of code to repeat`
`...`
	`...`

For...Next Key Words	Do While Key Words

`Next`	`Lines of code to repeat,`
	`[at least one of which`
	`must change loopCounter]`
	`...`
	`Loop`

`Do While` loops and `For...Next` loops have a significant difference in their use. The `For...Next` loop runs for a pre-specified number of times and no more, while the code between `Do While` and `Loop` continues to run for as long as your expression is true.

The second difference is the nature of the test to end the looping. `For...Next` has a variable for counting, a start point, and an end point. `Do While` has an expression test - at the beginning of each loop VB.NET checks the expression and if it is `True` it runs the loop. If the expression is `False`, the loop is not run and VB.NET jumps down in the code to the line after `Loop`.

There is a fatal trap into which most beginning programmers (and plenty of more experienced ones, too!) fall. If you start a loop and do not provide a means for it to stop, it will continue forever as an infinite loop. If you are working your way through a list of items (listbox values, database records, array members, and so on), be sure that within the loop you move to the next item on the list. Otherwise, you will forever perform the loop on the first item in the list.

Fortunately, most servers will eventually cut off a given ASP.NET page in an infinite loop, since the server needs to attend to other visitors and tries to optimize its resources. If a page seems to be hung up and not loading properly, it could be due to an unresolved loop, and it can cause your Web server not to respond.

Here is an example in pseudocode (code that explains the idea but does not use proper syntax). We want to print the names of all the members of our club. In *Chapter 8*, we will discuss how to connect to the database. Then we would write code along these lines:

```
... Code to connect to database
... Code to read the names into a set of records (RecordSet)
Do While Not EndOfRecordSet
  LblMEssage += (RecordSet.currentrecord.Name) & "<br/>"
  Move to next record
Loop
```

When we start the loop, we do not know how many cycles we will perform. However, at the beginning of each cycle we do a test as follows. First, we read the true/false property of the `EndOfRecordset`. If we are not at the end, this property returns a `False`. Since it is not at the end, we want to execute the loop, so we change the `False` into a `True` using `NOT`. With that `True` returned to VB.NET, it would execute the loop.

Note the very important second line within the loop – if we don't move to the next record we would just keep printing the name from the first record. However, with the `Move` we get, at some point, to the end of the records and `EndOfRecordSet` returns a `true`. That is turned into a `False` by the `NOT` and when the `Do While` sees a `False` in its text expression, it ends looping and jumps down to the next line of code below the loop.

We are not ready to read from databases, but we can code a page that involves chance and thus we do not know the number of loops to execute.

Try It Out Using Do While

We will write a page that simulates rolling a dice (by coming up with a random number between one and six) – and keeps rolling it until it gets a 6. A label on the page tells us the results of each try that was made. However, we don't know – at the time of writing our ASP.NET code, or even before we roll the first dice – how many times we'll have to roll the dice to get a 6. So we must use a `Do While` loop.

1. Create a new page `TIO-DoWhile.aspx` in `ch04` folder and type in the following:

```
<script language="vb" runat="server">
Sub Page_Load()
  Dim diceRoll As Integer
  Message1.text = "Lets begin. We'll keep trying until we get a six.<br/>"
  Do While diceRoll <> 6
    diceRoll = int(rnd * 6) + 1
    Message1.Text += "Rolled a: " & diceRoll & "<br />"
  Loop
  Message1.text += "Got it. Press page refresh to try again."
End Sub
</script>
<html><head><title>Do Loop Example</title></head>
<body>
  <asp:label id="message1" runat="server"/>
</body></html>
```

2. View this page in your browser as shown in Figure 4-9, and strike IE's refresh button several times:

Figure 4-9

How It Works

We started by declaring a variable that will hold the result of the `diceRoll`. Then we put some text into `Message1.text`. This line mainly demonstrates a line before a loop – it will only be executed once. When you start building complex pages, you will need to keep a clear idea of what is inside and outside of the loop:

```
Sub Page_Load()
   Dim diceRoll As Integer
   Message1.text = "Lets begin. We'll keep trying until we get a six.<br/>"
```

Then we run the loop. If the last dice roll was anything other than a 6, we want to roll again, so we use the inequality operator to tell VB .NET to keep running the loop, so long as the dice roll is not equal to six. We do this because we want the loop to stop once we have a 6:

```
Do While diceRoll <> 6
   diceRoll = int(rnd * 6) + 1
   Message1.Text += "Rolled a: " & diceRoll & "<br />"
Loop
```

When `diceRoll` equals 6, it will stop and not execute the contents of the loop, instead jumping to the next statement beyond the loop. In this case, it is our demonstration of a line outside the loop. It will be executed only once and that is after the loop is finished:

```
   Message1.text += "Got it. Press page refresh to try again."
End Sub
```

Modulo example

You came across the `modulo` operator in the last chapter and also earlier in this chapter. Recall that modulo returns the remainder of a division. You can refer to these sections to jog your memory about what modulo can do. Here we will apply this operator to our dice example.

Open `TIO-DoWhile.aspx`, change the code as shown and save as `Demo-Modulo.aspx`. This modification will give the user an encouragement message with every fifth roll:

```
Sub Page_Load()
      Dim diceRoll As Integer
      Dim bytRollCounter as byte
      Message1.text = "Lets begin. We'll keep trying until we get a six.<br/>"
      Do While diceRoll <> 6
        bytRollCounter +=1
        If bytRollCounter mod 5 = 0 Then
          Message1.Text += "   Keep trying!   "
        End If
        diceRoll = int(rnd * 6) + 1
        Message1.Text += "Rolled a: " & diceRoll & "<br />"
      Loop
      Message1.text += "Got it. Press page refresh to try again."
      End Sub
```

Test it with several refreshes until a try takes at least fives rolls. In this code, we start by creating a variable that will count our rolls. We can use byte data type with the assumption that we will roll a 6 in less then 255 tries. Then in each loop, we increase the value in `bytRollCounter`. Then we check if `bytRollCounter` is evenly divisible by 5, in other words the remainder is zero. If true, we concatenate the encouragement message as shown in Figure 4-10:

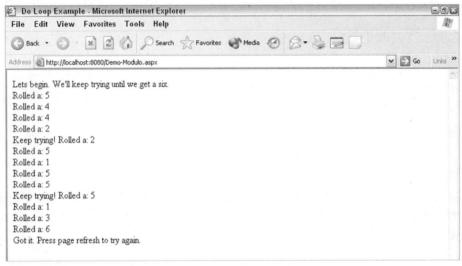

Figure 4-10

The Do...Until Structure

You are not restricted to placing the expression condition at the beginning of your loop. The `Do...Until` structure works as follows:

```
Do
   ...code here...
Loop Until a condition is True
```

So, if you went back to the previous example, it could be coded as follows (`DemoDoUntil.aspx`):

```
Sub Page_Load()
    Dim diceRoll As Integer
    Message1.text = "Lets begin. We'll keep trying until we get a six.<br/>"
    Do
        diceRoll = int(rnd * 6) + 1
        Message1.Text += "Rolled a: " & diceRoll & "<br />"
    Loop Until diceRoll = 6
    Message1.text += "Got it. Press page refresh to try again."
End Sub
```

The output and function will be the same as the `TIO-DoWhile.aspx` page. However, there is a very important difference – a `Do Until` loop is always executed *at least once*, because we don't check the condition *until the end of the loop*. Recall that a `Do While` does not execute if the condition was never met before the first loop.

> Use `Do Until` when actions within the loop absolutely have to occur at least once no matter what the result of the expression.
>
> Use `Do While` when there are actions within the loop that should not execute if the expression is false.

The For...Each Structure

VB.NET offers a cousin of the `For...Next` statement: `For Each...Next`. It works in a similar way to `For...Next`, except that it's only used for elements inside an array or a collection. It is like `Do While` in that we don't have to know the number of members in the collection. We've met several collections in the last chapter: `Arrays`, `ArrayLists`, `Hashtables`, and `SortedLists`.

```
Dim Item As String
Dim strCities As New ArrayList()
strCities.Add("London")
strCities.Add("Paris")
strCities.Add("Munich")
For Each Item In strCities
   Message.Text += Item & "<BR>"
Next
```

It looks almost identical to `For...Next` – the only difference is that you don't have to specify the number of items you want to loop through; VB .NET will simply start with the first item in the array and then repeat the loop until it reaches the last item.

With...End With

We'll finish with a structure that is not really a control structure but a way to change several properties of an object at once. `With...End With` allows you to perform several tasks on one object without re-typing the name of the object. The syntax also makes it easier to read and maintain the code. *Task* in this sense means make changes to properties or to execute a method (methods are discussed in *Chapter 7*).

The syntax for the structure is simple. We open it using `With` followed by the object to use. Then we can write lines starting with a period (full stop) and VB will assume the object is in front of that period. Finally, we close with `End With`. Note that all actions must be on one object. A simple example follows:

```
With MyObject
  .Property1 = Value1    ' works the same as MyObject.Property1=Value1
  .Property2 = Value2    ' works the same as MyObject.Property2=Value2
  .Property3 = Value3    ' works the same as MyObject.Property3=Value3
  .Method()              ' works for methods as well
End With
```

> The syntax of a control's property values in a `With...End With` is sometimes different from using the same properties in the attributes of an `<asp:control>` tag. Sometimes you must specify the value as a constant declared in the object's class. Use the class browser to find exact syntax. See the following exercise for some examples.

Try It Out   Using With...End With

We will write a page that demonstrates changing a number of attributes of a label using `With...End With`.

1.   Create `TIO-WithEndWith.aspx` in `ch04` folder and type in the following code. Observe that the generic label displays text as specified in the tag's attribute:

```
<%@ Page Language="VB" Debug="true" %>
<script runat="server">
Sub Page_Load
End Sub
</script>
<html>
<head><title>Example of With... End With</title></head>
<body>
    <form runat="server">
    <asp:textbox id="Mytext" runat="server" text="original text" />
    </form>
</body>
</html>
```

2.   Now add the following code:

```
<%@ Page Language="VB" Debug="true" %>
<script runat="server">
Sub Page_Load
  With MyText
    .text="This text comes from the With... End With block"
    .TextMode=textboxmode.multiline
    .rows="5"
    .columns="50"
    .backcolor=System.Drawing.Color.LightGray
  End With
End Sub
</script>
```

3. Save the page and view it in your browser as shown in Figure 4-11:

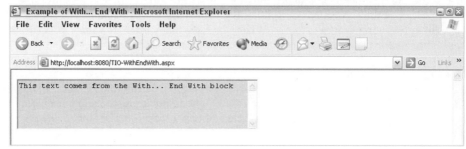

Figure 4-11

How It Works

In the first version, we had a simple label with all the default settings except the text. In the second version, we added a With...End With to change five properties. By using the With... End With we do not have to retype the object name on each line. It is also easier to see the overall purpose of the code. The trick is that the syntax of properties in this block is different then those same properties in an attribute tag. If we wanted to set the background to be light gray using an attribute in the tag we would have used:

```
<asp:textbox … BackColor="#E0E0E0"/ >
```

However, in With...End With we must use a value that comes from constants held in the namespaces.

Summary

This chapter introduced VB control structures, the tools used to determine the order of execution of lines of code. Sometimes we use a branching control to choose only one of several alternatives of lines to execute. At other times, we use a looping structure to repeat lines of code immediately after each other. Last, we may use jumping structures, which are covered in the next chapter.

We started with operators. The equal sign (=) assigns a value into a variable or object property. We can also use the += to add a value to the existing value in a variable or property. We also covered the concatenation operator, &, which appends a string of text onto an existing string of text.

We then covered the basic math operators for addition, subtraction, etc. Always keep in mind the precedence of execution if you have many terms: start in the parentheses, work left to right with multiplication and division, then left to right with addition and subtraction. Then VB.NET moves to the next higher level of parentheses. Using parentheses often makes the calculation easier to write and maintain. Modulo provides the remainder value from a division.

There are three commonly used logical operators. AND uses two complete expressions and requires both to be true in order to return a value of true. OR also uses two complete expressions but only one has to be true in order to get an overall answer of true. NOT changes the value of whatever follows it (best put in parenthesis if complicated).

If Then allows us to executed just one of two sets of code. The simplest form only takes one line, but can only execute one statement and only for the true case. Adding the END IF allows multiple lines to be executed in the case of the expression being True. If you also use ELSE then you can execute lines in the case where the expression resolves to False. When you have many possible values for a variable then you can use the Select Case structure rather then overly nesting If Thens.

When looping you must decide if you know, at the time the loop starts, how many loops you intend to execute. If you know then use For Next which requires a counter. Be careful of exactly which lines go in the loop and which should be before or after the loop. If you do not know the number of loops then you use one of the DO loops that perform a test each cycle and either loop again or stop. Do While may never execute a loop if its expression is false. Do Until always executes at least once because the test is not performed until the end of the first loop.

If you need to loop through code that affects each member of a collection (Arraylist, Hashtable, and so on), use For...Each. VB.NET will automatically perform the loop once on each member. Our last structure was the With... End With that allows you to type the name of the object once and then work on its properties and methods, thus making code faster to create and easier to maintain. However, you must provide values using a different syntax then you do in the tag attributes.

This chapter covered branching and looping structures. The next chapter will cover *Jumping Structures*.

Exercises

1. For each of the following Boolean expressions, say for what integer values of A each of them will evaluate to True and when they will evaluate to False:

   ❑ NOT A=0

   ❑ A > 0 OR A < 5

   ❑ NOT A > 0 OR A < 5

   ❑ A > 1 AND A < 5 OR A > 7 AND A < 10

   ❑ A < 10 OR A > 12 AND NOT A > 20

2. Suggest a loop structure that would be appropriate for each of the following scenarios and justify your choice:

   ❑ Displaying a set of items from a shopping list stored in an array

   ❑ Displaying a calendar for the current month

   ❑ Looking through an array to find the location of a specific entry

   ❑ Drawing a chessboard using an HTML table

3. Write a page that generates a few random numbers between two integers provided by the user in text boxes.

Jumping Structures –
Subroutines and Functions

In the last chapter, we discussed three ways to sequence the execution of the VB.NET code within your ASP.NET page: branching, looping, and jumping. We covered branching and looping, and will now discuss jumping structures in this chapter. *Jumping* is used when we want to leave the execution of our main code midway and jump over to execute another block of code. After executing the block, we return to our main code.

Jumping makes it easier to create and maintain code for many reasons, and thus is an important skill for programmers. This chapter will cover the following topics:

- ❑ Overview of jumping structures and procedures
- ❑ Subroutines
- ❑ Functions
- ❑ Passing parameters to procedures and functions
- ❑ Passing parameters by Ref and ByVal
- ❑ Good practices

A small note on vocabulary: one of the great things about the English language is that it is so widely spoken. But humans being what they are, this has lead to some divergences in word usage. The character ( ) is referred to as parentheses in the American and as brackets in European English. In America, brackets means [ ]. We will use the term parentheses in this chapter to refer to ( ) which are the characters of interest to use as we write procedures.

Overview of Jumping Structures

Jumping structures allow the programmer to pause the execution of the main code and jump to another block of code. After the block is done, execution returns to the main code again. For example, you may have written a block of code called `ShowOrder`, which produces lines to show the customer the goods that they ordered. For VB.NET to show those lines, you don't have to rewrite or copy all of that code into the body of code. Instead, just have VB.NET jump out of your current code, execute `ShowOrder`, and then come back and continue executing the original code.

There are two types of jumping controls, collectively known as *procedures*:

❑ **Subroutines:** These are also called *Subs* or *Routines* and can be called using the name of the subroutine, which will run the statements in the subroutine, and then return control to the line following the call.

❑ **Functions:** These can be used to execute some statements and can contain anything that's found in subroutines; the only difference is that they return a value to the main body of code.

Jumping Structures in Detail

As you write more and more ASP.NET code, you'll find that you want to use the same code in more than one place. ASP.NET allows you to write code once and run it as many times as needed to support the main body of your code. These mini-programs are called *procedures*. We want ASP.NET to jump away from execution of the main body of code, run through the commands of a procedure and then return to executing the main body of code.

For example, you may have some code to insert lines of text about how to contact the Sales department. If you would like to have these show up in various places on the page, but want to avoid having to rewrite the code separately each time, you can put them into a procedure; whenever you want the code to run, you can invoke the procedure rather than rewrite the code.

There are two types of procedures:

❑ Subroutines carry out an action. For example, a sub would be used to carry out the actions of putting text onto a page.

❑ Functions carry out an action and return an answer to your code. A function could be used to calculate a delivery date and return that answer to your main program.

You might think what are the benefits of using jumping structures? The following sections explore this aspect.

Modularization

The process of dividing one large program into several smaller, interlocking parts is called *modularization*. The term can be applied to several methods; for example, we already modularize our page into an HTML section and a script section. Within the script section we can further modularize our code by creating procedures as described in this chapter. Later, we will discuss moving code to its own page (covered in *Chapter 12* in the *Code-Behind* section). An additional level of modularization is to move code out into objects that exist completely independent of the page as we will cover in *Chapter 7*. Let's take a moment to discuss the advantages of modularization.

First, code that is modularized is much *easier to write*. Instead of trying to organize an entire project in your mind, you can focus on code to perform a specific job of a module. Then you can move on to the specific job of module number two. Many studies show that this type of programming, if properly planned, results in better code, with development done sooner and cheaper.

For the same reasons, it is easier to read and maintain modularized code. A programmer looking at the code for the first time can more quickly grasp the objectives of each section if sections are independent. Not only is each module clearer, but also a reader has an easier time tracing the flow of a program from section to section.

Modularized code is easier to test and troubleshoot. You can test modules independently without worrying about errors introduced by the rest of the code. If you know a particular module works without error and then plug it into an untested module, you can narrow the cause of any errors to the untested module or to the interface between the two.

Modularization allows multiple programmers to work together more efficiently. Each group of programmers can focus on one objective that will be self-contained within a module. The important management issue is to have each module clearly defined as to purpose, input, and output. In more advanced forms of modularization (particularly objects), different teams can even work in different languages. .NET provides for a common interface for modules to interchange information.

Obviously, there is the advantage of *code reuse*. Many tasks (such as the display of a shopping cart's current value) must be repeated at many points on a page or on a Web site. If you put 100 lines of code in one module and call it ten times in your code, that's 890 lines of code you've saved.

Finally, separating your code into procedures is a good stepping -stone for students. Ultimately you will want to use the more sophisticated techniques of code-behind and objects. Before tackling those levels of sophistication, it is good training to be thinking and acting modular within your simplescript tags.

Programmers must keep straight in their designs when code will call procedures and functions. These calls can be several layers deep and are easy to conceptualize with a diagram such as Figure 5-1:

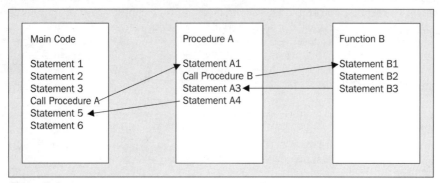

Figure 5-1

Subroutines

Subroutines are easy to write – in fact, we've written subroutines already, many times over in the earlier chapters. When putting code in our pages, it's been written in the following form:

```
<script language="vb" runat="server">
Sub Page_Load()
   ...
End Sub
</script>
```

`Page_Load()` is, in fact, a subroutine or sub. The code that we write inside this subroutine is executed by ASP.NET whenever our page is loaded – ASP.NET *calls* (or *invokes*) our subroutine. Call is the term for one line of code running another block of code, after which execution returns to the calling code.

You can write subroutines with any name (provided it begins with a letter, and only contains letters, numbers, and underscore characters), and call them from within your code. Write them in exactly the same way as the `Page_Load()` subroutine demonstrates. The first line consists of the `Sub` keyword and the name of your subroutine followed by parentheses. You then write the code to be executed on the subroutine being called. Finally, the subroutine ends with the `End Sub` line. In general:

```
Sub MySubroutine()
   ...Subroutine code...
End Sub
```

We cannot nest subroutine (or function) definitions within one another. Therefore, they go inside our script tags at the same level as our `Page_Load()` code. A procedure would *never* go in between the `Sub Page_Load()` and `End Sub` lines.

`Page_Load()` looks a lot like a subroutine. In fact it is, but of a special type because it is established by VB.NET. Microsoft has created several dozen subs for common purposes. They are executed at certain times without a call from your code. For example, `Page_Load()` is automatically called whenever a page is sent out from the IIS server. These pre-made routines are named *events*, and will be discussed in depth in the next chapter. Let's now look at how subroutines are called.

Our example subroutine can be called whenever needed, by using the `Call` keyword followed by the name of the subroutine:

```
<%@ Page Language="VB" Debug=true%>
<script runat="server">
Sub Page_Load()
   ...
   Call MySubRoutine()
   ...
End Sub

Sub MySubRoutine()
   ...
End Sub
</script>
```

Note that we call our subroutine, `MySubRoutine()`, from within the code in the `Page_Load()` subroutine. When the page is loaded, ASP.NET calls `Page_Load()`, and the first line of the code is executed. Then, when the second line is executed, control shifts to our subroutine. The line of code in the subroutine is executed, and control returns to the next line in the `Page_Load()` sub. This continues until the end of `Page_Load()` is reached, and control is handed back to ASP.NET.

You can also just skip the `Call` keyword and just use the name of the subroutine. The disadvantage, however, is that when you or other programmers read the code, it is sometimes confusing to know if a given name is a variable or a subroutine – the type of object must be determined by context. Using the `Call` keyword speeds up code comprehension and does not slow down execution of the code when deployed.

You can put the creation and calling of a subroutine together (available in code download as `ch05\Demo-SimpleSubRoutine.aspx`). For example, you might write a subroutine to insert a horizontal line and a line break at the end of a text string going into a label control, as follows:

```
<%@ Page Language="VB" Debug=true%>
<script runat="server">
Sub Page_Load()
   lblMessage.text = "First line"
   Call InsertLineBreak ()
   lblMessage.text += "Second line"
   Call InsertLineBreak ()
   lblMessage.text += "Third line"
   Call InsertLineBreak ()
End Sub

Sub InsertLineBreak()
   lblMessage.text += "<BR><HR>"
End Sub
</script>
```

```
<html>
<head><title>Simple SubRoutine Example</title></head>
<body>
    <form runat="server">
    <asp:Label runat="server" ID="lblMessage"/>
    </form>
</body>
</html>
```

Figure 5-2 shows the result of this code:

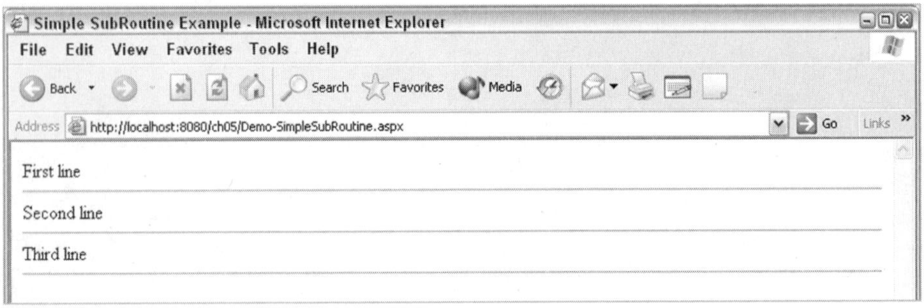

Figure 5-2

The code shown previously has a `Sub` named `InsertLineBreak()` within the `<script>` tags. Its single line concatenates a line break and horizontal line at the end of any text already in `lblMessage.text`:

```
Sub InsertLineBreak()
    lblMessage.text += "<BR><HR>"
End Sub
```

As the following lines show, this sub is called thrice when the page loads, thus leading to a longer `lblMessage.text` file. At the end of the page loading, we have the text, line breaks, and horizontal lines ready to display in `lblMessage`:

```
Sub Page_Load()
    lblMessage.text = "First line"
    Call InsertLineBreak ()
    lblMessage.text += "Second line"
    Call InsertLineBreak ()
    lblMessage.text += "Third line"
    Call InsertLineBreak ()
End Sub
```

Note that by using a sub you did not have to rewrite the line creation code thrice in the main code. Furthermore, if the pattern had to be changed to a gray line, you would have had to change the code in just one place. If the work of the sub was more complex, you might have turned it over to another programmer.

If you have more then one procedure in a `<script>`, you will help yourself by separating them with a line of apostrophes. Many programmers use a *flower box*, which is two lines of apostrophes enclosing comments about the procedure, its purpose, creation date, and author, demonstrated as follows:

```
<script runat="server">

'''''''''''''''''''''''''''''''''''''''''''''''''''''''''''''''''''
' Sets up label texts and horizontal lines
' version 7.8
' 01 January 2005
' Sylvia Johns
' note: (none)
'''''''''''''''''''''''''''''''''''''''''''''''''''''''''''''''''
Sub Page_Load()
   lblMessage.text = "First line"
   Call InsertLineBreak ()
   lblMessage.text += "Second line"
   Call InsertLineBreak ()
   lblMessage.text += "Third line"
   Call InsertLineBreak ()
End Sub
```

There is a weakness in the preceding code in that it is inflexible. We can't use it to insert two lines at once or to reuse it to change the contents of any other label. Also, the code will work only when we have a label control named `lblMessage`. The sub is of no use if we want lines added to the text of an `lblMessageTwo`. Passing parameters can solve this problem.

Passing Parameters

You can make subroutines more versatile by including parameters. A *parameter* (also called an *argument*) is a piece of data that is passed to the subroutine. This allows the behavior of the subroutine to be varied from one execution to the next. The result of calling the subroutine will depend on data sent from the place in your code where you make the call.

The basic syntax is not difficult. When creating a subroutine that uses a parameter, we simply give the parameter a name and type in the parentheses following the sub's name. In the following code, we establish a procedure-level variable called `MyParameter` that will be filled with a value from the calling code and will be available for use within the `Sub`:

```
Sub MySub(MyParameter as DataType)
... code that uses the value held in MyParameter
End Sub
```

When you call a subroutine that expects an argument, place the value of the argument in the parentheses after the subroutine name. In the following example, the string `"myText"` will be passed to `MySub()` and placed in the block variable named `MyParameter`:

```
Call MySub("myText")
```

Subroutines can receive more than one argument as long as a comma separates each combination of name and datatype. In the following example, the code at the bottom calls `MySub()`, and passes two values – the first, a string (in quotes), and the second, a number:

```
Sub MySub(MyParameter As String, MyParameter2 As Integer)
... code that uses the value held in MyParameter1 and myParameter2
End Sub
```

```
Call MySub("myText",myNumber)
```

As you can see, variables or strings both can be used as parameters for subroutines. In fact, you can use anything that can be evaluated to a value – mathematical or logical expressions, numbers, or an object's property (like the text property of a textbox Web control).

Try It Out   Using Subroutines with Parameters

Suppose we want the user to enter two words, which will be displayed (separated by horizontal lines) at the bottom of the page. The user, with the help of radio buttons and a list box, will determine the number of lines and their width. Since we will repeat the line building after each of the two input words, we will put the code for line building in a sub. The sub will need to get parameters for the width and number of horizontal lines. Consider this:

```
        Call InsertLineBreak(lblOut.text, _
            NumberOptions.SelectedItem.Value, _
            WidthOptions.SelectedItem.Value)
```

You can remove the underscores and type into your page on one line. Alternatively, you can type as shown here, but remember that the line continuation requires a space and underscore at the end of the line. An underscore alone will not work.

1.   Create a `TIO-SubWithParameters.aspx` file in the `ch05` folder and type the following:

```
<%@ Page Language="VB" Debug="true" %>
<script runat="server">

    '''''''''''''''''''''''''''''''''''''''''''''''''''''''''''''''''''''''''
    Sub Page_Load()
      If IsPostBack Then
      lblOut.text = txtWord1.text
      Call InsertLineBreak(lblOut.text, _
        NumberOptions.SelectedItem.Value, _
        WidthOptions.SelectedItem.Value)
      lblOut.text += txtWord2.text
      Call InsertLineBreak(lblOut.text, _
        NumberOptions.SelectedItem.Value, _
        WidthOptions.SelectedItem.Value)
      End If
    End Sub


    '''''''''''''''''''''''''''''''''''''''''''''''''''''''''''''''''''''''''
    Sub InsertLineBreak(TextIn as String, NumLines as byte, Width as short)
```

```
         Dim LineCounter as Byte
         For LineCounter=1 to NumLines
            lblout.text += "<BR><HR width='" & Width & "' align='left'>"
         Next
      End Sub

</script>
<html>
<head>
    <title>SubRoutine With Parameters Example</title>
</head>
<body>
    Enter two words and click on submit<br />
    <form runat="server">
        <asp:TextBox id="txtWord1" runat="server" text="default text 1"/>
        <asp:TextBox id="txtWord2" runat="server" text="default text 2"/>
        <asp:RadioButtonList id="WidthOptions" runat="server">
            <asp:listitem ID="w100" value="100" runat="server" />
            <asp:listitem ID="w300" value="300" runat="server" />
            <asp:listitem ID="w600" value="600" runat="server" />
        </asp:RadioButtonList>
        <asp:DropDownList id="NumberOptions" runat="server">
            <asp:listitem>1</asp:listitem>
            <asp:listitem>2</asp:listitem>
            <asp:listitem>3</asp:listitem>
        </asp:DropDownList>
        <asp:Button id="Button1" runat="server" Text="Button"></asp:Button>
        <br />
        <br />
        <asp:Label id="lblOut" runat="server" text="default output"></asp:Label>
    </form>
</body>
</html>
```

2.   View this in your browser; you will see a screen similar to Figure 5-3:

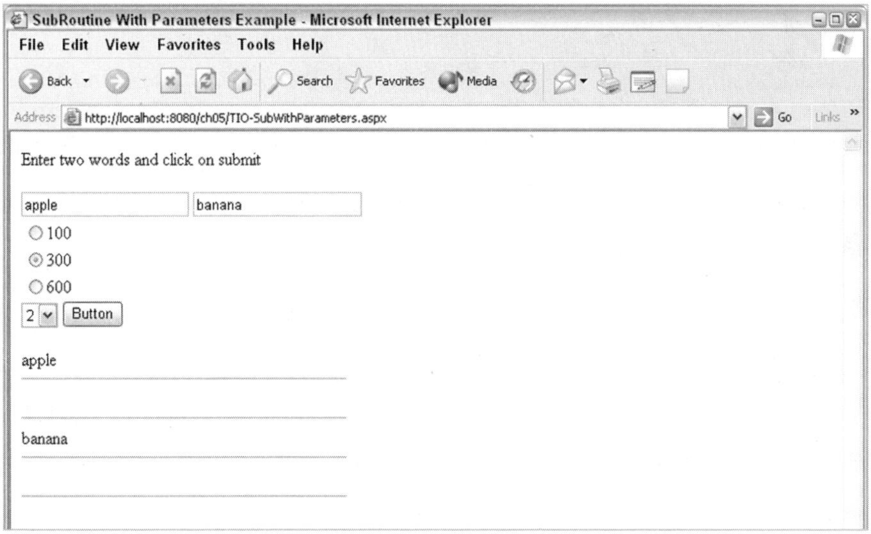

Figure 5-3

How It Works

At the bottom of the page is the form that has two simple text inputs:

```
<form runat="server">
    <asp:TextBox id="txtWord1" runat="server" text="default text 1"/>
    <asp:TextBox id="txtWord2" runat="server" text="default text 2"/>
```

We build more sophisticated input controls to get the user's preference for how to format the lining. (Later these will be passed into the sub that creates the lines.) The radio buttons offer a choice of widths. Note that the value is a number that is directly usable by the width attribute of an `<hr>` tag:

```
<asp:RadioButtonList id="WidthOptions" runat="server">
    <asp:listitem ID="w100" value="100" runat="server" />
    <asp:listitem ID="w300" value="300" runat="server" />
    <asp:listitem ID="w600" value="600" runat="server" />
</asp:RadioButtonList>
```

The drop-down list also gives three options, and again, they have values that we will be able to use directly in the loop that creates lines. This is more direct than offering text line "one" and "two" in the list:

```
<asp:DropDownList id="NumberOptions" runat="server">
    <asp:listitem>1</asp:listitem>
    <asp:listitem>2</asp:listitem>
    <asp:listitem>3</asp:listitem>
</asp:DropDownList>
```

The form finishes with a submit button and then a single output, and the label that will display a string that we build:

```
<asp:Button id="Button1" runat="server" Text="Button"></asp:Button>
<br /><br />
<asp:Label id="lblOut" runat="server" text="default output"></asp:Label>
</form></body></html>
```

Now let's take a look at the sub we built. Note that it is within the `<script>` tags but *not* inside any other subs. Furthermore, it begins and ends with Sub... End Sub. The first line is where our parameters are set up. We receive three parameters. The first parameter is *the text*. Then we pick up a small integer (byte data type), which will be used as the number of lines to create. Finally we receive another small integer (short data type) to set the line widths. Then within the sub we do a simple loop that concatenates more and more text to the end of lblOut.text.

Note how the values from the Width parameter is concatenated directly into the string so they will become valid HTML attributes of the `<hr>` tag:

```
''''''''''''''''''''''''''''''''''''''''''''''''''''''''''''''''''''
Sub InsertLineBreak(TextIn as String, NumLines as byte, Width as short)
  Dim LineCounter as Byte
  For LineCounter=1 to NumLines
    lblout.text += "<BR><HR width='" & Width & "' align='left'>"
  Next
End Sub
```

Now that we have input and output controls on the form and a sub, we are ready to actually call the sub from our main code. We do this from the Page_Load() since we know that will execute automatically. Page_Load() first checks if we are in postback mode, which means there needs to be some text in the textboxes. We then load the first textbox's text into lblOut.text and then call the sub to add our lines. We pass three parameters – the lblOut.text already has our first word in it.

The second parameter is *the value of the selection in the options buttons for line width*. Recall that in the sub that will be concatenated into the <hr> tag's Width attribute.

The third parameter is *the value of the item selected in the* DropDownList. That value will be a number, and will serve nicely in our sub to set the number of loops:

```
Sub Page_Load()
 If IsPostBack Then
 lblOut.text = txtWord1.text
 Call InsertLineBreak(lblOut.text, _
   NumberOptions.SelectedItem.Value, _
   WidthOptions.SelectedItem.Value)
```

We then add the word from the second textbox to lblOut.text and run our sub again:

```
 lblOut.text += txtWord2.text
 Call InsertLineBreak(lblOut.text, _
   NumberOptions.SelectedItem.Value, _
   WidthOptions.SelectedItem.Value)
 End If
End Sub
```

This example demonstrated several points. First, we looked at the syntax and location of a sub that uses parameters. We also looked at three ways (textbox, buttons, and DropDownList) to get information and pass it as a parameter. Within the sub, we saw how to use those data in lines of code such as a loop.

Web Controls as Parameters

There is one type of parameter that is useful but supported by a different syntax. The technique is used when you want to pass the name of a Web control object into a procedure as a parameter. For example, you can write a generic routine that will change the font size of a Web control. Its incoming parameter would be the name of the Web control. At first you might think that you could use the Web control name as string. But you really don't want the literal text lblMyLabel; rather, you want the reference to be to the Web control object itself.

When passing a Web control reference, you must declare its type as one of the Web controls as follows:

```
Sub MySub(Target as textbox)
Sub MySub(Target as label)
Sub MySub(Target as button)
Sub MySub(Target as checkbox)
```

Within the sub, after we declare a Web control type we can refer to the Web control by the name we gave it within parentheses. In the following case, that would be `Target`:

```
Sub MakeFancy(Target as label)
  Target.backcolor = drawing.color.red
  Target.font.size = fontunit.large
End Sub
```

Note that we have to use VB .NET syntax when referring to properties and values of the Web control inside the procedures code. We cannot use the same syntax as in the attribute of a tag. This is the same as when we studied the `With... End With` construction in *Chapter 4*. The exact syntax can be found in the class browser that is discussed in *Appendix B*.

Try It Out Using Web Controls as Parameters

We'd like to create a form with several labels, any of which can be changed to be italic according to checkboxes. The process of changing a label's style to italic should be coded once in a procedure. That one procedure can then be used to change to italics any of the three labels.

1. In the `ch05` folder, create a page named `TIO-ParameterWebControl.aspx` and enter the following:

```
<%@ Page Language="VB" Debug="true" %>
<script runat="server">

Sub Page_Load
  Call MakeItalic(label1, checkbox1.checked)
  Call MakeItalic(label2, checkbox2.checked)
  Call MakeItalic(label3, checkbox3.checked)
End Sub

Sub MakeItalic(TargetLabel as label, bolItalic as Boolean)
  Targetlabel.font.italic = bolItalic
End Sub

</script>
<html>
<head><title>Example</title></head>
<body>
  <form runat="server">
  <table><tbody>
  <tr>
    <td><asp:CheckBox runat="server" ID="Checkbox1" /></td>
    <td><asp:CheckBox runat="server" ID="Checkbox2" /></td>
    <td><asp:CheckBox runat="server" ID="Checkbox3" /></td>
  </tr>
  <tr>
    <td><asp:Label id="Label1" runat="server" text="apple" /></td>
    <td><asp:Label id="Label2" runat="server" text="banana" /></td>
    <td><asp:Label id="Label3" runat="server" text="carrot" /></td>
  </tr>
  </tbody></table>
  <asp:Button runat="server" Text="change font style"/>
```

```
  </form>
</body>
</html>
```

2.   View this page in your browser; Figure 5-4 shows the output:

Figure 5-4

How It Works

We start with a look at the form, which in this page sets up a table for formatting purposes. We have a column for each fruit. The first row consists of checkboxes:

```
<form runat="server">
  <table><tbody>
  <tr>
    <td><asp:CheckBox runat="server" ID="Checkbox1" /></td>
    <td><asp:CheckBox runat="server" ID="Checkbox2" /></td>
    <td><asp:CheckBox runat="server" ID="Checkbox3" /></td>
  </tr>
```

The second row has labels with the names of fruits. Make a mental note of the ID – it is how you refer to the control in your code:

```
  <tr>
    <td><asp:Label id="Label1" runat="server" text="apple" /></td>
    <td><asp:Label id="Label2" runat="server" text="banana" /></td>
    <td><asp:Label id="Label3" runat="server" text="carrot" /></td>
  </tr>
  </tbody></table>
  <asp:Button runat="server" Text="change font style"/>
</form>
```

Next we'll look at the `MakeItalic()` function in the `<script>` tags but outside all other procedures:

```
Sub MakeItalic(TargetLabel as label, bolItalic as Boolean)
  Targetlabel.font.italic = bolItalic
End Sub
```

The function receives two parameters. The first parameter is a reference to an ASP.NET label Web control. Therefore it must be typed as a label. The second parameter is a `True` or `False` Boolean that will be used to set the italicization of the text.

173

Within the sub, we can refer to the label by using the name assigned to it as a parameter – in this case, `TargetLabel`. Observe that we must use the VB.NET object model syntax to refer to the label's properties. Thus we use `Targetlabel.font.italic` rather than HTML attribute syntax like `<font-style: italic>`. Lastly, notice how the second parameter has been used. The `Italic` property only has two settings: `True` or `False`. Since a `Boolean` comes in as `True` or `False`, we can directly use that as the value for a Web control property.

Now it is time to actually use the function. As seen in the previous code snippet, we have to pass two variables to the sub. The first is the name of the label that the sub should modify. The second is a Boolean stating whether we want the italics turned on or off. Conveniently, the Web control `asp:checkbox.checked` property contains a `true` if the check is on and a `false` if the check is off. So we do not need to do any testing or transformation; we just type the `object.property` reference into the parameter, and its value will be passed to the sub:

```
Sub Page_Load
   Call MakeItalic(label1,checkbox1.checked)
   Call MakeItalic(label2,checkbox2.checked)
   Call MakeItalic(label3,checkbox3.checked)
End Sub
```

A good question arises when you study this code. In the form, instead of three independent checkboxes, why not use a `asp:CheckBoxList` and then have the three calls made to `MakeItalic` in a loop with the `counter = the checkboxlist.item()`? The problem is that we want to present the page in a table, and table tags like `<td>` do not co-exist well with code to add items to a `checkboxlist`. An alternate solution would be to use a datagrid bound to an array.

Functions

Recall that functions constitute code that performs a job and then sends a piece of information back to the calling code (whereas subs only do a job without returning a value). Functions are written in a syntax similar to subroutines, but with several special characteristics that handle the returning of information. Note that functions return a single piece of data. A common error that a beginning programmer makes is to attempt to write a function that delivers multiple values. A block of code that can return multiple values can be achieved with custom objects (see *Chapter 7*) that can have multiple properties.

The most frequent mistake seen with beginners developing functions is that they fail to handle the returned value. A function call cannot exist by itself on a line; the returned value *must* go into something. The most common receivers of a function's result are:

❑ A variable

❑ A property of an object

❑ An argument for another function

❑ An expression in a control structure

We will look at each of these in pseudo code and an exercise.

Defining Functions

When you write a function, you use Function (instead of Sub) on the first line and End Function (instead of End Sub) on the last line. The naming rules of functions are the same as for sub – start with a letter, use no spaces, and avoid symbols (except underscores). As with subroutines, we can declare functions that take any number of parameters or no parameters at all. Second, we must have a way to report the result back to the calling code (in other words, a way to return a value.) You simply use the Return keyword followed by the value to return. The data type of the returned value is established up in the first line of the function, where you use the As after the parameter's parentheses.
Consider an example:

```
Function MyFunction(myParam As String) As Integer
   Dim MyResult
   ... code which can use myParam and puts a value into MyResult
   Return MyResult
End Function
```

The preceding code creates a function named MyFunction(). That function expects a string parameter and names it myParam for internal use. When MyFunction() is finished it puts an integer value into MyResult. MyFunction() then returns to the caller the integer in MyResult.

You might see an older technique to specify the return value. You can simply set the name of the function equal to the value you want to return, such as the following:

```
Function MyFunction(myParam As String) As Integer
   Dim MyResult
   ... code that can use myParam and puts a value into MyResult
   MyFunction = MyResult
End Function
```

The preceding sample works and you are likely to see it in older code. However, using the Return keyword is the most appropriate way of specifying the return value of a function. This method makes the code more readable. Although it is an additional command, it does not decrease the performance of the function in any way.

Calling Functions

You can call a function just by typing its name followed by double a pair of parentheses:

```
MyVariable = MyFunction("Hello")
```

This line will call the MyFunction() function and send to it the parameter of value "Hello". The return value will be placed in MyVariable. You can also use the returned value in other situations, as the argument for another function, the value for an object's property, or as an expression.

Let's look at an example of each of the four ways to use a function's return value in pseudocode (that gives an idea of the code without perfect syntax) then we will try them in an exercise. To cut down on space we won't present the forms below. You can assume that there are various labels and textboxes in a form as needed by the code. In addition, the lower portion of each example would be within the `Sub Page_Load()` sub. Of course the functions would be outside the `Sub Page_Load()` because we cannot have one procedure inside another. However, the functions would be within the `<script>` tags. All the code will be used in the exercise.

The following example demonstrates putting the return value of a function *into a variable* named `decPriceWholesale`:

```
Function WholeSaleCostLookUp(CatalogNumber as integer) as Decimal
... code that takes a catalog number and looks up the price in the database
... code that will RETURN the price
End Function

Dim PriceWholeSale
DecPriceWholeSale = WholeSaleCostLookUp(txtCatalogNumber.text)
LblPriceRetail.text = decPriceWholesale*2
```

The following example demonstrates putting the return value of a function *into the value of an object's property*, namely the text property of `lblItemName`. Notice that the function expects an integer in the parameter. However, strictly speaking the `textbox.text` property is a string. So we run the value in `txtCatNumber` through the built-in function named `CInt` to convert it to an integer prior to using it as an argument for our custom-built `NameLookUp()` function:

```
Function NameLookUp(CatalogNumber as integer) as String
... code that takes a catalog number and looks up the item's name in the database
... code that will RETURN the name
End Function

LblItemName.text = NameLookUp( Cint(txtCatNumber.text) )
```

The following example demonstrates how the return value of a function can be used as *an expression in a control structure*. Note that the value returned is a Boolean, and thus can be used as a whole expression; there's no need for an additional `value=True` expression:

```
Function IsMember(MaybeNumber as integer) as Boolean
... code that looks up a number and determines if it is a true member number or
not.
... code that will RETURN a Boolean
End Function

If IsMember(SomeNumber) Then
   LblMember.text = "You are a member"
Else
   LblMember.text = "You are not a member"
End If
```

The following example demonstrates how the return value of a function can be used *as an argument for another function*. Our function replaces spaces in a string with underscores. In the lower code, the result of the function is used as an argument for the built-in function named LEN() that returns the number of characters in the string. The LEN() function , in turn, must have a receiver for its output, which in this case is the LengthOfString label:

```
Function Replacer(StringIn as String) as string
... code which replaces spaces with underscores
... code that will RETURN a string
End Function

LblLengthOfString.text = LEN( Replacer(txtFavoriteThings.text) )
```

Having seen pseudo code of several function examples, let's move on to a working exercise.

A Function Exercise

Good modularization requires good documentation, which we will do in this section before starting the exercise on using functions. Our objective in this exercise is to write and use four functions that will, each in their own way, modify some text provided by the user and put it into each of four output labels.

Each modification will demonstrate a different way of handling the result of a function: putting the results in a variable, putting the results into an object's property, using the result in the argument of another function, and using the result as an expression in a control structure. Note that the entire exercise is run in four parallel tracks: four functions, four output labels, and four sections of code that call the functions. For input, we just have two text boxes and a submit button.

The first function is named Blanker(), and its return will be put into a variable. Blanker() converts a string of characters into a string of blanks with a note at the end on the number of characters. The input parameters and output are of type string.

The second function is named JoinerDash(), and its return value will be put into an object's property. JoinerDash() takes two text strings and concatenates them with a dash in the middle. Input parameters and the output are of type string. We use JoinDash() to join the two strings in the textboxes and then we display the results in lblJoinedText.

The third function is named JoinerClean(), and its return will be put into the argument of another function. JoinerClean() takes two text strings and concatenates them with no blank or dash in the middle. Input parameters are of type string, and so is the output. We use JoinerClean() to join the two strings in the textboxes, and then use that long string as the argument for a VB.NET built-in function called LEN() which returns the number of characters in its argument. The result is displayed in lblTotalSize.

The fourth function is named IsBig(), and its return value will be put into a control structure's expression. IsBig() delivers a True or False – True if the input is larger then five characters. IsBig() has one input parameter of type string and its output is a Boolean. We use IsBig() as the expression in an If Then statement that sets the lblIsBig to either "…is large…" or "…is small…".

With that documentation we should be able to code the page as shown in the following example.

177

Try It Out   Using Functions

1.   In your `ch05` folder create a file named `TIO-Functions.aspx` and enter the following code. Although this is long, it is divided into clear sections, each of which is easy to type and understand:

```
<%@ Page Language="VB" Debug="true" %>
<script runat="server">

Sub Page_Load
If IsPostBack

' Put result of Blanker() into a variable named strWordBlanked
  Dim strWordBlanked as string
  strWordBlanked = Blanker(txtIn1.text)
  lblBlanks.text = strWordBlanked

' Put result of JoinerDash() into property of an object
  lblJoinedText.text = JoinerDash(txtIn1.text,txtIn2.text)

' Put result of JoinerClean into the arguement of another function LEN()
  lblTotalSize.text = LEN( JoinerClean(txtIn1.text,txtIn2.text) )

' Put result of IsBig() into the expression of a control structure
  If IsBig(txtIn1.text) then
    lblIsBig.text = "Box one has a large number of characters"
  Else
    lblIsBig.text = "Box one has a small number of characters"
  End If

End If
End Sub

'''''''''''''''''''''''''''''''''''''''''''''''''''''
' Returns a string of blanks, one for each character
'''''''''''''''''''''''''''''''''''''''''''''''''''''''''
      Function Blanker(String1 As String) As String
        Dim iCharCounter = 0
        Dim strOutput = " "
        For iCharCounter = 1 to LEN(String1)
          strOutput += "_ "
        Next
        stroutput += "(total characters = " & iCharCounter-1 & ")"
        RETURN strOutput
      End Function

'''''''''''''''''''''''''''''''''''''''''''''''''''''''
' Returns a concatenation of two texts with a seperating hyphen
'''''''''''''''''''''''''''''''''''''''''''''''''''''''''
      Function JoinerDash(String1 As String, String2 as String) As String
        RETURN String1 & " - " & String2
      End Function
```

```
'''''''''''''''''''''''''''''''''''''''''''''''''''''
' Returns a string concatenating two strings
'''''''''''''''''''''''''''''''''''''''''''''''''''''''
      Function JoinerClean(String1 As String,String2 As String) As String
        Return String1 & string2
      End Function

'''''''''''''''''''''''''''''''''''''''''''''''''''
' Returns a Boolean for longness of a string
'''''''''''''''''''''''''''''''''''''''''''''''''''''
      Function IsBig(String1 As String) As BOolean
        If LEN(String1)>5 Then
          RETURN TRUE
        Else
          RETURN FALSE
        End If
      End Function
</script>

<html>
<head><title>Functions Example</title></head>
<body>
    <form runat="server">
        <asp:TextBox id="txtIn1" runat="server"></asp:TextBox><br />
        <asp:TextBox id="txtIn2" runat="server"></asp:TextBox><br />
        <asp:Button id="Button1" runat="server" Text="Submit"></asp:Button><br />

        Function used in a variable:
        <asp:Label id="lblBlanks" runat="server" Font-Size="Medium"/><br />

        Function used as value for an object property:
        <asp:Label id="lblJoinedText" runat="server" Font-Size="Medium"/><br/>

        Function used as an arguement in another function: Total size =
        <asp:Label id="lblTotalSize" runat="server" Font-Size="Medium"/><br />

        Function used as an expression: Is word #1 big?
        <asp:Label id="lblIsBig" runat="server" Font-Size="Medium"/><br />
    </form>
</body></html>
```

2. View the page and enter two words. The results are shown in Figure 5-5:

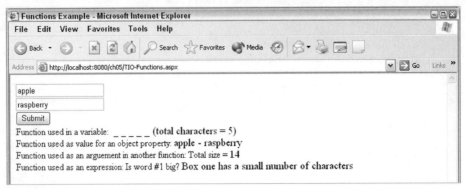

Figure 5-5

How It Works

First, be sure you have read the documentation in the earlier section, *A Function Exercise* , because that explains our overall purpose and approach. Remember that the code is written in four parallel tracks, one for each way to use a function's results.

Take a quick look at the form where we start with two textboxes for input and a submit button:

```
<form runat="server">
    <asp:TextBox id="txtIn1" runat="server"></asp:TextBox><br />
    <asp:TextBox id="txtIn2" runat="server"></asp:TextBox><br />
    <asp:Button id="Button1" runat="server" Text="Submit"></asp:Button><br />
```

Next let's look at the four functions and how they are used. In each case, we will look at how the function is called, the function itself, and then the label for output.

In the first case, our objective is to demonstrate how to use a variable as a receiver for the function. The function receives a string. Two variables are created; iCharCounter to count the number of characters contained in the input string, and strOutput to hold the output as we build it.

We start by inserting a space into the strOutput. Then we start a loop that adds an underscore and space to strOutput in each iteration. The additions are repeated once for each character in the input string. The For...Next loop will automatically increment the value in iCharCounter by one for each loop. This function is called by the code that takes the return from the function and puts it into a variable called strWordBlanked (at the top of the following snippet). strWordBlanked is then used as the source for the value in lblBlanks.text:

```
' Put result of Blanker() into a variable named strWordBlanked
  Dim strWordBlanked as string
  strWordBlanked = Blanker(txtIn1.text)
  lblBlanks.text = strWordBlanked
. . .
```

```
'''''''''''''''''''''''''''''''''''''''''''''''''''
' Returns a string of blanks, one for each character
'''''''''''''''''''''''''''''''''''''''''''''''''''''
        Function Blanker(String1 As String) As String
          Dim iCharCounter = 0
          Dim strOutput = " "
          For iCharCounter = 1 to LEN(String1)
            strOutput += "_ "
          Next
          stroutput += "(total characters = " & iCharCounter-1 & ")"
          RETURN strOutput
        End Function
  ...


Function used in a variable:
  <asp:Label id="lblBlanks" runat="server" Font-Size="Medium"/><br />
```

In the second example, we use the output of the `JoinerDash()` function to set the value in an object's property. Here our function performs the simple task of taking two string parameters and concatenating them with a hyphen in the middle. Therefore the text at the top of the following listing must pass two parameters to the function:

```
' Put result of JoinerDash() into property of an object
  lblJoinedText.text = JoinerDash(txtIn1.text,txtIn2.text)


'''''''''''''''''''''''''''''''''''''''''''''''''''
' Returns a concatenation of two texts with a seperating hyphen
'''''''''''''''''''''''''''''''''''''''''''''''''''''
        Function JoinerDash(String1 As String, String2 as String) As String
          RETURN String1 & " - " & String2
        End Function

        Function used as value for an object property:
        <asp:Label id="lblJoinedText" runat="server" Font-Size="Medium"/><br/>
```

The third example joins together the two input texts and uses the output as the argument of a built-in VB.NET LEN() function. This function requires a string as input. Instead of providing a literal string (like "apple") we provide our string as the return value from the `JoinerClean()` function:

```
' Put result of JoinerClean into the arguement of another function LEN()
  lblTotalSize.text = LEN( JoinerClean(txtIn1.text,txtIn2.text) )


'''''''''''''''''''''''''''''''''''''''''''''''''''
' Returns a string concatenating two strings
'''''''''''''''''''''''''''''''''''''''''''''''''''''
        Function JoinerClean(String1 As String,String2 As String) As String
          Return String1 & string2
        End Function

Function used as an arguement in another function: Total size =
        <asp:Label id="lblTotalSize" runat="server" Font-Size="Medium"/><br />
```

181

The last example is the most interesting because it uses the output of the function as a very small and clean expression. The function `IsBig()` takes in a string, counts the number of characters and then tests the size of the string. If the size is more then five characters, it returns a Boolean value of `true`. This value is used in the code at the top of the listing below. We do not have to write = or > in the expression of the `If . . . Then`. Since `IsBig()` returns either `True` or `False`, that is all that is needed for the `If . . . Then` to perform its branch:

```
' Put result of IsBig() into the expression of a control structure
  If IsBig(txtIn1.text) then
    lblIsBig.text = "Box one has a large number of characters"
  Else
    lblIsBig.text = "Box one has a small number of characters"
  End If


,,,,,,,,,,,,,,,,,,,,,,,,,,,,,,,,,,,,,,,,,,,,,,,,,,
' Returns a Boolean for longness of a string
,,,,,,,,,,,,,,,,,,,,,,,,,,,,,,,,,,,,,,,,,,,,,,,,,,
        Function IsBig(String1 As String) As BOolean
          If LEN(String1)>5 Then
            RETURN TRUE
          Else
            RETURN FALSE
          End If
        End Function

Function used as an expression: Is word #1 big?
        <asp:Label id="lblIsBig" runat="server" Font-Size="Medium"/><br />
```

Before we end our comparison of subs and functions, let's make a note on usage. Many times programmers write a procedure that performs a task as a function instead of a sub, even when there is no logical result to return.

Consider an example; a procedure would work fine for writing some values to a database. But typically a programmer would write it as a function. The return value of the function is used to send back a report on the success of the task (it might return a positive value for the number of records affected). However, if the task failed, it would return an error code of a negative value to reflect problems. When your main code runs the function, it checks the return for a positive or negative and either carries on or goes into an errorreporting mode.

Passing Parameters by Reference and by Value

We discussed passing parameters into both subroutines and functions earlier in the chapter. However, there are two ways that VB.NET can perform the passing. In the first case, passing *by value*, the value is copied and the copy is passed into the parameter and assigned to the internal variable. Any changes made to the value in the procedure have no effect on the value in the original source.

In the second method, the parameter is passed *by reference*, which means that instead of passing the actual value into the procedure, we just pass a pointer to the original value in the calling code. Any changes made to the value in the procedure are actually made to the value in the calling code. Let's look at examples and the implications for each of these techniques.

Passing Parameters by Value

By default, simple data values are passed to functions and subroutines by value in VB.NET. This means that when the parameter variables are created inside the function or subroutine, they are all set up to have the value that was passed in. This may seem like it goes without saying, but has some subtle consequences. Effectively, it means that inside a procedure, we are working with a *copy* of the original data. Look at the following code (available in code download as `Demo-ByVal.aspx`):

```vb
<script language="vb" runat="server">
  Sub Increment(Number as Integer)
    Number = Number + 1
  End Sub

  Sub Page_Load()
    Dim A As Integer
    A = 1
    Increment(A)
    Message.Text = A
  End Sub
</script>

<html>
<head><title>Demonstration of Passing a Parameter by Val</title></head>
<body>
  <asp:label id="Message" runat="server"/>
</body></html>
```

This is a subroutine that takes an integer as a parameter and increments it. When you use this subroutine from the `Page_Load()` subroutine, a variable containing the number 1 is passed in, but when you display the contents of this variable, you'll find that it hasn't been incremented. This is because the data is passed by value. Passing by value means that a copy is made for the subroutine or function to play with, and the data in the calling procedure is left untouched.

When `Increment(A)` is called in the code, the value stored in the variable A (which is 1) is copied into a new variable (called `Number`) inside the `Increment()` routine. The `Increment()` routine then adds 1 to the value stored in this variable, but the value stored in A is left untouched. If our `Number` variable were called A instead, it would still be a new variable. Using the `ByVal` keyword in the function or subroutine definition can make this default behavior explicit, as shown in the following snippet:

```vb
  Sub Increment(ByVal Number as Integer)
    Number = Number + 1
  End Sub
```

While this has no effect at all on the function and what it does, it does help to remind us of the manner in which the parameter is handled and thus is a good programming practice.

Passing Parameters by Reference

What happens if you wanted the calculation within your function to affect the calling code's contents? Well then you could pass the parameter by reference. Let's amend our `Increment` sample to use passing parameters by reference (available in code download as `Demo-ByRef.aspx`):

```
Sub Increment(ByRef Number as Integer)
    Number = Number + 1
End Sub
```

The preceding code results in the number 2 on the page. Now when the `Increment(A)` call is made, instead of a copy being taken of the value stored in `A`, a second variable is made which points to the variable `A`. This way, whenever the code inside the subroutine makes a change to the `Number` variable, it is actually changing the data in the `A` variable as well.

Try It Out Passing Values by Value and by Reference

We will create a simple page that demonstrates, sidebyside, the effects of using `ByVal` and `ByRef`.

1.   In the `ch05` folder, create a new file named `TIO-ByValRef.aspx` and enter the following:

```
<%@ Page Language="VB" Debug="true"%>
<script runat="server">
Sub Page_Load
  If IsPostBack

    Call myVal(txtInVal.text)
    lblOutVal.text = txtinVal.text

    Call myRef(txtInRef.text)
    lblOutRef.text = txtinRef.text

  End If
End Sub


''''''''''''''''''''''''''''''''''''''''''''''''''''''''''''''
Sub myVal(byVal strIn as string)
  strIn += " ending from myVAL"
End Sub


''''''''''''''''''''''''''''''''''''''''''''''''''''''''''''''
Sub myRef(byRef strIn as string)
  strIn += " ending from myRef"
End Sub
</script>
<html>
    <head><title>Example</title>
    </head>
    <body>
        <form runat="server">
    <asp:TextBox runat="server" ID="txtInVal"/>
    <asp:TextBox runat="server" ID="txtInRef"/><br/>
```

```
    <asp:Button runat="server" Text="Submit"/><br/>
    ByVal: <asp:Label runat="server" ID="lblOutVal" width=120/>
    ByRef: <asp:Label runat="server" ID="lblOutRef"/><br/>
    </form>
  </body></html>
```

2.   View this in your browser. You will see a screen similar to Figure 5-6:

Figure 5-6

3.   Add a third set of code that will show the result when the default value is used. Your output page should look like Figure 5-7:

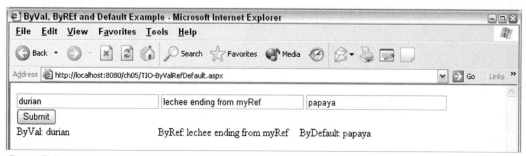

Figure 5-7

How It Works

Let's start with a quick glance at the form, which should be self-explanatory. We have two textboxes for input and two labels for output paired with names for `ByVal` and `ByRef`:

```
    <form runat="server">
      <asp:TextBox runat="server" ID="txtInVal"/>
      <asp:TextBox runat="server" ID="txtInRef"/><br/>
      <asp:Button runat="server" Text="Submit"/><br/>
      ByVal: <asp:Label runat="server" ID="lblOutVal" width=120/>
      ByRef: <asp:Label runat="server" ID="lblOutRef"/><br/>
    </form>
```

Now we'll take a look at the two routines written. They both concatenate a short bit of text to an incoming string parameter. However, they differ in how the parameter is passed to the sub.

The first sub receives its parameter by value. So the original value remains intact in the calling code. A copy of the value is created in the `strIn` block variable:

```
Sub myVal(byVal strIn as string)
  strIn += " ending from myVAL"
End Sub
```

The second sub receives its data by reference; in other words, `strIn` does not hold a string, rather it holds a pointer to a variable or object property in the calling code (in this case we will learn that it is `txtInRef.text`):

```
Sub myRef(byRef strIn as string)
  strIn += " ending from myRef"
End Sub
```

Now we can examine the code that uses the routines. Both pick up text from a textbox, run a function with the text as the parameter, and then set the results into the `lblOut`.

The first case (passing by value), shown in the following code, results in the sub modifying the copy of the string that was passed to it. The string in `txtInVal.text` remained unaltered, and so the result in `lblOutVal` is the same as the one typed into `txtinVal` by the user:

```
Call myVal(txtInVal.text)
lblOutVal.text = txtinVal.text
```

In contrast, the second call, shown in the following code, is by reference. Within the `myRef()` sub the concatenation occurs onto the actual text held in `txtInRef.text`. Therefore, we see a different result. The `lblOutRef` is modified first, followed by the text in `txtInRef`.

```
Call myRef(txtInRef.text)
lblOutRef.text = txtinRef.text
```

Here is the pertinent part of code to create a third display for the default case. In each case, they go right after the sections on `ByRef`:

```
...
     Call myDefault(txtInDefault.text)
     lblOutDefault.text = txtinDefault.text


...
     Sub myDefault(strIn as string)
        strIn += " ending from myDefault"
     End Sub
...
     <asp:TextBox runat="server" ID="txtInDefault" width=220/><br/>
```

Most people write their first procedures using `ByVal` and `ByRef`. Here are some generally overlooked points:

- ❑ The syntax of `ByVal` or `ByRef` is one word (different than `As String`, which is two words).
- ❑ `ByRef` or `ByVal` comes *before* the name assigned to the incoming value, and the type comes *after*.
- ❑ For multiple parameters, you must use the `By` and `As` for each parameter.

Here is a correct sample of the whole syntax for two parameters:

```
Sub MySub(ByVal strTextIn as String, ByRef intNumberIn as Integer)
```

ByVal versus ByRef: A Comparison

The default is `ByVal`. However, the default is `ByRef` for objects that are passed as parameters (for example, a Web control label object). In general there is no need to change those defaults.

`ByVal` makes a copy of the actual data to a variable within the block. If the data is large and thus uses a lot of resources, `ByRef` saves resources by simply pointing to the original holder of the data.

`ByVal` leads to fewer conflicts in complex pages. Several different functions using `ByRef` (perhaps written by different authors) could be changing the original contents of a variable. Programmers may not be sure at a given moment the actual value that is supposed to be in a variable.

For example, you may run a `DateDue` through a function which checks if the due date is a day the business is open. That would best be done `ByVal` so that when the date is modified, programmers are not confused when writing other processes that are looking at the date. On the other hand if you write a procedure that modifies the gray scale of a bit map image it would be better to pass the entire image `ByRef` to avoid multiple copies of the large file.

Modularization Best Practices

This section describes several guidelines for breaking your code into procedures and functions, a process referred to as modularization. *Chapter 7* covers custom objects, another form of modularization, for which many of these same ideas apply.

Modularization is good. Whenever practical, *divide your code into smaller parts* that each perform one part of the job. As you improve your skills, try to move your modularization practices into higher levels. Start with subs and functions, and then move to code-behind and custom objects.

Successful modularization requires *careful planning and definition*. You must ensure that each task in your project can be performed and that all modules have the same definition of data that is passed among them. Diagramming is often helpful in the planning stages. As part of the plan, there needs to be a clear statement of input and output of each module as well as the task that the module performs.

Good modules contain *extensive internal documentation* – at a minimum note the purpose of the module, its creation date, version number, and author. Code maintenance is cheaper if you also include notes on the purpose of variables. Comments do not slow down execution of code (they are removed at compilation) so there is no performance price for internal documentation.

Much of the planning for modularization can be done with *software design and authoring tools*. Basic tools come with Web Matrix, such as the ability to save a flower box template in your code and then insert that at the top of other procedures with a double click. More sophisticated tools are available in Visual Studio and third-party software.

Avoid using message boxes or other interfaces which pop-up outside of the HTML page. When you deploy your code on a server, you may have thousands of pop-ups occurring on a server that isn't even connected to a monitor.

Have a unique naming system and avoid variable name conflicts. Be especially wary of very common terms like *Price* and *Date*. Scope variables as narrowly as possible. Use `ByVal` to reduce the chances of a module making a change that is not expected by another module.

Within a procedure avoid specific reference to a Web control by name. It is almost always better to use a parameter to pass into the procedure a reference to the web control.

Passing a parameter `ByRef` is more likely to cause errors in the page as a whole. Therefore, explicitly *document in the code when `ByRef` is being used.*

In the end, the objective of your main code is to call a series of modules to go through a task. *The leaner the main code the better.* The only time to skip modularization is when there is a single, simple and short operation executed in the code of a page.

Summary

This chapter covered two of four techniques for modularization: subroutines and functions. The other two are code-behind (*Chapter 12*) and custom objects (*Chapter 7*). Subs and functions together are called procedures. In this chapter, we broke code into subs and functions.

Modularization is the process of breaking the code for a project into smaller, independent groups of code. The benefits include faster development, easier testing, and cheaper maintenance. Code that is used frequently is written and tested once, put in a module and then reused many times. Furthermore, advanced forms of modularization permit different programmers to work in different languages, according to their preferences or the best language to achieve a goal. This chapter introduced two ways to modularize: procedures and functions.

Procedures perform a task in a block of code separate from the main body of code. The code in procedures is executed when they are called. Subs merely perform a task, whereas functions perform a task and return some value to the calling code. For example a subroutine will perform a print job. A function will calculate a value and return the answer as the result. Many times a subroutine is written as a function with its return value being a report that the task was completed successfully or not.

The code for procedures must be written within a block starting with `Sub MyRoutine()` and ending with `End Sub` or starting with `Function MyFunction()` and ending with `End Function`. They are located within the `<script>` tags but outside any other `Sub`s (for example, the `Sub Page_Load()`). Good practice states that each procedure start with some comments identifying its purpose, creation date, and author, as well as restrictions on incoming data.

Subs are executed by using the `Call` command followed by the name of the routine. Function calls do not require the `Call` command. An important requirement of a function is that its return value must have a receptacle. A function cannot stand alone as a command. The receiver for a function's return can be a variable, an object property, an argument for another function, or an expression in a control structure. Functions that return a `Boolean` value can be an entire expression; there is no need to compare them to 'true' or 'false'.

Information can be passed into procedures by making use of parameters. Incoming values are assigned a name, data type, and a Val (Ref) designation upon receipt into the procedure. They are then available within the procedure as block-level variables. They decide when the procedure ends. Web controls such as label or textbox can be passed as a parameter into a procedure, and within the procedure their property values change. Objects passed into a procedure are always `ByRef`.

Data passed by value is copied into the block variable; any operations occur only on the copy. The original is untouched. Data passed into a procedure by reference creates a block variable that points to the original source of data. Operations within the procedure will actually modify the contents of the original holder of the data that is outside the procedure. `ByVal` is the default, and is generally best left unchanged unless there is a need to improve performance.

Exercises

1. Choose between using a sub and a function for each of the following scenarios, and justify your choice:

- ❑ Calculate the due date of a book being checked out of a library.

- ❑ Find out on which day of the week (Monday, Tuesday, and so on) falls a certain date in the future.

- ❑ Display in a label a string determined by the marketing department and stored in a text file.

2. List where and when values are held when a variable is used as a parameter passed `ByVal`. Do the same for `ByRef`.

3. Write a function that generates a set of random integers. Build an ASP.NET page that allows you to enter the lower and upper bounds, and generate a set of random numbers within that range.

Event-Driven Programming and Postback

A fundamental change from ASP to ASP.NET is the implementation of a robust event-driven programming model. In ASP we had to write many lines of code for reacting to a user's click on the submit button. With ASP.NET, much of that work is performed for us automatically and we can focus on writing just the code to implement our business goals.

ASP.NET supports three major groups of events. The first are events intrinsic to HTML and are executed on the browser. The second group are the ASP.NET page-level events that allow you to automatically run code at certain points while the page loads. A particularly important page-level event is the *postback*, triggered whenever a page is resubmitted to the server after the user clicks on submit. Lastly, you have many ASP.NET server control events that allow you to react to the user clicking or typing into controls on the Web page.

The great range of events available in ASP.NET improves the user experience, reduces the amount of code you write, and makes the resulting code much easier to maintain.

This chapter will look at:

- ❑ Definition of an event
- ❑ HTML events
- ❑ ASP.NET page events
- ❑ ASP.NET server control events
- ❑ Event-driven programming
- ❑ `IsPostBack`

What Is an Event?

Let's start by comparing an event to actions in real life. A fictional employee, Joe Public, sits in his cubicle in marketing department of his company, staring out the window. The phone rings. Joe reacts by picking it up and answering it with his name. A customer says, "We need to order ten cans of beans." Joe reacts by placing the order and hanging up the phone. Joe then goes back to staring out the window. Note the sequence of actions: the ringing of phone is an *event*, Joe responds to the event with a set of *actions* (answers the phone, states his name, takes the order), and then the event *concludes* (hangs up the phone). After the event is finished, Joe returns to a state of waiting for the next event to occur.

In event-driven programming, we have the same situation. Your page sits on the browser waiting for the user to interact. An event occurs when the user clicks on or types into the page. Your program reacts by executing code to perform some task in reaction to the event. When your code is finished, the page goes back waiting for the next event.

> *An event is an action taken on your application by some force outside of your code. This external force is usually the user, but could be another program. An event can hold code that will run when the action occurs.*

Therefore, you can break down your event-driven environment into four chronological sections:

❑ An event occurs – for example, the user clicks on a button

❑ The system detects the event – ASP.NET registers that an event has occurred

❑ The system reacts to the event – some code is executed

❑ The system then returns to its original state, waiting for the next event

Knowing this series of activities allows us to understand the usage of events when programming

What Is Event-Driven Programming?

Event-driven programming is a fundamental change in the nature of the traditional programming model. We leave behind the idea of sequential pages being processed on a server, and look at a model of programming where the server responds to events triggered by the user.

Before event-driven programming, your programs would execute from top to bottom as follows:

```
Line 1

Line 2

Line 3

Line 4
```

Broadly speaking, traditional programming languages (those over ten years old) start with the first line of your code, process it, move on to the second line, process that, and then move on to the third. There is no stopping, pausing, or waiting for interaction with the user. Even when functions and subroutines are used, they don't change the timing of execution as one procedure calls another, which calls another, and so on. There is still an uninterrupted sequence of execution.

The concept of event-driven programming changes all of this; with events, the sequential way of execution is no longer appropriate. The timing of code execution depends on interactions with the user. Consider the Windows operating system, which is event driven. It doesn't execute in a sequential fashion. Windows starts, then waits for an event to occur, like the user clicking on Start. As soon as an event occurs, Windows takes appropriate action to deal with that event. If you click on a menu, Windows provides the menu, and then waits for another user action. Windows is a collection of numerous sets of code, each waiting to be executed when called by an event.

Similarly, ASP.NET pages display in the browser and wait for user action. When the user types or clicks on the page, ASP.NET responds by executing some code. After the code execution ends, the page goes back to waiting for the next user action.

The term event has two further (and more subtle) meanings that are closely related and almost interchangeable. First, an event means something that happens to your page, such as a user's click, the user typing some text, or the page being served by IIS. Then we have the *event procedure*, the block of code that is run in reaction to the event.

There are two differences between an event procedure and the type of procedure we wrote in the last chapter. First, the naming syntax is different. You can use almost any name, such as `MyProcedure()`, for a plain procedure. An event procedure's name should specify the object and event separated by an underscore such as `MyButton_Click`. The second part, the event name like `Click` *must* be one of the standard event names established by Microsoft.

The second difference is how an event procedure is called. A non-event procedure is executed when it is called from other code. An event procedure is executed automatically in response to its event.

ASP.NET supports three groups of events:

❑ The first group contains HTML events that can occur on the page and are handled by the browser, completely on the client side. For example, pop-up tool tips or menu expansions that are typically run in client-side Javascripts. You'll see an example in this chapter.

❑ The second group contains several events that occur automatically when ASP.NET generates a page. There is no user involvement; they occur before the user even sees the page. We use these events to build the page.

❑ The last group is the largest, and contains all of the events that can occur by user interaction with the page.

HTML Events Executed on the Browser

The events that execute in HTML, on the browser (client) are not part of ASP.NET; however, let's briefly discuss them. Client-side events are written within pure HMTL tags such as <input>. The language is generally JavaScript or VB script. An interpreter built into the browser executes the code and there is no transfer of information to or action on the part of the server.

In the demonstration code that follows (ch06/Demo-BrowserEvent-OnClick.htm), we create a page that contains only HTML. For HTML input button tags there is an event called OnClick. When the user clicks on the button it executes the short line of code within the tag's onclick attribute. For this HTML event to work, you must be using a modern version of browser (*at least* IE 4.0, Netscape 6.0, or Opera 5.0).

```
<html>
<head><title>HTML Browser Event Example</title></head>
<body>
  <form>
    <input type="button"
      value="Click Me"
      onclick="alert('You have raised an event!')"
    >
  </form>
</body>
</html>
```

The code results in the screen shown in Figure 6-1:

Figure 6-1

Most HTML tags have events to which you can respond. The code inside the onclick attribute is known as an *event handler*. An event handler is simply the section of code that performs a suitable response to the event. HTML tags can react to many events, including:

❑   onmouseup: Occurs when a mouse button is released while clicking over an element.

❑   onmousedown: Occurs when a mouse button is pressed and held while clicking over an element.

❑   onmouseover: Occurs when a mouse is moved over an element.

❑   onmousemove: Occurs when a mouse moves over an element.

❑   onclick: Occurs when a mouse is clicked over an element.

❑   ondblclick: Occurs when a mouse is double-clicked while hovering over an element.

❑   onkeyup: Occurs when a key is released over an element.

❑   onkeypress: Occurs when a key is pressed and released over an element.

❑   onkeydown: Occurs when a key is pressed and held down while over an element.

You may want to try changing it to each of the events above to understand when they occur. For the events triggered by the keyboard, be sure to have the focus on the button before you strike the keys to test. We could change the code so that our button reacts to a different event; here, we've changed it to the OnMouseOver event (ch06/Demo-BrowserEvent-OnMouseOver.htm):

```
<html>
<head><title>HTML Browser Event Example</title></head>
<body>
  <form>
    <input type="button"
      value="Click Me"
      OnMouseOver="alert('You have raised an event!')"
    >
  </form>
</body>
</html>
```

ASP.NET can handle events similar to HTML. However, .NET gives us much greater functionality and the ability to utilize server-side resources such as database connections.

ASP.NET's Trace Feature

Before we dive into the two groups of ASP.NET events let's preview a technique for debugging, which will be discussed in detail in *Chapter14*. By adding trace="true" in the Page directive, we can have ASP.NET create a log of how it built the page. The log is appended to the bottom of the page. Trace does not conflict with Debug="true".

```
<%@ Page Language="VB" Debug="true" trace="true"%>
```

For example, open the TIO-ParameterWebControl.aspx page from *Chapter 5* and save it as Demo Trace.aspx in the ch06 folder. You can then turn on the trace by adding trace="true" in the Page directive and get the screenshot as depicted by Figure 6-2 (not all of the page is shown):

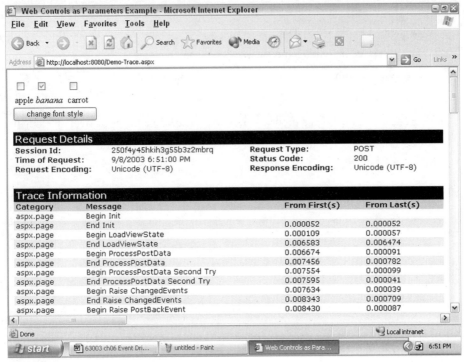

Figure 6-2

In the Trace Information, note the beginning and ending of events such as Init and PreRender under the Message column. We can put a custom message into the trace log with the following lines of code:

```
<script runat="server">
    Sub Page_Load
        Trace.Write("NOTE - First line of Page_Load")
        Call MakeItalic(label1,checkbox1.checked)
        Call MakeItalic(label2,checkbox2.checked)
        Call MakeItalic(label3,checkbox3.checked)
    End Sub

    Sub MakeItalic(TargetLabel as label, bolItalic as Boolean)
        Trace.Write("NOTE - First line of MakeItalic")
        Targetlabel.font.italic = bolItalic
    End Sub
</script>
```

Our `Trace.Write` notes will show up in the log in the order they are executed. As you can see in Figure 6-3, the "NOTE – First line of MakeItalic" occurs thrice as `MakeItalic()` was called three times:

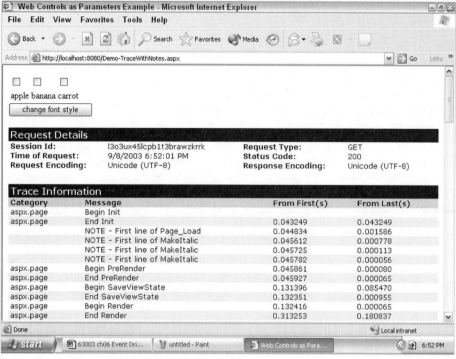

Figure 6-3

You can turn off trace by setting it to false in the `Page` directive, thus removing all of your diagnostic aids in one change. The `Trace.Write()` methods can remain in the code, they will have no effect on the output or performance of the page. This is a big improvement to those of us who programmed in classic ASP and had to remove scores of diagnostic `response.write` notes. We'll talk more about using Tracing in *Chapter 14*, but for now we just want to enter notes which will tell us when events occur and how our page reacts to those events.

ASP.NET Page Events

This section will address a group of events that are run by ASP.NET automatically when a page loads. Everything in ASP.NET comes down to objects, and in particular, the `page` object mentioned in *Chapter 2*. Each Web form you create is a page object in its own right. You can think of the entire Web form as an executable program whose output is HTML. Every time a page is called, the object goes through a series of stages – initializing, processing, and disposing of information. The page object performs these stages each time the page is called. Therefore, they occur every time a round trip to the server occurs. Each of these stages of page preparation generates an event, in the same way that clicking a mouse button does in Windows.

When you request your ASP.NET Web form, a series of events automatically occur on your Web server as follows:

❑ Page_Init() occurs when the page has been initialized. You can use the Sub Page_Init() subroutine associated with it to run code before .NET displays controls on the page. It works in a way similar to Page_Load(), but occurs earlier.

❑ Page_Render() and some additional events that occur to support advanced topics such as transactions. We will not discuss them in this book.

❑ Page_Load() occurs when the whole page is visible for the first time (that is, when the page has been read into memory and processed), but after some details about some of the server controls may have been initialized and displayed by Page_Init().

❑ Page_Unload() occurs when the page is unloaded from IIS memory and is sent out the wire to the browser. This occurs after any control events have been executed and so is an ideal place to shut down database connections. The name is misleading because this event does not occur when the user in the browser leaves the page or turns off the browser. The term *unload* is from the perspective of IIS, not the browser.

Notice the dual use of the word *event* in the preceding list. An *event* occurs – the page is served up by IIS. This event calls the Page_Load() *event procedure*.

The process of an event calling an event procedure has many slang terms, including to *fire* or *fire off*, *execute*, *start*, *invoke*, *initiate*, and, somewhat misleadingly, *call*.

If you want code to execute on your page before anything else occurs, you need to put it within a Page_Init() event procedure. The event of the page loading will automatically call the Page_Load() event procedure.

The syntax along with some trace writes (Demo-PageEvents.aspx) is as follows:

```
<%@ Page Language="VB" Trace="true" %>
<script runat="server">
    Sub Page_Init()
    Trace.Write("NOTE - First line of Page_Init")
    End Sub

    Sub Page_Load()
    Trace.Write("NOTE - First line of Page_Load")
    End Sub
</script>
<html>
<head><title>Demonstration of Page Events</title></head>
<body>
  <form runat="server">
    <asp:Button runat="server" Text="Submit"/><br/>
  </form>
</body>
</html>
```

The code results in the screen as shown in Figure 6-4:

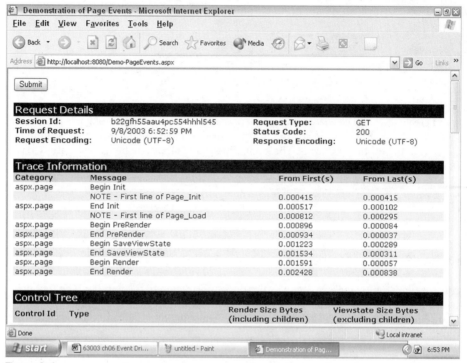

Figure 6-4

We've looked at `Page_Init()` and `Page_Load()`; that leaves us with the `Page_Unload()` event. Like the other two, this will occur automatically, but fires later, when IIS unloads the page from its working space and sends it out the wire to the browser. The `Page_Unload()` event will occur after all other tasks have been performed to create the page. Therefore `Page_Unload()` is a good place to end resource use, such as a database connection. As `Page_Unload()` is performed after the rest of the ASP.NET page has been completed, it is not possible to use `Page_Unload()` to change ASP.NET controls.

ASP.NET Web Controls Events

Now we reach the third and richest group of events – those that are associated with ASP.NET Web controls such as `<asp:textbox>` and `<asp:button>`. There are three important reasons why ASP.NET Web control events are much more powerful than HTML events run on the browser. Most importantly, you can execute the code in the event procedure on the server, which means that you have all of the server resources available to you, including custom-built objects and connections to other servers and databases. Second, you don't have to rely on the browser's capability to get HTML events to work because in ASP.NET the Web server only sends pure HTML back to the browser. Lastly, you can write code for the event procedure in any .NET enabled language, rather than just the scripts that run on browsers.

You add events to ASP.NET controls in two steps. First, in the control's tag you add an extra attribute with the name of the event and set its value to an event procedure. For example, in the following code, a sub named `Button1ClickEventHandler()` would run when the user clicks on `button1`.

```
<asp:button id="button1"
  runat="server"
  text="Click me"
  onclick="Button1ClickEventHandler"
  />
```

Second, you create the *event handler*, which is the procedure to run when invoked as mentioned. An event handler is almost the same as any other procedure; you just use the term to help humans understand what the routine performs. The small difference is that you have to specify two incoming parameters (arguments) with the *exact* syntax as follows:

```
<script language="vb" runat="server">
Sub ClickEventHandler(Sender As Object, E As EventArgs)
   ... ASP.NET code here...
End Sub

</script>
```

The arguments we provide for an event handler pass information to the handler. The first of these – `Sender` – provides a reference to the object that raised the event. The second, E, is an event class that captures information regarding the state of the event being handled, and passes an object that's specific to that event.

A common mistake is to not match the subroutine name with the name specified as the value for the event's attribute in the control's tag. The result is that *nothing* will happen when the event is triggered. You can call the subroutine whatever name you want, as long as you are consistent in using the same name in the server control and within the `<script>` tags. Adding `EventHandler` or EH to the name helps you remember the purpose of the procedure, as does providing a flowerbox as described in the previous chapter.

ASP.NET server controls have a reduced set (compared to HTML) of events that can be added to controls as extra attributes. These are as follows (note that these event names aren't case-sensitive):

Event Name	Description
onload	Occurs when the control has loaded into the window or frame
onunload	Occurs when a control has been removed from a window or frame
onclick	Occurs when a mouse button (or similar) is clicked when hovering over the `<asp: button>` control
oninit	Occurs when the Web page is first initialized
onprerender	Occurs just before the control is rendered

In addition to this, we also have the following events that can't be handled by the user in an event handler, but that occur in ASP.NET and cause actions within ASP.NET:

Event Name	Description
`selectindexchanged` `checkchanged`	These two occur when the contents of a control have been altered, such as a checkbox being clicked, or a list item being selected. These only apply to the appropriate controls, such as list items and checkboxes.

The difference between HTML controls and ASP.NET Web controls is in the way they're handled. With HTML form controls, when the event is raised, the browser handles it within itself. However, with Web controls, the browser raises the event, but instead of being dealt with by the browser, the client sends a postback message to the server to handle the event. It doesn't matter what kind of event was raised, the client will always return this single postback event to the server. However, some events such as key presses or mouseovers are impossible to deal with on the server. Hence there are no equivalent ASP.NET events for these. They will not be passed onto the server and will have to be handled by the client.

The ASP.NET Button Control

The `<asp:button>` control performs the HTML equivalent of a `<input type= Button>`. The button control has the following syntax:

```
<asp:button  id="id_name" event="event_handler_name" runat="server"/>
```

To get it to work, you need to specify an event. The ASP.NET button control supports the five events contained in ASP.NET Web controls, the most useful being `OnClick`. You need to create a subroutine, like the following, to handle the event:

```
<script language="vb" runat="server">
   Sub myButton_OnClickEH (Sender As Object, E As EventArgs)
     Code which can use Sender and E
   End Sub
</script>
```

We're going to consider the theory and practical application of postback in more detail, and then do an exercise that utilizes multiple buttons and event handlers.

Event-Driven Programming and Postback

So far, the issue of postback architecture has not been discussed in detail. Postback is the process by which the browser sends information back to the server so the server can handle the event. The server executes the code in the event handler and sends the resulting HTML back to the browser again. Postback only occurs with Web forms that have the `runat="server"` attribute, and only ASP.NET Web controls post information back to the server. Postback is not available in simple HTML and was implemented only weakly in classic ASP.

Note that ASP.NET doesn't look after the processing of all events. It is still necessary to handle some events (such as `OnMouseOver`) on the client-side because a round trip to the server couldn't possibly react to them as quickly as the user expects. Thus you should generally have a mix of server-side and client-side event procedures in your Web application.

Try It Out   Demonstrating Event Reaction in HTML and ASP.NET

We will create two pages. The first has only simple HTML events and you will see that there is no postback as the event is handled on the browser. We will then modify the page to support ASP.NET Web controls and see the postback to the server in effect.

1. In your `BegASPNET11` directory, create a `ch06` folder. Within this, create a page named `TIO-EventHTML.htm` and enter the following:

```
<html>
<head><title>Event - HTML</title></head>
<body>
   <h2>Event - HTML</h2>
   <form method="get">
   Select either A, B or C and click the button at the bottom<br/>
   A<input type="radio" value="a" name="test"><br />
   B<input type="radio" value="b" name="test"><br />
   C<input type="radio" value="c" name="test"><br /><br />
   <input type="submit" value="Click Me"
         onclick="alert('Button Click event occurred in HTML')">
   </form>
</body>
</html>
```

2. Save the page, making sure you remember the HTML suffix. View in your browser to arrive at Figure 6-5, and click on a choice. Notice that after the click you lose your selection:

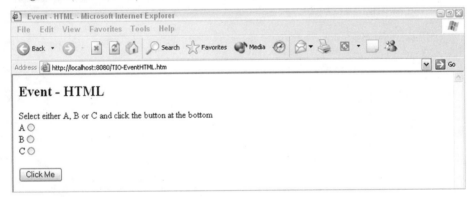

Figure 6-5

3. Go back to your editor and save the file as `TIO-PostbackAspNet.aspx`. Check that the file extension is `.aspx`. Make the following changes to convert the HTML code to ASP.NET code:

```
<%@ Page Language="VB" %>
<script runat="server">
</script>

<html>
<head><title>Event- ASP.NET</title></head>
<body>
  <h2>Event - ASP.NET</h2>
  <form runat="server">
    Select either A, B or C and click the button at the bottom<br/>
    <asp:radiobuttonlist id="test" runat="server">
    <asp:listitem id="option1" value="a" runat="server" />
    <asp:listitem id="option2" value="b" runat="server" />
    <asp:listitem id="option3" value="c" runat="server" />
    </asp:radiobuttonlist><br /><br />
    <input type="submit" value="Click Me"
           onclick="alert('Button Click event occurred in HTML')">
  </form>
</body>
</html>
```

4. Save (double check the extension) and surf to `TIO-PostbackAspNet.aspx` using your browser. Select an option and click the button to see that option remains selected. In other words, the state of the page is maintained by postback.

5. After clicking the button take a look at the Source (in IE, click on View | Source) as shown by Figure 6-6. Notice the presence of a VIEWSTATE tag containing a cryptic value.

```
TIO-PostbackAspNet[1] - Notepad
File  Edit  Format  View  Help
<html>
<head><title>Postback - ASP.NET</title></head>
<body>
  <h2>Postback - ASP.NET</h2>
  <form name="_ctl0" method="post" action="TIO-PostbackAspNet.aspx" id="_ctl0">
    <input type="hidden"
           name="__VIEWSTATE"
           value="dDwOMDk5MTgxNTU7Oz4PDGHD0RtpwsXjfPN87dGphxBp1Q==" />

    Select either A, B or C and click the button at the bottom<br/>
    <table id="test" border="0">
        <tr>
        <td><input id="test_0" type="radio" name="test" value="a" />
            <label for="test_0">a</label></td>
        </tr><tr>
        <td><input id="test_1" type="radio" name="test" value="b" />
            <label for="test_1">b</label></td>
        </tr><tr>
        <td><input id="test_2" type="radio" name="test" value="c" />
            <label for="test_2">c</label></td>
        </tr>
    </table>
        <br /><br />
    <input type="submit" value="Click Me" onclick="alert('Button Click event occured in HTML')">
    </form>
</body>
</html>
```

Figure 6-6

How It Works

In the first page, the HTML form, you noted the loss of selection when the button was clicked. However, the browser did append a query string to the request similar to the following:

http://localhost:8080/ch07/htmlevent2.htm?test=b

But the server has no intrinsic mechanism to pass that selection through to the refresh of the page. This is the normal behavior for HTML.

In our second page, we use ASP.NET postback. Postback is turned on because we use an ASPX extension on the file name, and our controls (form, radio, and button) use the runat="server" attribute. When you viewed the source, you saw a new <input> tag similar to the following:

```
<input type="hidden" name="__VIEWSTATE" value="dDw0MDk5MTgxNTU7Oz4=" />
```

When postback is used, information about the state of the form is sent back at the click in an associated hidden control called _VIEWSTATE. This information in _VIEWSTATE is generated by ASP.NET by encrypting the values of the old state of the form. That state includes user selections for each ASP.NET Web control. ASP.NET is able to look at the old version and compare it to the current version. With this information, the asp.dll can persist the state of ASP.NET server controls between page submissions. If there are differences, such as a different radio button being selected, internal events are generated by ASP.NET in response to the difference and the DLL runs code to create a *current* version of the form. The string of characters contained in the value attribute will differ as mentioned in *Chapter 3*.

There are three points to remember about _VIEWSTATE. First, it is crucial to ASP.NET being able to remember the state of controls between page submissions, without actually maintaining a page object or HTTP connection throughout. Second, you never have to program or interpret _VIEWSTATE at all; it is a fully automated part of ASP.NET. And third, _VIEWSTATE is passed to the browser as a standard HTML <input type=hidden>. There is no need for any special plug-in or interpretive software on the browser.

The IsPostBack Test

Let's discuss the IsPostBack test introduced in *Chapter 3*. This test determined whether a user had returned a form, together with data, or whether it was the first time the form had been displayed. In other words, our IsPostBack test just checks to see whether any postback information has been generated by an event. If it hasn't, this test generates false, otherwise it generates true. The syntax is as follows:

```
If Page.IsPostBack Then
    Code to run to check for and use data
Else
    Code to run assuming there is no data
End If
```

It is not necessary to have code to run in both cases. Many times we do not have code to run if `IsPostBack=false`. In other words an `IsPostBack=false` can be interpreted as absence of code to be run. This is logical since we probably don't have any data to feed into code.

Let's look at an example that draws together all of the things we've looked at in the chapter and utilizes event-driven programming. It contains two textboxes to take information from the user, and will perform a calculation depending on whether the user selects add, subtract, divide, or multiply button. Each of these options will have its own button; multiple button forms force us to write specific event handlers for each, rather than just making a single button perform a postback. In the second part of the example, we will tighten up the code by using a single event handler and testing parameters to determine how to manipulate the data.

Try It Out   Calculator

1. In your `ch06` folder create `TIO-Calculator1.aspx` and enter the following code:

```vb
<script runat="server" language="vb">

  Sub Page_Load
    btnAdd.backcolor = system.drawing.color.lightgray
    btnSubtract.backcolor = system.drawing.color.lightgray
    btnFactor.backcolor = system.drawing.color.lightgray
    btnRatio.backcolor = system.drawing.color.lightgray
  End Sub

    Sub Add(sender as object, e As EventArgs)
      lblAnswer.Text = CDbl(tbxInput1.text) + CDbl(tbxInput2.text)
      btnAdd.backcolor=system.drawing.color.yellow
    End Sub

    Sub Subtract(sender as object, e As EventArgs)
      lblAnswer.Text = CDbl(tbxInput1.text) - CDbl(tbxInput2.text)
      btnSubtract.backcolor=system.drawing.color.yellow
    End Sub

    Sub Factor(sender as object, e As EventArgs)
      lblAnswer.Text = CDbl(tbxInput1.text) * CDbl(tbxInput2.text)
      btnFactor.backcolor=system.drawing.color.yellow
    End Sub

    Sub Ratio(sender as object, e As EventArgs)
      lblAnswer.Text = CDbl(tbxInput1.text) / CDbl(tbxInput2.text)
      btnRatio.backcolor=system.drawing.color.yellow
    End Sub

  </script>
<html>
<head><title>Calculator Example version 1</title></head>
<body>
<h2>Calculator version 1</h2>
  <form runat="server">
    <asp:textbox id="tbxInput1" runat="server" />
    <asp:button id="btnAdd" runat="server" text=" + " Onclick="Add" />
    <asp:button id="btnSubtract" runat="server" text=" - " Onclick="Subtract" />
    <br/>
```

```
      <asp:textbox id="tbxInput2" runat="server" />
      <asp:button id="btnFactor" runat="server" text=" x " Onclick="Factor" />
      <asp:button id="btnRatio" runat="server" text=" ÷ " Onclick="Ratio" />
      <br/>
      <b>Answer = <asp:Label id="lblAnswer" runat="server" /></b>
   </form>
 </body>
 </html>
```

2.   The page in your browser will be as shown in Figure 6-7. Here, enter two numbers and select a button to perform a calculation. Note that only the operation corresponding to the button clicked was performed. Furthermore, notice that the executed operation's button is highlighted in yellow:

Figure 6-7

If you don't enter a number into one or other of the boxes before selecting an operator, you will get an error. Error handling will be discussed in *Chapter 14*.

---

3.   After doing a calculation, take a look at the source and note the existence of a `_VIEWSTATE` similar to that shown in Figure 6-8. You may want to take a look at the `_VIEWSTATE` after several calculations and notice the difference in the encrypted value. Do not try to discern a pattern, just note it is responding to changes in your activities as user of the page:

Figure 6-8

4. Now save the page as `TIO-Calculator2.aspx` and make the following changes. Start by deleting the four operator subs and then replacing them with the single one as follows:

```
<%@ Page Language="VB" Debug="true" %>
<script runat="server">

    Sub Page_Load
        btnAdd.backcolor = system.drawing.color.lightgray
        btnSubtract.backcolor = system.drawing.color.lightgray
        btnFactor.backcolor = system.drawing.color.lightgray
        btnRatio.backcolor = system.drawing.color.lightgray
    End Sub

    Sub Calc(sender as object, e As EventArgs)
        Select Case sender.Id
        Case "btnAdd"
          lblAnswer.Text = CDbl(tbxInput1.text) + CDbl(tbxInput2.text)
        Case "btnSubtract"
          lblAnswer.Text = CDbl(tbxInput1.text) - CDbl(tbxInput2.text)
        Case "btnFactor"
          lblAnswer.Text = CDbl(tbxInput1.text) * CDbl(tbxInput2.text)
        Case "btnRatio"
          lblAnswer.Text = CDbl(tbxInput1.text) / CDbl(tbxInput2.text)
        End Select
        sender.backcolor=system.drawing.color.yellow
    End Sub

</script>
<html>
<head><title>Calculator Example version 2</title></head>
<body>
<h2>Calculator version 2</h2>
```

```
<form runat="server">
    <asp:textbox id="tbxInput1" runat="server"></asp:textbox>
    <asp:button id="btnAdd"
        onclick="Calc" runat="server" text=" + "></asp:button>
    <asp:button id="btnSubtract"
        onclick="Calc" runat="server" text=" - "></asp:button><br />
    <asp:textbox id="tbxInput2" runat="server"></asp:textbox>
    <asp:button id="btnFactor"
        onclick="Calc" runat="server" text=" x "></asp:button>
    <asp:button id="btnRatio"
        onclick="Calc" runat="server" text=" ÷ "></asp:button><br />
    <b>Answer = <asp:Label id="lblAnswer" runat="server"></asp:Label></b>
</form>
</body>
</html>
```

5. View the `TIO-Calculator2.aspx` page in your browser. You'll notice that there is no change in behavior.

How It Works

This example works by using event-driven programming, as outlined previously. In `Calculator1`, we created a sub which fires automatically from the `Page_Load()` event. This sub merely returns all buttons to their original color:

```
Sub Page_Load
    btnAdd.backcolor = system.drawing.color.lightgray
    btnSubtract.backcolor = system.drawing.color.lightgray
    btnFactor.backcolor = system.drawing.color.lightgray
    btnRatio.backcolor = system.drawing.color.lightgray
End Sub
```

Next, look at how we set the events to be executed when there is a click on a button. These subroutines are called by the four ASP.NET button controls we have created:

```
<asp:button id="btnAdd" runat="server" text=" + " Onclick="Add" />
<asp:button id="btnSubtract" runat="server" text=" - " Onclick="Subtract" />
...
<asp:button id="btnFactor" runat="server" text=" x " Onclick="Factor" />
<asp:button id="btnRatio" runat="server" text=" ÷ " Onclick="Ratio" />
```

Each button has a symbol corresponding to its equivalent mathematical operation, and it calls the relevant subroutine. All four subroutines work in an identical way. Let's look at the sub `Add()` more closely:

```
Sub Add(sender as object, e As EventArgs)
    lblAnswer.Text = CDbl(tbxInput1.text) + CDbl(tbxInput2.text)
End Sub
```

The code you just saw is invoked by the `onclick` attribute of `btnAdd`, and passed two generic parameters. The first textbox is called `tbxInput1`, and the second textbox is `tbxInput2`. We can reference their contents by referring to their `text` attributes. As the `text` attribute returns its information as a string, we have to use CDbl, which converts the data type from a string to a double. Then we can perform a mathematical operation on these two pieces of data, effectively saying:

```
tbxInput1 + tbxInput2
```

We store our data in the <asp:label> control, lblAnswer. Once again, we can access its text attribute, but instead of getting the information, here we are setting it. So we are effectively saying:

```
lblAnswer.text = tbxInput1 + tbxInput2
```

This result is displayed on our screen. The remaining three subroutines work in the same way, and will only be executed in the event that the particular button associated with them is pressed.

In Calculator1, ASP.NET reacts in a different way to each of the buttons on the page by having four different event handlers. In Calculator2, we build a single event handler that is called by all four buttons. A click on btnAdd now invokes the Calc() event procedure, not an Add() event procedure:

```
<asp:button id="btnAdd"
        onclick="Calc" runat="server" text=" + "></asp:button>
```

Within this single handler named Calc(), as shown below, we do a Select Case to examine the sender parameter to determine who triggered the event. The value in sender.Id will be the value in the Id attribute of one of the buttons, so those values make up the possible answer in the Case lines. Depending on the matching case, the sub will use different operations on the two text boxes and put the answer into the lblAnswer.text, as follows:

```
' ' ' ' ' ' ' ' ' ' ' ' ' ' ' ' ' ' ' ' ' ' ' ' ' ' ' ' ' ' ' ' ' ' ' ' ' ' ' ' ' ' ' ' ' ' ' ' ' ' ' ' ' ' ' '
Sub Calc(sender as object, e As EventArgs)
   Select Case sender.Id
   Case "btnAdd"
      lblAnswer.Text = CDbl(tbxInput1.text) + CDbl(tbxInput2.text)
   Case "btnSubtract"
      lblAnswer.Text = CDbl(tbxInput1.text) - CDbl(tbxInput2.text)
   Case "btnFactor"
      lblAnswer.Text = CDbl(tbxInput1.text) * CDbl(tbxInput2.text)
   Case "btnRatio"
      lblAnswer.Text = CDbl(tbxInput1.text) / CDbl(tbxInput2.text)
   End Select
```

We change the background color of the object that fired the Calc() event as follows:

```
   sender.backcolor=system.drawing.color.yellow
End Sub
```

In this exercise, you saw two ways to handle multiple buttons. The first is to have different event handlers. If the different buttons have parallel tasks then we can employ the second technique where we create one handler that behaves differently depending on who triggers it.

Summary

This chapter presented the theory and practical aspects of event driven programming. Traditionally, code ran all at once and then the program was over. In event driven programming, different parts of our code are run at different times, as triggered by the user's interactions with the page.

We started with a brief look at HTML events that provide one way of handling user action. HTML events are executed on the browser and are generally written in VBScript or JavaScript. They are useful for implementing events reactions that would take too long to process in a round trip to the server, for example the display of tooltips. However, HTML events do not tap the power of the server. They are not part of ASP.NET and outside the scope of this book.

When you use ASP.NET event-driven programming, you execute your code on the server. You create blocks of code in procedures. The page loads and runs some procedures automatically. Then the page sits and waits for user action called *events*. Each event runs the code of an event handler to perform the desired tasks. When the event handler is finished, the page returns to a state of waiting for the next user-created event.

We looked at a group of events that occur automatically when a page is created on the server. The most commonly used event is `Page_Load()` to populate list boxes and to respond to the user input if the page is a postback. Postback pages have already been shown to the user and are now being refreshed, presumably with data entered by the user into the ASP.NET Web controls.

We saw another group of events that do not fire automatically. The Web control events are only executed when a user interacts with them. These controls will run whatever event handler is specified in their tag, typically an attribute like `OnClick="MyOnClickEH"`. A subroutine named `MyOnClickEH()` must exist on the page. These event handlers are subroutines and thus need the `Sub...End Sub` keywords and must be located outside any other sub but inside the `<script>` tags. They must also be written to handle two incoming parameters: `Sender` as `object` and e as `EventArgs`. The former contains a pointer (`ByRef`) to the object that invoked the event handler. The latter is used for passing of special parameters that we did not cover.

The `asp:button_OnClick` is the most commonly used event. It triggers a postback, which is a request to the server to refresh the page. Included in the request is a viewstate that defines, in a compact and encrypted form, the status of each ASP.NET Web control on the page. This process only works when the page's filename ends in `.aspx`, and each form and control contains the `runat="server"` attribute. Multiple buttons on a page can have their events handled by multiple event procedures or by one procedure which acts differently depending on the object which raised the event.

Exercises

1. Explain why event-driven programming is such a good way of programming for the Web.

2. Run the following HTML code in your browser (remember to save the page with a `.htm` suffix). Now translate it into a set of ASP.NET server controls so that the information entered into the form is retained when the Submit button is clicked. Add a function to the button to confirm that the details were received:

```
<%@ Page Language="VB" runat="server" %>
<script runat="server">
  Sub ClickHandler(Sender As Object, E As EventArgs)
    message.text = "Details received."
    questions.visible = False
  End Sub
</script>
<html>
<head>
  <title>ASP.NET</title>
</head>
<body>
  <asp:label id=message runat=server />
  <form id=questions runat="server">
    <h4>Please enter your name:</h4>
    <asp:textbox id=name runat="server" /><br /><br />
    <h4>What would you like for breakfast?</h4>
    <asp:checkboxlist id=food runat="server">
      <asp:listitem value="Cereal"/>
      <asp:listitem value="Eggs"/>
      <asp:listitem value="Pancakes"/>
    </asp:checkboxlist>
    <h4>Feed me:<h4>
    <asp:radiobuttonlist id=when runat="server">
      <asp:listitem value="Now"/>
      <asp:listitem value="Later"/>
    </asp:radiobuttonlist>
    <asp:button type="submit" id="btnSubmit" onclick="ClickHandler" text="Thank
                    you!" runat="server" />
  </form>
</body>
</html>
```

3. Add a `Page_Load()` event handler to the ASPX code you've just created, to confirm the selections made in the following format:

    > Thank you very much _____
    >
    > You have chosen _____ for breakfast, I will prepare it for you _____.

4. Create a very basic virtual telephone using an ASPX file that displays a textbox and a button named Call. Configure your ASPX file so that when you type a telephone number into your textbox and press Call, you are:

    ❑   Presented with a message confirming the number you are calling

    ❑   Presented with another button called Disconnect, which when pressed, returns you to your opening page, leaving you ready to type another number

5. Using the SELECT CASE or a collection, associate three particular telephone numbers with three names, so that when you press the Call button, your confirmation message contains the name of the person you are calling rather than just the telephone number.

Objects

When I started writing this chapter, I was struggling for a concise definition of what an object is. After all, everything is an object. A door is an object. So is an aardvark. So, being the computer geek I am, I went online to one of the numerous dictionary sites, and what I first got was the etymology:

> *Middle English, from Medieval Latin objectum, from Latin, neuter of objectus, past participle of obicere to throw in the way, present, hinder, from ob- in the way + jacere to throw*

I didn't understand any of that, so I tried elsewhere and got this:

> *\Ob"ject\, n.: That which is put, or which may be regarded as put, in the way of some of the senses; something visible or tangible.*

Ok, that makes a little more sense. So an object is something we can see, feel, hear, touch, taste or smell. Not much use in the virtual world of computer programming, so here's a more suitable definition:

> *An object is a self-contained entity that is characterized by a recognizable set of characteristics and behaviors.*

Taking this concept further, how do you tell the difference between various objects? Well, you do so through their recognizable characteristics and behaviors. Take a cow for an example where you could have the following:

Characteristics	Behaviors
They have four legs	They moo
They have udders	They eat grass
Size	They make milk
Color	
Breed	

These are fairly distinctive characteristics – if you described these, everyone should be able to tell you are describing a cow. What you are describing is not any single cow, but *all* cows – the template that specifies the characteristics of a cow. What you need to consider is what makes one cow different from another.

Classes and Instances

In the world of *Object-Oriented Programming* (*OOP*) the following two terms are used:

❑   **Class**: This is the template for an object, and defines the characteristics of the object. In our bovine example, it's what defines the characteristics of a cow.

❑   **Instance**: This is a real life object – the thing you can interact with. Thus you have only one class defining a cow, but many instances.

Therefore, cows don't exist until they have an instance created. This is when their characteristics come into play. A good analogy is making cookies – the cookie cutter is the class (it defines the size and shape of the cookie), and once cut, the cookie is the instance. In this case, multiple instances are a good thing.

Properties, Methods, and Events

In OOP, the following terms are used to describe the characteristics of an object:

❑   **Property**: This is a noun and describes some feature of an object. A cow has a `Breed` – this is a property that describes the breed to which a cow belongs, which in turn might imply other characteristics. For example, the Holstein breed produces beer instead of milk. Actually I made that up, but it's a nice idea, isn't it? In fact, the Holstein is the best milk-producing breed.

❑   **Method**: This is a verb and describes something an object can do, or that you want it to do. The cow can be milked and therefore might have a `Milk()` method.

❑   **Event**: This is also a verb and describes something that an object does in response to some stimuli. For example, your cow would have an event called `Moo`, which might happen when it is being milked. Or perhaps a `Sleep` event for when it's dark or the cow is tired.

The following sections show how these definitions apply to .NET.

Objects in .NET

.NET uses a lot of objects – in fact everything is an object in .NET. Even variables, which were discussed in *Chapter 3*, are objects in .NET. You don't really need to understand why or how (it's just the way .NET is built), but it's worth remembering that everything you deal with is an object. Consider the following:

```
Dim Name As String
```

You are actually declaring an object. Just like the real world, where objects are something specific, the Name variable is also something specific; it's a String – in fact, it's an instance of the String class. The String class defines the characteristics that our Name variable possesses, some of which are shown as follows:

Property	Method
Chars	ToUpper
Length	StartsWith
	Trim

It has a Length property so we can see how many characters make up the string, and a ToUpper() method to allow us to convert the characters to uppercase. These are just a few of the methods, but enough to give you the idea that a string is an object. Notice that there are no events – the String class doesn't have any events. This is an important point – classes don't *need* to have properties, methods, or events. In this chapter, we'll see how to build up a class in stages, adding the characteristics as needed.

Why Use Objects

In the programming world, objects are part of object-oriented programming and object-oriented design, and these bring great benefits. Many people think this is a complex subject, but in reality, it's quite simple and can be explained in four simple terms: *abstraction, encapsulation, polymorphism,* and *inheritance. Chapter 12* discusses encapsulation in detail, but it's worth having an idea about the other terms as well so that when you do more complex programming you'll understand the concepts:

❑ **Abstraction:** This is the process of hiding the complexity, the inner workings of a class, so that users don't have to know how it operates. For example, you don't have to know how a TV works if you only wanted to view picture; you just switch it on and get a picture. The On/Off switch abstracts the actual operation. In the String example, you have a Trim method that strips off any blank space at the beginning and end of a string. You don't need to know how it actually does it – just that it does.

❑ **Encapsulation:** Every object contains everything it needs to be able to operate – this feature is called encapsulation. Thus objects don't have to rely on other objects to be able to perform their own actions. For example, a cow contains everything it needs to produce milk – teeth to chew the grass, a stomach (four of them in fact), udders and so on. A String doesn't have to go elsewhere to convert all its characters into uppercase when you use the ToUpper() method.

However, encapsulation doesn't mean that you include absolutely everything in your class that it needs. For example, a class that uses strings would not define its own string object; it would reuse the standard one. This is acceptable because the String class it would reuse, is part of the base classes supplied by .NET. It wouldn't be sensible to rely on a class that might not be present.

❑ **Polymorphism**: This is the term given to different objects being able to perform the same action, but through their own implementation. For example, our cow might have a `Chew()` method. For that matter, even a `Person` class could have a `Chew()` method, but the implementation under-the-hood might be different.

❑ **Inheritance**: This defines how classes can be related to one another and share characteristics. Inheritance works by defining classes and subclasses, where the subclass inherits all of the characteristics of the parent class. For example, if an `Animal` class were to define the base characteristics of an animal, there could be subclasses of `Cow`, `Dog`, `Human`, and so on. Each subclass would not only inherit the characteristics of the `Animal` class, but could also define new characteristics.

The importance of inheritance is that it enforces conformance across classes of a similar type, and allows shared code. If you decide to create a new class called `Mouse`, you don't have to reinvent all of the characteristics of the parent class. Inheritance will be discussed in more detail later in the chapter.

Defining Classes

It's now time to put some of this theory into practice. We're going to create a `Person` class, with the following characteristics:

❑ Properties: `Name, Age, EyeColor`

❑ Methods: `Walk(), Talk(), Chew()`

This will be done in stages, so that you fully understand each part of the class before moving on. You'll create the class as part of an ASP.NET page, and look at how to create classes as separate file later in the chapter. You can use Web Matrix for these examples if you like, or any other editor as we're not using any specific Web Matrix features. However, using Web Matrix means you don't have to bother with any Web server settings as it handles it all for you.

Try It Out · Creating a Class

1. Create a new ASP.NET page called `FirstClass.aspx`. If you are using Web Matrix, you can pick the ASP.NET page template – make sure you pick the correct file Location and Filename, as shown in Figure 7-1:

Figure 7-1

2. In Web Matrix, then select the All tab and replace everything in the file with the following code:

```
<%@ Page Language="VB" %>
<script runat="server">
  Public Class Person

    Public Sub New()
    End Sub

    Private _Name As String
    Private _Age As Integer
    Private _EyeColor As String
    Public Property Name As String
```

```
        Get
            Return _Name
        End Get

        Set (ByVal Value As String)
            _Name = Value
        End Set
    End Property

    Public Property Age As Integer
        Get
            Return _Age
        End Get
        Set (ByVal Value As Integer)
            _Age = Value
        End Set
    End Property

    Public Property EyeColor As String
        Get
            Return _EyeColor
        End Get
        Set (ByVal Value As String)
            _EyeColor = Value
        End Set
    End Property

End Class

Sub Page_Load(Sender As Object, E As EventArgs)

    Dim myPerson As New Person()
    myPerson.Name = "Susan"
    myPerson.Age = "25"
    myPerson.EyeColor = "Blue"

    Name.Text = myPerson.Name
    Age.Text = myPerson.Age
    EyeColor.Text = myPerson.EyeColor

End Sub
</script>
<html>
<head>
</head>
<body>
  <form runat="server">
    Name: <asp:Label runat="server" id="Name" /><br />
    Age: <asp:Label runat="server" id="Age" /><br />
    Eye Color: <asp:Label runat="server" id="EyeColor" />
  </form>
</body>
</html>
```

3. Save this file and run it. Web Matrix users can hit the F5 key to run the file. You should see the result similar to Figure 7-2:

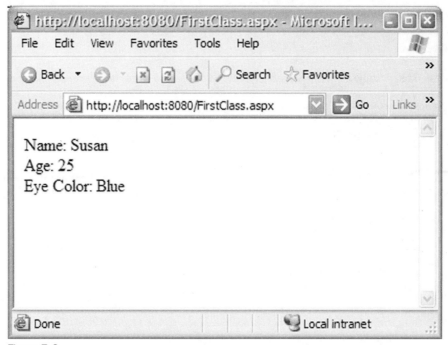

Figure 7-2

Nothing spectacular – it just shows the name, age, and eye color – but you are using a custom class. Let's see how this works.

How It Works

The first couple of lines define the language used in the page and the start of the server script. This is where your code will go:

```
<%@ Page Language="VB" %>
<script runat="server">
```

Next comes the definition of the class:

```
Public Class Person
```

Unlike variables, where the Dim statement defines a class, only the Class keyword followed by the class name (in this case, Person) has been used. If you refer to the discussion on variables in *Chapter 3*, Public means that the class will be available to all other programs. This is necessary, as an ASP.NET page will use it.

Next come the lines that initialize the class (this method is called the *Constructor*, and is always named `New()`). This procedure is run when you create an instance of a class, and is a good place to set default values, or perform any processing that the class itself requires. These will be discussed in more detail later.

```
Public Sub New()
End Sub
```

Next in the code are some `Private` variables that will be used to store the properties of the class such as the `Name`, `Age`, and `EyeColor`:

```
Private _Name As String
Private _Age As Integer
Private  EyeColor As String
```

As these variables are `Private`; they cannot be accessed from outside your class. In such a case, how would one allow external access to them? For this, the code uses the `Property` statement:

```
Public Property Name As String
  Get
    Return _Name
  End Get
  Set (ByVal Value As String)
    _Name = Value
  End Set
End Property
```

Let's break this statement down, starting with the declaration:

```
Public Property Name As String
```

As mentioned earlier, `Public` says that the property can be accessed from outside the class – that's what we need. The `Property` keyword indicates that a property is being declared, followed by the name of the property and its type. In this case, `Name` is a `String`.

Next we have the `Get` statement, which is the code that runs when the property is read. Here we just return the value of the private property variable:

```
Get
  Return _Name
End Get
```

The second part of the property is the `Set` statement, which is the code that runs when we want to store a value in the property:

```
Set (ByVal Value As String)
  _Name = Value
End Set
```

Here we just set the private property variable to the value passed in. The Set statement is a bit like a method call in that it has an argument. This argument is automatically assigned by .NET when we set the property. Consider the following:

```
Person.Name = "Susan"
```

The value Susan is passed into the property as the Value argument. Next we have the property definitions for the Age and EyeColor properties; these follow the same pattern as Name:

```
Public Property Age As Integer
  Get
    Return _Age
  End Get
  Set (ByVal Value As Integer)
    _Age = Value
  End Set
End Property

Public Property EyeColor As String
  Get
    Return _EyeColor
  End Get
  Set (ByVal Value As String)
    _EyeColor = Value
  End Set
End Property
```

Next we have the line that ends the class:

```
End Class
```

Now we come to the parts of the page that will use the class, starting with the Page_Load() method, which runs when the page is loaded:

```
Sub Page_Load(Sender As Object, E As EventArgs)
```

When the page loads, an instance of our Person class needs to be created; this is done in a manner similar to that of declaring variables:

```
Dim myPerson As New Person()
```

We use the Dim statement, give the class instance a name (myPerson), and then create a new instance by using the New keyword followed by the class name. At this stage, we have an instance of the class, but because it doesn't contain anything, we set the property values:

```
myPerson.Name = "Susan"
myPerson.Age = "25"
myPerson.EyeColor = "Blue"
```

Now the class instance has some values for its properties. We can read them out and display them in some label controls:

```
Name.Text = myPerson.Name
Age.Text = myPerson.Age
EyeColor.Text = myPerson.EyeColor
```

The last bit of code is the end of the `Page_Load()` routine and the end script tag:

```
End Sub
</script>
```

Finally, there are the HTML and Web controls – three `Label` controls used to display the property values:

```
<html>
<head>
</head>
<body>
  <form runat="server">
    Name: <asp:Label runat="server" id="Name" /><br />
    Age: <asp:Label runat="server" id="Age" /><br />
    Eye Color: <asp:Label runat="server" id="EyeColor" />
  </form>
</body>
</html>
```

That's all there is to it – you've now created and used your first custom class. Let's look at the reasons behind using private variables for properties.

Property Variables

Why is it that we have the variables that actually store the property values as `Private`, and then have the `Property` statement to allow access to them? Wouldn't it be easier to just have `Public` variables, like the following:

```
Public _Name As String
```

Yes it would, but this would break one of the key object oriented features mentioned earlier – abstraction. The whole idea is that we abstract the inner workings of the class, and this is not achieved with the above code doesn't do that. It explicitly exposes how the properties are stored. Therefore, we use `Private` variables and the `Property` statement, ensuring that all access to the property details is via that `Property` statement.

This also allows you to add any processing, such as validation, to the property. For example, consider the `Age` property, where you may wish to add validation:

```
Public Property Age As Integer
  Get
    Return _Age
  End Get
```

```
        Set (ByVal Value As Integer)
          If Value < 1 Then
            Value = 1
          Else
            _Age = Value
          End If

        End Set
      End Property
```

This validation checks whether the age is less than zero, and set it to 1 if it is. This sort of processing wouldn't be possible, had the `Property` statement not been used.

Property Types

As of now, the `EyeColor` property can be both read from and written to. In the real world, you can't change the color of your eyes (except by using contact lenses, but that's not really *changing* the color), so why should your class allow it? You'd certainly want some way of setting the eye color, but a property can't be the answer, as this would allow the eye color to be changed. However, the property can't be done away with either; we still want to be able to read the value.

One way to achieve a value that can only be read is to utilize a feature of properties that allows us to decide whether they can be read from or written to. To allow only reading of a property, we remove the `Set` section of the property and add the `ReadOnly` keyword. Similarly, to allow only writing to a property, we remove the `Get` section and add the `WriteOnly` keyword. For example, the following listings show how this could be applied to the `EyeColor` property. For a read-only property you would use:

```
      Public ReadOnly Property EyeColor As String
        Get
          Return _EyeColor
        End Get
      End Property
```

For a write-only property you would use:

```
      Public WriteOnly Property EyeColor As String
        Set (ByVal Value As String)
          _EyeColor = Value
        End Set
      End Property
```

Let's give this a go and turn `EyeColor` into a read-only property.

Try It Out **Read-Only Properties**

1. Edit `FirstClass.aspx`, and change the property for the `EyeColor` to the following:

```
Public ReadOnly Property EyeColor As String
   Get
      Return _EyeColor
   End Get
End Property
```

2. Save the file and run it; you should see something similar to Figure 7-3:

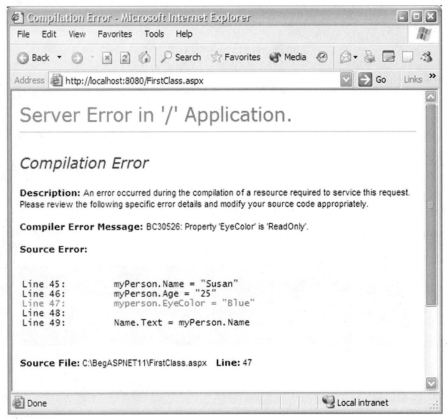

Figure 7-3

3. Oops, an error. If you think about it, this is fairly obvious – we've made the property read only, and thus can't set the value.

4.   Take out the line that sets the EyeColor and modify the class constructor so it looks like the following:

```
Public Sub New()
    _EyeColor = "Blue"
End Sub
```

5.   Save the file and run it. The error has disappeared and the eye color is displayed.

How It Works

The key to this is the ReadOnly keyword added to our property declaration:

```
Public ReadOnly Property EyeColor As String
    Get
        Return _EyeColor
    End Get
End Property
```

Adding ReadOnly means that we only need to have a Get section. Having a Set section with ReadOnly will cause an error. Thus, we can only read the value from the property, and not set it. To set the value we modify the constructor:

```
Public Sub New()
    _EyeColor = "Blue"
End Sub
```

Remember that the constructor is run when the class is instantiated. So when we do the following:

```
Dim myPerson As New Person()
```

The New keyword specifies that the object is being created, and therefore causes the constructor to be run.

Although we can set the eye color, it's not a very flexible object, as the color is hardcoded into the class. Thus, every person will have eyes of the same color (and think how dull that would be!). There needs to be some way to set the color as the object is created, and to do that you need to look at what happens when objects are initialized.

Initializing Objects

In the previous code, you've seen the following method of creating objects:

```
Dim myPerson As New Person()
```

You might also see this sort of coding:

```
Dim myPerson As Person()
myPerson = New Person()
```

This has the same effect as the single line version, but it is subtly different. The first line declares a variable of type Person, but doesn't instantiate it. It's only on the second line, when New is used, that the object instance is created. It's important to understand this so that you know when your object is actually created. For this example, an object that accesses a database and fetches a lot of data could take a long time to create, therefore knowing when it happens is important.

But none of this solves our problem of being able to set the eye color as the object is created. To do this you can create another constructor that allows you to specify the eye color.

Try It Out | Creating Another Constructor

1. Open the FirstClass.aspx file and add the following code, just below the existing constructor:

```
Public Sub New (EC As String)
    _EyeColor = EC
End Sub
```

2. Change the line that instantiates the class (the Dim myPerson As New Person() line) to:

```
Dim myPerson As New Person("Green")
```

3. Save the file and run it. Notice that the eye color is now displayed as Green.

How It Works

This technique works because .NET allows the same method to be declared more than once as long as the argument types are different (this is called the *signature*). In our case, we have the method declared twice – once with no arguments, and once with a single String argument. This is called *overloading*, and thus both of the following lines are valid:

```
Public Sub New ()
Public Sub New (EC As String)
```

What you can't have, however, is the following:

```
Public Sub New (NM As String)
```

The reason is that it has the same signature as the declaration that accepts the eye color as its argument. What you can do is this:

```
Public Sub New (NM As String, EC As String)
```

This has a different signature, and is therefore allowed.

> **Class constructors are always named New.**

Implementing Methods

Our class doesn't do much so we need to add some methods to round it out. You've already seen methods – the constructor is one. Adding a method is just the same, although unlike the constructor, you can pick the method name. A method is simply a `Public Function` or `Public Sub` within the class, and follows the same rules for those as discussed in *Chapter 6*, so we don't need to cover the basics again. However, it's worth looking at them within the context of a class, so let's give it a go.

Try It Out **Adding Methods to a Class**

1. Edit the `FirstClass.aspx` file, and remove the text and labels from the HTML `<form runat="server>` section. We are using a different form of displaying data in this example.

2. Add the following code to the `Person` class, just before the end of the class:

```
Public Function Walk() As String
   Return _Name & _
      ": you are now walking forwards"
End Function
```

3. Change the `Page_Load` event so that it looks like the following:

```
Sub Page_Load(Sender As Object, E As EventArgs)

   Dim Susan As New Person("Green")
   Susan.Name = "Susan"

   Response.Write(Susan.Walk())
   Response.Write("<br/>")

End Sub
```

4. Save the file and run it. You'll see a simple display that shows the name of the person and the direction they are travelling in, as shown in Figure 7-4:

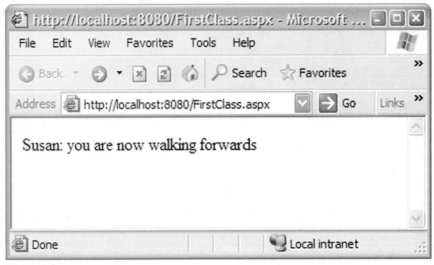

Figure 7-4

This is all very well, but what if you want to specify the direction of travel? You can use overloading for this (as you did with the constructor).

5. Switch back to your editor and add the following code, just underneath the previous `Walk()` method:

```
Public Function Walk(Direction As String) As String
   If Direction = "Back" Then
      Return _Name & _
         ": you are now walking backwards"
   Else
      Return _Name & _
         ": you are now walking forwards"
   End If
End Function
Public Function Walk(Direction As Integer) As String
   If Direction >0 Then
      Return _Name & _
         ": you are now walking backwards"
   Else
      Return _Name & _
         ": you are now walking forwards"
   End If
End Function
```

6. Change the `Page_Load` event so that it looks like the following:

```
Sub Page_Load(Sender As Object, E As EventArgs)

    Dim Susan As New Person("Green")
    Susan.Name = "Susan"
    Response.Write(Susan.Walk())
    Response.Write("<br/>")
    Dim Sam As New Person("Blue")
    Sam.Name = "Sam"
    Response.Write(Sam.Walk("Back"))
    Response.Write("<br/>")
    Response.Write(Sam.Walk(1))
    Response.Write("<br/>")

End Sub
```

7. Save the file and run it again, and you'll see the screen as in Figure 7-5:

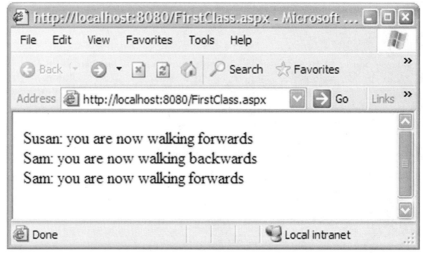

Figure 7-5

How It Works

The changes made to the `FirstClass.aspx` class were very simple – just the addition of an overloaded method. The first variant has no arguments, and just returns a string consisting of the name of the person and some text indicating the person is walking forwards:

```
Public Function Walk() As String
    Return _Name & _
        ": you are now walking forwards"
End Function
```

The second variant takes a string as its argument, and uses it to decide the direction of travel. If the string is `"Back"`, the person is deemed to be walking backwards, otherwise they are walking forwards:

```
Public Function Walk(Direction As String) As String
  If Direction = "Back" Then
    Return _Name & _
      ": you are now walking backwards"
  Else
    Return _Name & _
      ": you are now walking forwards"
  End If
End Function
```

The third variant also takes an argument to determine the direction of travel, but this time it's a number. A value greater than 0 is taken as travelling forwards, and a negative number as travelling backwards:

```
Public Function Walk(Direction As Integer) As String
  If Direction > 0 Then
    Return _Name & _
      ": you are now walking forwards"
  Else
    Return _Name & _
      ": you are now walking backwards"
  End If
End Function
```

This shows that overloading can be useful as you can provide several signatures for a method, allowing the method to be called in various ways. A good example is when looking up things in lists – you might have an overloaded method that allows lookup by name (a string) or by position in the list (a number).

Using these methods is simple, as seen in the Page_Load event:

```
Sub Page_Load(Sender As Object, E As EventArgs)

  Dim Susan As New Person("Green")
  Susan.Name = "Susan"

  Response.Write(Susan.Walk())
  Response.Write("<br/>")

  Dim Sam As New Person("Blue")
  Sam.Name = "Sam"
  Response.Write(Sam.Walk("Back"))
  Response.Write("<br/>")
  Response.Write(Sam.Walk(1))
  Response.Write("<br/>")
End Sub
```

Here we create two instances of the Person object – Susan and Sam. For the Susan instance, we use the first Walk() method without any arguments, and indicate that this instance is walking forwards. For the Sam instance, we use the other two Walk() methods (the string and the numeric ones).

This example uses Response.Write to output strings directly onto the page. Generally, you wouldn't use this method to interact with the page as you'd use server controls, but using Response.Write allows you to output any amount of text without worrying about creating controls.

Consolidating Overloaded Methods

Even though using overloaded methods can be beneficial, it may lead to the repeated use of code in the implementation. In our example, we have repeated code but also a potential problem – that is the use of the following (or similar) code in *all* methods:

```
Return _Name & _
    ": you are now walking forwards"
```

As developers, you'd want to minimize the amount of work to be done for the following reasons:

❑ It saves time – the quicker you can develop applications the better.

❑ If you want to change the functionality, you have to change it in all the methods.

❑ The more code there is, the greater are the chances of errors.

You could just create a fourth method, private and not accessible outside of the class, and then call this method from the three public methods. However, there is no need for this, since you can just call one overloaded method from another overloaded method. For example, the methods in the example could become:

```
Public Function Walk() As String
   Return Walk(1)
End Function

Public Function Walk(Direction As String) As String
   If Direction = "Back" Then
      Return Walk(-1)
   Else
      Return Walk(1)
   End If
End Function

Public Function Walk(Direction As Integer) As String
   If Direction > 0 Then
      Return _Name & _
        ": you are now walking forwards"
   Else
      Return _Name & _
        ": you are now walking backwards"
   End If
End Function
```

The actual functionality is contained within just one method – the one that takes an `Integer` as its argument – this is called by other methods. The code is all in one place, and thus can easily be tested or changed if required.

Advanced Classes

So far, this chapter has dealt with the basics of classes, which probably covers most of what you'll need and use. However, it would be worth mentioning a few infrequently used advanced topics here; they can be useful, and you may well see them used elsewhere.

Shared or Static Properties and Methods

The chapter began with a discussion on classes and instances, where you create an instance of a class before using it. However, the creation of an instance isn't actually necessary, as you can create properties and methods that can be used without a class instance. These are called *static* properties or methods, and are implemented using the `Shared` keyword in Visual Basic.NET. For example, consider a `Tools` class that contains some central methods, such as error logging. Using the techniques shown earlier, it could be defined as:

```
Public Class Tools
  Public Sub Log(error As String)
    ' error logging code goes here
  End Sub
End Class
```

To use this code, we'd have something as follows:

```
Dim t As New Tools()
t.Log("Something went wrong")
```

The use of a class here is just for abstraction and encapsulation purposes – providing a simple way to log errors, and hiding how it's actually done (writing to a file or database, for example). Since this is a single operation with no other properties or methods involved, the `Log()` method can be made static:

```
Public Class Tools
  Public Shared Sub Log(error As String)
    ' error logging code goes here
  End Sub
End Class
```

To use this static method, the object instance is no longer required, and the `Log()` method can be called directly:

```
Tools.Log("Something went wrong")
```

This technique should be restricted to method and properties that require no other references – properties that haven't yet been initialized. It is ideal for helper type methods, such as the `Log()` method shown above, where the class simply provides a wrapper for the method.

Inheritance

Inheritance was mentioned at the beginning of the chapter when describing why objects are used, and how you can create subclasses that inherit properties from the parent. This is best described with an example.

Consider an `Animal` class, which defines the `Legs` and `BodyHair` properties, and a `Walk()` method. Suppose you create two instances of this class as follows:

Property / Method	Instance 1	Instance 2
Legs	4	2
BodyHair	Yes	No
Walk	Yes	Yes

You can make an intelligent guess as to what these two instances could be. Something with lots of body hair and four legs could be a dog, and something without body hair and two legs is probably human. There could be other shared characteristics, but more importantly, there could be characteristics that aren't shared, and need to be different for each instance. Thus you need to create two new classes (`Dog` and `Person`) that inherit from `Animal`, but that also define distinct characteristics. For example:

Dog	Person
Bark	Talk
Bite	
Wag	

As you can see, dogs `Bark`, `Bite`, and `Wag` their tails, unlike people, who can `Talk`. However, since both classes inherit from `Animal`, they also both have the properties of the `Animal` class; `Legs`, `BodyHair`, and `Walk()`. Because `Dog` and `Person` inherit from `Animal`, they don't have to implement the methods and properties of `Animal`.

This has several benefits:

❑ You can create a hierarchy of objects, putting the functionality where it is most appropriate. For example, all the ASP.NET server controls inherit from a control called `WebControl`. This isn't used directly, and is simply a way to define all of the common functionality for the server controls. For example, it has a `BackColor` property to set the background color of a control, and `Height` and `Width` properties to set the height and width of the control. It doesn't however, have a `Text` property because not all server controls require text (the `Label` and the `TextBox` controls do, but the `Image` and the `Panel` controls don't).

❑ Functionality only needs to be implemented once, in the parent (or *base* class, as it is often called). This not only reduces development time, but also reduces the testing time and the possibility of errors.

❑ You can enforce functionality on subclasses by providing base functionality. For example, consider using a set of classes to provide access to databases. You can code all of the base functionality such as security into the base class, and enforce this so that classes inheriting from it have to use that base functionality. In the database example, this would ensure that all the data is accessed in a secure manner.

Although the remainder of the book doesn't make extensive use of inheritance, it is an invaluable technique – give it a go and see how easy it is.

Try It Out Inheritance

1. Create a new ASP.NET page called `Inheriting.aspx`.

2. Add the following class within the server code block just after the `<script runat="server">` line:

```
Public Class Animal
   Private _Legs As Integer
   Private _BodyHair As String

   Public Property Legs As Integer
     Get
        Return _Legs
     End Get
     Set (ByVal Value As Integer)
       _Legs = Value
     End Set
   End Property

   Public Property BodyHair As String
     Get
        Return _BodyHair
     End Get
     Set (ByVal Value As String)
       _BodyHair = value
     End Set
   End Property

   Public Function Walk() As String
     Return "I'm walking on " & _
       _Legs & _
       " legs"
   End Function
End Class
```

3. Add the `Dog` class underneath the `Animal` class:

```
Public Class Dog
   Inherits Animal
   Public Sub New()
```

```
      Legs = 4
   End Sub

   Public Function Bark() As String
      Return "Woof"
   End Function

   Public Function Bite() As String
      Return "Chomp Chomp"
   End Function

   Public Function Wag() As String
      Return "Wag Wag"
   End Function
End Class
```

4. Now add the class for the person, underneath the `Dog` class:

```
Public Class Person
   Inherits Animal

   Public Sub New()
      Legs = 2
   End Sub

   Public Function Talk() As String
      Return "yadda yadda yadda"
   End Function
End Class
```

5. Now add the `Page_Load` event, which is the code that will use our classes:

```
Sub Page_Load(Sender As Object, E As EventArgs)
   Dim Rover As New Dog()
   Response.Write(Rover.Walk())
   Response.Write("<br />")
   Response.Write(Rover.Bark())
   Response.Write("<br />")

   Dim Susan As New Person()
   Response.Write(Susan.Walk())
End Sub
```

6. Save the file and run it. You'll see the screen as depicted in Figure 7-6:

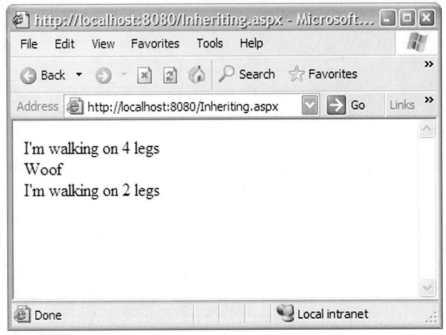

Figure 7-6

Here you see something walking on four legs and that woofs, and then something walking on two legs – someone taking his/her dog for a walk.

How It Works

Let's start by looking at the base class, the one for the animal. It has a couple of properties and one method (Walk()):

```
Public Class Animal
    Private _Legs As Integer
    Private _BodyHair As String

    Public Property Legs As Integer
      Get
        Return _Legs
      End Get
      Set (ByVal Value As Integer)
        _Legs = Value
      End Set
    End Property

    Public Property BodyHair As String
      Get
        Return _BodyHair
      End Get
      Set (ByVal Value As String)
```

```
        _BodyHair = value
      End Set
   End Property

   Public Function Walk() As String
      Return "I'm walking on " & _
         _Legs & _
         " legs"
   End Function
End Class
```

Next comes the class declaration for the Dog class:

```
Public Class Dog
   Inherits Animal
```

Notice the extra keywords added here. The second line states that we are inheriting from the Animal class, automatically giving us the properties and methods defined in that class. This is obvious when we look at the constructor:

```
Public Sub New()
   Legs = 4
End Sub
```

Notice that this class uses the Legs property without declaring it. That's because it's part of the base class. You can't use the Legs *variable* because that's private to the Animal class, but you can use the Legs *property*.

The methods are simple, each returning a string. These have been added to show that you can have methods additional to those provided by the base class:

```
Public Function Bark() As String
   Return "Woof"
End Function

Public Function Bite() As String
   Return "Chomp Chomp"
End Function

Public Function Wag() As String
   Return "Wag Wag"
End Function
End Class
```

We then defined the Person class, again inheriting from the Animal base class, with the Legs property set to 2:

```
Public Class Person
   Inherits Animal

   Public Sub New()
      Legs = 2
   End Sub
   Public Function Talk() As String
```

```
            Return "yadda yadda yadda"
        End Function
    End Class
```

Finally, the `Page_Load` event where the classes are used:

```
    Sub Page_Load(Sender As Object, E As EventArgs)
```

Within this event, we first create an instance of the `Dog` class, and then call the `Walk()` and `Bark()` methods:

```
    Dim Rover As New Dog()
    Response.Write(Rover.Walk())
    Response.Write("<br />")
    Response.Write(Rover.Bark())
    Response.Write("<br />")
```

Then we create an instance of the `Person` class and call the `Walk()` method:

```
    Dim Susan As New Person()
    Response.Write(Susan.Walk())
    End Sub
```

The `Walk()` method is called on both the `Dog` and the `Person` classes, even though it's not implemented by them. It's the base class that does the implementation, but because the `Dog` and the `Person`, both inherit from the base class they also get the `Walk` method. As you can see, the same functionality is available in multiple classes despite being implemented only once.

> **A class can inherit only from *one* other class.**

Interfaces

The term *interface* is used to describe the public view of a class – the public methods and properties. An interface is also a special type of class, but one that doesn't implement any methods or properties – it defines what a class *does*, rather than what a class *is*. Why is this useful? Well, when developing a large application, you may have a set of classes that all need to perform some similar action. The interface allows you to specify *what* that similar action should be, but *not how* it is implemented. Compare that with inheritance, where the implementation is at the base-class-level.

Some of the data-handling classes that .NET provide are good examples of this. Data can be stored in many different types of database, and there are special classes for handling data. There are two main sets of classes – one for Microsoft SQL Server, and one for other databases. Despite the fact that these databases might require special handling, the data-handling classes need to provide a common implementation. Why? This is to allow similar code to be used irrespective of the database. This reduces not only the techniques you need to learn, but also the complexity of code you need to write. Let's look at a simple example.

Try It Out **Creating an Interface**

1. Create a new ASP.NET page called `Interfaces.aspx`.

2. Add the following code to define the interface:

```
Public Interface IAnimal
    Property Legs() As Integer
    Function Walk() As String
End Interface
```

3. Now add the following code to define the `Person` class:

```
Public Class Person
    Implements IAnimal

    Private _Legs As Integer

    Public Sub New()
        _Legs = 2
    End Sub

    Public Property Legs As Integer Implements IAnimal.Legs
        Get
            Return _Legs
        End Get
        Set (ByVal Value As Integer)
            _Legs = Value
        End Set
    End Property

    Public Function Walk() As String Implements IAnimal.Walk
        Return "I'm walking on " & _
            _Legs & _
            " legs"
    End Function
End Class
```

4. Add the code for the `Dog` class:

```
Public Class Dog
    Implements IAnimal

    Public Property Legs As Integer Implements IAnimal.Legs
        Get
            Return 4
        End Get
        Set (ByVal Value As Integer)
        End Set
    End Property

    Public Function Walk() As String Implements IAnimal.Walk
        Return "I want to run"
    End Function
End Class
```

5. And finally, the code for using these classes:

```
Sub Page_Load(Sender As Object, E As EventArgs)

    Dim Rover As New Dog()
    Response.Write(Rover.Walk())
    Response.Write("<br />")


    Dim Susan As New Person()
    Response.Write(Susan.Walk())

End Sub
```

6. Save the file and run it – you'll see the output shown in Figure 7-7:

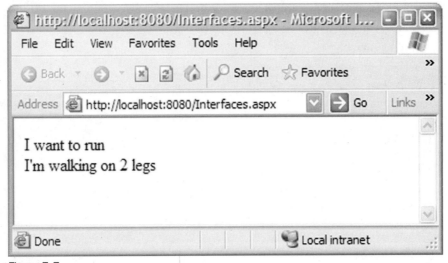

Figure 7-7

How It Works

The code is simple even if the concept seems a little strange. Let's start by looking at the `Interface`:

```
Public Interface IAnimal

    Property Legs() As Integer
    Function Walk() As String

End Interface
```

It's similar to the way a class is defined, except we use the `Interface` keyword before the interface name, which by convention, starts with an uppercase `I`. The properties and methods are defined within the interface. Notice that there is no implementation – all we are doing is defining what the interface does, *not* how it does it (that's for the class to decide).

Once the interface is defined, you can tell a class to implement it. This is done in a manner similar to inheritance, except for the use of the `Implements` keyword:

```
Public Class Person
    Implements IAnimal
```

This tells .NET we have a `Person` class, and that among its own properties and methods, it must also have the properties and methods defined by the `IAnimal` interface. So first we define the private variable to store the number of legs, and then the constructor to set that as follows:

```
Private _Legs As Integer

Public Sub New()
    _Legs = 2
End Sub
```

Now consider properties defined in the interface. The definition is the same as for normal properties except that the interface and property being implemented are specified:

```
Public Property Legs As Integer Implements IAnimal.Legs

    Get
        Return _Legs
    End Get

    Set (ByVal Value As Integer)
        _Legs = Value
    End Set

End Property
```

This code specifies that a property called `Legs` exists, and that it is defined by the interface. The same technique applies to the method:

```
Public Function Walk() As String Implements IAnimal.Walk
    Return "I'm walking on " & _
        _Legs & _
        " legs"
    End Function
End Class
```

Now let's look at the `Dog` class, which also implements our `IAnimal` interface:

```
Public Class Dog
    Implements IAnimal
```

The `Legs` property is implemented next. Note that the implementation is completely different from that of the `Person` class. There is no private variable to store the number of legs, setting the property doesn't do anything, and reading the value always returns 4:

```
Public Property Legs As Integer Implements IAnimal.Legs

    Get
        Return 4
    End Get

    Set (ByVal Value As Integer)
    End Set

End Property
```

The same applies to the `Walk()` method, which has an implementation different from that of the `Person` class:

```
Public Function Walk() As String Implements IAnimal.Walk
    Return "I want to run"
End Function
End Class
```

Finally, we have the code that uses the classes. Notice that we can still call the `Walk()` method on both classes in exactly the same manner as in previous examples:

```
Sub Page_Load(Sender As Object, E As EventArgs)

    Dim Rover As New Dog()
    Response.Write(Rover.Walk())
    Response.Write("<br />")


    Dim Susan As New Person()
    Response.Write(Susan.Walk())

End Sub
```

The key to this is remembering that the interface defines what a class can do, not how it does it. That's clearly seen by the implementation of the `Person` and `Dog` classes, where the `Legs` property and `Walk` method are implemented differently. The external view of these classes is the same.

Interfaces as Types

So, why are interfaces so useful? Suppose you are writing some generic routines to handle class instances; for example, a function that accepts an object as an argument, does some processing, and then calls a method on that object. Using your `Dog` class as an example, you could have something like the following:

```
Dim Rover As New Dog()
GoForAWalk(Rover)
Sub GoForAWalk(inst As Dog)
```

```
    ' do some processing
    ...
    ' go for a walk
    inst.Walk()
End Sub
```

Here, we created an instance of Dog, and passed that into the GoForAWalk() routine, which simply calls the Walk() method on the instance of the Dog class passed into GoForAWalk() as the inst argument. What happens if you now want to have the same sort of thing for a Person object? You could expand your code like the following:

```
Sub GoForAWalk(inst As Dog)
    ' do some processing
    ...
    ' go for a walk
    inst.Walk()
End Sub
Sub GoForAWalk(inst As Person)
    ' do some processing
    ...
    ' go for a walk
    inst.Walk()
End Sub
```

The difference in the second routine is the definition of the argument. All of the code is repeated.

A far better solution is to realize that both Dog and Person implement IAnimal, and we can use the interface name as our argument type:

```
Sub GoForAWalk(inst As IAnimal)
    ' do some processing
    ...
    ' go for a walk
    inst.Walk()
End Sub
```

We now have only a single routine that applies to both Dog and Person objects. In fact it applies to all objects that implement IAnimal, so if another class is created (Cat for instance), the GoForAWalk() routine doesn't need to be changed.

The key points are that interfaces:

❑ Provide an interface that is enforced upon classes that implement the interface. This means that all classes implementing the interface are guaranteed to have the minimum set of properties and methods defined in the interface.

❑ Don't enforce the implementation, as that is left to the individual class.

❑ Allow generic routines, because interfaces are data types. This means that instead of using the actual class as the data type, we can use the interface name, thus allowing the routine to work with any object that implements the interface.

The last point will be discussed in the next couple of chapters, where the topic of data access is addressed.

Implementing Interface Methods and Properties

One important point to remember is that when implementing an interface in a class, you *must* implement all methods and properties of that interface. For example, you cannot implement just the `Walk` method and not the `Legs` property. Everything defined in the interface has to be implemented in the class. If you don't, you'll see a compilation error as shown in Figure 7-8:

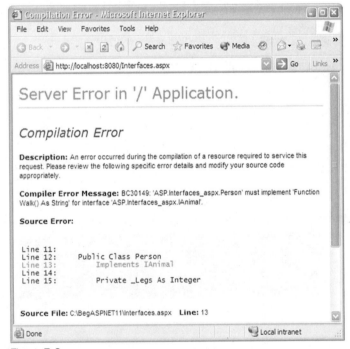

Figure 7-8

In this example, the `Implements IAnimal.Walk` was left off the `Walk()` method for the `Person` class.

.NET Objects

So far, this chapter has looked at creating classes and objects; early on, we talked about everything in .NET being an object. This is a core point to remember because it will aid you in understanding much of .NET. You'll know you are working with objects, so the use of properties and methods is easy to understand because it's exactly the same as classes you create yourself. Let's look at a couple of topics to understand how objects are organized and used within .NET.

Namespaces

The first stop in understanding objects in .NET is to understand namespaces. We've already explained that these provide a logical separation for classes, and when you look at the number of classes that come as part of .NET, you'll see why this is the case – there are more than 3000 classes. Having that number of classes without any form of structure would be really difficult to manage, especially when searching through documentation.

There are a couple of places where you can look at the available namespaces. The first is the documentation that comes with .NET, as shown in Figure 7-9:

Figure 7-9

Notice the number of namespaces and how they are broken down. Knowing which classes are in which namespace is essential not only to help look up documentation, but also to know which namespace to import into an ASP.NET page.

The Class Browser

Another useful tool is the class browser application, which is available if you have installed and configured the .NET Framework SDK samples. To access this, navigate to http://localhost/quickstart/aspplus and scroll to the bottom where you'll see a link to Sample Applications and A Class Browser Application. Running this sample shows Figure 7-10:

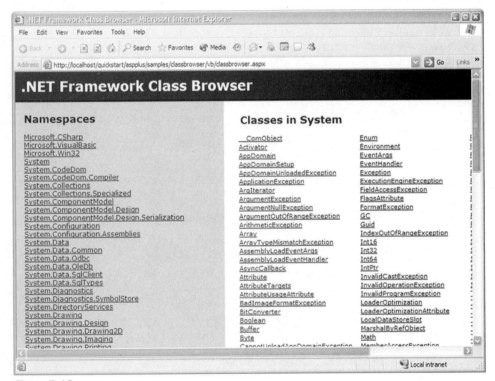

Figure 7-10

On the left you see the namespace, and selecting one of these displays the classes in the namespace on the right of the screen. Selecting an individual class will show its members. See for example, the `Button` control in the `System.Web.UI.WebControls` namespace as shown in Figure 7-11:

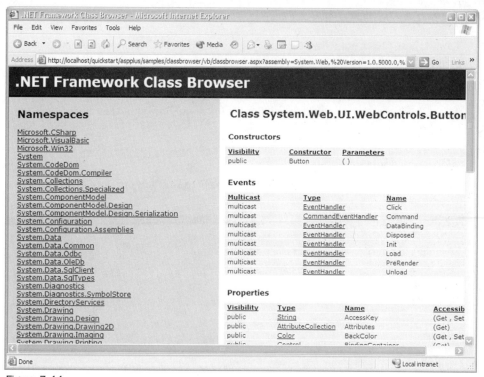

Figure 7-11

This shows all members for a class – the constructors, properties, methods, and the events. It also shows the object hierarchy (the inheritance used) and the implementation (classes implemented).

Summary

This chapter covered the fundamentals and some complex topics surrounding classes. It would have been easy to go deeper into objects and some more complex topics, but these are really outside the scope of the book. We looked at what objects are, and how object oriented programming is beneficial. Features such as inheritance and abstraction provide great benefits to programmers, such as reducing development time, improving stability of applications, and providing greater structure.

These techniques have been used for creating some sample classes to show how they work, and seeing how properties and methods can be easily added to a class. This chapter also discussed advanced topics such as overloading (that is, the same method can be implemented more than once) and interface (that is, where you define the structure of a class but not the implementation).

The chapter ended with a quick look at how classes are organized in .NET, and how you can find out what is in a namespace and a class. Now it's time to turn attention to data; the next chapter will look at how data can be retrieved from a database and displayed in your pages.

Exercises

1. Our examples have modelled some simple characteristics of real-world objects, such as animals. Think about other real-world objects that when turned into classes would be useful in programming.

2. In the `Animal` class, where the `Walk()` method accepts an argument of type `Integer`, expand it to use this Integer as the speed of walking. Think about how you'd store that speed and what you'd do with it.

3. Taking the results of *Exercise 2*, think about how you'd add validation to the speed, to ensure it didn't exceed some set limits.

4. Describe the main differences between class inheritance and interface. When would you use one over the other?

5. Create a class called `PieceOfString` with a single read/write property (of type `Integer`) called `Length`. Create an instance of the class and set the `Length` to `16`. Now you can answer that age old question "How long is a piece of string?"

Reading from Databases

So far in this book you've learnt a lot about programming, and seen those techniques in use in a variety of Web pages. Now it's time to turn our attention to one of the most important topics of building Web sites – data. Whatever the type of site you aim to build, data plays an important part. From a personal site (perhaps a vacation diary or a photo album), to a corporate e-commerce site, *data is key*.

There are many ways in which data can be stored, but most sites will probably use a *database*. So in this chapter we're going to look at data stored in databases, and show how easily it can be used on Web pages. For this we are going to use ADO.NET, which is the data access technology that comes as part of the .NET Framework.

If the thought of databases sounds complex and scary, don't worry. We're going to show you just how easy this can be. In particular, we'll be looking at:

- ❑ Basics of databases and how they work
- ❑ Creating simple data pages using Web Matrix
- ❑ Different ADO.NET classes used for fetching data
- ❑ Basics of ADO.NET and how it fetches data
- ❑ Using Web Matrix to simplify developing data access pages

Before we can head into these topics though, we need a little theory.

Understanding Databases

Understanding some basics about databases is crucial to using data in your pages. You don't need to be a database expert, but there are certain things you will need to know in order to work with data in .NET. For a start, you need to understand how data is stored. All types of data on a computer are stored in files of some sort. Text files, for example, are simple files and just contain the plain text. Spreadsheets, on the other hand, are complex files containing not only the entered text and numbers, but also details about the data, such as what the columns contain, how they are formatted, and so on.

Databases also fall into the category of complex files. When using Microsoft Access, you have an MDB file – this is a database file, but from the file itself you can't tell anything about the data inside. You need some way to get to the data, either using something such as Microsoft Access itself, or as we are going to do, using the .NET data classes.

Before you can access the data, you need to know how it is stored internally.

Tables

Within a database, data is stored in *tables* – these are the key to all databases. A table is like a spreadsheet, with *rows* and *columns*. You generally have multiple tables for multiple things – each distinct type of data is stored separately, and tables are often linked together.

Let's look at an example to make it easier to visualize. Consider an ordering system, for example, where you store details of customers and the goods they've ordered. The following table shows rows of customer orders, with columns (or *fields* as they are sometimes called in database terms) for each piece of order information:

Customer	Address	Order Date	Order Item	Quantity	Item Cost
John	15 High Street Brumingham England	01/07/2003	Widget	10	3.50
John	15 High Street Brumingham England	01/07/2003	Doodad	5	2.95
John	15 High Street Brumingham England	01/08/2003	Thingy	1	15.98
Chris	25 Easterly Way Cradiff Wales	01/08/2003	Widget	1	3.50
Dave	2 Middle Lane Oxborough England	01/09/2003	Doodad	2	2.95
Dave	3 Middle Lane Oxborough England	01/09/2003	Thingamajig	1	8.50

This is the sort of thing you'd see in a spreadsheet, but there are a couple of big problems with this. For a start, we have repeated information. John, for example, has his address shown thrice. What happens if he moves house? You'd have to change the address everywhere it occurs. Dave has two addresses, but notice they are slightly different. Which one is correct? Are neither correct?

To get around these problems we use a process called *Normalization*.

Normalization

Normalization is the process of separating repeated information into separate tables. There are whole books dedicated to database design, but we only need to look at the simplest case.

> *A good beginner book on database design is Database Design for Mere Mortals: A Hands On Guide to Relational Database Design, 2nd Edition (ISBN: 0-201-75284-0).*

What we need to do is split the previous table into three tables, one for each unique piece of information – Customers, Orders, and OrderDetails. To link the three new tables together, we create ID columns that uniquely identify each row. For example, we could create a column called CustomerID in the Customers table. To link the Customers table to the Orders table we also add this CustomerID to the Orders table. Let's take a look at our tables now.

The Customers table is as follows:

CustomerID	Customer	Address
1	John	15 High Street, Brumingham, England
2	Chris	25 Easterly Way, Cradiff, Wales
3	Dave	2 Middle Lane, Oxborough, England

The Orders table is as follows:

OrderID	CustomerID	OrderDate
1	1	01/07/2003
2	1	01/08/2003
3	2	01/08/2003
4	3	01/09/2003

The `OrderDetails` table is as follows

OrderDetailsID	OrderID	Order Item	Quantity	Item Cost
1	1	Widget	10	3.50
2	1	Doodad	5	2.95
3	2	Thingy	1	15.98
4	3	Widget	1	3.50
5	4	Doodad	2	2.95
6	4	Thingamajig	1	8.50

We now have three tables that can be linked together by their ID fields as shown in Figure 8-1:

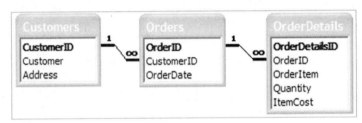

Figure 8-1

We now have links between the tables. The `CustomerID` field in the `Orders` table is used to identify which customer the order is for. Similarly, the `OrderID` field in the `OrderDetails` table identifies which order a particular order line belongs to.

The unique key in a table is defined as its *Primary Key* – it's what uniquely defines a row. When used in another table it is called the *Foreign Key*, so called because it's a key, but one to a foreign table. The foreign key is simply a column that is the primary key in another table. Because the values of the primary key and the foreign key will be the same, we can use them to link the tables together. This linking of the tables is done in *Structured Query Language (SQL)*, usually as a query or a stored procedure.

SQL and Stored Procedures

Queries are the way in which we deal with data in a database, either to extract data or to manipulate it. We can use an SQL statement or a stored procedure, which is an SQL statement wrapped to provide a simple name. It's worth to note that a stored procedure is actually more than just wrapping an SQL statement in a name, but that's a good enough description for what we need.

If you remember, in *Chapter 5* when we looked at functions, we had a function name encapsulating some code statements. Think of a stored procedure in a similar way – it wraps a set of SQL statements, allowing us to use the name of the stored procedure to run those SQL statements. We're not going to focus much on this topic as it's outside the scope of this book.

To learn more about SQL, read *SQL for Dummies (ISBN 0-7645-4075-0) by John Wiley & Sons*.

Here are a few reasons why you should always use stored procedures instead of direct SQL:

- ❑ **Security**: Using the .NET data classes with stored procedures protects you against certain forms of hacking.

- ❑ **Speed**: Stored procedures are optimised the first time they are called, and then the optimised code is used in subsequent calls.

- ❑ **Separation**: It keeps the SQL separate from your code.

During the rest of this book we'll actually be using a mixture of SQL and stored procedures, for the simple reason that sometimes it's easier to use SQL in the context of an example. Remember, our main focus is ASP.NET. We'll be using Microsoft Access for the samples, and although Access doesn't support stored procedures, its use of stored queries is equivalent.

Let's get on with some examples.

The Web Matrix Data Explorer

You've already seen how powerful Web Matrix is for creating Web pages, and this power extends to working with data. Where you've used the Workspace Explorer in the top right hand corner of Web Matrix to work with files, you can use the Data Explorer to work with data. This provides ways of creating databases, connecting to existing ones, and working with tables and queries. Let's give this a go.

Try It Out **Connecting to a Database**

1. Select the Data Explorer tab, and click the Add Database Connection button – the one that's second in from the right, and will be the only one highlighted, as shown in Figure 8-2, if you haven't already got a database connection open:

Figure 8-2

2. Select Access Database from the window that appears and press OK.

3. Enter the following into the Data File text area (we'll use a central location for the database, so that we can reuse it later in the book):

```
C:\BegASPNET11\data\Northwind.mdb
```

4. Press OK to connect to the database. This is the Northwind database, one of the sample databases that ships with Microsoft Access.

5. Figure 8-3 shows the tables contained in this database:

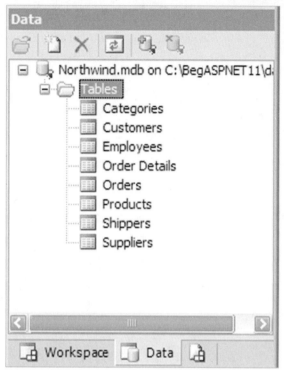

Figure 8-3

You can double-click on these to open the table, and see and change the data. One thing you might notice is that you don't see any queries – that's because Web Matrix doesn't support queries in Access. When connecting to SQL Server, you'll see the stored procedures – you can even create and edit them – but for Access, you are limited to tables only.

How It Works

There's nothing really to explain about how it works. What we are doing is simply creating a connection to a database that Web Matrix can use. This isn't required for ASP.NET to fetch data from databases, but Web Matrix has some great ways to generate code for you, so you don't have to do as much coding.

Creating Data Pages

Pages that display data can be created in a number of ways, and let's first look at the three ways that Web Matrix uses to save you coding. This is the quickest way to get data into your pages and saves a great deal of time. However, what it might not do is give you the knowledge to access databases without using Web Matrix. After we've seen the easy ways, we'll look at the .NET classes that deal with data. This way you'll have techniques to work with and without Web Matrix.

Displaying Data using the Data Explorer

You've already seen how easy connecting to a database is using the Data Explorer. Creating pages directly from this explorer is even easier – all you have to do is drag the table name and drop it onto a page. This will automatically create a connection on the page and a fully functional data grid. Let's give this a go.

Try It Out   Creating a Grid

1.   Create a new ASP.NET page called Grid1.aspx.

2.   From the Data Explorer, drag the Suppliers table onto your empty page as shown in Figure 8-4:

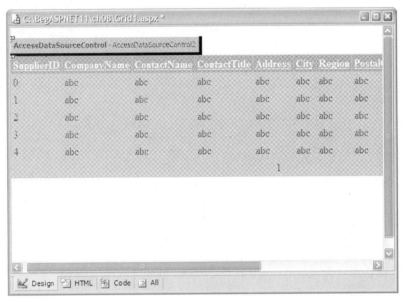

Figure 8-4

3.   Save the page and run it to see Figure 8-5:

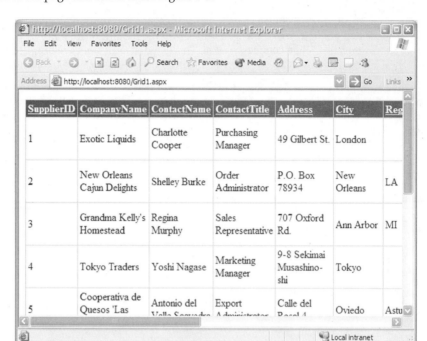

Figure 8-5

Amazing! A sortable grid full of data and you didn't have to write even a single line of code!

How It Works

Its workings rely on two controls: the `AccessDataSourceControl`, which provides the connection to the database, and an `MxDataGrid`, which is a Web Matrix control (also covered in *Chapter 10*) that displays the data. Looking at the HTML view for these controls gives you a good idea of what they do.

Let's start with the `AccessDataSourceControl`:

```
<wmx:AccessDataSourceControl id="AccessDataSourceControl2"
  runat="server" SelectCommand="SELECT * FROM [Suppliers]"
  ConnectionString="Provider=Microsoft.Jet.OLEDB.4.0; Ole DB Services=-4; Data
Source=C:\BegASPNET11\data\Northwind.mdb"></wmx:AccessDataSourceControl>
```

The first thing to notice is the way the control is declared. You're used to seeing `asp:` at the beginning of controls, but not `wmx:`. This prefix is the namespace – remember in the previous chapter where we said that namespaces provide a separation between classes. In this case, these controls are part of Web Matrix, and have thus been given a different namespace from the standard server controls.

Apart from the `id` and `runat`, there are two other attributes that provide the details regarding which database to connect to and what data to fetch:

❑ The `SelectCommand` defines the SQL that will return the required data – in this case, it's all rows and columns from the `Suppliers` table. This is the default since we dragged this table, but we can customize the `SelectCommand` to return only selected rows or columns.

❑ The `ConnectionString` defines the OLEDB connection string. You only need to worry about the bit with the path of the database file – the `Data Source` bit (if you move the file, you'll need to change this). The other parts of the `ConnectionString` just define the type of database and some database specific features. You don't need to know about these specifically (they are fully documented in the .NET help files); just copy them if you ever need to use them again.

At this stage you have enough details to connect to a database and fetch data, but don't have any way to *display* it. For that we are going to use the `MxDataGrid`:

```
<wmx:MxDataGrid id="MxDataGrid2" runat="server"
  DataSourceControlID="AccessDataSourceControl2" BorderColor="#CCCCCC"
  AllowSorting="True" DataMember="Suppliers" AllowPaging="True"
  BackColor="White" CellPadding="3" DataKeyField="SupplierID"
  BorderWidth="1px" BorderStyle="None">
    <PagerStyle horizontalalign="Center" forecolor="#000066"
      backcolor="White" mode="NumericPages"></PagerStyle>
    <FooterStyle forecolor="#000066" backcolor="White"></FooterStyle>
    <SelectedItemStyle font-bold="True" forecolor="White"
      backcolor="#669999"></SelectedItemStyle>
    <ItemStyle forecolor="#000066"></ItemStyle>
    <HeaderStyle font-bold="True" forecolor="White"
      backcolor="#006699"></HeaderStyle>
</wmx:MxDataGrid>
```

This seems complex but is actually very simple. Let's look at all of the attributes:

Attribute	Description
DataSourceControlID	This contains the ID of the data source control from which data will be fetched. In this case, it's the ID of the `AccessDataSourceControl` we described earlier.
BorderColor	This is the color of the grid border.
AllowSorting	Indicates whether or not the grid will support sorting.
DataMember	This contains the database table name.
AllowPaging	Indicates whether or not the grid supports paging. The default number of rows in a page is 10, and this can be changed with the `PageSize` attribute.
BackColor	This is the background color for the grid.
CellPadding	This defines the amount of padding between grid cells. A higher number means the cells will be spaced further apart.

Attribute	Description
DataKeyField	This is the primary key of the table.
BorderWidth	This is how wide the border of the grid is. Here it is 1 pixel (px stands for pixel), which is a thin border.
BorderStyle	This is the style of the border.

As part of the grid we also have some style elements:

❑ PagerStyle, which defines the style of the pager section. In our grid this is the last row, showing the page numbers, but it appears before the footer if a footer row is being shown.

❑ FooterStyle, which defines the style of the footer row. In our grid we aren't showing a footer, but the style is set so that the footer will look correct if it is shown.

❑ SelectedItemStyle, which defines the style of items when they are selected. Our grid isn't selectable by default, but like the FooterStyle the default style is set in case item selection is added.

❑ ItemStyle, which defines the style for each row of data in the grid

❑ HeaderStyle, which defines the style for the header row, where the column names are shown.

That's all there is to this example – two controls that are linked together. When the page is loaded, the AccessDataSourceControl connects to the database and runs the command. The MxDataGrid then fetches the data stored by the data source control and constructs a grid around it. In fact, the grid is the most complex piece of code here because of all the properties being set - purely to change the look. At its simplest you could have the following:

```
<wmx:MxDataGrid id="MxDataGrid2" runat="server"
  DataSourceControlID="AccessDataSourceControl2">
</wmx:MxDataGrid>
```

This contains just the attributes required to display data.

Displaying Data Using Web Matrix Template Pages

You've probably noticed a number of *template pages* when you add a new page in Web Matrix – some of those are for data reports. These provide a simple way to get more functionality into grids than the example earlier used.

The supplied template pages are as follows:

❑ Simple Data Report gives a simple grid without paging or sorting.

❑ Filtered Data Report gives a grid with a filter option, so you can select the rows displayed.

❑ Data Report with Paging gives a grid with paging enabled.

❑ Data Report with Paging and Sorting gives a grid with paging and column sorting enabled.

❑ Master – Detail Grids gives two grids, representing a master table and a child table.

❑ Editable Grid gives a grid allowing updates to the data.

❑ Simple Stored Procedure gives a grid that uses a stored procedure for its data source.

All of these supplied templates connect to a SQL Server database, and need modification if they are to be used with a different database. However, they provide a quick way to get pages constructed allowing you to make a few simple changes to get what you need, rather than coding from scratch.

Let's take a look at one of these, the report with paging and sorting.

Try It Out Creating a Data Page

1. Create a new page using the Data Pages templates. Pick the Data Report with Paging and Sorting, and call it SortPage.aspx.

2. In the design window, select the All tab and change this line:

```
<%@ import Namespace="System.Data.SqlClient" %>
```

to

```
<%@ import Namespace="System.Data.OleDb" %>
```

3. In the design window select the Code tab, find the BindGrid() subroutine, and change the code so it looks like the following:

```
Sub BindGrid()

    Dim ConnectionString As String = "Provider=Microsoft.Jet.OLEDB.4.0; " & _
                        "Data Source=C:\BegASPNet11\data\Northwind.mdb"
    Dim CommandText As String

    If SortField = String.Empty Then
        CommandText = "select * from suppliers order by CompanyName"
    Else
        CommandText = "select * from suppliers order by " & SortField
    End If

    Dim myConnection As New OleDbConnection(ConnectionString)
    Dim myCommand As New OleDbDataAdapter(CommandText, myConnection)

    Dim ds As New DataSet()
    myCommand.Fill(ds)

    DataGrid1.DataSource = ds
    DataGrid1.DataBind()

End Sub
```

Use a different path if you've installed the samples in a directory other than C:\BegASPNET11.

4. Save the file and run it; you'll see something like Figure 8-6:

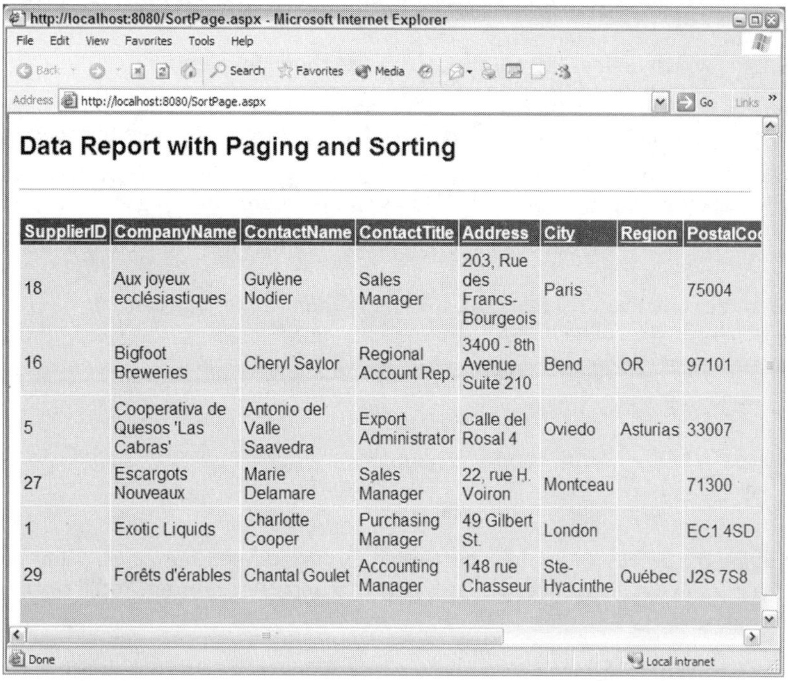

Figure 8-6

This isn't much different from the drag and drop approach we used in the first example, but it uses the .NET data classes and a `DataGrid` control, rather than the Web Matrix controls (`AccessDataSourceControl` and `MxDataGrid`). It means this technique will work even if Web Matrix isn't installed on the server running the page. Let's see how it works.

How It Works

The first thing to look at is the namespace change:

```
<%@ import Namespace="System.Data.OleDb" %>
```

By default the data pages are configured to use SQL Server and therefore use the `SqlClient` namespace. Since we are using Access, we have to use the `OleDb` namespace. Now let's look at the declaration of the grid itself. We won't show all of the properties as some are purely to do with the visual style. Instead, we'll concentrate on those that are related to the code we'll see:

```
<asp:datagrid id="DataGrid1" runat="server"
    AllowPaging="true" PageSize="6" OnPageIndexChanged="DataGrid_Page"
    AllowSorting="true" OnSortCommand="DataGrid_Sort">
```

Here we have the following properties defined:

❑   `AllowPaging`, which is `true`, allowing the grid to page the results. This works in a way similar to the `MxDataGrid` where the page numbers are shown at the bottom of the grid.

❑   `PageSize`, which defines the number of rows to show per page.

❑   `OnPageIndexChanged`, which defines the event procedure to call when the page number is changed. When a page number link is clicked, the procedure defined here is run.

❑   `AllowSorting`, which is `true`, allowing the grid to sort the rows on the basis of column selections. Setting this to `true` enables links on the column headings.

❑   `OnSortCommand`, which defines the event procedure to call when a column heading is clicked.

Now let's look at the code that uses this grid, starting with the `Page_Load` event:

```
Sub Page_Load(Sender As Object, E As EventArgs)

  If Not Page.IsPostBack Then
    BindGrid()
  End If

End Sub
```

Here we are calling the `BindGrid` routine, but only if this is the first time the page has been loaded. This ensures that the grid, in its initial state, displays data in a default sort order. You'll see how this works as we go through the code.

Next we have two events for the grid. The first is for when a page is selected on the grid, and is the event procedure defined in the `OnPageIndexChanged` attribute:

```
Sub DataGrid_Page(Sender As Object, e As DataGridPageChangedEventArgs)

  DataGrid1.CurrentPageIndex = e.NewPageIndex
  BindGrid()

End Sub
```

Notice that the second argument to this procedure is of type `DataGridPageChangedEventArgs`. This is automatically sent by ASP.NET and contains two properties, only one of which we are interested in – `NewPageIndex`. This identifies the number of the page selected, so we set the `CurrentPageIndex` property of the grid to the selected page number. We then call the `BindGrid` routine to re-fetch the data and bind it to the grid. Later, we'll look at why you need to do this.

The second event procedure is for sorting the grid, and is defined in the `OnSortCommand` attribute:

```
Sub DataGrid_Sort(Sender As Object, e As DataGridSortCommandEventArgs)

  DataGrid1.CurrentPageIndex = 0
  SortField = e.SortExpression
  BindGrid()

End Sub
```

The second argument for this procedure is of type `DataGridSortCommandEventArgs`, which contains the expression on which the grid is being sorted. In this case, this is automatically set by the `DataGrid` as the column headings are sortable, and so contains the column name.

The first line sets the `CurrentPageIndex` of the grid to 0, having the effect of starting the grid at page 1. We do this because we are re-sorting. We then set `SortField` to the sorted field, and rebind the grid.

Notice that `SortField` hasn't been declared as a variable – in fact it's a property. This might seem confusing because properties are always attached to objects, prompting the question what object is this one attached to. Well since it hasn't got a named object, ASP.NET takes this as being a property of the current `Page`. By default, a `Page` doesn't have a `SortField` property, so we define one:

```
Property SortField() As String

  Get
    Dim o As Object = ViewState("SortField")
    If o Is Nothing Then
      Return String.Empty
    End If
    Return CStr(o)
  End Get

  Set(ByVal Value As String)
    ViewState("SortField") = Value
  End Set

End Property
```

The interesting point is that we haven't defined a class. Because we are coding within an ASP.NET page, the `Page` *is* a class, so all we are doing is adding a property to the page (for the purpose of referencing the sorted field later when we bind the grid). When the page is run, ASP.NET adds your code to the class for the page. It's not like the examples in the previous chapter, where we were creating a separate class – here we want our property to be part of the same class as the rest of the code.

The `Get` part of the property first fetches the sort value from the `ViewState` into an object variable (all items in `ViewState` are returned as objects), and then checks to see if the object is `Nothing`. This would be the case if the sort hasn't been defined, such as the first time the page is loaded. If it is `Nothing`, then an empty string is returned, otherwise the object is converted to a string with `CStr` and that is returned. This is a perfectly safe conversion because we know that the `ViewState` for this item only contains a string, as that's what the `Set` part of the property does. `ViewState` was covered in *Chapter 6*.

> *Using `String.Empty` is a special way of defining an empty string, and avoids having to use open and close quotation marks next to each other, where it's often difficult to see if there is a space between the quotation marks.*

Now let's look at the `BindGrid()` routine:

```
Sub BindGrid()
```

The first two lines define string variables to hold the connection string and the text for the command to run. Notice that the connection string has been changed to an Access one:

```
Dim ConnectionString As String = "Provider=Microsoft.Jet.OLEDB.4.0; " & _
                    "Data Source=C:\BegASPNet11\data\Northwind.mdb"
Dim CommandText As String
```

Next we check the SortField property to see if we are sorting the data in the order selected by the user (that is, if the user has clicked one of the column headings). This is accessing the SortField property of the Page and therefore calls the Get part of the property. If the sort order hasn't been defined, the String.Empty is the value of SortField, so we set the command string to order by the CompanyName. If a sort string has been set then we use that as the sort order. In either case, we are simply selecting all rows and columns from the Suppliers table:

```
If SortField = String.Empty Then
   CommandText = "select * from suppliers order by CompanyName"
Else
   CommandText = "select * from suppliers order by " & SortField
End If
```

These commands use SQL statements, but we could equally have used stored queries or stored procedures. In practice you should use stored queries, but using SQL directly here means we don't have to create the stored query – since we're concentrating on ASP.NET we don't want to distract ourselves with the stored procedure. We'll be looking at stored procedures later in the chapter.

Now we come to the part where we connect to the database. Don't worry too much about this code – although we are going to explain it, we're not going to go into too much detail in this section, as we'll be going over the theory later. To define the connection we use an OleDbConnection object, and as part of the instantiation we pass in the connection string details. This tells ASP.NET which database to connect to, but doesn't actually open the connection. It just defines where to connect to when we are ready to connect:

```
Dim myConnection As New OleDbConnection(ConnectionString)
```

Now we use an OleDbDataAdapter to define the command to run – this will be the SELECT query to fetch the data. The data adapter performs two functions. It provides the link between the database and the DataSet. It is also how data is fetched from and sent to the database (we'll be looking at the DataAdapter in detail in the next chapter). The two arguments we pass in are the command text to run the SQL statement, and the connection object. These define which command to run and which database to run it against:

```
Dim myCommand As New OleDbDataAdapter(CommandText, myConnection)
```

Note that we still haven't connected to the database and fetched any data, as we've nowhere to store that data. For that we use a DataSet object, which you can think of as a mini database (it's not actually a mini database, but that descriptions works well for the moment). It provides a place for the data to be held while we manipulate it:

```
Dim ds As New DataSet()
```

Now that we have all of the pieces in place (the connection, the command to run, and a place to put the data), we can go ahead and fetch the data. For that we use the Fill method of the data adaptor, passing in the `DataSet`. This opens the database connection, runs the command, places the data into the `DataSet`, and then closes the database connection.

```
myCommand.Fill(ds)
```

The data is now in our `DataSet` so we can use it as the `DataSource` for the grid, and bind the grid:

```
DataGrid1.DataSource = ds
DataGrid1.DataBind()

End Sub
```

This may look like a complex set of procedures, but it's actually a simple set of steps that is used many times when you need to fetch data. You'll be seeing this many times during this book, and we'll go over its theory later so you really understand what's happening. For now though, let's look at another method of saving time, by using Web Matrix *code wizards*.

Displaying Data using the Code Wizards

There are times where both the drag and drop from the **Data Explorer** and the template pages cannot provide you with exactly what you need. Perhaps you'd like to customize the query, or just add a routine to fetch data to an already existing page. The code wizards allow you to add code routines to a page, giving you a finer control of the data being fetched or updated. Let's give this a go.

Try It Out   Creating a Data Page

1. Create a new blank ASP.NET page called `CodeWizard.aspx`.

2. Switch to **Code** view and you'll notice that the **Toolbox** now shows **Code Wizards** as in Figure 8-7:

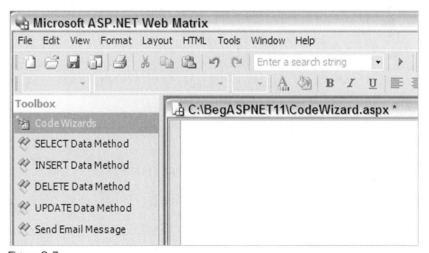

Figure 8-7

3. Pick the SELECT Data Method and drag it from the Toolbox, dropping it into your code window. This starts the wizard, and the first screen as shown in Figure 8-8 is where you pick the database to connect:

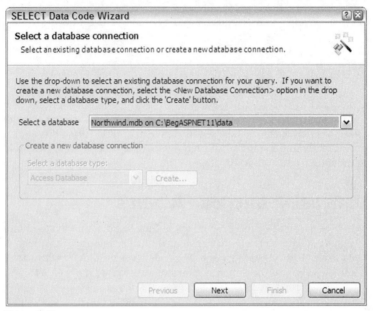

Figure 8-8

4. The drop down list shows configured data sources (from the Data Explorer) as well as an option to create a new connection. Pick the existing connection and press Next to go to the screen shown in Figure 8-9:

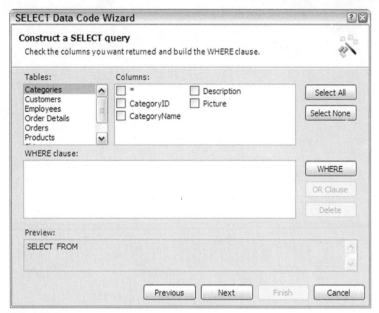

Figure 8-9

Now you can select the columns you wish to show. You can pick multiple columns (the * column means all columns from the table) from multiple tables. You simply select them individually. However, when picking columns from multiple tables, you must join the tables. Remember our discussion of linked tables and keys from the beginning of the chapter – you need the primary and foreign key to join the tables.

5. Select the Products table and the ProductName column, and the Categories table and the CategoryName column. Notice the Preview pane at the bottom of the window shows the SQL statement, but without the tables joined together, as shown in Figure 8-10:

Figure 8-10

6. To join these tables together, we need a WHERE clause, so press the WHERE button to open the WHERE Clause Builder window.

7. Select your options the same as shown in Figure 8-11:

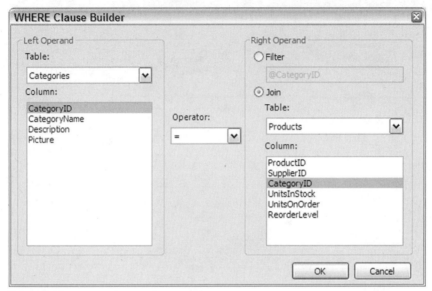

Figure 8-11

8. Click OK and you'll see the WHERE clause part of the window is filled in as shown in Figure 8-12:

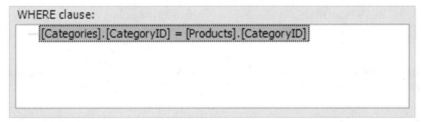

Figure 8-12

9. Press the Next button, and on the Query Preview window press the Test Query button (Figure 8-13 shows just the required columns):

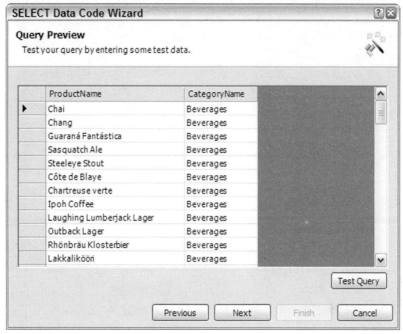

Figure 8-13

10. Press Next.

11. From the Name Method window, change the name textbox to `GetProductsDataSet`. Make sure the radio button at the bottom is set to DataSet and press Finish. We'll look at the `DataReader` later in the chapter.

12. Once the code has been added, you want a way to display it. You can do this by switching to Design view and dragging a DataGrid onto the page.

13. Switch to Code view and add the following code, after the `GetProductsDataSet` function:

```
Sub Page_Load(Sender As Object, E As EventArgs)
  DataGrid1.DataSource = GetProductsDataSet()
  DataGrid1.DataBind()
End Sub
```

14. Save the page and run it – you should see Figure 8-14:

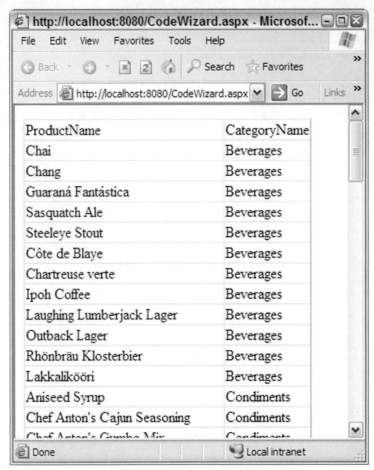

Figure 8-14

You can see how we've now only got two columns and from two different tables. Let's see how this works.

How It Works

The key to this is the wizard that allows you to build up an SQL statement. This is great if you are a to SQL as you don't have to understand how the SQL language works. Perhaps the most important part of this wizard is the WHERE Clause Builder shown in Figure 8-11.

This is where (pun intended) we add the WHERE part of the SQL statement, and this is what filters the rows and joins tables together. We've selected the Join option allowing us to specify the primary key (CategoryID in the Categories table) and the foreign key (CategoryID in the Products table). The WHERE clause becomes:

```
WHERE [Categories].[CategoryID] = [Products].[CategoryID]
```

If we wanted to add a third table, perhaps `Suppliers`, we could use an AND clause. Once you've declared one `WHERE` clause, the **WHERE** button has a different name – **AND Clause** as shown in Figure 8-15:

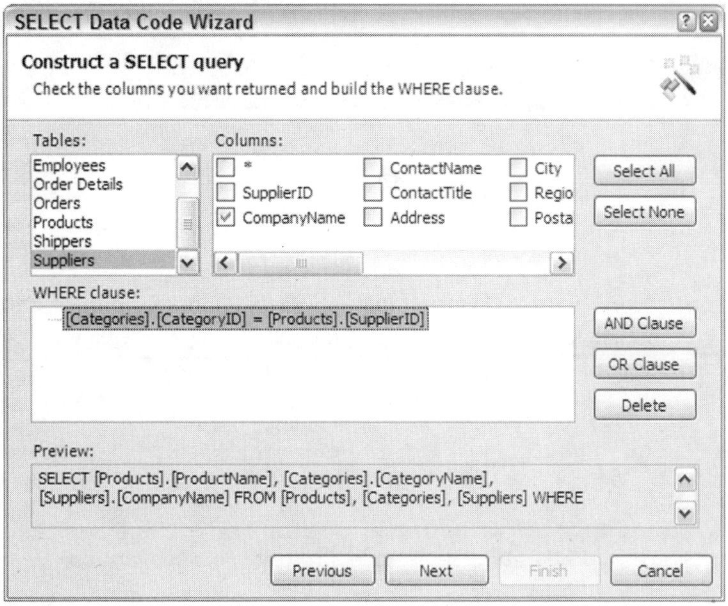

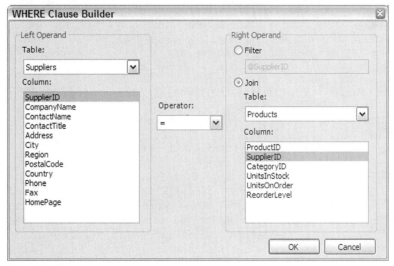

Figure 8-15

Pressing the **AND Clause** button shows the same **WHERE Clause Builder**, but this time you'd set the link between the `Suppliers` and `Products` tables as shown in Figure 8-16:

Figure 8-16

Now when you look at the WHERE clause section you see two tables joined together as in Figure 8-17:

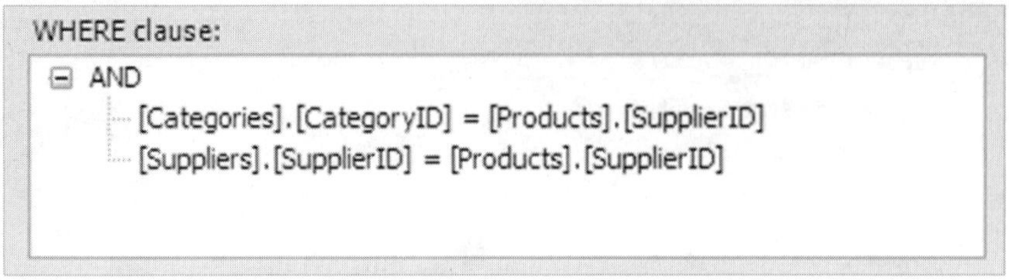

```
WHERE clause:

⊟ AND
    [Categories].[CategoryID] = [Products].[SupplierID]
    [Suppliers].[SupplierID] = [Products].[SupplierID]
```

Figure 8-17

The WHERE Clause Builder can also be used to filter data so that only *selected* rows are shown; we'll look at that later. For now though, let's move on to look at the code the wizard created for us (it may look slightly different in your page – we've wrapped it so it's easier to read):

```
Function GetProductsDataSet() As System.Data.DataSet
    Dim connectionString As String = "Provider=Microsoft.Jet.OLEDB.4.0; " & _
                "Ole DB Services=-4; Data Source=C:\BegASPNET11\" & _
                "data\Northwind.mdb"
    Dim dbConnection As System.Data.IDbConnection = _
        New System.Data.OleDb.OleDbConnection(connectionString)

    Dim queryString As String = "SELECT [Products].[ProductName], " & _
        "[Categories].[CategoryName] FROM [Products], "[Categories] " & _
        "WHERE ([Categories].[CategoryID] = [Products].[CategoryID])"
    Dim dbCommand As System.Data.IDbCommand = _
        New System.Data.OleDb.OleDbCommand
    dbCommand.CommandText = queryString
    dbCommand.Connection = dbConnection

    Dim dataAdapter As System.Data.IDbDataAdapter = _
        New System.Data.OleDb.OleDbDataAdapter
    dataAdapter.SelectCommand = dbCommand
    Dim dataSet As System.Data.DataSet = New System.Data.DataSet
    dataAdapter.Fill(dataSet)

    Return dataSet
End Function
```

Let's tackle this in stages. First we have the function declaration:

```
Function GetProductsDataSet() As System.Data.DataSet
```

This is defined as type System.Data.DataSet, which means it's going to return a DataSet (we'll look at this in detail in the next chapter). You'll notice that the declaration has the namespace System.Data before it. This is done because while declaring variables or functions, ASP.NET needs to know where the type is stored.

Normally we use the `<%@ import Namespace="..." %>` page directive to indicate the namespaces being used in a page, and thus we don't have to specify the namespace when declaring variables. The wizard isn't sure what namespaces have been set at the top of the page, so it includes the full namespace just in case, ensuring that the code will compile under all situations.

Next we have the connection string that simply points to our existing database:

```
Dim connectionString As String = "Provider=Microsoft.Jet.OLEDB.4.0; " & _
                  "Ole DB Services=-4; Data Source=C:\BegASPNET11\" & _
                  "data\Northwind.mdb"
```

Now we have the connection object:

```
Dim dbConnection As System.Data.IDbConnection = _
    New System.Data.OleDb.OleDbConnection(connectionString)
```

One thing that's immediately obvious is that this example is using the `IDbConnection` and not the `OleDbConnection` to define the connection to the database If this seems confusing, refer to the discussion of interfaces in the previous chapter, where we talked about generic routines.

`IDbConnection` is an interface that defines what the `Connection` class must do, and since the wizard is building a generic routine, it uses this interface. This is because the wizard allows you to connect to different database types. – tThhis is on the first screen and is the same as the **Data Explorer** allowing you to pick either Access or SQL Server database. To make the wizard simpler, it uses the generic interface as the type rather than having to use the type for a specific database.

> *The Interface simply enforces the correct signature on a class implementing the interface. There's no actual requirement for the implementation to do anything. You could have a class that implements the Open method but that actually does something else instead of opening a connection. It would be dumb, but it could be done.*

Next we have the SQL string, as built up by the wizard:

```
Dim queryString As String = "SELECT [Products].[ProductName], " & _
    "[Categories].[CategoryName] FROM [Products], "[Categories] " & _
    "WHERE ([Categories].[CategoryID] = [Products].[CategoryID])"
```

Now we have the definition of the command object. In previous examples we passed the command text directly into the `OleDbDataAdapter`. Underneath, ASP.NET actually creates another object – a `Command` object. But you don't see that `Command` object, as it is used internally. The wizard creates the `Command` object directly, by making use of the `CommandText` property to store the SQL command, and the `Connection` property to store the database connection. As with the connection, which used the interface as its type, the command is also defined as an interface type (`IDbCommand`).

```
Dim dbCommand As System.Data.IDbCommand = New System.Data.OleDb.OleDbCommand
dbCommand.CommandText = queryString
dbCommand.Connection = dbConnection
```

Now we have the definition of the data adapter, and as with the connection, the type of the variable is the interface type.

```
Dim dataAdapter As System.Data.IDbDataAdapter = _
    New System.Data.OleDb.OleDbDataAdapter
```

We mentioned that the data adapter is the link between our page and the data. As part of this link, the adapter provides not only data fetching, but also data modification. It does so with different command objects, exposed as properties of the adapter. These allow the different commands to run depending upon the action being performed. In this example, we are fetching data so we use the `SelectCommand` property (so named because we are selecting rows to view).

```
dataAdapter.SelectCommand = dbCommand
```

If you use the data adapter directly, this is what it does behind the scenes. To fetch the data, we then create a `DataSet` and use the `Fill()`. method of the adapter:

```
Dim dataSet As System.Data.DataSet = New System.Data.DataSet
dataAdapter.Fill(dataSet)
```

And finally, we return the data:

```
    Return dataSet
End Function
```

This code is more complex than the previous example, but it follows a similar path. It creates a connection, creates a command, creates a data adapter, and then a `DataSet`. A look at these objects and their relationships in more detail will give you a clearer picture of how they work together.

ADO.NET

All of the data access we've seen so far is based upon ADO.NET – the common name for all of the data access classes. We'll only be looking at a few of these, and the ones you'll use most are:

- ❏ `Connection`: to provide the details of connecting to the database
- ❏ `Command`: to provide the details of the command to be run
- ❏ `DataAdapter`: to manage the command, and fetch and update data
- ❏ `DataSet`: to provide a store for the data
- ❏ `DataReader`: to provide quick read-only access to data

ADO.NET is designed to talk to multiple databases, so there are different objects for different database types. To keep the separation, ADO.NET classes are contained within different namespaces:

- ❏ `System.Data`, which contains the base data objects (such as `DataSet`) common to all databases.
- ❏ `System.Data.OleDb`, which contains the objects used to communicate to databases via OLEDB. OLEDB provides a common set of features to connect to multiple databases, such as Access, DBase, and so on.
- ❏ `System.Data.SqlClient`, which provides the objects used to communicate with SQL Server.

For some of the objects there are two copies – one in the OleDb namespace, and one in the SqlClient namespace. For example, there are two Connection objects – OleDbConnection and SqlConnection. Having two objects means they can be optimized for particular databases. Look at figure 8-18 to see how they relate to each other:

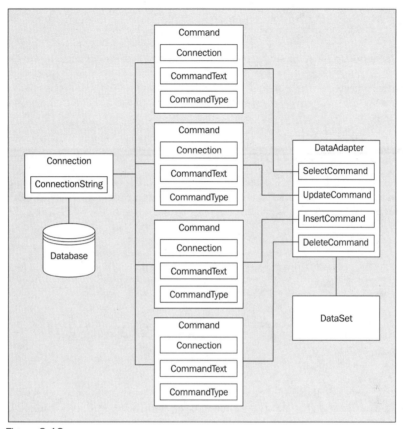

Figure 8-18

On the left we have the database and the connection, in the middle we have four Command objects, and on the right a DataAdapter and a DataSet. Notice that the DataAdapter contains four Command objects:

❑ SelectCommand, which fetches data.

❑ UpdateCommand, which updates data.

❑ InsertCommand, which inserts new data.

❑ DeleteCommand, which deletes data.

Each of these `Command` objects has a `Connection` property to specify which database the command applies to, a `CommandText` property to specify the command text to run, and a `CommandType` property to indicate the type of command (straight SQL or a stored procedure).

As we said earlier, if you don't explicitly create `Command` objects and use the `DataAdapter` directly, a `Command` is created for you using the details passed into the constructor of the `DataAdapter`, and this `Command` is used as the `SelectCommand`.

We'll be looking at the `UpdateCommand`, `InsertCommand`, and `DeleteCommand` in the next chapter.

Let's look at these objects in a bit more detail, concentrating on the `OleDb` ones, as we're using Access. If you want to use SQL Server, you can simply replace `OleDb` with `SqlClient` in the object names;, just change the connection string, and continue working.

The OleDbConnection Object

As we've said earlier, the `Connection` object provides us with the means to communicate to a database. Probably the only property you'll use is the `ConnectionString` property, which can either be set as the object is instantiated:

```
Dim connectionString As String = "Provider=Microsoft.Jet.OLEDB.4.0; " & _
            " Data Source=C:\BegASPNET11\data\Northwind.mdb"
Dim conn As New OleDbConnection(connectionString)
```

or with the property:

```
Dim connectionString As String = "Provider=Microsoft.Jet.OLEDB.4.0; " & _
            " Data Source=C:\BegASPNET11\data\Northwind.mdb"
Dim conn As New OleDbConnection()
conn.ConnectionString = connectionString
```

The two main methods you'll use are `Open` and `Close`, which (unsurprisingly) open and close the connection to the database. When used as we have so far, there is no need to do this explicitly since the `Fill` method of a `DataAdapter` does it for you.

The OleDbCommand Object

The `OleDbCommand` has several properties that we'll be looking at:

Property	Description
CommandText	Contains the SQL command or the name of a stored procedure.
CommandType	Indicates the type of command being run, and can be one of the `CommandType` enumeration values, which are: `StoredProcedure`, to indicate a stored procedure is being run. `TableDirect`, to indicate the entire contents of a table are being returned. In this case, the `CommandText` property should contain the table name. This value only works for Oledb connections. `Text`, to indicate a SQL text command. This is the default value.
Connection	The `Connection` object being used to connect to a database.
Parameters	A collection or `Parameter` objects, which are used to pass details to and from the command.

The three main methods of the command you'll use are the execute methods:

Method	Description
ExecuteNonQuery	This executes the command but doesn't return any data. It is useful for commands that perform an action, such as updating data, but doesn't need to return a value.
ExecuteReader	This executes the command and returns a `DataReader` object.
ExecuteScalar	This executes the command and returns a single value.

In the examples so far, we haven't used these methods, as the execution of the command is handled transparently for us. You'll see the `ExecuteReader` method in action when you look at the `DataReader`, and the `ExecuteNonQuery` method in action in the next chapter.

The Parameters Collection

A parameter is an unknown value – a value that ADO.NET doesn't know until the page is being run, and is often used to filter data based upon some user value. For example, consider a page showing a list of products, with a drop down list showing the product categories. The user could select a category so that only those categories are shown. The `Parameters` collection contains a `Parameter` object for each parameter in the query.

Thus, a command with three parameters would have objects looking like in Figure 8-19:

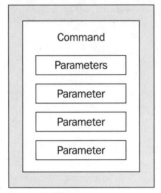

Figure 8-19

Let's look at an example to see how this works.

Try It Out Using Parameters

1. Create a new blank ASP.NET page called `Parameters.aspx`.
2. Add a Label and change the `Text` property to `Category:`
3. Add a DropDownList next to the label, and change the `ID` property to `lstCategory`.
4. Add a Button next to the DropDownList and change the `Text` property to `Fetch`.
5. Add a DataGrid underneath the other controls. Your page should now look like Figure 8-20:

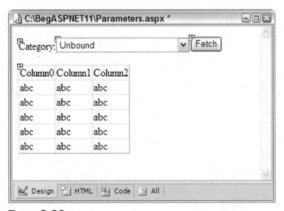

Figure 8-20

6. Double-click the Fetch button to switch to the `Click` event procedure. Add the following code:

```
Sub Button1_Click(sender As Object, e As EventArgs)
    DataGrid1.DataSource = GetProducts(lstCategory.SelectedValue)
```

```
        DataGrid1.DataBind()
End Sub
```

7. Underneath that procedure, add the following code:

```
Sub Page_Load(Sender As Object, E As EventArgs)

    If Not Page.IsPostback Then
        lstCategory.DataSource = GetCategories()
        lstCategory.DataValueField = "CategoryID"
        lstCategory.DataTextField = "CategoryName"
        lstCategory.DataBind()
    End If

End Sub
```

8. Underneath that, drag a **SELECT Data Method** wizard from the toolbox onto the page. Pick the current database connection and select the `CategoryID` and `CategoryName` columns from the `Categories` table. Call the procedure `GetCategories` and have it return a `DataSet`.

9. Underneath that, drag another **SELECT Data Method** wizard onto the page. Pick the current database connection, and select `ProductName`, `QuantityPerUnit`, `UnitPrice`, and `UnitsInStock` from the `Products` table.

10. Click the **WHERE** button and pick the `CategoryID` from the `Products` table making it **Filter** on `@CategoryID`, as shown in Figure 8-21:

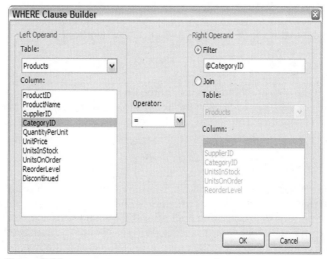

Figure 8-21

11. Click **OK** and **Next** to get to the **Name Method** screen.

12. Call the procedure `GetProducts` and have it return a `DataSet`. Press **Finish** to insert the code.

13. Save the file and run it.

14. Select a category and then click Fetch to see only products for that category shown in Figure 8-22:

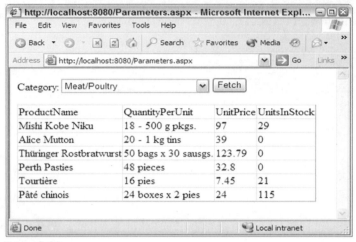

Figure 8-22

What you've achieved here is two things. First Yyou've first used two controls that are bound to data – the list of categories and the grid of products. Secondly you only fetched the products for a selected category – you've filtered the list. Let's see how this works.

How It Works

Let's start the code examination with the `Page_Load` event, where we fill the `Categories` list:

```
Sub Page_Load(Sender As Object, E As EventArgs)
```

We only want to fetch the data and bind it to the list the first time the page is loaded, so we use the `IsPostback` property of the `Page` to check if this is a postback. If it isn't, it must be the first load, so we fetch the data. We don't need to do this on subsequent page requests as the list itself stores the data.

```
If Not Page.IsPostback Then
    lstCategory.DataSource = GetCategories()
```

Instead of calling the `DataBind` straight away, we want to tell the list which columns from the data to use. A `DropDownList` stores two pieces of information – one is shown on the page (the text field), and the other is hidden (the value field). The text field is used for what the user needs to see, while the value field often contains an ID – what the user doesn't need to see. The `DropDownList` doesn't automatically know which columns contain these pieces of information, thus we use the `DataValueField` and `DataTextField` properties. The `DataValueField` is the `CategoryID`, the unique key for the category, and this will be used later in our code:

```
    lstCategory.DataValueField = "CategoryID"
    lstCategory.DataTextField = "CategoryName"
    lstCategory.DataBind()
    End If
End Sub
```

When the **Fetch** button is clicked, we need to get the value from the `DropDownList`. For this, we use the `SelectedValue` property, which is new to ASP.NET 1.1. This contains the ID of the selected category, and we pass this into the `GetProducts` routine, which will return a `DataSet` of the products. The returned `DataSet` is set to the `DataSource` of the grid and the `DataBind` method is called to bind the data:

```
Sub Button1_Click(sender As Object, e As EventArgs)

  DataGrid1.DataSource = GetProducts(lstCategory.SelectedValue)
  DataGrid1.DataBind()

End Sub
```

There are two routines to fetch data, but one of them is the same as we've already seen – using a simple `DataSet` to fetch data (in this case the `Categories`). What we want to see is the `GetProducts` routine, which gets *filtered* data. The first thing to notice is that it accepts an `Integer` argument – this will contain the `CategoryID`, passed in from the button click event:

```
Function GetProducts(ByVal categoryID As Integer) As System.Data.DataSet
```

Next we define the connection details, as we've seen in previous examples:

```
Dim connectionString As String = "Provider=Microsoft.Jet.OLEDB.4.0; " & _
      "Ole DB Services=-4; " & "Data Source=C:\BegASPNET11\data\Northwind.mdb"
Dim dbConnection As System.Data.IDbConnection = _
      New System.Data.OleDb.OleDbConnection(connectionString)
```

Then we define the query:

```
Dim queryString As String = "SELECT [Products].[ProductName], " & _
    "[Products].[QuantityPerUnit], [Products].[UnitPrice], " & _
    "[Products].[UnitsInStock] FROM [Products] " & _
    "WHERE ([Products].[CategoryID] = @CategoryID)"
```

Note that the `WHERE` clause is filtering on `CategoryID`. However, the value used for the filter (`@CategoryID`) is not a real value but a *placeholder*. This tells ADO.NET that the value will be supplied by a parameter.

Once the query string is set, we define our command to run the query, as follows:

```
Dim dbCommand As System.Data.IDbCommand = New System.Data.OleDb.OleDbCommand
dbCommand.CommandText = queryString
dbCommand.Connection = dbConnection
```

Now we come to the definition of the parameter. Like many of the other examples, this uses a database-specific object – an `OleDbParameter`, which defines what is being passed into the query:

```
Dim dbParam_categoryID As System.Data.IDataParameter = _
        New System.Data.OleDb.OleDbParameter
```

We then set the properties of the parameter. The `ParameterName` indicates the name of the parameter, and we set the value to be the same as the placeholder. The `Value` property stores the value for the parameter, and is set to the `CategoryID` passed into the procedure from the button click event – it's the ID of the category selected from the list. The `DbType` property indicates the database type – `Int32` is the database equivalent of an `Integer`:

```
dbParam_categoryID.ParameterName = "@CategoryID"
dbParam_categoryID.Value = categoryID
dbParam_categoryID.DbType = System.Data.DbType.Int32
```

At this point, even though we have a `Parameter` object, it's not associated with the command, so we add it to the `Parameters` collection of the command:

```
dbCommand.Parameters.Add(dbParam_categoryID)
```

When ADO.NET processes the command, it matches parameters in the collection with the placeholders in the query and substitutes the placeholder with the value in the parameter.

The rest of the code is as we've seen it before. We create a `DataAdapter` to run the command, and use the `Fill()` method to fetch the data into our `DataSet`:

```
Dim dataAdapter As System.Data.IDbDataAdapter = _
            New System.Data.OleDb.OleDbDataAdapter
dataAdapter.SelectCommand = dbCommand
Dim dataSet As System.Data.DataSet = New System.Data.DataSet
dataAdapter.Fill(dataSet)

Return dataSet
End Function
```

As you can see, there really isn't that much code; even though we've introduced a new object, much of the code remains the same, so you've added to existing knowledge.

Filtering Queries

There's a very important point to know about filtering data, as you may see code elsewhere that uses a bad method of doing it – it simply builds up the SQL string (as we've done), but instead of using parameters, it just appends the filter value to the SQL string. For example, you might see this:

```
Dim queryString As String = "SELECT [Products].[ProductName], " & _
    "[Products].[QuantityPerUnit], [Products].[UnitPrice], " & _
    "[Products].[UnitsInStock] FROM [Products] " & _
    "WHERE ([Products].[CategoryID] = " & CategoryID & ")"
```

This simply appends the `CategoryID` value (from the function argument) into the SQL string. Why is this bad when it achieves the same things, plus uses less code? The answer has to do with hacking. This type of method potentially allows what are known as *SQL Injection Attacks*, which are a 'very bad thing' (do a Web search for more details on SQL Injection). If you have a scale of 'bad things to do', then this is right there up at the top!

Using Parameters, on the other hand, protects you from this. Although it has the same effect, the processing ADO.NET does secure you against this type of attack.

So, even though using Parameters is a little more work, it's much safer and should always be used.

The OleDataAdapter Object

The `OleDbDataAdapter` contains the commands used to manipulate data. The four `Command` objects it contains are held as properties; `SelectCommand`, `UpdateCommand`, `InsertCommand`, and `DeleteCommand`. The `SelectCommand` is automatically run when the `Fill()` method is called. The other three commands are run when the `Update` method is called – we'll be looking at this in the next chapter.

The DataSet Object

While the other objects we've looked at have different classes for different databases, the `DataSet` is common to all databases, and is therefore in the `System.Data` namespace. It doesn't actually communicate with the database – the `DataAdapter` handles all communication.

The `DataSet` has many properties and methods, but we're not going to look at them until the next chapter. Since this chapter is concentrating on displaying data, all you need to remember is that when we fetch data it is stored in the `DataSet`, and then we bind controls to that data.

The DataReader Object

The `DataReader`, an object that we haven't come across yet, is optimised for reading data. When dealing with databases, connecting to them and fetching the data can often be the longest part of a page, therefore we want to do it as quickly as possible. We also want to ensure that the database server isn't tied up – we want not only to get the data quickly, but also stay connected to the database for as little time as possible.

For this reason we aim to open the connection to the database as late as possible, get the data, and close the connection as soon as possible. This frees up any resources, allowing the database to process other requests. This is the technique that the `DataAdapter` uses when filling a `DataSet`. If you manually open a connection, it isn't automatically closed.

Many times, when fetching data we simply want to display it as it is, perhaps by binding it to a grid. The `DataSet` provides a local store of the data, which is often more than we need, so we can use an `OleDbDataReader` to stream the data directly from the database into the grid. Let's give this a go.

Try It Out   Using a DataReader

1. Create a new blank ASP.NET page called `DataReader.aspx`.

2. Drag a DataGrid control from the Toolbox onto the page.

3. Switch to Code view and start the code wizard by dragging the SELECT Data Method onto the code page.

4. Select the existing database connection from the first screen and press Next.

5. Select the Products table, and from the Columns select ProductName, QuantityPerUnit, UnitPrice, and UnitsInStock.

6. Click Next, and Next again, to go past the Query Preview screen.

7. Enter `GetProductsReader` as the method name, and select the DataReader option on the Name Method screen.

8. Press Finish to insert the code into your page.

9. Underneath the newly inserted method, add the following:

```
Sub Page_Load(Sender As Object, E As EventArgs)
  DataGrid1.DataSource = GetProductsReader()
  DataGrid1.DataBind()
End Sub
```

10. Save the page and run it.

You'll see a grid containing just the selected columns. This isn't much different in look from other examples, but it's how the data is fetched that's important. Let's take a look at this.

How It Works

Let's start by looking at the code the wizard generated for us. The declaration of the function returns an `IDataReader` – the interface that data readers implement:

```
Function GetProductsReader() As System.Data.IDataReader
```

Next we have the connection details – these are the same as you've previously seen (although they might look different in your code file, as this has been formatted to fit on the page):

```
Dim connectionString As String = "Provider=Microsoft.Jet.OLEDB.4.0; " & _
    "Ole DB Services=-4; " & "Data Source=C:\BegASPNET11\data\Northwind.mdb"
Dim dbConnection As System.Data.IDbConnection = _
    New System.Data.OleDb.OleDbConnection(connectionString)
```

Next we have the query string and the command details:

```
Dim queryString As String = "SELECT [Products].[ProductName], " & _
                "[Products].[QuantityPerUnit], [Products].[UnitPrice], " & _
                "[Products].[UnitsInStock] FROM [Products]"
Dim dbCommand As System.Data.IDbCommand = New System.Data.OleDb.OleDbCommand
dbCommand.CommandText = queryString
```

```
dbCommand.Connection = dbConnection
```

Once the command details are set, we can then open the database connection:

```
dbConnection.Open
```

Even though the database connection has been opened for us when using a `DataSet`, we still have to open it manually because we are using an `OleDbCommand` and a data reader.

Next we declare the data reader. It is of type `IDataReader` and the object is created by the return value of the `ExecuteReader` method of the command:

```
Dim dataReader As System.Data.IDataReader = _
        dbCommand.ExecuteReader(System.Data.CommandBehavior.CloseConnection)
```

Remember that the command has the SQL statement, so `ExecuteReader` tells ADO.NET to run the command and return a data reader. The argument indicates that as soon as the data is finished with the connection to the database, the connection should be closed. When using `ExecuteReader`, you should always add this argument to make sure the connection is closed as soon as it no longer required.

Finally we return the reader object:

```
    Return dataReader
End Function
```

To bind to the grid, we simply use this function as the `DataSource` for the grid. Since the function returns a stream of data, the grid just binds to that data:

```
Sub Page_Load()

    DataGrid1.DataSource = GetProductsReader()
    DataGrid1.DataBind()

End Sub
```

DataReader Methods and Properties

The `DataReader` exists as `SqlDataReader` (for SQL Server) and `OleDbDataReader` (for other databases), as well as a common `IDataReader` interface. If you are not using generic code, you can create the reader as follows:

```
Dim dataReader As System.Data.OleDbDataReader = _
        dbCommand.ExecuteReader(System.Data.CommandBehavior.CloseConnection)
```

Using data readers is the most efficient way of fetching data from a database, but you don't have to bind to a grid. You can use the properties and methods to fetch the data directly. If you do this, it's best to use the `OleDbDataReader` rather than the interface, as the `OleDbDataReader` contains more properties that make it easier to use. For example, consider the following code:

```
Dim dataReader As System.Data.OleDbDataReader = _
        dbCommand.ExecuteReader(System.Data.CommandBehavior.CloseConnection)
```

```
If Not dataReader.HasRows Then
   Response.Write("No rows found")
Else
   While dataReader.Read()
      Response.Write(datareader("ProductName") & "<br/>")
   End While
End If
dataReader.Close()
```

This first uses the `HasRows` property to determine if there are any rows, and then uses the `Read` method to read a row. This is done within a loop, with `Read` returning the `True` if there is a current row and moving onto the next, and `False` if there are no rows.

Summary

The end results of the examples in this chapter have been relatively simple, but you've actually learned a lot. The first three main topics looked at how to use the Web Matrix to reduce your development time, taking away much of the legwork you'd normally have to do. We looked at the using the **Data Explorer** to drag and drop tables directly onto page, using the Web Matrix template pages, and using the code wizards.

After looking at the quick way of getting data, we looked at the theory behind it, examining the objects. Even though we still continued to use the wizards to generate code, we were now able to see how this wizard code worked (just because we understand how it works doesn't mean we abandon anything that makes our job easier.).

Now it's time to look at taking your data usage one step further by showing how to update data, and how to manage your data handling routines.

Exercises

1. In this chapter we created a page that showed only the products for a selected category. Try and think of ways to enhance this to show products for either a selected category or all categories.

2. In *Exercise 1* we wanted to bind data from a database to a `DropDownList` as well as manually add an entry. There are two ways to solve this issue – using techniques shown in this chapter, and using techniques not yet covered. Try and code the solution using the known technique, but see if you can think of a way to solve it using a new technique.

Advanced Data Handling

In the previous chapter we looked at various ways of reading data, how Web Matrix saves us writing code, and how ADO.NET objects work. Displaying data on a Web page is only half the story though, as there are many times when you want to update the data as well. Like we saw in the examples in the previous chapter, there are several ways this can be achieved; some more suitable to certain situations than others.

In this chapter we will look at ways of updating data, as well as some advanced topics that didn't really fit in the previous chapter. In particular, this chapter covers:

❑   A close look at the `DataTable` and `DataRow` objects.

❑   Updating data in a DataSet.

❑   Using the DataSet to update the original database.

Let's start with a detailed look at some of the ADO.NET objects.

More Data Objects

In the previous chapter we looked at the DataSet, but didn't really examine it in depth. It was used as a repository of data to which we could bind grids. In this chapter we will not only discuss DataSet in detail, but also look at the objects that the DataSet contains. In the examples until now, we've only fetched one set of data from a database, but the DataSet has the ability to hold more than one set of data. It does this by having a `Tables` collection containing a `Table` object for each set of data. Each table in turn has a `Rows` collection with a `Row` object for each row of data. Let's look at this in more detail.

The DataTable Object

The `DataTable` object is held in the `Tables` collection as part of the DataSet, as shown in Figure 9-1:

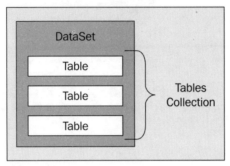

Figure 9-1

In the previous chapter, our DataSet contained just a single table; we need to know how to get more than one table into a DataSet. This is done by using different text for the command to run and calling the `Fill()` command of the data adapter again – if the table name in the command text is different then a new table in the DataSet will be created. For example, you can do this:

```
Dim connectionString As String = "Provider=Microsoft.Jet.OLEDB.4.0; " & _
          "Ole DB Services=-4; Data Source=C:\BegASPNET11\" & _
          "data\Northwind.mdb"
Dim dbConnection As System.Data.IDbConnection = _
    New System.Data.OleDb.OleDbConnection(connectionString)

Dim queryString As String = "SELECT * FROM Products"
Dim dbCommand As System.Data.IDbCommand = New System.Data.OleDb.OleDbCommand
dbCommand.CommandText = queryString
dbCommand.Connection = dbConnection

Dim dataAdapter As System.Data.IDbDataAdapter = _
    New System.Data.OleDb.OleDbDataAdapter
dataAdapter.SelectCommand = dbCommand
Dim data As System.Data.DataSet = New System.Data.DataSet
dataAdapter.Fill(dataset)

dataAdapter.SelectCommand.CommandText = "SELECT * FROM Employees"
dataAdapter.Fill(dataset)
```

Most of this code is exactly as you've seen it in the previous chapter – creating a connection and setting the command before using `Fill()`. However, we then change the `CommandText` of the `SelectCommand` to a new SQL command and call the `Fill()` method again. This gives two tables to our `Tables` collection, and we could access them as follows:

```
Dim tblProducts As DataTable = data.Tables(0)
```

Here we are just indexing into the `Tables` collection to get the first table. To make this easier to read we could name the tables as they are filled from the data adapter. For example:

```
dataAdapter.Fill(dataset, "Products")

dataAdapter.SelectCommand.CommandText = "SELECT * FROM Employees"
dataAdapter.Fill(dataset, "Employees")
```

This form of `Fill` takes two arguments. The first is the same as before – the DataSet into which the data is put, and the second is the name of the table, once it's in the collection. Realizing that each table in the DataSet has a name allows us to do the following:

```
Dim tblProducts As DataTable = data.Tables("Products")
```

There's no difference between this version and the one where we access the table by its index number, but this version is clearer – it's much easier to see which table you are dealing with in the collection. To use this method of accessing the `Tables` collection you don't have to specify the name when you use the `Fill` method. If you leave it out, the name of the source table is used as the name in the collection. Thus the SQL string `SELECT * FROM Products` would result in `Products` being used as the table name.

Since `Tables` is a collection, you can also loop through it if required:

```
Dim tbl As DataTable
For Each tbl In data.Tables
  DoSomethingToTable(tbl)
Next
```

So far in our examples we've used a DataGrid bound to a DataSet:

```
DataGrid1.DataSource = data
DataGrid1.DataBind()
```

This automatically binds to the first table in the collection. To bind to an explicit table simply specify the table name:

```
DataGrid1.DataSource = data.Tables("Products")
DataGrid1.DataBind()
```

In fact, because the DataSet contains multiple tables, they can each be bound to different controls:

```
DataGrid1.DataSource = data.Tables("Products")
DataGrid1.DataBind()

DataGrid2.DataSource = data.Tables("Employees")
DataGrid2.DataBind()
```

The DataRow Object

In the same way that the DataSet contains a `Tables` collection, each `DataTable` contains a `Rows` collection, as shown in Figure 9-2:

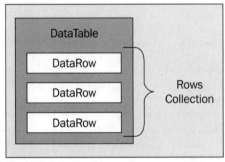

Figure 9-2

Like the `Tables` collection, the `Rows` collection can be indexed into:

```
Dim row As DataRow = data.Tables("Products").Rows(0)
```

Or enumerated in a loop:

```
Dim row As DataRow
For Each row In data.Tables("Products").Rows
   DoSomethingToRow(row)
Next
```

Let's now look at an example using these two objects.

Try It Out The DataTable and DataRow Objects

1. Create a blank ASP.NET page called `TableAndRow.aspx` into a new directory called `Ch09`.

2. In the All view, add the following code at the top of the page:

```
<%@ Import Namespace="System.Data" %>
<%@ Import Namespace="System.Data.Oledb" %>
```

3. Next, add the following code to the server code block:

```
Sub Page_Load(Sender As Object, E As EventArgs)

  Dim connectionString As String = "Provider=Microsoft.Jet.OLEDB.4.0; " & _
    "Data Source=C:\BegASPNET11\data\Northwind.mdb"
  Dim dbConnection As New OleDbConnection(connectionString)

  Dim queryString As String = "SELECT * FROM Categories"
  Dim dbCommand As New OleDbCommand

  dbCommand.CommandText = queryString
  dbCommand.Connection = dbConnection
  Dim dataAdapter As New OleDbDataAdapter
  dataAdapter.SelectCommand = dbCommand
  Dim data As DataSet = New System.Data.DataSet
  dataAdapter.Fill(data, "Categories")
  dataAdapter.SelectCommand.CommandText = "SELECT * FROM Shippers"
  dataAdapter.Fill(data, "Shippers")

  DataGrid1.DataSource = data.Tables("Categories")
  DataGrid1.DataBind()
  DataGrid2.DataSource = data.Tables("Shippers")
  DataGrid2.DataBind()

  Label1.Text = _
    data.Tables("Categories").Rows(1).Item("CategoryName").ToString()
  Label2.Text = data.Tables(1).Rows(2)(2).ToString()

End Sub
```

4. Switch to Design view and drag the two DataGrid controls onto the page. Also drag two the Label controls onto the page and position them as headings to describe the contents of the Datagrid controls.

5. Save the page and run it to see the result shown in Figure 9-3:

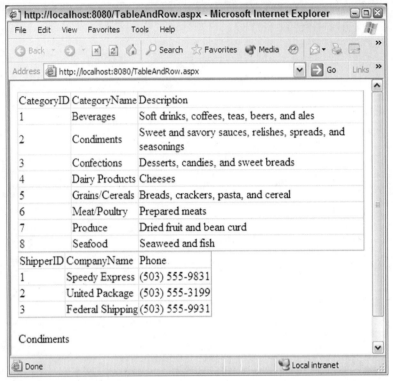

Figure 9-3

How It Works

You have seen most of this code in *Chapter 8*, so let's concentrate on the new bits of it, starting with the filling of the `DataSet`:

```
dataAdapter.Fill(data, "Categories")

dataAdapter.SelectCommand.CommandText = "SELECT * FROM Shippers"
dataAdapter.Fill(data, "Shippers")
```

Here, we fill the `DataSet` with the first table, change the `CommandText`, and then fill the `DataSet` with the next table, binding both tables to different grids:

```
DataGrid1.DataSource = data.Tables("Categories")
DataGrid1.DataBind()
DataGrid2.DataSource = data.Tables("Shippers")
DataGrid2.DataBind()
```

Next, we extract some details from the individual lines. The code demonstrates two different ways of indexing into the `Tables` and `Rows` collections, so you can see them in practice:

```
Label1.Text = data.Tables("Categories").Rows(1).Item("CategoryName").ToString()
Label2.Text = data.Tables(1).Rows(2)(2).ToString()
```

For the first line we use the table name to get to the correct table, and then pick the second row (remember that collections in .NET are zero-based). This gives us:

```
data.Tables("Categories").Rows(1)
```

At this stage we are pointing to an individual row. The `DataRow` has a property called `Item` that allows us to extract the column, so we just specify the column name and then use the `ToString()` method to convert this to a string. We could have used a column number instead of the name, but then we'd have to know the column order.

The second line does exactly the same thing, but in a different way:

```
Label2.Text = data.Tables(1).Rows(2)(2).ToString()
```

Instead of using names for collection indexes, we are using numbers. So we pick the second table in the `Tables` collection and find the second row. Notice that we *don't* specify the `Item` property or a column name. This is because the `Item` property is optional – you can leave it out. But you can't leave out the column *and* you have to either specify the name, or as in this case, the number. So, this is equivalent to:

```
Label2.Text = data.Tables(1).Rows(2).Item(2).ToString()
```

You can use either form. Explicitly using the `Item` property makes it clearer to read so it's probably best to stick to this form.

Updating Databases

Pages that display data are all very good, but we also often need to update data. There are two main ways to do this – by modifying data in the DataSet and using the DataAdapter to send the data back to the database, or by simply running a SQL command to update the data directly.

Which method you should pick depends on what you are doing. If you are making several changes to multiple rows, then the DataSet method is best. Using this translates into less work for you because you only have to specify the commands and tell the DataAdapter to perform the update. If you are only making changes to a single row, then the direct command method is often the best.

ADO.NET versus ADO

One thing that you have to know is that ADO.NET works in a disconnected manner. This means when you have a DataSet you are completely disconnected from the database. You can do changes, add rows, and so on, but you are only working within the DataSet, and until you explicitly force those changes back onto the database, it remains unchanged. This means that even in something like a grid, where it seems natural to use a DataSet because you might change multiple rows, you are only changing a single row at a time.

This is also similar to the way Web applications work – remember they are stateless, meaning that the server doesn't remember things between requests. Thus if you change some data in a DataSet and then post back to the server, those changes will be lost.

The reason for designing such a (disconnected) model is better performance – the less time you spend connected to the database, the better the database can run. This is not the way ADO worked, where (unless explicitly stated) you were always connected to the database, and thus the database generally had to do more work. Although you can work in a fully connected mode with ADO.NET, you can only read data this way, but cannot update data.

This disconnected model is an important point to remember about ADO.NET. Let's look at this in detail, starting with the DataSet method.

Updating Data in a DataSet

Updating data in a DataSet is a two-step process. First you need to know how to get access to the data within the DataSet and then alter it. This doesn't just mean changing values, but also adding and deleting rows. Then you have to know how to get those changes back into the database. We'll be doing the following example in stages, showing three simple ways to manipulate the data held in a table.

Try It Out   Adding, Editing, and Deleting Rows

1. Create a new file called EditingData.aspx in the Ch09 folder and add the following code in the All view:

```
<%@ Import Namespace="System.Data" %>
<%@ Import Namespace="System.Data.OleDb" %>
<script runat="server">

  Sub Page_Load(Sender As Object, E As EventArgs)

    Dim connectionString As String
    Dim queryString      As String
    Dim data             As New DataSet()
    Dim dbConnection      As OleDbConnection
    Dim dataAdapter       As OleDbDataAdapter
    connectionString = "Provider=Microsoft.Jet.OLEDB.4.0; " & _
                       "Data Source=C:\BegASPNET11\data\Northwind.mdb"
    queryString = "SELECT FirstName, LastName FROM Employees"

    dbConnection = New OledbConnection(connectionString)
    dataAdapter = New OledbDataAdapter(queryString, dbConnection)

    dataAdapter.Fill(data, "Employees")

    DataGrid1.DataSource = data.Tables("Employees")
    DataGrid1.DataBind()

    ' _____
    '
    ' Marker 1
    ' _____
    '
    ' Marker 2
```

```
        ' _____
        ' Marker 3

   End Sub

</script>

<html>
 <body>
  <table width="100%">
   <tr>
    <td>Original Data</td>
    <td>Data with new Row</td>
    <td>Data with edited Row</td>
    <td>Data with deleted Row</td>
   </tr>
   <tr>
    <td valign="top"><asp:DataGrid id="DataGrid1" runat="server" /></td>
    <td valign="top"><asp:DataGrid id="DataGrid2" runat="server" /></td>
    <td valign="top"><asp:DataGrid id="DataGrid3" runat="server" /></td>
    <td valign="top"><asp:DataGrid id="DataGrid4" runat="server" /></td>
   </tr>
  </table>
 </body>
</html>
```

The Marker 1, 2, and 3 comments will help you add code as we expand this example.

2.   Now run the file and you'll see the result shown in Figure 9-4:

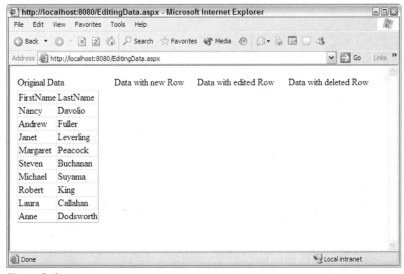

Figure 9-4

This is no different from some of the examples you saw in the previous chapter, but it serves as a foundation for showing the changes we'll be making.

3. Switch to **Code** view and add the following code at Marker 1. This will add a row to the table and display it in another grid:

```
Dim table  As DataTable
Dim newRow As DataRow

table = data.Tables("Employees")
newRow = table.NewRow()
newRow.Item("FirstName") = "Norman"
newRow.Item("LastName") = "Blake"
table.Rows.Add(newRow)

' bind the data grid to the new data
DataGrid2.DataSource = table
DataGrid2.DataBind()
```

4. In the browser, click the **Refresh** button (or F5) to see the new page, as shown in Figure 9-5:

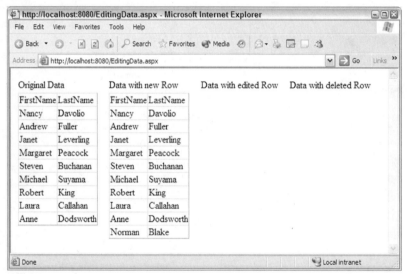

Figure 9-5

Here you can see that another row has been added to the end of the table.

5. Let's look at editing a row. Switch back to the code and add the following at `Marker 2`:

```
Dim selectedRows() As DataRow

' Find the row to change
selectedRows = table.Select("FirstName='Margaret' AND LastName='Peacock'")
selectedRows(0).Item("FirstName") = "John"
selectedRows(0).Item("LastName") = "Hartford"

' bind the data grid to the new data
DataGrid3.DataSource = table
DataGrid3.DataBind()
```

6. Back in the browser, click the **Refresh** button (or F5) to see the new page as shown in Figure 9-6:

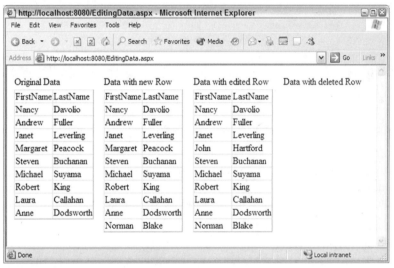

Figure 9-6

You can see that the row for **Margaret Peacock** has been changed to **John Hartford**.

7. Let's make the last addition to the code by adding the following at `Marker 3`:

```
' _____
' delete a row from the table

' The Rows collection is 0 indexed, so this removes the sixth row
table.Rows(5).Delete()

' bind the data grid to the new data
DataGrid4.DataSource = table
DataGrid4.DataBind()
```

8. Back in the browser, click the Refresh button (or F5) to see the new page as shown in Figure 9-7:

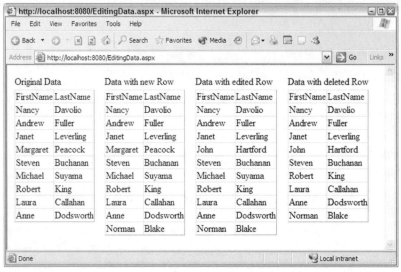

Figure 9-7

Here you can see that the row for Michael Suyama has been deleted, and doesn't appear in the fourth table.

Let's see how all this code works. We don't need to examine the code that gets the data from the database or binds it to the grid, as it's the same as the code we used in the previous example. We concentrate here on how we changed the data and the code fragments we put in the markers to do that.

How It Works – Adding Rows

The first section of code adds a new row to the table. The first thing we do is to declare two variables – one to point to the DataTable containing the data, and another to hold the data for the new row:

```
Dim table  As DataTable
Dim newRow As DataRow
```

We point the table variable to the Employees table:

```
table = data.Tables("Employees")
```

Next, we use the NewRow() method of the DataTable object to create a new DataRow:

```
newRow = table.NewRow()
```

This doesn't create a new DataRow in the table – it just provides a new DataRow object into which we can add data. We can then add this new row to the table once the data is filled. Note that you could add the empty row and then fill in the details – doesn't matter which way round you do it, but I prefer this way. The new row we've just created is empty, so we need to add some details. The rows in our table only hold first and last name information, but if you have tables with more columns, then you can just fill in their values too. The `DataRow` has only those columns requested in the `SelectStatement` when we filled the DataSet:

```
newRow.Item("FirstName") = "Norman"
newRow.Item("LastName") = "Blake"
```

Now that we've filled in the details, we need to add the new row to the existing table. Using the `NewRow()` method only creates a new `DataRow` object for us, and we have to add it to the table ourselves. This isn't done automatically as ADO.NET doesn't know what we want to do with the new row, so it leaves that choice to us. If you flip back to Figure 9-2 you'll notice that each `DataTable` has a `Rows` collection. The collection has an `Add` method, into which we pass the `DataRow` we want to add to the table:

```
table.Rows.Add(newRow)
```

Now we have the new row in the table, so all that's left to do is bind the table to the second DataGrid on the page, allowing us to see the results:

```
DataGrid2.DataSource = table.DefaultView
DataGrid2.DataBind()
```

One thing to remember is that you are still disconnected from the database. This means that if your database has constraints, they won't be enforced when adding the data to the DataSet. It's only when you update the original data store (which we'll discuss later) that this becomes an issue. You can also create constraints on the DataSet, but we won't be covering it in detail here.

> Constraints are rules held in the database to ensure that the data is correct. For example, a constraint would stop you from deleting an order if there were order lines attached to it.

How It Works – Editing Rows

The first thing we do in this code section is to declare a variable that can hold the rows we want to edit:

```
Dim selectedRows() As DataRow
```

Notice that this is an array, because the method we use to find selected rows returns an array of `DataRow` objects.

Next we use the `Select()` method of the table to find the row we want:

```
selectedRows = table.Select("FirstName='Margaret' AND LastName='Peacock'")
```

The string we pass is the same as a SQL `WHERE` clause.

Finally we update the data for the selected row. There could be many rows returned by the `Select()` method, so we index into the array. In our case we know that there is only one row returned:

```
selectedRows(0).Item("FirstName") = "John"
selectedRows(0).Item("LastName") = "Hartford"
```

It isn't necessary to use the `Select()` method, since you can edit the data directly, but using this method here makes it clear which row we are editing. What you can also do is just index into the `Rows` collection, using this code:

```
Dim row As DataRow

row = table.Rows(3)

row("FirstName") = "John"
row("LastName") = "Hartford"
```

First we declare a variable to hold the row to be edited:

```
Dim row As DataRow
```

Now you can point this variable at the row we are going to edit, by indexing into the `Rows` collection. It's important to note that the `Rows` collection (like any other collection) is zero-based, so the following line of code refers to the fourth row:

```
row = table.Rows(3)
```

Once the row variable is pointing to the correct row, we can just update the values for the appropriate columns:

```
row("FirstName") = "John"
row("LastName") = "Hartford"
```

Now that the data has been changed, we bind the data to a new grid so we can see the results:

```
DataGrid3.DataSource = table.DefaultView
DataGrid3.DataBind()
```

How It Works – Deleting Rows

Deleting a row from a table is simple; just use the `Delete` method of the `DataRow`. In the following code we index into the `Rows` collection (each member of which is a `DataRow`), specifying the row number as the index. Once again, remember that the `Rows` collection is zero-based, so this removes the sixth row:

```
table.Rows(5).Delete()
```

And as we saw before, we bind the data to a new grid:

```
DataGrid4.DataSource = table.DefaultView
DataGrid4.DataBind()
```

As you saw in the *Editing Rows* section of this Try-It-Out, we could have used the `Select` method of the table to return the rows to delete.

Updating the Original Data Source

Now that you've seen how to change data with a DataSet, you need to get that data back into the database, and to do that we use the DataAdapter. Remember in the previous chapter we said that the DataAdapter contains a `Command` object for each type of database operation, as shown in Figure 9.8:

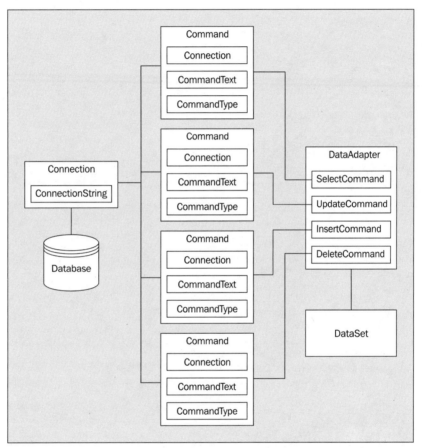

Figure 9-8

The question is how to set these commands, and what to set them to. You've seen the `SelectCommand` being used, but what about the other commands? Well, instead of learning SQL and worrying about this you can automate the process by using the `CommandBuilder`.

The `CommandBuilder` object automatically generates SQL commands using the `SelectCommand` as basis. This way you can concentrate on just coding without worrying about the actual way the commands are constructed. Let's see how easy this is.

The CommandBuilder is good for simple scenarios, but more advanced SQL code may be a problem. For a good description of these problems go to MSDN (http://msdn.microsoft.com/) and search for the article titled 'Weaning Developers from the CommandBuilder'.

Try It Out Auto-Generated Commands

1. Create a new blank ASP.NET page called `CommandObjects.aspx`.

2. Switch to All view and delete everything that's on the page.

3. Add the following code:

```
<%@ Import Namespace="System.Data" %>
<%@ Import Namespace="System.Data.OleDb" %>
<script language="VB" runat="server">

  Sub Page_Load(Sender As Object, E As EventArgs)

    Dim connectionString As String
    Dim strSQL           As String
    Dim data             As New DataSet()
    Dim dbConnection     As OleDbConnection
    Dim dataAdapter      As OleDbDataAdapter
    Dim commandBuilder   As OleDbCommandBuilder

    ' set the connection and query details
    connectionString = "Provider=Microsoft.Jet.OLEDB.4.0; " & _
                  "Data Source=C:\BegASPNET11\data\Northwind.mdb"
    strSQL = "SELECT EmployeeID, FirstName, LastName FROM Employees"

    ' open the connection and set the command
    dbConnection = New OledbConnection(connectionString)
    dataAdapter = New OledbDataAdapter(strSQL, dbConnection)

    ' create the other commands
    commandBuilder = New OleDbCommandBuilder(dataAdapter)
    dataAdapter.UpdateCommand = commandBuilder.GetUpdateCommand()
    dataAdapter.InsertCommand = commandBuilder.GetInsertCommand()
    dataAdapter.DeleteCommand = commandBuilder.GetDeleteCommand()

    ' now display the CommandText property from each command
    lblSelectCommand.Text = dataAdapter.SelectCommand.CommandText
    lblUpdateCommand.Text = dataAdapter.UpdateCommand.CommandText
    lblInsertCommand.Text = dataAdapter.InsertCommand.CommandText
    lblDeleteCommand.Text = dataAdapter.DeleteCommand.CommandText

  End Sub

</script>
<html>
 <body>
  <table border="1">
   <tr>
    <td>Command</td>
```

```
    <td>CommandText</td>
  </tr>
  <tr>
   <td>SelectCommand</td>
   <td><asp:Label id="lblSelectCommand" runat="server" />
  </tr>
  <tr>
   <td>UpdateCommand</td>
   <td><asp:Label id="lblUpdateCommand" runat="server" />
  </tr>
  <tr>
   <td>InsertCommand </td>
   <td><asp:Label id="lblInsertCommand" runat="server" />
  </tr>
  <tr>
   <td>DeleteCommand</td>
   <td><asp:Label id="lblDeleteCommand" runat="server" />
  </tr>
  </table>
 </body>
</html>
```

4. Save the file and run it to see the result shown in Figure 9-9:

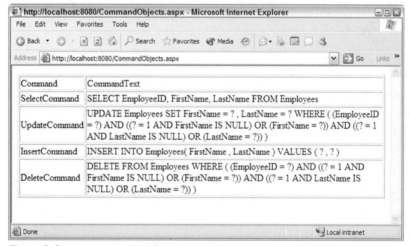

Figure 9-9

You can see the SQL statements to perform updates have been generated automatically. Let's see how that works.

How It Works

The start of this code is the same as we've seen before – creating a connection and an adapter. The only difference is the declaration of an `OleDbCommandBuilder` object. Like the DataAdapter, this deals directly with databases and therefore is in the `OleDb` namespace:

```
Dim commandBuilder    As OleDbCommandBuilder
```

Now create the `CommandBuilder` object, using the `dataAdapter` as the argument to the constructor. This ensures that the `CommandBuilder` picks up the `SelectCommand`:

```
commandBuilder = New OleDbCommandBuilder ( dataAdapter )
```

Next we use the `Get` methods to fill the other commands – there is a `Get` command for each type of `Command` object that we need to generate:

```
dataAdapter.UpdateCommand = commandBuilder.GetUpdateCommand()
dataAdapter.InsertCommand = commandBuilder.GetInsertCommand()
dataAdapter.DeleteCommand = commandBuilder.GetDeleteCommand()
```

Finally we display the `CommandText` for each of the `Command` objects:

```
lblSelectCommand.Text = dataAdapter.SelectCommand.CommandText
lblUpdateCommand.Text = dataAdapter.UpdateCommand.CommandText
lblInsertCommand.Text = dataAdapter.InsertCommand.CommandText
lblDeleteCommand.Text = dataAdapter.DeleteCommand.CommandText
```

You can see that the `GetUpdateCommand` simply generates a SQL UPDATE statement, and so on. Let's look at these in more detail.

The SelectCommand Property

You've already seen this before, but there is a reason we need to further talk about this. Our initial `SelectCommand` contains:

```
SELECT EmployeeID, FirstName, LastName FROM Employees
```

A unique key is required for the command builder to generate the other commands, so this time we have included the `EmployeeID` in the `SelectCommand`.

The UpdateCommand Property

The `UpdateCommand` is built to use a SQL UPDATE statement, for updating a row of data:

```
UPDATE Employees
SET FirstName = ?, LastName = ?
WHERE ((EmployeeID = ?)
AND ((? = 1 AND FirstName IS NULL)
  OR (FirstName =  ?))
AND ((? = 1 AND LastName IS NULL)
  OR (LastName = ?)) )
```

This consists of three parts:

- ❏ The UPDATE command followed by the table.

- ❏ The SET command, indicating fields that are to be updated. Here we are updating the FirstName and LastName fields (the EmployeeID field is a unique primary key and therefore can't be updated). The question marks are placeholders into which ADO.NET will place the updated values.

- ❏ The WHERE clause, which filters the data, ensuring that the correct row is updated.

The InsertCommand Property

The InsertCommand property is built to use a SQL INSERT statement, for inserting a new row of data:

```
INSERT INTO Employees(FirstName, LastName)
VALUES(?, ?)
```

This consists of two parts:

- ❏ The INSERT INTO statement, specifying the table name and, in parenthesis, the columns being updated.

- ❏ The VALUES statement, where the question marks are placeholders into which ADO.NET will place the column values for the new row.

The DeleteCommand Property

The DeleteCommand is built to use a SQL DELETE statement, for deleting a row of data:

```
DELETE FROM Employees
WHERE ((EmployeeID = ?)
AND ((? = 1 AND FirstName IS NULL)
  OR (FirstName =  ?))
AND ((? = 1 AND LastName IS NULL)
  OR (LastName = ?)) )
```

This consists of two parts:

- ❏ The DELETE FROM statement followed by the table name.

- ❏ The WHERE clause, which filters the data, ensuring that the correct row is deleted.

Updating the Database

Our examples so far have shown us how to modify data within a DataSet and how to generate the commands that will force these changes back to the database. What we now need to consider is how the database is actually updated. We've previously said the DataAdapter does this, and it's the Update method we need to use. So let's combine the examples in this page.

In the following try-it-out you'll update some data, use the CommandBuilder to generate the update commands, and then send those changes back to the database.

Try It Out Updating the Database

1. Create a new blank ASP.NET page called `UpdateDatabase.aspx`.

2. Switch to All view and delete everything that's there.

3. Add the following code (or if you're all fingers and thumbs like me, download it from www.wrox.com):

```
<%@ import Namespace="System.Data" %>
<%@ import Namespace="System.Data.OleDb" %>
<script runat="server">

    Sub Page_Load(Sender As Object, E As EventArgs)

        Dim connectionString As String
        Dim queryString As String
        Dim data As New DataSet()
        Dim dbConnection As OleDbConnection
        Dim dataAdapter As OleDbDataAdapter

        ' set the connection and query details
        connectionString = "Provider=Microsoft.Jet.OLEDB.4.0; " & _
                           "Data Source=C:\BegASPNET11\data\Northwind.mdb"
        queryString = "SELECT EmployeeID, FirstName, LastName FROM Employees;"

        ' open the connection and set the command
        dbConnection = New OledbConnection(connectionString)
        dataAdapter = New OledbDataAdapter(queryString, dbConnection)

        ' fill the dataset with the data
        dataAdapter.Fill(data, "Employees")

        ' bind the data grid to the data
        DataGrid1.DataSource = data.Tables("Employees")
        DataGrid1.DataBind()

        ' _____
        ' add a new row to the table
        Dim table  As DataTable
        Dim newRow As DataRow

        table = data.Tables("Employees")
        newRow = table.NewRow()
        newRow("FirstName") = "Norman"
        newRow("LastName") = "Blake"
        table.Rows.Add(newRow)

        ' add another new row. We'll be deleting the one above later.
        ' we can't delete existing rows from the database because of
        ' referential integrity (every employee also has Orders)
        newRow = table.NewRow()
        newRow("FirstName") = "Kasey"
        newRow("LastName") = "Chambers"
```

```vb
table.Rows.Add(newRow)


' bind the data grid to the new data
DataGrid2.DataSource = table
DataGrid2.DataBind()
' _____
' edit an existing row in the table
Dim objRow As DataRow

' The Rows collection is 0 indexed, so this changes the fourth row
objRow = table.Rows(3)
objRow("FirstName") = "John"
objRow("LastName") = "Hartford"

' bind the data grid to the new data
DataGrid3.DataSource = table
DataGrid3.DataBind()


' _____
' delete a row from the table

' The Rows collection is 0 indexed, so this removes the sixth row
table.Rows(table.Rows.Count - 2).Delete()

' bind the data grid to the new data
DataGrid4.DataSource = table
DataGrid4.DataBind()


' ================================================================
' generate the update commands
Dim commandBuilder    As OleDbCommandBuilder

commandBuilder = New OleDbCommandBuilder(dataAdapter)
dataAdapter.UpdateCommand = commandBuilder.GetUpdateCommand()
dataAdapter.InsertCommand = commandBuilder.GetInsertCommand()
dataAdapter.DeleteCommand = commandBuilder.GetDeleteCommand()


' ================================================================
' update the data store
dataAdapter.Update(data, "Employees")


' ================================================================
' refresh the data in the DataReader and bind it to a new grid
' to prove that the data store has been updated

queryString = "SELECT EmployeeID, FirstName, LastName FROM Employees"
dbConnection.Open()
Dim command As New OleDbCommand(queryString, dbConnection)
DataGridUpdated.DataSource = _
```

```
            command.ExecuteReader(CommandBehavior.CloseConnection)
        DataGridUpdated.DataBind()

    End Sub

</script>
<html>
<head>
</head>
<body>
    <table width="100%">
        <tbody>
            <tr>
                <td>
                    Original Data</td>
                <td>
                    Data with new Row</td>
                <td>
                    Data with edited Row</td>
                <td>
                    Data with deleted Row</td>
            </tr>
            <tr>
                <td valign="top">
                    <asp:DataGrid id="DataGrid1" runat="server"></asp:DataGrid>
                </td>
                <td valign="top">
                    <asp:DataGrid id="DataGrid2" runat="server"></asp:DataGrid>
                </td>
                <td valign="top">
                    <asp:DataGrid id="DataGrid3" runat="server"></asp:DataGrid>
                </td>
                <td valign="top">
                    <asp:DataGrid id="DataGrid4" runat="server"></asp:DataGrid>
                </td>
            </tr>
        </tbody>
    </table>
    <hr />
    Data fetched from database after the update:<br />
    <asp:DataGrid id="DataGridUpdated" runat="server"></asp:DataGrid>
</body>
</html>
```

4. Save the page, run it, and you'll see the results, as shown in Figure 9-10:

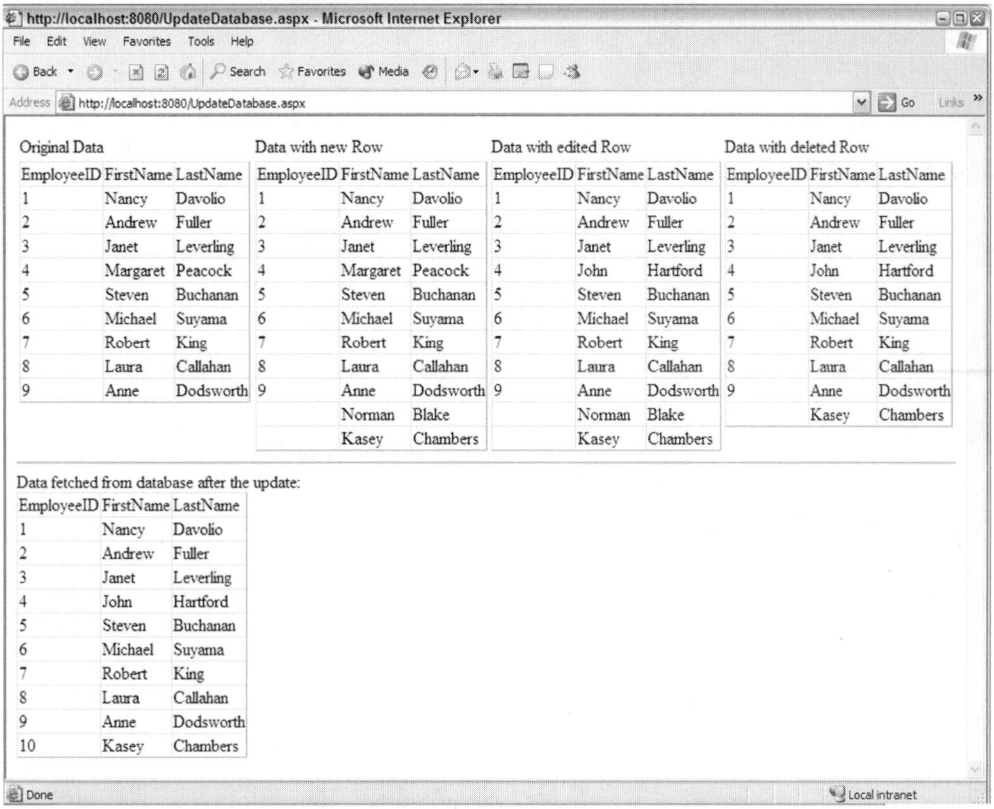

http://localhost:8080/UpdateDatabase.aspx - Microsoft Internet Explorer

File Edit View Favorites Tools Help

Back • Search Favorites Media

Address http://localhost:8080/UpdateDatabase.aspx   Go   Links »

Original Data		
EmployeeID	FirstName	LastName
1	Nancy	Davolio
2	Andrew	Fuller
3	Janet	Leverling
4	Margaret	Peacock
5	Steven	Buchanan
6	Michael	Suyama
7	Robert	King
8	Laura	Callahan
9	Anne	Dodsworth

Data with new Row		
EmployeeID	FirstName	LastName
1	Nancy	Davolio
2	Andrew	Fuller
3	Janet	Leverling
4	Margaret	Peacock
5	Steven	Buchanan
6	Michael	Suyama
7	Robert	King
8	Laura	Callahan
9	Anne	Dodsworth
	Norman	Blake
	Kasey	Chambers

Data with edited Row		
EmployeeID	FirstName	LastName
1	Nancy	Davolio
2	Andrew	Fuller
3	Janet	Leverling
4	John	Hartford
5	Steven	Buchanan
6	Michael	Suyama
7	Robert	King
8	Laura	Callahan
9	Anne	Dodsworth
	Norman	Blake
	Kasey	Chambers

Data with deleted Row		
EmployeeID	FirstName	LastName
1	Nancy	Davolio
2	Andrew	Fuller
3	Janet	Leverling
4	John	Hartford
5	Steven	Buchanan
6	Michael	Suyama
7	Robert	King
8	Laura	Callahan
9	Anne	Dodsworth
	Kasey	Chambers

Data fetched from database after the update:

EmployeeID	FirstName	LastName
1	Nancy	Davolio
2	Andrew	Fuller
3	Janet	Leverling
4	John	Hartford
5	Steven	Buchanan
6	Michael	Suyama
7	Robert	King
8	Laura	Callahan
9	Anne	Dodsworth
10	Kasey	Chambers

Done   Local intranet

Figure 9-10

How It Works

You've seen all of this code before; the only new part is the update:

```
dataAdapter.Update(data, "Employees")
```

Calling the Update method of the dataAdapter sends any pending changes back to the database. The two arguments are:

❑ The DataSet containing the pending changes.

❑ The name of the table within the DataSet.

This actually looks through the table for rows that have changed, and then executes the appropriate Command object. If a new row has been added, the InsertCommand is run with values from the new row. In reality you wouldn't update your data in the Page_Load() event – you'd probably have a button on the page allowing the users to send their edits back to the database, and you'd have an event procedure for that button. It's at that stage you'd update the data. However, this example works fine for the purpose of explaining how simple it is to send the changes back to the database.

Updating Databases Using a Command

The preceding examples show the modification of data by use of a DataSet and a DataAdapter, but this isn't the only way it can be done. In the previous chapter you saw the use of the Command object for running SQL commands and we mentioned the use of the ExecuteNonQuery method. Let's take a look at how to use this.

Try It Out Executing Commands Directly

1. Create a new blank ASP.NET page called CommandExecute.aspx.

2. Add a Label and a TextBox control. Change the Text property of the Label to First Name, and the ID property of the TextBox to txtFirstName.

3. Underneath the first two controls add a second Label and a second TextBox control. Change the Text property of the Label to Last Name, and the ID property of the TextBox to txtLastName.

4. Underneath these add a button, changing the Text property to Run and the ID property to btnRun. Your page should look like Figure 9-11:

Figure 9-11

5. Double-click the Run button to create the event handler and add the following code:

```
Dim connectionString As String = "Provider=Microsoft.Jet.OLEDB.4.0; " & _
                                  "Data Source=C:\BegASPNET11\data\Northwind.mdb"
Dim dbConnection As New OleDbConnection(connectionString)
dbConnection.Open()

Dim commandString As String = "INSERT INTO Employees(FirstName, LastName) " & _
                              "Values(@FirstName, @LastName)"

Dim dbCommand As New OleDbCommand(commandString, dbConnection)
Dim firstNameParam As New OleDbParameter("@FirstName", OleDbType.VarChar, 10)
firstNameParam.Value = txtFirstName.Text
dbCommand.Parameters.Add(firstNameParam)
Dim lastNameParam As New OleDbParameter("@LastName", OleDbType.VarChar, 20)
LastNameParam.Value = txtLastName.Text
```

```
dbCommand.Parameters.Add(LastNameParam)

dbCommand.ExecuteNonQuery()

dbConnection.Close()
```

6. Switch to **All** view and add the following, either at the top of the page, or underneath the
    `<%@ Page %>` directive:

```
<%@ Import Namespace="System.Data.OleDb" %>
```

7. Save the file and run it.

8. Enter a first and last name and press the button.

9. Switch to Web Matrix and open the **Data Explorer**. Pick the `Employees` table, open it, and you'll
    see the newly added data, as shown in Figure 9-12:

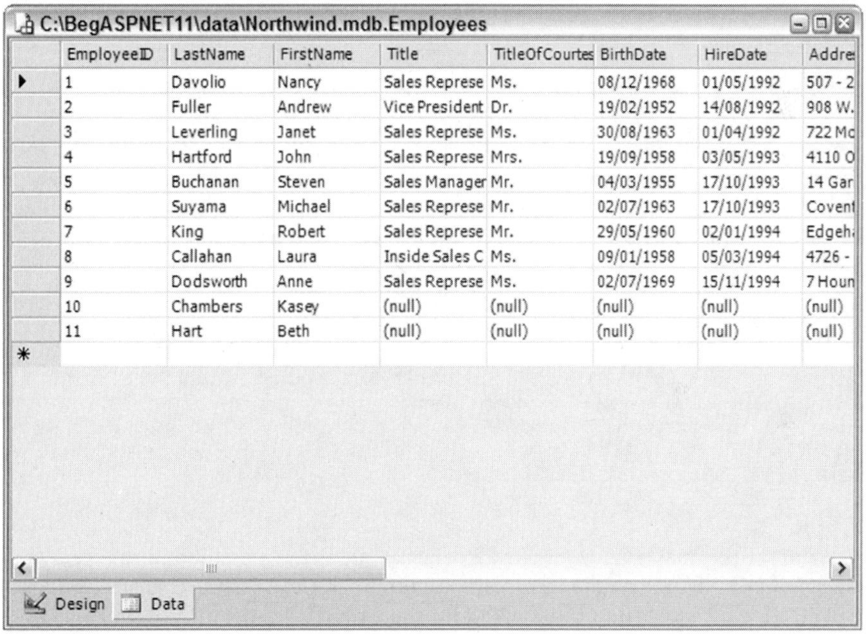

EmployeeID	LastName	FirstName	Title	TitleOfCourtesy	BirthDate	HireDate	Addre
1	Davolio	Nancy	Sales Represe	Ms.	08/12/1968	01/05/1992	507 - 2
2	Fuller	Andrew	Vice President	Dr.	19/02/1952	14/08/1992	908 W.
3	Leverling	Janet	Sales Represe	Ms.	30/08/1963	01/04/1992	722 Mc
4	Hartford	John	Sales Represe	Mrs.	19/09/1958	03/05/1993	4110 O
5	Buchanan	Steven	Sales Manager	Mr.	04/03/1955	17/10/1993	14 Gar
6	Suyama	Michael	Sales Represe	Mr.	02/07/1963	17/10/1993	Coventr
7	King	Robert	Sales Represe	Mr.	29/05/1960	02/01/1994	Edgeh
8	Callahan	Laura	Inside Sales C	Ms.	09/01/1958	05/03/1994	4726 -
9	Dodsworth	Anne	Sales Represe	Ms.	02/07/1969	15/11/1994	7 Houn
10	Chambers	Kasey	(null)	(null)	(null)	(null)	(null)
11	Hart	Beth	(null)	(null)	(null)	(null)	(null)

C:\BegASPNET11\data\Northwind.mdb.Employees

Design   Data

Figure 9-12

You can see that I entered **Beth Hart** as my names (I just happen to be listening to her album at the moment!).

How It Works

You've seen most of the code before, but there are a couple of differences. We first start with the connection, which we open explicitly. That's because we are going to run a command directly, which needs the connection to be open:

```
Dim connectionString As String = "Provider=Microsoft.Jet.OLEDB.4.0; " & _
  "Data Source=C:\BegASPNET11\data\Northwind.mdb"
Dim dbConnection As New OleDbConnection(connectionString)
dbConnection.Open()
```

We then define the command we are going to run. Notice that it's an SQL INSERT statement, but one that uses placeholders for parameters. We do so because the user is going to supply the values, and using parameters is the secure method of doing this:

```
Dim commandString As String = "INSERT INTO Employees(FirstName, LastName) " & _
    "Values(@FirstName, @LastName)"
```

We then create the Command object, using the command string shown earlier and the already opened connection:

```
Dim dbCommand As New OleDbCommand(commandString, dbConnection)
```

Now we can define our parameters. The first argument defines the parameter name and must match one of the parameter names defined in the SQL statements. The second argument defines the type of the parameter, and in this case they are both character strings (VarChar is what we use for general strings that have a variable length). The final argument is the length of the column.

Once the parameter object has been created, we set the Value property to be the contents for that parameter, and these are the values of the TextBox controls:

```
Dim firstNameParam As New OleDbParameter("@FirstName", OleDbType.VarChar, 10)
firstNameParam.Value = txtFirstName.Text
dbCommand.Parameters.Add(firstNameParam)
Dim lastNameParam As New OleDbParameter("@LastName", OleDbType.VarChar, 20)
LastNameParam.Value = txtLastName.Text
dbCommand.Parameters.Add(LastNameParam)
```

Now we can run the command, so we use the ExecuteNonQuery() method of the command. This simply instructs ADO.NET to run the command but not to expect a result. This way it doesn't have to worry about creating a DataSet or a DataReader for the data. This gives us a slight performance increase – if no data is going to be returned, there's no point creating an object just in case some data is returned.

```
dbCommand.ExecuteNonQuery()
```

Finally, we close the connection:

```
dbConnection.Close()
```

As you can see, this method is much simpler than the DataSet method of updating data, and is certainly the best method to use for small amounts of data.

Summary

In this chapter we extended our knowledge of ADO.NET, moving from data reading to advanced handling. We looked at the DataSet in more detail, seeing how it's really a container object, having a collection of `Tables`, and it's these tables, which provide us with access to the data by way of the `Rows` collection. We also saw that data can be updated within the DataSet, but is still disconnected from the database.

We then looked at ways in which to update the data in database, first using the changes made to a DataSet, and then by using commands to directly update data.

Now it's time to combine the techniques we've seen in this book, as we move on to creating a sample application.

Exercises

1. Load a DataSet with the `Shippers` table from Northwind and add the following data into it:

   ❑   Company Name: FastShippers

   ❑   Phone: (503) 555-9384

2. Using the `CommandBuilder` object, create an `InsertCommand` to insert this new data, and send the changes back to the database.

3. Using direct SQL commands change the phone number of FastShippers to (503) 555-0000.

4. Use the Web Matrix data templates to create an Editable DataGrid. Have a look at the code and see how many familiar techniques you see.

10

ASP.NET Server Controls

Up to this point in the book, we have covered a lot of theory about how to create Web pages, and we've used .NET's object-oriented approach to create some interesting pages, including some that display data from a database, as in the previous chapter. While creating these pages, we've used a few of the most popular server controls (the `Button` and `Label` controls for example). However, we haven't explored their characteristics in great detail – now's our chance! In this chapter, we'll start to build up a simple Web site, using a wide variety of controls.

Having worked through the previous chapters, you will now be familiar with the fact that ASP.NET has a *control-based*, *event-driven* architecture. Pages are built using controls (textboxes, buttons, data lists or grids), and these controls generate and can react to events (the clicking of a hyperlink, the selecting of items). This chapter concentrates on two key concepts, *controls* and *events*, and how they are at the core of every ASP.NET application you will write.

Server controls are reusable components that can render plain output to the browser, just like standard HTML tags, but they have the additional ability to be processed on the server, and can be accessed just like any other .NET object. They can respond to events, get and set properties, and so on. These controls are processed on the server where, for example, data from a data source is retrieved and combined with the server control when the page is compiled. When that page is requested, the appropriate HTML or JavaScript content is sent back to the browser, which displays the finished page. This process is known as *rendering*.

There are two main types of server controls available to us: *Web controls* (like the `<asp:button ... >` control) and *HTML server controls* (simple HTML elements with a `runat="server"` attribute). This chapter will concentrate on Web controls for the most part, though we'll briefly discuss how HTML server controls work.

Like normal HTML tags, but with a stronger adherence to XML formatting rules, Web controls are declared using tag syntax. The following example declares an ASP.NET `Button` control and assigns values to three of the control's properties:

```
<asp:Button id="SampleButton" runat="server"
            Text="I'm A Sample Button!"/>
```

One of the unique qualities of Web controls is that even though their tag syntax is different from that of HTML tags, every Web control is rendered (processed and converted) to standard HTML after being processed on the server. Each control renders in a different way, but they all have the full set of standard HTML tags at their disposal when they are rendered. Some of the Web controls provide the ability to render rich Web content – for example, a Calendar control for displaying dates, a `DataGrid` control for displaying data, as well as other controls that we will explore throughout this chapter.

As we delve into the world of controls and events, you would benefit greatly from having a copy of ASP.NET Web Matrix installed on your system. Web Matrix is a superb tool for putting together simple sites, like the one we will create soon.

In this chapter, we'll look at:

❑ A review of the syntax and benefits of Web controls

❑ A brief recap of the lifecycle of an ASP.NET page

❑ Using a variety of Web controls on a Web form that starts the Wrox United application that we'll be developing in the following chapters

❑ Introducing data rendering controls – a very powerful group of controls for displaying data

❑ Using rich controls like the `Calendar` control to render complex HTML, adding a minimum of code

❑ The extra controls offered by Web Matrix that we can use in our applications

❑ Validating user input using validation controls

Server controls are such a major part of ASP.NET that we won't be able to cover everything here, but you will gain a good understanding of how they work and how to use them.

The Wrox United Application

Whether you call it soccer or football, you'll no doubt be familiar with this game – eleven players, a ball, two goals, and a legion of dedicated supporters! Our application will be the Web site of a fictitious soccer team, known as Wrox United, who compete in a small league. Figure 10-1 shows the finished application:

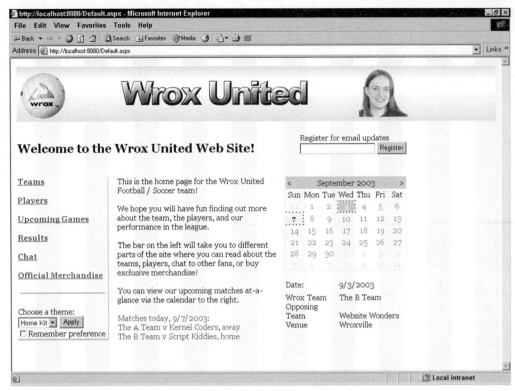

Figure 10-1

As we work through this chapter and the following three chapters, we'll build up the core of this site using Web Matrix. In *Appendix D*, we duplicate some of the features of the Wrox United application when we discuss creating Web applications using Visual Studio.NET.

ASP.NET Web Controls

Day-to-day usage of the different types of controls is possibly the best way to realize how useful they are. Whenever we add a single line of code to an ASP.NET page to add a simple control, we're actually adding a lot of functionality that has been hidden away from us. The end result is that the complicated inner workings of the control are abstracted away from us, leaving us to worry about day-to-day tasks like designing pages, without having to write mountains of code to make pages functional. Anyone who has experience of developing with older Web technologies like ASP will appreciate how simple Web development becomes when they have a full set of controls at their fingertips! ASP.NET has a broad set of Web controls that can be grouped into four broad categories:

❑ **Basic controls**: (sometimes referred to as *intrinsic* controls) This group contains controls that when rendered, look and feel like standard HTML elements, but are processed on the server, and have a standard set of properties and events that can be accessed by the server which are common to all of these controls. Examples include the `Button`, `CheckBox`, and `TextBox` controls, which all have `Text`, `Font`, `ForeColor`, and `Visible` properties, among many others.

❑ **Data-list controls**: These controls are used for binding and displaying data from a data source, for example, the `DataGrid` and `DataList` controls.

❑ **Rich controls**: These controls have no direct HTML counterparts. Rich controls like the `Calendar` control are made up of multiple components, and the HTML generated will typically consist of numerous HTML tags (as well as client-side script) to render the control in the browser.

❑ **Validation controls**: These controls are designed to improve user interaction with pages. They can be used in a wide range of situations, from ensuring that a password is entered correctly, to ensuring that only valid data is entered into textboxes and submitted to a database server. Textboxes used to get data into databases without any validation logic can be used by hackers to bring down entire sites! Examples of validation controls include the `RequiredFieldValidator`, which can be used to ensure that data is provided in all mandatory fields. We'll see these controls in action in the next chapter.

As you start to build the example in this chapter, you will be working with each of the different types of controls listed here. You will also learn to write event handlers for the various events raised by each of these controls, for example, the clicking of a button, or the selection of an item in a drop-down box.

The introduction briefly mentioned that you can add a `runat="server"` attribute to HTML tags to process them on the server, so let's take a look now at what this means and how it works. We'll then compare HTML server controls with Web controls.

HTML Server Controls

HTML server controls are simple HTML tags with a `runat="server"` attribute, which enables developers to access them programmatically and work with them in a manner similar to Web controls. So, why include these types of controls when we have Web controls? Well, HTML server controls do have some advantages over Web controls, including:

❑ Web developers coming from an ASP3 or similar background may prefer to work with the HTML style of control that they're used to.

❑ Developers can convert existing HTML tags to HTML server controls fairly easily, thus gaining some server-side programmatic access to the control.

When a `runat="server"` attribute is added to an HTML tag, the tag *becomes* a control. Each of these controls derives its functionality from the `System.Web.UI.HtmlControls.HtmlControl` base class.

Compare the following lines of code:

```
<input id="MyHTMLTextBox" type="text"
       name="MyHTMLTextBox">
```

and

```
<input id="MyHTMLTextBox" type="text"
       name="MyHTMLTextBox" runat="server">
```

The first tag is a simple HTML tag that the server doesn't particularly care about. It will be rendered exactly as it appears here. The second snippet of code adds the magic words `runat="server"`, which means we can add the following code to our page:

```
Sub Page_Load
    MyHTMLTextBox.Value = "Hello world!"
End Sub
```

This would produce the output shown in Figure 10-2:

Figure 10-2

There is an HTML server control object for every corresponding HTML tag, so any standard HTML tag, from a `<div>` to an `<img>`, can be processed on the server.

> Note, however, that you always need to add an identifier for all server-side controls (in our example, we used `id="MyHTMLTextBox"`), to provide a unique name for the object, enabling you to reference it in your server-side code.

Like Web controls, HTML server controls offer a variety of features that include:

❑ **Programmatic Object Model**: HTML server controls can be accessed programmatically on the server. Each HTML server control is an object and, as such, you can access its various properties as well as get and set them in your method or event-handler code.

❑ **Event Processing**: HTML server controls provide a mechanism to write event handlers in much the same way you would for a client-based form. The only difference is that the event is handled in the server code.

❑ **Automatic Value Caching**: When form data is posted to the server, the values that the user entered into the HTML server controls are automatically maintained when the page is sent back to the browser. The magic behind this functionality is the result of a property called `ViewState` that all ASP.NET Web controls inherit.

❑ **Custom Attributes**: You can add any attributes you need to an HTML server control. The .NET Framework will render them to the client browser without any changes. This enables you to add browser--specific attributes to your controls.

❑ **Validation**: You can actually assign an ASP.NET validation control to do the work of validating an HTML server control. Validation controls are covered in the next chapter.

One situation where you might consider using HTML server controls in your ASP.NET pages is when you have an existing HTML page that you would rather not rewrite from scratch, but still would like to write some server-side code to access properties of the various controls on the page.

> **A neat trick – if you want to edit the properties of a plain HTML tag on your Web page using the Web Matrix properties editor, you can add a runat="server" attribute to the tag you want to edit, making the control appear in the list of available controls in the Properties pane. All you have to do then is select the control and edit the properties. When you have finished, you can simply remove the runat="server" attribute to change the control back into a tag.**

HTML Server Controls versus Web Controls

Given that Microsoft has provided two distinct categories of server controls (HTML and Web controls), with both sets of controls sharing some degree of overlapping functionality, you may be a bit confused as to which set of controls you should use within your Web forms. The short answer is simply this: you can use both! It's perfectly fine to mix the usage of HTML server controls and ASP.NET server controls within your Web forms – using one set of controls does not restrict you to that control type. Despite the overlap in functionality, there are some clear distinctions between these controls that you should be aware of when developing your ASP.NET pages:

Control Feature	HTML Server Control Behavior	ASP.NET Web Control Behavior
Control Abstraction	HTML server controls provide a one-to-one mapping with a corresponding HTML tag and offer no real abstraction.	ASP.NET Web controls offer a high level of abstraction – they don't necessarily map directly to any existing HTML control. For example, an ASP.NET `Calendar` control has no single HTML control equivalent – it's actually made up from a collection of several controls. As such, you will often hear the phrase *rich control* associated with many ASP.NET server controls.

Control Feature	HTML Server Control Behavior	ASP.NET Web Control Behavior
Object Model	HTML server controls utilize a very HTML-centric object model. Additionally, the HTML attribute convention is not strongly typed, so you could set `<div width="huge" ...>`. This would be sent to the browser, but the browser would not be able to render it to be "huge" (there is no such attribute), so it would revert to a standard width.	ASP.NET Web controls provide a consistent and type-safe programming model, meaning that the server will prevent an invalid page from being rendered. An error page will be displayed when you run a page that contains a control with a property that is set to an invalid value. Additionally, code design environments like Web Matrix or Visual Studio won't let you set the properties in the Properties panel to an invalid value (for example, attempting `<asp:panel width="huge"...>` will cause an error message to be displayed in the designer). All ASP.NET Web controls inherit a set of base properties and methods (such as `ForeColor`, `BackColor`, `Font`, and so on.)
Target Browser	HTML server controls do not automatically detect the capabilities of the browser loading the page. It's up to you to make sure the HTML controls you use are compatible with the browsers that might be consuming your page.	ASP.NET Web controls automatically detect the client browser requesting the page and render the controls based on the browser's capabilities.
How the Control Renders	HTML server controls provide you with complete control over what gets rendered and sent to the client browser.	ASP.NET web controls provide a higher level of abstraction in terms of how the controls are rendered. The properties you choose to set for a control may play a role in controlling how and what is actually rendered, but the process of rendering is handled by the ASP.NET runtime. If you really do want or need full control over the output you can dig deep into .NET and customize controls or write your own – a topic which is briefly covered in *Chapter 13*.

Web Controls

ASP.NET's Web controls are the building blocks for creating ASP.NET Web forms. Like their HTML counterparts, Web controls provide all the basic controls necessary for building Web forms (`Button`, `ListBox`, `CheckBox`, `TextBox`, and many more), as well as a collection of rich controls, like the `Calendar` and `DataGrid` controls. As we discussed above, these controls have a rich object model, the ability to detect which browser is displaying them, and a set of properties and events that we can use as we develop sites.

Rich Object Model

Web controls draw from the rich features of the .NET Framework. As such, they inherit their base methods, properties, and events from either the `System.Web.UI.WebControls.Control` or `System.Web.UI.WebControls.WebControl` base classes.

As discussed in *Chapter 7*, inheritance is a key feature of object-oriented design and programming. When instantiating a Web control, you're really creating an instance of an object that gives you access to the properties, methods, and events of its base class and interfaces. Web controls have style properties, which are instances of `CssStyle` objects. We can set colors using standard .NET `Color` objects, and specify dimensions using strongly typed Web measurement objects. By comparison, HTML controls generally have weakly-typed properties mapping to their attributes, allowing any string to be set as a value.

Automatic Browser Detection

Web controls detect client browser capabilities and create the appropriate HTML and client-side script for the client browser. The difference in rendering won't be apparent with a control such as a `Button` control, but you may find that a script-rich control like a validation control may render differently on different browsers. Or you may find that older browsersthat aren't CSS-compliant may have style rendered as old-style attributes, instead of `style=""` attributes. The HTML (or the script) rendered for the different browsers is all handled by the Web control, and by and large, the developer does not have to worry too much about client browser capabilities or limitations.

Properties

All Web controls share a common set of base properties, as well as their own class-specific properties. These properties allow you to change the look and behavior of the control. Some of the more common base class properties shared by all ASP.NET server controls include:

❑ `BackColor`: The background color of the control; for example, `AliceBlue`, `AntiqueWhite`, or even a hexadecimal value like `#C8C8C8`.

❑ `ForeColor`: The foreground color of the control.

❑ `BorderWidth`: The width of the border of the control, in units of either exs, ems, pixels, points, picas, inches, centimeters (or millimeters), or a percentage value.

❑ Visible: If set to True (the default for all controls) the control will be displayed. If set to False, the control will be hidden. This property is useful for when you want to hide a particular control on the Web form. For example, if you were obtaining details from a user, and in one control they had declared their nationality as British, you might want to hide another control that asks them for their Social Security Number (or SSN; only US residents have a SSN), while displaying a third that asks for their National Insurance number (only UK residents have an NI number).

❑ Enabled: Whether on not the control is enabled. If set to False, the control will appear grayed out, and will not process or respond to events until its Enabled property is set to True.

❑ Height: The height of the control.

❑ Width: The width of the control.

❑ ToolTip: Hover text displayed dynamically on mouse rollover. Typically used to supply additional help without taking up space on the form.

❑ Font-Size: Size of the control's font.

The above properties are merely an abbreviated listing; many more common properties are available (you can investigate these in depth in the SDK documentation).

The following is an example of an ASP.NET Button Web control with several of the common base class properties assigned, to give it a rather distinctive look:

```
<asp:Button id="MyButton" runat="server"
            Text="I'm an ASP.NET server control Button!"
   BackColor="purple"
   ForeColor="white"
   BorderWidth="4"
   BorderStyle="Ridge"
   ToolTip="Common Properties Example!"
   Font-Name="Tahoma"
   Font-Size="16"
   Font-Bold="True"
/>
```

When rendered and displayed in the client browser, the button will look something like Figure 10-3:

I'm an ASP.NET server control Button!

Figure 10-3

The HTML generated for this control (for Internet Explorer 6.0) looks like this:

```
<input type="submit" name="MyButton"
       value="I'm an ASP.NET server control Button!"
       id="MyButton" title="Common Properties Example!"
       style="color:White;background-color:Purple;
              border-width:4px;border-style:Ridge;
              font-family:Tahoma;font-size:16pt;font-weight:bold;" />
```

Have a go yourself – to look at the HTML, just select View | Source from your browser.

As an alternative method of adding styling, all Web controls have a `style` property. This property acts in a similar manner to the `style` attribute of an HTML tag, and makes it possible to apply any CSS-compatible style to a control. Using this property, the code used to generate this control would be as follows:

```
<asp:Button id="MyButton" runat="server"
            Text="I'm an ASP.NET server control Button!"
            style="color:White;background-color:Purple;
                   border-width:4px;border-style:Ridge;
                   font-family:Tahoma;font-size:16pt;font-weight:bold;"/>
```

Note that this code looks very similar to the code produced when the control is rendered.

Finally, you can also use the `CssClass` attribute of any Web control to specify that the control inherits styling information from the appropriate class in the underlying stylesheet for the page. As an example of this, the button could have been written as follows:

```
<asp:Button id="MyButton" runat="server"
            Text="I'm an ASP.NET server control Button!"
            CssClass="StylishButton"/>
```

The appropriate CSS stylesheet would then need to contain the following declaration:

```
.StylishButton{
  color:White;
  background-color:Purple;
  border-width:4px;
  border-style:Ridge;
  font-family:Tahoma;
  font-size:16pt;
  font-weight:bold;
}
```

These three variations on the same button are included in the code download for this chapter, along with a very simple stylesheet. They demonstrate that despite the code written in each of the three cases being different, the rendered appearance is the same.

Events

As seen in *Chapter 3*, an event handler is essentially the code you write to respond to a particular event. For example, a `Button` control raises a `Click` event after being clicked; a `ListBox` control raises a `SelectedIndexChanged` event when its list selection changes; a `TextBox` control raises a `TextChanged` event whenever its text has changed and the active focus on the form changes, and so on. ASP.NET Web controls support the ability to assign event handlers that execute specific code in response to particular events raised by an ASP.NET Web control.

Events and event handlers are extremely useful to us Web developers, because they provide a mechanism for responding dynamically to events in our Web pages. For example, let's say you were asked to write a page that contained a button that listed the current date and time to the latest second. For demonstration purposes, when the user clicks on the button, you might want the date and time to be displayed as the button's new text. To achieve this result, you'll need to *wire up* an event handler for your `Button` control. Let's do this in Web Matrix.

Try It Out   Creating an Event Handler

1.   Fire up Web Matrix and create a new `SimpleButton.aspx` ASP.NET page called within your `C:\BegASPNET11\Ch10` folder. Switch to HTML view, and enter the following code:

```
<form runat="server">
  <asp:Button id="CurrentTimeButton" runat="server"
      Text="Click for current time..." OnClick="UpdateTime" />
</form>
```

2.   Now switch to Code view and add the following method to handle the clicking of the button:

```
Public Sub UpdateTime (sender As Object, e As EventArgs)
   ' update the button text with current time
   CurrentTimeButton.Text = DateTime.Now.ToLongTimeString ()
End Sub
```

3.   If you run the code in your browser, you'll see the button we created, and when you click on it, you'll see the current time, as shown in Figure 10-4:

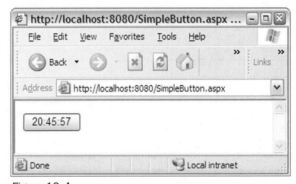

Figure 10-4

How It Works

In this example, we added a `Button` control to a form, and named it `CurrentTimeButton`. We also set its `Text` property to `Click for current time...`, which is the first thing you see when you run the page:

```
<asp:Button id="CurrentTimeButton" runat="server"
    Text="Click for current time..." OnClick="UpdateTime" />
```

Additionally, we set the `OnClick` property to `UpdateTime()`, the method that we added to handle the `Click` event. We then added the event handler to update the button text with the current time whenever the button is clicked:

```
Public Sub UpdateTime (sender As Object, e As EventArgs)
    ' update the button text with current time
    CurrentTimeButton.Text = DateTime.Now.ToLongTimeString ()
End Sub
```

The body of this method has just one line of code, which assigns the value
`DateTime.Now.ToLongTimeString ()` to the `Text` property of the `CurrentTimeButton`. This is
basically saying, "when the `UpdateTime()` method is run, display the current time in the `Text` property
of `CurrentTimeButton`, which is a string datatype".

> *The `DateTime` class is a standard .NET class, which has a `Now()` method that returns the current date
> and time. This date/time value can be displayed in many ways, using different methods, including
> `ToShortDateString()` and `ToLongTimeString()`.*

Page Lifecycle

Let's take a moment to briefly consider the series of stages that happen whenever an ASP.NET page is
requested, how that page is loaded, when events are raised, and when controls are rendered. When you
create a page, you are really creating a new `Page` object (instantiating a new instance of the `Page` class).
The `Page` class defines a series of methods, properties, and events that are available to all ASP.NET
pages. When loading a page for the first time, you might, for example, want to preload the `Page` object's
controls with values from a database, or set property values of various controls on the page dynamically.

Let's quickly look at the order of events that happen on the server every time a page is requested. This is
shown in Figure 10-5:

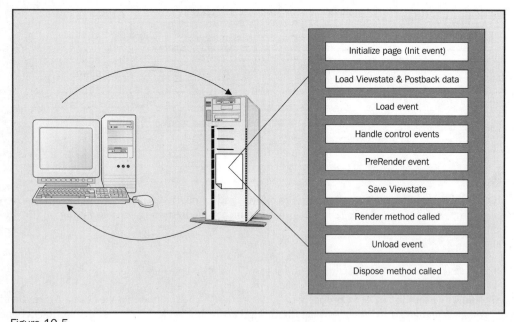

Figure 10-5

When a page is requested, the server runs through the page lifecycle as it prepares the page for the browser. Let's quickly run through the main items in this list:

❏ **Init event**: This is the first stage in the life of the page. If you wanted to, you could add code to the `Page_Init()` method to handle this event. The code in this method will then be processed before any code in the `Page_Load()` method, and before any event handlers are processed. You can use it to initialize variables or objects that you may need later.

❏ **Load event**: The `Page_Load()` method handles the `Load` event of the page, and is used to contain any code that needs to be processed each time the page is loaded. We'll look at this in more detail soon.

❏ **Handle control events**: From the clicking of a button to the selection changing in a listbox, this stage is where any event handler methods are processed. We've seen many of these events in action already, and we'll soon meet many more. At this point, remember that any code in your `Page_Load()` method will have already been run.

❏ **PreRender event**: The `Page_PreRender()` method is processed when this event is fired. You can add code here to perform any last minute processing after all the control events are processed. We'll see an example of how to use this in the next chapter.

❏ **Render method called**: At this stage, the ASP.NET processor starts converting the ASP.NET code into HTML. It's this stage that produces the HTML that is sent to the browser. It's possible to add code to cause controls to be rendered differently, thereby customizing their appearance. We'll look at this in detail when we learn more about creating custom server controls in *Chapter 13*.

❏ **Unload event**: This stage is used for last minute cleanup of any objects that you may have used, like database connections. We'll see an example of this in just a moment. Note that, because this event is handled *after* the render method is called, you can't now affect the appearance of the page.

❏ **Dispose method called**: This is where the page object that was processed is removed from the .NET managed memory space in the Web server. This is called behind the scenes when any .NET object falls out of scope and is no longer needed. Hence, once a page is sent to the client, the server can forget about how that page was rendered on that occasion, and free up memory.

The following listings provide an overview of some of these methods that are commonly overridden in your ASPX `Page` object implementation that allow you to perform processing during the various stages of the page's lifetime.

Page_Load()

The `Page_Load()` method is invoked anytime the ASP.NET page is requested – in other words, when the page is loaded for the first time, when it is refreshed, or when it is reloaded in response to the clicking of a button. The following is an example implementation of the `Page_Load()` method:

```
Sub Page_Load(Sender As Object, e As EventArgs)
  If Not Page.IsPostback Then
    ' First time page loads -
    ' perform initialization here!
  End If
End Sub
```

The most interesting part of the preceding listing is the reference to the `Page` object's `IsPostback` property. The `IsPostback` property is significant because it can be used to distinguish whether or not a page is being loaded for the very first time, or if it's being loaded as the result of what is commonly referred to as a *Postback*. In other words, if a `Button` control was clicked, a `Click` event would be raised and the form data would be posted (sent) *back* to the server – hence the term Postback. You have seen this technique several times in the past few chapters.

The most common uses for implementing the `Page_Load()` method in your ASPX pages are to:

❑ Check whether this is the first time the page is being processed, or to perform processing after the page is refreshed

❑ Perform data binding the first time the page is processed, or re-valuate data-binding expressions on subsequent round trips to, for example, display the data sorted differently

❑ Read and update control properties

You'll often use the `If Not Page.IsPostback` construct in your pages when binding data to controls on a page. Minimizing the amount of times you have to query a database is essential if you want a site with good performance, and in many cases, you will only want to bind data once, because that data will be stored in the page's *ViewState*.

Event Handling

The next major part of a page's lifecycle is the event handling stage. After an ASPX page is loaded and displayed, additional event handlers will be invoked when control events are raised. For example, after a user clicks an ASP.NET `Button` control, the `Click` event will be raised, thus causing a postback to the server so that the event can be handled. If an event handler is written and assigned to process the `Click` event for that particular control, it will be invoked whenever the `Button` control is clicked.

Not all controls perform this type of automatic posting-back to the server when an event is raised. For example, the `TextBox` control does not, by default, post back notification to the server when its text changes. Similarly, the `ListBox` and `CheckBox` server controls do not, by default, post back event notifications to the server every time their selection state changes. For these particular controls, their `AutoPostBack` property (which can be set to either `True` or `False`) would need to explicitly be set to `True` in the control's declaration (or set programmatically within the code) to enable automatic post back of events/state changes to the server for processing.

If you create an ASP.NET Web control that performs server-side processing whenever the control's state changes (such as when a `CheckBox` is checked) and you don't seem to be getting the results you expect, check if the control has an `AutoPostBack` property, and if so, set it to `True`. This property typically defaults to `False` if not explicitly declared when the control was defined.

Page_Unload()

`Page_Unload()` serves the opposite purpose to the `Page_Load()` method. The `Page_Unload()` method is used to perform any cleanup just prior to the page being unloaded. You would want to implement the `Page_Unload()` method in cases where any of the following actions need to be performed:

- ❏   Closing files

- ❏   Closing database connections

- ❏   Any other cleanup or discarding of server-side objects or resources

The following is an example implementation of the `Page_Unload()` method:

```
Sub Page_Unload(Sender As Object, e As EventArgs)
    ' Perform any post-load processing here!
End Sub
```

One thing to note is that the unloading of a page doesn't happen when you close the browser or move to another page. The `Page_Unload()` event happens when the page has finished being processed by ASP.NET, and before it's sent to the browser, when it is too late to do anything that will affect the appearance of the page.

Right – now that we've spent time looking at how pages and basic controls work, let's put it together by starting our Wrox United example.

Understanding Web Controls: The Wrox United Application

The Wrox United application that we'll be building up over the next few chapters has a database with some sample data, and a series of pages that query and display that data. We'll be using a variety of controls and events, and we'll examine each of these in turn as we encounter them.

Let's take a quick look at the database structure for the application. This is shown in Figure 10-6:

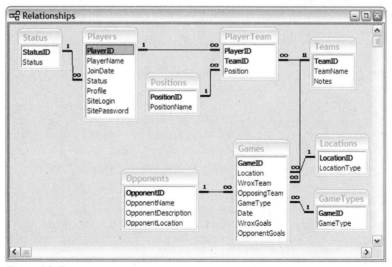

Figure 10-6

The most obvious tables in this database are `Players`, `Teams`, `Games`, and `Opponents`. Players have a status (Active, Injured, or Retired), and can play in different positions in more than one Wrox team (they can be a forward in one team, and a goalkeeper in another). Each team has many players. Games take place between one of the Wrox teams and an opposing team. Each game can take place either home (at the Wrox location) or away (at the opposing team's ground). Finally, games can be either friendly or league games.

For a more thorough investigation of the Wrox United database, how to create it, and its data structures, please refer to *Appendix C, The Wrox United database*. There is an Access and an MSDE version of this database available for download from the Wrox Web site. So, let's have a go at displaying some of this data using some server controls.

> **To run this code, you need to have installed the Wrox United database. Download whichever version of the database you prefer (the samples in the book assume you are using the Access version) before starting this exercise.**

Try It Out Wrox United Main Page – Default.aspx

The first page we'll build in our site is the `Default.aspx` page. This page will be the first thing our visitors will see when they come to the site. For now, we won't worry too much about styling – as you work through these chapters, we'll refine this page step by step until it looks and feels like a Web site. For now, let's start by adding a heading or two and some links to other pages that we'll be building.

1. Open up your ASP.NET Web Matrix editor, and create a new ASP.NET page called `Default.aspx` in a folder that lives within your `BegASPNET11` directory (`C:\BegASPNET11\WroxUnited`, for example), as shown in Figure 10-7. Web Matrix will then display this page in the main window, ready to be worked on:

Figure 10-7

2. In Design view, type in Wrox United and make this text Heading 1 style, using the block format drop-down menu on the main toolbar at the top of the environment. On a new line, change the paragraph style back to Normal and type in Welcome to the Wrox United Website! Please select one of the following:

3. Next, select the Web Controls tab on the left (if it isn't already selected), and drag four Hyperlink controls onto your form, pressing the Return key after each link to place them on separate lines. Your page should look like Figure 10-8:

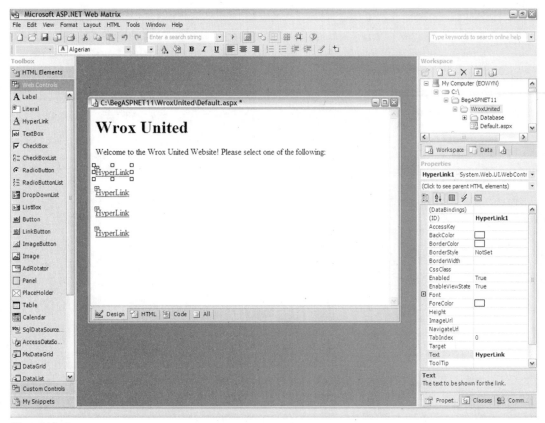

Figure 10-8

4. Notice that when you select one of the Hyperlink controls, the properties available for that control appear in the Properties pane in the right hand side. Select each one of the Hyperlink controls in turn and assign the following properties using the Properties pane:

Property	Link 1	Link 2	Link 3	Link 4
Text	Teams	Players	Upcoming Games	Results
ID	lnkTeams	lnkPlayers	lnkGames	lnkResults
NavigateUrl	Default.aspx	Default.aspx	Default.aspx	Default.aspx

5. As we continue to build pages in this site, we'll add a separate `NavigateUrl` property for each of these controls, but, for now, keep them all pointing to the same page. If you run this page now, you will see that these controls are rendered almost exactly like an HTML `<a href ...>` hyperlink would be; see Figure 10-9:

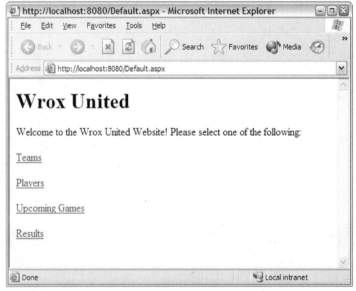

Figure 10-9

How It Works

Let's take a look at the code that has been generated for us. In Web Matrix, go to the HTML view, and you will see that the following code has been created:

```
<h1>Wrox United
</h1>
<p>
Welcome to the Wrox United Website! Please select one of the following:
</p>
<p>
  <asp:HyperLink id="lnkTeams" runat="server"
            NavigateUrl="Default.aspx">Teams</asp:HyperLink>
```

```
</p>
<p>
  <asp:HyperLink id="lnkPlayers" runat="server"
                 NavigateUrl="Default.aspx">Players</asp:HyperLink>
</p>
<p>
  <asp:HyperLink id="lnkGames" runat="server" NavigateUrl="Default.aspx">
    Upcoming Games
  </asp:HyperLink>
</p>
<p>
  <asp:HyperLink id="lnkResults" runat="server"
                 NavigateUrl="Default.aspx">Results</asp:HyperLink>
</p>
```

This isn't a lot of code, and we could have typed it all in by hand, but we've saved time by using the Web Matrix editor, with the added advantage that there are no typos.

Now, view the page in your browser, and select View | Source from the main menu. You will see the following generated code:

```
<h1>Wrox United
</h1>
<p>
Welcome to the Wrox United Website! Please select one of the following:
</p>
<p>
  <a id="lnkTeams" href="/Default.aspx">Teams</a>
</p>
<p>
  <a id="lnkPlayers" href="/Default.aspx">Players</a>
</p>
<p>
  <a id="lnkGames" href="/Default.aspx">Upcoming Games</a>
</p>
<p>
  <a id="lnkResults" href="/Default.aspx">Results</a>
</p>
```

The ASP.NET **Hyperlink** control is one of the most simple Web controls in our toolbox, and acts in a very similar way to the `<a href ... >` HTML anchor control. As you can see, the changes between the code we've created and the rendered code are very small, but this will not always be the case.

When you click on each link in turn, notice that the browser window flickers as it follows the link to the page. Note that these controls don't cause a postback to the server in the same way as a `Button` control does – these controls simply transfer you to a new page, without firing any server-side events. We didn't need to add an `OnClick` attribute, like we did with a `Button` control.

So what's so useful about the ASP.NET `Hyperlink` control? Well, firstly they have the same basic set of properties that every Web control has. Secondly, they're simple, and just as easy to use as a normal anchor tag. Later on, you'll be using the `Visible` property of the `Hyperlink` controls to display or hide links, depending on whether you're a logged in user or not – a very useful trick!

Let's take a quick look at several other simple controls available to you for developing ASP.NET pages.

Intrinsic Controls

These are controls that correspond directly to HTML tags, and include the `Button`, `Checkbox`, `DropDownList`, and `TextBox`. We are familiar with these controls now, as we've been using them throughout the book.

Here is a list to remind you of which controls fall into the intrinsic controls' group:

Control	Purpose
Button	General-purpose button – you typically write a `Click` event handler
CheckBox	Single checkbox
DropDownList	Drop-down listbox, also known as a combo box, for selecting from a list of items
Hyperlink	Similar to the HTML `<a></a>` tag for displaying a hyperlink
Image	Displays an image file, GIF, JPG, or other image file
Label	Provides a way to display text on a page; corresponds to the HTML `<span>` tag
ListBox	Provide a scrollable list of items, single or multiple selection
Panel	Similar to the HTML `<DIV>` tag – typically serves as a container for other controls
RadioButton	Single radio button, similar to a checkbox, except you must handle deselect programmatically
Table	Similar to an HTML table
TableCell	A cell within a table
TableRow	A row within a table
TextBox	Text box – single or multiple lines, it is similar to an `<input ... >` or a `<textarea ... >` control

Let's take a look at some more interesting controls. You'll create the `Teams.aspx` page, and examine a different type of control, the `DataList` control. This control enables you to display repetitive elements on a page, based on rows of data that are stored in a database.

Try It Out   **Wrox United – Teams.aspx**

1. Create a new ASP.NET page and call it `Teams.aspx`. On this page, in Design view, add a Heading 1 that again displays the text **Wrox United**. Underneath that, add a Heading 2 that displays the text **Teams**. On a new line, switch back to the Normal paragraph style. Now you can add some content.

2. You can add a simple table to the form to lay out the form a bit more clearly. Navigate to the **HTML** menu and select **Insert Table**. Create a 1 row, 2 column table, with no specified width or height, as shown in Figure 10-10:

Figure 10-10

3. Drag a `DataList` control into the first cell of the table from the **Web Controls** panel on the left, as shown in Figure 10-11:

Figure 10-11

4. Let's do some work on the code in the page. First, switch to HTML view and enter the following code:

```
<asp:DataList id="TeamList" runat="server">
  <ItemTemplate>
    <asp:linkbutton text='<%# Container.DataItem("TeamName") %>'
        CommandArgument='<%# Container.DataItem("TeamID") %>'
        id="TeamNameLink" style="color:darkred" runat="server" />
```

```
      <br />
      <asp:Label text='<%# Container.DataItem("Notes") %>'
          id="teamnotes" runat="server" />
    </ItemTemplate>
    <SeparatorTemplate>
      <br />
      <hr color="#b0c4de" width="200px"/>
    </SeparatorTemplate>
  </asp:DataList>
</asp:DataList>
```

We've entered some data binding expressions in step 4, but not yet created a data source for this control. Next, grab the name of each of the teams from the database, and an ID for each team. This ID will come in handy when you need to find out more information about each of the teams. Also, you'll need to grab data from the Notes field that describes each of the teams.

> If you are using Access, ensure that a copy of the database is placed into the
> BegASPNET11\WroxUnited\Database folder (you need to create this folder if it
> doesn't yet exist).

5. You can now start to add some data source information to our page. We're going to use a neat feature of Web Matrix to generate some database access code. In Code view, drag a SELECT Data Code Wizard onto the page from the Code Wizards panel on the left, as shown in Figure 10-12:

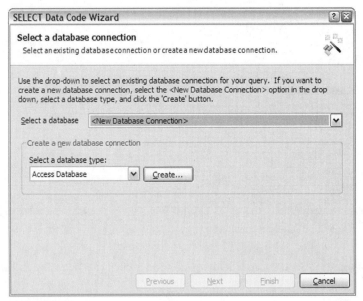

Figure 10-12

6. Create a new database connection to the Wrox United database by selecting your preferred database type, and clicking the Create button. If you are using Access, you will be prompted to enter the path to the database. If you are using MSDE, you will be prompted to select the WroxUnited database from your database list; see Figures 10-13, 10-14, and 10-15:

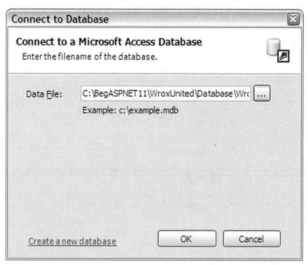

Figure 10-13

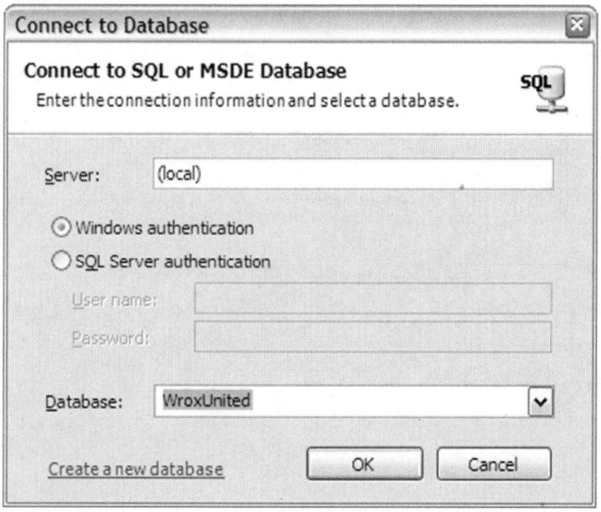

Figure 10-14

In this book, the examples use the Access version of the database, but you can obviously use the SQL Server version. In fact, in *Appendix D*, a SQL Server connection is used instead.

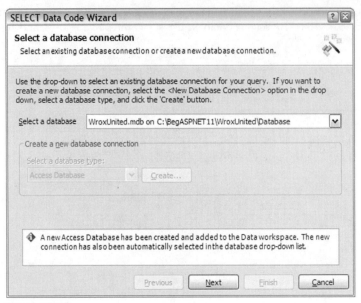

Figure 10-15

Now that you have a connection to your database, you can go ahead with the code wizard.

7. Click Next, and the Code Wizard is launched. You need to select data from the Teams table. After this, select each field from the table, as shown in Figure 10-16:

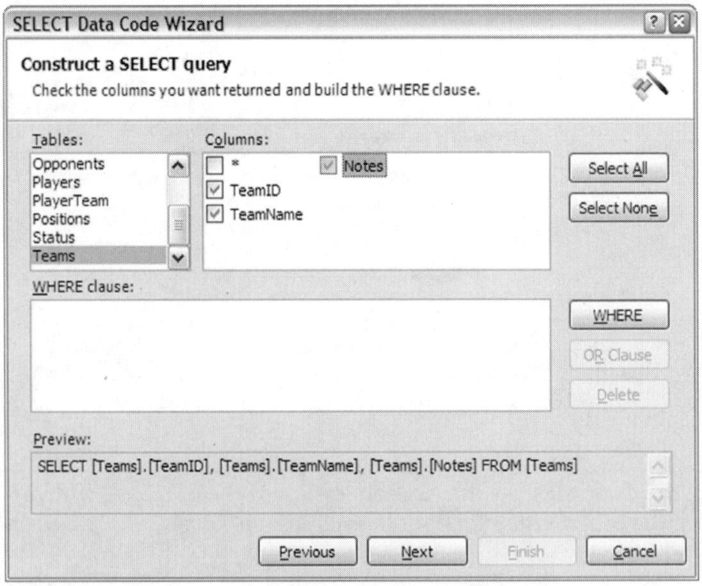

Figure 10-16

8. Click Next, and you can test out the query. You should see a screen similar to Figure 10-17:

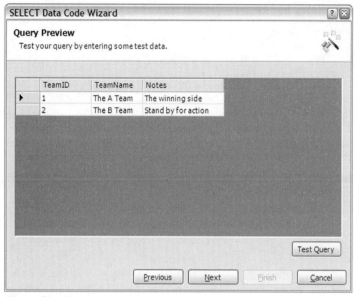

Figure 10-17

9. In the final screen, save this method as `GetTeams()`, ensure that the **DataReader** type is selected, and then click **Finish**, as shown in Figure 10-18:

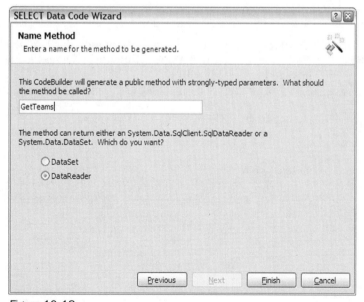

Figure 10-18

Back in **Code** view, you will now see the following:

```
Function GetTeams() As System.Data.IDataReader
  Dim connectionString As String = & _
    "Provider=Microsoft.Jet.OLEDB.4.0;"& _
    "Ole DB Services=-4;"& _
    "Data Source=C:\BegASPNET\WroxUnited\Database\WroxUnited.mdb"
  Dim dbConnection As System.Data.IDbConnection = _
    New System.Data.OleDb.OleDbConnection(connectionString)
  Dim queryString As String = "SELECT [Teams].[TeamID], "& _
    "[Teams].[TeamName], [Teams].[Notes] FROM [Teams]"
  Dim dbCommand As System.Data.IDbCommand = New System.Data.OleDb.OleDbCommand
  dbCommand.CommandText = queryString
  dbCommand.Connection = dbConnection

  dbConnection.Open
  Dim dataReader As System.Data.IDataReader = _
    dbCommand.ExecuteReader(System.Data.CommandBehavior.CloseConnection)

  Return dataReader
End Function
```

Phew – that's a lot of code! These code builders are very useful, and we'll be using these quite often as we build up the site. We now have a function that returns a DataReader object that we can use to populate the `DataList` control. However, before we continue, we need to change this code a bit. The database connection string can be stored in a central location in the `web.Config` file. Since we'll be doing a fair amount of database work for this application, let's change the code so that we use this technique.

10. Create a new `web.Config` file for your Wrox United application, and in the code that is generated, add the highlighted line of code.

> **Due to page width limitations, the following line is too long to fit on one line in the following listing. You must ensure that the following statement is not wrapped in your code, and is all on one line!**

```
<?xml version="1.0" encoding="UTF-8" ?>

<configuration>
  <appSettings>
    <add key="ConnectionString"
         value="Provider=Microsoft.Jet.OLEDB.4.0; Ole DB Services=-4;
                Data Source=C:\BegASPNET11\WroxUnited\Database\WroxUnited.mdb" />
  </appSettings>

    <system.web>
```

11. Now modify the `GetTeams()` method as follows to make use of this global connection string:

```
Function GetTeams() As System.Data.IDataReader
   Dim connectionString As String = _
     ConfigurationSettings.AppSettings("ConnectionString")
   Dim dbConnection As System.Data.IDbConnection = New
System.Data.OleDb.OleDbConnection(connectionString)
```

12. Add the following code block above the `GetTeams()` function:

```
Sub Page_Load()

   TeamList.DataSource = GetTeams
   TeamList.DataBind()

End Sub
```

That's it for this page. Run the page; the output is similar to Figure 10-19:

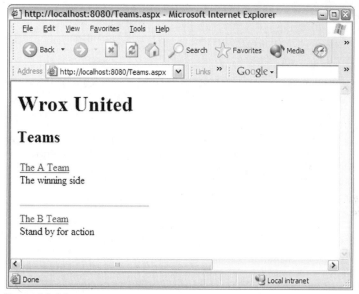

Figure 10-19

How It Works

This exercise used many different types of ASP.NET controls in order to display team information on the page. Let's look at each of these controls in turn, starting with the `DataList` control.

The `DataList` control is a powerful way to display repeated values from a database. It uses templates to present the data. In this example, we added content for the `ItemTemplate` and `SeparatorTemplate` elements within the `DataList`.

The `ItemTemplate` section is used to display each row of data retrieved, and gives you the option of adding some layout and styling code:

```
<asp:DataList id="TeamList" runat="server">
  <ItemTemplate>
    <asp:linkbutton text='<%# Container.DataItem("TeamName") %>'
      CommandArgument='<%# Container.DataItem("TeamID") %>'
      id="TeamNameLink" style="color:darkred" runat="server" />
    <br />
    <asp:Label text='<%# Container.DataItem("Notes") %>'
      id="teamnotes" runat="server" />
  </ItemTemplate>
```

The `SeparatorTemplate` is where we added a horizontal line to clearly separate the results:

```
  <SeparatorTemplate>
    <br />
    <hr color="#b0c4de" width="200px"/>
  </SeparatorTemplate>
</asp:DataList>
```

Inside the `ItemTemplate`, we used two different controls – an ASP.NET `LinkButton` control, and a `Label` control. Let's first look at the `LinkButton` control:

```
<asp:linkbutton text='<%# Container.DataItem("TeamName") %>'
  CommandArgument='<%# Container.DataItem("TeamID") %>'
  id="TeamNameLink" style="color:darkred" runat="server" />
```

The `Text` property is set to display the value stored in the `TeamName` field for each row in the database. The `CommandArgument` property stores the `TeamID` that represents the currently selected team. This property will be very useful later on when we use the `LinkButton` control to display more information on the page. Later in this chapter, we'll use it to retrieve a list of players that play for the selected team.

Now, let's look at the `Label` control:

```
<asp:Label Text='<%# Container.DataItem("Notes") %>'
  id="teamnotes" runat="server" />
```

This control is a little simpler than the `LinkButton` control. The interesting bit is the `Text` property, which is set to the value stored in the database for the notes for the currently selected team.

Each of these controls will be rendered once for each row in the database. Six teams would result in six links and six sets of notes. Each result will have the same separator between items.

The code used for accessing the data stored on the database should be familiar to you from working through the exercises in *Chapters 8* and *9*. The Web Matrix data wizard lessens a lot of your work and produces neat functions that you can use in your code. However, the Web Matrix wizards don't allow for specifying a centralized database connection string, we added a line to the default `Web.Config` file created for this exercise:

```
<add key="ConnectionString"
     value="Provider=Microsoft.Jet.OLEDB.4.0; Ole DB Services=-4;
            Data Source=C:\BegASPNET11\WroxUnited\Database\WroxUnited.mdb" />
```

Once this was added, the `connectionString` created by the data access wizard was changed as follows:

```
Dim connectionString As String = _
   ConfigurationSettings.AppSettings("ConnectionString")
```

This line of code looks up the value stored in the central `Web.Config` file and uses that value to connect to the database.

Linking to the Teams.aspx Page

Before you finish this example completely, flick back to `Default.aspx` and change the following line of code as shown:

```
<asp:HyperLink id="lnkTeams" runat="server" NavigateUrl="Teams.aspx">
   Teams
</asp:HyperLink>
```

Changing the `NavigateUrl` property means that you can link to the newly created `Teams.aspx` page from the main front page.

The `DataList` control is one of the numerous data controls available to ASP.NET developers. Here's a quick look at the other controls available to us.

Data Rendering Controls

These controls are extremely feature-rich (they have numerous properties to choose from) and greatly simplify the work of displaying a variety of data, particularly database-related data. The definition of *data* in the context of these controls is very broad. It could include database records, an `ArrayList`, an XML data source, or even custom collection objects containing custom class instances. There are two important concepts you need to know:

❑ **Data Binding:** This is the term used to describe the process of associating a server control with information in a data store. Binding data to a server control is a two-step process in ASP.NET – first assign the server control's `DataSource` property to the data you want to bind to, and then call the control's `DataBind()` method. Controls can be bound to a variety of data sources, from tables retrieved from the database to values stored in an object like an Array or Hashtable.

❑ **Templates:** This is a way to define the various layout elements of a particular control. Templates describe how data is displayed in the browser.

The following table lists the available data controls:

Control	Purpose
DataGrid	Creates a multi-column, data-bound grid. This control allows you to define various types of columns, for laying out the contents of the grid and to add specific functionality (edit button columns, hyperlink columns, and so on).
DataList	Displays items from a data source, using templates, and renders as a structured table. You can customize the appearance and the contents of the control by manipulating the templates that make up its different components.
Repeater	The Repeater control is very similar to the DataList, except that results are not rendered in a table. Each row in the data source is rendered in a format that you specify in the ItemTemplate. Given the lack of structure in the rendered output, you may find you use the ItemSeparatorTemplate more often. Unlike DataList, the Repeater control does not have any built-in selection or editing support.

The DataGrid Control

The DataGrid control provides a wealth of functionality for displaying data in columns and rows, and has many properties that you can use to control the layout of your grid. For example, you could alternate the colors for the rows of data being displayed. Some useful properties for the DataGrid control include:

❑   AllowSorting: Allows you to dynamically sort and re-display the data based on the values in a selected column. For example, if you had a table in a database containing employees' surnames and salaries, enabling sorting would allow you to sort the rows in your table according to either column.

❑   AllowPaging: The ability to view subsets of the data called by the DataGrid control on different pages. The number of items displayed on the page is determined by the PageSize property.

❑   AlternatingItemStyle: The style (such as background color) of every other item listed

❑   ItemStyle: The style of individual items. If no AlternatingItemStyle is defined, all the items will render with this style.

❑   FooterStyle: The style of the footer (if any) at the end of the list

❑   HeaderStyle: The style of the header (if any) at the beginning of the list

To use the DataGrid control, declare it like the other server controls you've seen (using the <asp:DataGrid> start tag and </asp:DataGrid> end tag), set the relevant properties, define the columns in your table, and then apply the relevant template for those columns. Within the template tags, include the information to which the template must be applied:

```
<asp:DataGrid id="EventData"
  AllowSorting="true"
    <Columns>
      <asp:TemplateColumn HeaderText="Column1">
        <ItemTemplate>
          <%# Container.DataItem("ShortDesc") %>
        </ItemTemplate>
      </asp:TemplateColumn>
      <asp:TemplateColumn HeaderText="Column2">
        <ItemTemplate>
          <%# Container.DataItem("DetailDesc") %>
        </ItemTemplate>
      </asp:TemplateColumn>
    </Columns>
</asp:DataGrid>
```

DataList

The DataList control used in the previous example is useful for displaying rows of database information (which can become columns in DataGrid tables) in a format that you can control using *templates* and *styles*. Manipulating various template controls changes the way your data is presented. The DataList control enables you to select and edit the data that is presented. The following is a list of the supported templates:

Templates	Purpose
ItemTemplate	Required template that provides the content and layout for items referenced by DataList.
AlternatingItemTemplate	If defined, this template provides the content and layout for alternating items in the DataList. If it is not defined, ItemTemplate is used.
EditItemTemplate	If defined, this template provides editing controls, such as text boxes, for items set to 'edit' in the DataList. If it is not defined, ItemTemplate is used.
FooterTemplate	If defined, the FooterTemplate provides the content and layout for the footer section of the DataList. If it is not defined, a footer section will not be displayed.
HeaderTemplate	If defined, this provides the content and layout for the header section of the DataList. If it is not defined, a header section will not be displayed.
SelectedItemTemplate	If defined, this template provides the content and layout for the currently selected item in the DataList. If it is not defined, ItemTemplate is used.
SeparatorTemplate	If defined, this provides the content and layout for the separator between items in the DataList. If it is not defined, a separator will not be displayed.

You can actually make a DataList render like a DataGrid, arranging data in columns, by changing the RepeatDirection property from Vertical to Horizontal. We recommend checking this out yourself, and taking a look at the source for the rendered page – you'll soon see where you need to add or remove layout data to customize the appearance of your data.

The Repeater Control

The Repeater control is very similar to the DataList control with one very important distinction: the data displayed is always *read only*. You cannot edit the data being presented. It is particularly useful for displaying repeating rows of data. Like the DataGrid and DataList controls, it utilizes templates to render its various sections. The templates it uses are generally the same as the ones used with the DataList control, with a similar syntax. The next Try It Out shows an example of the Repeater control in action.

We've completed the first part of the Teams page, but it would be really useful to see which players are on each team. For that part of the example, we'll work with some more Web controls (including a Repeater control) that bind to data.

Try It Out   Wrox United – Teams.aspx Part 2

In this example, we'll make the `TeamNames` from the previous example clickable, so that when a team is selected, the players of that team are listed in the right hand side of the table.

1.   Reopen `Teams.aspx`, and go straight to **Code** view. We need to get some more data from the database. Start by dragging another `SELECT` query onto the page, launching the wizard.

2.   This time, select `PlayerName` from the `Players` table, and `PositionName` from the `Positions` table as the two columns to display, as shown in Figure 10-20:

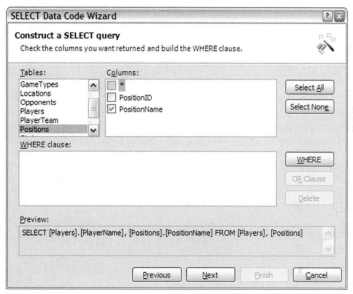

Figure 10-20

3.   Before you can exit the wizard, you need to add some `WHERE` clause data to link up the data you're gathering. This data comes from two different tables, `Players` and `Positions`. You also need to ensure that player data is only retrieved for the specific team you're interested in.

4.   Click the **WHERE** button to start adding a `WHERE` clause to select only rows where the **PlayerID** column in the **PlayerTeam** join table matches the **PlayerID** column in the **Players** table, as shown in Figure 10-21:

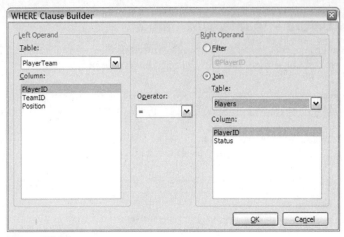

Figure 10-21

5. Repeat the process to join the following sets of tables and columns: the Position column in the PlayerTeam table to the PositionID column in the Positions table, and the TeamID column in the PlayerTeam table to the TeamID column in the Teams table.

6. Finally, set the TeamID column in the PlayerTeam table to be equal to the TeamID parameter, as shown in Figure 10-22. This will be passed in when the function is called:

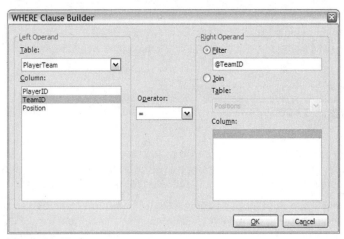

Figure 10-22

You should now see the screen in Figure 10-23:

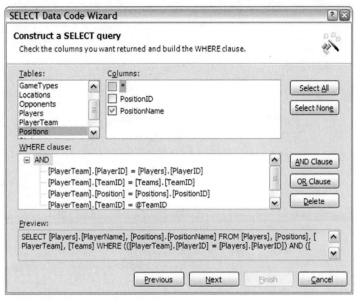

Figure 10-23

7. Click Next to test out the query. When prompted, enter an integer that corresponds to a valid `TeamID`, as shown in Figure 10-24 (1 is a safe bet!):

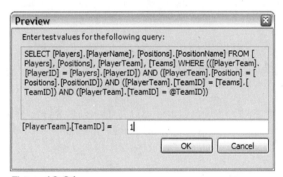

Figure 10-24

You should see the screen in Figure 10-25:

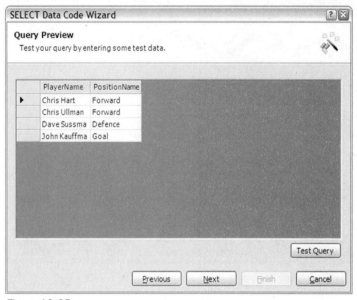

Figure 10-25

8. Save the query as a **DataReader** called `GetPlayersByTeam`. You can now exit the wizard. The following code should have been inserted:

```
Function GetPlayersByTeam(ByVal teamID As Integer) As System.Data.IDataReader
  Dim connectionString As String = _
    "Provider=Microsoft.Jet.OLEDB.4.0;Ole DB Services=-4;" & _
    "Data Source=C:\BegASPNET\WroxUnited\Database\WroxUnited.mdb"
  Dim dbConnection As System.Data.IDbConnection = _
    New System.Data.OleDb.OleDbConnection(connectionString)

  Dim queryString As String = _
    "SELECT [Players].[PlayerName], [Positions].[PositionName]" & _
    "FROM [Players], [Positions], [PlayerTeam], [Teams]" & _
    "WHERE (([PlayerTeam].[PlayerID] = [Players].[PlayerID])" & _
      "AND ([PlayerTeam].[Position] = [Positions].[PositionID])" & _
      "AND ([PlayerTeam].[TeamID] = [Teams].[TeamID])" & _
      "AND ([PlayerTeam].[TeamID] = @TeamID))"
  Dim dbCommand As System.Data.IDbCommand = New System.Data.OleDb.OleDbCommand
  dbCommand.CommandText = queryString
  dbCommand.Connection = dbConnection
  Dim dbParam_teamID As System.Data.IDataParameter = _
    New System.Data.OleDb.OleDbParameter
  dbParam_teamID.ParameterName = "@TeamID"
  dbParam_teamID.Value = teamID
  dbParam_teamID.DbType = System.Data.DbType.Int32
  dbCommand.Parameters.Add(dbParam_teamID)
  dbConnection.Open
```

```
    Dim dataReader As System.Data.IDataReader = _
        dbCommand.ExecuteReader(System.Data.CommandBehavior.CloseConnection)

    Return dataReader
End Function
```

Again, the wizard has done a great job of creating complex code with only a few mouse clicks! You need to make one slight adjustment though, so that the code uses the centralized connection string added to the `web.config` file earlier. Change the following highlighted line of code to use this central connection string:

```
Function GetPlayersByTeam(ByVal teamID As Integer) As System.Data.IDataReader
    Dim connectionString As String = _
        ConfigurationSettings.AppSettings("ConnectionString")
    Dim dbConnection As System.Data.IDbConnection = _
        New System.Data.OleDb.OleDbConnection(connectionString)
```

Now, add some controls that can use this code. Switch back to HTML view and add another cell to the table that contains a `Repeater` control:

```
</td>
<td style="vertical-align:top">
  <asp:Repeater id="PlayersList" runat="server">
    <ItemTemplate>
      <asp:linkbutton text='<%# Container.DataItem("PlayerName") %>'
                      style="color:darkred" runat="server"
                      width="120"/>
        
      <asp:Label text='<%# Container.DataItem("PositionName") %>'
                      id="playerposition" runat="server" /><br/>
    </ItemTemplate>
    <headerTemplate>
      Players in: <%= SelectedTeam %>
      <hr color="#b0c4de" width="200px">
    </headerTemplate>
    <footerTemplate>
      <hr color="#b0c4de" width="200px">
    </footerTemplate>
  </asp:Repeater>
</td>
</tr>
</table>
```

So, you've got a `Repeater` control, and a function to fill it with data. However, a few things are missing. The `Repeater` control should only be filled with data when a team is selected. We do this in three steps. First you wire up an event handler so that when the name of the team is clicked, the players will be displayed. Then pass in the `TeamID` parameter to the `GetPlayerByTeam()` function. Here you should remember the name of the team that has been selected, so that you can display it in the Repeater's header template.

9. Head back to the `DataList` control and edit the `LinkButton` control:

```
<asp:linkbutton text='<%# Container.DataItem("TeamName") %>'
       CommandArgument='<%# Container.DataItem("TeamID") %>'
       id="TeamNameLink" style="color:darkred"
       CommandName="ShowTeam" runat="server" />
```

10. Add the following to the `DataList` control tag:

```
<asp:DataList id="TeamList" runat="server"
               OnItemCommand="TeamList_ItemCommand">
```

11. Add the following line of code outside of all the methods on the page (this is a public variable):

```
Dim SelectedTeam as String
```

12. Finally, add the following code to **Code** view of the page:

```
Sub TeamList_ItemCommand(sender As Object, e As DataListCommandEventArgs)

  If e.CommandName.equals("ShowTeam") Then
    SelectedTeam = CType(e.CommandSource, LinkButton).Text
    PlayersList.DataSource = GetPlayersByTeam(e.CommandArgument)
    PlayersList.DataBind()
  End If

End Sub
```

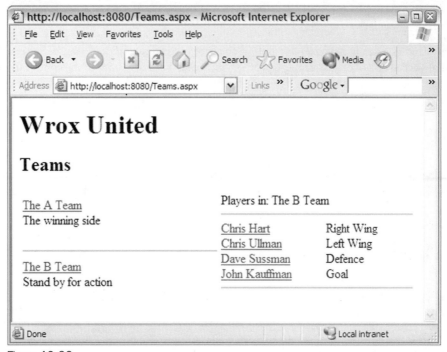

Figure 10-26

How It Works

We extended the first part of the example to incorporate an event handler that runs some specific code when the name of a team is clicked. This code is used to populate the Repeater control. Let's run through it piece-by-piece:

```
<asp:DataList id="TeamList" runat="server"
            OnItemCommand="TeamList_ItemCommand">
```

Adding the OnItemCommand property to the DataList control ensures that when the LinkButton within the DataList is clicked, the ItemCommand event of the Repeater is raised, and some code in the TeamList_ItemCommand() event handler is run. However, we need to pass in the CommandArgument of the LinkButton, so we assign a CommandName property to the LinkButton:

```
<asp:linkbutton text='<%# Container.DataItem("TeamName") %>'
    CommandArgument='<%# Container.DataItem("TeamID") %>'
    id="TeamNameLink" style="color:darkred"
    CommandName="ShowTeam" runat="server" />
```

In the event handler that runs when the `ItemCommand` event is fired, we can use the `CommandArgument` property of the `LinkButton`:

```
Sub TeamList_ItemCommand(sender As Object, e As DataListCommandEventArgs)
```

The event handler takes two parameters. `e` is an object of type `DataListCommandEventArgs`. This means that we can access certain properties of `e` in our code that relate back to the control that originally fired the event.

Firstly, we can use the `CommandName` property of the `LinkButton` that was set to `ShowTeam` earlier:

```
If e.CommandName.equals("ShowTeam") Then
```

We test whether the argument passed into the event handler has a `CommandName` set to `ShowTeam`. If it has, we process some more code. The next line sets the public string variable that stores the name of the team currently selected:

```
SelectedTeam = CType(e.CommandSource, LinkButton).Text
```

The next section binds to the `PlayersList` `Repeater` control. In here, we access the `CommandArgument` property of the `e` object – this is the argument that is passed into the event handler, which is the `CommandArgument` property of the `LinkButton` control that raised the event.

```
PlayersList.DataSource = GetPlayersByTeam(e.CommandArgument)
PlayersList.DataBind()
End If

End Sub
```

> This event handler is quite complicated, but is a great example of how to handle events raised by child controls (the **LinkButton**) via a parent control (the **DataList**). This is a process known as *Event Bubbling*, where the events raised by the child control *bubble up* to their parent control, where they can be intercepted and handled.

We've seen how the event is handled. Now let's look at the control that is populated when the event handler runs:

```
<asp:Repeater id="PlayersList" runat="server">
    <ItemTemplate>
        <asp:linkbutton text='<%# Container.DataItem("PlayerName") %>'
                        style="color:darkred" runat="server"
                        width="120"/>
```

This control contains a `LinkButton` and a `Label` control in its `ItemTemplate`:

```
  
<asp:Label text='<%# Container.DataItem("PositionName") %>'
                  id="playerposition" runat="server" /><br/>
</ItemTemplate>
```

We also define a header and footer for our player list. Notice that the string value stored in the `SelectedTeam` variable adds the name of the team to the header of the control:

```
<headerTemplate>
  Players in: <%= SelectedTeam %>
  <hr color="#b0c4de" width="250px">
</headerTemplate>
 <footerTemplate>
  <hr color="#b0c4de" width="250px">
</footerTemplate>
</asp:Repeater>
```

The data for the items in the `Repeater` control comes from the `GetPlayersByTeam()` method:

```
Function GetPlayersByTeam(ByVal teamID As Integer) As System.Data.IDataReader

 Dim connectionString As String = _
    ConfigurationSettings.AppSettings("ConnectionString")
  Dim dbConnection As System.Data.IDbConnection = _
    New System.Data.OleDb.OleDbConnection(connectionString)
```

This method contains a large SQL statement to retrieve the data we're interested in:

```
Dim queryString As String = _
  "SELECT [Players].[PlayerName], [Positions].[PositionName]" & _
  "FROM [Players], [Positions], [PlayerTeam], [Teams]" & _
  "WHERE (([PlayerTeam].[PlayerID] = [Players].[PlayerID])" & _
   "AND ([PlayerTeam].[Position] = [Positions].[PositionID])" & _
   "AND ([PlayerTeam].[TeamID] = [Teams].[TeamID])" & _
   "AND ([PlayerTeam].[TeamID] = @TeamID))"
```

This query is followed by some code that creates a `Command` object, and a parameter that passes in the `TeamID`.

```
Dim dbCommand As System.Data.IDbCommand = New System.Data.OleDb.OleDbCommand
dbCommand.CommandText = queryString
dbCommand.Connection = dbConnection

Dim dbParam_teamID As System.Data.IDataParameter = _
  New System.Data.OleDb.OleDbParameter
dbParam_teamID.ParameterName = "@TeamID"
dbParam_teamID.Value = teamID
dbParam_teamID.DbType = System.Data.DbType.Int32
dbCommand.Parameters.Add(dbParam_teamID)
```

> **Using a parameter ensures that the data passed into the method doesn't violate any database constraints. For example, using a parameter removes our obligation to escape text that would be invalid in a SQL statement, or worry about converting dates to a suitable format, and so on.**

Finally, the data is read from the database, and the `DataReader` object is passed back from the function:

```
    dbConnection.Open
    Dim dataReader As System.Data.IDataReader = _
      dbCommand.ExecuteReader(System.Data.CommandBehavior.CloseConnection)
    Return dataReader
  End Function
```

Our page is a bit more interesting now. Try clicking on different teams and see how the list of players changes. Note that we could also add more code to react to the clicking of the link button in the `PlayersList` control to transfer the reader to more information about the selected player, but that's something you can do yourselves.

The `Repeater` control has produced results similar to the `DataList` control, and in many cases, you will find yourself wondering which controls to use for different purposes. The end result is subtly different. The `DataList` control actually renders as an HTML table, with cells for each item in the template. The `Repeater` is much less structured, and simply spits back rendered versions of exactly what was put into the templates with no extra hidden tags. This is why we had to add a line break to this control to split the content onto different lines (although we could have used a separator template.)

The only functionality difference between the two is that the `DataList` can be used to edit data, whereas the `Repeater` is always read only. For more information and some great examples, refer to *Professional ASP.NET 1.1, Special Edition, Wiley, ISBN 0-7645-5890-0.*

> **These data-oriented controls have many different properties and events that we could discuss in depth here, but it's time to move on to look at some different topics in this chapter. I highly recommend that you play with these controls and experiment. Check out the rendered HTML in your browser using View | Source – you'll find it's a great way to understand how the rendering process works, and how to optimize your code to work with, not against, the ASP.NET compiler to produce the results you want.**

You've now gained some experience of using a `DataList`, a `Repeater`, and a `LinkButton` while putting together one of the pages in the site. As you saw at the end of the previous example, the `DataList` control is a data rendering control. The `LinkButton` control, however, is a rich control. Let's find out more about this type of control.

Rich Controls

Rich controls are compound in nature, and provide extended functionality. In other words, rich controls are typically combinations of two or more simple or *intrinsic* controls that compose a single functional unit, say, an `AdRotator` control. Another distinguishing trait of these controls is that they don't have a direct correlation to any single HTML control, although they do render to HTML when displayed in the client browser.

The following table discusses various rich controls and their functions:

Control	Purpose
AdRotator	Displays advertisement banners on a Web form. The displayed ad is randomly changed each time the form is loaded or refreshed.
Calendar	Displays a one-month calendar for viewing/selecting a date, month, or year.
CheckBoxList	Multiple-selection checkbox group. Can be dynamically generated with data binding.
ImageButton	Provides a clickable image with (optional) access to the clicked coordinates to support image-map functionality.
LinkButton	Hyperlink-style button that posts back to the page of origin. We've seen a couple of these in action already.
RadioButtonList	Mutually exclusive radio button group. Can be dynamically generated with data binding.

The nice thing about this family of rich controls is that they are just as easy to use as the other ASP.NET server controls. They may boast more features and properties, but the basic way of defining them and interacting with them is programmatically the same as for all the other ASP.NET server controls.

The Calendar Control

The Calendar control produces some really complex HTML when rendered, but you'll find that adding this control to a Web page is as simple as adding any other Web control! This control is designed to present date information in the form of a calendar, and allows a user to select a particular date. You can configure the control via the SelectionMode property to allow the user to select a range of dates. You can also completely customize how this control is presented using the many different properties that it has access to. Let's take a quick look at some of those properties:

```
FirstDayOfWeek=[Default|Monday|Tuesday|Wednesday|
                Thursday|Friday|Saturday|Sunday]
```

The FirstDayOfWeek property enables you to choose the day of the week your calendar starts from. Some calendars default to Sunday as the first day of the week; for business purposes, however, it's more practical to view the week starting from Monday.

```
SelectionMode=[None|Day|DayWeek|DayWeekMonth]
```

By default, the Calendar control's SelectionMode defaults to Day. This is useful when you want your user to be able to select only a single day. However, you can select multiple days by setting the SelectionMode property to either DayWeek, which will allow you to select a single day or an entire week, or DayWeekMonth, which will allow you to select a single day, an entire week, or the entire month.

The Calendar control's SelectMonthText and SelectWeekText properties enable you to customize the HTML that is rendered at the browser – use these properties if you're really going for a customized look:

```
SelectMonthText="HTML text"
SelectWeekText="HTML text"
```

You need not define all of the properties of the ASP.NET Calendar control to display the control. In fact, the following declaration will create an efficient ASP.NET Calendar server control that looks good and displays quite well:

```
<asp:Calendar id="MyCalendarControl" runat="server" />
```

When delivered to the client browser, the result is an HTML calendar that enables you to navigate through the various days, months, and years, as shown in Figure 10-27:

Figure 10-27

Have a look at the HTML that ASP.NET produced to create this page – over 100 lines of HTML and JavaScript, yet you wrote only a single line!

Let's now add a calendar that will highlight the days on which matches are scheduled and then display the details of those matches when that date is selected.

Try It Out **Wrox United – Default.aspx Part 2, the Event Calendar**

1. Reopen `Default.aspx` and add the following HTML table in HTML view to help to lay out the new and improved front page:

```
<p>
  Welcome to the Wrox United Website! Please select one
  of the following:
</p>
<table style="WIDTH: 800px">
  <tr>
    <td style="WIDTH: 200px">
      <p>
        <asp:HyperLink id="lnkTeams" runat="server"
                       NavigateUrl="Default.aspx">
          Teams
        </asp:HyperLink>
      </p>
      ...
      <p>
        <asp:HyperLink id="lnkResults" runat="server"
                       NavigateUrl="Default.aspx">
          Results
        </asp:HyperLink>
      </p>
    </td>
    <td style="VERTICAL-ALIGN: top; width: 350px;"> </td>
    <td style="VERTICAL-ALIGN: top; width: 250px;"></td>
  </tr>
</table>
</form>
```

2. Switch to **Design** view and drag a `Calendar` control into the third cell of the table, as shown in Figure 10-28. Name this calendar `EventCalendar`:

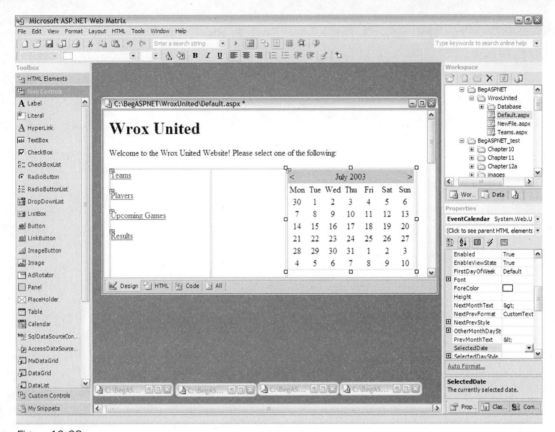

Figure 10-28

3. Now click the lightning bolt in the Properties pane to display the available events, and double-click on the `DayRender()` event's textbox to be taken back to **Code** view, where you need to enter more code. Before filling in the `DayRender()` event handler, let's take a moment to consider what we're trying to achieve. We want to highlight the days of the games and store dates of the games in the `Games` table in the database. If we want to display more information about a particular day, we also need to store the `GameID`, so that we can again query the database later.

4. The next task is to add another data reader to this page using the wizard, and then store that data in a Hashtable (where we can store details of dates and games in key-value pairs, as we saw in *Chapter 8*). At the top of the page, add the following line of code:

```
public DateList as New System.Collections.Hashtable()
```

5. Next, drag a SELECT Data Wizard onto the page. Select the **GameID** and **Date** fields from the `Games` table, and save this function with the name `Dates()`, and specify that it returns a `DataReader` object:

```
Function Dates() As System.Data.IDataReader
  Dim connectionString As String = _
        "Provider=Microsoft.Jet.OLEDB.4.0; Ole DB Services=-4;" & _
        "Data Source=C:\BegASPNET\WroxUnited\Database\WroxUnited.mdb"

  Dim dbConnection As System.Data.IDbConnection = _
    New System.Data.OleDb.OleDbConnection(connectionString)

  Dim queryString As String = _
    "SELECT [Games].[Date], [Games].[GameID] FROM [Games]"
  Dim dbCommand As System.Data.IDbCommand = New System.Data.OleDb.OleDbCommand
  dbCommand.CommandText = queryString
  dbCommand.Connection = dbConnection

  dbConnection.Open
  Dim dataReader As System.Data.IDataReader = _
   dbCommand.ExecuteReader(System.Data.CommandBehavior.CloseConnection)

  Return dataReader
End Function
```

6. Change this code to use the central connection string stored in `web.config`:

```
Function Dates() As System.Data.IDataReader
  Dim connectionString As String = _
    ConfigurationSettings.AppSettings("ConnectionString")

  Dim dbConnection As System.Data.IDbConnection = _
    New System.Data.OleDb.OleDbConnection(connectionString)
```

7. Add a `Page_Load()` event handler to the page, just below the Hashtable's declaration:

```
Sub Page_Load()

  ' we need to run this each time the page is loaded, so that
  ' after a date is selected and the page is posted back, the
  ' active dates will still be highlighted.
  Dim DateReader as System.Data.iDataReader
  DateReader = Dates()

  While DateReader.Read()
  DateList(DateReader("Date")) = DateReader("Date")

  End While
  DateReader.Close()

End Sub
```

8. Finally, add code to the `DayRender()` event handler to check if a match has been scheduled for a specific day, and highlight it in such a case:

```
Sub EventCalendar_DayRender(sender As Object, e As DayRenderEventArgs)

  If Not DateList(e.day.date) is Nothing then

    e.cell.style.add("font-weight", "bold")
    e.cell.style.add("font-size", "larger")
    e.cell.style.add("border", "3 dotted darkred")
    e.cell.style.add("background", "#f0f0f0")

  Else
    e.cell.style.add("font-weight", "lighter")
    e.cell.style.add("color", "DimGray")
  End If

End Sub
```

9. Run the page. You should see the screen in Figure 10-29:

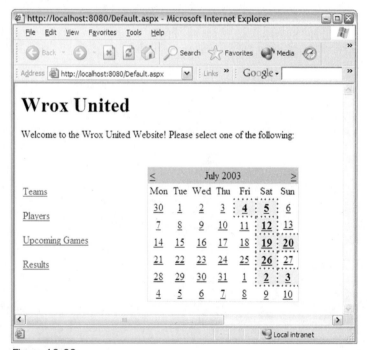

Figure 10-29

How It Works

The `Calendar` control is one of the most complex controls in the ASP.NET toolbox, and without writing too much code, we've managed to get the calendar to highlight dates that are stored in a database! Let's have a look at how we did this, and consider how this code can be improved.

First, we added a `Calendar` control to our page by simply dragging it onto the page, and then wired it up to an event handler:

```
<asp:Calendar id="EventCalendar" runat="server"
            OnDayRender="EventCalendar_DayRender"></asp:Calendar>
```

The `OnDayRender` property ensures that when each day is rendered in the calendar, the event handler is fired. This means that we can test each date as it's rendered, and compare it with the dates stored in the database. Let's take a look at the event handler:

```
Sub EventCalendar_DayRender(sender As Object, e As DayRenderEventArgs)

  If Not DateList(e.day.date) is Nothing then
```

We need to check whether the date being rendered (`e.day.date`) matches a date in the `DateList` Hashtable that is declared at the top of the page. Let's continue with the event handler:

```
        e.cell.style.add("font-weight", "bold")
        e.cell.style.add("font-size", "larger")
        e.cell.style.add("border", "3 dotted darkred")
        e.cell.style.add("background", "#f0f0f0")
```

If a matching date is found, some formatting is added to the cell. We make it bold, slightly larger, with a border, and background shading.

However, if the date being rendered doesn't match, we apply different formatting:

```
    Else
      e.cell.style.add("font-weight", "lighter")
      e.cell.style.add("color", "DimGray")
    End If

  End Sub
```

At the top of the page, as mentioned earlier, is the Hashtable declaration:

```
public DateList as New System.Collections.Hashtable()
```

Adding this to the top of the page means that all methods in the code have access to the data stored in the Hashtable for as long as the page exists.

```
Sub Page_Load()

    ' we need to run this each time the page is loaded, so that
    ' after a date is selected and the page is posted back, the
    ' active dates will still be highlighted.
    Dim DateReader as System.Data.iDataReader
    DateReader = Dates()
```

The first part of the `Page_Load()` method is where we create a new `DataReader` using the `Dates()` function built using the wizard. We can then loop through this data, and store key and value pairs in the Hashtable. In this case, we can store just the date information in both the key and the value parts of the Hashtable:

```
    While DateReader.Read()

        DateList(DateReader("Date")) = DateReader("Date")

    End While
    DateReader.Close()

End Sub
```

> As the comment in the code states, we need to run this code each time the page is loaded, because the values in the Hashtable are not saved (persisted) between postbacks. The problem with this method is that every time the page is loaded, we have to go back to the database to get the same data over and over again, which isn't very efficient! In the next chapter, we'll look at a better way to store this data, when we introduce the `Cache` object.

The function that retrieves the data from the database is really quite simple and looks very similar to the code we've seen previously – let's just recap the SQL that was generated to get the data we're interested in:

```
    Dim queryString As String = _
        "SELECT [Games].[Date], [Games].[GameID] FROM [Games]"
```

In the final example of this chapter, we'll extend the calendar example so that details of the match are displayed whenever the selected date corresponds to a match day.

Try It Out Wrox United – Displaying Fixture Details

In this example, we need to respond to a different type of event in order to display the details of a match. The `Calendar` control has many different events that can be handled, and the one we need to handle in this example is the `SelectionChanged` event, which fires whenever a date is selected. The user will expect to be able to click on a highlighted date in the calendar, and view the details of any matches scheduled for that day. Clicking on a different date will cause the `SelectionChanged` event to fire, which we can handle and add code to display data for the selected day.

1. Let's start by adding some more controls to the page for displaying the results. Start by adding a paragraph and an ASP.NET `Panel` control. Set the `Panel` ID to `pnlFixtureDetails`, and its `Visible` property to `False`:

```
<asp:Calendar id="EventCalendar" runat="server"
              OnDayRender="EventCalendar_DayRender"></asp:Calendar>
<p>
  <asp:Panel id="pnlFixtureDetails" runat="server" visible="false">
  </asp:Panel>
</p>
```

2. Inside the `Panel` control, add the following `Repeater` control to the page:

```
<asp:Repeater id="MatchesByDateList" runat="server">
  <headertemplate>
    <span style="width:110px;height:25px">Date: </span>
    <span style="width:135px;height:25px">
      <%# EventCalendar.SelectedDate.ToShortDateString %>
    </span> <br />
  </headertemplate>
  <itemtemplate>
    <span style="width:110px">Wrox Team</span>
    <span style="width:135px">
      <%# Container.DataItem("TeamName") %>
    </span> <br />
    <span style="width:110px">Opposing Team</span>
    <span style="width:135px">
      <%# Container.DataItem("OpponentName") %>
    </span> <br />
    <span style="width:110px">Venue</span>
    <span style="width:135px">
      <%# venue(Container.DataItem("OpponentLocation"), _
                Container.DataItem("Location")) %>
    </span> <br />
  </itemtemplate>
  <separatortemplate>
    <hr color="#b0c4de" width="200" />
  </separatortemplate>
</asp:Repeater>
```

We will bind this control to some data to display it on the page. As there could be more than one match on a certain day, we need to use a repeater control to display all the matches on that day. One last item to note at this stage is the last span in the `ItemTemplate`:

```
<span style="width:135px">
  <%# venue(Container.DataItem("OpponentLocation"), _
            Container.DataItem("Location")) %>
</span> <br />
```

One of the other pieces of code we're going to have to add will do some work to render an appropriate value for the venue for the match. We'll add a venue function in just a moment, and we'll examine why we need this in the *How It Works* section.

3. While you're in HTML view, modify the `Calendar` control to add an event handler for the `SelectionChanged` event:

```
<asp:Calendar id="EventCalendar" runat="server"
              OnDayRender="EventCalendar_DayRender"
              OnSelectionChanged="EventCalendar_SelectionChanged">
</asp:Calendar>
```

4. Add the following event handler to the page:

```
Sub EventCalendar_SelectionChanged(sender As Object, e As EventArgs)

    pnlFixtureDetails.Visible = True
    MatchesByDateList.DataSource = _
      GamesByDate(EventCalendar.SelectedDate.ToShortDateString)
    MatchesByDateList.DataBind()

End Sub
```

5. Add the `Venue()` function:

```
Function Venue(OpponentLocation as string, MatchVenue as integer) as string

    If matchvenue = 1 then
      ' match is at home
      return "Wroxville"

    else
      return opponentlocation

    end if

end function
```

6. Finally, we need to add a function that gets the data that we're interested in. We need to display:

  1. The name of the team (the `TeamName` field from the `Teams` table)

  2. The name of the opposing side (the `OpponentName` field from the `Opponents` table)

  3. The location of the game (the `Location` field from the `Games` table)

  4. The home location of the opposing team (the `OpponentLocation` from the `Opponents` table)

We also need to add some WHERE clauses to link together the related tables, so select the WHERE clause and add the following relationships:

  1. OpponentID from the Opponents table is equal to the OpposingTeam field in the Games table

  2. TeamID from the Teams table is equal to the WroxTeam field in the Games table

  3. Date from the Games table is equal to a parameter that we input called @Date

Save the method as `GamesByDate()`, and have it return another `DataReader` object. If it all goes to plan, you will end up with the following code:

```
Function GamesByDate(ByVal [date] As Date) As System.Data.IDataReader
  Dim connectionString As String = _
    "Provider=Microsoft.Jet.OLEDB.4.0; Ole DB Services=-4; " & _
    "Data Source=C:\BegASPNET\WroxUnited\Database\WroxUnited.mdb"
  Dim dbConnection As System.Data.IDbConnection = _
    New System.Data.OleDb.OleDbConnection(connectionString)

  Dim queryString As String = _
    "SELECT [Teams].[TeamName], [Opponents].[OpponentName], " & _
          "[Games].[Location], [Opponents].[OpponentLocation] " & _
    "FROM [Teams], [Opponents], [Games] " & _
    "WHERE ((([Opponents].[OpponentID] = [Games].[OpposingTeam]) " & _
    "AND ([Teams].[TeamID] = [Games].[WroxTeam]) " & _
    "AND ([Games].[Date] = @Date))"
  Dim dbCommand As System.Data.IDbCommand = _
    New System.Data.OleDb.OleDbCommand
  dbCommand.CommandText = queryString
  dbCommand.Connection = dbConnection

  Dim dbParam_date As System.Data.IDataParameter = _
    New System.Data.OleDb.OleDbParameter
  dbParam_date.ParameterName = "@Date"
  dbParam_date.Value = [date]
  dbParam_date.DbType = System.Data.DbType.DateTime
  dbCommand.Parameters.Add(dbParam_date)

  dbConnection.Open
  Dim dataReader As System.Data.IDataReader = _
    dbCommand.ExecuteReader(System.Data.CommandBehavior.CloseConnection)

  Return dataReader
End Function
```

7. Change this code to use the central connection string as follows:

```
Function GamesByDate(ByVal [date] As Date) As System.Data.IDataReader
  Dim connectionString As String = _
    ConfigurationSettings.AppSettings("ConnectionString")
  Dim dbConnection As System.Data.IDbConnection = _
    New System.Data.OleDb.OleDbConnection(connectionString)
```

8. Run the page and take a look at the results; they should be similar to Figure 10-30:

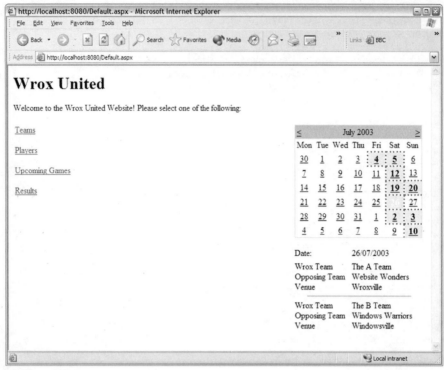

Figure 10-30

How It Works

We've added another panel to the page to display details of matches on a specific day. We first added the `Panel` control itself, and then started to build up another `Repeater` control:

```
<asp:Panel id="pnlFixtureDetails" runat="server" visible="false">
  <asp:Repeater id="MatchesByDateList" runat="server">
    <headertemplate>
      <span style="width:110px;height:25px">Date: </span>
      <span style="width:135px;height:25px">
        <%# EventCalendar.SelectedDate.ToShortDateString %>
      </span> <br />
    </headertemplate>
```

To write out the selected date in the header of the control, we use the `SelectedDate` property of the calendar, and write it out as a short date. After the header template comes the item template. Here, to render the results, we add plain HTML `<span>` tags as follows:

```
<itemtemplate>
  <span style="width:110px">Wrox Team</span>
  <span style="width:135px">
    <%# Container.DataItem("TeamName") %>
  </span> <br />
```

Notice how the text within the span contains a data binding expression that takes the `TeamName` column from the data source and places it as text within the control.

We repeat the process of building up the template for the rest of the columns:

```
<span style="width:110px">Opposing Team</span>
<span style="width:135px">
  <%# Container.DataItem("OpponentName") %>
</span> <br />
<span style="width:110px">Venue</span>
<span style="width:135px">
  <%# venue(Container.DataItem("OpponentLocation"), _
             Container.DataItem("Location")) %>
</span> <br />
```

In the final item in the list, we call the `Venue()` function that we declared in our code, which will display some text detailing the location of the game (depending on whether it's a home or away match). We pass two parameters into the function – the location of the opponent's pitch and the location flag from the `Games` table that states whether the game is at home (Wrox location) or whether it is away (opponent's location).

Finally, after finishing with the items in the repeater, we add a `SeparatorTemplate`:

```
    </itemtemplate>
    <separatortemplate>
      <hr color="#b0c4de" width="200" />
    </separatortemplate>
  </asp:Repeater>
</asp:Panel>
```

Let's head back to the `Venue()` function and look at how it works:

```
Function Venue(OpponentLocation as string, MatchVenue as integer) as string
```

The function takes two input parameters – the location of the opposing team's pitch, and the flag that states whether the match is at home or away. It returns a string that writes out either the name of the home pitch, or the name of the opposing teams pitch:

```
If matchvenue = 1 then
  ' match is at home
  return "Wroxville"

else
  return opponentlocation

end if

end function
```

The rest of the code for this exercise deals with getting the match data from the database, and displaying it when an event happens. We want to display details when the currently selected date in the calendar changes, so we added an `OnSelectionChanged` attribute to the calendar control:

```
OnSelectionChanged="EventCalendar_SelectionChanged">
```

Then we added the event handler code:

```
Sub EventCalendar_SelectionChanged(sender As Object, e As EventArgs)

    pnlFixtureDetails.Visible = True
    MatchesByDateList.DataSource = _
      GamesByDate(EventCalendar.SelectedDate.ToShortDateString)
    MatchesByDateList.DataBind()

End Sub
```

In this event handler, we call the `GamesByDate()` function to retrieve the match details, passing in the selected date as a parameter. That function will then retrieve the information, and the resulting `DataReader` will be used as the data source for the `MatchesByDateList` repeater control.

The actual code that retrieved the data included quite a substantial `SELECT` query:

```
Dim queryString As String = _
    "SELECT [Teams].[TeamName], [Opponents].[OpponentName], " & _
           [Games].[Location], [Opponents].[OpponentLocation] " & _
    "FROM [Teams], [Opponents], [Games] " & _
    "WHERE (([Opponents].[OpponentID] = [Games].[OpposingTeam]) " & _
    "AND ([Teams].[TeamID] = [Games].[WroxTeam]) " & _
    "AND ([Games].[Date] = @Date))"
```

We are gathering data from multiple tables, so the query used is a bit long-winded, but the end result is that we retrieve the required data fields from these three tables, and can display them on the page.

There are two more examples to look at in this chapter. First, we're going to look at Web Matrix-specific controls, and produce another quick and simple ASP.NET page. In the second example, we'll take a quick look at validation controls.

Web Matrix Controls

There are some extra controls that you can use when working with Web Matrix to develop Web applications. They are designed to make life very simple when you want to create data-driven pages.

The MX DataGrid

This control is a lot like a normal `DataGrid` control, except that you can use it in conjunction with a Web Matrix `DataSource` control. There are two data source controls, one for SQL Server connections, and one for Access connections. There is only one extra property on the MX `DataGrid` control; the `DataSourceControlID` property. This how you tell the MX grid to get its data from the appropriate data source control.

The Data Source Controls

These controls have three simple properties:

❑ `ConnectionString`: The string for connecting to the database

❑ `SelectCommand`: The SQL used to get the data into the grid

❑ `EnableViewState`: Determines if data stored in the control has persisted between postbacks

Let's see a quick example of this in action.

Try It Out Wrox United – Players.aspx and the Web Matrix MX DataGrid

1. Create a new ASP.NET page and call it `Players.aspx`. On this page, in Design view, add a Heading 1 that again displays the text Wrox United. Underneath this, add a paragraph in Heading 2 that displays the text Players. On a new line, switch back to Normal paragraph style. Now we can add some content.

2. In the Workspace | Data panel at the top left of the Web Matrix environment, switch to Data view. Now drag the `Players` table onto the form, below the two headings, as shown in Figure 10-31:

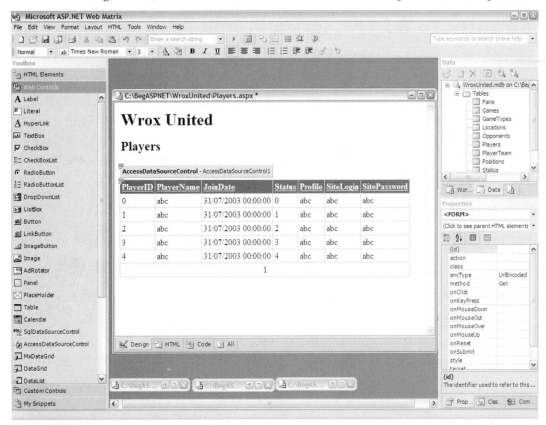

Figure 10-31

You can actually run the page at this stage – with one click and drag operation, you can display an entire table of data on the screen. If you run the page now, you will see the screen in Figure 10-32:

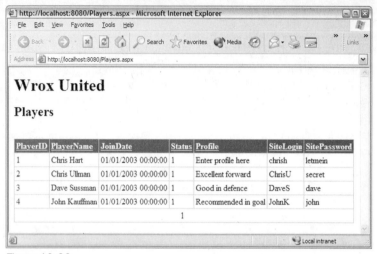

Figure 10-32

Although this is very cool, we don't necessarily want just anyone to view the site login or password details. Also, a status flag of 1, 2, or 3 doesn't mean much whereas **Active**, **Injured**, or **Retired** would mean more to visitors. Let's amend the example slightly.

3. Back in Web Matrix, switch to **Design** view, select the `DataSource` control, and in the **Properties** panel set the `SelectCommand` to the following:

```
SELECT PlayerID, PlayerName, Profile, JoinDate FROM [Players]
```

4. Now select the `MxDataGrid` control, and change the `AutoGenerateFields` property to `False`, then back to `True` to refresh the grid. Run the page again to see the screen in Figure 10-33:

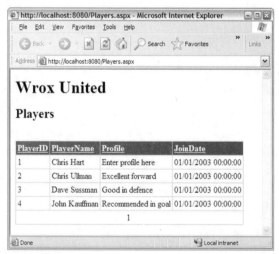

Figure 10-33

How It Works

This simple example demonstrates how Web Matrix can make life easy for us! The results of this quick and simple page aren't exactly brilliant, but the information we want to display is on the form with a minimum of fuss. The MxDataGrid control can be customized quite heavily, like the full .NET DataGrid control, so you can better control how the data is rendered.

Let's take a quick look at the code that was generated for us:

```
<wmx:AccessDataSourceControl id="AccessDataSourceControl1"
  runat="server"
  ConnectionString="Provider=Microsoft.Jet.OLEDB.4.0; Ole DB Services= - 4;
    Data Source=C:\BegASPNET\WroxUnited\Database\WroxUnited.mdb"
  SelectCommand="SELECT PlayerID, PlayerName, Profile, JoinDate FROM [Players]">
</wmx:AccessDataSourceControl>
```

The first control added to the page was the DataSourceControl (which is either a SQLDataSourceControl or an AccessDataSourceControl, depending on what database you are using). This control contains a connection string, and a SQL SELECT statement to retrieve the data we're interested in. This control was accompanied by the MxDataGrid:

```
<wmx:MxDataGrid id="MxDataGrid1" runat="server" BorderStyle="None"
  BorderWidth="1px" DataKeyField="PlayerID"
  CellPadding="3" BackColor="White" AllowPaging="True"
  DataMember="Players" AllowSorting="True"
  BorderColor="#CCCCCC"
  DataSourceControlID="AccessDataSourceControl1">
  <SelectedItemStyle font-bold="True" forecolor="White"
    backcolor="#669999">
  </SelectedItemStyle>
  <ItemStyle forecolor="#000066"></ItemStyle>
  <FooterStyle forecolor="#000066" backcolor="White"></FooterStyle>
  <HeaderStyle fontbold="True" forecolor="White"
    backcolor="#006699"></HeaderStyle>
  <PagerStyle horizontalalign="Center" forecolor="#000066"
    backcolor="White" mode="NumericPages"></PagerStyle>
</wmx:MxDataGrid>
```

As you can see, this control contains templates just like any other repetitive databound control. Notice that this grid has a few different properties compared to the DataGrid control:

❑ DataKeyField: The unique identifier for each row in the table

❑ DataMember: The name of the table you want to view

❑ DataSourceControlID: The name of the control that contains the data

Also included in the default implementation of this grid is a considerable amount of styling information that you may want to remove (when we come to styling the site, we will remove this information to ensure that all pages correctly follow the stylesheet we will use).

To further improve on this page, you could manually specify the columns that appear in the grid and add formatting information for the `JoinDate` field. For example, you could remove the time portion of the date (unnecessary in this application).

To try this out, you can either manually set the `AutoGenerateFields` property to `False`, and then specify each field individually using the `Fields` collection editor, or you can alter the code as follows:

```
<wmx:MxDataGrid id="MxDataGrid1" ...
AutoGenerateFields="False">
  <SelectedItemStyle font-bold="True" forecolor="White"
    backcolor="#669999"></SelectedItemStyle>
  <ItemStyle forecolor="#000066"></ItemStyle>
  <FooterStyle forecolor="#000066" backcolor="White"></FooterStyle>
  <HeaderStyle font-bold="True" forecolor="White"
    backcolor="#006699"></HeaderStyle>
  <PagerStyle horizontalalign="Center" forecolor="#000066"
    backcolor="White" mode="NumericPages"></PagerStyle>
  <Fields>
    <wmx:BoundField Visible="False" DataField="PlayerID">
    </wmx:BoundField>
    <wmx:BoundField DataField="PlayerName" HeaderText="Name">
    </wmx:BoundField>
    <wmx:BoundField DataField="Profile" HeaderText="Profile">
    </wmx:BoundField>
    <wmx:BoundField DataField="JoinDate" HeaderText="Join Date"
      DataFormatString="{0:d}">
    </wmx:BoundField>
  </Fields>
</wmx:MxDataGrid>
```

This will change the appearance, as shown in Figure 10-34:

Figure 10-34

If you want to use the centralized connection string, you could alter the code as follows:

```
<wmx:AccessDataSourceControl id="AccessDataSourceControl1" runat="server"
    SelectCommand="SELECT PlayerID, PlayerName, Profile, JoinDate FROM [Players]"
    ConnectionString='<%# ConfigurationSettings.AppSettings("ConnectionString") %>'>
</wmx:AccessDataSourceControl>
```

For this code to work correctly, you need to call the `DataBind()` method of the page object – you can do this by adding a simple `Page_Load()` method to your page:

```
Sub Page_Load
    Page.DataBind()
End Sub
```

Before we finish this section, flick back to `Default.aspx` and alter the following line of code:

```
<asp:HyperLink id="lnkPlayers" runat="server"
        NavigateUrl="Players.aspx">
    Players
</asp:HyperLink>
```

We can now link to the `Players.aspx` page from the main page of the site.

Let's move on to the final part of this chapter, where we take a brief look at validation controls.

Validation Controls

Validation controls are designed to help ensure that data entered into a form conforms to some specific criteria. This reduces the chances of random gibberish being sent back to the server. Validation controls also demonstrate how ASP.NET Web controls abstract common tasks. Without validation controls, we would typically need to write our own client-side validation code (for example, client-side JavaScript) – a time consuming task indeed!

By using validation controls within ASP.NET Web forms, our work is greatly simplified. Although validation involves a bit of overhead and some thought (for instance, what type of validation control to use and some knowledge of how to implement it) the benefits are that we end up with:

- ❑ Easier code base to maintain

- ❑ Better control over the user interface and the data that gets passed to our servers

- ❑ Better experience for our users or customers

For example, using these controls, you can ensure that a user registration form contains data in all appropriate fields. This is done using the `RequiredFieldValidator` control before posting it to the server. You can also verify that an email address is in a valid format.

The following is a complete list of validation controls that will give you an idea of what is possible:

Control	Purpose
CompareValidator	Compares a user's entry against a constant value (less than, equal, greater than, and so on). For example, you can use this to check that a Password and a Confirm Password textbox contain identical data.
CustomValidator	Checks the data entered by the user using validation logic from a custom method that you write – processed on the server or the client.
RangeValidator	Checks that data entered by the user falls between specified lower and upper boundaries. Checks ranges within pairs of numbers, alphabetic characters, and dates. Boundaries can be expressed as constants, or as values derived from another control.
RegularExpressionValidator	Checks that the entry matches a pattern defined by a regular expression. This type of validation allows you to check for predictable sequences of characters, such as those in social security numbers, e-mail addresses, telephone numbers, postal codes, and IP addresses.
RequiredFieldValidator	Ensures that the user does not skip an entry.

Let's take a quick look at how we can add validation controls to the site.

Try It Out   Wrox United – Registering for Email Updates (Default.aspx)

We are going to add a textbox to the front page of the website to collect email addresses of fans who may want to receive information about upcoming events, or emails containing match reports. In this example, we will simply add the textbox, a button for submitting the data, and some validation controls. We won't store the email address in this part of the example, since we'll be coming back to this example in the next chapter.

1. Start by reopening `Default.aspx`. At the moment, we have code that displays a welcome message:

```
<p>
   Welcome to the Wrox United Website! Please select one of the following:
</p>
```

2. Change this section of code as follows:

```
<table width="800">
  <tr>
```

```
    <td width="580">
      <h2>Welcome to the Wrox United Website! Please select one of the following:
      </h2>
    </td>
    <td width="220" border="1">
    </td>
  </tr>
</table>
```

3. Switch back to Design view and you will see the screen in Figure 10-35:

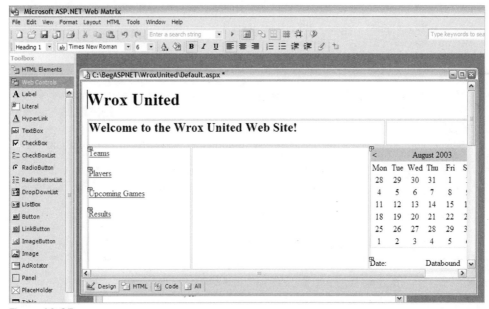

Figure 10-35

4. Drag a Label control into the second cell of the top table, then a TextBox control, a Button control, and finally a RegularExpressionValidator control. Set their properties as follows:

Control	Property	Value
Label	Id	lblRegister
	Text	Register for email updates
TextBox	Id	txtEmailAddress
Button	Id	btnRegister
	Text	Register
	Width	60

377

Control	Property	Value
RegularExpressionValidator	Id	validEmail
	ErrorMessage	Please enter a valid email address
	ControlToValidate	txtEmailAddress

Notice that when you set the `ControlToValidate` property of the `RegularExpressionValidator`, the property box displays a combo box that lists all available controls that can be validated (in this case, the only control that can be validated by this control is `txtEmailAddress`).

5. We need to enter a validation expression, or else not much will happen when we run the page. In the properties for the `validEmail` control, select the `ValidationExpression` property and click the ... button in the box to go to the expression builder.

Select **Internet E-mail Address** from the list, as shown in Figure 10-36, and click **OK**:

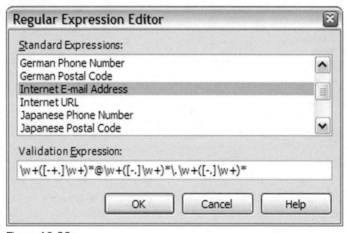

Figure 10-36

You should now have the following code on your page:

```
<asp:Label id="lblRegister" runat="server">Register for email updates</asp:Label>
<asp:TextBox id="txtEmailAddress" runat="server"></asp:TextBox>
<asp:Button id="btnRegister" runat="server" Text="Register"
        Width="60px"></asp:Button>
<asp:RegularExpressionValidator id="validEmail" runat="server"
    ErrorMessage="Please enter a valid email address"
    ControlToValidate="txtEmailAddress"
    ValidationExpression="\w+([-+.]\w+)*@\w+([-.]\w+)*\.\w+([-.]\w+)*">
</asp:RegularExpressionValidator>
```

6. Run the page and try to enter different values into the textbox. You'll notice that if you enter some text that is clearly not a valid email address, an error message appears when you click the button, as shown in Figure 10-37. Also notice that the page doesn't reload when you click the button – the error message is being generated using client-side script!

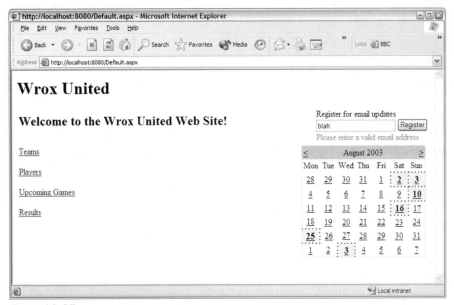

Figure 10-37

Alternatively, if you enter a valid email address, you will notice that a postback occurs when you click the button but no new information displays on the form. This is because we haven't yet handled the button click event on the server.

How It Works

Once again, we managed to create quite an interesting result using a minimum of code. Let's look at the code that was created when we added the validation control:

```
<asp:RegularExpressionValidator id="validEmail" runat="server"
    ErrorMessage="Please enter a valid email address"
```

The first interesting property is the `ErrorMessage` property, which contains the text that is displayed if validation fails.

```
ControlToValidate="txtEmailAddress"
```

The `ControlToValidate` property is quite self explanatory. Notice, that the only control we could select in the Web Matrix **Properties** pane was the textbox. The textbox is the only control on the form that allows free text input, so it is the only one that can possibly be validated by this control.

```
ValidationExpression="\w+([-+.]\w+)*@\w+([-.]\w+)*\.\w+([-.]\w+)*">
```

The final property contains the validation expression that we saw briefly when we were using the expression browser. The `RegularExpressionValidator` control works by comparing text that has been entered against this pattern. If it matches the rules specified by the pattern, validation is successful. If the text does not match this pattern, validation will fail.

A full explanation of regular expressions would take a long time, so let's quickly look at what this expression means:

- ❏   \w+ match one or more alphanumeric characters
- ❏   (...) * match zero or more instances of the contents of the brackets:

    [+.] match a hyphen, a plus sign, or a period

    \w+ match one or more alphanumeric characters

- ❏   @ match an @ sign
- ❏   \w+ match one or more alphanumeric characters
- ❏   (...) * match zero or more instances of the contents of the brackets:

    [.] an instance of a hyphen or a period

    \w+ match one or more alphanumeric characters

- ❏   \. match a period
- ❏   \w+ match one or more alphanumeric characters
- ❏   (...) * match zero or more instances of the contents of the brackets:

    [.] an instance of a hyphen or a period

    \w+ match one or more alphanumeric characters

Ok, so no one said these things were going to be too easy! However, a lot of this expression is repeated, and it means that all the following (and many more) are valid:

- ❏   me@here.com
- ❏   someone-else@somewhere.co.uk
- ❏   thing.2@elsewhere-thing.com

> **If you are a full time developer, it's definitely worth spending time looking at how regular expressions work – they are extremely powerful and extremely useful. The .NET Framework SDK includes information on all of the regular expression patterns available to .NET developers.**

Summary

In this chapter we have spent a fair bit of time looking at different types of controls and how they work. We've started putting together a small Web site using these controls, and we'll be building on this Web site in the next few chapters. Let's take a look at what we've achieved in this chapter:

❑ We looked at what a Web control is, and we discussed the relative merits of both the Web control and the HTML control (the HTML tag with a `runat="server"` attribute).

❑ We saw how a page is rendered, and looked at when (and how) events are handled.

❑ We looked at some simple intrinsic controls, particularly the `Hyperlink` control, which we used to add some links to the rest of the site. We returned to this control twice to add links to the `Players` and `Teams` pages.

❑ We used a `DataList` control and a `Repeater` control to display information about teams, and we learned how to handle events raised by controls that live within other controls.

❑ We used the `Calendar` control to display date information on our pages, and learned about two of the events it raises that we can handle, thus providing a customized appearance and behavior.

❑ We looked at the validation controls, particularly the `RegularExpressionValidator` control. We'll be learning more about these controls in the following chapters.

We've covered a lot of information, but given that ASP.NET is designed to work around controls and events, it's understandable that there's still a lot to discuss! The built-in controls provide us with a lot of rich functionality that we can use in our sites to display data, arrange information, and make the site user friendly.

In the next chapter, we'll look at different methods of storing information outside of the scope of a page (including that hashtable of dates from the `Calendar` control that we saw earlier). We'll also look at adding other validation controls, as well as extending the `Default.aspx` page to actually store an email address when the `Register` button is clicked.

Exercises

1. Consider a use for an HTML tag with `runat="server"` in the Wrox United application in place of one of the existing Web controls and explain why the HTML control is able to achieve the same result as the Web control.

2. Add another event handler to the `Teams.aspx` page that reacts to the selecting of the name of a player, and takes the reader to the `Players.aspx` page.

3. Amend the code in `Default.aspx` so that if the user selects a date in the calendar for which there are no matches, nothing is displayed in the panel below.

4. Have a go at customizing `Players.aspx` to change the field hat displays the name of the player into a hyperlink that, when clicked, will reveal a panel lower down the page that lists the team or teams that the selected player is a member of. You will find that the Fields editor of the `MxDataGrid` is very useful for this (select the Fields property builder when in **Design** view). You need to ensure that the clicking of the player name is handled correctly. You also need to add another method to extract team information (you may find that the `DataReader` function that returned the list of teams from the `Teams.aspx` page is useful here).

Users and Applications

Moving from a series of Web pages connected together by links, to a fully functional Web application is an essential step when developing a site. Once you can share information across all the pages in a site, the term *application* really starts to take hold. From the users' perspective, whenever they log in to a site, they receive some amount of personalization in the pages they view. From a developer's point of view, once users log in, certain details related to them can be tracked as they navigate the site. This is all made possible using centralize configuration settings with reusable code, thus reducing development time and increasing reusability.

This chapter will look at tracking users across pages using sessions, and will start to add some application-specific configuration. We will work with the Wrox United application started in the previous chapter, adding extra functionality and features to demonstrate key concepts.

ASP.NET stores information about a user session in a Session object. From the moment the user first starts to browse the site, you can access any code with Session scope, and use this, for example, to store information about the currently logged-in user. You can also add code that will remain in memory for as long as the application is running. This could contain some in-memory data objects that are accessed frequently but don't often change. This technique protects the database from repeat requests for the same data, thereby improving the performance of the application.

Another means of remembering information is cookies – small text files that are created and stored on the client computer (assuming cookies are enabled on the client). A cookie can store information such as the number of times that user has visited a site, whether the user has registered to receive email notifications, and so on. You can also add Application or Session scope configuration information that can store global settings, such as the length of a session until it expires, or the connection string to a database. This information is stored in a file known as the `web.config` file. In addition, the application's security model can be configured using the information stored in this file.

This chapter will look at:

❑   Using a cookie to store user-related information

❑   Remembering information relating to the actions of users as they browse the Web site

- ❑ Storing data in a variable that is accessible by any piece of code in the Web application
- ❑ Storing commonly used data in memory to improve the application's performance
- ❑ Writing code that will respond to any application or session events
- ❑ Adding some skinning functionality to the Wrox United site by using the state management techniques discussed in the chapter

Remembering Information in a Web Application

When you browse to a Web page, you establish a connection with the Web server for a brief moment while the page is sent to your browser. After this happens, the Web server forgets all about you. This is because HTTP, the protocol used for surfing the Web, is a *stateless* protocol. A stateless protocol, like HTTP, is used where it is impractical to maintain a constant link between the server and the client. Messages are sent back and forth, using request-response mechanism. The client makes requests and the server sends a response. After each response is fully sent by the server, the connection is dropped.

Unless some external mechanism is in place to associate the client with a known list of clients stored on the server, client-specific proactive communication from the server is not possible. One of the reasons HTTP is stateless is that it would be impossible for a Web server to remember everything about every single visitor to the site – imagine how the BBC news Web site would cope with remembering details of every one of the millions of readers that visit to catch up with the headlines! Statelessness essentially means that you cannot log in to a site using only HTTP. Thankfully, there are tools available that make it possible for the Web server to remember information.

When you browse any Web site, you leave a trail of information with the Web server about the pages you are viewing, and where you are connecting from. This information, combined with some code on the server (and some help from the client), enables Web servers to remember some information about visitors. What those Web servers do with that data depends on how you configure them, but as a user, you are most likely to see the result of this process in the form of a personalized browsing experience. For example, you can buy stuff from online stores, and you can log in to community Web sites and participate in online forums. Personalization is a natural side effect of being able to remember information about users and making it useful.

It's not just information about users that needs to be remembered – often you will want to be able to access some common code that has data stored in memory from every page in the site. This data could be any kind of object, from a simple string variable to a `DataSet` object. Because of the mechanism used to serve pages to browsers (via the stateless HTTP protocol), pages only have a limited lifespan. Thus, persisting information is a problem you are likely to encounter as you develop ASP.NET sites. Learning how to overcome the statelessness of HTTP is important and not very difficult, as you'll see when you work through examples in this chapter.

There are four different mechanisms for remembering information:

- ❑ **Cookies**: Identifying previous visitors to a site by storing small amounts of data on the client machine
- ❑ **Sessions**: Remembering information for as long as a user is browsing the site

❑ **Applications**: Remembering information that exists for as long as the application is running

❑ **Caching**: Remembering data for as long as is necessary to improve performance

Each of these mechanisms fulfills a different purpose, so it is important to understand *which* mechanism should be used to remember information, and not just *how* each mechanism works. Let's start the discussion by looking at how cookies work.

Cookies

Cookies are used throughout the Web to store small pieces of information on the client machine. They are small text files that usually store persistent data that is useful whenever you revisit a site. This can be information like user preferences, user login tokens, whether a user has voted in an online poll, details of the last time you browsed a site, and so on. They are designed such that only the site that created them can read them. In short, cookies contain information that allows a Web server to identify users based on their visiting history.

If you look at the `<drive>\Documents and Settings\<UserName>\Cookies` folder on your hard drive, you'll notice that hundreds of cookies reside on your system. Each of them has some kind of identifier in their name that indicates what site created them.

Figure 11-1 shows that I've visited Web sites for the BBC, Computer Manuals, and Firebox.com. You can open a cookie using MS Notepad. The information contained in any of these cookies, normally some text, will give you clues about the site that created it.

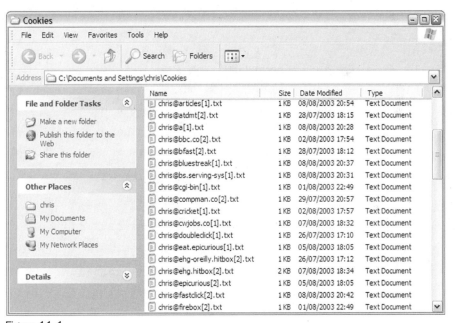

Figure 11-1

Taking the BBC news site as an example, I know that in the past I've checked a button to say that I'm in the UK (so I get the UK front page instead of the World front page by default, every time I visit the site). I've also specified that when I view the http://www.bbc.co.uk/weather site, my hometown should be set to Birmingham, UK. If I look inside the BBC cookie, I can see bits and pieces of text (among the rest of the text) that look as if they correspond to those choices:

```
... BBCNewsAudienceDomestic ... BBCWEACITYuk1045 ...
```

If I change the default page preference to BBC News Audience International, and the hometown to Nottingham, the relevant information in the cookie will change as follows:

```
... BBCNewsAudienceInternational ... BBCWEACITYuk2803 ...
```

By modifying preferences on the Web site, a file on my hard drive has been updated. This means that when I next visit the site, it will remember my preferences. Let's look at how this happens.

How Do Cookies Work?

Cookies are linked to the request-response mechanism of HTTP and are passed back and forth along with other data between the client and the server. Let's look at a situation where a site uses cookies to remember whether a user wants to tell a Web server to not display a certain popup when they visit a site:

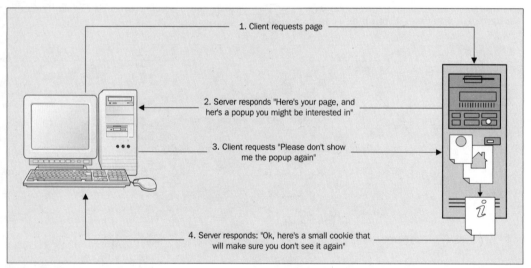

Figure 11-2

In Figure 11-2, Stage 1 corresponds to a user browsing to a site. Stage 2 will be the contents of that site sent to the browser. These contents happen to include a popup. At stage 3, anyone browsing the site could check a box on a form that states "Do not show the advert popup again". When they click a button to submit their request, they send data back to the server. Finally, the server sends a small cookie to the client machine. Figure 11-3 represents what happens when the user requests the page again.

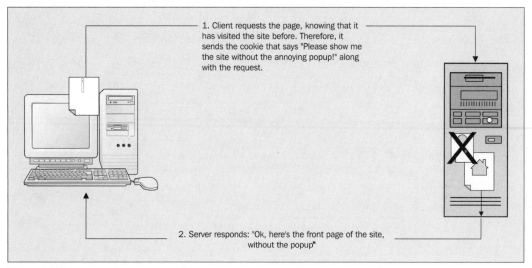

1. Client requests the page, knowing that it has visited the site before. Therefore, it sends the cookie that says "Please show me the site without the annoying popup!" along with the request.

2. Server responds: "Ok, here's the front page of the site, without the popup"

Figure 11-3

This time round, the user won't see the popup ad when browsing the site because the server will have read their cookie's value and know that the user expressed a preference not to see the popup. The client will send this cookie each time the user visits the site.

At this point, you need to understand that the client can never be trusted. The client may not send the cookie, send a dodgy cookie, or the cookie may have prematurely expired. Different Internet settings and browsers mean that you can't always rely on cookies. If they were reliable, you could store all kinds of logon data in a cookie, but in practice, treat them as "it would be nice if you could remember this". For more secure and reliable storage of information, use cookies in combination with things like sessions and data stored in a database.

When you save a cookie onto the client machine, you can specify how long it should exist. Cookies can live on indefinitely, or they can be set to expire after a certain time. In the popup example, you could specify that the cookie will expire after a month, by which time a new advert will have appeared. The user would then have to recreate the cookie if they wanted to block the popup.

Not only can cookies expire after a certain time, but users also can forcibly delete cookies from their system. If you have Internet Explorer, you can delete all of the cookies on your machine by selecting Tools | Preferences from the main IE window, then clicking Delete Cookies, as shown in Figure 11-4:

Figure 11-4

Of course, by doing this, I would have to again tell the BBC site that I wanted the UK version of the site and the weather details for Birmingham. Moreover, if you try this yourself, you may find you have to log back on to all sorts of sites where you had once clicked **Remember my details**.

As the earlier lifecycle diagrams hinted, you can set the cookie state using the `Response` object and read the existing cookie state using the `Request` object. It's quite simple to do this, so let's look at an example, and see these objects working their magic!

Try It Out   Using Cookies

In this example, we're going to add to the `WroxUnited` application once again. In the previous chapter, we added a box that enabled the user to register for email updates to the `Default.aspx` page, but didn't do anything with this information other than validate it. Let's get this working now.

1.   Open up `Default.aspx` in Web Matrix, and you will see the page in its current state, as shown in Figure 11-5:

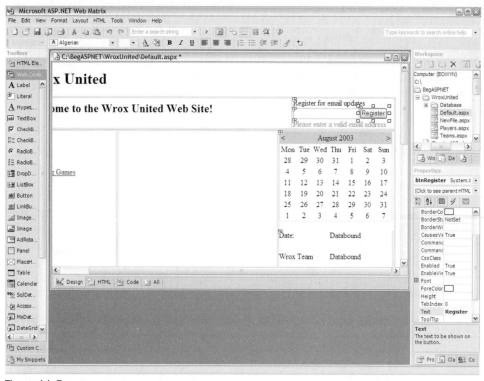

Figure 11-5

In the `WroxUnited` database there is a simple table called `Fans` that will contain email addresses of fans of the team. When the **Register** button is clicked, we need to do three things:

❑ Check that the address hasn't already been added to the database. If it has, create a cookie and update the display to indicate that the user has registered for updates.

❑ If the address hasn't already been added, add it to the database, create a cookie, and indicate that the user has registered for updates.

❑ When the page is loaded, if the client has a cookie indicating that they have already registered for updates, simply display a message confirming this.

2. Switch to **Code** view – it's time to add some database code to check whether a user has registered already or not. Drag a `Select` data wizard onto the page and select the `FanEmail` field from the `Fans` table where the `FanEmail` field matches a parameter, `@FanEmail`. Call this method `CheckFanEmailAddresses()` and save it as a **DataReader**. Pass this into the function:

```
Function CheckFanEmailAddresses(ByVal fanEmail As String) As
System.Data.IDataReader
  Dim connectionString As String = _
    "Provider=Microsoft.Jet.OLEDB.4.0; Ole DB Services=-4;" & _
    "Data Source=C:\BegASPNET\WroxUnited\Database\WroxUnited.mdb"
```

```
    Dim dbConnection As System.Data.IDbConnection = _
      New System.Data.OleDb.OleDbConnection(connectionString)
    Dim queryString As String = "SELECT [Fans].[FanEmail] FROM [Fans] "& _
      "WHERE ([Fans].[FanEmail] = @FanEmail)"

    Dim dbCommand As System.Data.IDbCommand = New System.Data.OleDb.OleDbCommand
    dbCommand.CommandText = queryString
    dbCommand.Connection = dbConnection

    Dim dbParam_fanEmail As System.Data.IDataParameter = _
      New System.Data.OleDb.OleDbParameter
    dbParam_fanEmail.ParameterName = "@FanEmail"
    dbParam_fanEmail.Value = fanEmail
    dbParam_fanEmail.DbType = System.Data.DbType.String
    dbCommand.Parameters.Add(dbParam_fanEmail)

    dbConnection.Open
    Dim dataReader As System.Data.IDataReader = _
     dbCommand.ExecuteReader(System.Data.CommandBehavior.CloseConnection)

    Return dataReader
End Function
```

This code needs to be altered slightly to fit our needs. Firstly, we need to change the connection string to use the database connection details stored in the `web.config` file. Then, all we need is to find out if a user has already registered, so let's modify this code to retrieve only a count of the number of times that particular email address appears in the database. If all goes well, this should never exceed 1. We can then use this value to return a Boolean true (if the user already exists) or false.

3. To alter this code, change the following highlighted lines:

```
Function CheckFanEmailAddresses(ByVal fanEmail As String) As Boolean
  Dim connectionString As String = _
    ConfigurationSettings.AppSettings("ConnectionString")
  Dim dbConnection As System.Data.IDbConnection = _
    New System.Data.OleDb.OleDbConnection(connectionString)
  Dim queryString As String = _
    "SELECT COUNT([Fans].[FanEmail]) FROM [Fans]" & _
    "WHERE ([Fans].[FanEmail] = @FanEmail)"
  Dim dbCommand As System.Data.IDbCommand = _
    New System.Data.OleDb.OleDbCommand
  dbCommand.CommandText = queryString
  dbCommand.Connection = dbConnection
  Dim dbParam_fanEmail As System.Data.IDataParameter = _
    New System.Data.OleDb.OleDbParameter
  dbParam_fanEmail.ParameterName = "@FanEmail"
  dbParam_fanEmail.Value = fanEmail
  dbParam_fanEmail.DbType = System.Data.DbType.String
  dbCommand.Parameters.Add(dbParam_fanEmail)
  Dim Result As Integer = 0
  dbConnection.Open
  Try
```

```
      Result = dbCommand.ExecuteScalar
   Finally
      dbConnection.Close
   End Try

   If Result > 0 then
      Return true
   Else Return false
   End If
End Function
```

Notice the changes made to the return type of the function, the SQL, and the method used to query the data source. This will be discussed in a moment.

4. Switch back to the Design view and double-click the Register button at the top left to create an event handler for the Click event of the button. Add the following code:

```
Sub btnRegister_Click(sender As Object, e As EventArgs)
   Dim FanEmail as String = txtEmailAddress.Text

   'Check whether the email address is already registered
   'If not, we need to register it by calling the AddNewFanEmail() method
   If CheckFanEmailAddresses(FanEmail) = false Then

       AddNewFanEmail(FanEmail)

     End If

   ' Email has been registered, so update the display and attempt to set a
   ' cookie
   txtEmailAddress.Visible = False
   lblRegister.Text = "You have successfully registered for email updates"
   btnRegister.visible = False

   Dim EmailRegisterCookie as New HttpCookie("EmailRegister")
   EmailRegisterCookie.Value = FanEmail
   EmailRegisterCookie.Expires = now.AddSeconds(20)
   Response.Cookies.Add(EmailRegisterCookie)
End Sub
```

If you look through this code, you will notice a function call to a function called AddNewFanEmail() – let's create this now.

5. Drag an Insert Data Method code wizard onto the page, select the Fans table, click Next and save the method as AddNewFanEmail().

> **Do not check the box next to the FanEmail field when you are building this method. The correct parameter information will be created for you automatically if you just ignore the field completely. All you need to do is select the Fans table, click Next and save the method.**

Let's take a look at the code:

```
Function AddNewFanEmail(ByVal fanEmail As String) As Integer
  Dim connectionString As String = _
    "Provider=Microsoft.Jet.OLEDB.4.0; Ole DB Services=-4; " & _
    "Data Source=C:\BegASPNET\WroxUnited\Database\WroxUnited.mdb"
  Dim dbConnection As System.Data.IDbConnection = _
    New System.Data.OleDb.OleDbConnection(connectionString)

  Dim queryString As String = "INSERT INTO [Fans] ([FanEmail]) " & _
                               "VALUES (@FanEmail)"
  Dim dbCommand As System.Data.IDbCommand = New System.Data.OleDb.OleDbCommand
  dbCommand.CommandText = queryString
  dbCommand.Connection = dbConnection

  Dim dbParam_fanEmail As System.Data.IDataParameter = _
  New System.Data.OleDb.OleDbParameter
  dbParam_fanEmail.ParameterName = "@FanEmail"
  dbParam_fanEmail.Value = fanEmail
  dbParam_fanEmail.DbType = System.Data.DbType.String
  dbCommand.Parameters.Add(dbParam_fanEmail)

  Dim rowsAffected As Integer = 0
  dbConnection.Open
  Try
    rowsAffected = dbCommand.ExecuteNonQuery
  Finally
    dbConnection.Close
  End Try

  Return rowsAffected
End Function
```

6. Change the connection string to use the central connection string:

```
Function AddNewFanEmail(ByVal fanEmail As String) As Integer
  Dim connectionString As String = _
    ConfigurationSettings.AppSettings("ConnectionString")
  Dim dbConnection As System.Data.IDbConnection = _
    New System.Data.OleDb.OleDbConnection(connectionString)
```

7. The last thing you need to do is check whether a cookie is present when the page is loaded so that you can change the display if the user has already registered. Add the following to the Page_Load() method:

```
If Not Request.Cookies("EmailRegister") is nothing Then

  txtEmailAddress.Visible = False
  lblRegister.Text = "You have registered for email updates"
  btnRegister.visible = False

End If
```

Run the page , enter your email address, and click Register. The message will change (so long as you enter a valid email address) to indicate that you've registered, as shown in Figure 11-6.

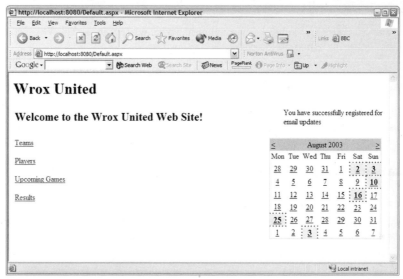

Figure 11-6

Note that the expiration time on the cookie was set to 20 seconds, resulting in your email not being remembered for long. Quickly close your browser and reopen the page. You should see the message shown in Figure 11-7:

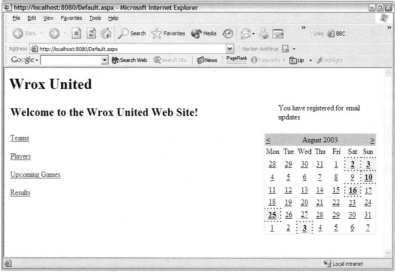

Figure 11-7

If you keep clicking **Refresh**, after about 20 seconds the textbox and button will reappear, along with a message asking you to register.

How It Works

Let's start the discussion by looking directly at what happens when a user clicks the **Register** button. This is when the cookie is created on the client:

```
Sub btnRegister_Click(sender As Object, e As EventArgs)
   Dim FanEmail as String = txtEmailAddress.Text

   'Check whether the email address is already registered
   'If not, we need to register it by calling the AddNewFanEmail() method
   If CheckFanEmailAddresses(FanEmail) = false Then

     AddNewFanEmail(FanEmail)

   End If
```

If the email address is already stored in the database, the `CheckFanEmailAddresses()` method will return `True`. However, if it returns `False`, the email address is new, and needs to be added to the database.

Once the email has been stored in the database, we can go ahead and change the displayed text on the screen:

```
' Email has been registered, so update the display and attempt to set a
' cookie
txtEmailAddress.Visible = False
lblRegister.Text = "You have successfully registered for email updates"
btnRegister.visible = False
```

Next, we attempt to add a cookie to the client's collection of cookies:

```
Dim EmailRegisterCookie as New HttpCookie("EmailRegister")
EmailRegisterCookie.Value = FanEmail
EmailRegisterCookie.Expires = now.AddSeconds(20)
Response.Cookies.Add(EmailRegisterCookie)
```

The first line of code creates a new instance of the `HttpCookie` class, and names it `EmailRegister`. Once the cookie has been successfully created on the client, you can refer to the cookie by name later on in the code. The value of the cookie was set to be the email address entered into the textbox, and the `Expires` property was also set. In this example, the cookie was set to expire 20 seconds from the time at which it was created, which isn't practical in a real world application! The `Expires` property can be any `DateTime` value, so you could, for example, change this to `AddMonths(6)` to refresh your email address list every 6 months.

The `now()` function is a good way to specify that a cookie will expire in a set amount of time from when it was created. For example, you may want to display this box every 6 months to fans in case their email address has changed, to ensure that they are registered correctly. Alternatively, you can hard-code a date (for example, if you wanted to create something like the monthly special offers example discussed earlier).

We also added two data methods to check the status of the cookie. The first method was used to add a new email address to the database:

```
Dim queryString As String = "INSERT INTO [Fans] ([FanEmail]) " & _
                             "VALUES (@FanEmail)"
```

The second data method queried the database to check whether the email address exists in the database. Let's look at the lines of code:

```
Function CheckFanEmailAddresses(ByVal fanEmail As String) As Boolean
```

The first thing altered was the return type of the function. After all, you don't want a DataReader in this case – you want a simple yes or no answer to whether the email address exists already, so the return type is set to return a boolean true or false.

The next change is to the query used:

```
Dim queryString As String = _
  "SELECT COUNT([Fans].[FanEmail]) FROM [Fans]" & _
  "WHERE ([Fans].[FanEmail] = @FanEmail)"
```

The COUNT statement literally counts the number of results matched by the SELECT statement. You should never end up with the result of a count being more than one because this check is performed every time we attempt to add a new email address. To be on the safe side, return true to the calling code if you retrieve any rows at all:

```
Dim Result As Integer = 0
dbConnection.Open

Try
  Result = dbCommand.ExecuteScalar
Finally
  dbConnection.Close
End Try

If Result > 0 then
  Return true
Else Return false
End If
```

The last thing done was adding a quick test to the Page_Load() event handler to check whether a cookie has already been stored on the client:

```
If Not Request.Cookies("EmailRegister") is nothing Then
```

The Request object is used to read the cookie. Notice that you can refer to a cookie by the name given to it earlier. If the cookie exists, this will return True and you can hide the unnecessary registration:

```
  txtEmailAddress.Visible = False
  lblRegister.Text = "You have registered for email updates"
  btnRegister.visible = False
End If
```

Ok, so you've learned a lot about cookies and seen how to use cookies in your site. To recap, the general rules of thumb for using cookies are:

❑ Use them to store small pieces of data that aren't crucial to your application.

❑ Use them wisely – don't be tempted to store large objects in a cookie, because every request a client makes of your site will be accompanied by the cookie data.

❑ Don't rely on them for storing secure user details; instead keep them simple to help with preliminary identification. The Amazon Web site is a good example of how to use cookies. It uses cookies to remember some information about who you are when you visited the site, but to actually *buy* stuff, you need to retype your password details; these are passed to secure servers that authenticate you.

Sessions

A session can be thought of as the total amount of time you spend browsing a site. For example, in an online store, you first visit the site, log on and buy some stuff, and then leave. The term session applies per user, so each user session relates to the interactions that occur when a user browses a site. Information in a session is accessible for as long as the session is active, so you could for example store the name of the currently logged in user in the session object relating to that user, and any of the pages in the site could then take this value and display it.

Sessions are commonly used for things like shopping baskets, or any application that stores information on whether or not a user is logged in. They are tied in to a specific instance of a browser, so a second browser on the same machine would not be able to access the same data.

It's a bit tricky to evaluate when a session ends, since when a browser closes, this information is not usually sent to the server (imagine having to wait for a "close" signal to be sent whenever you closed a Web page!) To solve this problem, you can specify a timeout value for sessions. The default value is normally 20 minutes, which means that the session ends after 20 minutes of inactivity. You can change this value. For example if you created a financial Web site, you may want sessions to end after five minutes of inactivity. This would minimize the chances of sensitive information leaking even if a user forgot to log out or left his browser window open after a banking transaction.

How Do Sessions Work?

When a session starts, you can store data that will exist during that session. This could be simple text information about a user, or an object such as an XML file. A 120-bit session identifier identifies each session. This session identifier is passed between ASP.NET and the client either by using cookies or by placing the identifier in the URL of the page:

```
http://www.mysite.com/(vgjgiz45ib0kqe554jvqxw2b)/Default.aspx
```

Embedding the session identifier in the URL, as demonstrated above, is only necessary when the client has cookies turned off. The actual data stored in the session is held on the server – only the identifier is passed between the client and the server. After the user logs on to an online store, the server knows who the user is, and can relate each request from that user to any of the details stored in the session that relate to that user. Therefore, the server can maintain a shopping basket and checkout functionality without asking the user to log back in with every request. Once the user has finished browsing the site, the server will eventually destroy the information stored in session memory and free up resources that it may need to address other clients. Take a look at Figure 11-8:

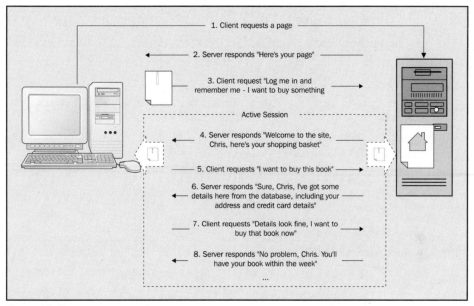

Figure 11-8

ASP.NET by default stores session information in memory in the same process as ASP.NET itself. This means that if the application crashes, the session data will be lost. However, you do have the ability to store session state information in a different process, on a different machine, or even in a database. This flexibility allows you to make your applications more robust in large-scale deployment scenarios.

The `Session` object has quite a few methods that you can use:

❑ `Session.Add`: Adds a new item to the `Session` object.

❑ `Session.Remove`: Removes a named item from the session.

❑ `Session.Clear`: Clears all values from the session, but leaves the session active.

❑ `Session.Abandon`: Ends the current session.

Perhaps the simplest way to add data to a session is to use the following syntax:

```
Session("ItemName") = Contents
```

After creating a new item in the session, you can use the name of the item to refer to the contents of its corresponding object. The item is the identifying feature for the contents of the session, so you could store all the following in the session:

```
Session("Name") = "Chris"
Session("Email") = txtEmailAddress.Text
Session("ShoppingBasket") = HashtableOfBasketItems
```

397

The first item is a simple string, the second is the string entered into a textbox, and the third is a Hashtable object. Let's look at sessions in action using an example.

Try It Out Using Session State – Wrox United, Merchandise.aspx

Before you run this example, you will need three images – shirt.gif, hat.jpg, and mascot.jpg. These three files are available along with the rest of the source code for this book from the Wrox Web site.

1. This example will add another new page called Merchandise.aspx to the site. Add this new blank ASP.NET page to the Wrox United application folder.

2. Add a heading 1 with the text Wrox United at the top of the page, and directly underneath that, add a heading 2 with the text Official Merchandise Store:

```
<form runat="server">
  <h1>Wrox United</h1>
  <h2>Official Merchandise Store</h2>
```

3. Add an HTML table of width 600 pixels to the page, with three columns and three rows. In each row, add in turn an ASP.NET Image control, some text, and an ASP.NET Button, with the following properties:

	Column 1	Column 2	Column 3
Row 1	Image control: **ImageUrl**="images/shirt.gif"	Text: "The Wrox United shirt, available in one size only"	Button Control: **id**="btnBuyShirt" **onclick**="AddItemToBasket" **width**="100px" **text**="Buy a shirt!" **CommandArgument**="Shirt"
Row 2	Image control: **ImageUrl**="Images/hat.jpg"	Text: "The official Wrox United hat!"	Button Control: **id**="btnBuyHat" **onclick**="AddItemToBasket" **width**="100px" **text**="Buy a hat!" **CommandArgument**="Hat"
Row 3	Image control: **ImageUrl**="images/mascot.jpg"	Text: "The Wrox United cuddly mascot – a must-have for the younger supporters!"	Button Control: **id**="btnBuyMascot" **onclick**="AddItemToBasket" **width**="100px" **text**="Buy a Mascot!" **CommandArgument**="Mascot"

You should see the Design view as shown in Figure 11-9:

Figure 11-9

4. In HTML view, you should have the following code generated for you automatically (alternatively, instead of dragging and dropping, you could type this lot in by hand if you wanted to):

```
<table width="600">
  <tr>
    <td><asp:Image id="imgCap" runat="server" ImageUrl="images/shirt.gif">
        </asp:Image></td>
    <td>The Wrox United shirt, available in one size only</td>
    <td><asp:Button id="btnBuyShirt" onclick="AddItemToBasket"
                    runat="server" Text="Buy a shirt!" Width="100px"
                    CommandArgument="Shirt"></asp:Button> </td>
  </tr>
  <tr>
    <td><asp:Image id="imgShirt" runat="server" ImageUrl="images/hat.jpg">
        </asp:Image></td>
    <td>The official Wrox United hat!</td>
    <td><asp:Button id="btnBuyHat" onclick="AddItemToBasket"
                    runat="server" Text="Buy the hat!" Width="100px"
                    CommandArgument="Hat"></asp:Button> </td>
  </tr>
  <tr>
    <td><asp:Image id="imgMascot" runat="server" ImageUrl="images/mascot1.jpg">
        </asp:Image></td>

    <td>The Wrox United cuddy mascot - a must-have for the younger supporters!

    </td>
```

```
        <td><asp:Button id="btnBuyMascot" onclick="AddItemToBasket"
                    runat="server" Text="Buy the mascot!" Width="100px"
                    CommandArgument="Mascot"></asp:Button> </td>
    </tr>
  </table>
```

5. Now add the following code below the table, while still in HTML view:

```
<br/>
  <p>
    Your basket contains:
    <asp:label id="lblBasketMessage" runat="server"></asp:label>
  </p>
  <p>
    <asp:Repeater id="basketlist" runat="server">
      <itemTemplate>
        <asp:Label width="70" runat="server"
                  text='<%# Container.DataItem.Key & "s: " %>'>
          </asp:Label>
         
        <asp:Label runat="server" text='<%# container.Dataitem.Value %>'>
          </asp:Label>
        <br />
      </itemTemplate>
    </asp:Repeater>
  </p>
  <p>
    <asp:Button id="btnCheckOut" runat="server" Text="Checkout"></asp:Button>
    <asp:Button id="btnEmptyBasket" onclick="btnEmptyBasket_Click"
              runat="server" Text="Empty Basket"></asp:Button>
  </p>
</form>
```

6. That's it for the HTML side of things! Switch to the **Code** view and enter the following methods:

Note that the method signature for the `AddItemToBasket()` *sub is already generated for you, so make sure you don't add another copy of this or the page won't compile properly.*

```
Sub Page_Load

  If Session("Basket") is Nothing Then
    ' Call the InitializeBasket method to create a new empty basket
    InitializeBasket()
  End If

End Sub

Sub btnEmptyBasket_Click(sender As Object, e As EventArgs)
  ' Call the InitializeBasket method to clear out any existing items
  InitializeBasket()

End Sub
Sub AddItemToBasket(sender As Object, e As EventArgs)
  ' Each time this is run, get the CommandArgument property of the button that
  ' fired the event, and use this to populate the Session object
```

```
    Dim itemName as String = sender.CommandArgument
    Dim basketTable as System.Collections.Hashtable = Session("Basket")

    ' If the item has never been added to the session before, add a new empty entry
    ' into the hashtable for this item
    If basketTable(ItemName) Is Nothing
      basketTable(ItemName) = 0
    End If

    ' Increment the counter for the selected item
    Dim itemCount as Integer = basketTable(ItemName)
    basketTable(ItemName) = itemCount + 1

End Sub
Sub InitializeBasket()

    ' Clear out the session object and fill it with a new, empty hashtable
    Dim basketTable as new System.Collections.Hashtable()
    Session("Basket") = basketTable

End Sub

Sub Page_Prerender

    ' Run the following code immediately before the page is displayed, after all
    ' other events have been processed
    Dim basketTable as System.Collections.Hashtable = Session("Basket")
    basketlist.DataSource = basketTable
    basketlist.databind()

    If basketTable.Count = 0 then
      lblBasketMessage.Text = "nothing - please buy something!"
    else
      lblBasketMessage.Text = ""
    End If

End Sub
```

You'll notice that there are quite a few methods in here that we'll look at in detail in just a moment; these are designed to help your application become more scalable Let's see how the page works, then the purpose of these methods will be a bit more clear. It's time to run the page and try it out! You should see the screen depicted in Figure 11-10:

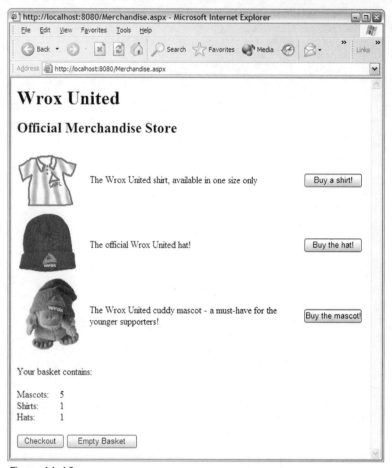

Figure 11-10

How It Works

This simple example uses quite a few techniques to store data about the items in the shopping basket. The data stored in the session object is a hashtable that stores pairs of names and values. The key field for the hashtable is the name of the item added to the basket and the value is the quantity of that item. The event handlers on that page all perform different actions on the data stored in the session.

Let's start by looking through the added code.

First, we added an HTML table and some simple controls to the page. Notice that the `onclick` attribute of each button in the table was set to fire the same event handler – `AddItemToBasket()`. Each button has a unique `CommandArgument` property that describes what is added to the basket:

```
<table width="600">
  <tr>
    <td><asp:Image id="imgCap" runat="server" ImageUrl="images/shirt.gif">
```

```
      </asp:Image></td>
    <td>The Wrox United shirt, available in one size only</td>
    <td><asp:Button id="btnBuyShirt" onclick="AddItemToBasket"
                runat="server" Text="Buy a shirt!" Width="100px"
                CommandArgument="Shirt"></asp:Button> </td>
  </tr>
  <tr>
    <td><asp:Image id="imgShirt" runat="server" ImageUrl="images/hat.jpg">
        </asp:Image></td>
    <td>The official Wrox United hat!</td>
    <td><asp:Button id="btnBuyHat" onclick="AddItemToBasket"
                runat="server" Text="Buy the hat!" Width="100px"
                CommandArgument="Hat"></asp:Button> </td>
  </tr>
  <tr>
    <td><asp:Image id="imgMascot" runat="server" ImageUrl="images/mascot1.jpg">
        </asp:Image></td>
    <td>The Wrox United cuddy mascot - a must-have for the younger supporters!
    </td>
    <td><asp:Button id="btnBuyMascot" onclick="AddItemToBasket"
                runat="server" Text="Buy the mascot!" Width="100px"
                CommandArgument="Mascot"></asp:Button> </td>
  </tr>
</table>
```

Next, we added some more controls to display the contents of the basket and to provide the option of either clearing the basket or checking out via a checkout and payment process:

```
<br/>
  <p>
    Your basket contains:
    <asp:label id="lblBasketMessage" runat="server"></asp:label>
  </p>
  <p>
    <asp:Repeater id="basketlist" runat="server">
      <itemTemplate>
```

The `basketlist Repeater` control will be databound to a `Hashtable` object (as we'll see in just a moment). This enables us to do some interesting databinding in this control. The first label in this control includes an interesting statement:

```
<asp:Label width="70" runat="server"
            text='<%# Container.DataItem.Key & "s: " %>'>
  </asp:Label>
```

Notice that the `text` property has a databinding statement in it. Here, the currently selected `Key` of the current item in the Hashtable used to populate this control is displayed in this label, along with some text. In this way, we take the name of each item, and can pluralize it by adding "s" to the end of it. The colon is there to add a neat grammatical separator between the name of the item and the quantity (so we have "Mascots: 3" as the displayed text, having obtained the key "Mascot" from the Hashtable).

```
         
        <asp:Label runat="server" text='<%# container.Dataitem.Value %>'>
          </asp:Label>
        <br />
    </itemTemplate>
  </asp:Repeater>
</p>
<p>
  <asp:Button id="btnCheckOut" runat="server" Text="Checkout"></asp:Button>
  <asp:Button id="btnEmptyBasket" onclick="btnEmptyBasket_Click"
             runat="server" Text="Empty Basket"></asp:Button>
</p>
```

Note that the `Checkout` button hasn't been implemented in the code – that's a bit beyond the scope of this chapter. For more information on online payments, you may want to consult `www.paypal.com;` *one of many online payment service providers.*

It's time to work through the methods in the code. They are presented here in roughly the same order in which they will be processed when a page is sent to the browser (following the chain of events as they correspond to the page lifecycle).

Firstly, the `Page_Load()` event handler:

```
Sub Page_Load

  If Session("Basket") is Nothing Then
    ' Call the InitializeBasket method to create a new empty basket
    InitializeBasket()
  End If

End Sub
```

Each time the page is loaded, this method will check whether the Session object contains a basket. If it doesn't, a new empty basket is created. We'll look at the `InitializeBasket()` method that does this in just a moment.

```
Sub btnEmptyBasket_Click(sender As Object, e As EventArgs)

  ' Call the InitializeBasket method to clear out any existing items
  InitializeBasket()

End Sub
```

The `btnEmptyBasket_Click()` method also calls the `InitializeBasket()` method to clear out any existing basket data. The `AddItemToBasket()` method comes next, and this one is quite interesting.

For starters, all three item buttons not only called *this* method, but also passed along a
CommandArgument property.

```
Sub AddItemToBasket(sender As Object, e As EventArgs)

    ' Each time this is run, get the CommandArgument property of the button that
    ' fired the event, and use this to populate the Session object
    Dim itemName as String = sender.CommandArgument
```

This single line of code is all that's needed to get the string information that specifies which button the
user clicked. Once you have this string (which, as you may recall, was set to either Shirt, Hat, or
Mascot), you can use it to add data to the session.

First, create a local Hashtable object to temporarily store the contents of the Session's basket item. This
will make the code easier to understand.

> **Note that the New keyword is not included in the Hashtable's declaration – this is
> very important, as you'll see in a moment!**

```
Dim basketTable as System.Collections.Hashtable = Session("Basket")
```

The remainder of the code for this method uses the basketTable hashtable representation of the
contents of the Session object's Basket item to add items to the session. Now, the fun thing is that
because you didn't add a New keyword to the basketTable, you don't get a *new* Hashtable object.
Instead, you *refer* to an existing Hashtable object, specifically the one that is stored in the Session object.
This is an example of working with *reference* types. Because you are working with the contents of the
Session's Basket item via the basketTable Hashtable, anything you do to the basketTable will affect
the contents of the Session.

A full discussion of value and reference types is a bit beyond this chapter. For more information, you
should read Professional ASP.NET 1.1 Special Edition, ISBN: 0-7645-5890-0.

We check to see if the item being added to the basket has been added before:

```
    ' If the item has never been added to the session before, add a new empty entry
    ' into the hashtable for this item
    If basketTable(ItemName) Is Nothing
        basketTable(ItemName) = 0
    End If
```

If the item has never been in the basket before, the item is added to the basket with a quantity of zero to
initialize to make it ready to receive a new quantity. In the next piece of code, one more of the selected
item is added to the basket. Thus, if there were already three Mascots in the basket, clicking this button
will add another one to the basket, resulting in a basket that contains four fluffy mascots. If, however,
this were the first mascot bought, you would end up with one mascot (0 + 1):

```
    ' Increment the counter for the selected item
    Dim itemCount as Integer = basketTable(ItemName)
    basketTable(ItemName) = itemCount + 1
End Sub
```

Let's look at the `InitializeBasket()` method mentioned earlier:

```
Sub InitializeBasket()

  ' Clear out the session object and fill it with a new, empty hashtable
  Dim basketTable as new System.Collections.Hashtable()
  Session("Basket") = basketTable

End Sub
```

In just two lines of code, a new Hashtable is created, and the Session's `Basket` item is set to point to this new Hashtable object. The new object doesn't have any items in it, so it will be an *empty* basket. If this method was called in response to clicking the **Empty Basket** button, it's likely that you originally had a full basket, so where do all the original contents of the basket go?

Well, the answer is that by changing which Hashtable the Basket item is pointing to, we change which Hashtable is referenced by the Session. Thus, the old Hashtable is no longer pointed to by anything, and the .NET garbage collector will come along and sweep the Hashtable away. The poor old Hashtable is no longer wanted and no one is using it. The garbage collector gets rid of unreferenced objects on a regular basis, and it's very efficient in how it does it. The memory that the old Hashtable object was taking up is completely recycled anew, meaning that you are less likely to run out of memory.

Right, there is one last event handler to look at. This one handles the `Prerender` event of the page. This event is always fired when a page is loaded, and is your last chance to change anything just before the page is displayed:

```
Sub Page_Prerender

  ' Run the following code immediately before the page is displayed, after all
  ' other events have been processed
  Dim basketTable as System.Collections.Hashtable = Session("Basket")
  basketlist.DataSource = basketTable
  basketlist.databind()
```

This piece of code also uses the same Hashtable that is stored in the Session object's `Basket` item, by pointing another Hashtable towards the same data. This data is all stored in your computer's memory, so what you're doing is telling your program where to find that data. Again, any changes made to the `basketTable` will change the contents of the `Basket` (because you are changing the same object!). The `basketList` control is a simple `Repeater` control, like the ones used in the previous chapter. You can bind the contents of a Hashtable to a `Repeater` to display its contents on the page. You can display the contents of the page by binding the contents of a Hashtable to a `Repeater`:

```
  If basketTable.Count = 0 then
    lblBasketMessage.Text = "nothing - please buy something!"
  else
    lblBasketMessage.Text = ""
  End If

End Sub
```

Lastly, a message is displayed if the basket is empty (if the count of all the items in the `basketTable` Hashtable is `0`, the Hashtable is empty).

All this is done in the `Prerender()` event handler to ensure that only the most recent data is displayed, after any items that may have been added as a result of clicking a button. If this was done in the `Page_Load()` event, you would not be displaying the current data, but the data of what happened that last time the button was clicked. Try this out for yourself – if you move all the contents of this method into the `Page_Load()` event handler, you'll see that the basket list is one behind the actual count, because `Page_Load()` is handled *before* the button click events are handled.

> **The actual order of events is: Page_Load —> Control Events —> Prerender**

That's it for now – Sessions will be back later when we put together a fun example that adds some style to the Wrox United site. Let's move on to applications.

Applications

One step up from the session is the application. From the time an ASP.NET application is first loaded, to when the application is restarted, which could be due to a configuration change or the restarting of the Web server, you can store information relating to that application in the `Application` object. When the application is restarted, any information stored in the `Application` object will be lost, so you need to decide carefully what to store in application state.

> **It's best to store small amounts of data in application state to minimize memory usage on the server. Small bits of information that change frequently but don't need to be saved when the application is restarted are best kept in a `Session` object. For larger data or for data that doesn't often change, the ASP.NET `Cache` object can be very useful, as you'll see in the *Caching* section later in the chapter.**

How Do Applications Work?

Applications are a bit simpler than sessions, since they run entirely on the server. When the application is running, you can use the same method of storing data in an application object as used with sessions. All you need to do is enter an identifier and a value, which can be of any type, even a dataset.

Perhaps the best way to look at how application state can be used is through an example. Let's take this opportunity to add to your site another page that has more interactivity than the previous pages!

Try It Out **Using Application State: Wrox United, Chat.aspx**

In this example you will construct the world's simplest chat room! All you need is a new ASP.NET page on the Wrox United site, a few controls, a bit of code and you can chat with anyone around the world.

1. The first step is to reopen `Default.aspx` and add a new hyperlink to the list of links on the left. Call it `lnkChat`, and set its `NavigateUrl` property to `Chat.aspx`.

2. Next, create a new ASP.NET page called `Chat.aspx`. Switch to HTML view and enter the following code within the `<form>` tags:

```html
<h1>Wrox United
</h1>
<h2>Online Chat
</h2>
<asp:TextBox id="txtChatBox" runat="server"
             TextMode="MultiLine"
             Height="200px" Width="550px" ReadOnly="True">
</asp:TextBox>
<br />
<br />
<table width="550">
  <tbody>
    <tr>
      <td width="150">
        Enter your name:
      </td>
      <td>
        <asp:TextBox id="txtName" runat="server"></asp:TextBox>
      </td>
    </tr>
    <tr>
      <td width="150">
        Enter your message:
      </td>
      <td>
        <asp:TextBox id="txtMessage" runat="server"
                 MaxLength="100" Width="402px">
        </asp:TextBox>
      </td>
    </tr>
    <tr>
      <td>
         
      </td>
      <td>
        <asp:Button id="btnPost" onclick="btnPost_Click"
                 runat="server" Text="Post message">
        </asp:Button>
        <asp:Button id="btnClearLog" onclick="btnClearLog_Click"
                 runat="server" Text="Clear log">
        </asp:Button>
      </td>
    </tr>
  </tbody>
</table>
```

Quickly flick to the Design view and look at the page; it should be as shown in Figure 11-11:

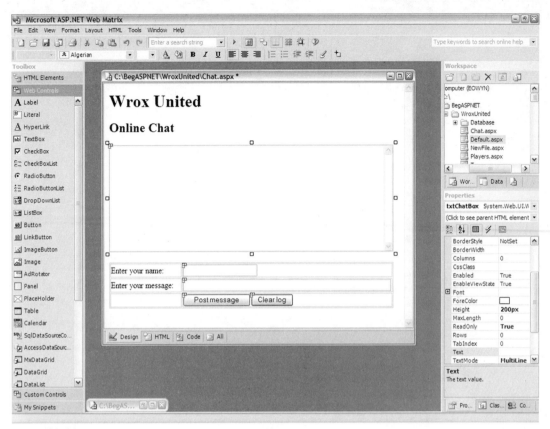

Figure 11-11

3. Switch to the Code view and enter the following code:

```
Sub btnPost_Click(sender As Object, e As EventArgs)

  Dim newmessage as string = txtName.Text & ":" & _
            Microsoft.VisualBasic.vbtab & txtMessage.Text & _
            Microsoft.VisualBasic.vbCrLf & Application("ChatLog")

  If newmessage.Length > 500 then
    newmessage = newmessage.substring(0,499)
  end if


  Application("ChatLog") = newmessage

  txtChatBox.Text = Application("ChatLog")
  txtMessage.Text = ""

End Sub
```

This event handler runs whenever someone clicks the Post message button on the page. This method will save the name of the person who posted the message and the message itself in the `Application` object.

4. Now add the following two methods. The first is a `Page_Load()` event handler that loads in the details of the current chat. The second clears the log when the Clear log button is pressed:

```
Sub Page_Load

  txtChatBox.Text = Application("ChatLog")

End Sub

Sub btnClearLog_Click(sender As Object, e As EventArgs)

  Application("ChatLog") = ""
  txtChatBox.Text = Application("ChatLog")

End Sub
```

Run the page and you will be able to have a conversation with yourself (Figure 11-12)!

Figure 11-12

Notice that new messages in the chat will always be added to the top of the window. If you increased the size of the chat log, you could store a lot more text, which would start to disappear off the bottom of the textbox (which you could view by scrolling down the box). Keeping the newly added messages at the top means that new content is always visible.

Also notice that after a certain amount of text has appeared in the main chat window, characters start to disappear from the end of the chat – this is intentional, and saves on server resources, as we'll see in a moment. Additionally, clicking the Clear log button will wipe the entire chat log instantly. New browsers to the page will see the current chat as soon as they get to the page.

How It Works

We've constructed a page that any visitor to the site can use to chat to their friends. There isn't a permanent store for chat logs, but you can at least get instant communication working, which could be really useful for a quick Internet team chat (especially if one member of the team works at an office where instant messaging programs like MSN Messenger or AOL Instant Messenger are banned!)

Let's look through the added code. The front end of the site is quite simple, so let's directly look at the properties of the three textboxes on the form:

```
<asp:TextBox id="txtChatBox" runat="server"
             TextMode="MultiLine"
             Height="200px" Width="550px" ReadOnly="True">
</asp:TextBox>
```

Because the first textbox holds the entire chat transcript so far, we've made it a ReadOnly, MultiLine textbox that has a specified width and height. The second textbox is very simple indeed:

```
<asp:TextBox id="txtName" runat="server"></asp:TextBox>
```

The third textbox has an interesting feature:

```
<asp:TextBox id="txtMessage" runat="server"
             MaxLength="100" Width="402px">
</asp:TextBox>
```

We specified that this textbox has a maximum length, to prevent anyone from entering really long messages.

In the Code editor, we added two button-click event handlers and a Page_Load() event handler. Let's look at them in turn:

```
Sub btnPost_Click(sender As Object, e As EventArgs)

Dim newmessage as string = txtName.Text & ":" & _
            Microsoft.VisualBasic.vbtab & txtMessage.Text & _
            Microsoft.VisualBasic.vbCrLf & Application("ChatLog")
```

The first event handler reacts to the posting of a new message. A new String object is created to hold the message, some formatting, and the name of the person posting the message. The string is made up of the name of the person posting the message, followed by a colon:

```
txtName.Text & ":"
```

Then a tab character is added to space out the name from the message, before adding the message itself:

```
Microsoft.VisualBasic.vbtab & txtMessage.Text
```

Finally, we added a carriage return (or line feed character), followed by the current contents of the chat log, so the new message will always appear at the top of the textbox, one line above the previous message:

```
Microsoft.VisualBasic.vbCrLf & Application("ChatLog")
```

The existing chat log is saved in the `Application` object and is retrieved using the following syntax:

```
Application("ChatLog")
```

If there is no data in the log yet, this value will be null, and the new message will simply contain a formatted version of the new post. You can refer to the contents of the item in the Application store by its name, in this case `ChatLog`. This will return the contents of the item, which in this example is the string of the existing messages.

Note that you don't want to store too much data in the Application object or your Web server will grind to a halt! In the example, this has been brutally limited to 500 characters. Any text beyond this point is removed (working from oldest to newest text):

```
If newmessage.Length > 500 then
   newmessage = newmessage.substring(0,499)
end if
```

The `substring()` method grabs all the string data between the two specified points, in this case, from the first character (at index 0) to the 500th character (at index 499). If you want a longer log of chat transcript, increase the two larger numbers to higher values (note that the end point of the substring is always one less than the length of the message because the items in the string are zero indexed).

Finally, the new transcript is saved back to the Application object:

```
Application("ChatLog") = newmessage
```

In addition, the new transcript is displayed in the transcript textbox:

```
txtChatBox.Text = Application("ChatLog")
txtMessage.Text = ""

   End Sub
```

The application works quite well, but without some mechanism to refresh the page, other people browsing the page would have to either keep refreshing the page manually, or post new messages to see any new messages. The most common solution to this problem would be to split the page into two frames. The top frame would contain the chat box and the bottom frame would contain the textboxes and buttons. Then an auto-refresh could be added to the top page to force it to refresh every 10 seconds or so.

Application state is quite a useful feature, as is session state, but one of the coolest things that ASP.NET has to offer when it comes to applications and sessions is the ability to react to events raised by both of these. The next section looks at this process in more detail.

Reacting to Application and Session Events

An event is fired every time an application or a session starts, ends, or when an error occurs. As an ASP.NET developer, you have the ability to intercept these events and write event handlers for them.

These event handlers have numerous useful features. For example, when an application starts, you can create in the application state an item with a default value that can be updated later. Event handlers are placed in a special application-specific file called Global.asax.

Global.asax

This file exists at the root of a Web application, and can contain event handlers for all the application and session level events that are fired when an application is run. If you open up Web Matrix and create a new Global.asax file, you will see the following:

```vb
<%@ Application language="VB" %>

<script runat="server">

  Sub Application_Start(Sender As Object, E As EventArgs)
    ' Code that runs on application startup
  End Sub

  Sub Application_End(Sender As Object, E As EventArgs)
    ' Code that runs on application shutdown
  End Sub

  Sub Application_Error(Sender As Object, E As EventArgs)
    ' Code that runs when an unhandled error occurs
  End Sub

  Sub Session_Start(Sender As Object, E As EventArgs)
    ' Code that runs when a new session is started
  End Sub

  Sub Session_End(Sender As Object, E As EventArgs)
    ' Code that runs when a session ends
  End Sub

</script>
```

The helpful comments in the code give you an idea of what belongs in each part of the file. Note that you can add code that runs in one of five event handlers. Suppose you add the following line to the `Application_Start` event handler:

```
Sub Application_Start(Sender As Object, E As EventArgs)
   Application("ChatLog") = "Welcome to the Wrox United chat page!"
End Sub
```

Adding this one line means that the very first time the application is started, there will be some default text in the chat page.

The event handlers available in the `Global.asax` page mean that you could, for example, add some global event handling code to the `Application_Error()` event handler, or add some cleanup code to the `Session_End` section to ensure that all memory is freed up when a session ends.

Let's add a `Global.asax` page to the application now and have a go at adding global code.

Try It Out   Global.asax – Wrox United Global Settings

1. Head back into Web Matrix and create a new file. Select the `Global.asax` file type from the options, as shown in Figure 11-13:

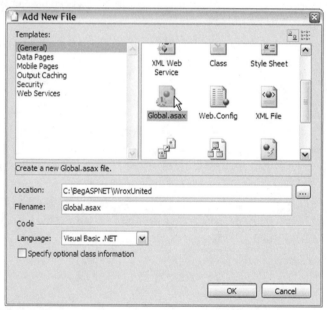

Figure 11-13

2. You'll find that Web Matrix automatically creates the skeleton of the file, so you don't need to add much code. In your `Global.asax` page, add the following highlighted lines of code in the appropriate event handlers:

```
<%@ Application language="VB" %>
<script runat="server">

  Sub Application_Start(Sender As Object, E As EventArgs)
    Application("ChatLog") = "Welcome to the Wrox United chat page!"
  End Sub
...
  Sub Session_Start(Sender As Object, E As EventArgs)

    Dim basketTable as new System.Collections.Hashtable()
    Session("Basket") = basketTable
  End Sub
...
</script>
```

Shut down the Web Matrix Web server (by right-clicking on the Web Matrix Web Server icon in the System tray in the bottom right of the screen, then clicking Stop). Relaunch the Chat.aspx page, and the application will restart and fire the Application's Start event. Notice that default text appears when you open the chat page for the first time, shown in Figure 11-14:

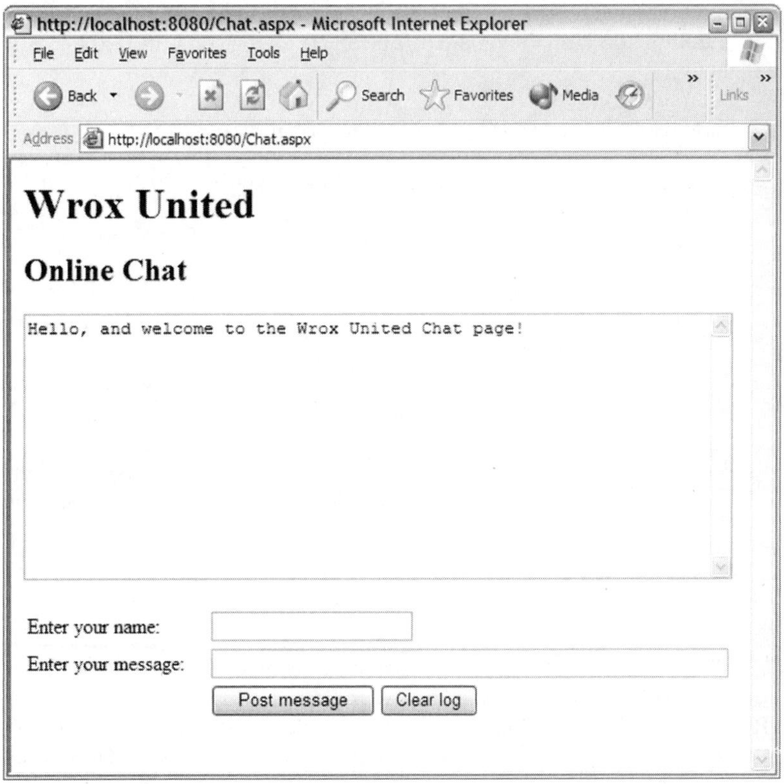

Figure 11-14

The other change made doesn't really have a discernable impact on the basket example, except that it handles creating a new instance of the basket Hashtable that was used in the Merchandise.aspx page for us. This means that you could theoretically remove the code from the Page_Load() event for that page that checks whether the basket exists or not (it will always exist, even for new sessions, if this code runs as intended) without affecting the basket.

3. Once you have added the code to Global.asax, remove the contents of the Page_Load event handler for the Merchandise.aspx page and you will find that the page will still run without errors.

How It Works

Let's quickly run through the newly added code:

```
Sub Application_Start(Sender As Object, E As EventArgs)
    Application("ChatLog") = "Welcome to the Wrox United chat page!"
End Sub
```

In the Application_Start() event handler, we set the Application object's ChatLog item to have some default text. Whenever the application is restarted, there will be some text in the chat room. Note that when you click the Clear log button on that page, the default text will not be displayed, because the application is still running. Clicking the Clear Log button clears the contents of the existing object, without reinitializing it.

The next change made was to the Session_Start() event handler:

```
Sub Session_Start(Sender As Object, E As EventArgs)
    Dim basketTable as new System.Collections.Hashtable()
    Session("Basket") = basketTable
End Sub
```

In this case, we duplicated the code that used in the InitializeBasket() method in the Merchandise.aspx page's code, and placed it in the event handler. This means that every new session will run this code before the user even browses to that page, so the basket will always exist for each session until the session ends (when all session objects will be cleared out).

Global.asax is a very useful tool for storing default application-wide settings, but there is another way to remember information for the entire duration of an application, which is to *cache* information.

Caching

In addition to Application state, ASP.NET offers us another way to share objects across an application – the Cache object. Any object, from XML data to a simple variable can be stored in the Cache object. If you are thinking that this sounds quite similar to the Application object, you'd be right. In general terms, you can use the Cache object in exactly the same way. However, the Cache object also has some additional features, notably the ability to store data about *dependencies*.

So, what are dependencies? Well, imagine you wanted to store the contents of a hashtable in the cache. For example, this hashtable could hold a set of dates corresponding to the dates when a soccer team is playing a match. You could save this to the cache with a dependency set to the value of a global variable; this could be a `DateTime` field representing when the list of dates was last updated. If the contents of that variable change (if a new match was scheduled), the cached hashtable would immediately expire and need to be regenerated to display the new date.

ASP.NET allows you to have dependencies between items placed in the cache and files in the file system. If a file targeted by a dependency changes, ASP.NET automatically removes dependent items from the cache. This allows for the development of fast applications where developers do not have to worry about stale data remaining in the cache.

To add an object to the cache, all you need to do in the simplest case is:

```
Cache("MyCachedThing") = ThingToBeCached
```

An example of this would be:

```
Cache("TeamNickname") = txtNickname.Text
```

In this example, you created a new item that stores a value that comes from the `Text` property of a textbox, and stored it in the `Cache` collection.

As you might be able to tell, the `Cache` stores data in the form of a collection of name / value pairs. To retrieve the value of an item in the `Cache`, all you need to do is refer to the item by its name:

```
lblDisplayNickname.Text = Cache("TeamNickname")
```

To add a dependency to the object being cached, you need to add some more parameters when adding the item to the cache.

There are two methods for adding an object to the cache with a dependency or a specified expiration (which works in a similar way to the other state management mechanisms encountered in this chapter).

The `Insert()` method adds an item to the cache. The `Add()` method also adds an item to the cache, but it also returns an object representing the item you add to the cache. Let's see what this means:

```
Cache.Insert("TeamNickname", txtNickname.Text, null, _
             DateTime.Now.AddMinutes(20), NoSlidingExpiration)
```

This statement will add a new entry to the cache called `TeamNickname`. The value will come from the `Text` property of a TextBox. There are no dependencies for this item (which is why you include null in the parameter list). The last two options are where the expiration for the item is set. In this example, the expiration is set to an absolute value (using the `DateTime` object) whereas the second parameter accepts sliding time values (specified using the `TimeSpan` object).

The Add() method works exactly the same way, except that it returns an object representing the cached item. So, instead of inserting the new item into the cache on one line and using it on a following line of code, you could do the following:

```
lblDisplayNickname.Text = Cache.Add ("TeamNickname", _
                           txtNickname.Text, null, _
                           DateTime.Now.AddMinutes(20), _
                           NoSlidingExpiration)
```

You can't add a new item to the cache using the Add() *method if an item with the same key already exists – in that situation, you would need to use the* Insert() *method.*

Finally, you can be notified when an item in the cache expires, enabling you to code event handlers that react to this, a feature that could come in very handy! Let's say you cache that Hashtable of match dates in a cache object – you could intercept the event that fires when the cache expires, and repopulate the cache with an updated set of data automatically. Scheduling these sorts of actions for times when the site is at its most lightly loaded means that visitors will be less likely to be inconvenienced by any of these sorts of updates.

We won'tt be looking at how to implement this in the examples in this book, so if you are interested in learning more about this process, you should consult the documentation and learn about using the CacheItemRemovedCallback *delegate. Refer to Professional ASP.NET 1.1 Special Edition, Wiley ISBN: 0-7645-5890-0 for more on this subject.*

Let's look at an example.

Try It Out Wrox United – Caching Objects

Cast your mind back to the previous chapter and you will recall that the calendar control added to the front page of the site used a Hashtable to store the list of dates on which there were matches scheduled. This Hashtable had to be refreshed every time the page was hit, which meant that each request opened up a fresh connection to the database to retrieve the active dates. However, the list of dates isn't likely to change all that often, so remembering that data for subsequent hits would be a great idea, which is what we'll implement here.

1. Reopen Default.aspx in Web Matrix and amend the following lines of code in the Page_Load() event:

```
Sub Page_Load()
  If Cache("DateList") is Nothing Then
    Dim DateReader as System.Data.iDataReader
    DateReader = Dates()

    While DateReader.Read()
      DateList(DateReader("Date")) = DateReader("Date")
    End While
    DateReader.Close()
```

```
     Cache.Insert("DateList", DateList, nothing, DateTime.Now.AddMinutes(1), _
                  Cache.NoSlidingExpiration)

  Response.Write ("Added to cache")
Else
 Response.Write ("Already in cache - nothing added")

End if
```

```
If Not Request.Cookies("EmailRegister") is nothing Then

...

  End If
End Sub
```

Notice that a couple of `Response.Write` statements were added to the code – these are crude but effective ways of quickly testing whether some code worked or not, and since the caching won't really produce any visible results, you can use these to confirm that the newly implemented caching mechanism is working.

2. Amend the following highlighted line of code from the `DayRender()` event handler for the `Calendar` control:

```
Sub EventCalendar_DayRender(sender As Object, e As DayRenderEventArgs)

    If Not Cache("DateList")(e.day.date) is Nothing then

      e.cell.style.add("font-weight", "bold")
...

  End Sub
```

3. Run the code and you should see Figure 11-15 the first time the page is loaded:

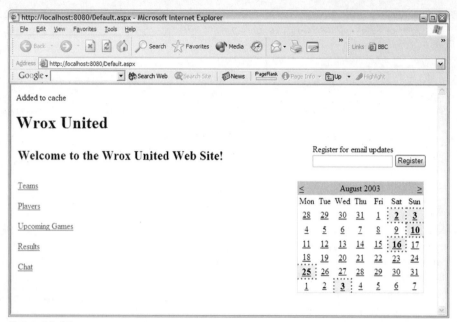

Figure 11-15

Now refresh the page, or even launch a new browser instance to view the page as shown in Figure 11-16:

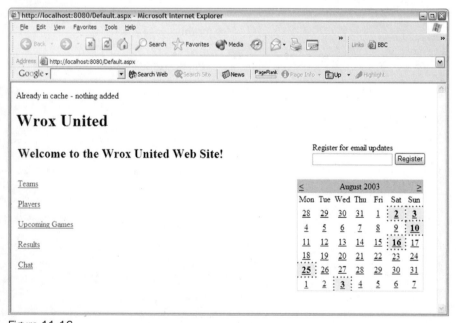

Figure 11-16

This message will appear in the top left of the page if you keep refreshing the page for a whole minute. Any hits received by the server after that minute is over will reload the Hashtable into the cache.

How It Works

Every connection opened to a database is a costly maneuver; reducing the frequency of actions like this is essential for any site to perform well under load. Therefore, this simple example could considerably improve the performance of the Wrox United application.

So what did we actually do? Look at the code added to the `Page_Load()` event handler:

```
If Cache("DateList") is Nothing Then
```

The first addition checks whether there is an object called `DateList` in the cache. If there isn't one, we populate the Hashtable object like before:

```
Dim DateReader as System.Data.iDataReader
DateReader = Dates()

While DateReader.Read()
  DateList(DateReader("Date")) = DateReader("Date")
End While
DateReader.Close()
```

Then you can add this newly created Hashtable to the cache:

```
Cache.Insert("DateList", DateList, nothing, DateTime.Now.AddMinutes(1),_
             Cache.NoSlidingExpiration)
```

In this example, we specified that the `DateList Hashtable` object should be stored in the cache with the name `DateList`. We didn't specify a dependency for this object, but we *did* specify that it only exists for one minute before expiring. In a real life situation, you could increase this to whatever you like – once every couple of hours, once a day, whatever is appropriate – depending on how often the data changes.

Finally, we added some quick 'n dirty debugging statements to the code to help see what was going on. Remove these or at least comment them out once you're happy with the way your code works.

```
  Response.Write ("Added to cache")
Else
 Response.Write ("Already in cache - nothing added")
End if
```

The only other change made was to the `DayRender()` event handler for the `Calendar` control:

```
If Not Cache("DateList")(e.day.date) is Nothing then
```

Instead of referring to the Hashtable directly, you can now refer to the version stored in the `Cache` object, substituting `Cache("DateList")` for `DateList` in the code.

State Recommendations

In this chapter, we looked at several different methods for storing state information, but the question is, which is the right one to use? Well, the answer is that it depends on what you want to achieve. The Microsoft MSDN documentation has a great discussion on this topic available to view online at http://msdn.microsoft.com/library/default.asp?url=/library/enus/vbcon/html/vbconchoosingserverstateoption.asp .However, to round off this chapter, let's look at a quick overview of the most important considerations when choosing which method to use.

When to Use Cookies

Cookies are great for storing small pieces of identification data but not complete authentication details. They can be configured to expire after any length of time, but most of the cookies on your system are likely to last a long time. Once you log on to Amazon.com for the first time, on every subsequent trip you make to the site, you will be presented with a personalized front page. Cookies are also stored on the client, which takes the burden off the server a bit.

Cookies, however, can be blocked at the client end, so you can't rely on your users being able to use them. Also, cookies should never be used to store sensitive information, since cookies can be tampered with – all you have to do is open a cookie, change its contents and save it again, and the Web site that created the cookie may not be able to use that cookie any more.

When to Use Sessions

Sessions are used to maintain information about users across a series of pages in a site. The `Session` object can store any object you choose, and is thus a very flexible way to remember information. If you need to remember any information relating to a user session, the `Session` object is the right choice for you. You can also react to session-wide events, which gives us even more flexibility.

However, extreme flexibility comes with a price – you must take care not to store too much information in the `Session` object, because you'll quickly find it can be a drain on server resources. Store only essential data in a session.

When to Use Applications

Applications are very powerful and flexible, just like sessions. You can store any object in application state. Also, you can react to events raised (such as the `Start` and `End` of the application, as well as a global `Error` event) and add custom event handler code so that you can store information globally, and have it accessible by any code in the application.

The main disadvantages of applications are that they too can drain your server's resources, and since they don't exist after the application ends, they shouldn't be used to store anything you need to keep. You can specify default values for both the `Session` and `Application` objects using `Global.asax`, but if you need to store data, use something more permanent, such as a database.

When to Use Caching

When you find yourself spending many precious server resources accessing the same data over and over, use caching instead! Caching data can bring huge performance benefits, so whenever you find that you have frequently accessed data that doesn't often change, cache it in the `Cache` object and your application's performance will improve.

The trick with caching is to use the highest possible value that won't negatively impact the required behavior of the page. Taking the example we looked at earlier (caching match dates) to both extremes, specifying that the cache never expires (or has a very long duration) would mean that newly added dates would not be visible to visitors to the site unless the application was restarted. On the other hand, using a very small length of time before the cache expires would mean that the performance improvements gained by using caching are reduced, since the code has to keep going back to the database to get new data.

Caching is often considered more of a performance tool than a way to store application data, but since that's essentially what you are doing when you cache an object, it's just another way to remember data across pages.

Other State Management Techniques

Aside from the main state management methods used in this chapter, there are several other ways to remember data. Let's take a quick look at these now.

Viewstate

Viewstate is a concept first discussed back in *Chapter 3*, and it's been with us on every page that has server controls on it! If you use the View > Source command on any page with a Web control, you'll see a large block of code:

```
<input type="hidden" name="__VIEWSTATE" value="dDw0MTMzOTEzMDM7O2w8Y2hrUmVt ...
```

Viewstate can be enabled or disabled on a control-by-control basis. The more controls you have on your page that have viewstate enabled, the more data your page will have to store in this hidden field. On complex pages, this field can grow to be quite large, increasing download times, so take care to only enable viewstate on those controls that need it. For example, if you wanted to disable viewstate on a `TextBox` control, you could do so using the following syntax:

```
<asp:textbox id="myTextBox" runat="server" EnableViewState="false" />
```

You'll soon find out if you need to enable viewstate for a control or not if you try disabling it for all controls on a page. If you try this and run your page, you may find that it no longer behaves as expected. At this point, you can start re-enabling it control by control (using `EnableViewState="true"`), until your site behaves as intended, which will help you to understand which controls require viewstate on your site, and which don't.

Hidden Form Fields

Viewstate uses this mechanism to store its data, but by default, a standard hidden control is sent to the client unencrypted. Even if you do encrypt this data, the encryption methods available for hidden form fields are not the most rigorous available, so you should never store sensitive data in these fields.

Database

Never underestimate the power of the database! Storing bits and pieces of data that relate to the session or application is one way to move away from the standard server-based state management models. However, too much reliance on the database for this type of information could cause bottlenecks at the database end instead of the server end!

As you can see, most of the drawbacks to each of the methods discussed here boil down to performance. Performance enhancement techniques will be covered in *Chapter 15*.

Using Multiple State Management Techniques on a Page

Right, we've looked at quite a lot of different concepts in this chapter, so let's put together one more example using a couple of those concepts. This example will use both Sessions and Cookies to add some simple skinning functionality to the Web site. Once you complete this example, you will be able to add stylesheets to improve the look of every page on the site. If you've not worked with CSS before, don't worry – it's all quite simple, and once you complete this exercise, you'll be able to alter the look of the entire site by altering the values stored in one central location.

Try It Out   Wrox United – Adding Some Style!

In this example, we're going to add some styling to the Wrox United site, and at the same time, make use of session state. It's going to take a bit of preparation, so let's work through it piece by piece.

1. Start by re-opening `Default.aspx`. Switch to **Code** view and add the following line of code near the top of the page:

```
<html>
<head>
    <link id="css" href='<%= Session("SelectedCss") %>' type="text/css"
        rel="stylesheet" />
</head>
```

2. Now add the following code further down the page, after the last `HyperLink` control:

```
<p>
   <asp:HyperLink id="lnkChat" runat="server" NavigateUrl="Chat.aspx">
     Chat</asp:HyperLink>
</p>
<hr /><br/><br/>
<p>
   Choose a theme: <br/>
   <asp:DropDownList id="ddlTheme" runat="server">
     <asp:ListItem Value="WroxUnited.css" Selected="True">Home Kit</asp:ListItem>
     <asp:ListItem Value="WroxUnited2.css">Away Kit</asp:ListItem>
```

```
    </asp:DropDownList>
    <asp:Button id="btnApplyTheme" onclick="btnApplyTheme_Click"
            runat="server" Text="Apply"></asp:Button>
    <br />
    <asp:CheckBox id="chkRememberStylePref" runat="server"
                Text="Remember preference"></asp:CheckBox>
</p>
  </td>
```

3.   Switch to the Design view; Figure 11-17 shows what you should see in the left hand column:

Figure 11-17

4.   Double-click on the Apply button to switch back to the Code view. Notice that Sessions and Cookies have both been used in this event handler:

```
Sub btnApplyTheme_Click(sender As Object, e As EventArgs)

    Session("SelectedCss") = ddlTheme.SelectedItem.Value

    If ChkRememberStylePref.Checked Then

      Dim CssCookie as New HttpCookie("PreferredCss")
      CssCookie.Value = ddlTheme.SelectedItem.Value
      CssCookie.Expires = now.AddSeconds(20)
```

425

```
      Response.Cookies.Add(CssCookie)

    End If

  End Sub
```

5.   We need to add some code to the `Page Load()` method to set the style for the page when it is first loaded:

```
Sub Page_Load()
    If Not Page.IsPostback

      If Session("SelectedCss") is Nothing Then
        If Request.Cookies("PreferredCss") is Nothing Then
          Session("SelectedCss") = "WroxUnited.css"

        Else
          Session("SelectedCss") = Request.Cookies("PreferredCss").Value

        End If
      End If

    End If
```

That's quite a lot of `If`s! Don't worry – we will come to this in just a moment. However, before you can run the code, you need to include some stylesheets, or else nothing will be displayed! You will also need to make some minor adjustments to some of the code on the page, notably to the `Calendar` control's `DayRender` event handler, to make the page look a bit nicer when the stylesheet is applied.

6.   First, change the `DayRender` event handler as follows (removing the original style settings and replacing them with a single class statement):

```
Sub EventCalendar_DayRender(sender As Object, e As DayRenderEventArgs)
  If Not Cache("DateList")(e.day.date) is Nothing then
    e.cell.cssclass = "selecteddate"
    ' The following line will exist in your code if you completed the exercises
    ' at the end of the last chapter
    e.day.isselectable = true

  Else
    ' This line of code is part of the solution to one of the exercises at the end
    ' of chapter 10
    e.day.isselectable = false
  End If
End Sub
```

7.   Amend the code for the calendar:

```
<asp:Calendar id="EventCalendar" runat="server"
              OnSelectionChanged="EventCalendar_SelectionChanged"
              OnDayRender="EventCalendar_DayRender" CssClass="calendar">
  <DayStyle cssclass="normaldate"></DayStyle>
  <OtherMonthDayStyle cssclass="othermonthdate"></OtherMonthDayStyle>
</asp:Calendar>
```

8. Now create a new blank stylesheet, and call it `WroxUnited.css`, as shown in Figure 11-18:

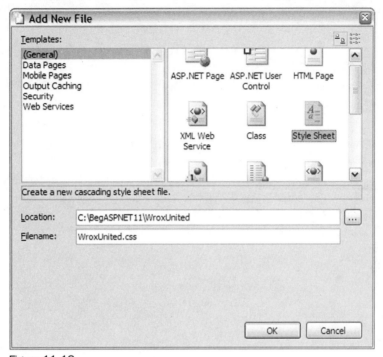

Figure 11-18

9. In this new stylesheet, enter the following code:

```
BODY {
  background-image:url(images/background.gif);
  color:"#000000";
  font-family: georgia;
}

a {
  color:"#8b0000";
  font-weight:bold;
}

.selecteddate{
  font-weight: bold;
  font-size: larger;
  border: 3 dotted darkred;
  background:#f0f0f0;
}

.normaldate{
  font-weight:lighter;
  color:dimgray;
```

```
     }

   .calendar a{
     text-decoration:none;
     font-size: 10pt;
   }

   .othermonthdate{
     font-weight:lighter;
     color:#d3d3d3;
   }
```

10. Save this as `WroxUnited.css` in the `WroxUnited` folder. Then, change the following lines, and save the file with a different name, `WroxUnited2.css`:

```
BODY {
background-image:url(images/awaybackground.gif);
color:"#ffffff";
font-family: georgia;
}
a {
color:"yellow";
font-weight:bold;
}
.calendar a{
 text-decoration:none;
}
.selecteddate
{
 font-weight: bold;
 font-size: larger;
 border: 3 dotted white;
 background:#c0c0c0;
}
.normaldate
{
 font-weight:lighter;
 color:#d3d3d3;
}
.othermonthdate
{
 font-weight:lighter;
 color:dimgray;
}
```

11. Finally, you need to get hold of the two background images that are used in the two stylesheets, `background.gif` and `awaybackground.gif`. Both are available for download from the Wrox site. They are extremely small images, so they will not take long to download.

12. It's that time – run the page and try it out for yourself! The first style you'll see is the *home-style* page, as shown in Figure 11-19:

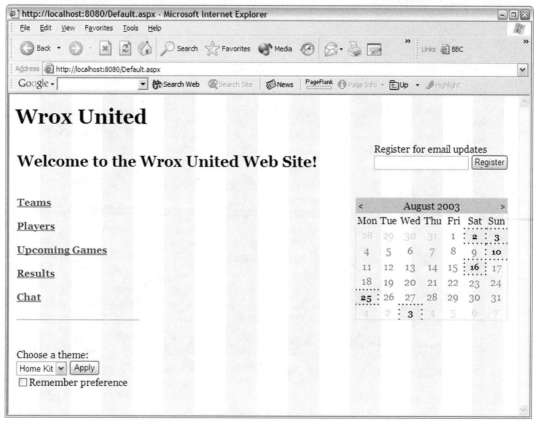

Figure 11-19

The Away Kit is fairly different, as you'll notice in Figure 11-20:

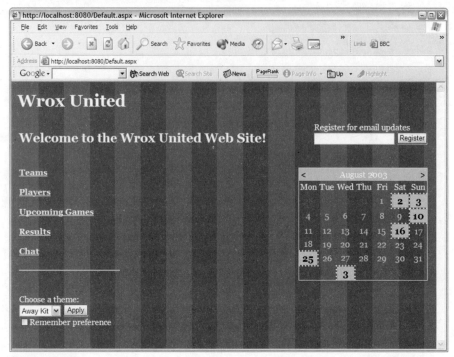

Figure 11-20

13. If you check the Remember Preference box before clicking Apply, the style you are applying will be remembered for you in a cookie. Next time you open the site, that stylesheet will be the default.

How It Works

This example rolled together two different techniques, sessions and cookies, and gave a unified look and feel that you can apply to all the pages in this site.

The first thing done was to use the contents of the session object to provide a filename for the `<Link ... >` tag in the head section of the ASP.NET page:

```
<html>
<head>
    <link id="css" href='<%= Session("SelectedCss") %>' type="text/css"
        rel="stylesheet" />
</head>
```

You'll recall that the `<%= ... %>` syntax is used to access ASP.NET objects from the HTML side of the page. This technique is certainly adequate for this example, and is a simple way to get to the contents of the session object.

The next step was to add some controls to the page to select and apply the stylesheet to the page:

```
<hr /><br/><br/>
<p>
  Choose a theme: <br/>
  <asp:DropDownList id="ddlTheme" runat="server">
    <asp:ListItem Value="WroxUnited.css" Selected="True">Home Kit</asp:ListItem>
    <asp:ListItem Value="WroxUnited2.css">Away Kit</asp:ListItem>
  </asp:DropDownList>
  <asp:Button id="btnApplyTheme" onclick="btnApplyTheme_Click"
              runat="server" Text="Apply"></asp:Button>
  <br />
  <asp:CheckBox id="chkRememberStylePref" runat="server"
                Text="Remember preference"></asp:CheckBox>
</p>
```

Note that we set the details of the drop down list manually, assigning each item a `Text` property and a `Value` property. The `Text` property (the bit between the tags) is the text that displayed in the control. The value is the underlying value for the selected item, and we use this value to update the session. Clicking the `Apply` button will fire the `Click` event of the button, taking you neatly to the event handler for this event:

```
Sub btnApplyTheme_Click(sender As Object, e As EventArgs)

  Session("SelectedCss") = ddlTheme.SelectedItem.Value
```

Set the value of the session to be the *value* of the currently selected drop-down list item (not the text). This value is the filename for the stylesheet.

```
  If ChkRememberStylePref.Checked Then

    Dim CssCookie as New HttpCookie("PreferredCss")
    CssCookie.Value = ddlTheme.SelectedItem.Value
    CssCookie.Expires = now.AddSeconds(20)
    Response.Cookies.Add(CssCookie)

  End If

End Sub
```

If the `ChkRememberStylePref` checkbox is checked when the button is clicked, a cookie is added to the user's machine, specifying their preference for subsequent visits to the site. Again, we set a short expiry time for this cookie so you could see it working, and see what happens when it expires. You can set this to be whatever time interval you prefer.

Ok, so you have a session and a cookie – the next stage is to read those values in when the page is loaded:

```
Sub Page_Load()

    If Not Page.IsPostback

      If Session("SelectedCss") is Nothing Then
```

If the Session does not yet exist, we set a default value for the selected stylesheet using the value in the cookie if the cookie exists on the client machine, or set it to a specific value if there is no cookie present:

```
        If Request.Cookies("PreferredCss") is Nothing Then
          Session("SelectedCss") = "WroxUnited.css"

        Else
          Session("SelectedCss") = Request.Cookies("PreferredCss").Value
        End If
      End If

    End If
```

Now that we have applied the stylesheet, we need to manually alter the styling of the Calendar control (if you have skipped this step, you'll notice that the calendar doesn't follow the stylesheet like the rest of the page):

```
Sub EventCalendar_DayRender(sender As Object, e As DayRenderEventArgs)
  If Not Cache("DateList")(e.day.date) is Nothing then
    e.cell.cssclass = "selecteddate"
    e.day.isselectable = true

  Else
    e.day.isselectable = false
  End If
End Sub
...
  <DayStyle cssclass="normaldate"></DayStyle>
  <OtherMonthDayStyle cssclass="othermonthdate"></OtherMonthDayStyle>
```

Finally, we declare some stylesheet information. Let's run through the values of just a couple of these definitions:

```
BODY {
  background-image:url(images/background.gif);
  color:"#000000";
  font-family: georgia;
}
```

The BODY tag controls the way the bulk of the page is rendered, including any background coloring or styling, as well as the font color and style.

The `.selecteddate` style is the style added in the `DayRender` event handler for the calendar:

```
.selecteddate{
  font-weight: bold;
  font-size: larger;
  border: 3 dotted darkred;
  background:#f0f0f0;
}
```

Notice how the styles here are similar to the styles used in the code for the `DayRender` event handler previously? Well, that's the joy of stylesheets! You've now centralized this code so that you only have to alter it in one place.

Summary

We covered quite a bit of ground in this chapter. We used cookies, sessions, and applications, and cached data for fast retrieval from the database. We also had some fun with interactive examples in this chapter that demonstrated these concepts.

The important points covered in this chapter are:

❑ Cookies are a neat way to store small pieces of identifying data, but cannot be relied upon (users may have them disabled in their browser preferences).

❑ Sessions are an extremely powerful way to store data that exists for as long as a user is connected to the site, and you can use them to store shopping basket data.

❑ Application-scope objects are accessible by any page in an application, and are a great way to centralize objects that need to be shared.

❑ Caching data is crucial to improve application performance, but it's also a very similar method to storing data in the Application object. However, the Cache object has some neat features such as linking to a dependancy, and you can control when items in the cache expire, and react to the event raised when those items expire.

The next chapter will look at encapsulating commonly used page elements into reusable secions, known as user controls. You'll also learn how the code-behind technique can be used to cleanly separate HTML code from VB.NET code.

Exercises

1. Add some text, Current Topic, and a label control to the Chat.aspx page, above the main chat box, which contains the text of the current topic (stored in the Application object). Add some default topic text to the Global.asax file, and also another box and a button to the page, allowing you to change the current topic.

2. Add the session initialization code from the Stylesheet example to your Global.asax file.

3. Add a link to the Merchandise.aspx page from the front page of the site, then apply the stylesheet used in the Default.aspx page to all the other pages in the site. You will need to add the <link ... > tag to the <head ... > section of each page, and you will need to ensure that the session initialization code is correctly configured in the Global.asax file from the previous exercise.

Reusable Code for ASP.NET

So far, most of the ASP.NET pages we've built have been quite specialized and self-contained. We've put a lot of functionality into each one, but only really retained the benefits of our hard work from one page to another by copying the entire contents into a new ASPX page.

This isn't really an ideal way to write functionality-rich Web sites, particularly if you're on a salary and expected to deliver results before the next millennium. We're now going to look at how to write reusable code for ASP.NET. Note that we're not just talking about objects here (although, yet again, objects play a crucial role in the reusability story) but about code *components* – totally independent files that encapsulate groups of useful functionality.

This chapter will look at two specific ways of using components in ASP.NET:

❑ **User control**: A Web form that is encapsulated in a reusable server control

❑ **Code-behind**: Used for separating HTML user interface design (color, aesthetics, and so on) from page code

First, let's take a careful look at what is meant by components, and consider the various advantages they offer.

Encapsulation

As discussed in *Chapter 7*, an object essentially is a software construct that bundles together data and functionality. You can define a few very specific interfaces on an object to use the functionality it contains, for example, by creating methods and properties that can be accessed programmatically.

By hiding away absolutely everything that doesn't concern task-specific usage of an object, implementation details are hidden from the consumer, making it a lot easier to plug it together robustly with other objects. This makes it far easier for large teams of developers to build complex applications that don't fall prey to lots of low-level weaknesses.

Crucial information needed for making an object is held in the class definition, and any code with access to this class should be able to instantiate an instance of our class, and store this in an object. The way in which the object works is *encapsulated*, so that only the public methods and properties are available to the consumer of the class.

In a similar way, a component is a set of reusable code stored in a location that makes it accessible to many applications. Like an object, it encapsulates functionality, but the difference is that while an object is an implementation unit, a component is a deployment or packaging unit. A component could be a single class, or it could hold multiple class definitions. Let's take a quick look at an example of this:

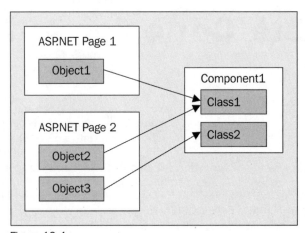

Figure 12-1

As shown in Figure 12-1, the first ASP.NET page creates a new object of type Class1, which resides within the Component1 component. The second ASP.NET page creates two new objects: one of type Class1 and one of type Class2. Class2 also resides within the Component1 component.

All the code written so far has been held in specific ASPX pages. So, why have all this reusable code if it can be reached only from within a single page? We need to break our reusable code into separate components that we can reference from our ASPX pages.

A component packages up a set of classes and interfaces to isolate and encapsulate a specific set of functionality, and can provide a well-specified set of publicly available services. It is designed for a specific *purpose* rather than for a specific *application*.

Components

A component is a self-contained unit of functionality, with external interfaces that are independent of its internal architecture. In other words, it's a bunch of code packaged as a blackbox that can be used in as many different applications as required.

We're all familiar with Microsoft Windows, which is an example of componentization. If you spend a lot of time working with Windows, you're almost certain to have come across DLL files – *Dynamic Link Libraries*. Many of these files contain components that define most of the functionality you're likely to come across in Windows, including that of any applications you've installed.

> *DLLs are classified as system files, which are hidden by default. They can only be seen in Windows Explorer if your Folder Options are set to 'Show hidden files and folders'.*

For example, every time you fire up an instance of Internet Explorer, you're actually running a small program called `iexplore.exe`. This program accesses numerous DLLs that reside in your system directory (if you have Windows 2000 or XP running on your `C:` drive, this will probably be `C:\WINNT` or `C:\Windows`), and most of the browser's functionality is defined within these files. This directory also contains the file `Explorer.exe`, which is the executable for Windows Explorer. Note that both these applications feature an identical **Address** bar, where you type in the URL of a Web site or the path to a local directory. This user interface element has been implemented once, packaged inside a component, and is now being used by both programs.

What's more, if you enter the URL for a Web page in the Windows Explorer address bar, you can view that page and even browse the Web in the main pane without having to use `iexplore.exe` at all. Likewise, you can use `iexplore.exe` to view and browse your files, simply by entering a file path in the address bar. What we can deduce from this is that either there's a lot of duplication between the two EXE files, or the two sets of browser functionality are actually implemented as standalone components that can be accessed by both applications.

Another case to consider is the Microsoft Office suite, which features many components that are shared among the individual Office applications and throughout Windows itself. For example, there is a component that handles the **Save As** dialog used by Word, Excel, Outlook, and the rest – this is why the **Save** dialog looks the same, no matter which application you run it from. This component is actually a Windows component, but the Office package makes use of it whenever you save or load a file. You can also use this from any other application that will let you save or load files; for example, Internet Explorer or even Notepad as shown in Figure 12-2:

Figure 12-2

In this component, there's probably some presentation code for all of the buttons, and some logic that understands what to do when you click on each of those buttons. For example, changing the selection in the Save in drop-down box will change the files listed in the main window to show the contents of the selected directory.

Throughout this book, we've been using the `aspnet_isapi`, which has been working away behind IIS to process all of our ASP.NET pages. When IIS spots that someone is requesting a page with a `.aspx` extension, it uses this component to process the page and communicate with the .NET Framework.

The DLLs in these examples are COM DLLs. A .NET DLL differs slightly in what it contains, but the concept of componentization is the same, whatever the underlying technology.

Why Use Components

You should start thinking of components as small, self-contained nuggets of functionality that can potentially make life a lot simpler when building any sort of non-trivial application. In this respect, they are similar to objects, but a component is reusable code whose behind-the-scenes functionality is encapsulated, so that only certain interfaces are available to the programmer. It can contain one or more class definitions that tell which objects can be created and which can be used for behind-the-scenes code. The benefits of using components are:

❑ An individual component is a lot simpler than a full-blown application. It is restricted to a set of predefined functionality.

❑ As components are self-contained, they can be seamlessly upgraded (or fixed) simply by replacing one component with another that supports the same interfaces (methods, properties, and so on).

❑ Since using components is a good way of dividing your application into serviceable chunks, sometimes the functionality a component contains may be reusable elsewhere. You might even make it available to other programmers, or incorporate some of their components into your applications.

Ultimately, components reduce the amount of code you write and make your code easier to maintain. Once you've written one, you can reuse it within as many different applications as you like. Moreover, you can even obtain components from third party component vendors, which is a very popular way to enhance the functionality of ASP.NET sites. If, for example, you need components that utilize the drawing capabilities of .NET to their limit, and your existing knowledge does not cover this, you can consider looking for a third-party solution that you can bolt onto your application.

Applying Component Theory to Applications

Let's look at how componentization relates to our application models. So far, in this book, we've made ASP.NET pages that do all sorts of things from working with information input via a form through to connecting to a database and working with data. Throughout, you've been encouraged to keep your code separated into distinct blocks – namely dynamically generated content (ASP.NET code) and presentation (HTML and various controls), so that it's easy to change the look of your page without affecting what it does.

Web Matrix really helps with this process, with its separate HTML and Code views. In addition, we've written a lot of VB.NET code in our pages for accessing and working with data stored in a central database. In this sense, the VB.NET code has provided a framework of logical operations between the data and presentation code.

Let's look at an example. Imagine a team of developers creating a Web site that sells books. Some of these developers would probably be concerned with the look, feel, and ease of use of the site. They'd be responsible for the public image of the company on the Web, so they'd be most concerned with design, color, and usability. These are our designers who are probably using HTML, and perhaps some graphics tools like Flash for fancy loading screens.

There would probably also be another set of developers whose main interest lay in providing nifty blocks of code that did, when you clicked a button, cool things such as validating the information entered into a form by the customers. These developers might also be responsible for generating the code required for connecting to the database of different books, and preparing the information on individual titles for display on the site. The designers would then make use of that information and display it in an aesthetically pleasing fashion.

If you were constantly to use ASP.NET pages that had all of the code, and HTML on the same page, it would be awkward for both sets of people to work on the site at once. Simple mistakes would easily be made if people overwrote each other's code. In addition, every page would have to be hand-made, and code would have to be copied, pasted, and amended as appropriate. If you made one change to the functionality of your site, you'd have to remember to make that change to all the appropriate pages.

However, if you could separate out the HTML and design-focused code from the ASP.NET code blocks, and then reuse bits of that code, it would be much easier to update a single piece of code to change functionality – every page that used it would be automatically updated.

This style of work would make everyone happy. Web designers get to play with color and layout as much as they like, and the ASP.NET developers can fine-tune their code without affecting the look and feel of the site. Code separation and reuse means that the designers and developers can work in parallel, allowing applications to be developed much more quickly. This is called *Rapid Application Development*.

This chapter will look at two ways of dividing code into reusable sections – *user controls* and *code-behind* files. In the next chapter, we'll take this one step further and look at compiled components and custom server controls.

Let's now look at user controls, the first application of this code separation concept.

User Controls

When the ASP.NET team first devised the concept of user controls, they were called *pagelets*, a term that many people disliked. They were later renamed, but many felt that the term pagelet, which implies a mini-page, was a good descriptive term for these controls.

User controls are Web forms encapsulated into a reusable control. They hold repetitive blocks of code that are needed by many of the pages in a Web site. For example, consider the Microsoft Web site, where each page has the same header style – a menu bar and a logo. This is a very common feature for many Web sites; even our own http://www.wrox.com/ shown in Figure 12-3 has this kind of style:

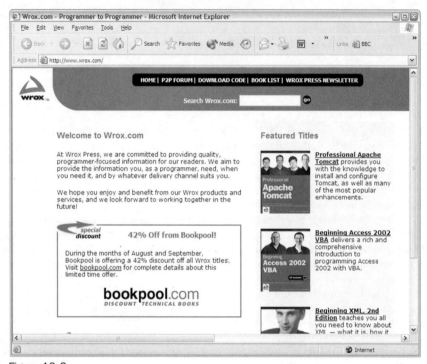

Figure 12-3

The Wrox site has the same kinds of menu bars visible on the screen at all times. These panes, panels, or frames (depending on what you call them) and how you code them, together form just one example of what user controls can provide programmatically. Instead of having to copy and paste chunks of repeated code to provide the header on all of our pages, we can create a simple user control that will have this code inside it, ready to be used. It's a way of accessing the same functionality repeatedly throughout an application.

> *If you've ever programmed with ASP 3.0, you'll probably be familiar with* include *files. User controls are similar to include files, but because ASP.NET is different from ASP 3.0, these controls are now created and used in a different manner and include advanced features such as caching (covered in Chapter 11).*

User controls can also do a lot more than simply produce headers and footers. We can give these controls the ability to look and behave a bit like ASP.NET Server controls. We can code properties so that the control can adapt depending on which attributes have been set on it. A user control can be used anywhere on a site to provide a repository for repetitive code blocks when many pages have similar blocks of functionality. Take for example a user login control. This control could be created as a user control, using a couple of textboxes and labels.

Another example is a menu control that applies different formatting to a link representing the page currently being viewed, or even displays a submenu for that page. A user control is saved with a `.ascx` file extension, and can be called from any of the ASP.NET pages in our application using just two lines of code. The main principle of user controls is that you essentially cut out a portion of code from your ASP.NET page and paste it into a user control, where it will work just fine as long as the ASP.NET page knows where to find the code, and where to put it.

Let's look at a few pros and cons of using user control in your applications.

User controls are ideal for:

❏   Using repetitive elements (such as headers, menus, login controls, and so on) on pages

❏   Reducing the amount of code per page by encapsulating these repetitive elements

❏   Improving page performance by using caching functionality available to user controls to cache frequently viewed data

However, some situations aren't ideal for using user controls. These include:

❏   Separating presentation HTML from the code blocks (use code-behind, discussed later in this chapter)

❏   Encapsulating data access methods in a reusable package (use pre-compiled assemblies, discussed in the next chapter)

❏   Creating a control that can be reused more widely than in just your application (use custom server controls, discussed in the next chapter)

It's time to start looking at code. This chapter and the next will look at creating custom reusable elements in ASP.NET pages, showing how these elements can all be plugged together with a minimum of fuss to produce a very clean `.aspx` file, hiding the advanced functionality within reusable components. The next example demonstrates user controls in action.

Try It Out   Our First User Control

In this section, we will discuss a very basic example (to show the theory), which will be followed by a more complex example. We'll add a simple header control to the default page of the Wrox United application.

1.   Start by creating a new ASP.NET user control within the Wrox United folde, and name it `SimpleHeader.ascx` (Note the different file extension – `.ascx`, not `.aspx`); see Figure 12-4

Figure 12-4

2. In the new file that appears, switch to HTML view – notice that there is hardly anything in the file when it's first created! All you need to do here is add one line of code:

```
<h1>Wrox United</h1>
```

3. Save this file, and then reopen `Default.aspx` from the Wrox United application. We're going to replace the heading in this page with the newly created user control.

4. Switch to All view – notice that there are some *yellow colored* statements (which aren't visible in any other view) at the top of the file. This is where you need to add the first piece of code. Add the following highlighted line of code:

```
<%@ Page Language="VB" %>
<%@ Register TagPrefix="WroxUnited" TagName="SimpleHeader"
                Src="SimpleHeader.ascx" %>
<%@ import Namespace="System.Web.Caching" %>
```

5. Switch back to HTML view. Replace the `<h1>` ... `</h1>` section with the following highlighted line of code:

```
<form runat="server">
    <WroxUnited:SimpleHeader id="HeaderControl" runat="server"/>
    <table width="800">
...
```

6. That's about all you need to add to the code! If you switch over to Design view as shown in Figure 12-5, you'll see that the control has been added:

Figure 12-5

7. It's time to try it out – run the page and you should see the familiar front page of the site, as shown in Figure 12-6:

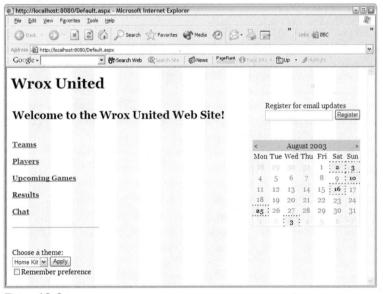

Figure 12-6

Notice that the front page looks exactly same as before, and the new title has the correct style applied to it, as if it were still a part of the main page.

How It Works

Having completed this example, you won't see any difference in the rendered page when it is run and the page that we built in the last chapter. However, the technique that we implemented behind the scenes (changing the hardcoded HTML to a reusable control) in this example will prove to be very powerful, as you'll see for yourself later in this chapter.

If you open up `SimpleHeader.ascx` in the All view in Web Matrix, you'll see the following:

```
<%@ Control Language="VB" %>
<script runat="server">

    ' Insert user control code here
    '

</script>
<!- Insert content here ->
<h1>Wrox United
</h1>
```

The default code that Web Matrix added is quite light. There are a couple of comments, an unused script block, and a special directive at the top of the code. The first line of code tells the compiler that we wrote this control in VB.NET. The only code added to the page was the `<h1>Wrox United</h1>` line. This line of code can be displayed on any code that uses this control.

Let's look at the *consumer* of our ASCX user control, the `Default.aspx` page:

```
<%@ Page Language="VB" %>
<%@ Register TagPrefix="WroxUnited" TagName="SimpleHeader"
                Src="SimpleHeader.ascx" %>
<%@ import Namespace="System.Web.Caching" %>
```

The first line of code links the ASCX control to the ASPX page. This tag must appear at the top of your page, before any HTML code, in order for it to work. Two attributes have been set for the `Register` tag:

❑   `TagPrefix`

❑   `TagName`

`TagPrefix` is the collective name for our group of controls. `TagName` is the name of this specific control. For example, to use an ASP.NET textbox control on an ASPX page, use the syntax `<asp:textbox />`. `TagPrefix` precedes the colon, and `TagName` follows the colon. For an ASP.NET textbox, `<asp:...>` would be `TagPrefix`, and `<...:textbox>` would be `TagName`.

In this example, the `TagPrefix` for the new user control was set to `WroxUnited`, and `TagName` was set to `SimpleHeader`. When the control is used on the page, it's added using `<WroxUnited:SimpleHeader />`. You could have a whole library of `WroxUnited` tags, each identified by different `TagNames`, in the code. The final part of the line specifies the source file of our user control. Note that ASP.NET expects this file to be in the same place as the `.aspx` file. If this is not the case, then add either a relative or an absolute path here.

The other change made was to embed the user control into the page:

```
<WroxUnited:SimpleHeader id="HeaderControl" runat="server"/>
```

Here you can see the `WroxUnited:SimpleHeader` syntax discussed earlier – `TagName` and `TagPrefix` that were assigned earlier to call our user control have been used. The control is added to the page using `TagName` and `TagPrefix` specified in the attribute declaration at the top of the page.

Web Matrix can provide a preview of pages that include user controls, so you could see the output of the user control that you added in **Design** view. The result is that the page is rendered in exactly the same way as before. The HTML code from the control is rendered within the HTML of the page.

While this user control could be implemented on every page in the site easily, this isn't exactly the most exciting control that we could use. Let's work on a visually more appealing header control that can be displayed at the top of every page in the site.

Try It Out **Wrox United: Simple Header Control Example**

Let's create a user control that forms a header for the Wrox United Web site. Our example used a few images, including a team logo and pictures of the players. These images are available for download, along with the rest of the code for the book, from **www.wrox.com**.

1. Open up Web Matrix, create a new ASP.NET user control, and enter the following code:

```
<table width="100%">
  <tr style="BACKGROUND-IMAGE: url(images/headbg.gif);"><td>
      <table width="800">
        <tr style="VERTICAL-ALIGN: middle">
          <td style="TEXT-ALIGN: left" width="200">
            <a href="default.aspx"><img src="images/logo.gif" border="0" /></a>
          </td>

          <td style="TEXT-ALIGN: center" width="400">
            <img src="images/teamlogo.gif" />
          </td>

          <td style="TEXT-ALIGN: right" width="200">
            <asp:AdRotator id="AdRotator1" runat="server"
                       Height="95px" Width="100px"
                       AdvertisementFile="faces.xml"></asp:AdRotator>
          </td>
        </tr>
      </table>
  </td></tr>
</table>
<h2><%= PageTitle %></h2>
```

2. Switch to Code view and enter the following line of text:

```
public PageTitle as String = "'
```

3. Save this file as `header.ascx`. You'll notice an ASP.NET `AdRotator` control in this file. This control depends on the content of an XML file. Let's create this.

4. Create a new blank XML page, add the following code, and save as `faces.xml`:

```xml
<?xml version="1.0" encoding="utf-8" ?>
<Advertisements>

  <Ad>
    <ImageUrl>images/chrish_s_t.gif</ImageUrl>
    <NavigateUrl>players.aspx</NavigateUrl>
    <AlternateText>Player: Chris Hart</AlternateText>
    <Impressions>80</Impressions>
    <Keyword>ChrisH</Keyword>
  </Ad>

  <Ad>
    <ImageUrl>images/chrisu_s_t.gif</ImageUrl>
    <NavigateUrl>players.aspx</NavigateUrl>
    <AlternateText>Player: Chris Ullman</AlternateText>
    <Impressions>80</Impressions>
    <Keyword>ChrisU</Keyword>
  </Ad>

  <Ad>
    <ImageUrl>images/dave_s_t.gif</ImageUrl>
    <NavigateUrl>players.aspx</NavigateUrl>
    <AlternateText>Player: Dave Sussman</AlternateText>
    <Impressions>80</Impressions>
    <Keyword>Dave</Keyword>
  </Ad>

  <Ad>
    <ImageUrl>images/john_s_t.gif</ImageUrl>
    <NavigateUrl>players.aspx</NavigateUrl>
    <AlternateText>Player: John Kauffman</AlternateText>
    <Impressions>80</Impressions>
    <Keyword>John</Keyword>
  </Ad>

</Advertisements>
```

We'll examine how the `AdRotator` control works in just a few moments, but for now, just add the new header control to the default page by altering a couple of lines.

5. Change the declaration at the top of the page in `Default.aspx`:

```
<%@ Page Language="VB" %>
<%@ Register TagPrefix="WroxUnited" TagName="Header" Src="Header.ascx" %>
<%@ import Namespace="System.Web.Caching" %>
```

6. Now change the code that embeds the header control in the page:

```
<form runat="server">
    <WroxUnited:Header id="HeaderControl" runat="server"></WroxUnited:Header>
    <table width="800">
...
```

7. Save the file again and view it in your browser. The page should appear as shown in Figure 12-7:

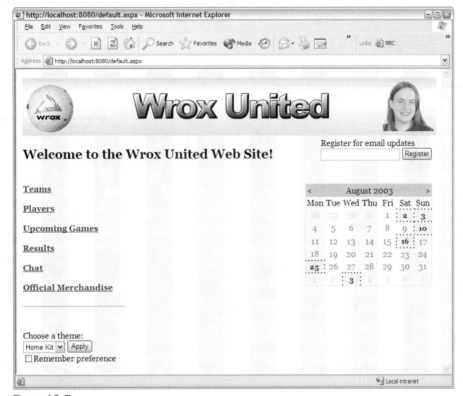

Figure 12-7

How It Works

In this example, we implemented another simple user control and introduced another type of server control that's available. The `AdRotator` control is traditionally used to store banner adverts and rotate the visible advert according to a random algorithm. Each time the page is refreshed, an advert is selected for displaying. The relative frequency with which each advert appears on the page depends on the weighting we give to each advert. In this example, each advert is given equal weighting, so adverts display quite randomly upon refresh.

The control was used to display images of the members of the team (instead of displaying adverts) and to change which image appears on subsequent visits to the site. The information that controls which images to display and how often to display them is stored in an XML file.

Let's break down the code and work through what we did. First, the header.ascx control:

```
<table width="100%">
  <tr style="BACKGROUND-IMAGE: url(images/headbg.gif);"><td>
      <table width="800">
        <tr style="VERTICAL-ALIGN: middle">
          <td style="TEXT-ALIGN: left" width="200">
            <a href="default.aspx"><img src="images/logo.gif" border="0" /></a>
          </td>

          <td style="TEXT-ALIGN: center" width="400">
            <img src="images/teamlogo.gif" />
          </td>

          <td style="TEXT-ALIGN: right" width="200">
            <asp:AdRotator id="AdRotator1" runat="server"
                           Height="95px" Width="100px"
                           AdvertisementFile="faces.xml"></asp:AdRotator>
          </td>
        </tr>
      </table>
  </td></tr>
</table>
<h2><%= PageTitle %></h2>
```

This control is made up of one large table that contains a sub-table with three cells. We applied a style to the single row in the parent table. The addition of a background image to this row resulted in this style being applied as a solid background for the whole header. The inner table helps to lay out the contents of the header. The items in the row are centered along a horizontal axis:

```
<tr style="VERTICAL-ALIGN: middle">
```

Each of the three cells were aligned to the left, center, or right of the vertical axis of each cell respectively:

```
<td style="TEXT-ALIGN: left" width="200">
```

In the first two cells, a couple of static images were added. Notice that the image in the first cell is wrapped in an HTML <A . . . > tag, which will turn the image into a hyperlink. In this case, clicking the first image would take the user to the front page, thus making it a handy *home* button that users can use to return to the default page.

In the third cell, we added an AdRotator control:

```
<asp:AdRotator id="AdRotator1" runat="server"
               Height="95px" Width="100px"
               AdvertisementFile="faces.xml"></asp:AdRotator>
```

The control declaration is very simple, but the most interesting part is the link to the `AdvertisementFile` XML file, which controls how `AdRotator` works.

Let's look at an extract of `Advertisements` XML:

```xml
<?xml version="1.0" encoding="utf-8" ?>
<Advertisements>

  <Ad>
    <ImageUrl>images/chrish_s_t.gif</ImageUrl>
    <NavigateUrl>players.aspx</NavigateUrl>
    <AlternateText>Player: Chris Hart</AlternateText>
    <Impressions>80</Impressions>
    <Keyword>ChrisH</Keyword>
  </Ad>


  <Ad>
...
  </Ad>

</Advertisements>
```

The settings that control what is displayed and what functionality is available each time the page is loaded are contained within an `<Advertisements> ... </Advertisements>` tag. Each displayed item is defined within an `<Ad> ... </Ad>` element. In this example, you can see the element definition for `Chris Hart`. Let's work through each of the tags for this player. The first tag controls which image is displayed for this player. Here, the image is a small one with a transparent background; available along with the code downloads for this book:

```xml
<ImageUrl>images/chrish_s_t.gif</ImageUrl>
```

The `<NavigateUrl>` tag controls where the browser will navigate to, when the image is clicked. Here, we specified the `Players.aspx` page:

```xml
<NavigateUrl>players.aspx</NavigateUrl>
```

The `<AlternateText>` tag controls the text that is displayed when the mouse is hovered over the image, as well as the text that is read out to assist visually impaired surfers understand the content of the site:

```xml
<AlternateText>Player: Chris Hart</AlternateText>
```

The `<Impressions>` tag controls the weighting that affects how often this advert is displayed compared to other advertisements. In this example, all players have equal weighting, but you could indicate a preference for your favorite player by increasing the number for that particular advertisement element. An amusing point to note is that you must keep the total of all of the values in the `<Impressions>` tags under 2 billion so as to avoid a runtime error:

```xml
<Impressions>80</Impressions>
```

449

The last tag controls the keyword for the advert. This element is optional, but you can use it to filter advertisements by including a `KeywordFilter` attribute to the `<ASP:AdRotator ... >` tag in your ASP.NET pages:

```
<Keyword>ChrisH</Keyword>
```

The last piece of the puzzle involves including this header on the `Default.aspx` page. You only need to make a couple of minor changes (including adding a directive at the top of the page) to specify that you want to use the new header file in the page:

```
<%@ Register TagPrefix="WroxUnited" TagName="Header" Src="Header.ascx" %>
```

You can then use the control in the page by including the following line of code:

```
<WroxUnited:Header id="HeaderControl" runat="server"></WroxUnited:Header>
```

Before we move on, don't forget that you could include this header control on all the pages of the Wrox United site in the same way. With this in mind, we added an interactive element to this header control. Recall the last line in the header control itself:

```
<h2><%= PageTitle %></h2>
```

This line of text will create a Heading 2 style paragraph, and add the text contents of the `PageTitle` public variable to the page:

```
public PageTitle as String = ""
```

Take the chat page as an example; add two lines of code to the `Chat.aspx` page to see this in action (assuming that you've already added code to add the selected CSS theme to the page.) First, at the top of the page, add the following:

```
<%@ Register TagPrefix="WroxUnited" TagName="Header" Src="Header.ascx" %>
```

Then add the following highlighted line of code (instead of the Heading 1 and 2 tags) to the HTML view of the page:

```
<form runat="server">
  <WroxUnited:Header id="HeaderControl" runat="server" PageTitle="Online Chat">
  </WroxUnited:Header>
  <asp:TextBox id="txtChatBox" runat="server" TextMode="MultiLine"
            Height="200px" Width="550px" ReadOnly="True"></asp:TextBox>
```

When you view this page in your browser, it should appear as shown in Figure 12-8:

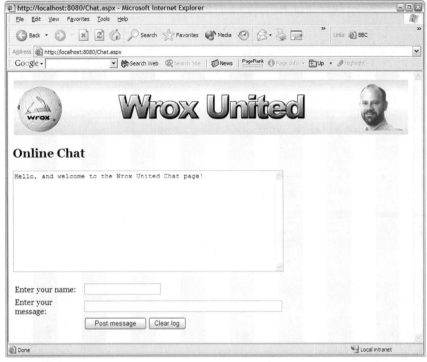

Figure 12-8

Notice that the Heading 2 text has been included on the page, thanks to the `PageTitle` attribute in the control's declaration. This is a neat trick for making header controls a bit more interactive, removing more standard code from the main pages, and further ensuring that the look and feel of all pages is maintained centrally.

Let's look at a slightly different type of user control now. This control can be used as a navigation bar, like the links on the left of the front page. An advantage is that it can be added to all the pages in the site with less fuss, and minimal code reuse.

Try It Out   Wrox United: Navigation User Control

In this example, we will take the ASP.NET hyperlink controls from `Default.aspx`, along with any associated code from the left-hand side of the page, and place it in a user control.

1. Create a new user control and call it `Navbar.ascx`. Add the following code:

```
<div class="navbar">
</div>
```

We will add code between these tags in just a moment.

451

2. Reopen `Default.aspx` and head straight to All view. Add the following highlighted line of code to the top of the page:

```
<%@ Page Language="VB" %>
<%@ Register TagPrefix="WroxUnited" TagName="Header" Src="Header.ascx" %>
<%@ Register TagPrefix="WroxUnited" TagName="NavBar" Src="NavBar.ascx" %>
```

3. Back in HTML view, find the section that contains all the left hand column of content (the first `<td>` element in the big layout table). This column contains the links and the CSS selector. Copy this section and paste it into `Navbar.ascx` within the `<div>` tag:

```
<div class="navbar">
<p>
  <asp:HyperLink id="lnkTeams" NavigateUrl="Teams.aspx" runat="server">
  Teams</asp:HyperLink>
</p>
<p>
  <asp:HyperLink id="lnkPlayers" NavigateUrl="Players.aspx" runat="server">
  Players</asp:HyperLink>
</p>
<p>
  <asp:HyperLink id="lnkGames" NavigateUrl="Default.aspx" runat="server">
  Upcoming Games</asp:HyperLink>
</p>
<p>
  <asp:HyperLink id="lnkResults" NavigateUrl="Default.aspx" runat="server">
  Results</asp:HyperLink>
</p>
<p>
  <asp:HyperLink id="lnkChat" NavigateUrl="Chat.aspx" runat="server">
  Chat</asp:HyperLink>
</p>
<p>
  <asp:HyperLink id="lnkMerchandise" NavigateUrl="Merchandise.aspx" runat="server">
  Official Merchandise</asp:HyperLink>
</p>
<hr width="95%"/>
<br />
<p>
  Choose a theme:<br />
  <asp:DropDownList id="ddlTheme" runat="server">
    <asp:ListItem Value="WroxUnited.css" Selected="True">Home Kit</asp:ListItem>
    <asp:ListItem Value="WroxUnited2.css">Away Kit</asp:ListItem>
  </asp:DropDownList>
  <asp:Button id="btnApplyTheme"
              onclick="btnApplyTheme_Click" runat="server" Text="Apply">
  </asp:Button>
  <br />
  <asp:CheckBox id="chkRememberStylePref" runat="server"
              Text="Remember preference"></asp:CheckBox>
</p>
</div>
```

4. Now replace the original left-hand column of the main layout table in `Default.aspx` with the following:

```
<table style="WIDTH: 800px">
  <tr>
    <td style="VERTICAL-ALIGN: top; WIDTH: 200px">
        <WroxUnited:NavBar id="NavigationLinks" runat="server"></WroxUnited:NavBar>
    </td>
```

5. You will need to copy across the event handler for the button that applies different themes. Cut and paste the `btnApplyTheme_Click()` method from `Default.aspx` and place it in the **Code** view of `Navbar.ascx`:

```
Sub btnApplyTheme_Click(sender As Object, e As EventArgs)

    Session("SelectedCss") = ddlTheme.SelectedItem.Value

    If ChkRememberStylePref.Checked Then

        Dim CssCookie as New HttpCookie("PreferredCss")
        CssCookie.Value = ddlTheme.SelectedItem.Value
        CssCookie.Expires = now.AddSeconds(20)
        Response.Cookies.Add(CssCookie)

    End If

End Sub
```

In the last part of this exercise, we'll add some styling to the control. We don't have a stylesheet declaration in the code for this control, but that's not a problem. Once the control is added to a page, the control will inherit the current stylesheet information from the parent page.

6. Reopen `WroxUnited.css` and add the following style declaration to the bottom of the stylesheet definition:

```
.navbar{
  width:185px;
  border-bottom-width:4;
  border-bottom-color:#c0c0c0;
  border-bottom-style:solid;
  border-right-width:2;
  border-right-color:#c0c0c0;
  border-right-style:solid;
  padding-right:1;
  padding-bottom:0;
  padding-top:0;
}
```

7. Run the page and you should now see the page looking pretty much the same as it did before, except that it now has a border around the control, as shown in Figure 12-9:

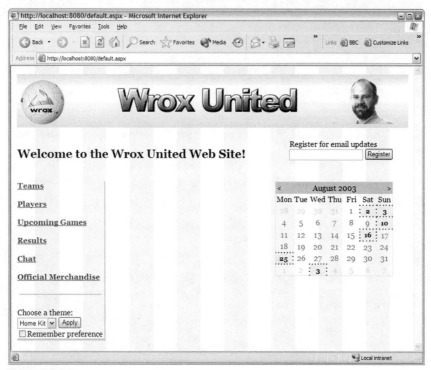

Figure 12-9

8. Add the control to the Chat.aspx page in exactly the same way as before. First, add the following line to the top of the page:

```
<%@ Register TagPrefix="WroxUnited" TagName="NavBar" Src="NavBar.ascx" %>
```

9. Then add the navigation bar control to the page. Note, however, that you need to add a layout table to make space for this control:

```
<form runat="server">
<WroxUnited:Header id="HeaderControl" runat="server" PageTitle="Online Chat">
</WroxUnited:Header>
<table width="800">
  <tr>
    <td width="200">
      <WroxUnited:NavBar id="NavigationBar" runat="server"></WroxUnited:NavBar>
    </td>
    <td>
      <asp:TextBox id="txtChatBox" runat="server" TextMode="MultiLine"
                   Height="200px" Width="550px" ReadOnly="True"></asp:TextBox>
        </td>
  </tr>
</table>
</form>
</body>
```

10. Once the control has been added, you can view the results of your hard work as shown in Figure 12-10:

Figure 12-10

How It Works

Once again, we've seen how to encapsulate some useful code into a reusable control, and with a minimum of fuss, add it to our pages. Also notice in this example how we added a full event handler to our control to handle the clicking of the stylesheet selector button in the navigation bar control – go ahead and try out this button for yourself, and you'll see the stylesheet selection changes appropriately. You can then navigate back to Default.aspx and see that your selection has been saved in the Session object. If you check the box, you can also add a cookie to the client machine, as long as they allow cookies.

Just like the previous examples, all you need to do to add a user control to a page is include two extra lines in the .aspx page:

```
<%@ Register TagPrefix="WroxUnited" TagName="NavBar" Src="NavBar.ascx" %>
...
<WroxUnited:NavBar id="NavigationBar" runat="server"></WroxUnited:NavBar>
```

In our example, the code in the ASP.NET user control contained an event handler that was taken from `Default.aspx`. This event handler is run whenever the button in the user control is clicked. It changes in the same way the stylesheet used on the page, on every page that includes the control. This holds true as long as each of these pages contains a stylesheet reference in the HTML view of the page:

```
<link id="css" href='<%= Session("SelectedCss") %>' type="text/css"
      rel="stylesheet" />
```

Next, we're going to move on to look at code-behind, and how to neatly separate our code into separate, manageable sections.

Code-Behind

When we were creating simple forms in *Chapter 3*, we simply created textboxes and worked with buttons that sent data on a round trip to the server. To enhance these forms, we added code to handle things such as validating input. The extra code that enabled validation in small functions was put at the bottom of our pages to avoid cluttering up the presentation code. However, there is a cleaner way of doing this – move all of this code into a *code-behind* file.

A code-behind file can be used to store all of the script blocks of an ASP.NET page. While it's perfectly possible to include this in the same page as the presentation HTML code, separating out the script blocks is a good way to cleanly separate presentation from the code. All the presentation code remains in one ASPX file (or, if you've got a couple of user controls for repetitive presentation elements, it can reside in part in ASCX files), and the code-behind code lives in a language-specific file, for example, `.vb` for a Visual Basic.NET code-behind file or `.cs` for a C# code-behind file. The ASPX file is the central point for the application from which the code-behind file and any user controls are referenced.

Code-behind files are easy to deploy – all you need to do is copy over the code-behind file along with the ASPX page. You can even compile your code-behind files into an assembly to reuse the functionality contained within them over more than one page or application. In the next chapter, we'll introduce compilation, and you'll learn how to compile components and why this is a useful technique to employ in your applications.

A code-behind file can be written in any .NET-compatible language, some good examples being VB.NET (which we've used throughout this book so far), C#, JScript .NET. This concept will be explored in the next chapter, when we talk about .NET assemblies – don't worry if you haven't got any experience with the other languages, as we'll stick with VB .NET for this chapter and the majority of the next.

> *If you have Visual Studio .NET, Web Forms applications are always created with a code-behind file, instead of placing your code on the same page. In addition, code-behind files in Visual Studio .NET are named the same as the ASPX page, with an additional .vb or .cs on the end of the filename. For example, `MyPage.aspx` would have an associated VB .NET code-behind page named `MyPage.aspx.vb`.*

Let's look at a simple example of a code-behind file.

Try It Out   Our First Code-Behind File

In this example we're going to create a very simple Web form with a textbox and a button, and give this simple arrangement extra functionality by adding a code-behind file.

1. In Web Matrix, create a new Visual Basic.NET class file and call it `SimpleCodeBehind.vb`. Set the class name to be `MyCodeBehind` and the namespace to be `Wrox` as shown in Figure 12-11:

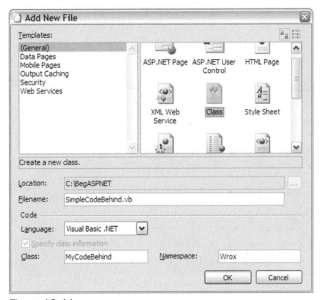

Figure 12-11

2. In the file, you will see the following generated code:

```vb
Imports System

Namespace Wrox

  Public Class MyCodeBehind
    Public Sub New()

    End Sub
  End Class
End Namespace
```

3. Change this code by adding the following lines:

```
Imports System
Imports System.Web.UI
Imports System.Web.UI.WebControls

Namespace Wrox
  Public Class MyCodeBehind : Inherits Page
  Public Name as Textbox
  Public Message as Label
  Public Sub SubmitBtn_Click(Sender As Object, E As EventArgs)
    Message.Text = "Hello " & Name.Text
  End Sub

  End Class
End Namespace
```

4. The `Public Sub New()` method needs to be removed (notice that this method has already been removed in the preceding code listing.)

The `Public Sub New()` method is a constructor, a type of method often used when creating full classes. However, we don't need this method in a code-behind file.

5. Next, create a new ASP.NET page called `SimpleCodeBehind.aspx`, and save it in the same directory as the code-behind page. Switch to All view and add the following code:

```
<%@ Page Inherits="Wrox.MyCodeBehind" Src="SimpleCodeBehind.vb" %>

<html>
<head><title>Simple Code-Behind Page</title>
</head>
<body>
  <form runat="server">

  Please enter your name then click the button below:<br /> <br />

  <asp:textbox id="Name" runat="Server" />
  <asp:button text="ClickMe!" OnClick="SubmitBtn_Click" runat="server" />
   <br /><br />
  <asp:label id="Message" runat="Server" />
  </form>
</body>
</html>
```

6. Run the ASP.NET page. You should see the page in your browser as shown in Figure 12-12:

Figure 12-12

How It Works

This example did a very basic job of passing information from the `.aspx` file to the `.vb` file and back again. We inputted a name into a textbox on the `.aspx` page; the `.vb` code-behind file took this name and passed it into a string along with some text, and then outputted this string to a label control that was sitting almost invisibly on our page. Look at the stages step-by-step to fully understand this process.

```
<%@ Page Inherits="Wrox.MyCodeBehind" Src="SimpleCodeBehind.vb" %>
```

This line of code is essential when working with code-behind. The first part of the statement specifies that we will be using the functionality in the `MyCodeBehind` class, which is a member of the `Wrox` namespace. The page will inherit the functionality defined in the `MyCodeBehind` class (refer to *Chapter 7* for more information on inheritance.) The second part of this statement specifies where to find the class – in this case, in the `SimpleCodeBehind.vb` file. Only one of these declarations can be used for any given `ASPX` page.

The rest of this ASP.NET page is simple, with a `textbox`, a `button`, and a `label` control. These controls are the same as the ones introduced in *Chapter 3*:

```
<form runat="server">

Please enter your name then click the button below:<br /> <br />

<asp:textbox id="Name" runat="Server" />
<asp:button text="ClickMe!" OnClick="SubmitBtn_Click" runat="server" />
  <br /><br />
<asp:label id="Message" runat="Server" />
</form>
```

Let's move on to the code-behind file and see how this works. The syntax in this file looks different from the sort of code used so far because this is a purely VB .NET file, and not an ASP.NET page.

```
Imports System
Imports System.Web.UI
Imports System.Web.UI.WebControls
```

This first block of code lays the foundation for the code-behind file. These three lines of code import important namespaces from the .NET *Class Library*. These namespaces are used to access all of the functionality of ASP.NET pages. Actually, these are loaded by default in any ASP.NET page, though we never get to see this ourselves because it's all done behind the scenes. As mentioned in *Chapter 7*, these namespaces provide easy access to the classes they contain. To make use of one of their classes, you can simply refer to the class by name instead of typing out the full path that includes all of the namespace.

The next line of code assigns a `Namespace`, and names the class in the code-behind file. If you remember, the first line in our ASP.NET page mentioned `Wrox.MyCodeBehind`. Well, this is what the ASP.NET page is looking for – the `MyCodeBehind` class in the `Wrox` namespace.

```
Namespace Wrox
    Public Class MyCodeBehind : Inherits Page
```

The second part of this line indicates that the `MyCodeBehind` class is inheriting functionality from the ASP.NET `Page` object. This means, "take the `Page` class, combine it with the one defined below, and call it `MyCodeBehind`". Essentially, both `Inherits` statements in the two files are like a kind of glue – they make the two files stick together as if they were one single file. This statement is essential when working with code-behind on an ASP.NET page.

```
    Public Name as Textbox
    Public Message as Label
```

These lines are simply variable declarations, and mimic the names of the controls on the ASP.NET page. This is a technique you need to use for any code-behind file – all controls on a page that you want interacting with the code-behind file need to have a corresponding local variable.

```
    Public Sub SubmitBtn_Click(Sender As Object, E As EventArgs)
        Message.Text = "Hello " & Name.Text
    End Sub
```

We then move on to the practical details of the code-behind file. The preceding block of code is where the action happens. A method is created to handle the `Click` event of our **Click Me!** button. A welcome message string is built by adding some standard text to the string object, and then appending the value entered and held in the textbox by the user. The `text` attribute of the `label` control can then be changed to display the welcome message that is constructed whenever the button is clicked.

```
    End Class
End Namespace
```

The last two statements close the class and the namespace blocks, respectively.

This example was very simple, and it didn't really show off the capabilities of the code-behind style of coding to its fullest. However, it did illustrate the principle of encapsulation. This technique can be used to encapsulate a lot of logic to deal with user input, thereby separating out the jobs of the designer and the programmer, which is one of the goals of ASP.NET.

Code-behind can be used on any `ASPX` page with a `<script...>` block on it. The code portion of the page can be cleanly moved out to the code-behind file.

If you use or intend to use Visual Studio .NET, you will notice that this is the default behavior. Using code-behind is good practice since it neatly separates presentation from code – using it outside of the Visual Studio.NET environment is optional, but it's still a good idea.

The key steps to remember when switching to using code-behind are:

❑ Reference the code-behind file from your ASPX page using that single line at the top of the page, specifying the class which the ASPX page is inheriting from, and the source file that contains that class definition.

❑ In the code-behind file, ensure to add : `Inherits Page` on the same line as the class definition, after the name of the class.

❑ Again, in the code-behind file, add variable declarations corresponding to each of the controls on the page that you will be working with programmatically (ensuring that you make each variable `Public` in scope.)

❑ Finally, in the code-behind file, enter the code that formerly resided in the script block on the ASPX page. Ensure that any appropriate `Imports` statements are added at the top of the page, so that the appropriate class libraries are referenced, so that the code runs as intended.

It's worth noting that the principle of code-behind can be applied to user controls in exactly the same manner as to normal ASPX pages. All you need to do is add a statement to the top of the ASCX control, with the same syntax that the ASPX statement used in the preceding example, to link the .ascx to an associated .ascx.vb code-behind file.

Let's try using code-behind in the Wrox United site. In the next example, we'll look at how we could separate the script code contained in the Default.aspx page into a separate file.

Try It Out Using Code-Behind in Wrox United

1. Create a new class file called Default.aspx.vb with a namespace of Wrox, and a class name of DefaultCodeBehind.

2. In this file, you will need to copy over all the lines of code from **Code** view of Default.aspx. These are mostly methods and one public Hashtable. These lines are not highlighted in the following listing (we've not included all the code from the methods in this listing; just their signatures, to give you an idea how many methods we're moving). The highlighted lines below need to be added to the code-behind page to make it work:

```
Imports System
Imports System.Web
Imports System.Web.UI
Imports System.Web.UI.WebControls
Imports System.Web.Caching
Imports System.DateTime

Namespace Wrox
   Public Class DefaultCodeBehind : Inherits Page

      Public DateList as New System.Collections.Hashtable()
      Public txtEmailAddress as Textbox
      Public lblRegister as Label
```

```
      Public btnRegister as Button
      Public pnlFixtureDetails as Panel
      Public MatchesByDateList as Repeater
      Public EventCalendar as Calendar

   Sub Page_Load()
      ...
   End Sub

   Sub EventCalendar_DayRender(sender As Object, e As DayRenderEventArgs)
      ...
   End Sub

   Function Dates() As System.Data.IDataReader
      ...
   End Function

   Sub EventCalendar_SelectionChanged(sender As Object, e As EventArgs)
      ...
   End Sub

   Function Venue(OpponentLocation as string, MatchVenue as integer) as string
      ...
   End Function

   Function GamesByDate(ByVal [date] As Date) As System.Data.IDataReader
      ...
   End Function

   Function CheckFanEmailAddresses(ByVal fanEmail As String) As Boolean
      ...
   End Function

   Sub btnRegister_Click(sender As Object, e As EventArgs)
      ...
   End Sub

   Function AddNewFanEmail(ByVal fanEmail As String) As Integer
      ...
   End Function
  End Class
End Namespace
```

3. Once you've created the code-behind page, save the file. Ensure that you have removed all code from **Code** view of the `Default.aspx` page, and then add the following line to the top of the page while in All view:

```
<%@ Page Inherits="Wrox.DefaultCodeBehind" Src="Default.aspx.vb" Language="VB" %>
```

That's it! Run the page and you shouldn't notice any difference – the page will look and feel the same, but we now have two files that store the code for the page, instead of one.

How It Works

This example is a great demonstration of moving a large amount of code to a code-behind page. The main additions that had to be made were the inclusion of some additional namespace directives at the top of the file, and the addition of declarations referring to the controls on the page:

```
Imports System
Imports System.Web
Imports System.Web.UI
Imports System.Web.UI.WebControls
Imports System.Web.Caching
Imports System.DateTime

Namespace Wrox
  Public Class DefaultCodeBehind : Inherits Page

    Public DateList as New System.Collections.Hashtable()
    Public txtEmailAddress as Textbox
    Public lblRegister as Label
    Public btnRegister as Button
    Public pnlFixtureDetails as Panel
    Public MatchesByDateList as Repeater
    Public EventCalendar as Calendar
```

Once these additions were made, all that remained was to transfer all the methods.

The successful transfer of the code for the `Default.aspx` page into a code-behind page was achieved with minimum fuss. However, if you were to now switch back to `Default.aspx`, you will find that you can't flick to **Code** view to edit the methods that handle events like you have in the past. Instead, you have to open the code-behind file and edit it separately. This is a bit of a pain – why bother separating the code?

Well, for creating Web applications, a natural progression is to switch to Visual Studio.NET from using Web Matrix. Visual Studio.NET uses code-behind by default. Using code-behind is also good practice if you have multiple developers working on an application, because it forces you to keep presentation code separate from functionality code, such as methods and event handlers, resulting in cleaner, more understandable code.

Summary

This chapter introduced two methods of encapsulating sections of code into separate files, so that our code remains as maintainable as possible:

- ❑ User controls, designed to hold code for sections of ASPX files that are repeated on numerous pages in a site

- ❑ Code-behind, designed for containing all of the script code in one file, leaving the ASPX file purely for the HTML and control placement to be done by designers

These two methods are relatively straightforward, and simply involve moving code into different areas to improve readability, reduce complexity, and reduce errors caused by mixing presentation and script.

The next chapter will look at more advanced methods of encapsulating code functionality into reusable components, namely .NET assemblies and custom server controls.

Exercises

1. Add the header control and navigation bar control to each page in the site. Remember to add the following code at the top of each page:

```
<%@ Register TagPrefix="WroxUnited" TagName="Header" Src="Header.ascx" %>
<%@ Register TagPrefix="WroxUnited" TagName="NavBar" Src="NavBar.ascx" %>
```

2. Move the VB.NET code for each page (visible in the **Code** view in Web Matrix) into an associated code-behind file, making sure each control has a corresponding declaration in the code-behind file.

3. Move the VB.NET code from the navbar.ascx control (which contains an event handler) into an associated .ascx.vb code-behind file, following exactly the same technique as you used for the other pages on the site.

4. Create a user control for the Merchandise.aspx page that enables you to easily add new items to the list. You will need to copy a row of the table from Merchandise.aspx into a new ASCX user control file. Make the properties on the image and button controls generic, then add some public properties to programmatically set the values on each Web control in the user control. Here's some code to get you started.

Firstly, here's some code that is currently in Merchandise.aspx which could be placed in the control:

```
<tr>
  <td>
    <asp:Image id="imgCap" runat="server" Height="100px"
      ImageUrl="images/shirt.gif" Width="100px"></asp:Image>
  </td>
  <td>
    The Wrox United shirt, available in one size only</td>
  <td>
    <asp:Button id="btnBuyShirt" onclick="AddItemToBasket" runat="server"
      Width="100px" CommandArgument="Shirt" Text="Buy a shirt!"></asp:Button>
  </td>
</tr>
```

If you change the ImageUrl of the image, the Text of the button, and the CommandArgument to empty strings ", then you can set those in the Page_Load event. Consider the previous example – the word "shirt" features in all three of these attributes, so you could add a property like the following that would store the name of the item (in this case, shirt), then use this value to construct the appropriate values for these attributes:

```
Private _itemName as string = "
Public Property ItemName As String
  Get
    Return _itemName
  End Get
  Set(ByVal Value As String)
    _itemName = Value
  End Set
End Property
```

Here's an example of using this property to update another private variable:

```
If _imageName = " Then _imageName = _itemName & ".jpg"
```

This could be used, for example, to provide a default image name.

You would also need to move the `AddItemToBasket` sub to the control because the buttons now reside within this control. Since the name of the session is globally available, it's possible to set or update session values from the control just as easily as from a page.

You will need three properties in all. The first, `ItemName` is shown above. You can include an optional property, to override the default value (in case you want to use a .gif, for example). Finally, you need to store the text that describes the item in a `Text` property, and include the value stored in this property in the page using the following syntax:

```
<td><%=Text%></td>
```

All that remains then is to add the item to the page:

```
<WroxUnited:Product id="Shirt" runat="server"
  ItemName="Shirt"
  ImageName="shirt.gif"
  Text="The Wrox United shirt, available in one size only"/>
```

5. Move the new code in `Product.ascx` into a code-behind file.

.NET Assemblies and Custom Controls

In the previous chapter we discussed user controls and code-behind as two different ways to break up our code into manageable sections. These two methods are used for encapsulating commonly used chunks of ASP.NET code, and for separating the script sections of our page into separate files. In this chapter, we will concentrate on some more advanced techniques of componentization, namely, creating *.NET assemblies* and *custom server controls*.

.NET gives us the ability to pre-compile code *components* into a central location that we can then access from all the pages in a site. Each component can contain one or more classes encapsulated into a compiled *assembly*. .NET assemblies can be written in any .NET-compliant language, and are pre-compiled into a file with a `.dll` extension. ASPX pages can then reference this file to gain access to the classes and methods contained within the assembly.

An assembly can store one or many different components within one physical file on your system. You can create a separate assembly for each component if you require, enabling you to distribute your components separately. Alternatively, you can compile all of your components into one central assembly if you prefer to have fewer files to distribute with your application.

Assemblies can contain any kind of required functionality. They can be used, for example, to store a set of classes relating to accessing and working with data, all compiled into one file. They can even store a custom server control, which is designed to render a custom user interface element that can be used on an ASPX page as easily as an ASP.NET Datagrid control. An assembly is a .NET construct that contains reusable functionality required in your applications, and applies to all kinds of .NET applications, not just Web forms.

> **.NET assemblies are groups of related classes and interface definitions encapsulated in a compiled file that can be accessed programmatically from ASP.NET Web Forms, Windows forms, or any .NET application.**

In this chapter we will discuss:

❑   What assemblies are and how they work, including details of how to compile assemblies.

❑   Creating an assembly that contains a data access component. This component will contain all of the methods we've used so far for accessing the database and retrieving or updating data.

❑   Creating a simple custom server control that adds a Match of the Day message to the site.

❑   Customizing the default `calendar` control using a *composite control*.

We'll take a closer look at what assemblies are and how they're created after we consider why and when we'd want to use them.

Three-Tier Application Design

Let's take the concept of separation of content from presentation one step further. Once we've separated the elements of an application into distinct purpose-specific categories (often referred to as layers), it becomes much easier to structure them efficiently. In many respects, everything we've said in the book so far about structured code has served as a preparation for what we're about to do – breaking out this *application logic* code into separate components that we can use both here and elsewhere. So, in traditional application design terms, our ASP.NET pages comprise the top *presentation layer*, a *data layer* (where a database stores contents) at the bottom, and components sit in between to marshal the flow of data between them. These components provide the core logic of our application, and are usually referred to collectively as the *application logic layer*:

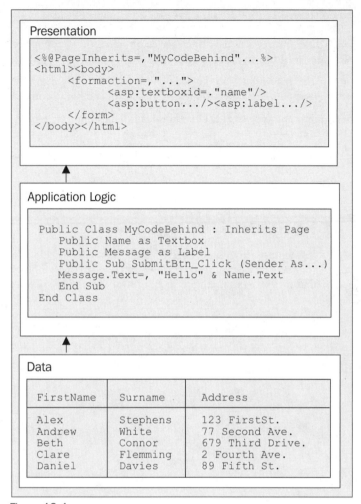

Figure 13-1

Figure 13-1 represents the *three layers* we've just described – in fact, an application built using this sort of architecture is often referred to as a *three-tier application*. So, how do these fit together? Consider a Web site offering low priced holidays. A user might click a button on this Web site that says "Show me all available hotels in Gran Canaria", which, in a two-tier situation, would call a class in one of our application logic components that is connected to the database, and query it for all hotels matching the criterion.

In a three-tier scenario, this application logic may talk to data logic that, in turn, talks to the database. In either case, we're looking for hotels in Gran Canaria, but we could expand this to match hotels available on a certain date, or hotels of a certain style.

The three tiers in generic three-tier applications can be broken down as follows:

- ❑ **Presentation** – This comprises all user interface code, containing a mixture of static HTML, text and graphics, user controls, and server controls.

- ❑ **Application Logic** – This contains all the code that is used to query the database, manipulateretrieved data, pass data to the user interface, and handle any input from the UI.

- ❑ **Data** – This could be any type of data store, for example, a database, an XML file, an Excel work sheet, or even a text file.

So how does this relate to the concepts we've met so far, and how do assemblies and server controls fit into the picture?

ASP.NET Application Design

User controls are used to encapsulate frequently used sections of ASP.NET code into separate files to improve manageability and make it easier to reuse code within one application. In the previous chapter, we chose to use code-behind files to separate the code that processed our Web Form. Look at figure 13.2:

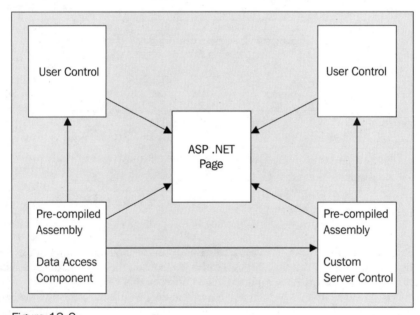

Figure 13-2

In this structure, each ASPX page can have a code-behind file and each user control can have a code-behind file. These user controls can be used by any of your ASP.NET pages. You can create data access components stored in assemblies that can be used by any of your user controls, ASP.NET pages, or custom server controls. You can also create custom server controls that can be used again by any of your user controls or ASP.NET pages. Your data access code can be accessed and used in your other assemblies, code-behind files, ASP.NET pages, server controls, or user controls, so the traditional three-tier application design paradigm doesn't really seem so clear. However, once you decide how you're going to structure your application, the process becomes much clearer:

1. First, you need to decide what part of your code does what. One scenario is that you keep your ASPX files purely for HTML and control elements.

2. You then use code-behind to handle any page-level events (the clicking of a button, or the loading of a page).

3. You can then apply exactly the same process to the user controls, separating presentation and code as appropriate.

4. Then you create data access components that will plug in to the ASPX and ASCX pages that contain all your data connectivity and data processing code.

5. Finally, server controls could also make use of data-handling classes from another assembly, so you're left with a very interlinked but compact model.

You could theoretically keep all of your code in ASPX pages, but this isn't recommended, given the benefits that encapsulating functionality into different components can bring to your applications, including increased ease of manageability, increased portability, and so on.

Since we've looked at the user interface design using ASPX and ASCX files, and we've seen how we can encapsulate page logic into a code-behind file, let's now look at how to encapsulate some of our application logic into a .NET assembly.

.NET Assemblies

An assembly is a logical grouping of functionality contained in a physical file. Assemblies are designed to solve the problem of versioning and make your code extremely simple to deploy. An assembly consists of two main parts:

❏ **The Assembly Manifest** – This contains the assembly metadata. This can be thought of as a table of contents that describes what's in the assembly and what it does, including the version number and culture information. It is generated when the assembly is compiled.

❏ **The MSIL (Microsoft Intermediate Language) code** – The source code (pre-compilation) is written in a .NET language, for example, VB.NET, or C#. At compile time, this source code is translated into MSIL code, which is the language .NET uses to communicate.

In the remainder of the chapter, we'll look at some examples of what can be put into assemblies. This ranges from very basic components through to components containing classes that can be used to work with data. We'll also look at a simple custom server control that renders its own custom user interface. We'll do this by writing code in Visual Basic .NET, compiling it into DLLs using the Visual Basic .NET compiler (vbc.exe), and calling it from our applications. We'll also look at how we can create an assembly in a different language that can be used in exactly the same way, so the language difference is transparent in the end result.

In our first ASP.NET assembly, we'll create a component with just one method – the SayHello() method.

Try It Out   Our First ASP.NET Component

To start with, let's create a simple component outside of the Wrox United application to demonstrate how components can be created and compiled into assemblies.

1. Ensure that you have a Chapter13 folder within your BegASPNET11 directory and then open up Web Matrix.

2. Create a new Class file called HelloWorld.vb. Set its Class property to HelloVB, and its Namespace property to WroxComponents as shown in Figure 13-3:

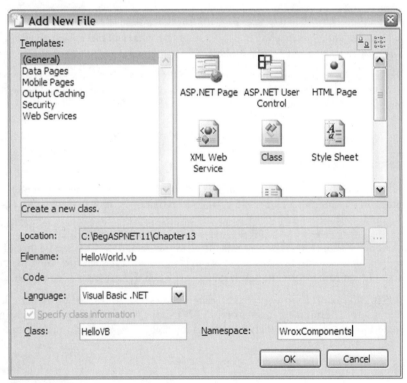

Figure 13-3

3. The file will be created when you click **OK**. The following code is generated automatically:

```
'HelloWorld.vb
'
Imports System
Namespace WroxComponents

    Public Class HelloVB
        Public Sub New()
        End Sub
    End Class

End Namespace
```

4. We need to make one modification to finish this example. Add the following method to the code:

```
Imports System
Namespace WroxComponents
  Public Class HelloVB
    Public Sub New()
    End Sub
    Public Function SayHello() As String
      Return "Hello World - I'm a VB.NET component!"
    End Function
  End Class
End Namespace
```

5. Save the file. Let's pause for a moment and look at how this code works before continuing with the example.

How It Works

This is a very simple component; let's take a brief look at what it does. The first line qualifies all of the following classes into a namespace, which we'll use to corral together components under a single banner:

```
Namespace WroxComponents
```

You can use the same namespace for each of your components – as long as each method name in each component is unique, this is a good way of combining specific groups of functionality.

In this example, we've used the `WroxComponents` *namespace. In the Wrox United application, we'll use* `WroxUnited` *as the root namespace for all of the components in the later examples.*

Once the component is compiled, other pages and applications can import this namespace, and all the classes it contains can easily be accessed. It doesn't matter which DLL contains each class, since ASP.NET automatically loads all the classes for each application, as long as they reside in a specific location (the `/bin` directory) when the application is started.

The next line declares the first and only class in our component, which is called `HelloVB`. Once you have imported the `WroxComponents` namespace in an ASPX page and created a new instance of this class, you will be able to access the `HelloVB` class from within an ASP.NET page:

```
Public Class HelloVB
```

Speaking of creating instances of the class, let's look at the next part of the code:

```
Public Sub New()
End Sub
```

The `New()` method shown in the preceding code snippet is a *constructor*, and is called whenever a new instance of this class is created. If you wanted to, you could add code here to set some default properties or to run specific initialization code. Let's move on and look at the custom method added:

```
Public Function SayHello() As String
   Return "Hello World - I'm a VB.NET component!"
End Function
```

These lines are where our method is created. The `SayHello()` function is declared, and we specified that it will return a `string`. By declaring this function as `Public`, we're making it available to the outside world as an interface. We'll be able to call a `SayHello()` method on any object derived from this class once we're in our ASPX page. We're going to be really simplistic and explicitly tell our function to return the text "Hello World – I'm a VB.NET component!" whenever the method is called, but in a more complex component, you can obviously do a lot more, as you will see later.

The last lines of code in our component simply close up the class declaration and the namespace declaration:

```
   End Class
End Namespace
```

This component must now be *compiled*, and the compiled version must be saved to the `bin` directory of your Web application. If the directory isn't there already, don't worry – the code you will use to compile the component will create this automatically.

> *Previously, when using COM, any components created had to be registered with the system registry. With .NET, all you need to do is save your files in the right place and compile them.*

Let's take a closer look at what is meant by *compile* before compiling the component.

What Is Compilation?

When we create an ASP.NET page, we write code using an editor, and save the code as an ASPX file somewhere on our system. When that ASPX page is requested, the code is compiled into *Intermediate Language (IL)* behind the scenes when the page is first run, and stored in a cache until the Web server is restarted, or until the page (the ASPX file) has been changed in some way (for example, if you added some code and re-saved the file). The cached Intermediate Language code is then *Just-In-Time (JIT)* compiled into the native machine code at runtime.

When we use an ASP.NET page, we suffer a performance hit the first time the page is accessed because the page has to be compiled to IL, and then JIT compiled. Once the page has been accessed, the process of accessing the page is much quicker because all that needs to be done then is for the JIT compiler to run. However, when we create a .NET assembly, we do the compilation to IL in advance, saving us from even more of this initial performance hit. This means that components are slightly faster than an ASPX page the first time a page is run – though subsequent page hits will perform about the same. The compiled assembly is more discrete than the raw source code we put into it – it's much harder now to simply look through the compiled code and see how the classes are structured in the assembly without using a specialist tool – simply opening the DLL in Notepad will display gibberish, so alternative methods have to be used to see the code in its true IL form (although we'll not be looking at these in detail here because they are outside the scope of this book).

Now let's move on to compiling our first component.

Try It Out Compiling Our First ASP.NET Component

To compile our component, we need to create a file that will perform this compilation by running a series of specified commands.

1. Open Notepad, type in the following code, and save the file in the C:\BegASPNET11\Chapter13 folder as Compile.bat. Remember to set the **Save as type:** to **All Files**, otherwise the file will be saved as a text file and not a batch file. We can use this batch file to execute the shell commands within it:

```
cd c:\BegASPNET11\Chapter13
md bin
vbc /t:library /r:System.dll /out:bin/HelloWorld.dll HelloWorld.vb
pause
```

2. Double-click this file and you should see the following window:

Figure 13-4

We'll examine how this works in just a moment. However, if you received any error messages when you ran this command, and the output looked different from what you can see in Figure 13-4, double-check your code to make sure it's typed-in correctly (especially the spacing in the .bat file).

If this doesn't solve your problem or if you're getting an error that reads System Cannot find file vbc.exe then you will need to check whether your environment variables are configured correctly. There is a tutorial on how to do this, with accompanying code, available for download from www.wrox.com.

How It Works

So, what did this do? Let's first look at what's been created, and then we'll look at the compilation batch file in detail.

If you browse your hard drive and look at the `C:\BegASPNET11\Chapter13\bin` directory, you'll notice that there's a new file in here – `HelloWorld.dll` as shown in Figure 13-5. This is our compiled assembly, ready for use!

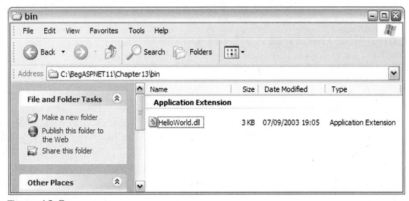

Figure 13-5

Let's look through the compilation batch file, step-by-step. First, here's the code we entered:

```
cd c:\BegASPNET11\Chapter13
md bin
vbc /t:library /r:System.dll HelloWorld.vb /out:bin/HelloWorld.dll
pause
```

Let's start at the beginning. The first line of code sets the active directory for the following commands to be the directory containing the code we're using. This line means that you could place the `compile.bat` physical file anywhere on your system and run it successfully:

```
cd c:\BegASPNET11\Chapter13
```

The next line of code creates a sub-directory (if one doesn't already exist) that will contain the compiled code. This location is quite important in that it must be named `bin` and be a folder within the root of a Web application for the assemblies to be loaded correctly:

```
md bin
```

In this example, the application directory is `C:\BegASPNET11\Chapter13`, and this line of code will create a folder within here that resides at `C:\BegASPNET11\Chapter13\bin`.

The next line of code actually performs the compilation. The first part of the command is the name of the Visual Basic .NET compiler – `vbc.exe`:

vbc /t:library /r:System.dll /out:bin/HelloWorld.dll HelloWorld.vb

The next part provides additional information that the compiler needs:

vbc /**t:library** /r:System.dll /out:bin/HelloWorld.dll HelloWorld.vb

This is known as a *switch* or an *option*. We're telling the VB compiler that when it compiles, we want it to produce a *library* file or assembly, and not an executable. If we'd not included this switch, the default value would have been used instead, and the compiler would have attempted to produce an executable.

> *Attempting to create an executable file in this situation would have failed since EXE files must be coded so that they have a method called Main() in them, that is called when the EXE is run. Our code doesn't have this method in it, so we would see an error.*

Next, we have a reference to the main .NET library file, `System.dll`:

vbc /t:library /**r:System.dll** /out:bin/HelloWorld.dll HelloWorld.vb

The /r: switch indicates to the compiler that any DLL files immediately following this switch are to be referenced in the final compiled file, because they contain functionality that is necessary to the compiled assembly. The assembly referenced in this example, `System.dll`, is one of the core .NET assemblies that are installed along with .NET itself. In this example, the VB file that was compiled doesn't actually use any of the System classes, so this part could have been omitted, but to demonstrate a more complete example, we've kept this reference in:

vbc /t:library /r:System.dll **/out:bin/HelloWorld.dll** HelloWorld.vb

This statement includes the /out: switch, which indicates that the code that immediately follows it is the name and location of the compiled assembly. In this case, we're creating `HelloWorld.dll` and placing it in the `bin` directory that we created earlier.

The last part of the statement is the name of the file we are compiling, which in our case is `HelloWorld.vb`:

vbc /t:library /r:System.dll /out:bin/HelloWorld.dll **HelloWorld.vb**

The last statement in the file, `pause`, tells the operating system to wait for the user to press a key before closing the command prompt window that's popped up. This gives us the chance to wait and see what happens before the window disappears so we know that our code executed correctly, or if not, get a chance to read the error message.

When we're working with the .NET command line compiler, there are several options available to us other than those we've already seen. When we compiled our component, we used the /t parameter to specify the type of output the compiler would create – in our case, we used /t:library switch to produce a DLL library file. This option, a shortened form of /target, can also take the following arguments:

Option	Effect
/target:exe	Tells the compiler to create a command-line executable program. This is the default value, so if the /target parameter is not included, an EXE file will be created.
/target:library	Tells the compiler to create a DLL file that will contain an assembly consisting of all of the source files passed to the compiler. The compiler will also automatically create a manifest for this assembly.
/target:module	Tells the compiler to create a DLL, but not to create a manifest for it. This means that in order for the module to be used by the .NET Framework, it will need to be manually added to an assembly using the Assembly Generation tool (al.exe). This tool allows you to create the assembly manifest information manually, and then add modules to it.
/target:winexe	This tells the compiler to create a Windows Forms application. This is not covered in this book. (For more information about Windows Forms, you can refer to *Professional C#, ISBN 0-7645-4398-9*)

Two other compilers supplied by default with the .NET Framework are used to compile C# and JScript components. These compilers are in the same directory as the vbc.exe compiler, and are called csc.exe and jsc.exe, respectively. They take the same parameters.

Accessing a Component from Within an ASP.NET Page

So far, we've got a simple component that contains code that displays Hello World – I'm a component! Let's access this from a simple ASP.NET page.

Try It Out — Using a Compiled Component

1. Create a new ASP.NET page in Web Matrix called `HelloWorldExample.aspx` in the `C:\BegASPNET11\Ch13` directory. In HTML view, enter the following code:

```
<form runat="server">
  <p>Our component says:</p>
  <p><asp:Label id="lblMessage" runat="server" /></p>
</form>
```

2. Switch to Code view and enter the following code:

```
Sub Page_Load
   Dim MyVBComponent as New WroxComponents.HelloVB()
   lblMessage.Text = MyVBComponent.SayHello()
End Sub
```

3. Save the page and then run it in your browser to see Figure 13-6:

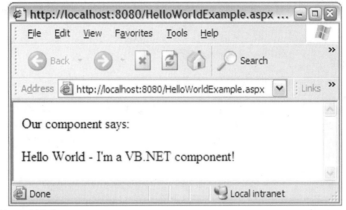

Figure 13-6

How It Works

Let's take a look at our ASP.NET page, starting with the code we added in HTML view:

```
<form runat="server">
  <p>Our component says:</p>
  <p><asp:Label id="lblMessage" runat="server" /></p>
</form>
```

Within the two paragraph tags on the form, we added some text and a label control, respectively. The label control's ID property was set to `lblMessage`.

In **Code** view, we added a `Page_Load()` event handler method:

```
Sub Page_Load
   Dim MyVBComponent as New WroxComponents.HelloVB()
```

The first line of code in this method creates a new instance of the HelloVB() class within the WroxComponents namespace. Recall that we've used syntax like this previously, whenever we created new Hashtable objects or DataReader objects. Since the HelloVB() class is a .NET class, and since the method within the class is an instance method, an active instance of the class needs to be created before the method within the class can be run. We instantiated a new instance of the HelloVB() class by creating an object, in this case VBComponent, and specifying that this object will hold a new instance of the HelloVB() class. VBComponent now has all the functionality of our class available to it as its own methods and properties. In this case, it has only one method – the SayHello() method.

The next line of code calls this method (which, as you will recall, returns a string) and uses the string value to populate the Text property of the Label control:

```
    lblMessage.Text = MyVBComponent.SayHello()
End Sub
```

Returning briefly to the line of code that created the new instance of the HelloVB() class, you will notice that we prefixed the HelloVB() class with the namespace in which it resides. However, this could have been omitted by adding one simple line of code to the top of the page. If you switch to All view, you could add the following code:

```
<%@ Page Language="VB" %>
<%@ Import Namespace="WroxComponents" %>
<script runat="server">
...
```

Remember that this line refers to the namespace declared in the component. Back in the component, we had the following lines of code:

```
Namespace WroxComponents
...
End Namespace
```

This is what we are referring to here. The namespace declaration is different from the class declarations in that a namespace can contain more than one class. These classes can then be referenced with the notation namespace.class, but if you use the Import Namespace command, you can simply refer to the class by name. It's a form of shorthand, and is exactly the same as the syntax we used in the previous chapter when we imported System.Web.UI and similar namespaces. They act as shortcuts to commonly used classes. Note that if you use a code-behind file in conjunction with the ASPX page, the namespace would have to be imported into the code-behind file.

Once this is added, you can change the line of code that creates the object as follows:

```
    Dim MyVBComponent as New HelloVB()
```

No doubt some of you will be using Visual Studio. Creating and using an assembly in Visual Studio is a little different from the command line method. For a discussion on how to create components from Visual Studio .NET, please refer to Appendix D.

XCopy Deployment

If you've ever worked with Windows in detail, you've probably heard of the *Registry*. The registry is a database that holds all the information about your computer, the hardware, the setup, and the software. It provides Windows with a way of locating DLL files or components. In this sense, it's a bit like the Yellow Pages of your computer. Any traditional DLL that is created has to have an entry in the registry so that the computer can locate it when it's needed. This process is called *Registration*. With basic ASP.NET components, there's no longer any need to do this – all you need to do is have the right directory in the right place, and ASP.NET will know where to look and what to do with it.

When we created our DLL, we had to place our compiled component into a /bin directory. This is a subdirectory of our Web application, or virtual directory.

> **Any time you need to use an assembly with .NET Web applications, the easiest way is to place your assembly in a /bin directory, and your ASP.NET application will now be able to use it.**

In the good old days of DOS, copying from one location to another was done with a command called xcopy; hence the term that is often used when referring to deploying .NET assemblies is *xcopy deployment*.

When a component is created, it can be accessed by any Web pages in that application space. All you need to do is place the component in the correct directory, create a new instance of the component, and include an <%@ Import Namespace . . . > declaration in your code if you want to add a shortcut to the classes contained within that namespace. If, however, you need to alter the functionality in the component in any way, all you need to do is go back to your original source file, alter the code, and recompile it. Once that process is complete, the new component will be used by any Web site hits that require it. This is totally different to the scenario faced by developers of classic ASP, who had to stop and restart their Web application to update components, thereby losing uptime.

When a change is made to a component, ASP.NET allows any requests that are currently executing to complete, and directs all new incoming requests to the new component, so the users of a site barely notice any change.

Accessing Assemblies in Other Locations

In the previous example, we stated that all we needed to do to access our assembly was to place it within the /bin directory in the root of our Web application. But what if we wanted to use an assembly in another location?

ASP.NET has a default configuration setup so that each created application knows how to access its required functionality. Occasionally, we may want to override or alter this default functionality to tailor it more to our specific application configuration. We can accomplish this using the web.config file. This file, as you will recall, resides within the root of our Web application. It can be used to help pages to find the required components.

To recap briefly, `web.config` is an XML-based file that specifies important configuration information that every ASP.NET application will need. It can store everything from information on debug settings and session state timeout values, to references and ASP.NET components. Being XML-based, it's human-readable, and this makes it very easy to add, remove, and change settings. Any changes to configuration that we make are instantaneous; they take effect as soon as the file is saved.

Let's take a quick look at an example of a `web.config` file with a directive detailing where to find an assembly:

```
<configuration>
  <system.web>
    <sessionState timeout="10" />
    <compilation>
      <assemblies>
        <add assembly="AssemblyName" />
      </assemblies>
    </compilation>
  </system.web>
</configuration>
```

> A quick word of warning: `web.config` files are case sensitive, so all the tag names must be typed in with care.

This simple configuration file sets the session state timeout of a page to be 10 minutes, and it references an assembly called `AssemblyName` using the `<add assembly="AssemblyName" />` tag. Here, `AssemblyName` refers to the assembly we require that resides outside of the `bin` directory. For example, we could reference `System.Data` if we wanted to use the classes within the `System.Data` namespace on a regular basis throughout our application, or `c:\somedirectory\somefile.dll` to locate a custom assembly in a different directory to the current working directory.

Writing Code in Other Languages

Since the .NET Framework is happily language-agnostic, we can write our components in any language. Throughout this book, we've been writing code in Visual Basic .NET. Indeed, our first component in this chapter was written in Visual Basic. Now we'll look at that first component again, but this time written in C#, to show how easy it is to work with any language to create your components.

Although the following example is written in C#, don't panic if you've never looked at C# code. It's just to illustrate the cross-language compatibility of .NET and, as you'll see, there are a lot of similarities between the two languages since they have to follow the same sorts of rules in order to be .NET compliant.

Try It Out **Writing a Component in C#**

1. Create a new class file `HelloWorld.cs` in Web Matrix. Set the language to C# in the drop-down box, the **Class** name to be `HelloCS`, and the **Namespace** to be `WroxComponents` as shown in Figure 13-7:

Figure 13-7

2. A chunk of standard code will be created. In this code, enter the following highlighted lines:

```
// HelloWorld.cs
//
namespace WroxComponents {
  using System;
  /// <summary>
  /// Summary description for HelloCS.
  /// </summary>
  public class HelloCS {
    /// <summary>
    /// Creates a new instance of HelloCS
    /// </summary>
    public HelloCS() {
```

```
      }

      /// <summary>
      /// Custom method that returns a string
      /// </summary>
      public String SayHello() {
        return "Hello World, I'm a C# component!";
      }
    }
}
```

Note that because C# is case sensitive, you must take particular care to copy this example letter-by-letter.

3. We need to compile this code. A simple way to do this is to reopen `Compile.bat`, amend some of the code, then save it with a new name. Amend the following code and save it as `CompileCS.bat`:

```
cd c:\BegASPNET11\Chapter13
md bin
```

```
csc /t:library /r:System.dll /out:bin/HelloWorldCS.dll HelloWorld.cs
pause
```

4. Double-click this batch file from an Explorer window and you should see Figure 13-8:

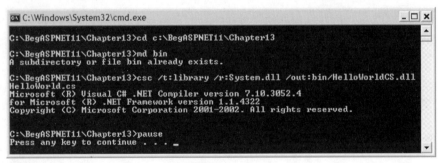

Figure 13-8

5. Let's import the namespace for the components in this example. Open up `HelloWorldExample.aspx` and amend the file by inserting the highlighted line to the top of the page in All view:

```
<%@ Page Language="VB" %>
<%@ Import Namespace="WroxComponents" %>
```

6. Next, add the following line of code while in HTML view:

```
<form runat="server">
  <p>Our component says:</p>
  <p><asp:Label id="lblMessage" runat="server" /></p>
```

```
    <p><asp:Label id="lblMessageCS" runat="server" /></p>
</form>
```

7.   Switch to **Code** view, modify (or add) the following highlighted lines, and save the file:

```
Sub Page_Load
    Dim MyVBComponent as New HelloVB()
    Dim CSComponent as New HelloCS()
    lblMessage.Text = MyVBComponent.SayHello()
    lblMessageCS.Text = CSComponent.SayHello()
End Sub
```

Notice that we've removed the `WroxComponents` before the `HelloVB` class name and `HelloCS` class name since we added a reference to the namespace at the top of the file.

8.   Reopen `HelloWorldExample.aspx` in your browser to see Figure 13-9:

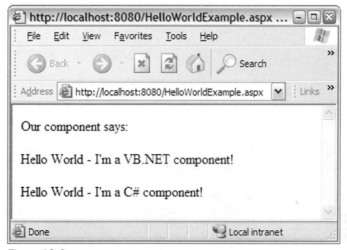

Figure 13-9

How It Works

Although the syntax was somewhat unfamiliar in this example, it's not too hard to compare the two versions of our component. The lines prefixed by `//` and `///` are comment lines, so ignoring those, let's look at the actual code in this example:

```
namespace WroxComponents{
    using System;
```

The namespace declaration is now case sensitive (since C# is case sensitive), and there's a curly bracket at the end of the line. Under this is a `using` statement – this statement is the C# equivalent of the VB.NET `imports` clause.

```
public class HelloCS{
```

There is one default method in this class, which is the default constructor:

```
public HelloCS() {
}
```

Our class definition is also case sensitive, and it also has a curly bracket at the end of the line. This is followed by the contents of the method – essentially the same line of code as the VB example with some changed wording, and a semicolon at the end of the line. C# doesn't need to know what kind of method is being created, so we can omit the word `Function` from our declaration. Instead of saying `As String`, we simply include the word `string` before the name of our method – this is the C# way to specify that the method must return a string. Again, there's a curly bracket at the end of the line:

```
public String SayHello() {
```

The next line is the body of the method:

```
return "Hello World - I'm a C# component!";
```

The `return` statement has barely changed, except for the content of the message. You'll notice a semicolon at the end of the line. VB automatically assumes each command takes up only one line, and you have to use an underscore (_) to continue on a new line. C#, on the other hand, doesn't end a line until it sees a semicolon. This removes the need for a continuation character.

We finish with a rather alien bit of curly bracket frenzy – this is simply C# closing up our method, our class, and finally our namespace in exactly the same way as we did in VB:

```
}
}
}
```

The difference is that the VB syntax is `End Function`, `End Class`, and `End Namespace`. In C#, because of the use of curly brackets (braces), the compiler knows that everything between each nested set of braces is a separate block.

Let's briefly look at the new lines we encountered in our ASP.NET page:

```
<p><asp:Label id="lblMessageCS" runat="server" /></p>
```

We need to add another paragraph containing another label, which we'll use to store the output of our component, just as we did with the VB component. We also added the namespace import directive to the top of the page:

```
<%@ Import Namespace="WroxComponents" %>
```

This means that we can declare the two instances of the components without having to explicitly mention which namespace the classes reside in:

```
Dim MyVBComponent as New HelloVB()
Dim CSComponent as New HelloCS()
```

Finally, we set the second label control to display the string returned by the C# component:

```
lblMessage.Text = MyVBComponent.SayHello()
lblMessageCS.Text = CSComponent.SayHello()
```

As you'll see, the ASP.NET page hardly looks any different – there are no braces or semicolons in here, because that's all held in the C# component. We have referenced two components, one written in VB, another written in C#, by using just one namespace import statement in our ASPX, and they've both been integrated seamlessly into our page, which only contains VB.NET code in the script section. We could have written other components in other languages, and the results would be the same.

This is one of the cool features of .NET, and it's one that many developers have grown to love. Imagine, if you're a Visual Basic .NET developer, working on a project with a C# developer, and a JScript .NET developer – you could all write components to be used in ASP.NET pages, with no need to worry about which language the original component code was written in, as long as it has been compiled into Intermediate Language code.

The only way this is possible is to have a compiler that is supported by the CLR. The .NET Framework only includes a handful of compilers by default (VB.NET, C#, JScript .NET, and J#), but there are many languages that already have compilers for .NET, and many more are planned. For information on the status of the Perl, Python, Fortran, Cobol, and all the other languages planned for use with the .NET Framework, check out the languages section of www.gotdotnet.com.

Data Access Components

A common use for components is to contain code for accessing data, or application logic. Our previous example of using an assembly didn't exactly push the boundaries very far, so in the next example, we're going to be slightly more adventurous and include some code to work with a database.

In the following example, we will create a component that combines the data access methods we've been using in the Wrox United application, into a central component that can be accessed by all pages in the site. This will mean that we can reuse standard data access methods stored in this central component from any of the pages on the site, which could save us time in the long run. And it also means that to change the data that is returned, you only need to change the code once in the central component, and not in every single page that needs to access that data.

Try It Out Encapsulating Data Access Code into a Component

In this example we will move some of the data access code used in the `Default.aspx` and `Teams.aspx` pages from the Wrox United site into a component. If you recall, in the previous chapter we moved a lot of data access code from `Default.aspx` into a code-behind file called `Default.aspx.vb`. This file contains most of code that we'll be putting in the component. The rest of the methods will come from `Teams.aspx`.

1. Start by creating a new class file called `DataAccessComponent.vb` within the `BegASPNET11\WroxUnited` directory. Set its **Class** name to `DataAccessCode`, and its **Namespace** to be `WroxUnited` as shown in Figure 13-10:

Figure 13-10

2. You will see that the following code has been automatically generated for you:

```
' DataAccessCode.vb
'

Imports System

Namespace WroxUnited
   Public Class DataAccessCode
```

```
        Public Sub New()
        End Sub

    End Class
End Namespace
```

3. The next step is to move over all the data access methods from the code-behind file to this new class. Reopen `Default.aspx.vb` and copy the following four methods into this class - `Dates()`, `GamesByDate()`, `CheckFanEmailAddresses()`, `AddNewFanEmail()`.

4. You should now have the following code in your new class file (the body of each method has been omitted from the following listing to save space):

```
Imports System
Imports System.Data
Imports System.Collections
Imports System.Configuration
Namespace WroxUnited
    Public Class DataAccessCode
        Public Sub New()
        End Sub
        ' From Default.aspx:
        ' Dates() returns a datareader containing the date and ID of every game
        Function Dates() As System.Data.IDataReader
        ...
        End Function

        ' GamesByDate(date) returns all games scheduled for a specified date
        ' The date parameter is a Date datatype

        Function GamesByDate(ByVal [date] As Date) As System.Data.IDataReader
        ...
        End Function

        ' CheckFanEmailAddresses(fanEmail) verifies if an email address exists
        ' already in the Fans table in the database. If the email already exists, a
        ' boolean true is returned, otherwise, boolean false is returned.
        ' The fanEmail parameter is a string.

        Function CheckFanEmailAddresses(ByVal fanEmail As String) As Boolean
        ...
        End Function

        ' The AddNewFanEmail(fanEmail) function adds a new email address to the
        ' Fans table in the database.
        ' The fanEmail parameter is the email address to be added, in the format
        ' of a string datatype.

        Function AddNewFanEmail(ByVal fanEmail As String) As Integer
        ...
        End Function
        ' That's the last of the functions taken from Default.aspx
    End Class
End Namespace
```

In the preceding code, comments have been added before each method. It is a great idea to make data components easy to use by other developers in a team, and it only takes a few minutes.

5. `Teams.aspx` also contains several methods for retrieving data, so let's add those now. You will be transferring the following methods - `GetTeams()`, `GetPlayersByTeam()`.

Note that if you successfully completed the exercises at the end of the previous chapter, these methods will have been moved to `Teams.aspx.vb`.

6. Add these two methods to the component, below the ones added previously:

```
...
' That's the last of the functions taken from Default.aspx
' From Teams.aspx:
' The GetTeams() function retrieves the ID, name and notes regarding each
' team from the database and returns them in a datareader object.

Function GetTeams() As System.Data.IDataReader
...
End Function

' The GetPlayersByTeam(teamID) function searches the database for all the
' players in a specified team. It returns a DataReader containing the
  name,
' position, and team name for each player.
' The teamID parameter is an integer that contains the unique identifier
' for the appropriate team.

Function GetPlayersByTeam(ByVal teamID As Integer) As
System.Data.IDataReader
...
End Functio
' End of Teams.aspx methods.
End Class
End Namespace
```

7. All of these methods consume methods from the .NET Framework stored in the `System.Data` namespace, so you need to add a line to the top of this class to make it possible to use these methods without prefixing them with a full namespace declaration each time:

```
Imports System
Imports System.Data
Namespace WroxUnited
...
```

8. `Default.aspx.vb` now only contains event handler methods and just one other method, `Venue()`, which is used to display the correct fixture location for either home or away matches. `Teams.aspx.vb` now only contains event handler methods.

9. The next stage is to compile this component. The easiest way to do this is to create a batch file, as we did before. Open Notepad and enter the following lines of code. Save the file as `compile.bat`, making sure that the **Save as type** is set to **All Files**.

```
cd c:\BegASPNET11\WroxUnited
md bin
vbc /t:library /r:System.dll,System.Data.dll
/out:bin/DataAccessCode.dll DataAccessCode.vb
pause
```

Note that the two lines starting vbc *shown in the preceding code snippet should all be typed on one line with no line break in your code.*

10. Back in Windows Explorer, double-click on this file and you should see Figure 13-11:

Figure 13-11

11. If you re-run this code, you'll see a message stating that the bin directory already exists, but this won't affect the compile process at all, so it's worth keeping that line in to ensure that the bin directory always exists.

12. The data access component is now compiled, so it's time to make some changes to the ASP.NET pages so that they can still find the functions that they need! Reopen Default.aspx.vb and add the following lines of code:

```
Imports System.Web.Caching
Imports System.DateTime
Imports WroxUnited
Namespace Wrox
    Public Class DefaultCodeBehind : Inherits Page
        public DateList as New System.Collections.Hashtable()
        public txtEmailAddress as Textbox
        public lblRegister as Label
        public btnRegister as Button
        public pnlFixtureDetails as Panel
        public MatchesByDateList as Repeater
        public EventCalendar as Calendar
        public Data as New DataAccessCode()
        Sub Page_Load()
...
```

The first two lines are a simple namespace import; however the third changed line of code creates a new instance of the data component that we've just created. We need to have an instance of this component before we can call any methods on this object, in the same way that we need to have instances of Web controls before we can call methods on those.

13. Now that there is an active instance of the `DataAccessCode` component on the page, we can call methods on that object. The method names are the same as they were before, but you will need to prefix each method call with the name of this object (because we are now calling methods of that object). We will consider each method individually:

In the `Page_Load()` method:

```
If Cache("DateList") is Nothing Then
   Dim DateReader as System.Data.iDataReader
   DateReader = Data.Dates()
```

In the `calendar` control's `SelectionChanged()` event handler:

```
Sub EventCalendar_SelectionChanged(sender As Object, e as EventArgs)
  pnlFixtureDetails.Visible = True
  MatchesByDateList.DataSource = _
    Data.GamesByDate(EventCalendar.SelectedDate.ToShortDateString)
  MatchesByDateList.DataBind()
End Sub
```

And in the `btnRegister_Click()` method:

```
If data.CheckFanEmailAddresses(FanEmail) = true Then
  ...
Else
   data.AddNewFanEmail(FanEmail)
```

14. At this stage, you can view `Default.aspx` (we've not yet amended `Teams.aspx`). If you run the page, you should see the screen in Figure 13-12:

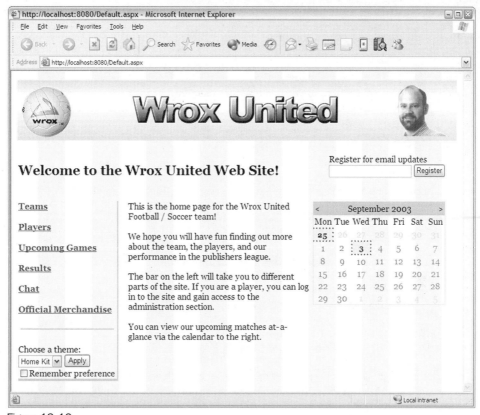

Figure 13-12

15. You need to make a couple of small adjustments to `Teams.aspx` and then the whole site should be up and running. In the code of this page (whether it's still in your ASPX page or in a code-behind page) you need to make the following changes:

```
dim SelectedTeam as String
public data as New DataAccessCode()
...
Sub Page_Load()
  TeamList.DataSource = data.GetTeams()
  TeamList.DataBind()
End Sub

Sub TeamList_ItemCommand(sender As Object, e As DataListCommandEventArgs)
  If e.CommandName.equals("ShowTeam") Then
    SelectedTeam = ctype(e.commandsource, LinkButton).Text
    PlayersList.DataSource = data.GetPlayersByTeam(e.commandargument)
    PlayersList.DataBind()
  End If
End Sub
```

16. At this point, you can run the `Teams.aspx` page, and it should look the same as before.

How It Works

This example didn't introduce any new functionality in the Wrox United site, but it did succeed in centralizing the data access methods and removing clutter from the pages themselves. Let's look through the most important parts.

At the top of the component, the necessary namespaces were imported:

```
Imports System
Imports System.Data
Imports System.Collections
Imports System.Configuration
```

The next bits of code declared the namespace and class name for the component:

```
Namespace WroxUnited
    Public Class DataAccessCode
```

After the default constructor was added to the code, we added all the different data access methods we've used so far. We won't look through these again here.

In the compilation file, we used the following statement to compile the component:

```
vbc /t:library /r:System.dll,System.Data.dll
    /out:bin/DataAccessCode.dll DataAccessCode.vb
```

In this example, because we are using classes that do a lot of work with data, we need to reference the .NET `System.Data.dll` component that contains class definitions for things like the `IDataReader` interface that we've used quite often.

In the ASPX pages, we made a few changes. We imported the `WroxUnited` namespace so that we could access the `DataAccessCode` class without having to prefix it with the name of the namespace:

```
Imports WroxUnited
```

We then created an instance of the new class so that we could call methods on this new object:

```
        public Data as New DataAccessCode()
```

Whenever we needed to call data access methods, we added the name of the object to the line of code, indicating that we were calling methods on that object:

```
        DateReader = Data.Dates()
        ...
        Data.AddNewFanEmail(FanEmail)
        ...
```

If you actually compare what we did in this example with what we've done in the two previous examples, you will notice that the bulk of the work has been the same – create the component, compile it, add it and instantiate it in the page, and then call methods on that object. That's all there is to it, really. Components are a convenient way to break up the code we work on to make it more maintainable and developer friendly. If you work as a full time developer, you probably encounter many components on a daily basis, so it's important to document them by adding comments, as we did in this example.

Once you understand how to put together components using class files, you can take this knowledge one step further and create custom controls. It takes a bit more coding, but the results are not just reusable code (as shown in the examples in this chapter so far), but reusable *visual* components.

Custom Server Controls

ASP.NET pages revolve around the concept of server controls. Controls-based development is the new 'big thing', as you may have gathered by now. The previous chapters discussed how to use the built-in ASP.NET server controls, and we saw how to create our own user controls for reuse in Web pages. Now we're going to look at what ASP.NET custom controls are, how they differ from user controls and standard components, and how they are created.

What Are Custom Controls?

Custom controls are a specific type of component – they also contain classes and are compiled. However, the main difference between a custom control and an application logic or data access component is that a custom control generates a visible user interface. When we place a server control on our page, we can see it and hopefully interact with it. As an example, consider the simple `TextBox` server control that is available to us out of the box when we create Web applications. This control was originally developed by someone at Microsoft who coded the methods and properties available to instances of that control. The .NET Framework enables us to create custom controls, which gives us the flexibility to create controls like these ourselves.

How Are Custom Controls Different from User Controls?

User controls encapsulate user interface elements of a site into easily reusable portions. However, they are usually site specific – they aren't meant to be used outside of the application in which they're based, and this is where the more universal custom control fits in. Custom controls inherit from the `System.Web.UI.Control` namespace, and are compiled. These controls can combine the functionality of other pre-existing server controls (in which case they are referred to as *composite controls*), or can be completely new controls, developed from ground up. They are fully compiled and have no UI code contained in an ASPX page, as all rendering is controlled programmatically. They are designed to provide functionality that can be reused across many applications; for example, a tree view control for representing file systems or XML file structures.

> If you use Visual Studio .NET, you'll notice a difference between these two types of controls. Whereas a user control does not display fully in design view, and you can't set properties on this control via the property tab, a custom control can be coded to work with Visual Studio .NET so that you see a visual representation of the rendered page at design-time and you are able to make use of the property toolbox to work with the control at design-time. While we won't be looking at how to achieve this in this book, you can see it in action whenever you drag a TextBox, DataGrid, or any other .NET Web control onto a page – these may be built-in controls, but the theory behind them is the same as a custom control.

How Are Custom Controls Different from Standard Components?

While a standard component is designed to hold application logic or database access methods, custom controls are designed to produce viewable output. They are compiled to make it easier to deploy components on other systems or applications. They can also inherit from other assemblies and components themselves, yet their visual appearance is defined by the control-specific code they contain. A lot of functionality that is taken for granted when working with existing ASP.NET server controls, such as the ability for a control to maintain its visual state (known as its viewstate) across a postback, has to be coded by hand. This does mean a lot of coding when you get into advanced controls, but it gives the developer a very powerful reusable tool that works the way you want, rather than having to hack about to produce a less-than-ideal solution.

Let's have a go at creating a simple custom control and displaying it in an ASP.NET page.

Try It Out Our First ASP.NET Custom Control

We're going to create a simple custom control that will output some text to the `Default.aspx` page on Wrox United. The text that will be displayed will be a "Match of the Day" message. We will add a small method to the `DataAccessCode.vb` class that we created earlier and recompile it. This method can then be called from within the server control, which formats the message and renders it in the browser.

1. Fire up Web Matrix and reopen `DataAccessCode.vb`. Add the following method to the class, which we'll look at in more detail once we finish the example:

```
' GetMotd() builds an Arraylist containing strings that detail any
' scheduled matches for the current day.
' If there are no matches, an appropriate message is added instead.

Function GetMotd() As ArrayList
  Dim myReader As IDataReader

  ' Call the GamesByDate function in this class to retrieve fixture
  ' information for today

  myReader = GamesByDate(System.DateTime.Now.ToShortDateString)
  Dim motdMessage As new ArrayList
  Dim individualMessage as String
  Dim resultCount as Integer = 0

  While myReader.Read()
    individualMessage = myReader("TeamName") & " v " & _
                        myReader("OpponentName")

    If myReader("Location") = 1 Then
      individualMessage += ", home"
    Else
      individualMessage += ", away"
    End If

    motdMessage.Add(individualMessage)
    resultCount = resultCount + 1
  End While

  If resultCount < 1 then
    motdMessage.Add("No games scheduled today.")
  End If

  Return motdMessage
End Function
```

2. If you like, you can recompile this class now by simply double-clicking on `Compile.bat` from explorer as you did before. If all goes well, no errors will be produced. After building the custom control in this exercise, we'll add some more commands to `Compile.bat`, enabling us to compile all custom controls and classes in one step.

3. Time to build the control itself. Create a new class in Web Matrix, call it `CustomMotdControl.vb`, and specify that it belongs to the `WroxUnited` namespace.

4. Enter the following code into the newly created file:

```vb
Imports System
Imports System.Collections
Imports System.Web.UI

Namespace WroxUnited

  Public Class MotdControl
    Inherits System.Web.UI.Control

    private _name As String = "MOTD"

    Public Property Name As String
      Get
        Return _name
      End Get
      Set(ByVal Value As String)
        _name = Value
      End Set
    End Property
    Protected Overrides Sub Render(writer as HtmlTextWriter)
      Dim data as new DataAccessCode
      Dim motdMessages as new ArrayList()

      motdMessages = data.GetMotd()
      writer.Write("<div class='motd'>" & _name & ", " &_
        DateTime.Now.ToShortDateString() & ": <br/>")

      Dim message as string
      For Each message in motdMessages
        writer.Write(message & "<br/>")
      Next

      writer.Write("</div>")
    End Sub

  End Class
End Namespace
```

5. Make sure that you save this code before you continue. Now, reopen `Compile.bat` and add the following highlighted line of code (again, make sure it is all on one line in your code):

```
cd c:\BegASPNET11\WroxUnited
md bin
vbc /t:library /r:System.dll,System.Data.dll
  /out:bin/DataAccessCode.dll DataAccessCode.vb
vbc /t:library /r:System.dll,System.Web.dll,bin/DataAccessCode.dll
  /out:bin/CustomMotdControl.dll CustomMotdControl.vb
pause
```

Make sure you keep the statement that compiles the `DataAccessCode.vb` file – this is needed in the custom control. You'll notice that we've added the `DataAccessCode.dll` file in the compile statement for the custom control – this will ensure that we can access the methods stored in the data access component from the server control.

6. Run this file by double-clicking it in Explorer view.

7. Open `Default.aspx` and at the top of the file, add the following line:

```
<%@ Register TagPrefix="WroxUnited" TagName="NavBar" Src="NavBar.ascx" %>
<%@ Register TagPrefix="WroxUnitedMotd" Namespace="WroxUnited"
             Assembly="CustomMotdControl" %>
```

8. Then, in the central table cell (which you can use to store general introductory text), enter the following highlighted line of code:

```
The bar on the left will take you to different parts of the site. If you are a
player, you can log in to the site and gain access to the administration
section.
<br /><br />
You can view our upcoming matches at-a-glance via the calendar to the right.
<br /><br/>
<WroxUnitedMotd:MotdControl id="WuMotd" Name="Matches today" runat="server" />
```

9. So, the extra data method has been added, the control has been created, and both components have been compiled. We've also added code to use this control from `Default.aspx`, so it's nearly time to run the page and see the results. However, before you do so, reopen `WroxUnited.css` (and `WroxUnited2.css`) and add a new element to the stylesheet.

In `WroxUnited.css`, add the following:

```
.motd {
   color: #8b0000;
}
```

In `WroxUnited2.css`, add the following:

```
.motd {
   color: "yellow";
}
```

10. Now it's time to run the page! If you run the page on a day when there is a game (or several games) scheduled, you'll see something like in Figure 13-13:

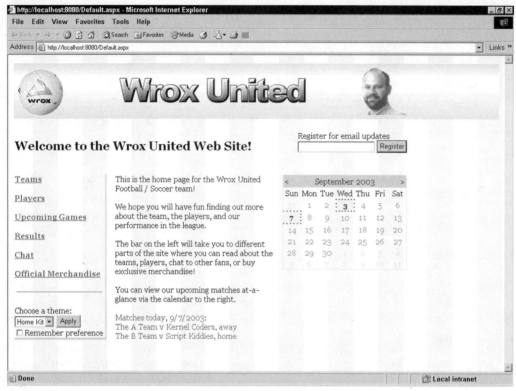

Figure 13-13

11. However, if you run the code on a day when no matches are scheduled, you'll see a default message saying **No games scheduled today**.

You can edit the contents of the `Games` *table in the* `WroxUnited` *database if you want to see different results. If matches are scheduled for the current day, you will see a message on the* `default.aspx` *page. However, if you change the date of each match, you can change the message that is displayed on the front page accordingly. In the above example, I manually changed the date of two scheduled matches to the previous day, in order to demonstrate what is displayed on days when there are no matches scheduled.*

How It Works – The Control

We created a control with a property that rendered very limited output to demonstrate how simple custom controls can be created. Let's take a look at how we put it together:

```
Imports System
Imports System.Collections
Imports System.Web.UI
```

We imported three namespaces at the top of the file. We will be using an `ArrayList` in this example, hence the `Imports System.Collections` statement. We will also be creating a Web control; hence we've added an `Imports` statement for the `System.Web.UI` namespace (because we'll probably want to use classes within this namespace).

The next part of the code declares the namespace for the control, and also the `MotdControl` class:

```
Namespace WroxUnited
   Public Class MotdControl
      Inherits System.Web.UI.Control
```

Notice that there is an `Inherits` statement immediately after the class definition. This is an important part of custom control development, because all custom controls must inherit from either the `System.Web.UI.Control` or `System.Web.UI.WebControl` namespace. The `Control` class is the leaner class of the two, and while it provides a lot of basic functionality behind the scenes that any control needs in order to work, it doesn't provide many methods implemented in the `WebControl` class. This isn't a problem here, because we don't need any of these methods in this example. Inheriting from `Control` means that we have more control over how the control is rendered at runtime.

The next part of the code creates the only public property of the control:

```
private _name as string = "MOTD"

Public Property Name As String
  Get
     Return _name
  End Get
  Set(ByVal Value As String)
    _name = Value
  End Set
End Property
```

The first line of code creates a private variable called `_name`, which is only accessible by the rest of the code in this class. The next block is where the public property is declared. This property can be set programmatically (`MyControl.Name = thing`), and also read programmatically (`thing = MyControl.Name`). The `Get` and `Set` blocks are used to specify how this works. Each time a new value is set via the public property, the private variable is updated. Conversely, whenever the public property is read, the returned value is stored in the private variable. The public property sits between the outside world and the internal variable. In this case, we are setting or getting the value of a string variable with some text that we'll use as we build up the displayed message. If we don't set the property in our code, the `_name` variable will store the default value of `MOTD`.

```
Protected Overrides Sub Render(writer as HtmlTextWriter)
```

We're creating one method in this class. There are a couple of new terms in here that you may be unfamiliar with. There is a method in the `Control` class called `Render`. What we're doing here is altering how that method works by *overriding* its functionality with our own functionality. While we don't want to go too far into the world of VB programming here, you need to know that this statement is required to provide the output we specify, instead of the default output from the `Control` class. We will be using an `HtmlTextWriter` to display the output of our control.

The only difference between this example and the previous one is that the control is rendering (writing) the text directly to the page, while our previous tests required a label control or similar to display any returned text from our components. Note, however, that we can render much more than just plain text using these controls. In this example, the output contains some HTML tags.

The next part of the code gets the complete set of daily match details from the data access component:

```
Dim data as new DataAccessCode
Dim motdMessages as new ArrayList()
motdMessages = data.GetMotd()
```

We created a new object called `data` and set it to contain a new instance of the `DataAccessCode` class. We then created a new `ArrayList` called `motdMessages` and retrieved the `ArrayList` of the day's fixtures from the database using the `GetMotd()` method.

The next line is where the magic starts – the `Write()` method of the `writer()` object that was declared in the method signature is used to write the required output to the Web page when the control is rendered:

```
writer.Write("<div class='motd'>" & _name & ", " &_
   DateTime.Now.ToShortDateString() & ": <br/>")
```

This first line builds up an HTML string and inserts the string stored in the `_name` private variable (the one that is set programmatically using the public `Name` property), and also the current date. Notice that this HTML string is in the form of a `<div ... >` element, which has an associated class definition – this enables us to style the output of the control in a CSS file.

The remainder of this method loops through the individual strings in the `ArrayList` and adds them (and a line break after each one) to the output. The last call to the `Write()` method writes the closing `</div>` tag to the browser (a sample of the rendered HTML output is shown in just a moment):

```
Dim message as string
For Each message in _motd
   writer.Write(message & "<br/>")
Next
writer.Write("</div>")
End Sub
```

All that's left is to close up the class and the namespace:

```
   End Class
End Namespace
```

If you view the source of `Default.aspx` you will find the following text about halfway down the page:

```
<div class='motd'>Matches today, 07/09/2003: <br/>No games scheduled
today.<br/></div>
```

This should give you a clear indication of how this code fits together. The result is clean and simple, and has been produced programmatically.

The Component

The `GetMotd()` method that we added to the `DataAccessCode` component provides the custom control with details of any matches on that particular day in the form of an `ArrayList`:

```
Function GetMotd() As ArrayList
```

The first part of this function retrieves all fixture details for the current day by passing in the `DateTime.Now()` method to the `GamesByDate()` method that was created earlier:

```
Dim myReader As IDataReader
' Call the GamesByDate function in this class to retrieve fixture
information
' for today
myReader = GamesByDate(System.DateTime.Now.ToShortDateString)
```

Next, we created some variables to hold various items of data, including the `ArrayList` of messages, the individual messages, and a count of how many matches are happening on the current day:

```
Dim motdMessage As new ArrayList
Dim individualMessage as String
Dim resultCount as Integer = 0
```

Looping through the results stored in the `myReader()` object, we built up a string containing details about the fixture:

```
While myReader.Read()
  individualMessage = myReader("TeamName") & " v " & _
                      myReader("OpponentName")

  If myReader("Location") = 1 Then
    individualMessage += ", home"
  Else
    individualMessage += ", away"
  End If

  motdMessage.Add(individualMessage)
  resultCount = resultCount + 1
End While
```

At this point, if there are no matches on the current day, the count of the results will still be zero; hence we can output a specific message to the array instead of match details:

```
If resultCount < 1 then
  motdMessage.Add("No games scheduled today.")
End If
```

Finally, we return the `ArrayList` of messages to the calling code:

```
  Return motdMessage
End Function
```

The Batch File

The command that we used to compile this component is very similar to the command that we used to compile the `DataAccessCode.vb` file:

```
vbc /t:library /r:System.dll,System.Web.dll,bin/DataAccessCode.dll
    /out:bin/CustomMotdControl.dll CustomMotdControl.vb
```

Notice that we have referenced `System.Web.dll` this time around (we needed this so that we could use the classes it contains, including the `System.Web.UI.Control` class). We also referenced the `DataAccessCode.dll` compiled assembly – needed as a reference so that the `GetMotd()` method could be called to return the required `ArrayList`. Since the `DataAccessCode` compilation statement should still be in this file, this will be compiled before the custom control is compiled, hence the custom control will be able to make use of any changes to the `DataAcccessCode` when the custom control itself is compiled.

The ASPX Page

We didn't make too many changes to the `Default.aspx` page itself – all the hard work was kept completely separate from this code file, which is exactly what we're after! Firstly, we registered the custom control so that the page knows about the assembly and the code it contains:

```
<%@ Register TagPrefix="WroxUnitedMotd" Namespace="WroxUnited"
            Assembly="CustomMotdControl" %>
```

We set a `TagPrefix` like we did with user controls, however, we do not set a `TagName` – we'll see why in a moment. We specified the namespace to be used as the `WroxUnited` namespace, and that we're using the `CustomMotdControl` assembly. Later in the code, we added the control to the page:

```
<WroxUnitedMotd:MotdControl id="WuMotd" Name="Matches today" runat="server" />
```

This is where we place our control on the page. We call it by the `TagPrefix` we set earlier, followed by the class name we specified in the control. We specify a `runat="server"` attribute, set the `Name` of the control, and close the tag. The `Name` property relates directly to the `Name` property we added to the custom control, so when we set this property, the `Set` block in the property in the custom control is run, and the local `_name` property has its value changed to the string we specify here. This value is then added to the output string, and hey presto! – we've just used our first custom control.

We mentioned earlier that one of the main reasons for using custom server controls was reusability, well, as long as our control can access a `GetMotd()` method in a class called `DataAccessCode`, we can use this control to display "message of the day" notices on a site. It's a good thing that MOTD could be an acronym for either "match" or "message" of the day!

Composite Custom Controls

In the last example, we created a totally new control that inherited some basic functionality from the `Control` base class, but the rest of the control was completely our own work. While it's possible to create all custom controls in this way, there are situations where you might find yourself saying "wouldn't it be great if I had a textbox that only allowed numeric input?" or perhaps "I'd really like a custom calendar that highlighted specific dates instead of having to add event handlers and code every time!"

Composite controls will solve these problems for you. A composite control is a custom control that contains an existing control within its definition, and allows you to customize how that existing control is rendered.

Let's have a look at this in action by creating a neat custom calendar class that will highlight specific dates for us automatically, and then use this as part of Default.aspx.

Try It Out Wrox United – Custom Composite Control

1. Start the example by creating a new class file, setting its namespace to WroxUnited, and its class name to CustomCalendar. Save the file as CustomCalendar.vb.

2. In the file, add the following code:

```
' CustomCalendar.vb
'
Imports System
Imports System.ComponentModel
Imports System.Web.UI
Imports System.Collections

Namespace WroxUnited

Public Class CustomCalendar
   Inherits System.Web.UI.Control
   Implements INamingContainer
   Private WithEvents calendar As WebControls.Calendar
   Public Event SelectionChanged As EventHandler
   Private _dateList As Hashtable

   Public Property DateList() As Hashtable
     Get
       Return _dateList
     End Get
     Set(ByVal Value As Hashtable)
       _dateList = Value
     End Set
   End Property
   Public ReadOnly Property SelectedDate() As DateTime
     Get
       Return calendar.SelectedDate
     End Get
   End Property

   Protected Overrides Sub CreateChildControls()
     calendar = New WebControls.Calendar
     calendar.CssClass = "calendar"
     calendar.DayStyle.CssClass = "normaldate"
     calendar.OtherMonthDayStyle.CssClass = "othermonthdate"
```

```
      Me.Controls.Add(calendar)
   End Sub

   Sub EventCalendar_DayRender(ByVal sender As Object, _
      ByVal e As WebControls.DayRenderEventArgs) Handles calendar.DayRender
      If Not _dateList Is Nothing Then
         If Not _dateList(e.Day.Date) Is Nothing Then
            e.Cell.CssClass = "selecteddate"
            e.Day.IsSelectable = True
         Else
            e.Day.IsSelectable = False
         End If
      Else
         e.Day.IsSelectable = False
      End If
   End Sub
   Sub EventCalendar_SelectionChanged(ByVal sender As Object, _
      ByVal e As EventArgs) Handles calendar.SelectionChanged
      RaiseEvent SelectionChanged(Me, e)
   End Sub

End Class
End Namespace
```

3.   Now, we need to compile this control. In the `Compile.bat` file, add the following line of code:

```
vbc /t:library /r:System.dll,System.Web.dll
  /out:bin/CustomCalendar.dll CustomCalendar.vb
```

4.   Compile the control by double-clicking `Compile.bat` from an Explorer window.

5.   To add this control to the page, add the following directive to the top of the In `Default.aspx`:

```
<%@ Register TagPrefix="WroxUnitedCalendar" Namespace="WroxUnited"
             Assembly="CustomCalendar" %>
```

6.   Next, add the following code in place of the original `calendar` control:

```
<td style="VERTICAL-ALIGN: top; WIDTH: 250px">
    <WroxUnitedCalendar:CustomCalendar id="EventCalendar" runat="server"
      OnSelectionChanged="EventCalendar_SelectionChanged" />
    <p>
      <asp:Panel id="pnlFixtureDetails" runat="server" visible="false">
```

7.   Switch to the code-behind for this page and alter the `calendar` control declaration to refer to the new `CustomCalendar` class:

```
    public pnlFixtureDetails as Panel
    public MatchesByDateList as Repeater
    public EventCalendar as WroxUnited.CustomCalendar
```

8.   Further down the page, in the `Page_Load()` method, add the following line of code:

```
    Cache.Insert("DateList", DateList, nothing, _
                 DateTime.Now.AddMinutes(1), _
                 Cache.NoSlidingExpiration)
    End if
    EventCalendar.DateList = Cache("DateList")
```

9. Delete the `EventCalendar_DayRender` from the code-behind page – we don't need this method any more because the functionality it contained is now encapsulated in the new custom control.

10. Run `Default.aspx` in your browser and you will see the same results as before, shown in Figure 13-14. You will be able to click on the different match dates in the calendar, and see the fixture details for a particular day:

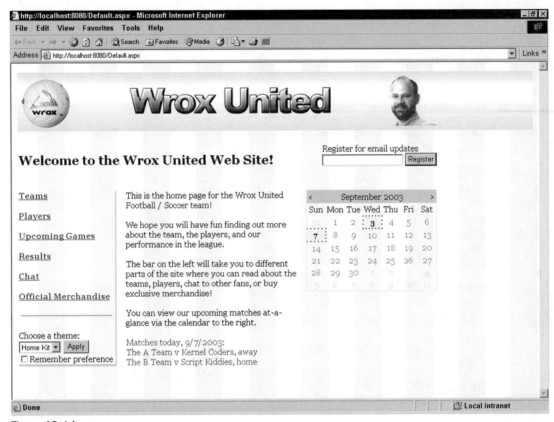

Figure 13-14

How It Works – The Control

This control may appear a bit complex at first, so let's step through it piece by piece. We start with some `Imports` statements and a `Namespace` declaration:

```
Imports System
Imports System.ComponentModel
Imports System.Web.UI
Imports System.Collections
Namespace WroxUnited
```

Next, we declared the class:

```
Public Class CustomCalendar
    Inherits System.Web.UI.Control
    Implements INamingContainer
```

Notice that in addition to inheriting the functionality in the `Control` class, we have implemented an interface (a special type of class) called `INamingContainer`. This interface enables ASP.NET to assign a name to the calendar that we'll be adding to this control in just a moment. Interfaces are discussed in *Chapter 7*.

The next line of code creates a new object called calendar of type `WebControls.Calendar`. This object is created using the VB.NET `WithEvents` keyword, which makes it simple for us to intercept and work with the events raised by this control when we use it. One such event, the Selection Changed event, is handled by an event handler called `SelectionChanged`:

```
Private WithEvents calendar As WebControls.Calendar
Public Event SelectionChanged As EventHandler
```

Next comes some more familiar code. We declare a private `Hashtable` (which we'll use to store the dates that will be highlighted in the calendar). This `Hashtable` has its value set via the public property `DateList`:

```
Private _dateList As Hashtable
Public Property DateList() As Hashtable
  Get
    Return _dateList
  End Get
  Set(ByVal Value As Hashtable)
    _dateList = Value
  End Set
End Property
```

The next block of code creates a second property, but this time, we're only going to allow consumers of this control to read the value in this property. The `ReadOnly` keyword specifies that this property is, as its name suggests, read only. When you declare a property to be read only, you should omit the `Set` block:

```
Public ReadOnly Property SelectedDate() As DateTime
  Get
    Return calendar.SelectedDate
  End Get
End Property
```

This property returns the value of the currently selected date in the calendar, which allows us to use this value to populate the panel below the calendar on the `Default.aspx` page.

The next part of the code is where we add the `calendar` control to the main `Parent` container. The `calendar` control is what is known as a `Child` control (it has a parent control; the custom control). To add this `Child` control, we override the `CreateChildControls` method of the `Control` class:

```
Protected Overrides Sub CreateChildControls()
  calendar = New WebControls.Calendar
```

The first part of the body of this method is where we instantiate a new `calendar` control. The reason we have added the `WebControls` prefix is that we have only imported `System.Web.UI`, not `System.Web.UI.WebControls`. Next, we specify three CSS class properties:

```
calendar.CssClass = "calendar"
calendar.DayStyle.CssClass = "normaldate"
calendar.OtherMonthDayStyle.CssClass = "othermonthdate"
```

Adding these properties to this control mean that, as long as we include a CSS stylesheet with the appropriate definitions in our pages, we'll be able to style our `calendar` control automatically. The last part of this method adds this control to the `Controls` collection of the parent control:

```
Me.Controls.Add(calendar)
End Sub
```

The second method in this file is very similar to the `DayRender` event handler that we saw previously:

```
Sub EventCalendar_DayRender(ByVal sender As Object, _
  ByVal e As WebControls.DayRenderEventArgs) Handles calendar.DayRender
```

The method signature has a `Handles` statement at the end of it, indicating that we want this method to be processed whenever the `DayRender` event is fired via the child `calendar` control.

Next, we test whether any date information has been passed into the control. If it has, then `_dateList` will contain *something* (not `Nothing`), and we can proceed to test whether the day that is being rendered matches any of the days in the `_dateList` Hashtable:

```
If Not _dateList Is Nothing Then
  If Not _dateList(e.Day.Date) Is Nothing Then
    e.Cell.CssClass = "selecteddate"
    e.Day.IsSelectable = True
  Else
    e.Day.IsSelectable = False
  End If
Else
```

If the `_dateList` Hashtable is empty, then we ensure that the dates are not selectable:

```
    e.Day.IsSelectable = False
  End If
End Sub
```

The final method in this control is the `SelectionChanged` event handler. This method is fired whenever the `calendar` control's `SelectionChanged` event is fired. Whenever this event is fired, we pass that event to the public `SelectionChanged` event object that was declared earlier. This ensures that the `SelectionChanged` event exists for the newly created custom control, and can be handled in the consuming page:

```
Sub EventCalendar_SelectionChanged(ByVal sender As Object, _
  ByVal e As EventArgs) Handles calendar.SelectionChanged
```

```
        RaiseEvent SelectionChanged(Me, e)
    End Sub
```

After this method closes, we close up the last of the control:

```
    End Class
    End Namespace
```

So, time to compile the control!

The Batch File

The compile statement for this file isn't too different from the statements we've used in the other controls and components in this chapter:

```
vbc /t:library /r:System.dll,System.Web.dll
    /out:bin/CustomCalendar.dll CustomCalendar.vb
```

This time, we only needed to reference the `System.Web.dll` in addition to the `System.dll` assembly. We didn't access any data in this example.

The ASPX Page

We made only a couple of changes to the `Default.aspx` page to use this new calendar. First, we added a reference to the new control:

```
<%@ Register TagPrefix="WroxUnitedCalendar" Namespace="WroxUnited"
Assembly="CustomCalendar" %>
```

Next, we changed the code in the page to use the custom calendar in place of the default calendar, which turned out to involve less code than before (we've added a lot of this code to the custom control already):

```
<WroxUnitedCalendar:CustomCalendar id="EventCalendar" runat="server"
        OnSelectionChanged="EventCalendar_SelectionChanged" />
```

Notice that we still set the `OnSelectionChanged` attribute as we did before to point to the event handler that fires whenever the selection in the calendar changes.

In the code-behind page itself, we changed the `EventCalendar`'s data type from `Calendar` to `CustomCalendar`:

```
    public EventCalendar as WroxUnited.CustomCalendar
```

Then we added a line to the `Page_Load()` event handler that passed in the `DateList` Hashtable (stored in the cache) to the `CustomCalendar` control. This is the data that we need to highlight specific dates!

```
    EventCalendar.DateList = Cache("DateList")
```

Summary

In this chapter we have continued the thread from the previous one, and discussed creating .NET assemblies that can be used to store classes that handle data access code, or custom server control code. We've even seen an example of using a C# component from within a VB.NET ASPX page, demonstrating how .NET handles components written in different languages. We've also created two different custom server controls, and taken a first look into the world of custom control creation.

In this chapter, we looked at:

❑ Compiling a .NET assembly

❑ Using classes contained in a compiled assembly on a page

❑ Encapsulating data access code into a compiled component

❑ Creating simple custom controls that render custom HTML to the browser

❑ Enhancing an existing ASP.NET control using a composite control

Exercises

1. Explain the benefits of using components, and what sorts of things we should encapsulate in a .NET assembly. When should we use compiled `.dlls` instead of code-behind files and user controls?

2. Create a new component that converts from imperial units to metric and back again. You'll need four methods: Celsius to Fahrenheit temperatures, Fahrenheit to Celsius, Kilometers to Miles, and Miles to Kilometers. You'll need the following data:

❑ Fahrenheit temperature = Celsius temperature `* (9/5) + 32`

❑ Celsius temperature = (Fahrenheit temperature `- 32) * (5/9)`

❑ 1 Mile = `1.6039` Kilometers (to 4 decimal places)

❑ 1 Kilometer = `0.6214` Miles (to 4 decimal places)

3. Create an ASP.NET page that uses this functionality. One example might be a page about holiday destinations. Users in other countries might want to know distances in metric instead of imperial, or temperatures in Celsius, rather than Fahrenheit.

4. Additionally, you might want to access this functionality from a completely different type of site, for example, one that has some scientific purpose that requires unit conversion, a route planner that will provide results in both miles or kilometers, or a weather site that needs to provide today's temperatures in both Celsius and Fahrenheit. A completely different situation would be a cookery site that displayed instructions for cooking a meal in an oven set to either Celsius or Fahrenheit temperatures.

Debugging and Error Handling

One of the fundamental truths of organized systems is that the more complex they become, the more likely they are to go wrong. While most of the examples we've looked at so far in this book have been quite simple, the principles behind the .NET Framework make it easier for you to build larger and more complex systems.

Once you have planned and created your program, the steps involved in ensuring that your code runs smoothly at all times can be broken down into two main categories:

❏   **Debugging:** No matter the painstaking attention to detail that we give to our code, mistakes will occur. We can minimize their ill effects by identifying the portions of our code that are most prone to errors, and by adhering to good coding practices that facilitate troubleshooting.

❏   **Error Handling:** Even if we produce flawless code, there is no guarantee that everything will operate smoothly at runtime. Things can (and at times *do*) go wrong. Problems such as network connection failures or power failures may occur in the operating environment. There may be problems with unexpected data types or data may not have been properly prepared. Third-party programs may return unexpected data. Good programming practices dictate that we anticipate as many problems as we can *before* they occur so that we may apply a graceful solution.

This chapter will provide information to help you identify problems, fix them, and prevent them from occurring in future. Specifically, we'll look at the following topics:

❏   Good coding practices

❏   Different types of errors

❏   Locating errors in the page

❏   Tracing

❏   Exceptions

❑   Handling Exceptions

❑   Handling errors

❑   Notifying and logging errors

A Few Good Habits

Whether you're an expert developer or a beginner, you can significantly reduce the probability of an error's occurrence by adopting some very straightforward habits. Finding an error in your application is not a cause for panic – it just indicates that an effective error handling strategy is needed. We will provide you with the information needed to design and implement an effective error handling strategy.

Before getting into detail about the different kinds of errors that may afflict your code, let's talk about how you may reduce the time and effort required to identify and fix an error.

❑   **Understand your code**: Make clean distinction between serverside and client-side functionality. Adopt, and consistently use, naming conventions. Write headers for methods that explicitly state their purpose. Give variables meaningful names. These habits will go a long way to producing self-documenting code. If sections or routines in your code are still unclear after these practices have been implemented, then document some more. Clear and concise code will be an invaluable asset when it is time to locate where, and understand why, an error has occurred.

❑   **Identify where it might break:** Before even loading the page and testing its functionality, identify the potential problem areas. For instance, say you have developed a page that communicates with a database and pulls a set of records. You must create a connection to the database, formulate a query, and then execute that query to retrieve the records. Connecting to the database or the execution of the query may throw an error. You need to look out for potential problems at an early stage (we will discuss different kinds of errors later in this chapter).

❑   **Amend identified error conditions:** Once you have identified areas that could break within your page, the next step is to make sure the conditions under which your error might occur are as stable as possible. Remember the old adage: an ounce of prevention is worth a pound of cure.

Mistakes in your code are not the end of the world. What matters is how quickly you can identify them and fix them. With that in mind, let's start by looking at the habits that should be cultivated.

Good Coding Practice

It may not be feasible to expect perfect, completely error-free programs, but there are some precautions we *can* take to reduce or avoid the most common mistakes. There are a lot of things that we can do such as indenting and structuring the code or adding comments to increase its comprehensibility. We will take a look at these and other good coding practices.

Indent Your Code

This is quite an obvious and straightforward step. Although it won't ensure an error-free program, this will really help to improve the readability of your code, for yourself *and* for others. Indenting your code will help you detect many kinds of errors faster. The following example lays out some code that we will be using later, in two different ways. See the difference for yourself:

```
<html>
<head>
<title>Syntax Error Example </title>
</head>
<body>
<form method="post" action="sytntaxerror.aspx" runat="server">
  <asp:TetBox id="txtQuantity" runat="server" />
</form>
</body>
</html>

<html>
  <head>
   <title>Syntax Error Example </title>
  </head>
  <body>
    <form method="post" action="sytntaxerror.aspx" runat="server">
      <asp:TetBox id="txtQuantity" runat="server" />
    </form>
  </body>
</html>
```

Structure Your Code

Use subroutines and functions in your code to implement specific tasks. This is even more important for tasks that are used several times in your applications. For instance, consider a situation when you need to format the display of a date. The database might store a date in the form "CCYYMMDD", whereas you might need to display it on the screen as MM/DD/CCYY. You could then create a subroutine, such as the one shown below:

```
Public Function FormatDate(ByVal CCYYMMDD As String) As String
  Dim intYear, intMonth, intDay
  intYear = left(CCYYMMDD,4)
  intMonth = mid(CCYYMMDD,5,2)
  intDay = right(CCYYMMDD,2)
  return (Cstr(intMonth) &"/"& Cstr(intDay) &"/"& Cstr(intYear))
End Sub
```

If you need to format the display of your date at different places in your program, you can simply call this subroutine to format the display, rather than writing the whole process repeatedly. Not only does this save time; if there's an error in the code (or you need to change it), you only need to change the code once.

Comment Your Code

Commenting your code is another simple and easy-to-implement technique. It also increases readability of the code. Your code, unless adequately commented, will look extremely confusing, even to you, after a period of time (maybe a few months, weeks, or even days). Writing comments in your code will help you remember exactly what your code is doing, which will be invaluable when you try to debug or modify it. Look again at the method from the previous section:

```
'***********************************************************************
Public Function FormatDate(CCYYMMDD as String) As string
'*Purpose: convert date from CCYYMMDD format to MM/DD/CCYY format
'*Input:  String     date in the format CCYYMMDD
'*Returns: string    string that represents a date in the format MM/DD/CCYY
'***********************************************************************
Dim intYear as integer  'year value (CCYY)
Dim intMonth as integer  'month value (MM)
Dim intDay as integer  'day value (DD)
  intYear = left(CCYYMMDD,4)
  intMonth = mid(CCYYMMDD,5,2)
  intDay = right(CCYYMMDD,2)
  return(Cstr(intMonth) &"/"& Cstr(intDay) &"/"& Cstr(intYear))
End Sub
```

The commenting in this example may seem excessive for such a little method. But the small investment in time that it takes to adequately comment your code will pay huge dividends when revisiting that code. Also, habits such as writing method headers and providing general comments facilitate the reuse of code.

Use the Page Explicit Setting

One of the options that can be set in the `Page` directive at the top of an ASPX page is:

```
<%@ Page language="VB" runat="server" explicit="True" %>
```

If you set `explicit` to `True` and try using a variable that hasn't been defined, you'll find that your code throws an error. This can actually save you falling foul of various logical errors that occur because of a typo in a variable name – otherwise, these are very hard to find. For instance, look at the following code:

```
Dim DepositAmount, AccountBalance
  AccountBalance = 5000 ' the initial balance is $5000
  DepositAmount = 2000 ' Customer deposits $2000
'adding the deposit to the balance to get the new balance
  AccountBalance = AccountBalance + DepostAmount
```

You'd expect to see the new account balance as $7000, but actually, the balance will still be $5000. This is because the `DepositAmount` variable is misspelled in the line in which it is added to the `AccountBalance` variable. This will throw an error if `explicit` is used, since the `Depost Amount` variable is not defined.

Use the Page Strict Setting

This is another level of protection that you can opt for, also set from the `Page` directive:

```
<%@ Page language="VB" runat="server" strict="True" %>
```

Using setting will prevent any implicit type conversion that results in data loss.

Convert Variables to the Correct Data Types (Validation)

Converting the values provided in your Web page to an appropriate data type before using them in your program will prevent Type Mismatch errors when you're using the `Strict` setting. For example, if the user provides 12.23 for a numeric field for which you're expecting an integer, assigning this value to the integer variable will result in an error. To prevent this error convert the value entered to an integer before assigning the value to a variable of integer data type. You could use one of the following conversion functions provided by VB.NET:

Conversion Function	Return Datatype
Cbool	Boolean
Cbyte	Byte
Cchar	Char
Cdate	Date
CDbl	Double
Cdec	Decimal
Cint	Integer
CLng	Long
Cobj	Object
CShort	Short
CSng	Single
CStr	String

The following lines show the syntax for using this conversion function:

```
Condtion = CBool(SomeVariable) ' Converts to a Boolean
Number = CInt(AnotherVariable) ' Converts to an Integer
```

You could use the `Convert` class in the `System` namespace provided by the .NET Framework. The following shows the syntax of using the `ToString()` method of the `Convert` class:

```
SomeVariable = Convert.ToString(SomeInteger)
'Convert Integer to String
```

Try to Break Your Code

This can be a more difficult task than expected. It is often difficult for the developer of an application to anticipate all the unusual things a user might attempt to do with the application, such as accidentally type in letters when numbers are required, or supply an answer that was longer than anticipated, or even deliberately try to break it. So, when it is time to test your application, try to think like a user who is only a little computer literate. You can break down your testing strategy into two main approaches:

❑ **Be nice to your program:** Supply your program with legal values, or values that your program is designed to expect and handle. For instance, if your program contains an age field, supply only numbers, not letters. Watch how your program behaves – does it respond as you expect it to with the legal values supplied to it?

❑ **Try to break your program:** This is the fun part. Supply your program with illegal values. For instance, provide string values where integers are expected. This ensures that your program handles all illegal values appropriately. Depending on the kind of data you are expecting in your program, you could to do anything from a simple numeric or alphabetic check to a validity check (such as inserting invalid dates into a date field). If your program spans several pages, then surf to some of the pages out of the expected sequence.

Both these techniques can be used to help standardize and improve the readability of your code. Many basic errors can be avoided in this way. However, even if you follow all these suggestions, your code still can't be guaranteed to be bug-free. Let's look at some of the specific errors that may plague your code.

Where Do Errors Come from?

The errors that occur in an ASP.NET page can be grouped into four categories:

❑ **Parser errors:** These occur because of incorrect syntax or bad grammar within the ASP.NET page.

❑ **Compilation errors:** These are also syntax errors, but they occur when using statements that are not recognized by the language compiler, rather than ASP.NET itself. For example, using `endif` to close an `if` block in VB.NET, or not providing `Next` to close a `For` loop, will result in a compilation error. The difference between the parser error and compilation error is that the parser error occurs when there is a syntax error in the ASP.NET page, and the ASP.NET parser catches it, whereas the compilation error occurs when there is a syntax error in the VB.NET code block and the VB.NET compiler complains about it.

❑ **Configuration Errors:** These occur because of the incorrect syntax or structure of a *configuration file*. An ASP.NET configuration file is a text file in XML format, and contains a hierarchical structure that stores application-wide configuration settings. There can be one configuration file for every application on your Web server. These configuration files are all named `web.config`, irrespective of the application's name. There is also a single configuration file called `machine.config` that contains information that applies to every application on a single machine. We will discuss configuration files in detail in *Chapter 15*, although we do touch upon them again later in this chapter.

❑ **Runtime or logical errors:** As the name implies, these errors are not detected during compilation or parsing, but are caught during execution. For example, when the user enters letters into a field that expects numbers, and your program assigns the user entry to an integer variable, you will get a runtime error when the code tries to execute. These are also known as logical errors.

Now let's look at some specific examples that fall into the above categories.

Syntax Errors

As the name suggests, these errors occur when there are problems in the syntax of the code. Parser and compilation errors fall under this category. These are usually the first errors encountered when developing ASP.NET pages. There are several reasons why these errors occur:

❑ **A typo or bad grammar in the code syntax:** For example, instead of typing `<asp:textbox>` for creating a textbox control in your page, you type `<asp:textbx>`. The browser shows an error.

❑ **Incorrect code syntax:** For instance, when creating a textbox control, you might forget to close the tag (as `<asp:TextBox id="txtName" runat="server">` when it should actually be `<asp:TextBox id="txtName" runat="server" />`)

❑ **Combining or splitting keywords between languages:** I make this error quite a lot. If you switch coding between JScript.NET and VB.NET, you encounter it even more often. A good example is the `ElseIf` keyword. So what is the correct syntax? It depends on the language you are using. In VB.NET, the correct syntax is `ElseIf`, whereas in JScript.NET the correct syntax is `Else If`.

❑ **Not closing a construct properly:** This error occurs if we forget to close a construct, such as a `for...next`, or a nested `if...then...else...end if` statement. Take a look at this example:

```
If condition1 Then
 'do this
ElseIf condition2 Then
  'do this
If condition2a Then
  'do this
Else
  'do this
End if
```

Did you catch the error in the above code? An `end if` is missing. Imagine how difficult it would be to spot this if we had the above code block set amongst hundreds of other lines of code. It's another good argument for formatting your code correctly too. If it had been formatted, it would've been easier to spot the error.

Try It Out Syntax Error

Let's have an example of creating a syntax error (a parser error) and see how ASP.NET responds to the error:

1. Open Web Matrix and type the following lines of code into the All Window. Make a spelling mistake when creating the textbox control, as highlighted in the following code:

```
<html>
  <head>
    <title>Syntax Error Example </title>
  </head>
  <body>
    <form method="post" action="syntaxerror.aspx" runat="server">
      <asp:TetBox id="txtQuantity" runat="server" />
    </form>
  </body>
</html>
```

2. Save this file as `syntaxerror.aspx` and load the file using a browser. You expect to see a textbox in the browser, as shown in figure 14-1:

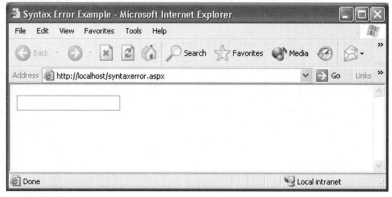

Figure 14-1

However, what you actually see is Figure 14-2:

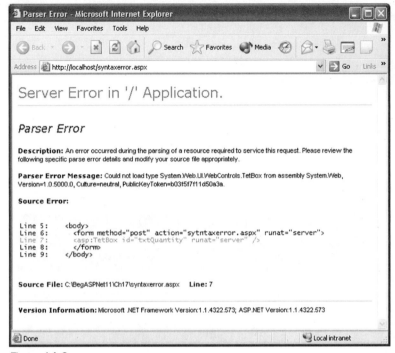

Figure 14-2

How It Works

As the error message clearly states, the ASP.NET parser points to Line 7, and asks us to check the details. You can see that a spelling mistake exists, `Tetbox` (which should be `TextBox`). If you correct the spelling mistake and rerun the code, you'll get the expected result.

Errors of this kind are very common, but are usually quick and easy to fix, since the error message provides a detailed breakdown of the error and the line on which it occurs.

Now we will look at a syntax error that will generate a compilation error.

Try It Out **Generate a Compiler Error**

1. Create a new file called `compilationerror.aspx`, and type the following code into the Web Matrix `All` window:

```
<%@ Page language="VB" Debug="true" %>
<script language="vb" runat="server">
Sub CompleteOrder(sender As Object, e As EventArgs)
  if txtQuantity.Text = "" then
    lblOrderConfirm.Text = "Please provide an Order Quantity."
  else if CInt(txtQuantity.Text) <= 0 then
    lblOrderConfirm.Text = "Please provide a Quantity greater than 0."
```

```
    else if CInt(txtQuantity.Text) > 0 then
        lblOrderConfirm.Text = "Order Successfully placed."
    endif
End Sub
</script>
<html>
  <head>
    <title>Compiliation Error Example</title>
  </head>
  <body>
    <form method="post" action="manualtrapping.aspx" runat="server">
        <asp:Label text="Order Quantity" runat="server" />
        <asp:TextBox id="txtQuantity" runat="server" />
      <br />
        <asp:Button id="btnComplete_Order" Text="Complete Order"
                                   onclick="CompleteOrder"
                                         runat="server"/>
      <br />
        <asp:Label id="lblOrderConfirm" runat="server"/>
    </form>
  </body>
</html>
```

2. Save and view the `compilationerror.aspx` file with a browser. The page displayed is as shown in Figure 14-3:

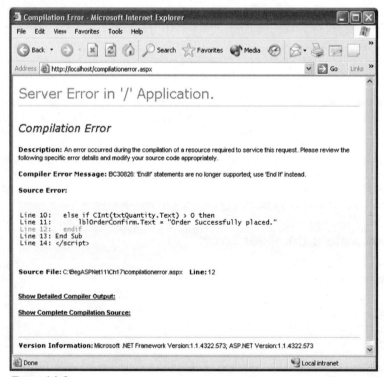

Figure 14-3

How It Works

We typed `endif` at the end of our control block instead of `end if`. As expected, when we tried to run the new `compilationerror.aspx` file in the browser, we got an error message. It tells us we have a compiler error in Line 12 and even tells us how to fix it!

These are just a few common examples of syntax errors. There is no way we could provide a list of all possible syntax errors that you might encounter, but the good news is that syntax errors are usually easy to find and fix.

Logical (Runtime) Errors

The second type of error is the *Logical Error*, unfortunately relatively difficult to find and fix. Logical errors become apparent during runtime. As the name implies, these errors occur due to mistakes in programming logic. Some of the more common reasons for these errors are:

❑ **Division by zero**: This is the dreaded error that has been around since the days of valve-based computers. This error occurs when your program ends up dividing a number by zero. But why in the world do we divide a number by zero? In most cases, this occurs because the program divides a number by an integer that should contain a non-zero number, but for some reason, contains a zero. For instance, this could happen if you do not use the `Explicit` setting in your program and make a spelling mistake in the variable name that is in the denominator.

❑ **Type mismatch**: Type mismatch errors occur when you try to work with incompatible data types and inadvertently try to add a string to a number, or store a string in a date data type. It is possible to avoid this error by explicitly converting the data type of a value before operating on it. We will talk about variable data type conversion later in this chapter.

❑ **Incorrect output**: This type of error occurs when you use a function or a subroutine that returns a different output from what you are expecting in your program.

❑ **Use of a non-existent object**: This type of error occurs when you try to use an object that was never created, or when an attempt to create the object failed.

❑ **Mistaken assumptions**: This is another common error, and should be corrected during the testing phase (if one exists). This type of error occurs when the programmer uses an incorrect assumption in the program. This can happen, for instance, in a program that adds withdrawal amounts to a current balance, instead of subtracting them.

❑ **Processing invalid data**: This type of error occurs when the program accepts invalid data. An example of this would be a library checkout program that accepts a book's return date as February 29, 2003, in which case, you may not have to return the book for a while!

While this is far from being an exhaustive list of possible logical errors, it should give you a feel for what to look out for when testing your code.

Try It Out Generate a Runtime Error

1. Open `compilationerror.aspx` in Web Matrix, go to the All Window, and make the following change by adding a space:

```
Sub CompleteOrder(sender As Object, e As EventArgs)
  If txtQuantity.Text = "" Then
    lblOrderConfirm.Text = "Please provide an Order Quantity."
  Else If Not IsNumeric(txtQuantity.Text) Then
    lblOrderConfirm.Text = "Please provide only numbers in Quantity field."
  Else If CInt(txtQuantity.Text) <= 0 Then
    lblOrderConfirm.Text = "Please provide a Quantity greater than 0."
  Else If CInt(txtQuantity.Text) > 0 Then
    lblOrderConfirm.Text = "Order Successfully placed."
  End If
End Sub
```

2. Save the file as `runtimeError.aspx`.

3. View the `runtimeError.aspx` file using the browser. Provide a non-numeric value, such as ABC, to the order quantity textbox, and click the **Complete Order** button. Figure 14-4 shows the result:

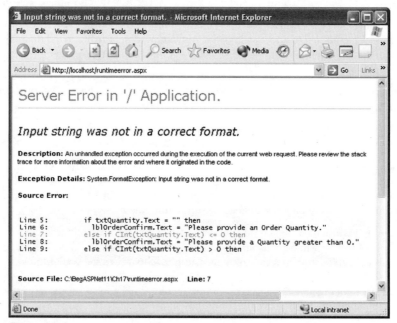

Figure 14-4

How It Works

Our control block validates input for null values, and for numeric values that are equal to or less than zero. It does not check input for other non-numeric input values. The code generated a runtime error when the `CInt` function tried to convert a non-numeric entry to an integer field. The process of checking for this type of errors is known as validation. To validate the data entry values, your control block should have an extra couple of lines as follows:

```
else if not IsNumeric(txtQuantity.Text) then
    lblOrderConfirm.Text = "Please provide only numbers in Quantity field."
```

Let's take a closer look at validating user input.

Trapping Invalid Data

Testing your code by supplying both legal and illegal values is crucial for the proper functioning of your program. Your program should return expected results when providing legal values, and handle errors when supplied with illegal values. In this section, we'll talk about ways to handle the illegal values supplied to your program. We have two objectives here:

❑ Prevent the occurrence of errors that may leave you with many disgruntled users.

❑ Prevent your program from accepting and using illegal values.

There are two main techniques that are used to fulfill these objectives: *manual trapping* and *validation*.

Manual Trapping

When building the application, you could create error traps to catch illegal values before they get into the page processing, where they might halt the execution of the page or provide invalid results. How do you block illegal values from sneaking into page processing? Let's develop a page that accepts order quantity from the user.

Try It Out Catching Illegal Values

1. Open `compilationError.aspx` in Web Matrix and make the following changes in the All Window:

```
Sub CompleteOrder(sender As Object, e As EventArgs)
  If txtQuantity.Text = "" Then
    lblOrderConfirm.Text = "Please provide an Order Quantity."
  Else If Not IsNumeric(txtQuantity.Text) Then
    lblOrderConfirm.Text = "Please provide only numbers in Quantity field."
  Else If CInt(txtQuantity.Text) <= 0 Then
  lblOrderConfirm.Text = "Please provide a Quantity greater than 0."
    Else If CInt(txtQuantity.Text) > 0 Then
      lblOrderConfirm.Text = "Order Successfully placed."
    Else
      lblOrderConfirm.Text = "Please provide a valid Order Quantity."
    End If
End Sub
  <head>
    <title>Compiliation Error Example</title>
  </head>
```

2. Save the file as `manualTrapping.aspx`.

3. Load this file using your browser. Figure 14-5 shows the result of providing an order quantity of 10:

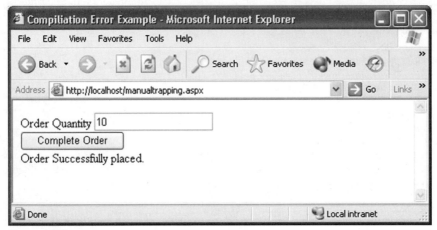

Figure 14-5

4. Supply different values to the order quantity textbox and check whether the page behaves as expected.

How It Works

Notice that we have added an extra directive to the page calls:

```
<%@ Page language="VB" Debug="true" %>
```

This will enable us to view detailed error messages throughout the course of the chapter. How this works will become clearer as we progress.

We are using two label controls: a textbox control and a button control. The first label control is the label for the order quantity textbox:

```
<asp:Label text="Order Quantity" runat="server" />
```

The second label control called `lblOrderConfirm` is used to display a message after processing the order, indicating whether the order was successfully placed or not:

```
<asp:Label id="lblOrderConfirm" runat="server"/>
```

The textbox accepts an entry from the user – the order quantity:

```
<asp:TextBox id="txtQuantity" runat="server" />
```

The button calls the `CompleteOrder` procedure when clicked:

```
<asp:Button id="btnComplete_Order" Text="Complete Order"
        onclick="CompleteOrder"
        runat="server"/>
```

Within the `CompleteOrder` sub, we create a series of checks to avoid illegal values. First, we check for no entry to the textbox:

```
if txtQuantity.Text = "" then
    lblOrderConfirm.Text = "Please provide an Order Quantity."
```

This is followed by numeric check:

```
else if not IsNumeric(txtQuantity.Text) then
    lblOrderConfirm.Text = "Please provide only numbers in Quantity field."
```

Next, we check for a negative number or zero:

```
else if CInt(txtQuantity.Text) <= 0 then
    lblOrderConfirm.Text = "Please provide a Quantity greater than 0."
```

Finally, we check if the number is greater than zero. If it is not (as verified by the checks so far) we display a message to enter a valid value:

```
else if CInt(txtQuantity.Text) > 0 then
    lblOrderConfirm.Text = "Order Successfully placed."
else
    lblOrderConfirm.Text = "Please provide a valid Order Quantity."
end if
```

Using Validation Controls

The second technique is to use one or more of the different validation controls provided by ASP.NET (refer to *Chapter 10* for a detailed discussion on using validation controls.)

Validation controls are used to validate user input. For instance, you could use the `RequiredFieldValidator` control to ensure that users enter a value to a textbox. By doing this, you could avoid runtime errors that occur because of your program using a null (unknown value), when it is expecting *an entry* from the user.

By using one of the many validation controls provided by ASP.NET and shown in the following section, you could present the users with a message informing them about the incorrect value supplied, and the value your program is expecting. This prevents the program from processing an illegal value and developing an error.

Let's look at an example to demonstrate how to use these controls. In the following Try It Out, we'll use the `RequiredFieldValidator` to ensure that the user provides a value for the `Order Quantity` field.

Try It Out Using RequiredFieldValidator

1. Open `manualtrapping.aspx` (from the previous exercise) in Web Matrix, and make the following changes in the `All` Window:

```
<form method="post" action="usingvalidationcontrol.aspx" runat="server">
<asp:Label text="Order Quantity" runat="server" />
<asp:TextBox id="txtQuantity" runat="server" />
<asp:RequiredFieldValidator ControlToValidate="txtQuantity" runat="server"
        ErrorMessage="Please enter a value in the Order Quantity Field">
</asp:RequiredFieldValidator>
<br />
<asp:Button id="btnComplete_Order" Text="Complete Order"
                            onclick="CompleteOrder" runat="server"/><br>
<asp:Label id="lblOrderConfirm" runat="server"/>
</form>
```

2. Save this file as `usingvalidationcontrol.aspx`.

3. Use your browser to open `usingvalidationcontrol.aspx`. When you try to complete the order without entering anything, you're presented with the request that you see in Figure 14-6:

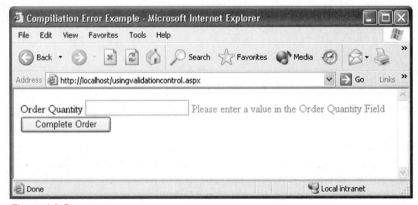

Figure 14-6

How It Works

In this example, we have used a `RequiredFieldValidator` control. The `ControlToValidate` property is used to specify the control we are validating:

```
<asp:RequiredFieldValidator ControlToValidate="txtQuantity" runat="server"
```

In this case, we are validating the order quantity textbox. The `ErrorMessage` property is used to provide an error message when the user does not enter a value to the order quantity field:

```
ErrorMessage="Please enter a value in the Order Quantity Field">
```

The validation control saves us the extra *second-guessing* of typical mistakes a user might make.

System Errors

These errors are generated by ASP.NET itself. They may be due to malfunctioning code, a bug in ASP.NET, or even one in the Common Language Runtime. Although you could find this type of error, rectifying it is usually not possible – particularly if it is an ASP.NET or CLR error.

Other errors that can be placed in this category are those that arise due to the failure of a Web server or component, a hardware failure, or a lack of server memory.

When an error occurs in an ASP.NET page, the details about the error are sent to the client. However, ASP.NET by default shows detailed error information only to a *local client*.

A local client is a browser running on the same machine as the Web server, and therefore only viewable by the site administrator. For instance, if you create the ASP.NET examples from this book on a machine running a Web server, and access them using a browser on the same machine, as you would do with Web Matrix, then the browser is a local client. While *you* might see the error, if this was deployed on a network using IIS then no-one else viewing the page on the network would – they would just receive a generic "something's wrong" kind of message.

So, the fact that ASP.NET sends detailed information about errors to local clients is actually very helpful to the developer during the development phase.

Finding Errors

Even though we have adopted the good coding practices listed earlier in our program and have used different techniques to trap the invalid data, why are we still talking about finding errors? Even after taking the precautions, our program might still end up with an error page. It could be because we did not cover all possible error scenarios in our testing (point the fingers at the testers), or another program did not behave as expected (refer it to the other team) or worse, the server administrators did not set up the server right (blame it on the network administrators.)

However well you plan ahead, it is always difficult, if not impossible, to catch every bug in advance. So, what do we do if our well-constructed code still doesn't work? We will discuss this topic next.

Let's go back to the local client scenario. ASP.NET displays a *call-stack* when a runtime error occurs. A call-stack contains a series of procedure calls that lead up to an error. Before you do this, delete (or rename) any `web.config` files residing with your samples; otherwise all errors generated will be handled by this file.

Let's create a page that leads up to a runtime error.

Try It Out **Viewing the Call-stack**

1. Open Web Matrix and create a file called `callstack.aspx`. Then type the following code into the `All` Window:

```
<%@ Page Language="VB" Debug="true" %>
<script language="VB" runat="server">
  Sub CreateRunTimeError
```

```
      dim intCounter as integer
      intCounter = "Test"
      Response.Write ("The value of counter is :" & intCounter)
      End sub
</script>
<%
  CreateRunTimeError()
%>
```

2.   Save the file and open it in your browser. You should see something like Figure 14-7 (as long you haven't got a `web.config` file in the same folder as the `.aspx` file):

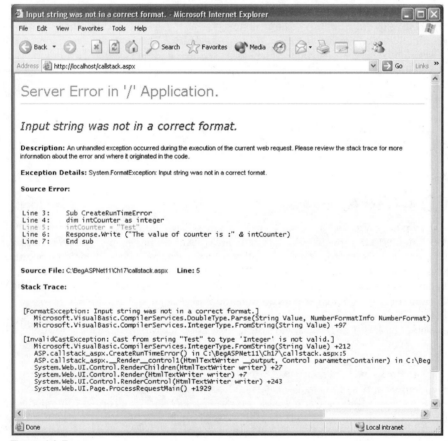

Figure 14-7

How It Works

In the block of code, we created a variable called `intCounter`, an integer, and then assigned a string to this variable:

```
dim intCounter as integer
intCounter = "Test"
```

On running this code, an error was generated when the program tried to execute an integer data type containing a string. We were presented with the previous error page. The error page contains different sections, such as Exception Details (we'll discuss exceptions shortly), Source Error, Stack Trace, and so on. The Stack Trace contains the call-stack, which says that the value we are trying to assign to an integer variable is not valid. If you look through the call-stack, you can see the series of procedures that led to the exception.

Try the same example with just one modification. Change the value assigned to `intCounter` from `Test` to `123`. Executing this page will no longer generate an error because `123` can be cast to an integer data type.

The information provided under the Source Error section is useful in locating the line in which the error occurred. Displaying this information is controlled by the *Debug mode*.

Debug Mode

If `Debug` mode is enabled, then the Source Error section of the error message is displayed as part of the error message that pinpoints the location in the code that generated the error. If `Debug` mode is disabled, then the Source Error section is not displayed.

Now the question is: where and how can we set the value for `Debug` mode?

It can be set in two different places. The first place should be familiar as we have used it twice already within this chapter. You can set it at every page within the `Page` directive at the top of the page, as shown below:

```
<%@ Page Debug="true" %>
```

To disable it you can set it to `false`:

```
<%@ Page Debug="false" %>
```

If the `Debug` mode is set like this, at the page level, the setting is applied *only* to that specific page.

Let's return to our previous example, and disable the `Debug` mode at the page level:

Try It Out   Disable the Debug Mode

1. Open the `callstack.aspx` file in Web Matrix, and in the `All` window, insert the following line at the top of the page – don't replace the existing declaration:

```
<%@ Page Language="VB" Debug="false" %>
```

2. Save the file as `debugmode.aspx`, and access the page using the browser. You will see an error page that looks like the one shown in Figure 14-8:

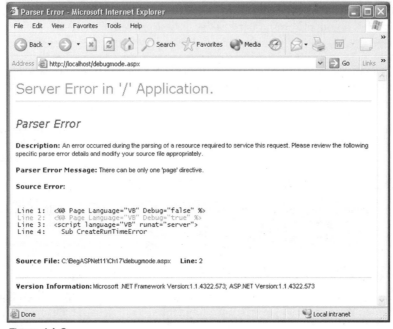

Figure 14-8

How It Works

We disabled the `Debug` mode in our `debugmode.aspx` by adding the following line at the top of the page:

```
<%@ Page Debug="false" %>
```

Then on running our new file in the browser, we saw a new error message. In this error message, under the **Source Error** section, there are instructions to enable the `Debug` mode for displaying the source code that generated the exception, but the actual source code is not there.

As mentioned a moment ago, there are two ways to set the `Debug` mode. The second way is to set it at the *application level*, using the `<compilation>` configuration section in the configuration file (see *Chapter 15*).

Setting the `Debug` mode at the application evel will display the **Source Error** section in the error message for all the files under the application. This has a performance overhead though, so before moving your application to a production environment, make sure you disable the `Debug` mode.

Tracing

When developing an application, we execute the page at different levels of development, and for effective debugging we always need to see the values assigned to variables and the state of different conditional constructs at different stages of execution. In *classic* ASP, developers used the ubiquitous `Response.Write` statement to display this information. The downside of doing this is that when completing the application development, the developer has to go to every page and either comment or remove the `Response.Write` statements they created for testing purposes. ASP.NET provides a new feature to bypass all of this, by using the `Trace` capability.

The tracing feature provides a range of information about the page, including request time, performance data, server variables, and most importantly, any message added by the developers. It is disabled by default. Like the `debug` mode, tracing can be either enabled or disabled at either the page (or application) level. We'll now discuss these levels and tracing in more detail.

Page-Level Tracing

Tracing can be enabled at the page level to display trace information using the `Page` directive's `Trace` attribute, as shown below:

```
<%@ Page Trace = "true" %>
```

Tracing can be disabled using:

```
<%@ Page Trace = "false" %>
```

When tracing is enabled, the trace information is displayed underneath the page's contents. Let's create a simple ASP.NET page with a textbox and a label control, and enable tracing at the page level.

Try It Out Enabling Trace at the Page Level

1. Open Web Matrix, create a page called `pageLevelTracing.aspx`, and type in the following code to the All Window:

```
<%@ Page Trace="true"%>
<html>
  <head>
    <title>Page Level Tracing</title>
  </head>
  <body>
    <form method="post" action="pageleveltracing.aspx" runat="server">
      <asp:label text="Name" runat="server" />
      <asp:textbox name="txtName" runat="server" />
    </form>
  </body>
</html>
```

2.   Save this file and view it using the browser. Figure 14-9 shows how this page should look:

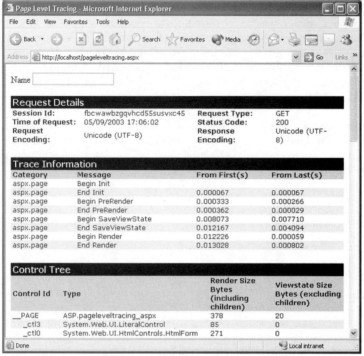

Figure 14-9

How It Works

First, we enabled the page trace with the line:

```
<%@ Page Trace="true"%>
```

We then created a textbox with some text beside it. What we got was the textbox plus a whole load of tracing. Let's look at each section of the trace output to get a fuller understanding of 'what they display:

❑   **Request Details**: This section contains information pertaining to the page request, such as the Session ID for the current session, the request type (whether it is GET or POST), the time at which the request was made, the encoding type of the request among others, as shown in Figure 14-10:

Request Details			
Session Id:	fbcwawbzgqvhcd55susvxc45	Request Type:	GET
Time of Request:	05/09/2003 17:06:02	Status Code:	200
Request Encoding:	Unicode (UTF-8)	Response Encoding:	Unicode (UTF-8)

Figure 14-10

❑ **Trace Information**: This is the section in which the actual trace information is displayed. It is also the section where the messages written by developers are displayed. As shown in Figure 14-11, this section displays the category, the message, the time since the first message was displayed, and the most recent message displayed:

Trace Information

Category	Message	From First(s)	From Last(s)
aspx.page	Begin Init		
aspx.page	End Init	0.000067	0.000067
aspx.page	Begin PreRender	0.000333	0.000266
aspx.page	End PreRender	0.000362	0.000029
aspx.page	Begin SaveViewState	0.008073	0.007710
aspx.page	End SaveViewState	0.012167	0.004094
aspx.page	Begin Render	0.012226	0.000059
aspx.page	End Render	0.013028	0.000802

Figure 14-11

❑ **Control Tree**: This section displays details about the different controls used in the page. The details include the ID provided for the control, the type of control used, and its position among other controls, as shown in Figure 14-12:

Control Tree

Control Id	Type	Render Size Bytes (including children)	Viewstate Size Bytes (excluding children)
__PAGE	ASP.pageleveltracing_aspx	378	20
_ctl3	System.Web.UI.LiteralControl	85	0
_ctl0	System.Web.UI.HtmlControls.HtmlForm	271	0
_ctl4	System.Web.UI.LiteralControl	7	0
_ctl1	System.Web.UI.WebControls.Label	17	0
_ctl5	System.Web.UI.LiteralControl	7	0
_ctl2	System.Web.UI.WebControls.TextBox	49	0
_ctl6	System.Web.UI.LiteralControl	6	0
_ctl7	System.Web.UI.LiteralControl	22	0

Figure 14-12

❑ **Cookies Collection:** This section displays all cookies used in the page. Figure 14-13 shows only the `SessionID` because it is the only member of the cookies collection used in our page:

Cookies Collection

Name	Value	Size
ASP.NET_SessionId	fbcwawbzgqvhcd55susvxc45	42

Figure 14-13

❑ **Headers Collection**: As shown in Figure 14-14, this section displays the various HTTP headers sent by the client to the server, along with the request:

Headers Collection	
Name	**Value**
Connection	Keep-Alive
Accept	*/*
Accept-Encoding	gzip, deflate
Accept-Language	en-gb
Host	localhost
User-Agent	Mozilla/4.0 (compatible; MSIE 6.0; Windows NT 5.1; .NET CLR 1.1.4322)

Figure 14-14

❑ **Server Variables**: This section displays all the members of the Server Variables collection as shown in Figure 14-15:

Server Variables	
Name	**Value**
ALL_HTTP	HTTP_CONNECTION:Keep-Alive HTTP_ACCEPT:*/* HTTP_ACCEPT_ENCODING:gzip, deflate HTTP_ACCEPT_LANGUAGE:en-gb HTTP_HOST:localhost HTTP_USER_AGENT:Mozilla/4.0 (compatible; MSIE 6.0; Windows NT 5.1; .NET CLR 1.1.4322)
ALL_RAW	Connection: Keep-Alive Accept: */* Accept-Encoding: gzip, deflate Accept-Language: en-gb Host: localhost User-Agent: Mozilla/4.0 (compatible; MSIE 6.0; Windows NT 5.1; .NET CLR 1.1.4322)
APPL_MD_PATH	
APPL_PHYSICAL_PATH	C:\BegASPNet11\Ch17\
AUTH_TYPE	
AUTH_USER	
AUTH_PASSWORD	
LOGON_USER	
REMOTE_USER	
CERT_COOKIE	
CERT_FLAGS	
CERT_ISSUER	
CERT_KEYSIZE	
CERT_SECRETKEYSIZE	
CERT_SERIALNUMBER	
CERT_SERVER_ISSUER	
CERT_SERVER_SUBJECT	
CERT_SUBJECT	
CONTENT_LENGTH	0

Figure 14-15

Now that we've introduced the information displayed in the trace page, let's talk about techniques you can use to write a message to the Trace Information section, and get updates on what' goes on behind the scenes as your code is executed.

Writing to the Trace Log

Each ASP.NET page provides a `Trace` object that can be used to write messages to the trace log. You can use two methods to write messages to the trace log (note, however, that the messages are only displayed when tracing is enabled):

❑ `Trace.Write()`

❑ `Trace.Warn()`

Both methods are used to write messages to the trace log, but when using the `Trace.Warn()` method, the messages are displayed in red. You may want to use `Trace.Warn()` for writing unexpected results or incorrect values for variables in your program, to highlight them. Let's create an example that shows how to use these two methods.

Try It Out   Writing to the Trace Log

1. Open Web Matrix, create a file called `writetotrace.aspx`, and type the following code into All Window:

```
<%@ Page Trace="true"%>
<script language="VB" runat="server">
  Sub WriteToTrace()
     ' This is where messages are written to Trace Log
     ' Syntax as follows:
     ' Trace.Write ("Category", "Message to be displayed")
     ' Trace.Warn ("Category", "Message to be displayed")

     Dim intCounter as integer
     intCounter=1
     Trace.Write ("FirstCategory", "Variable is initialized")
     do while intCounter > 10
       intCounter = intCounter + 1
     loop
     if intCounter < 10 then
        Trace.Warn("ErrorCategory", "Value of intCounter is not incrementing")
     end if
  End Sub
</script>
<%
 WriteToTrace()
%>
```

2. Save this file and then open it in your browser. The message we wrote using the `Trace.Warn()` method is shown in figure 14-16 (displayed in red - it's the **Error Category** line; red doesn't show up in black and white):

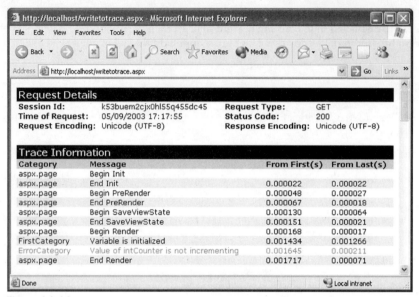

Figure 14-16

How It Works

The first thing we do is to use `Dim` to declare `intCounter` (which we're using as a label), and type it as an integer data type. We then assign a value of 1 to `intCounter`:

```
Dim intCounter as integer
intCounter=1
```

We write a message saying our variable has been initialized to the `Trace` object:

```
Trace.Write ("FirstCategory", "Variable is initialized")
```

The next three lines of code is a loop that says that `intCounter` is greater than 10, and that it should have 1 added to it. This function is then looped back to the beginning, so 1 is continually added:

```
do while intCounter > 10
 intCounter = intCounter + 1
loop
```

This is obviously going to generate an error, because we have specified that `intCounter=1`, so it cannot be greater than 10. We then introduce a `Trace.Warn()` statement, by saying that if `intCounter` is less than 10 (which it is), we should display a warning message:

```
"Value of intCounter is not incrementing"
```

This is true – for the incrementation loop to work, `intCounter` must be greater than `10`:

```
if intCounter < 10 then
Trace.Warn("ErrorCategory", "Value of intCounter is not incrementing")
```

It gives us an easy way of spotting logical errors where they might otherwise be difficult to find.

Application-Level Tracing

As stated earlier, tracing can also be enabled or disabled at the application level, in which case the tracing information is processed for all the pages under the application.

A page-level tracing setting always overrides the application level tracing setting. For instance, if tracing is enabled at the application evel but disabled for a page, then the tracing information will not be displayed for that page.

Application level tracing is set using the `<trace>` section in the configuration file discussed earlier (`web.config`). The following code is an example of the `<trace>` section:

```
<configuration>
  <system.web>
    <trace enabled="false" requestLimit="10" pageOutput="false"
    traceMode="SortByTime" localOnly="true" />
  </system.web>
</configuration>
```

The use of tracing in `web.config` is discussed in more detail in *Chapter 15*.

Trace.axd: The Trace Information Log

When application level tracing is enabled (there has to be a `web.config` file present for this – you can copy the previous code and save it as `web.config` just to test it), the trace information is logged to the `Trace.axd` file. This file can be accessed using the URL for your application, followed by `trace.axd` – for example, http://yourwebservername/applicationname/trace.axd

The following Figure 14-17 shows how the `trace.axd` file looks in the browser, after another browser has made a request to `manualtrapping.aspx` and received a response from the server:

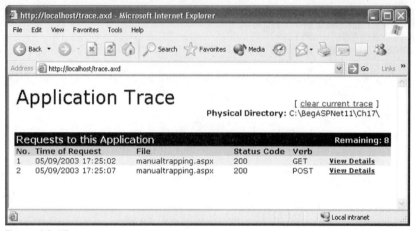

Figure 14-17

`trace.axd` provides a summary of each page requested, and for each, a View Details hyperlink takes to the trace information page for that particular screen.

Handling Errors

We've seen what kind of errors can occur, how to avoid them, and how to find them if things do go wrong, but what if the errors just won't go away? Annoyingly, this happens all the time! Don't worry, though, because there is a way of dealing with this – we can use an error handling technique to catch them, and even though we can't write a wonder program to fix on the fly all bugs, we can let users know that there is a bug and not to worry if things don't look right. In this section, we will talk about different error handling techniques that can be used to catch errors.

Unstructured Error Handling

The first technique that we are going to talk about is *unstructured error handling*. Unstructured error handling uses the `On Error` statement and the `Err` object. The `On Error` statement is used to spot errors when the code is run, and is able to respond to them as dictated – it handles them. There are two dialects of `On Error` that you can use – one allows you to continue execution on the line after the one that has generated an error, and the second directs execution to a custom-made error handler. Let's look at the former.

Using the On Error Resume Next Statement

A very common error handling approach in ASP has been to use the `On Error Resume Next` statement. When using this statement in your page, the page continues its execution from the line following the line in which the error occurred. By just using `On Error Resume Next`, you could avoid displaying an error message to the users of your application.

The following Try It Out is based on our last example with the loop, and shows an ASP.NET page using the `On Error Resume Next` statement.

Try It Out Using On Error Resume Next

1. Open Web Matrix, create a new file called `unstructurederror.aspx`, and then replace the existing code in the All Window with the following:

```
Sub UnstructuredError ()
  Dim intCounter as integer
  intCounter =1
  For intCounter=1 To 10
    intCounter = intCounter+1
  Next
  Response.Write ("The value of the counter is:" & intCounter & "<br>")
  intCounter = "Storing a string to an integer"
End Sub
Sub Page_Load()
  On Error Resume Next
  UnstructuredError ()
  Response.Write ("The Page Execution is completed")
  End Sub
```

2. Save the file and view it using a browser. Figure 14-18 shows the result:

Figure 14-18

It works! All we see is the value of the counter as `11` and the Page Execution is completed message.

How It Works

Again, we're creating the `intCounter` integer, and initializing it to a value of `1`:

```
Dim intCounter as integer
intCounter =1
```

This time we use a `for loop` construct to increment the value of `intCounter` 10 times:

```
for intCounter=1 to 10
intCounter = intCounter+1
```

The reason we didn't use the `do...while` loop from the Trace Log Try It Out is that at the end of our loop construct, we want to display the value of `intCounter`. Therefore, we need this value to be at a fixed point – the `do...while` loop construct will increment `intCounter` indefinitely, as each time the function is performed, it is looped and performed again, so `intCounter` would never reach that fixed point. Once we have displayed the value of `intCounter`, we come to an important line. In this line, we are storing a string to a variable of integer data type. "Houston, we have a problem...":

```
intCounter = "Storing a string to an integer"
```

Then, we call the procedure and return a message that the page execution is completed, to the browser:

```
On error resume next
UnstructuredError ()
Response.Write ("The Page Execution is completed")
```

Note that the `On Error Resume Next` statement is placed before the call to the sub. This is because any errors occurring within the sub will be stacked up to the calling sub. As the first line in the calling procedure is the `On Error Resume Next` statement, the rest of the page (from the `Next` keyword) is instructed to execute. So when our error occurs within the `UnstructuredError` subroutine call, everything underneath our `next` marker is still executed.

This may not be prudent in all cases. For instance, consider an online shopping application. Say this application is placing an order for ten items to be delivered next week. An error occurs during the order processing. However, we have used the `On Error Resume Next` statement to continue the execution. So the page execution is continued, and the customer is informed that the order is completed. Unfortunately, the items ordered by the customer will never reach them, since the order process was *not* completed in the first place.

What do we need to do in this case? Instead of displaying an incorrect message that the order is completed, we should inform the customer that there was an error completing the order (and perhaps provide a toll-free number to call and place the order).

Using the On Error Goto Handler Statement

It is also possible to link the `On Error` statement with the `Goto` keyword. This keyword will indicate either a line number or a label which points to a piece of code we want to run when our `On Error` statement has been triggered by an error. The following code shows an example of using the `On Error Goto` statement inside the `Page_Load()` subroutine (although it can be used inside any subroutine):

```
Sub Page_Load()
   On Error Goto OurHandler
   'do something
Exit Sub
OurHandler:
   'Handle the error. Display a message to the user
End Sub
```

The error handler is bolted on to the subroutine after an `Exit Sub` statement. The handler name is followed by a colon, followed by the code that is run in the event of an error. The name specified in the `On Error Goto` and the name of the handler itself must be the same for the code to work as intended.

Let's go back and modify our previous example to catch the error and handle the error ourselves by displaying a message saying that an error has occurred instead of displaying that the page execution is completed.

Try It Out **Using On Error**

1. Open the `unstructurederror.aspx` in Web Matrix, go to the All Window, and modify it as follows:

```
<script language="VB" runat="server" >
  Sub UnstructuredError ()
    Dim intCounter As Integer
    intCounter =1
    For intCounter=1 To 10
      intCounter = intCounter+1
      Response.Write ("The value of the counter is:" & intCounter & "<br>")
    Next
    intCounter = "Storing a string to an integer"
  End Sub
  Sub Page_Load()
    On Error Goto OurHandler
    UnstructuredError ()
    Response.Write ("The Page Execution is completed")
    Exit Sub
    OurHandler:
    Response.Write ("An error has occurred while executing this code")
  End Sub
</script>
```

2. Save the file as `unstructurederror2.aspx`, and run it in your browser to get results as shown in figure 14-19.. You will see the following :

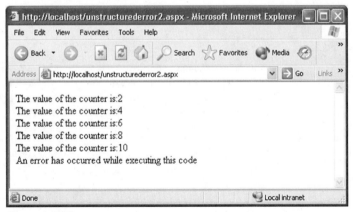

Figure 14-19

Note that we see 2, 4, 6 rather than 1, 2, 3 because every time the value of `intCounter` is incremented by 1 in the `for` loop, it also has 1 added to it. This time, the error in our code triggered our `Handler` message, and did not continue executing the rest of the program.

How It Works

The code has remained almost exactly the same as it was in `unstructurederror.aspx`. All we have done is taken out the `On Error Resume Next` statement and replaced it with a simple `On Error` one. We've also moved the `Response.Write` from outside of the loop to inside so we can confirm that the loop is indeed being executed.

Notice that the `On Error` statement is placed at the top of a code block – this tells the program that the `On Error` command applies to the whole page of code. This time, when the error occurs, the `On Error` command that points to our `Handler` message is triggered. This message is then displayed on the screen, and our imaginary user knows what has happened. The execution of this subroutine is terminated once the error is encountered, and as a result the Page Execution is completed message is never displayed.

There is another way we can inform the user that an error has occurred, but still continue to run the rest of the script. We do this by using the `On Error Resume Next` command in conjunction with the `Err` object.

Using the Err Object

The `Err` object (only available in VB.NET) contains information about runtime errors. Every time an error occurs during page execution, the properties of this object are populated with information pertaining to that error. The following sections summarize the various properties and methods of the `Err` object.

The `Err` object only contains information about the most recent error; it cannot hold multiple sets of error information at the same time.

Member	Description
`Err.Number`	This property exposes a numeric value representing an error value. It's like an ID field for your error, and associated with it are all the other properties and methods of the `Err` object. Apart from being used to set a numeric value to an error, the `Number` property can also be used to retrieve one that you set previously.
`Err.Description`	This property exposes a descriptive message about the error, and can be used to read or write a description.
`Err.Source`	This property exposes information about the application that generated the error.
`Err.Clear`	This method is used to clear any information stored in the different properties of the `Err` object. This method can be used to clear the error information after the error has been handled.

Member	Description
Err.Raise	This method is used to generate a runtime error message. When using the Raise() method, you need to provide the Number you used to identify the error. You also have the option to provide a description, and source information for the error.
	If you do not provide values for the optional parameters, the values for those parameters are supplied from the existing information in the Err object, which could be from a previous error. This is a good reason to use the Clear property after each time you use the Err object.

The following example uses the Raise() method to generate an error message:

```
Err.Raise (vbObjectError + 1000,"Source of the error","Error occurred")
```

We add the error number to the vbObjectError constant. As we saw in earlier chapters, a constant is an item that contains a constant value throughout the execution of a program. This ensures that the error number we raise does not conflict with the numbers of pre-established specific system errors in VB.NET.

Let's take a look at a worked example. We'll modify the previous example and add the Err object code to handle the error.

Try It Out Using the Err Object

1. Open unstructurederror.aspx in Web Matrix and make the following changes to the code in the All Window:

```
<script language="VB" runat="server" >
  Sub UsingErrObject()
    dim intCounter as integer
    intCounter =1
    for intCounter=1 to 10
      intCounter = intCounter+1
     next
    Response.Write ("The value of the counter is : " & intCounter & "<br>")
    intCounter = "Storing a string to an integer"
  End Sub
Sub Page_Load()
  on error resume next
  UsingErrObject()
  if Err.Number <> 0 then
        Response.Write ("Error occurred : " & "<br>")
        Response.Write ("Error Description : " & Err.Description & "<br>")
        Response.Write ("Error Number : " & Err.Number & "<br>")
  End if
  Err.Clear
  Response.Write ("The Page Execution is completed")
  End Sub
</script>
```

2. Save this file as `usingerrobject.aspx`, and view it in your browser. What you see should should resemble Figure 14-20:

The value of the counter is : 11
Error occurred :
Error Description : Cast from string "Storing a string to an integer" to type 'Integer' is not valid.
Error Number : 13
The Page Execution is completed

Figure 14-20

How It Works

The first new line we added creates the new sub, `UsingErrObject`:

```
Sub UsingErrObject()
```

The code itself functions in exactly the same way as `unstructurederror.aspx`, until we come to call our sub in the HTML block. Here we encounter our `Err` object:

```
if Err.Number <> 0 then
  Response.Write ("Error occurred : " & "<br>")
  Response.Write ("Error Description : " & Err.Description & "<br>")
  Response.Write ("Error Number : " & Err.Number & "<br>")
End if
```

First, the number for the error is evaluated. An error *will* occur, because we have entered a string into our integer field. But because we don't know the `Number` of that particular error, we look for any error that is greater or less than zero – that is, anything but zero.

If this number is found, the following three `Response.Write` statements will execute. The first one just displays the text Error Occurred. The second one requests the error description of the error that occurred, and the third line prints the number of the error.

Finally, we clear our `Err` object:

```
Err.Clear
```

Structured Error Handling

Now that we've looked at unstructured error handling using the `On Error` statement and the `Err` object, let's talk about structured error handling. This feature is new to VB.NET, but has been available for a while in languages such as C++, C#, and Java.

So what do we mean by structured error handling? Pretty much just that: handling errors via a particular structure. Lines of code are grouped together, and different handlers are provided to handle different errors within those groups. The following list shows the sequence of events that take place when using structured error handling:

1. We execute one or more lines of code in a group. They might execute without an error, or they might generate one or many different kinds of errors.

2. If errors are generated, a handler (which you will have defined) corresponding to the error will be called. If there is no error, no handler will be called.

You might have defined a generic handler, which will handle any errors for which you did not define a specific handler.

So, two important things need to be done if you want to use structured error handling effectively:

❑ Creating a group of lines, or block of code

❑ Creating handlers for the different kinds of errors that could occur when the code block is executed

Before launching into this subject, we need to introduce the concept of exceptions.

Exceptions

An *exception* is any error condition or unexpected behavior that occurs during the execution of a program, and consequently disrupts the normal flow of instructions – in fact, the term is just shorthand for *exceptional event*. If an error occurs within a method call, the method creates an exception object and hands it off to the runtime system – this object contains information detailing the type of exception that was raised and the state of the program at the time.

> **Depending on whether the exception originates from the program itself or from the CLR, you may or may not be able to recover from the exception. While you can recover from most application exceptions, you can seldom recover from a runtime exception.**

The exception event is *thrown* by the code that calls the event. The code can either catch the exception (and try and handle the problem), or pass it on up to the code that called that code, and so on up the invocation stack. If it reaches the top of the stack without being caught by a handler along the way, the program will crash. Before talking about how to handle exceptions, we'll briefly introduce you to the exception object, and its properties.

The Exception Class

.NET Framework provides a `System.Exception` class, which acts as the base class for all exceptions. The `Exception` class contains properties that inform our understanding of the exception. The following list summarizes the different properties within `Exception` class:

Property	Description
StackTrace	This property contains the stack trace (which shows the sequence of nested procedure calls your program has executed). This can be used to determine the location of the error occurrence.
Message	This property contains the message about the error.
InnerException	This property is used to create and store a series of exceptions during exception handling. For example, imagine if a piece of your code threw an exception. The exception, and its handler, could be stored in the `InnerException` property of that handler. You could then reference the exception, see how it was handled, and, based on that information, perhaps create a more effective handler. This can be very useful when you are reviewing the execution of a piece of troublesome code. `InnerException` can also be used to store an exception that occurred in a previous piece of code.
Source	This property contains information about the application that generated the error.
TargetSite	This property contains information about the method that throws the exception.
HelpLink	This property is used to provide the URL for a file containing help information about the exception that occurred.

The two important exception classes that inherit (derive methods and properties) from `System.Exception` are `ApplicationException` and `SystemException`. The `SystemException` class is thrown by the runtime, and the `ApplicationException` class is thrown by an application.

With this introduction, let's look at some actual code that makes structured error handling possible.

Using Try...Catch...Finally to Catch Exceptions

For structured error handling, we will use the `Try...Catch...Finally` statement. As explained earlier, the first task in error handling is to group one or more lines of code. This group must be placed within the `Try` block.

The block of code within the `Try` is then executed. This may or may not generate an error. If an error does occur during the execution, the `Catch` block comes into action. The `Catch` block will contain handlers for the different exceptions that could occur within the code in the `Try` block. VB.NET executes the exception handler for whatever exception occurs. If a specific handler is not provided, VB.NET will execute a generic handler. If a generic handler is not found, an error is sent to the client.

The `Finally` block will be executed after either the error has been handled or the code in the `Try` block has been executed. The `Finally` block is typically used to do clean up tasks, such as releasing resources, closing objects, initializing variables and so on.

> When using the `Try` block, follow it with a `Catch` block and a `Finally` block, otherwise the code will result in a syntax error.

The following example shows the structure of the `Try...Catch...Finally` statement:

```
Try
   'group of one or more lines
   intSum = intNumber1 + intNumber2
Catch
   'handle the error that might occur in the try block
   intSum = 0
Finally
   'clean up code goes here
   intNumber1 = 0
   intNumber2 = 0
End Try
```

Let's get deeper into the details of each block.

The Try Block

There is not a lot more to say about the `Try` block, except that it can contain nested `Try...Catch` blocks inside each other. If an exception occurs within a nested `Try` block and is not handled by the nested `Catch` block, then the exception is tacked up to the outer `Try` block, where the exception might be sorted by the handler provided in the outer `Catch` block. This means multiple handlers can be established and activated within a nested `Try...Catch` block.

The Catch Block

You can utilize a similar technique to `Try...Catch` nesting, just within the `Catch` block. If you want to handle five different types of exceptions you will write five `Catch` blocks -, one to handle each specific exception.

The `Catch` block is executed in the order it's written, so provide the catch blocks to handle specific exceptions first and follow these with your generic exceptions.

The following code block shows an example of handling specific exceptions using the `Catch` block (e represents an exception):

```
Catch e as IndexOutOfRangeException
Response.Write (e.ToString)
```

In this example, we are handling the `IndexOutOfRangeException`. This exception occurs when accessing a member of an array that does not exist in that array – in other words, its index is out of the specified range. This can happen, for instance, if you create an array with four elements, but for some reason your code is trying to access the fifth element in the array.

Once we have caught the exception, we use the `ToString()` method of the `Exception` class to send information about the exception back to the browser. This method provides information such as the error message, the name of the exception, and the stack trace.

Note that the preceding `Catch` block will only handle the `IndexOutOfRangeException`. As we have indicated, it is best to provide exception handlers for all possible exceptions that could occur within the `Try` block, and provide a generic handler to handle unexpected exceptions. The following example shows a generic exception handler:

```
Catch excep as Exception
   Response.Write ("Exception Occurred")
```

The `Catch` block can also be used with a `when` clause, which handles exceptions when the condition specified in the `when` clause is `true`. The following example shows the usage of the `when` clause:

```
Catch when Err.Number <> 0
   Response.Write ("Error Occurred: " & "<br>")
   Response.Write ("Error Number: " & Err.Number & "<br>")
   Response.Write ("Error Occurred: " & Err.Description & "<br>")
```

In the above example, the `when` clause checks if the `Err` object number property is not equal to zero. If the answer to this is `True`, then a detailed message is sent to the client via the `Response.Write` statements.

Finally Block

As we have seen, this block contains cleanup code that should be executed at the end, after the `Try` or `Catch` block is executed.

Exit Try

We haven't seen this statement yet, but it's very simple – it's just used to exit the `Try` block:

```
If intCounter=11 Then
Response.Write ("Exiting the Try Block" & "<br>")
Exit Try
End If
```

Any errors that occur after this block are effectively ignored, as we have jumped out of the `Try` block and cannot handle them any more.

Now we've done the theory, let's try a practical!

Try It Out Using Try...Catch...Finally

1. We're going to modify our `unstructurederror.aspx` code file again. Open it in Web Matrix and make the following changes within the All Window:

```VB
<script language="VB" runat="server" >
  Sub StructuredErrorHandling ()
  Try
    Dim intCounter As Integer
    intCounter =1
    for intCounter=1 To 10
      intCounter = intCounter+1

    Next
    Response.Write ("The value of the counter is:" & intCounter & "<br>")
   intCounter = "Storing a string to an integer"
     'Handler for InvalidCast Exception
  Catch excep As InvalidCastException
    Response.Write ("Error Occurred"& "<br>" & excep.ToString & "<br>")
     'Catch block using when clause and generic exception handler
  Catch When Err.Number <> 0
    Response.Write ("Generic Error Occurred" & "<br>")
  Finally
    Response.Write ("The Page Execution is completed" & "<br>")
  End Try
  End sub
</script>
<%
  StructuredErrorHandling ()
  Response.Write ("Procedure call completed" & "<br>")
%>
```

2. Save this file as `structurederrorhandling.aspx`, and load it into your browser. Figure 14-21 shows the result:

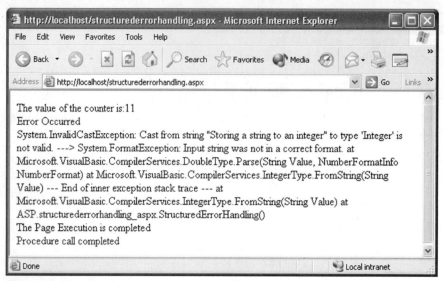

Figure 14-21

How It Works

We began by creating a new subroutine, and initiating the `Try` block:

```
Sub StructuredErrorHandling ()
Try
```

We then used the `intCounter` loop as we have done in the past few exercises:

```
Dim intCounter As Integer
intCounter =1
for intCounter=1 To 10
  intCounter = intCounter+1
Next
Response.Write ("The value of the counter is:" & intCounter & "<br>")
```

The loop has executed correctly, because the line that follows the loop and displays the contents of the loop counter has worked. After this, we have our problem line, which generates an error. This line is followed by two `Catch` blocks. The first `Catch` block looks out for incorrect casts in the code, and if one is found, returns a line of text and the error information to the browser:

```
Catch excep As InvalidCastException
    Response.Write ("Error Occurred"& "<br>" & excep.ToString & "<br>")
```

Because we cast a string to an integer variable, this error is indeed generated, and our line of text as well as the error information appears in our browser window. The second `Catch` block is a generic exception handler, which returns the line **Generic Error Occurred**, if any error number is encountered:

```
Catch when Err.Number <> 0
   Response.Write ("Generic Error Occurred" & "<br>")
```

Because our only error has already been handled, this Catch statement is not triggered. Then comes the Finally block, which returns a line to the browser:

```
Finally
   Response.Write ("The Page Execution is completed" & "<br>")
```

At the end, once the sub has been called, a line is sent to inform the user that the whole procedure is complete:

```
Response.Write ("Procedure call completed" & "<br>")
```

Again, we see both of these lines in the browser window, which shows that the Finally block was executed despite the error in our code, as was the Response.Write statement within the HTML tags.

Handling Errors Programmatically

We can now handle errors using the On Error statement, Err object, and Try statements, but there is still a possibility that some exceptions will sneak through. Among other reasons, this might happen because we did not handle all possible exceptions, or we did not provide a generic exception handler. ASP.NET provides us with two more methods that can be used to handle any errors unaccounted for, and provide a friendly message to the user, instead of the default runtime error screen.

The two methods are:

- ❑   Page_Error() method
- ❑   Application_Error() method

Page_Error() Method

The Page class provides this method. Refer to *Chapter 10* for more information on the Page class and its members.

The Page_Error() method can be used to handle errors at the page level. Every time an unhandled exception occurs, this event is called. To see how it works, let's take our previous example and modify it to use the Page_Error() method.

In the example, we created an error by storing a string to an integer datatype, and we used the Try statement to handle exceptions. This time, we'll just use the Page_Error() method to handle the exception:

Try It Out   Using Page_Error

1.   Open structurederrorhandling.aspx in Web Matrix, and make the following adjustments within the **All** Window:

```
<script language="VB" runat="server">
  Sub PageLevelErrorTest()
    Dim intCounter as integer
    intCounter =1
    For intCounter=1 To 10
```

```
        intCounter = intCounter+1
      Next
      Response.Write ("The value of the counter is:" & intCounter & "<br>")
      intCounter = "Storing a string to an integer"
  End Sub
  Sub Page_Error(sender As Object, exc As EventArgs)
    Response.Write("Error occurred: " & Server.GetLastError().ToString())
    Server.ClearError()
  End Sub
  Sub Page_Load()
    PageLevelErrorTest()
  End Sub
</script>
```

2. Save the file as `pagelevelerror.aspx`, and open it in your browser. You should see something like Figure 14-22:

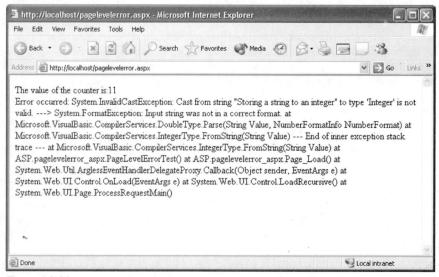

Figure 14-22

How It Works

We already know about the first half of this code; it's the `Page_Error()` sub that we're interested in. When we create the sub, we specify several things in parentheses:

```
Sub Page_Error(sender As Object, exc As EventArgs)
```

Within the `Page_Error()` method, we are writing a message to the user to say that an error has occurred, and detailed error information is provided using the `GetLastError()` method of the `Server` object:

```
Response.Write("Error occurred: " & Server.GetLastError().ToString())
```

After displaying the message, we free up the server by using the `ClearError()` method of the `Server` object.

The `Page_Error()` method is called whenever an unhandled exception is thrown within the page. This method could be used to catch the error, log the error to a log file, notify the administrator of the error using e-mail, or to store the error information to a database. This will be discussed in a moment, in the *Notification and Logging* section.

Application_Error() Method

This method too can be used to handle any errors unaccounted for. The `Application_Error()` method is similar to the `Page_Error()` method – if it is enabled, it is called whenever an unhandled exception is thrown, from *any page under the application*. This method is part of the `global.asax` file. Another similarity with the `Page_Error()` method is that `Application_Error()` can also be used to log the errors to a log file, notify an administrator using email, or store the error information to a database.

The following example shows the usage of this method:

```
Sub Application_Error(sender As Object, exc As EventArgs)
  'Handle the Error
  'Provide code to log the error or send an email
End Sub
```

Notification and Logging

In this section, we will talk about the techniques that are used to log errors to the Windows event log, and notify a site manager or administrator of the occurrence of the error.

Customized Error Messages

The next question is: what if the development server is on a different machine? ASP.NET allows you to specify whether you want the detailed message to be displayed on the local client or remote clients, or both. You can specify this information using the `<customErrors>` section in the Web configuration file, `web.config`. We'll discuss `web.config` later in the book (see *Chapter 15* for more details); for now, just create a new file in your application folder called `web.config`, so that you can demonstrate how to handle custom errors in this chapter. The following example shows a sample setting for the `<customErrors>` section:

```
<configuration>
  <system.web>
    <customErrors defaultRedirect="userError.aspx" mode="On">
    <error statusCode="404" redirect="PagenotFound.aspx" />

  </customErrors>
  </system.web>
</configuration>
```

All settings in `web.config` have to be enclosed with `<configuration>` and `<system.web>` tags. Also make sure that you copy the upper and lower case of this code exactly, as `web.config` is case-sensitive.

As shown, the `<customErrors>` configuration section has two attributes. The first is the `defaultdirect` attribute, and specifies the URL for the page to be redirected to when an error occurs. The above configuration setting will redirect the user to a default error page, `userError.aspx` when an error occurs.

The second attribute is the `mode` attribute, which takes three values: `On`, `Off`, and `RemoteOnly`. `On`, specifies that the custom error is enabled; the users will be redirected to the custom error page specified in the `defaultdirect` attribute. `Off` specifies that the custom error is disabled; the users will *not* be redirected to a customized error page, but to a general non-informative one. `RemoteOnly`, the default setting, specifies that only remote (and not local) clients should be redirected to the custom error page.

The `<customError>` configuration section contains an `<error>` sub tag, which is used to specify error pages for different errors. In the above example, I have specified `PagenotFound.aspx` page as the error page when error HTTP 404 occurs. You could provide multiple `<error>` subtags for different error codes.

Let's create the two friendly error pages, `userError.aspx` and `PagenotFound.aspx`, specified in the configuration file.

Try It Out   Creating Error Pages

1. Create a Web configuration file in `BegASPNet11/ch14`. To do this, go to Web Matrix and choose the **Web.config** option in the third row of the **Add New File** dialog. Don't worry if there is already a `web.config` file there; it is OK to overwrite it.

2. Delete all of the code that is automatically generated, as it only needs to consist of the following `<customErrors>` section, which you should type in:

```
<configuration>
  <system.web>
    <customErrors defaultRedirect="userError.aspx" mode="On">
     <error statusCode="404" redirect="PagenotFound.aspx" />
    </customErrors>
  </system.web>
</configuration>
```

3. Now create the `userError.aspx` page. Open up Web Matrix, and enter the following code into the **All** Window:

```
<html>
  <head>
  <title> Friendly Error Page</title>
  </head>
  <body>
  <h2> An error has occurred in executing this page. Sorry for the
inconvenience. The site administrator is aware of this error occurrence.</h2>
  </body>
</html>
```

4. Next you create the `PagenotFound.aspx` page. Create another new file in Web Matrix and enter the following code into the All Window:

```
<html>
  <head>
  <title> Friendly Error Page</title>
  </head>
  <body>
  <h2> Sorry, the resource you are requesting is not available. Please verify the
address. </h2>
  </body>
</html>
```

5. Now, load the `RuntimeError.aspx` file, using your browser. Figure 14-23 shows the result:

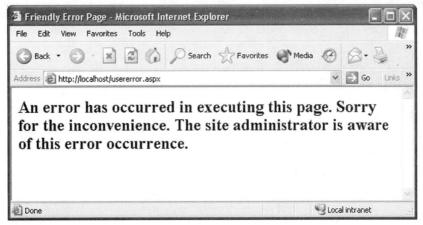

Figure 14-23

What you see in here is the `userError.aspx` file, and not the detailed error message showing the runtime error.

6. Now, try to access a file that does not exist in your application folder. Type into the URL address section of your browser something like `thispagedoesntexist.aspx`. Figure 14-24 shows the result of accessing a file that is not found in the application:

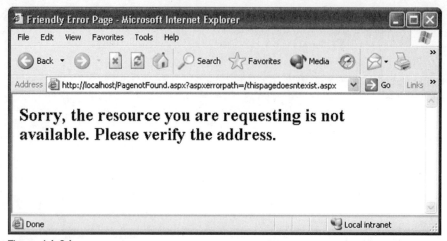

Figure 14-24

What you see is the file with the friendly error message and *not* the default Page not found message from the Web server.

How It Works

We created a `<customErrors>` section in the Web configuration file. This section pointed to the correct file. We did this by setting the default error page displayed to `userError.aspx`, and the error page for status code 404 to `PagenotFound.aspx`:

```
<customErrors defaultRedirect="userError.aspx" mode="RemoteOnly">
 <error statusCode="404" redirect="PagenotFound.aspx" />
</customErrors>
```

Once this was done, we created our own text for the error messages in `userError.aspx` and `PagenotFound.aspx` files. If we had been using a pre-existing `web.config` file, we would have also had to ensure that `<customErrors>` was set to `On`, so that our new error pages were sent to the local browser. Otherwise, we wouldn't have been able to view them when we triggered them by using files containing mistakes.

In the example, we saw how to redirect users to a friendly error page using the different attributes in the `<customErrors>` section of `web.config`. There is a way to redirect users to different friendly error pages based on which page the error has occurred on, by using the `ErrorPage` property in the `Page` directive as shown below:

```
<% @ Page ErrorPage="ErrorPage.aspx" %>
```

If you have this directive in `runtimeerror.aspx`, then the users will be redirected to `ErrorPage.aspx` when an error occurs in `runtimeerror.aspx`.

Now let's go back to the local client scenario. ASP.NET displays a call-stack (a series of procedure calls that lead up to an error) when a runtime error occurs. Before doing this, we suggest you delete the `web.config` file; if you don't all errors generated will be handled by this file.

Writing to the Event Log

We now know that any exceptions that are not handled can call the `Application_Error()` and `Page_Error()` methods. There is another step we can take in handling these unforeseen errors, which involves finding out when they occurred, or logging them, as this could provide vital clues as to how we handle them in the future.

For instance, say a customer who is ordering a few items from your online shopping center receives an error that the order could not be completed. The site manager should be able to see that an error *has* occurred, so they can take steps to avoid this error in the future.

To achieve this, errors can be logged in to the Windows event log that can then be reviewed on a periodic basis. Depending on the nature of the application, the event log could be reviewed every hour, day, or week.

System.Diagnostics Namespace

The tool that the .NET Framework provides for us here is the `System.Diagnostics` namespace, which contains classes that can be used for reading and writing to event logs. Before using the class for accessing event logs, we have to import the `System.Diagnostics` namespace into the program, as follows.

```
<%@ Import Namespace="System.Diagnostics" %>
```

This line goes at the very top of your code page.

EventLog Class

We use the `EventLog` class to read and write to the event log. We can create a new log, or write entries to an existing log.

First, you need to create a log that you can write to, and then you need to specify an event *source*. A source is a string identifying an individual entry to the log. Creating an event source opens some space in the log for the entry to be recorded. The `CreateEventSource()` method can be used to create both a source and a log. In the following example, we create a log called `MyApplicationLog`, and a source called `MyApplicationSource`.

To actually write an entry to the log, we use the `WriteEntry()` method, and as in our last example, provide detailed error information by using the `GetLastError()` method of the `Server` object.

Try It Out | Writing to the Windows Error Log

1. Type the following code into Web Matrix into the All Window:

```
<%@ Import Namespace="System.Diagnostics" %>
<script language="VB" runat="server" >
  Sub EntrytoLog()
```

```
      dim intCounter as integer
      intCounter =1
      for intCounter=1 to 10
       intCounter = intCounter+1
      next
      Response.Write ("The value of the counter is:" & intCounter & "<br>")
      intCounter = "Storing a string to an integer"
    End sub
    Sub Page_Error(sender As Object, exc As EventArgs)
      dim errorMessage as string
      errorMessage = "Error occurred" & Server.GetLastError().ToString()
      Server.ClearError()
      Dim LogName As String = "MyApplicationLog"
      Dim SourceName As String = "MyApplicationSource"
      If (Not EventLog.SourceExists(SourceName))
      EventLog.CreateEventSource(SourceName, LogName)
      End If
      'Insert into Event Log
      Dim MyLog As New EventLog
      MyLog.Source = LogName
      MyLog.WriteEntry(errorMessage, EventLogEntryType.Error)
    End Sub
  </script>
  <%
    EntrytoLog()
  %>
```

2. Save this file as `entrytolog.aspx`, and load it in the browser. After the page has loaded, you will see the results as seen in Figure 14-25:

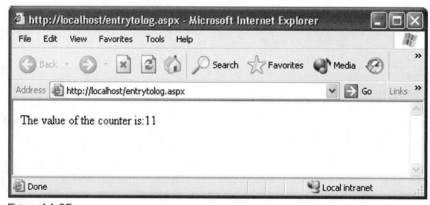

Figure 14-25

3. However, it's not really the display we interested in, but the fact that it has written to a log. To view the contents of the log, you will need to open the Event Viewer. Click Start from the Windows tool bar, and then select Settings. Select Control Panel and double click on the Administrative Tools icon. This will launch the Administrative Tools window. Double-click on the Event Viewer icon to open the Event Viewer window. Figure 14-26 shows the Event Viewer on my machine:

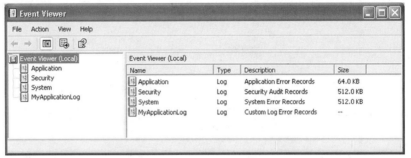

Figure 14-26

4. Double-click on the MyApplicationLog (listed under the Name column after System Log) to open it. You will see the Error entry that we made. Figure 14-27 shows the entry:

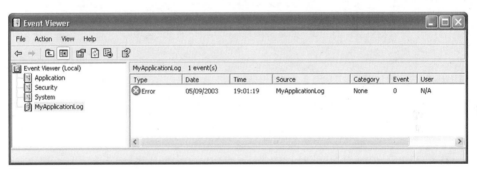

Figure 14-27

5. Double-click on the Error entry to open the Event Properties window, as shown in Figure 14-28. This shows the date and time the entry was made, and the description we provided using the `WriteEntry()` method:

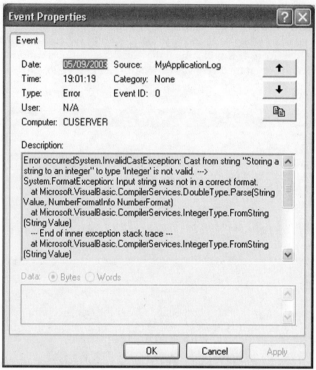

Figure 14-28

How It Works

The opening line imports the namespace we will use:

```
<%@ Import Namespace="System.Diagnostics" %>
```

We then establish and loop our familiar `intCounter` variable. Next we build the `Page_Error()` sub and start it by creating our `errorMessage` variable as a string and supplying the variable with a line of text to display, along with error information from the server. The next line of code erases all mention of the error from the server:

```
Sub Page_Error(sender As Object, exc As EventArgs)
    dim errorMessage as string
    errorMessage = "Error occurred" & Server.GetLastError().ToString()
    Server.ClearError()
```

Now we define the name of our log and this particular source, but before creating these two items, we check to see if the source already exists:

```
Dim LogName As String = "MyApplicationLog"
Dim SourceName As String = "MyApplicationSource"
If (Not EventLog.SourceExists(SourceName))
    EventLog.CreateEventSource(SourceName, LogName)
```

If the source doesn't already exist, we proceed to write an entry to the log:

```
Dim MyLog As New EventLog
MyLog.Source = LogName
MyLog.WriteEntry(errorMessage, EventLogEntryType.Error)
```

In this example, we have used the `EventLog` class to make an entry to the log file under the `Page_Error()` method. Alternatively, you could use the `EventLog` class within the `Application_Error()` method in the `global.asax` file. If you place it in the `Application_Error()` method, then the `EventLog` class will create an entry to the log files for any unhandled errors that occur at any point throughout the pages within the application.

Mailing the Site Administrator

In the last example, we made an entry to a log file after the occurrence of an error. In the real world, a Web site manager or administrator could review this log file at regular intervals. However, this may not be prudent for certain applications. Depending on the nature of the application, the manager or administrator may need to be informed of an error right away. To do this, we could notify the site administrator by sending an e-mail with the details of the error as soon as it occurs.

System.Web.Mail Namespace

The .NET Framework provides a namespace with a set of classes to do this. The `System.Web.Mail` namespace contains three classes that can be used to create and send an e-mail using SMTP:

❏   `MailMessage`

❏   `MailAttachment`

❏   `SmtpMail`

Before using these classes in our page, we need to import the `System.Web.Mail` namespace, just as we did with the `System.Diagnostics` namespace in the last example. Let's look at our three classes in more detail.

MailMessage

The `MailMessage` class provides properties that are used to create an e-mail. The following table lists the name and purpose of some of the more commonly used members of this class:

Name	Use
From	This property specifies the sender's e-mail address
To	This property specifies the recipient's e-mail address.
Subject	This property specifies the subject line for the e-mail message.
Body	This property is used to set the body of the e-mail message.

The syntax when using this class looks like this:

```
mailMessage.From = "senders email address"
mailMessage.To = "recipients email address"
mail.Message.Subject = "subject line"
mailMessage.Body = "body of email message"
```

MailAttachment

This class contains members that are used to create an attachment that is to be sent with the e-mail message.

Name	Use
Encoding	This property specifies the type of encoding of the e-mail attachment.
Filename	This property specifies the file name of the mail attachment.

SmtpMail

This class provides properties that are used to send an e-mail using the SMTP Service. The method we are interested in, at the moment, is the Send() method of this class. This method is used to send an e-mail, and the code looks like this:

```
SmtpMail.Send(mailMessage)
```

To show you how a working piece of code based on the System.Web.Mail namespace, would look, we have modified the previous example to send an e-mail, instead of writing to the log file:

```
<%@ Import Namespace="System.Web.Mail" %>
<script language="VB" runat="server" >
  Sub sendMailTest()
    dim intCounter as integer
    intCounter =1
    for intCounter=1 to 10
    intCounter = intCounter+1
    Response.Write ("The value of the counter is:" & intCounter & "<br>")
    intCounter = "Storing a string to an integer"
  End sub
  Sub Page_Error(sender As Object, exc As EventArgs)
    dim errorMessage as string
    errorMessage = "Error occurred " & Server.GetLastError().ToString()
    Server.ClearError()
    'Create an email message
    Dim newMail As New MailMessage
    newMail.From = "fromaddress@yourserver.com"
    newmail.To = "administrator@yourserver.com"
```

```
      newMail.Subject = "Error Occurred"
      newMail.Body = errorMessage
      'send the mail to the administrator.
      SmtpMail.Send(newMail)
   End Sub
</script>
<%
   sendMailTest()
%>
```

This code allows e-mail to be sent to the administrator of the server in the event of an error being generated. We haven't stepped through this code in Try It Out fashion, because unless you have a working SMTP server on your machine, it won't send emails from to your address.

Summary

In this chapter, we talked about error handling techniques that can be used when developing ASP.NET applications.

We discussed the different kinds of errors that can occur, techniques for handling errors (including the new tracing features), handling exceptions using unstructured and structured error handling, and finally, techniques to log the error messages to a log file and notify the site administrator through e-mail.

We saw that adopting good coding practice helps reduce the number of errors in your code, and that the time spent in testing helps us create handlers for recurring errors before the application is moved to the production environment. Using different error handling techniques helps us to develop applications with fewer bugs, which are, therefore, more successful and competitive.

Exercises

1. How are parser errors different from compilation errors? Is there any difference between the ways they are displayed by ASP.NET?

2. Here are three portions of code – what is wrong with each section and what type of error does it contain? How would you fix it?

❑ Section A:

```
<html>
  <head>
    <title>Syntax Error Example </title>
  </head>
  <body>
    <form method="post" action="syntaxerror.aspx" runat="server">
    <asp:TextBox id="txtQuantity" runat="Server />
    </form>
  </body>
</html>
```

❑ Section B:

```
<script language="vb" runat="server">
Sub Page_Load()
Dim intCounter, intLoop as Integer
intCounter=0
intLoop=0
do while intCounter<10
 intLoop = intLoop +1
End While
End Sub
</script>
```

❑ Section C:

```
 <script language="vb" runat="server">
Sub Page_Load()
Dim a As String
Dim b As Integer
Dim c As String
a = "Hello"
b = "World"
c = a + b
End Sub
</script>
```

3. Create a form with four textboxes and a submit button. Make one textbox take a user name, another take an e-mail, another take a phone number, and the last take the user's gender. Use validation controls to make sure there are no blank entries, that you can only enter numbers into the phone field, and that you can only enter a number between 1 and 140 in the age field. Also, but not necessarily with validation controls, make sure that the gender textbox only accepts controls, make sure that the gender textbox only accepts male or female and that the email address contains a "@". In what ways could this form be improved further?

4. Write a try...catch error handler that will handle errors specifically for a divide by zero handler (as we did for invalid casts).

Hint: We haven't mentioned the specific class involved, you can find a list of class using the class browser.

5. Create a custom error page for an HTTP 403 error Access is forbidden and get it working for this chapter's code folder.

15

Configuration and Optimization

ASP.NET makes some important and dramatic changes to the way in which configuration is managed. With ASP, a lot of configuration was done via the Web server's interface, whereas in ASP.NET, the configuration information is located within XML files separately from the Web server. These configuration files are directly accessible from ASP.NET and offer the user greater control over the workings of both the Web server and the Web page. They even remove the need for restarting your Web server, because once you alter the configuration files and recompile your application code, the change has already been made. Also you don't have to worry about whether you are running Web Matrix or IIS; you have the ability to easily alter the configuration settings.

With the greater levels of customization that we can exercise over our applications, it is crucial that our code runs quickly and efficiently. In addition to the configuration aspects, optimization of your code is equally vital to ensure that everything runs as expected on the Web server. Up until now we've only really been concerned with demonstrating a particular concept and the ways it can be used, but from now on we need to be concerned also with the efficiency of our code.

This chapter will look at how to configure your applications in ASP.NET, and also how to increase the performance of your pages through general optimization techniques. We will consider the effects of the installation of .NET Framework 1.1 since it doesn't replace the old version of the .NET Framework but runs alongside it. We will also look at other aspects of optimization to improve security, user-friendliness, and to make debugging and managing applications easier. In particular, this chapter will look at:

❑   The structure and function of the ASP.NET configuration files `machine.config` and `web.config`

❑   Customization of `machine.config` and `web.config` files to increase performance, security, and usability

❑   How to use caching to improve the performance of your server

❑   How to monitor the resources your application is taking up, and gather basic statistics about its operation

To learn more about the advanced topics presented in this chapter, refer to Professional ASP.NET 1.1 Special Edition, Wiley ISBN: 0-7645-5890-0.

Configuration Overview

IIS (Internet Information Services) has long been a powerhouse for ASP and continues that role in ASP.NET. In the earliest days of ASP, IIS offered only very limited functionality beyond the ability to switch on and off its Web serving capabilities. This is because initially IIS was only expected to vend static HTML pages. Everything was different about it, right down to the name. IIS used to stand for "Internet Information Server". However, just as the jump from the early browsers that couldn't display tables or frames, to the multimedia-saturated monsters we see today, IIS has had to adapt to the changing environment and the changing needs of its users.

It quickly grew to control many of the features of ASP via a point-and-click interface, such as those normally accessed by the Server and Response objects, so a name change was in order. To alter aspects of the Web server's operation in classic "ASP", you pointed and clicked via IIS's management console and then restarted the IIS service to refresh and resume operations. You started being able to assign permissions for different users, implement security policies and it was able to handle e-commerce transactions and much more than it was ever designed for. However if you were running ASP via Personal Web Server though then your ability to make changes was severely restricted by the rudimentary interface, which offered you little more than a "stop-start" button.

ASP.NET has made configuration even more powerful and more flexible by removing the reliance of the Web server front-end by the adoption of XML-based configuration files. These files can be used to configure any component of ASP.NET by editing the file in a text editor. Now you just write a piece of code to explain how you'd like ASP.NET to perform a certain operation, and then configure ASP.NET to run your code instead of its built-in code. No longer do you have to worry about understanding IIS and its different settings, as you can alter the code itself.

You're not restricted to just defining configuration settings at design or run time, either. You can add or change them at any time. The new configuration settings you have supplied will simply be activated, with no loss of efficiency for the server.

This chapter will look at two types of configuration files:

- ❑ The Machine Configuration File – `machine.config` – for machine specific settings
- ❑ The Application Configuration File – `web.config` – for application specific settings

> **The .NET Framework has two other configuration files, which are beyond the scope of this book. They are the Security Configuration Files enterprisesec.config and security.config that deal with the tiers of a Web server's security policy.**

Let's take a look at how you can view configuration files using Internet Explorer.

Browsing .config Files

The configuration files stored as XML documents in plain text format. This means you can view them with any text editor. When viewed in Internet Explorer, you have the ability to expand and collapse the different nodes of the document to make the tree easier to read. Type in the location of the configuration file into Internet Explorer's address bar to view it.

A Quick Word on .Net Framework Versions 1.0 and 1.1

Before taking a look at the `machine.config` file, you need to ascertain the exact location of the configuration file on your machine, and its version. This book assumes that you are using .NET Framework 1.1.

> *When .NET Framework 1.1 is installed on a machine that already has .NET 1.0, the older installation is not removed automatically. To remove the older version, uninstall it manually.*

Having both versions of the .NET Framework (1.0 and 1.1) installed is not a problem because .NET gives us the ability to run an application against a particular version of the .NET Framework. This is, in fact, very important because as the .NET Framework evolves, certain aspects of a class could be removed entirely, which may cause older applications built with a particular version of the framework to malfunction. If you have more than one version of `machine.config` on your machine, you need to ascertain which version of the Framework the Web Matrix is using, and therefore which version of the file you need to use.

It is already mentioned in *Chapter 1* that you need to alter settings in the `WebServer.exe.config` file. It's possible (although unlikely) that you didn't do this and got this far. However, in this chapter it will be essential to do this if you have both versions 1.0 and 1.1 installed. If you haven't already changed settings then find `Webserver.exe.config` that should be located in something like `C:\Program Files\Microsoft ASP.NET Web Matrix\v.0.6812` (the version number is liable to change). Open it in Web Matrix and add the following settings after the `</configSections>` and before the `<runtime>` section (roughly around line 17):

```
<startup>
    <supportedRuntime version="v1.1.4322" />
</startup>
```

Save the changes and restart the Web Matrix Web server.

Finding the Correct machine.config

Right – having ensured that everybody is using the same version, let's now take a look at the `machine.config` file. You can find this file at the following location:

```
%SystemRoot%\Microsoft.NET\Framework\v1.1.4322\CONFIG\machine.config
```

> **If you have both versions of the Framework installed, you will also find a second machine.config in this location:**
> `%SystemRoot%\Microsoft.NET\Framework\v1.0.3705\CONFIG\machine.config`.
> **Ignore this version, as it is now redundant for examples in this book.**

If you copy this file and save it as `machine.config.xml` anywhere on your system, and then open it in your browser, you'll see your `machine.config` file displayed in the same way as an XML document as depicted in Figure 15-1.

> Important: Do not rename the original `machine.config` — ASP.NET relies on this file for its configuration, and will not run properly without it!

If you collapse the major nodes, you'll get a graphical display of the basic elements:

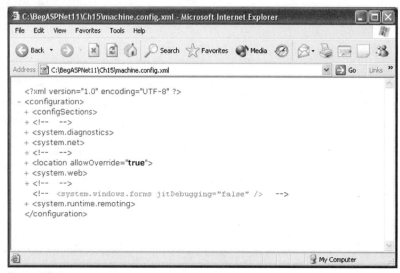

Figure 15-1

The Configuration Files

Your system will have only one file called `machine.config` on it (per installation of the .NET Framework), but possibly many `web.config` files. The `machine.config` file contains any machine-specific settings that ASP.NET needs to function, whereas `web.config` contains configuration information for a *specific* Web application, and can override default functionality defined in the base `machine.config` file to provide a customized environment for each application that you produce.

The configuration sequence of events runs as follows. When a page is initialized, the information in `machine.config` is read. Once this has been done, ASP.NET descends to the next level of the hierarchy and reads the individual `web.config` files stored in your Web application's root directories. These files supply additional configuration information to augment or override settings inherited from `machine.config`. Then, ASP.NET will descend to the next level and read the `web.config` files stored in your application's child directories below the root. These will be used to augment or override information given either in `machine.config` or in the root `web.config`. Next, any `web.config` files in child directories below these will be read and acted on in a similar manner.

This will continue until all `web.config` files in the tree have been processed. Some of your directories may not have a `web.config` file – in this case, they will inherit their settings from the closest configuration file node in the tree above them.

This can be seen more clearly in Figure 15-1 that shows the virtual directories in IIS (don't worry if you are using Web Matrix – this diagram is purely for illustrative purposes as it demonstrates the hierarchical organization of a `.config` file):

A well-structured setup would store general settings you want taken into account at a machine-wide level in the `machine.config` file, and then override them when necessary, using `web.config` files specific to the application page(s) that need to do so. This approach is beneficial because if changes need to be made to the general structure of your application, you only need to make alterations to the `machine.config` file. Likewise, if an individual page needs special settings to function, it can be placed in a child directory with its own `web.config` file, and any changes you make there will affect just that page and not your whole application or machine.

At runtime, ASP.NET uses the information provided by the configuration files to compute the settings for each application or URL resource. The settings are then cached (see later in the chapter) to allow faster access on subsequent calls. ASP.NET can detect changes made to the configuration files while the Web server is running, and will apply the altered version immediately without having the server stopped or rebooted.

Configuration files are protected from unauthorized snooping because both Web Matrix and IIS are automatically configured to prevent HTTP access to them. A server error will be returned if any attempt is made to browse these files over HTTP, even if the file does not exist. You can try this for yourself by directing your browser to http://localhost/web.config, where you will see the following message as depicted in Figure 15-2:

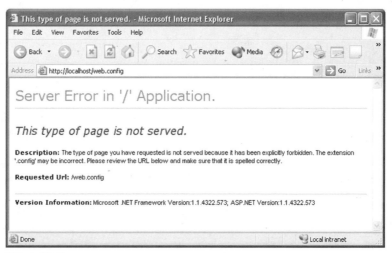

Figure 15-2

You'll get the same result if you try to browse to `global.asax`, or any file that has the following extensions: `.ascx`, `.cs`, `.csproj`, `.vb`, `.vbproj`, and `.webinfo` as they're set up the same way.

Configuration File Rules

Let's look at the basic rules of XML that are applied to configuration files.

❑ They must have a single unique root element that encloses all other elements within it. The root element for both `machine.config` and `web.config` is `<configuration>`.

❑ Elements must be enclosed between the corresponding start `<tag>` and end `</tag>` tags. These tags are case-sensitive so `<Tag>` and `<tag>` will be treated differently.

❑ Any attributes, keys, or values must be enclosed in double quotes - `<add key="data" />`.

❑ Elements must be nested and should not overlap.

In the configuration files you will also find that a couple of rules of thumb follow (in other words not XML rules, but general methods that are applied throughout the config files)

❑ Tag names and attribute names are camel-cased, in other words the first character of a tag name is lowercase and the first letter of any subsequent concatenated word is uppercase.

❑ Attribute values are Pascal-case , that is the first character is uppercase and the first letter of any subsequent concatenated words is uppercase. An exception is `true` and `false`, which are lowercase.

> **Be very careful when editing configuration files, as they affect your server's behavior – always make a backup before modifying them.**

Configuration File Format

Now that we've refreshed our memory about the basic XML rules that apply to configuration files, let's look at the way these files are structured.

As the .NET Framework uses a set of XML classes to access and alter the configuration files, it forces developers to use a common structure for each of the configuration files. The XML structure is most noticeable in `machine.config`, where all of the XML elements are declared and their values set. `web.config` is a smaller file because it only contains a subset of the settings already found in `machine.config`.

The configuration files are structurally divided into two main areas:

❑ A **declarations** section, where individual classes are defined to manipulate information. This section is delimited by `<configSections>` tags.

❑ A **settings** section where values are assigned to the classes declared in the first section. This is delimited by `<sectionGroup>` tags.

In `web.config` files, we can override the values of classes defined in the `machine.config` declarations section. Within these two main groups there are several subgroups that divide the information into manageable chunks. Let's now consider the `system.web` group, because this is the only one that contains the ASP.NET specific material.

Figure 15-3 shows a screenshot of the declarations section, with the `system.web` group expanded:

Figure 15-3

Beneath the declarations sections in the hierarchy, you will find a settings section. This section establishes the attributes and properties for each of the declared classes, such as `CustomError`. The settings of the elements don't have to be declared in the same order as they are found in the `<configSections>` tags, but there must be settings defined for every handler declared, otherwise exceptions will be thrown when applications are run.

> **All tags must be properly closed and nested, and any values specified must fall within the correct range.**

Configuration File Structure

As mentioned earlier, the structures of `machine.config` and `web.config` are similar. In fact, the `web.config` file is a strict subset of the `machine.config` file. To explain the subset division, let's first consider the `machine.config` file.

machine.config

A typical `machine.config` file has an outline like this:

```
<?xml version="1.0" encoding="UTF-8" ?>
<configuration>
    <configSections>
    </configSections>
    <appSettings>
    </appSettings>
    <system.diagnostics>
    </system.diagnostics>
    <system.net>
    </system.net>
    <system.web>
    </system.web>
    <system.runtime.remoting>
    </system.runtime.remoting>
</configuration>
```

The different sections deal with matters such as how the settings at runtime are specified, and the settings used to define the elements used for tracing and routing.

Most of the settings within the `machine.config` file have some preliminary explanation/example within comment tags demonstrating the use of the element involved. For example, under the page settings section, you'll find the following:

```
<!-- pages Attributes:
  buffer="[true|false]"                         // Default: true
  enableSessionState="[true|false|ReadOnly]"    // Default: true
  enableViewState="[true|false]"                // Default: true
  enableViewStateMac="[true|false]"             // Default: false
  smartNavigation="[true|false]"                // Default: false
  autoEventWireup="[true|false]"                // Default: true
  pageBaseType="[typename]"        //Default: System.Web.UI.Page
  userControlBaseType="[typename]"//Default: System.Web.UI.UserControl
-->
<pages buffer="true" enableSessionState="true" enableViewState="true"
       enableViewStateMac="true" autoEventWireup="true" />
```

This should give you a reasonable idea as to how each of the settings work, and how they may be The top-level `system.net` section deals with .NET network class settings, while the `system.web` section deals with all the ASP.NET class settings. We're only really interested in the `system.web` section because it deals specifically with ASP.NET configuration and controls all of the aspects of the behavior of a typical ASP.NET application.

Settings of system.web

There are over thirty settings in the `system.web` section; some of most commonly used settings are:

- ❑ **Page settings**: Allows the user to alter the options relating to the ASP.NET page, such as Web page buffering

- ❑ **Session handling**: Handles options relating to sessions, such as the length of a session or whether cookie-less support should be enabled

- ❑ **Application settings**: Allows the user to create name-value pairs within this section and access the data from within a specific application

- ❑ **Tracing**: Sets the level to which execution should be traced, (used in debugging)

- ❑ **Custom errors**: Allows the user to create error pages for particular situations or change settings altering whether users can see different types of error messages

- ❑ **Web Services**: Stores options that affect the operation of the Web service such as the method of transmission of the Web service (i.e. whether to use HTTPGET, HTTPPOST or SOAP)

- ❑ **Security**: Alters many security related aspects such as modes of authentication, encryption, whether particular users are denied access or not

- ❑ **Compilation**: Sets options for setting (or altering) the default language for ASP.NET, as well as the way in which the page is compiled

- ❑ **Globalization**: Sets options for character encoding used in the requests to and responses from the server

- ❑ **General settings**: Contains general information relating to the request and options affecting what happens to the page at run time

There is a great deal more structure and detail in these files than we've covered here. Our aim has been to give you a general idea of what these files are and what they look like, so that when we move on to the next section you'll be able to find your way around and tune your system.

web.config

As `web.config` files govern the settings of particular applications, they are much smaller than the `machine.config` file.

The sections of a typical `web.config` file are as follows:

```
<?xml version="1.0" encoding="utf-8" ?>
<configuration>
  <system.web>
    <compilation  />
    <customErrors  />
    <authentication />
    <trace  />
    <sessionState  />
    <globalization  />
  </system.web>
</configuration>
```

Here you find only a `<system.web>` section present within the `<configuration>` element, and it has a much-reduced set of elements. As you can deduce from this, it is possible to set only these attributes independently for each application.

Let's see a quick overview of five of the most useful settings, and point out some of the simple alterations that you can make to improve the functioning of your Web application. Let's look in order at general configuration settings, page configuration, application settings, custom errors settings, and trace settings.

General Configuration

This section of our configuration files contains general application configuration settings, such as how long a request is processed for before it is timed out, the maximum size of a request, and whether or not to use a fully qualified URL when redirecting pages. They are contained within the `<httpRuntime>` tags, and occur within the `<system.web>` tags. Here's how you'd set them up in your `web.config` file:

```
<configuration>
  <system.web>
    <httpRuntime executionTimeout="120"
    maxRequestLength="8192"
    useFullyQualifiedRedirectUrl="false"
    />
  </system.web>
</configuration>
```

Let's look at these settings in more detail:

❑ `executionTimeout` controls the time in seconds for which a resource is allowed to try to execute before ASP.NET cancels (times out) the execution of the request. The default value is 90 seconds. If you know that a process (like a complex database query) is likely to take longer than 90 seconds to execute, you should increase this value. This is a very useful feature, because if your database returns an error during the code's execution, ASP.NET knows how long to wait before delivering an error message – it will not wait forever!

❑ `maxRequestLength` specifies the maximum length of a request. The default value is 4MB. If the content requested is larger than 4MB, increase this value. If the content requested never exceeds a lesser value, use that instead. This can be a useful precaution. If your code has a bug, this will prevent it from dumping great quantities of data to your client, as it will stop when it hits the `maxRequestLength`. It also stops clients trying to request too much information at once and hogging all your server's processing time dealing with their requests at the expense of other users.

❑ `useFullyQualifiedRedirectUrl` is not often used. One example of when you need to use this parameter is when you are working with mobile controls. It indicates whether client-side redirects are fully qualified, or whether relative redirects should be used (which is the default). Certain mobile controls require that you use fully qualified redirects.

Using these settings you can control certain aspects of the way your application executes. There are also settings for `minFreeThreads`, `minLocalFreeThreads`, `appRequestQueueLimit`, and `enableVersionHeader`, but these are beyond the scope of the book. Once again, if you wish to know we recommend looking at *Professional ASP.NET 1.1 Special Edition, Wrox Press ISBN: 0-7645-5890-0.*

Page Configuration

The page configuration settings give us control over the default behavior of ASP.NET pages. This can include things such as whether we should buffer output before sending it, and whether or not `session` state is enabled for pages within your application. The information is housed within the `<pages>` element in your configuration files. Here's how you'd set it up in your `web.config` file. All values are set to their defaults:

```
<configuration>
  <system.web>
    <pages buffer="true"
    enableSessionState="true"
    enableViewState="true"
    autoEventWireup="true" />
  </system.web>
</configuration>
```

Let's take a closer look at what these settings do:

❑   `buffer` indicates the code execution processing mode. When it is set to `true`, all code is executed before any HTML data in the page is rendered. When it is set to `false`, all code is rendered as it executes. For example, you could turn off buffering if you're running a complex data query that returns results with a slight delay between each record – you could display a table line-by-line while the page is loading, so that the user is aware that something is happening.

❑   `EnableSessionState` indicates whether server `session` variables are available. The default value is `true`, enabling `session` state. To disable it, set the value to `false`. We recommend that you set it to `true` only if you need to use `session` variables in your page, as disabling `session` state improves performance.

❑   `EnableViewState` indicates whether server controls maintain state when the page request ends. This is a global setting for all server controls used on the page. You can, however, control the viewstate setting of individual server controls by changing the property value. When `EnableViewState` is set to `true` the server controls maintain state (they 'remember' their value). This is the default setting. If it is set to `false`, the server controls don't maintain state. Only set it to `true` if you need your controls to maintain state, as disabling it improves performance.

❑   `AutoEventWireup` indicates whether ASP.NET fires page events like `Page_Load()` automatically or not. `True` is the default setting. Changing it to `false` allows custom assemblies to control the firing of page events. `False` is the default setting for the Visual Studio.NET IDE, as it uses an internal mechanism to control event firing. If you are not using VS.NET you should leave it at the default `True`.

Application Settings

Application settings allow us to store application configuration details in configuration files without the need to write our own custom section handlers for them. The data is stored in the form of key-value pairs. You've come across them earlier in the book, so we won't linger too long on them. Here we have a typical add tag:

```
<add key="XMLFileName" value="myXmlFileName.xml" />
```

You can see that the add tag has both a key attribute and a value attribute. The key attribute is like the name of the variable and the value attribute can be whatever you wish to set it to. In this example, you are assigning the key XMLFileName a value of myXmlFilenName.xml, just like the line XMLFileName = "myXmlFileName.xml" would do so in ASP.NET code.

We can use key-value pairs to store the Connection String for database access. This connection string typically contains the database user Id and password that can be accessed from within our applications. This is a great benefit; configuration files are not accessible over HTTP so it keeps your database connection strings, and so on away from prying eyes. Here's how you'd set it up in web.config:

```
<configuration>
 <appSettings>
 <add key= "DSN"
  value="server=LSERV; uid=user; pwd=password; database=data" />
 </appSettings>
</configuration>
```

Here a key called DSN is being added to the table, and the values in the value section are being associated with it. We would now be able to access this information from inside our application. This is done in your ASP.NET script as follows:

```
strDataSource = ConfigurationSettings.AppSettings("DSN")
```

Custom Errors

While every developer does their best to ensure their pages are thoroughly tested before they are deployed in a full application, errors still happen. When a page has errors that are caught during compilation by a .NET Framework compiler (remember that ASP.NET pages are compiled), ASP.NET generates a syntax error report with information about the error, and sends this information to the browser. On the other hand, if an error occurs while a page is being executed, ASP.NET sends a Stack Trace containing information about the error to the browser. This Stack Trace contains information about what was going on when the error occurred.

While this information is convenient for the developer to debug his code, it's not something you'd want visitors to your site to see, not least because it can reveal detailed information about how your code works – potentially allowing malicious types to find loopholes and exploit them.

That aside, we don't want this information to be displayed to our users because this 'raw' information is going to disconcert them and bring the quality of our coding into question. It's spoiling our client's experience. Furthermore, they have no way of finding out whether the error is in the application or their computer. Thus if there is a friendly, plain English message with a similar look and feel to your site, they know that there *is* a problem and that the problem is *not* with themselves but with the application. This means it is far better for us to make some changes to the way our application handles errors, so that the user can be redirected to elsewhere on our site.

You can configure custom error pages for your application using the <customErrors> section of your web.config file, inside the <system.web> tags:

```
<customErrors
  defaultRedirect="url"
  mode="On|Off|RemoteOnly">
```

```
    <error statusCode="statuscode" redirect="url"/>
  </customErrors>
```

Let's look at the important settings in this section:

❑   `defaultRedirect` indicates the default URL where the browser is redirected if an error occurs. This allows your application to recover if a page fails by sending your users elsewhere, so they're not confronted with a broken page.

❑   `mode` indicates whether custom errors are `On`, `Off`, or `RemoteOnly`. `On` shows your custom error to everyone when it occurs, regardless of where they are. `Off` never shows a custom error to anyone, and `RemoteOnly` shows your custom error to browsers that are *not* located on your server.

> **You'll need to set `mode` to `On` in order to test your custom error pages (unless you've access to a browser off the server). After this, we recommend you change it to `RemoteOnly`, so your users will see the custom error page while you'll still get the standard error page with all the useful debugging information that it contains.**

❑   `error` subtags can appear as often as required throughout your custom error element. They are used to define special conditions above and beyond the default redirect we set up with the `defaultRedirect` value. They are given an HTTP status code to react to and an URL to redirect to if that status code occurs. This gives you the flexibility to react to different errors differently, for example reacting to 404 Page Not Found and 403 Access Forbidden errors differently.

The default `customErrors` configuration option for ASP.NET is `RemoteOnly`, which means that detailed ASP.NET error information is only shown on the browsers on the server and remote users are directed to a custom error page. However, as no redirect page is specified in the defaults, so the redirection won't work until you set it up in `web.config`, like this:

```
<configuration>
  <system.web>
    <customerrors
      defaultRedirect = "customerror.aspx"
      mode = "RemoteOnly"
    />
  </system.web>
</configuration>
```

Trace Settings

Chapter 14 discussed how Tracing was a very useful feature that enables you to follow the execution of your code and review it afterwards. It helps you tighten up loose coding and fix bugs. Tracing can also be set up in your `web.config` files like this:

```
<configuration>
  <system.web>
    <trace
      enabled="true"
      requestLimit = "10"
```

```
         pageOutput="false"
         traceMode="SortByTime"
         localOnly = "true"
      />
   </system.web>
</configuration>
```

When we set up tracing in this way, (the default value for trace, inherited from `machine.config`, is `false`) we can view our trace output using a special tool called `trace.axd` that was discussed in the last chapter. This file is a log file that can be used to store the trace results for the last page viewed. It can be called from your browser in the directory for which you have enabled tracing. This method is useful if you don't want to display the actual trace information at the bottom of your page, but want to keep a record of it in a separate file, which is overwritten each time a page is called. Setting the `pageOutput` directive back to `true` appends this information back to the bottom of your page.

The options for the `web.config` file are:

❑ `enabled` switches tracing on, when set to `true`, or off, when set to `false`, at the application level. When it is switched off, you can still set traces for individual pages using the page directive. By default, this is set to `false` in `machine.config`.

❑ `requestLimit` is the total number of trace requests to keep for viewing later with `trace.axd`. By default, this is set to 10.

❑ `pageOutput` allows you to decide whether you want trace information displaying on every page, as well as being available through `trace.axd`. When it is set to `true`, the tracing information is added to every page. By default it is set to `false`.

❑ `traceMode` allows you to specify if the trace information is sorted by time or by category. If you sort by category, it will be group information based on the system and `Trace.Write()` settings. By default, this is set to `SortByTime`.

❑ `localOnly` specifies that only requests made through http://localhost/ will be allowed to see the trace information. By default it is set to `true`. This stops your users from viewing your trace information, while letting you see exactly what's going on at the same time.

You can embed `Trace.Write` statements in your code while you're debugging your pages, to provide useful information when you view a trace on the page. If you turn tracing off on the page, these statements get hidden; these do not need to be removed because they do not affect the final page output. However, if you find that your application isn't actually performing as it should, all you need to do is re-enable tracing, and these statements will be used again.

Performance Optimization

Some of the options discussed in the previous section help improve your system's security (for example, using configuration files to house database connection strings). Others increase user friendliness (creating customized error pages). Some simply improve the speed at which your applications perform (enabling page buffering, while disabling `session` state will speed up your pages).

Let's focus on some more ways to make your application perform faster.

Caching

Caching is a process of storing frequently accessed Web pages (or data) that are faster to access than accessing it from the original medium. What effect does this have on you? Well, imagine that you're working on your home PC, and it's connected to the Internet via a modem - when you browse a Web page for the first time, you may find that the page takes a while to load. Subsequent visits to that page may well be a lot quicker, because the page has been cached on your machine.

In a similar way, if a person on a corporate network visits a Web site, the page may take a while to load. But, if someone else visits the same page, depending on the settings on the network, they may find the page loads a lot more quickly because it has been cached by a network proxy. Caching is used by ASP.NET to store frequently used portions of ASP.NET pages on the Web server so they don't need to be compiled every time a page is accessed.

However, you probably don't want certain items to be cached indefinitely – for example, if you're running a news site, you want the content on your site to be refreshed at regular intervals, perhaps to display any new items of news. Depending on the nature of your news, you might want it to refresh every half an hour, ten minutes, or even every minute. Any requests that get served during the cached period see the same page, but after the cache duration expires, the old cache is destroyed and a new page is generated with updated content. Simply checking for the absence of the item in the cache causes the re-creation of the data in the cache. This content is then cached for the required duration and the cycle starts again.

Setting the appropriate time period is very important. A list of cities or ZIP codes won't need a short expiration period, while a list of clients, or a product list, will need regular refreshing over relatively short periods of time.

> **Keep in mind that anything you place in the cache consumes memory, so use this feature judiciously.**

Now let's look at the three different types of caching that you can set up. These are:

❑   Output caching

❑   Fragment caching

❑   The Cache object

Output Caching

Output caching allows caching of any response generated by any request for any application resource. It is very useful when you want to cache contents of an entire page. On a busy site, caching frequently accessed pages for even as little as a minute can result in substantial performance gains. While the page lives in the output cache, additional requests for that page are served from the cache without executing and recompiling the code that created the page. Output caching is especially useful for static pages on busy sites.

The complete syntax for the Output Cache is as follows:

```
<%@ OutputCache Duration="#ofseconds" Location="Any | Client |
    Downstream | Server | None" VaryByControl="controlname"
    VaryByCustom="browser | customstring" VaryByHeader="headers"
    VaryByParam="parametername" %>
```

Let's look at some of the most important parameters in more detail:

❏   Duration specifies the duration in seconds that the content be allowed to cache for.

❏   Location is used to specify the locations that are allowed to cache the page. When set to Server, only the server running the application is allowed to cache the page. A setting of Downstream means that any intervening network proxies are allowed to cache a copy of the page. When set to Client, the browser is allowed to cache the page locally. When set to Any, any of these caches may be used. Alternatively, you could specify a setting of None, which stops caching from being used.

❏   VaryByControl allows controls to be cached on the server, so that they do not have to be rendered every time a page is requested. Using this parameter caches the control specified as it appears on the page. For example, if you have a control that displays a list of news items, these could be cached for ten minutes, simply by caching the control for that long.

❏   VaryByCustom allows you to specify whether you want to store different versions of the cache for different browser, or to vary by a specified string. If this parameter is given the value browser, different caches are created by browser name and major version, which allows you to have different cached versions of a page for different pages. This is particularly useful when you need to target output differently for different browsers or different devices. It allows you to specify in detail the parts of a page that you want to cache. If the browser is given the setting CustomString, then you can use VaryByCustom to distinguish between different versions of cached pages by using the Vary HTTP header's content. It works by matching any word you store there against a semicolon-separated list contained with VaryByCustom. Whenever VaryByCustom finds a match, it will cache a new version of the page.

❏   VaryByHeader enables you to cache pages specified by different HTTP headers, using a semicolon-separated list. When this parameter is set to multiple headers, the output cache will contain a different version of the requested document for each specified header.

❏ `VaryByParam` allows you to vary the caching requirements by specific parameters in the form of a semicolon-separated list of strings. By default, these strings correspond to a query string value, or to a parameter sent with the `POST()` method. When this parameter is set to multiple values, the output cache will contain a different version of the requested document for each specified value. Possible values include `none`,`*`, and any valid query string or `POST()` parameter name. This attribute is required when you output cache ASP.NET pages or user controls. A parser error will occur if you don't include it. If you want the complete page cached at all times then set the value to `none`. If you want to have a new output cache created for each of the possible setting of the parameters, then set the value to `*`.

Let's quickly look at how this works.

Try It Out   Output Caching

1. Open Web Matrix, create a new ASPX file, and call it `Servertime.aspx`. Type the following code into the All window:

```
<%@ Page Language="VB" %>
<script  runat = "server">
Function ServerTime() As String
   ServerTime = System.DateTime.Now.ToLongTimeString()
End Function
</script>

The time on your web server is : <% Response.Write(ServerTime)%>
```

2. This code displays the current time on your Web server. Call it up in your browser and verify that the code is working as depicted in Figure 15-4. After a couple of seconds, click your browser's refresh button and watch the numbers change:

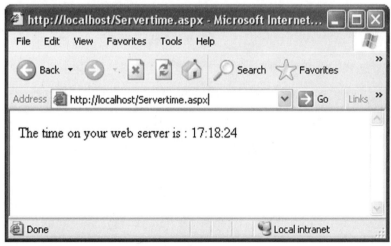

Figure 15-4

3. Now, add the following page directive at the top of your code:

```
<%@ OutputCache Duration="60" VaryByParam="none" %>
<%@ Page Language="VB" %>
<script  runat = "server">
Function ServerTime() As String
  ServerTime = System.DateTime.Now.ToLongTimeString()
End Function
</script>

The time on your web server is : <% Response.Write(ServerTime)%>
```

4. Save your file as `CachedServerTime.aspx` and call it up in your browser again. To begin with, everything looks the same; the code displays the time as before. But when you click the refresh button, the time *doesn't* change, it remains the same. In fact it will remain the same for 60 seconds. Try it and see!

How It Works

The `Servertime.aspx` code example is very simple. It runs a function called `ServerTime()` on your server to get the server's time, and then returns it formatted as a string. This returned information is then displayed on the screen using a line of HTML and some in-line ASP.NET tags:

```
<script runat = "server">
Function ServerTime() As String
  ServerTime = System.DateTime.Now.ToLongTimeString()
End Function
</script>

The time on your web server is : <%=ServerTime %>
```

This code does not specify that the page should be cached, so the server processes it anew each time the page is called. When you click your browser's refresh button, it processes the code and gives you the newly processed result. The time changes each time you press the refresh button.

When the page directive is added as follows, this is no longer the case:

```
<%@ OutputCache Duration="60" VaryByParam="none" %>
```

We're instructing the server to cache the output generated by your request for a period of 60 seconds. Any subsequent page requests within that period will be served with the cached version, so the time will remain the same until the cached page expires and it is processed anew. The `VaryByParam` attribute you saw earlier is set to `"none"` in this example, meaning that the same page will be delivered from the cache regardless of the parameters delivered with the request (our example is quite basic; it doesn't have any parameters).

Fragment Caching

This allows the caching of portions of a response generated by any request that includes user controls. Sometimes it's not practical to cache an entire page. For example, you may have a section for ad vertisements on a page, or some personalization features that have to be unique to every user). In such cases you may still want portions of the page to be cached and the remainder to be generated programmatically for each user. If this is the case, it is worthwhile to create user controls frequently for those portions that do not change, so that they can be created once and cached for a defined time period.

For example, to cache all the controls defined in an ASCX (user control) source file, just include this directive in the control itself:

```
<%@ OutputCache Duration="60" VaryByParam="none" %>
```

You don't have to place the `OutputCache` directive in the page in which the controls are called (the ASPX page). All other controls included in the ASCX will automatically be cached for 60 seconds.

If you wanted to cache each of the possible variations of your control's properties, you'd use this directive:

```
<%@ OutputCache Duration="60" VaryByParam="*" %>
```

The asterisk (*) directs the Output Cache to cache a page for every parameter property returned by your control.

The Cache Object

The third and most complex method of caching is to use the ASP.NET Cache object. Unlike the first two methods, the Cache object doesn't store pages, instead it stores data, which is viewed frequently and doesn't change that frequently between views.

The Cache object came into being as developers continually used the Application object as a cache. This was because classic ASP provided little support for caching mechanisms over and above the Application and Session objects. When developers used the Application or Session objects, they had to write code to manage the creation and disposal of data. In ASP.NET more advanced caching capabilities are introduced in the form of a programmable Cache object. Efficient use of ASP.NET's caching capabilities can allow you to balance the use of resources such as PC memory and database connections against the need to generate client pages quickly.

In ASP.NET a Cache object was introduced to provide a temporary repository for information. This comes along with the ability to refresh the cache and expire old information from it via a number of possible policies. The first policy is based on a date or timestamp – when a particular date or time is reached, the cache is expired. The second involves linking the Cache to a file and then expiring it if the file is updated or amended in anyway. The third policy is to link the Cache to another Cache via a master key, and then expire the items in all linked caches if an item changes in just one of them.

As the Cache object has quietly "sneaked" in the backdoor in ASP.NET, we'll take a little time discussing it now.

Cache Creation

When creating a cache, you'll find that the Cache object uses the same intuitive syntax as the other ASP objects:

```
Cache("NewCache") = "Confidential Information"
```

Here we create a Cache called NewCache and store the value Confidential Information in it. However, it's more effectively used when it stores objects. If we created a class Addressbook that contains the properties name, address, phone, and email, we could store the contents of this class in our Cache as follows:

```
Dim newAddressBook as New AddressBook()
newAddressBook.name = "Rheingold Cabriole"
newAddressBook.address = "673 Chellingworth Place, Morningtown"
newAddressBook.email = "Rheingold.Cabriole@fabemails.com"
newAddressBook.phone = "333-444-555"
Cache("address") = newAddressBook
```

One major application of the Cache object is to use it to store datasets. For example, the Cache object could point to the contents of an XML document, such as the following address.xml file:

```
<?xml version="1.0"?>
<address>
 <name> Rheingold Cabriole </name>
 <address>673 Chellingworth Place, Morningtown </address>
 <email>Rheingold.Cabriole@fabemails.com</email>
 <phone>333-444-555</phone>
</address>
```

If this was saved on the root of the C:\ drive, then the following code could be used to store it in the Cache object:

```
Dim XMLFileDataSet As DataSet
XMLFileDataSet.ReadXML("C:\address.xml")
Cache("XMLDoc") = XMLFileDataSet
```

This is known as the *implicit* method of insertion, where key-value pairs are inserted into the cache – the key being XMLDoc and the value being the contents of XMLFileDataset. However, there is also another method of insertion, known as *explicit* insertion. To do an explicit insert, use the Cache.Insert() method to add the XML file you created:

```
Dim XMLFileDataSet As DataSet
XMLFileDataSet.ReadXML("C:\address.xml")
Cache.Insert("XMLDoc", XMLFileDataSet, nothing)
```

It does exactly the same thing as the implicit method, but uses a more powerful syntax. You might notice that there is a third argument present in the method. This third parameter allows us to specify and set up a dependency (in this example we set it to nothing). Dependencies allow us to create expiration policies for the cache. We're also not just restricted to inserting datasets; we can add files or any other objects or items that don't change regularly. Next, let's talk about retrieving information from the cache.

Cache Retrieval

When retrieving information, all you need to do is follow the exact reverse of the procedure we just outlined. With our `AddressBook` class, you'd create an instance of the class and read the contents of the cache into it:

```
Dim newAddressBook as New AddressBook()
newAddressBook = CType(Cache.Item("address"), AddressBook)
```

The `CType()` function converts the Cache Item into something that can be stored in the Address book class. Here we assume that the contents of the cache are appropriate for storage in that class you have to store something in the class of the correct type.

You could then display the contents of the Cache object in a label control called `MyLabel1`, as follows:

```
myLabel1.Text = newAddressBook.Name & "<br>" & newAddressBook.Address & "<br>" &
newAddressBook.Phone & "<br>" & newAddressBook.Email
```

However, due to the transient nature of caches, it is best that you first check to see if anything is already in the cache:

```
If Not Cache.Item("address") Is Nothing Then
  newAddressBook = CType(Cache.Item("address"), AddressBook)
myLabel1.Text = newAddressBook.Name & "<br>" &
newAddressBook.Address & "<br>" & newAddressBook.Phone & "<br>" &
newAddressBook.Email
Else
  myLabel1.Text = "Cache is Empty"
End If
```

Having seen how we can place and retrieve items from the cache, it's time to move on to the crux of the tutorial – how things can be removed from the Cache object.

Cache Removal

To remove items from the Cache object, you just need to specify the `Cache.Remove()` method:

```
Cache.Remove("address")
```

However, this would mean using the Cache object just like an Application object and nullifying the main advantages that the Cache object enjoys over the Application object – expiration policies. It is more beneficial to be able to tell the Cache object when to expire, or under what circumstances to expire the contents of the cache.

Expiration Information

There are three common ways in which information can be expired and we shall look briefly at each of them:

- ❏ **Timestamp Expiration**: Information is removed when a pre-specified time (or date) is reached.

- ❏ **File Dependency**: Information is expired when a file is updated or amended in some way.

- ❏ **Key Dependency**: Cache items are commonly linked together and when information is expired in one cache then it is often desirable that information in your own linked cache should also be jettisoned. This linking can be achieved via a set of cache keys.

TimeStamp Expiration

The most straightforward type of expiration policy is via the timestamp. There are two separate ways in which information can be removed via timestamp. The first is by the setting of an absolute date (or time) when the cache must be expired. The second is by the means of a timescale within which the cache must be updated, for instance you can specify that this is to be 30 minutes after the object was last updated or accessed.

The absolute method of expiration takes two extra arguments. One is for the absolute time of expiration and the second specifies the time within which the cache must have been last visited. To insert our XML file into the Cache and expire it in 5 minutes, no matter what, would look like this:

```
Cache.Insert("XMLDoc", XMLFileDataSet, nothing, DateTime.Now.AddMinutes(5),
TimeSpan.Zero)
```

We have five parameters specified here – the syntax for `Cache.Insert` is as follows:

```
Cache.Insert(FileName, DataSet, Dependency, DateTime, TimeSpan)
```

- ❏ `FileName` specifies the name of the XML document.
- ❏ `DataSet` specifies the name of the DataSet.
- ❏ `Dependency Type` specifies the type of Dependency.
- ❏ `DateTime` specifies the date and time of when to expire the cache.
- ❏ `TimeSpan` specifies the period of time elapsed after the cache was last accessed, before the cache should be expired.

After specifying the file name and dataset contents, the dependency type is set to `nothing` once again, as there are no dependencies. We use the `AddMinutes()` method to specify a time 5 minutes in advance of the current time. As we don't wish to expire the cache if it isn't updated, the second argument is set to `TimeSpan.Zero`, which is just the syntax used to indicate that we don't wish to use a time period within which the cache must have been last updated.

When specifying a time within which the cache must have been visited, the method looks very similar, it's just that we tweak the last two argument's values as follows:

```
Cache.Insert("XMLDoc", XMLFileDataSet, nothing, Cache.NoAbsoluteExpiration,
TimeSpan.FromSeconds(300))
```

Here the absolute expiration value is set to NoAbsoluteExpiration (in other words it will never expire) while the maximum value is set to 300 seconds (5 minutes) from when the cache was last refreshed. In this way the cache will expire when it hasn't been accessed within the last five minutes. If it is accessed (even if at 4 minutes 59 seconds) again it will have a lifespan of 5 minutes. This is called *sliding time expiration*.

File Dependency

With *file dependency*, things get a little more complex. You have to create a CacheDependency object. This object is given an argument that specifies the file you wish to associate with your cache. We can set up this dependency by creating an instance of the CacheDependency object and reading the filename into it. We then must also read the contents of the file into the dataset:

```
Dim FileDepend As New CacheDependency("C:\address.xml")
Dim XMLDataSet As New DataSet
XMLDataSet.ReadXML("C:\address.xml")
Cache.Insert("address", XMLDataSet, FileDepend)
```

Instead of setting the third argument to nothing, as in the time expiration policy, we set it to the name of our CacheDependency object. In this way, whenever the time or date the file was last amended, the contents of the cache expired as well. We can demonstrate the use of file dependency now. In the next example we will cache an XML document relating to our fictitious entrant, Rheingold Cabriole, then change the document, and use a file dependency to force the expiration of the contents of the cache.

Try It Out   Creating a File Dependency

1. Open up Web Matrix and create an XML document called address.xml in the C:\BegASPNet11\ch15 folder. Enter code as follows:

```
<?xml version="1.0"?>
<address>
 <name>Rheingold Cabriole</name>
 <address>673 Chellingworth Place, Morningtown </address>
 <phone>333-444-555</phone>
 <email> Rheingold.Cabriole@fabemails.com</email>
</address>
```

2. Next create the following ASP.NET page and name it cachefile.aspx:

```
<%@ Page Language="vb" Debug="true" %>
<%@ Import Namespace="System.Data" %>
<%@ Import Namespace="System.XML" %>
<html>
<head>
<script language="vb" runat="server">

Sub Create(sender As Object, e As EventArgs)
 Dim XMLFileDataSet As New DataSet
 XMLFileDataSet.ReadXML("C:\BegASPNet11\ch15\address.xml")
 Dim filedependency As New CacheDependency("C:\BegASPNet11\ch15\address.xml")
 Cache.Insert("address",XMLFileDataSet, filedependency)
 MyLabel1.Text="Cache Full"
End Sub
```

```
Sub Display(sender As Object, e As EventArgs)
  Dim myAddressBook as New DataSet()
  If (IsNothing(Cache("address"))) Then
          grid1.DataSource = nothing
          grid1.DataBind()
          myLabel1.Text = "Cache Empty"
  Else
          myAddressBook = CType(Cache.Item("address"), DataSet)
          grid1.DataSource = myAddressBook
          grid1.DataBind()
  End If
End Sub

</script>
</head>
<body>
<form id="form1" runat="server">
<asp:label id="mylabel1" runat="server" />
<asp:datagrid id="grid1" runat="server" />
<br/>
<input type="submit" Value="Create Cache" OnServerClick="Create" runat="server" />
<input type="submit" Value="Display Cache" OnServerClick="Display" runat="server"
/>
</form>
</body>
</html>
```

3. Run this on your browser and press the Create Cache button followed by clicking of the Display Cache button and you will see the screen depicted in Figure 15-5:

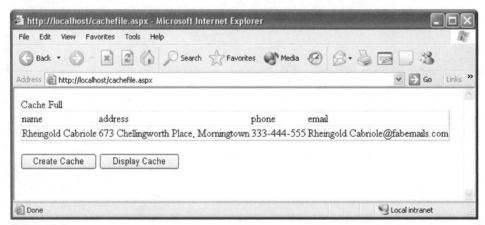

Figure 15-5

4. Keeping the browser open, go back and change the code in address.xml to read as follows:

```xml
<?xml version="1.0"?>
<address>
 <name>Rheingold Cabriole</name>
 <address>135 Tabletop Drive, Workville </address>
 <phone>333-444-555</phone>
 <email>Rheingold.Cabriole@fabemails.com</email>
</address>
```

5. Save it and now go back and click the Display Cache button only (without refreshing). View the browser and you will see the screen depicted in Figure 15-6:

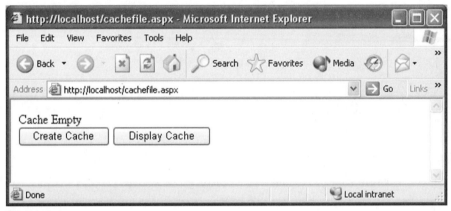

Figure 15-6

As you have updated the file, it automatically expired the contents of the cache. You must then reload the cache object using Create Cache to see the updated contents.

How It Works

Basically, the code is very straightforward. For the event code for the **Create Cache** button, we create a dataset and read into it the contents of our file `address.xml`:

```
Dim XMLFileDataSet As New DataSet
XMLFileDataSet.ReadXML("C:\BegASPNet11\ch15\address.xml")
```

We then create a `CacheDependency` object and link it to this file:

```
Dim filedependency As New CacheDependency("C:\BegASPNet11\ch15\address.xml")
```

We then create an item called "address" using the dataset and file dependency, and set the label control text to `cache full`:

```
Cache.Insert("address",XMLFileDataSet, filedependency)
MyLabel1.Text="Cache Full"
```

For the code for the **Display Cache** button, we create a new dataset called `Addressbook` and then check to see if there is an item in the cache:

```
Dim myAddressBook as New DataSet()
If (IsNothing(Cache("address"))) Then
```

If there is no item, we bind the grid to nothing and display `cache empty`:

```
grid1.DataSource = null
grid1.DataBind()
myLabel1.Text = "Cache Empty"
```

If there is an item in the cache, we convert into a dataset and bind it to our data grid control:

```
Else
        myAddressBook = CType(Cache.Item("address"), DataSet)
        grid1.DataSource = myAddressBook
        grid1.DataBind()
End If
```

It's only a small use, but you can see how the Cache object can be used to monitor an XML document and see when it has been changed, to make sure the cache is expired if the document is updated. In fact, in this example the cached object is created from XML file and file dependency is also placed on the same XML file. It is also possible to cache content from a different file, as it is not always dependent on the same source file.

It is possible to use file and key dependencies together, so that if the contents of one file changed and several files were affected, then *all* files could be expired automatically from the cache. This is beyond the scope of our tutorial, but you now have a solid grounding in the fundamentals of the Cache object.

Key Dependency

The last method of expiration is *key dependency*. It is similar to file dependency, but is slightly more complex. It is known as key dependency because it is based upon a key rather than the cached item itself. If you wanted to expire something from the cache when another related item in the cache had been changed, you would use a key dependency. It is done in two stages:

❑ Creating the key based upon a cached item

❑ Mapping the key to another dependent item

For instance, if you had an address and a phone number for that address in the cache, if the address changed, then in all likelihood, you'd want the phone number changed as well. You could use a key dependency to do this.

The following code would create a key dependency:

```
Cache("addressKey") = "1273 Abledown Road "
Dim keydepend(0) As String
keydepend(0) = "addressKey"
Dim keydependency As New CacheDependency(nothing, keydepend)
Cache.Insert("phone","123-456-789", keydependency)
```

We create a cache item for the phone number and then link this to a cache address item. This means that if the phone item changes then the address item should also be expired. You don't have to create one key dependency, you could create many dependencies, so that other details such as fax number and postcode are removed automatically when the address item in the cache is changed.

To create a key dependency, once again you have to create a `CacheDependency` object, but this time by passing it two parameters. The second parameter is passed an array containing the dependency key, the key itself being the name of the first cache we created ("address"). The first parameter is left blank because it is used normally to pass a file name or path and this information isn't need here. Then you can insert a name-value pair into the Cache along with an argument that specifies our `CacheDependency` key. In effect, when we create a second cache item, we add the `CacheDependency` key to specify a link to the first cache item

Let's transperse this code into a fully working example.

Try It Out   Creating A Key Dependency

Let's create an ASPX page with three buttons: one which fills the cache with the two items, one that displays the contents, and one that removes one of the cache items.

1. Open Web Matrix, create an ASP.NET page called `cachekey.aspx` and enter the following code into the All view, removing all existing code:

```
<%@ Page Language="vb" Debug="true" %>
<html>
<head>
<script language="vb" runat="server">

Sub Create(sender As Object, e As EventArgs)
```

```
Cache("address") = "444 Horror House"
Dim keydep(0) As String
keydep(0) = "address"
Dim keydependency As New CacheDependency(nothing, keydep)
Cache.Insert("phone","123-456", keydependency)
MyLabel1.Text="Cache Full"
End Sub

Sub Display(sender As Object, e As EventArgs)
 If (IsNothing(Cache("phone"))) Then
        myLabel1.Text = "Cache Empty"
 Else
        myLabel1.Text = "Address:" & Cache("address") & "<br>Phone: " &
Cache("phone")
 End If
End Sub

Sub Change(sender As Object, e As EventArgs)
 Cache.Remove("address")
 myLabel1.Text = "Address removed"
End Sub
</script>
</head>
<body>
<form id="form1" runat="server">
<asp:label id="mylabel1" runat="server" />
<br/>
<input type="submit" Value="Create Cache" OnServerClick="Create" runat="server" />
<input type="submit" Value="Display Cache" OnServerClick="Display" runat="server"
/>
<input type="submit" Value="Change Cache" OnServerClick="Change" runat="server" />
</form>
</body>
</html>
```

Take care that `Cache("address")` and `keydepend(0)="address"` both have the same case, otherwise you will get an error.

2. Run this page in the browser and you should see the screen depicted in Figure 15-7. Click the Create Cache and Display Cache buttons in turn:

Figure 15-7

3. You can see quite clearly that there are two items in the cache. Click Change Cache followed by Display Cache, and you will see that nothing is in the cache now as depicted in Figure 15-8:

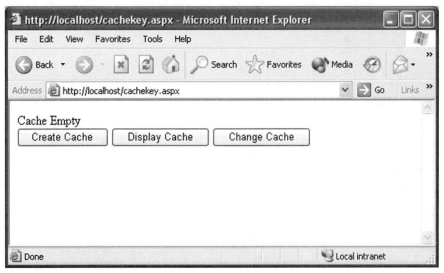

Figure 15-8

How It Works

Our Create Cache event handler starts by creating a cache ("address") item:

```
Cache("address") = "444 Horror House"
```

Next we create a key dependency based on Cache("address"):

```
Dim keydep(0) As String
keydep(0) = "address"
Dim keydependency As New CacheDependency(nothing, keydep)
```

We create a second cache item "phone" and link it to the first and display the message "Cache Full" in your text control:

```
Cache.Insert("phone","123-456", keydependency)
MyLabel1.Text="Cache Full"
```

The Display Cache item just checks to see if there is anything in the cache phone item and displays it if there is something or the message "Cache Empty" if nothing is found:

```
Sub Display(sender As Object, e As EventArgs)
  If (IsNothing(Cache("phone"))) Then
        myLabel1.Text = "Cache Empty"
  Else
        myLabel1.Text = "Address:" & Cache("address") & "<br>Phone: " &
Cache("phone")
  End If
End Sub
```

The third event handler deletes one of the cache items. Clicking the Change Cache button removes the Address item only:

```
Sub Change(sender As Object, e As EventArgs)
  Cache.Remove("address")
  myLabel1.Text = "Address removed"
End Sub
```

However, when we click Display Cache, we check only the contents of the phone item:

```
...
If (IsNothing(Cache("phone"))) Then
        myLabel1.Text = "Cache Empty"
  Else
  ...
```

Nothing is displayed; the key dependency has ensured that both items have been deleted from the cache.

Cache Priorities

On top of the expiration policies, it is also possible to set the relative importance of items within the cache to each other, so that items can be quickly dumped if memory is low or if performance is really dragging. When you create an item, there are an extra couple of arguments you can add that specify in relative terms, the priority of the cache item and how slowly that priority should decline:

```
Cache.Insert("XMLFile", XMLDataSet, nothing, DateTime.Now.AddMinutes(5),
TimeSpan.Zero, CacheItemPriority.High, CacheItemPriorityDecay.Slow)
```

The items in the cache Priority can be set in order either as `Low`, `BelowNormal`, `Normal`, `AboveNormal`, `High`, and `NotRemovable`. The speed at which they decay can be set as follows: `Fast`, `Medium`, `Default`, `Slow`, and `Never`. This means that the cache expiration can be determined separately from the expiration policies by the system if necessary, and contents of the caches can be managed dynamically.

The Cache object offers a lot of features over and above the Application object, such as the creation of dependencies on files or other caches as well as the setting of priorities. It's possible to link together file dependencies and key dependencies, so that, say when an item in one file was changed, a whole load of files could be expired from the cache. Judicious use of this object in place of the Application object could make your applications a whole lot faster and more efficient.

Tips and Tricks

No configuration guidelines would be complete without offering a list of optimization tips. Here's a brief listing of the tips and examples included in the Microsoft QuickStart samples. If you've not got these installed, they're available from the following sites:

- ❑   http://www.gotdotnet.com/quickstart/aspplus/

- ❑   http://docs.aspng.com/quickstart/aspplus/default.aspx

- ❑   http://aspalliance.com/quickstart/aspplus/

- ❑   http://www.dotnetjunkies.com/quickstart/default.aspx

Don't worry if you don't understand them all! They are included here so that you can refer back to them throughout your development as a programmer. Think of them as a quick reference guide, that you'll still be able to use as a refresher in the years to come.

- ❑   *Disable Session State when it is not needed*. Maintaining session state consumes memory and processing time. If you don't need to recall or modify session variables in a page, disable session state for that page.

- ❑   *Choose your Session State provider carefully*. If you are running just one Web server, the fastest and most economical mode of maintaining state is In-Process. Only if you are running a Web farm on more than one machine should you even consider using SQL Server or the State Server.

- ❑   *Avoid excessive round trips to the server*. Round tripping to the server takes time and server resources. You should only round-trip to the server when storing or retrieving data. You can program your controls to generate client-side code, and still use ASP.NET's efficient server controls. Use client-side processing to save server-processing time as much as you can.

❑ *Use Page.IsPostback to avoid extra work on a round trip.* For example, you can use `IsPostback` to determine whether a dataset needs to be generated. Generating data is expensive in terms of processing time. Generating one query on first access and another one on a `POST` can cost you processing time.

❑ *Use server controls sparingly and appropriately.* Even though server controls are very cool and afford you incredible event-handling capabilities, for simple displays a simple rendering using `Response.Write` will be far more efficient.

❑ *Avoid excessive server control viewstate.* The more data you're passing back and forth between the client and the server, the larger the viewstate gets, and the longer it takes for the more resources you're consuming. Like session state, turn this feature off if you don't need to keep state on a page.

❑ *Use System.Text.StringBuilder for string concatenation.* When you modify a string object using the traditional concatenation methods, you add a new string object for every modification made. This adds up! The new `StringBuilder` object is much more efficient because you use only one object no matter how many modifications you perform on the string.

❑ *Use the page Strict setting.* The line `<%@ Page Language="VB" Strict="true" %>` can be your best friend! This forces early-binding of your code, which in turn forces your code to be more efficient. In other words, all of the variables are checked to see if they have been declared up front. By having correct typing enforced you prevent costly, inefficient, late-binding (waiting until a variable is used before checking to see it is bound to a data type). A side benefit is that `Strict` forces you to declare your variables, preventing misplaced values in your code.

❑ *Use SQL stored procedures for data access.* In the .NET Framework, the `SqlConnection` class allows you to have even larger performance gains, since it can actually execute native SQL Server code. Now, not only do you gain the speed of stored procedures but, also, they are executed natively. Performance gains are estimated at 200 to 300% over `OleDb` or `Odbc` connections!

❑ *Use SqlDataReader for a fast-forward, read-only data cursor.* `SqlDataReader` provides what was known in the ASP world as a 'firehose' cursor, which is much faster than other cursors available. In addition, `SqlDataReader` reads data directly from a database connection using Tabular Data Streams (TDS), and allows you to bind server controls directly to data.

❑ *Use Caching features wherever possible.* In high-traffic situations, caching data can save you a lot of processing time, since the data will be served from RAM instead of using precious processing cycles.

❑ *Enable Web gardening for multiprocessor computers.* Hey, why encourage idleness? Enabling the use of all processors available makes sense, since the more processing power available to your applications, the more efficient your Web server will be.

❑ *Do not forget to disable Debug mode.* Having a compiler watching for errors is the most expensive process that a processor can undertake! Never enable debugging on a production box!

Summary

This chapter has covered a lot of ground in the vast topic of configuration and optimization. We looked at `machine.config` and `web.config` and saw how they were structured and their settings hierarchically inherited. Then we looked in more detail at some of the specific settings within those files that you can use to improve the performance, security, and user friendliness of your applications.

Next, we moved on to look at how we could increase our server's performance through the use of output and fragment caching so that our pages didn't need to be compiled as frequently, before looking at how the cache object can be used to store information that is frequently visited. The chapter concluded with a reference list of recommended performance optimization tips.

Exercises

1. If you didn't know how a particular setting of an element in the `config` file where would you look to find them?

2. Create a "friendly" custom error page for a file not found error and set the relevant `config` file so that it appears whenever a 404 error message is generated.

3. Create a page with two label controls that both display the time and create an output cache that lasts for 30 minutes and caches just one of the controls.

4. Create a cache that stores the following information "MyFavouriteColour = Orange" and expires it if it hasn't been updated for 3 minutes.

5. Create a cache that will expire whenever the contents of one of three files `XMLDoc1.xml`, `XMLDoc2.xml`, and `XMLDoc3.xml` is changed. Note they can all contain the following code:

```xml
<?xml version="1.0"?>
<address>
 <name>Rheingold Cabriole</name>
 <address>673 Chellingworth Place, Morningtown </address>
 <phone>333-444-555</phone>
 <email> Rheingold.Cabriole@fabemails.com</email>
</address>
```

16

Web Services

In the days before the Internet, if you wanted to research a subject, you would visit a library to find a book on the topic, or browse the relevant periodicals to find the latest articles. While this is still quite possible (if you like that sort of thing), it isn't usually necessary. As the Internet connects computers containing all sorts of different data sources, it frequently provides us with a one-stop-shop for whatever information we might need. In a sense, the Internet has become a *virtual library* for Web users.

Over the years, Web developers created isolated Web applications and would often produce code merely duplicating what many other programmers had already done elsewhere in their own applications. To overcome this, many developers began using technologies (such as COM and DCOM) that would allow them to build code components once and bundle them up so they could be shared across multiple applications by many developers. However, in practice these components had some fundamental drawbacks, since they had to be physically distributed and then explicitly registered on each user's machine. It was possible to share logic around, but it wasn't easy.

The logical next step for the Web was to use the infrastructure to make specific bits of the information available without requiring a user to download a whole component or application. The ASP.NET Web Services model provides a simple, straightforward way to do precisely this. For example, if a developer wanted a weather forecast for their flight simulator, or the latest currency rates for their economic models, rather than having to program the logic, or download a component to do this, they can access the relevant Web Service and glean the necessary information for their own application.

Web Services enable developers to share application logic and therefore reduce the overall amount of code duplication. They also provide us with the ability to easily access information from different sources, because Web Services make information available as pure text. Thus, Web Services truly make the Web a 'virtual library' for Web developers.

This chapter will show how easy it is to create and use ASP.NET Web Services. The topics covered are:

❑ What is a Web Service and its role in the .NET Framework

❑ How to create and use a Web Service

❑ How to describe a Web Service's behavior using *Web Services Description Language* (*WSDL*)

❑ How users can discover which Web Services are available using *Universal Description, Discovery, and Integration* (*UDDI*)

❑ What you need to consider when building a Web Service

What Is a Web Service?

Technically speaking, a Web Service is a component of programmable application logic that can be accessed using standard Web protocols. It's quite similar to the server controls considered earlier on in the book. The big difference is that it lets you access all of its functionality across the Web, whereas server controls only access functionality on the *local* Web server. For example, if I browsed a calendar control, this would be all done on the local Web server, whereas if I accessed a stock price, this could come from any remote Web site that listed stock prices as a Web Service. In principle, anyone who can browse the Web can see and use a Web Service.

Think of a Web Service as a *black box* resource that accepts requests from a consumer (an application running on the Web client), performs a specific task, and returns the results of that task. In some respects, a search engine such as Google (www.google.com) is a kind of Web Service – you submit a search expression, and it compiles a list of matching sites, and returns the list to your browser.

Currently the term Web Service is something of a buzzword within the sphere of software development, thanks to a number of new protocols that have opened up the scope of what we can expect Web Services to do. XML plays a central role in all these technologies. Most of the time, you'll find that when people talk about Web Services, they're implicitly referring to XML Web Services. This is now so prevalent that many people believe that all Web Services use XML by definition. *XML Web Services* are something you can expect to hear a great deal about, now and well into the future.

There's a very important distinction between a Web Service like Google and the kind of XML Web Service that will be discussed here: on Google, *you* submit the search expression, and *you* read the list of sites that gets sent back. The browser provides you with a textbox, and parses the response stream so that it looks nice – it doesn't actually *understand* the information you've submitted, let alone the HTML that Google sends back.

If you're using an XML Web Service, you can assume the results will be returned as some kind of XML document, with information that's explicitly structured and self-describing. It's therefore quite straightforward to write a program that interprets these results and perhaps even uses the results to formulate a new submission.

ASP.NET makes it very easy to build XML Web Services, and just as easy to use them – ultimately you only need to reference the Web Service in your code, and you can use it just as if it were a local component. As with normal components, you don't need to know anything about how the service functions, only the tasks it can do, the type of information it needs to do them, and the type of results you'll be getting back.

You can use Web Service methods to do just about anything from adding two numbers together to writing information to a database. The logic they use can be as simple or as complex as you need it to be.

Let's create a simple Web Service to demonstrate just how easy it is.

Try It Out Creating Our First Web Service

In this example, we'll make a Web Service that takes a string input and returns a greeting that includes the name specified in the input.

1. Open up Web Matrix and choose the **XML Web Service** option. Replace `NewFile.asmx` (seen in Figure 16-1) with `greetings.asmx` and enter Greetings into the **Class** textbox and Ch16 into the namespace textbox:

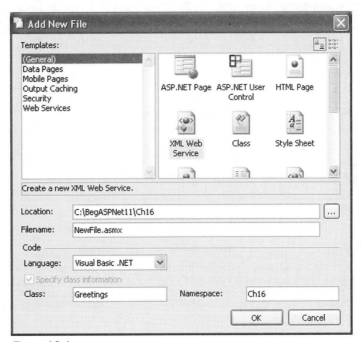

Figure 16-1

2. In the window that opens up, add the following code:

```vb
<%@ WebService Language="vb" Class="Greetings"%>
Imports System
Imports System.Web.Services
Imports System.Xml.Serialization
Public Class Greetings
    <WebMethod(Description:="Returns a greeting using the name passed in")> _
    Public Function Hello(ByVal Name As String) As String
        Return "Hello, " & Name & ". Have a great day!"
    End Function
End Class
```

3. Open the file in your browser, and you should see something like Figure 16-2:

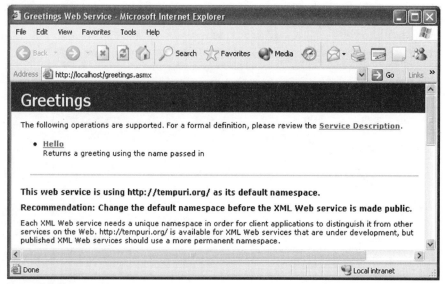

Figure 16-2

4. Following the Hello hyperlink, this page will also include a warning message about using the http://tempuri.org default namespace. It will also display information on how to use the Web Service directly from SOAP, and from HTTP GET and HTTP POST requests.

5. Click on the bulleted Hello hyperlink – this is the name of the method defined in the Greetings class. A new page will be displayed; this allows us to enter a name; see Figure 16-3:

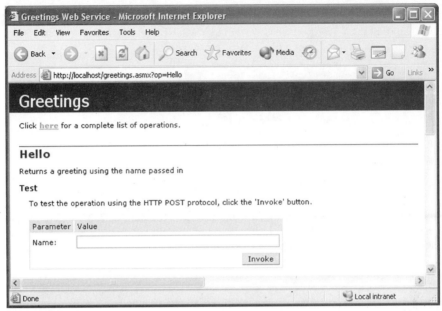

Figure 16-3

6. Enter your name in the textbox adjacent to the Name parameter, and click the Invoke button to call your Web Service's `Hello` method. The following result (Figure 16-4) should now appear in a new browser window:

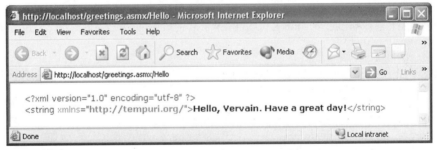

Figure 16-4

7. That's it! The Web Service is now working on our local machine.

How It Works

The first line shows that the Web Service is written in VB .NET. We also declare our class name as `Greetings`, which will be important when a consumer wants to use it:

```
<%@ WebService Language="vb" Class="Greetings"%>
```

The next lines give us access to objects that are needed to build a Web Service:

```
Imports System
Imports System.Web.Services
Imports System.Xml.Serialization
```

Next, we have some logic to actually define the Web Service's functionality. Within the `Public Class Greetings` declaration (notice the name here matches the one in the `WebService` declaration), we define a `Hello` function that simply returns a string based on the parameter `Name`. We prefix this method declaration with a `<WebMethod()>` attribute – this is how we specify that it's to be exposed as a Web method, making the function visible to the outside world:

```
Public Class Greetings
  < WebMethod ()> _
  Public Function Hello(Name As String) As String
    Return "Hello, " & Name & ". Have a great day!"
  End Function
End Class
```

With just a few lines of code, we've created a functioning Web Service. We didn't need to specify a format for the result, or write any code to handle any network connections. We didn't even have to register it on the client – all we needed to know was the URL.

To conclude the first example, let's touch upon the warning message that appeared on the first page of the Web Service. It read as follows:

This Web Service is using http://tempuri.org/ as its default namespace. Recommendation: Change the default namespace before the XML Web Service is made public.

This warning means that if you do not make a practice of changing this namespace, your Web Service will be organized within the default `tempuri.org` namespace, which can become difficult to manage if there are multiple developers on a project who all use this default.

Namespaces were discussed in detail back in *Chapter 7*, but let's recap here. A namespace allows us, as developers, to organize our programming components into categories. For instance, imagine multiple Web Services that perform various tasks for specific parts of an application. If you were working on a 'Purchasing' module for an accounting system, you could specify a `Purchasing` namespace within all of your Web Service files pertaining to purchasing-related tasks.

That way, if you, in the *Purchasing* module, have a Web Service called `Reporting`, and Joe, in *Accounts Receivable* module, has a similarly named service, you can declare your namespace in applications that use it as `Purchasing.ReportingWS` while Joe can declare `AccountsReceivable.ReportingWS` and the two will not conflict.

Now, let's take a quick look at how the requests and responses are sent to and from a Web Service.

HTTP, XML, and Web Services

Chapter 3 discussed the basic mechanism by which information is passed back and forth across the Web, so that we can pop a URL in our browser's address bar and request a Web page from a remote server. We also pointed out that ASP.NET Web Services rely on the same mechanism – namely the HTTP Request-Response system. All the information submitted to a Web Service is sent as an HTTP Request. Likewise, any information received from the Web Service is sent as an HTTP Response as shown in Figure 16-5:

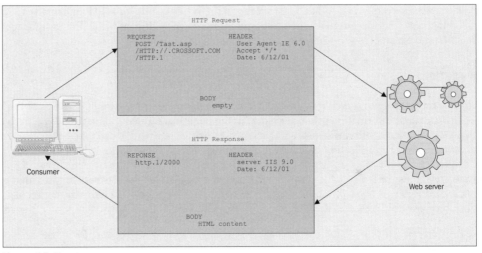

Figure 16-5

You've already seen that a typical Web Service operates by accepting input from a consumer and using it to produce a result that is sent back to the consumer as XML. When a consumer makes use of a Web Service's logic, it takes the form of an HTTP Request – that's why it's so easy to access from a Web browser, which is tailor-made for such requests. An HTTP Request consists of packets of information that are sent to the Web Service (wherever it may reside). These packets contain:

❑   Vital information such as the Web Service's URL and the fact that we're submitting a Request (that is, initiating a data exchange that requires a Response, rather than simply responding to someone else's Request)

❑   Details of the amount of information being sent

609

❏   The type of document we require back from the Web Service

❏   Information about the consumer, the request date, general configuration statistics, and the data itself

The Web Service will return an HTTP Response with:

❏   A return address for the consumer, and the fact that it's submitting a Response and so doesn't expect any further action from the recipient

❏   A success or failure status code indicating whether or not the Web Service received a valid Request from the consumer

❏   Configuration information

❏   Any appropriate data

We can transmit HTTP Requests and Responses between a Web Service and a consumer as many times as we like, depending on how the interaction between the two has been designed.

So, how exactly does our submitted data get wrapped up in this bundle of HTTP information? As discussed in *Chapter 3*, there are two ways to submit information within an HTTP Request, using the GET and POST methods respectively – let's take a quick recap:

HTTP GET

This is the simplest way to send data to the client, and probably the most familiar to users of the Web. Simple unstructured information is bundled in with the page as a sequence of *name-value pairs*. These pairings are a simple way to combine all the values into a single string. We can use the Request.QueryString collection in our ASP.NET code to access these name-value pairs on the server.

When you tested the Greetings.Hello Web method, the built-in testing mechanism provided by ASP.NET used HTTP GET to submit the string Vervain to the Web Service. Here's the actual GET request that your browser used to access the Web Service:

```
GET /BegASPNET11/Ch16/greetings.asmx/Hello?Name=Vervain HTTP/1.1
Host: localhost
```

It specifies the GET method, states the requested page (including the directory path) along with your query string, and declares that it has structured the HTTP Request according to version 1.1 of HTTP. It then states the name of the host to which it wants the request submitted – in this case, the local machine. The resource requested is:

```
/BegASPNET11/Ch16/greetings.asmx/Hello?Name=Vervain
```

and using this path along with the Host value, we have a full URL:

```
localhost/BegASPNET11/Ch16/greetings.asmx/Hello?Name=Vervain
```

The corresponding Response simply specifies the content type we're returning (text/xml) along with the character set and content length. The body of the Response then contains the XML we saw earlier:

```
HTTP/1.1 200 OK
Content-Type: text/xml; charset=utf-8
Content-Length: 112

<?xml version="1.0" encoding="utf-8"?>
<string xmlns="http://tempuri.org/">
Hello, Vervain. Have a great day!</string>
```

> **Notice that the Response contains our desired message within a string, which is the return type specified in the function.**

The Response from the server is a 200 message, which is HTTP's success message.

> **Another common return code is 404, which indicates 'File not found'. Our HTTP Response from the server can also tell us information such as the Web server software, the number of bytes to expect, content type, and the type of cookie that will be set.**

Note that it's very easy to make a new request to our Web Service by simply editing the query string in the browser's address bar. You might like to try calling up your page again as follows:

http://localhost/BegASPNET11/Ch16/greetings.asmx/Hello?Name=my%20fine%20fellow

HTTP POST

While HTTP GET uses the end of the URL to pass its information from resource to resource, HTTP POST uses the body of the Request to carry the same name-value pairs. You can retrieve these values using the Request.Form collection in ASP.NET. If you use the POST method to send the information, it means that the information isn't visible in the URL. This provides a slightly more secure method, since it is possible to manipulate the name-value pairs when using the GET method, by just typing names and values into the query string in the address bar.

Here is an example of an equivalent POST message being sent to the Web server:

```
POST /5040/ch16/greetings.asmx/Hello HTTP/1.1
Host: localhost
Content-Type: application/x-www-form-urlencoded
Content-Length: 15
Name=Vervain
HTTP/1.1 200 OK
```

This time, the HTTP Request specifies the `POST` method before stating the page requested and the HTTP version. It states the host name and content type (usually this is `application/x-www-form-urlencoded`) and the content length, which now tells the server how many bytes' worth of name-value pairs are there. This is followed by the name-value pairs themselves, which are placed on a separate line. The corresponding response from the Web server is exactly the same as you saw when using the GET method, returning a simple XML document in the Response body, along with the result that our Web method placed inside a `<string>` element.

That's all well and good so far as it goes, but using either HTTP POST or GET is still rather limited. Since we ultimately want to use these Web methods to replace various local method calls in applications, we surely need to be able to pass things like data sets and other complex objects.

This is where XML comes into the picture. XML plays a vital role in Web Services, as it allows us to send simple, structured, self-describing data between many different computer platforms and setups.

Web Services therefore use XML to describe data sent from the consumer as well as that being returned. It can also be used to describe the parameters a Web Service expects, and how to find information on Web Services available to consumers on the Internet. Let's look into these topics in detail later in the chapter.

While XML is very easy to read and understand – handy when you debug the code – it can often be verbose. This is because even the simplest of data exchanges requires a significant amount of description (since while exchanging all types and structures of data, we must cater to the lowest common denominator). With a common protocol (HTTP/ HTTPS, or even SMTP) and a common language (XML) that transcends individual machine platforms and operating systems, Web Services can be a potentially powerful tool.

However, a drawback is that the common protocol HTTP was designed in mind for calling up only Web pages, and returning information as HTML. As already discussed, Web Services were built with the aim of returning more complex information than just Web pages. To handle the call and response of Web services, another protocol was needed.

Simple Object Access Protocol (SOAP)

The *Simple Object Access Protocol* provides an effective way to call Web Services remotely and to return information whether in the form of numeric, string variables, datasets, images, or even files. It wraps up the information inside an XML element known as a *SOAP envelope*, and frees us from most of the structural limitations imposed by the HTTP methods discussed earlier. You can send a request using a SOAP envelope and also receive a response with a SOAP envelope. Here's what a SOAP envelope making a request looks like:

```
POST /7337/ch16/greetings.asmx HTTP/1.1
Host: localhost
Content-Type: text/xml; charset=utf-8
Content-Length: length
SOAPAction: "http://tempuri.org/Hello"
<?xml version="1.0" encoding="utf-8"?>
<soap:Envelope
```

```
        xmlns:xsi="http://www.w3.org/2001/XMLSchema-instance"
        xmlns:xsd="http://www.w3.org/2001/XMLSchema"
        xmlns:soap="http://schemas.xmlsoap.org/soap/envelope/">
    <soap:Body>
      <Hello xmlns="http://tempuri.org/">
        <Name>Vervain</Name>
      </Hello>
    </soap:Body>
  </soap:Envelope>
```

As seen, the submitted string value `Vervain` is held in a `<Name>` element (identifying the specific parameter being specified in the Web method call) and this is nested within a `<Hello>` element (identifying the name of the method called). Admittedly, at this stage it hardly looks more complex than our previous Requests, but that's largely due to the fact that you're only passing a single string value. Once you start sending more complex items of data there will be more to see. When items such as data sets are sent, the SOAP envelope needs to be larger and more detailed to describe the information contained within.

Aside from being somewhat more explicit about your request, this approach also allows you to submit data in a well-defined structure. Even if you wanted to submit a huge array of complex data objects, the flexibility inherent within this SOAP envelope allows you to do it. Although the SOAP Request is submitted as part of an HTTP POST Request, it's totally separate and selfcontained.

> **As SOAP allows us to use other protocols, we're not tied to HTTP as a transport protocol. For example, it's quite possible to send this envelope to the Web Service via SMTP (that is, simply email it to the Web Service). While this is a fascinating and extremely useful option, it's beyond the scope of this book. If you're interested in finding out more, refer to *Professional ASP.NET 1.1*, Wiley (ISBN 0-7645-5890-0).**

The SOAP response takes a form similar to our request:

```
HTTP/1.1 200 OK
Content-Type: text/xml; charset=utf-8
Content-Length: length
<?xml version="1.0" encoding="utf-8"?>
<soap:Envelope
    xmlns:xsi="http://www.w3.org/2001/XMLSchema-instance"
    xmlns:xsd="http://www.w3.org/2001/XMLSchema"
    xmlns:soap="http://schemas.xmlsoap.org/soap/envelope/">
  <soap:Body>
    <HelloResponse xmlns="http://tempuri.org/">
      <HelloResult>Hello, Vervain. Have a great day!</HelloResult>
    </HelloResponse>
  </soap:Body>
</soap:Envelope>
```

You can see that the response string is the result of a call to the `Hello` method. Again, this result could just as easily take the form of some sort of structured data, and isn't tied into the HTTP response in any way.

When you use Web Services within your ASP.NET logic, SOAP is used as the default protocol. Although it seems a little more bulky than the other options, it's the only mechanism that makes it possible to use Web methods directly, flexibly, and seamlessly from within the code.

Building an ASP.NET Web Service

Let's take a more detailed look at how a Web Service is put together. We'll also start to explore the enormous range of possible uses for Web Services.

You can define a Web Service by simply writing a few lines of code and placing them inside a file with an ASMX extension. This extension tells Web Matrix that a Web Service is being defined. You can create a Web Service just like a standard ASP.NET page, using Web Matrix (as we did earlier in the chapter) or any text-based editor. When creating a Web Service, it must contain four essential parts:

- ❏ Processing directive
- ❏ Namespaces
- ❏ Public class
- ❏ Web methods

Let's take a look at each of these, in turn.

Processing Directive

Within the empty ASMX file, which is the required file type for an ASP.NET Web Service page, you must let the Web server know that you're creating a Web Service. To do this, enter a directive at the top of your page (in fact, Web Matrix creates this automatically based on the information submitted in the startup dialog):

```
<%@ WebService Language="language" Class="classname"%>
```

This statement appears at the top of an ASP.NET source file to tell the .NET Framework about any settings or constraints that should be applied to whatever object is generated from the file. In this case, the directive tells the compiler the language in which the Web Service is written, and the name of the class in which it is defined. This class might reside in the same file (as it will in this example) or within a separate file (which must be in the \bin directory immediately beneath the Web Application root in which the Web Service lives).

Namespaces

Just as is possible with an ASPX, you can make use of other files' logic within your ASMX page by specifying appropriate namespaces. In this case, you can use the VB.NET `Imports` command:

```
Imports System
Imports System.Web.Services
Imports System.Xml.Serialization
```

Web Services require importing these namespaces as an absolute minimum, because they contain the classes needed for Web Services to handle network connection issues and other OS-related tasks.

Public Class

A `Public Class` acts as a container for the methods in our Web Service:

```
Public Class ClassName
...
End Class
```

> Note that the name of this class is effectively the name of the Web Service, and should therefore correspond to the class value specified in the processing directive.

Essentially, we're just defining an object whose methods will be exposed over the Web. This will ultimately allow us to make remote method calls over the Internet that, to our server, will look like method calls to the same machine that the consuming application resides on.

Web Methods

The methods exposed for consumption over the Internet are known as *Web-callable methods* or simply *Web methods*. By definition, a Web Service will expose one or more Web methods – of course it can have other non-Web methods as well, and these can be protected as needed so that consumers cannot use them directly. The syntax varies slightly depending upon the language used, but they all tend to follow a similar structure; in VB.NET, it is the following:

```
<WebMethod()> Public Function Name(Input As DataType) As DataType
```

> We place the `WebMethod` declaration only before functions we wish to expose to consumers. Those without this declaration cannot be seen.

You may have noticed the set of parentheses following the `WebMethod` declaration. These are available for providing **attributes**. This allows you to customize your Web methods in various ways – for example, you can use the `CacheDuration` attribute to set the number of seconds for which the `WebMethod` will cache its results. If a consumer requests a result from the Web Service, the `WebMethod` will retrieve the cached copy of these values, instead of retrieving them from original source, for the time specified.

For example:

```
<WebMethod(CacheDuration:= 5)> Public Function Hello(Name As String) As String
```

> **For more information on WebMethod attributes, such as `CacheDuration`, please visit: www.microsoft.com/library/default.asp.**

When you build a Web Service, the majority of the time will be spent creating a Web method for the Web Service. It is possible to include more than one Web method in an ASMX file, as you'll see in the next example.

Try It Out Creating a Web Service with Multiple Web Methods

This Web Service contains four Web methods that convert inches to centimeters, centimeters to inches, miles to kilometers, and kilometers to miles.

1. Create an XML Web Service in Web Matrix called `MeasurementConversions.asmx` and enter `MeasurementConversions` as the class, `Ch16` as the namespace, and add the following code:

```
<%@ WebService language="VB" class="MeasurementConversions" %>
Imports System
Imports System.Web.Services
Imports System.Xml.Serialization
Public Class MeasurementConversions
    <WebMethod(Description:="Convert Inches to Centimeters")> _
    Public Function InchesToCentimeters(decInches As Decimal) As Decimal
        Return decInches * 2.54
    End Function
    <WebMethod(Description:="Convert Centimeters to Inches")> _
    Public Function CentimetersToInches(decCentimeters As Decimal) As Decimal
        Return decCentimeters / 2.54
    End Function
    <WebMethod(Description:="Convert Miles to Kilometers")> _
    Public Function MilesToKilometers(decMiles As Decimal) As Decimal
        Return decMiles * 1.61
    End Function
    <WebMethod(Description:="Convert Kilometers to Miles")> _
    Public Function KilometersToMiles(decKilometers As Decimal) As Decimal
        Return decKilometers / 1.61
    End Function
End Class
```

2. Call it up in your browser and you should see something like Figure 16-6:

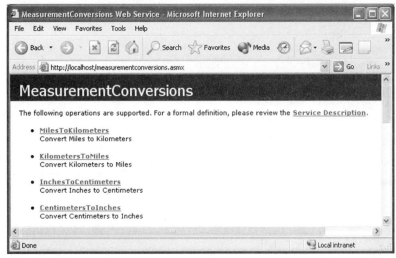

Figure 16-6

Let's break off here for a moment to look at the code. We'll pick up afterwards to consider the testing of our Web Service.

How It Works

In this example, we created a Web Service that converts between Imperial (English) measurements and Metric measurements. Now let's look at the code. The first line tells us that the file is a Web Service written in VB .NET. We have a class name of `MeasurementConversions` that will be used by consumers to make reference to the Web Service:

```
<%@ WebService Language="VB" Class="MeasurementConversions"%>
```

Next, we import the namespace that allows us to refer to Web Service objects without using fully qualified names:

```
Imports System.Web.Services
```

We then name our class to match the processing directive class name. When we are ready to make remote calls to the Web Service through a consumer, we'll need to know this:

```
Public Class MeasurementConversions
```

Finally, consider the actual Web methods. These are separate functions that can be called within a Web Service to return a result.

The first Web method receives a `Decimal` value in inches and converts it to a `Decimal` value in centimeters using the standard conversion formula. The second receives a `Decimal` in centimeters and converts it to inches in the same manner:

```
<WebMethod(Description:="Convert Inches to Centimeters")> _
Public Function InchesToCentimeters(decInches As Decimal) As Decimal
   Return decInches * 2.54
End Function
<WebMethod(Description:="Convert Centimeters to Inches")> _
Public Function CentimetersToInches(decCentimeters As Decimal) As _
            Decimal
   Return decCentimeters / 2.54
End Function
```

The third and fourth Web methods perform similar conversions from miles to kilometers and kilometers to miles respectively:

```
<WebMethod(Description:="Convert Miles to Kilometers")> _
Public Function MilesToKilometers(decMiles As Decimal) As Decimal
   Return decMiles * 1.61
End Function
<WebMethod(Description:="Convert Kilometers to Miles")> _
  Public Function KilometersToMiles(decKilometers As Decimal) As Decimal
     Return decKilometers / 1.61
  End Function
```

We've now created a complete Web Service using the *processing directive*, adding *namespaces* and creating *Web methods*. Now the big question is 'How do we know it works?' It's time to put it through its paces.

Testing Your Web Service

To test Web Services, all you need is an Internet connection and a browser. In the browser address window, just enter the URL of the Web Service in the following format:

http://[path]/[webservice].asmx

The first time the Web Service is accessed, the code will compile on the Web server, and a new browser window will appear containing some very helpful diagnostic information. This Web Service Description page allows us to impersonate a consumer and enter input values to send to the Web Service. The page contains the following information about the Web Service:

❑   Names of the Web Service's Web-callable functions

❑   Request Parameters: The names of all the inputs that the Web Service expects a consumer to supply

❑ Response Type: The datatypes of the result sent by the Web Service to a consumer (such as `integer`, `string`, `float`, and `object`)

❑ Fields to enter test values

You'll also see the following message at the top of the test page:

The following operations are supported. For a formal definition, please review the Service Description.

The *Service Description* is a comprehensive technical description of all the functionality exposed by the Web Service. You'll be taking a closer look at it later on in the chapter. For the time being, however, we're just interested in testing our Web Service. Let's now go back and see what happens when we test our `MeasurementConversions` Web Service.

Try It Out Browse to the Conversions Test Page

1. Assuming your browser is still open, just click on the MilesToKilometers hyperlink and enter a test value of 60 in the decMiles value field, as shown in Figure 16-7:

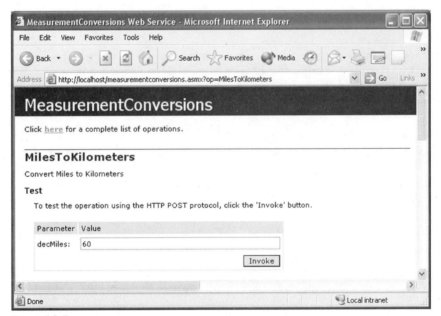

Figure 16-7

2. Click on Invoke, and a new browser window appears, as shown in Figure 16-8, containing our result in kilometers in XML format:

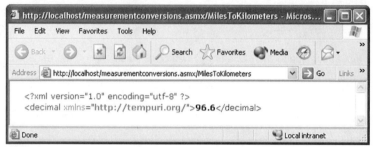

Figure 16-8

3. In the original .asmx, click on the word here at the top of the test page, and you'll return to the original test screen. You can now repeat this procedure for the other methods shown on the page.

How It Works

When we browse to the test page, we see a screen containing the name of our Web Service and underneath it, a list of the methods that it exposes. These method names are hyperlinks. When we click on MilesToKilometers, the Web method test section will appear in the browser window. We are given the name of the parameter, decMiles, and an associated field to enter the test value in.

> Remember that the datatype for **MilesToKilometers** is a decimal. This is the value that our **MeasurementConversions** Web Service expects from a consumer.

Once the value is entered, we can press the Invoke button to execute the Web method. We are impersonating a consuming application when we do this. The entered test value 60 is passed, using HTTP as a request, to the `MilesToKilometers` Web method. The value will be multiplied by 1.61 and returned as a `Decimal`. The result is in XML.

You might say "Sure, our test page tells *us* what the Web Service's expectations are. But how would a consumer know what they are?" This consumer might not necessarily be another user, it could be an application and then the expectations need to be explicitly defined.

The next section discusses how to know what a Web Service requires, what it produces, and how a consumer can communicate with it.

Using Your Web Service

As you've learned, it's essential for consumers to know what parameters to send to a Web Service and what values to expect it to return. To accomplish this, a *Web Service Description Language (WSDL)* file is used. This is an XML file that sets out how the interaction between a Web Service and its consumer will occur. WSDL is a standard managed by the W3 standards organization, and you can find more details about it at http://www.w3.org/TR/wsdl.

The impact of this WSDL standard is enormous. WSDL is able to define all the interactions of a Web Service regardless of whether the service is running in ASP.NET, Java, and regardless of whether it is running on Windows or UNIX.

It means that in future you won't need to be concerned with whether our services, or languages, are compatible across platforms, but can instead concentrate on the real issue of writing robust, functional code. WSDL will take care of declaring the interaction for us.

For instance, if a Web Service expects two specific parameters and returns a single value, the WSDL defines the names, order, and data types of each input and output value. Since we know where to find the Web Service using its URL, we don't need to know the physical location or the internal logic of the Web Service. With WSDL, we have all the information necessary to begin making use of the Web Service functionality within our applications. It's really that simple!

Let's take a quick look at what a WSDL contract looks like using our `MeasurementConversion` Web Service.

Try It Out   Viewing the WSDL Contract

1. Open up your browser and enter the path http://localhost/MeasurementConversions.asmx and click on the Service Description hyperlink at the top of the page. You should see a screen similar to Figure 16-9:

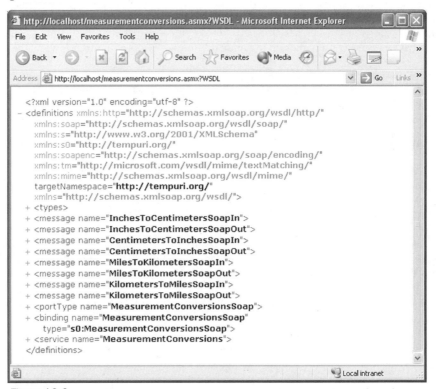

Figure 16-9

How It Works

As you can see, there's a lot of information in here and this is just the collapsed view! Our Web method message names are there and the various HTTP GET, HTTP POST, and SOAP message structures are laid out. These message formats contain the requirements for a consumer to know what parameters are needed to communicate with a Web Service using each message structure.

At the top, the following declaration indicates that the WSDL file is in XML format:

```
<?xml version="1.0" encoding="utf-8" ?>
```

Below that declaration is the `<definitions>` element, which contains various namespaces. Most of these namespaces make reference to SOAP, which we discussed earlier. These must be included in the file for SOAP to work correctly:

```
<definitions xmlns:http="http://schemas.xmlsoap.org/wsdl/http/"
xmlns:soap="http://schemas.xmlsoap.org/wsdl/soap/"
xmlns:s="http://www.w3.org/2001/XMLSchema" xmlns:s0="http://tempuri.org/"
xmlns:soapenc="http://schemas.xmlsoap.org/soap/encoding/"
xmlns:tm="http://microsoft.com/wsdl/mime/textMatching/"
xmlns:mime="http://schemas.xmlsoap.org/wsdl/mime/"
targetNamespace="http://tempuri.org/" xmlns="http://schemas.xmlsoap.org/wsdl/">
```

Next, the `<types>` element defines each of the data types that the Web Service expects to receive and return after completion. This is very complex, and almost a science in itself. It is written in *XML Schema Definition* (*XSD*) language. You can't see the definitions in the screenshot as its section is collapsed (like the others). All you need to do is click on the node in Internet Explorer in order to view them.

After this are the various one-way transmissions from a consumer to the Web Service and back again. Our Web method message names are in here, and the various SOAP message structures are laid out. For example, on expanding the `message` element, we can see the `InchesToCentimeters` Web method message structures for SOAP:

```
<message name="InchesToCentimetersSoapIn">
<part name="parameters" element="s0:InchesToCentimeters" />
</message>
<message name="InchesToCentimetersSoapOut">
<part name="parameters" element="s0:InchesToCentimetersResponse" />
</message>
```

In short, this file contains all of the information necessary to communicate with our Web Service. Now that you've seen the process of building and communicating with XML Web Services in detail, let's create something a bit more complex.

The next example will accept a value, and return a result using ADO.NET to retrieve data from an Access database.

Try It Out ISBN Search Web Service

Let's create a Web Service that returns the title of a book, based on an ISBN that the consumer provides. This will allow our librarian to add a function on the library's Web page to enable users to search by consuming the Web Service.

This particular service will access a database of books. The database contains information on ISBN and book titles. Once the details are received from the database, the results will be inserted into a DataReader and returned to the consumer in XML.

This example uses the Library.mdb Access database, which you can download along with the code samples for this book from www.wrox.com. You should ensure that the file is in the same path as the Web Service that you create.

1. Create a XML Web Service called ISBN.asmx in Web Matrix, with the class name ISBN and the Namespace Ch16.

2. Add the following Imports statements to the beginning of the file:

```
<%@ WebService Language="vb" Class="ISBN" %>
Imports System
Imports System.Web.Services
Imports System.Xml.Serialization
Imports System.Data
Imports System.Data.OleDb
```

3. Add the following code to enable the Web Service:

```
'Inherit the WebService class that provides all the built-in features
'that are needed to create a Web Service.
Public Class ISBN
    Inherits System.Web.Services.WebService
<WebMethod()> Public Function BookDetail(ByVal Isbn As String) As String
   Return GetBookDetails(Isbn)
End Function
```

4. Enter the following code directly after the `BookDetail` Web method. This function performs the database lookup and returns the book title string:

```
Private Function GetBookDetails(ByVal Isbn As String) As String 'Declare the
database access objects
 Dim LibraryDr As OleDbDataReader
 Dim LibraryConn As OleDbConnection
 Dim LibraryCmd As OleDbCommand
'Declare the connection string that grants access to the database
 Dim Conn As String ="Provider=Microsoft.Jet.OLEDB.4.0;Data Source=" & _
                Server.MapPath("Library.mdb") & ";"

 'Declare the SQL that will be executed. Dim SQL As String = "SELECT Title FROM
Books WHERE ISBN = '" & Isbn & "'"
```

```
 Dim BookTitle As String
 'Open the connection to the database.  LibraryConn = New OleDbConnection(Conn)
 LibraryCmd = New OleDbCommand(SQL, LibraryConn)
 LibraryConn.Open()
 'Create a DataReader that will return our Book information.
 LibraryDr = _
  LibraryCmd.ExecuteReader(CommandBehavior.CloseConnection)
 If LibraryDr.Read() Then    'A row was returned; our book exists!
   BookTitle = LibraryDr(0)
 Else    'A row was not returned; this book does not exist.
   BookTitle = "Book not found in the database"
 End If
 LibraryDr.Close()
 Return BookTitle
End Function
End Class
```

5. Once you have completed this code entry, test your Web Service. Save the file, and then browse to http://localhost/isbn.asmx.

6. Within the Isbn field, enter the ISBN 0764557076. A new browser window will appear, containing the XML as shown in Figure 16-10:

Figure 16-10

How It Works

Our Web Service provides what is technically known as a 'level of abstraction'. This means that the code to do the work of finding our information isn't taken care of by the Web-callable `BookDetails` method. Instead, `BookDetails` calls another internal function that consumers can't see. This function, `GetBookDetails`, does the work of finding the book information, and then returns it to `BookDetails`, which returns it to us:

```
<WebMethod()> _
Public Function BookDetail(ByVal Isbn As String) As String
    Return GetBookDetails(Isbn)
End Function
Private Function GetBookDetails(ByVal Isbn As String) As String
...
End Function
```

This is done because the job of the `GetBookDetails` function remains the same, regardless of the source making the request. The same function may be called from a non-Web Service source. Also, we certainly wouldn't want to maintain two separate functions that do the same thing, the difference being only the `<WebMethod>` declaration.

We're using ADO.NET to connect to the `Library.mdb` database, retrieve a book title from its `Books` table based on the ISBN, and store it in a `String` variable. Keeping the data request simple, we define a connection string (`Conn`), and then open the connection to the database (with `LibraryConn`):

```
LibraryConn = New OleDbConnection(Conn)
LibraryCmd = New OleDbCommand(SQL, LibraryConn)
LibraryConn.Open()
```

Using the `LibraryCmd` object, we execute the query for a specific ISBN, placing the results in the `LibraryDr` DataReader:

```
LibraryDr = LibraryCmd.ExecuteReader(CommandBehavior.CloseConnection)
```

We then check whether a row was returned, by calling the `Read` method of our `DataReader`, `LibraryDr`. If it returns `True`, we take the first column (column zero, the `Title` column of the database) from the `DataReader` and place it into `BookTitle`. If it returns `False`, we know that the book was not found, and we place a 'not found' message in the title value. Then we close our DataReader and return the book title string:

```
If LibraryDr.Read() Then
  BookTitle = LibraryDr(0)
Else
  BookTitle = "Book not found in the database"
End If
LibraryDr.Close()
Return BookTitle
```

For more information on working with data sources, please refer to *Chapters 8* and *9*.

Consuming a Web Service

You've created some Web Services from start to finish using a variety of technologies. The next step is to understand how to include this functionality within a consumer application. To do this, you must first create an interface that will allow the consumer to see all of the Web-callable methods and properties exposed by the Web Service. This saves the headache of ensuring that your parameters are the correct type and having to create our own protocol request and response handlers. This interface is called a Web Service *proxy*.

How Does a Proxy Work?

A proxy resides on the consumer's machine and acts as a relay between the consumer and the Web Service. When building a proxy, we use a WSDL file (we'll examine the source shortly) to create a map that tells the consumer what methods are available and how to call them. The consumer then calls the Web method that is mapped in the proxy, which in turn, makes calls to the actual Web Service over the Internet. The proxy (and not the consumer) handles all of the network-related work, the sending of data, as well as managing the underlying WSDL. When we reference the Web Service in the consumer application, it looks as if it's part of the consumer application itself.

Figure 16-11 illustrates this process:

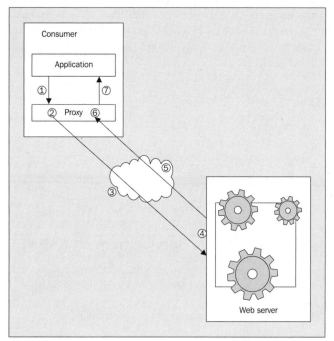

Figure 16-11

The procedure works as follows:

1. The application executes a function in the proxy code, passing any appropriate parameters to it, without being concerned that the proxy is going to call a Web Service.

2. The proxy receives this call, and formulates the request that will be sent to the Web Service, using the parameters the consumer has specified.

3. This function call is sent from the proxy to the Web Service. This call can be within the confines of the same machine, across a *Local Area Network (LAN)*, or across the Internet. The method of calling remains the same.

4. The Web Service uses the parameters provided by the proxy to execute its Web-callable function and build the result in XML.

5. The resulting data from the Web Service is returned to the proxy at the consumer.

6. The proxy parses the XML returned from the Web Service to retrieve the individual values generated. These values may be as simple as `integers` and strings, or they may define more complex data types.

7. Your application receives the expected values from the proxy function, completely unaware that they resulted from a Web Service call.

To make use of a Web Service from an ASP.NET page, your proxy must be created and compiled appropriately. You can create a proxy to a Web Service using either Web Matrix or a tool called WSDL.exe which is provided in the .NET Framework SDK. Both of these methods make use of WSDL to create a proxy, built in the language of your choice. As it's undeniably simpler to use Web Matrix than it is to use the command line tool WSDL.exe, we'll create a new ASP.NET application that will access our new ISBN Web Service using Web Matrix.

Creating a Proxy

Building a proxy is a two-step process:

1. Generate the proxy source code automatically

2. Compile the proxy into a runtime library

In the following example, we will look at how to do this.

Try It Out Accessing the ISBN Web Service from an ASP.NET Page

In this example, you will build the proxy and a simple page for retrieving book titles from the ISBN Web Service, demonstrating how quickly your Web Service applications can be up and running.

1. Open the ISBN.asmx file you just created in Web Matrix.

2. Go to the Tools menu and choose select Web Service Proxy Generator.

3. Fill in the dialog that appears, as shown in Figure 16-12:

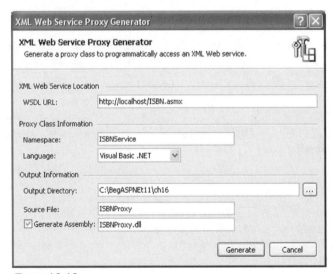

Figure 16-12

4. You've created the proxy class in VB.NET, and defined the ISBNService namespace. By selecting a namespace, you will be able to reference your proxy class from within your consuming application. The proxy is contained in a file called ISBNProxy.vb. At the same time, Web Matrix has also performed the second stage. It has taken the ISBNProxy.vb and compiled it to create a DLL file that can be referenced within the code. Once this process is finished, you should see the dialog in Figure 16-13:

Figure 16-13

5. Now that we have a proxy class and a DLL, we're ready to make use of the ISBN Web Service from within an ASP.NET page. We'll call the BookInfo.aspx page, and use it to call the Web-callable function BookDetail in ISBN.asmx. By using a proxy, the reference to the function's namespace will appear as if it were a function within the same page. So, create a new ASPX file called BookInfo.aspx in Web Matrix, in the folder C:\BegASPNET11\Ch16.

6. Click on the All window and enter the following code:

```
<%@ Page Language="vb" Debug="true"%>
<%@ Import namespace="ISBNService" %>

<script language="vb" runat="server">
Private Sub RetrieveBook(ByVal sender As System.Object, ByVal e As _
                        System.EventArgs)
  Dim ws As New ISBNService.ISBN()
  lblBookTitle.Text = ws.BookDetail(txtISBN.Text)
End Sub
</script>

<html>
  <body>
    <form id="Form1" method="post" runat="server">

      Enter an ISBN number to search on:
      <br />
      <asp:TextBox id="txtISBN" runat="server"></asp:TextBox>
      <br />
      <asp:Button id="Button1" runat="server" Text="Submit" _
            OnClick="RetrieveBook"></asp:Button><br />
      <asp:Label id="lblBookTitle" runat="server" Width="152px" _
            Height="23px"></asp:Label>

    </form>
  </body>
</html>
```

7. Save the file and call it in your browser. You should see a page similar to Figure 16-14:

Figure 16-14

8. Enter an ISBN that we know is in the Books table, like the ISBN for this book (0764557076), as shown in Figure 16-15:

Figure 16-15

9. Now try an ISBN that you know will not be found, to ensure that the proxy is actually working; see Figure 16-16:

Figure 16-16

How It Works

Before Web Matrix came along, we had to use WSDL.exe, which comes as part of the .NET Framework SDK to both to generate a proxy class and use a command line compiler to compile the proxy class and to create the ISBNProxy.dll. This is no longer the case; we can now use Web Matrix to perform these two distinct operations in one step. Set the options in the dialog as follows:

❑   WSDL URL: This indicates where to find the Web Service.

❑   Namespace: The name by which you can reference the Web Service in your ASP.NET code.

❑   Language: The language the proxy class should be generated in.

❑   OutputDirectory: The place where both the proxy class and the assembly should be placed.

❑   SourceFile: The name of the proxy class.

❑   GenerateAssembly: The name of the DLL.

These options ensured that we create the DLL so that it works correctly and can be added to our ASP.NET page.

In our ASP.NET page, we made use of Web Form controls. These controls – <asp:TextBox>, <asp:Label>, and <asp:Button> make up the simple form that makes a very specific call to the BookDetail subroutine.

Upon clicking the Submit button, the RetrieveBook event fires, as specified in the OnClick attribute of <asp:Button>:

```
<asp:Button id="Button1" runat="server" Text="Submit" _
OnClick="RetrieveBook" /></asp:Button>
```

Within the `RetrieveBook` subroutine, first of all, we create an instance of the proxy class that we'll be using:

```
Dim ws As New ISBNService.ISBN()
```

Then it's simply a matter of calling the `BookDetail` function of the `ws` object. Remember the previous example where we created the Web `method`:

```
Public Function BookDetail(ByVal Isbn As String) As String
   Return GetBookDetails(Isbn)
End Function
```

Here we are actually accessing the same Web method from our ASPX page. `ISBNService.ISBN` refers to our automatically created DLL file, which is used to communicate with the ASMX Web Service file created from the previous example. So once we've created our `ws` object using the DLL, we can use all the Web methods of the object as though they were normal methods.

With a single line of code, we pass the string contents of `txtISBN.text` to the Web service and receive the book title, placing that string into the label `lblBookTitle.text`:

```
lblBookTitle.Text = ws.BookDetail(txtISBN.Text)
```

Once again, this example proved the simplicity and power of Web services.

Creating a Web Service for the Wrox United Application

The process for creating a Web Service, while relatively easy, can be quite lengthy. So far the examples have been kept as simple as possible. In fact the previous example might seem like a long winded way to go about just returning a single string from our database. The power of Web Services lies in the ability to return more complex items than just single items of data.

We'll now build a Web method that links back to the Wrox United application and use it to return a set of results. In fact, the Web Service will take the name of a team from you, scour the database for the score from the most recent game, and return that to the user. For the sake of simplicity and compatibility, we'll still take these results and output them as a single string, but this string will be created from a concatenation of both integer and string values that have been gleaned from the database. It is possible to return this information as a dataset. However, there isn't a standard way to return a dataset, so by returning our information as a string, we make it easily consumable to users on all platforms, because a dataset on Windows can be completely different to a dataset returned from a database on a UNIX server.

Before building the Web method though, we're going to add a results page to the Wrox United application. This page's functionality is unrelated to Web Services, so let's see how it works. We'll borrow some of the data-reading routines from this page and use this within our Web method to extract a single result from the database.

Try It Out Adding a Results Page

1. Open up Web Matrix and create a new `.aspx` page called `results.aspx`.

2. Next, download the code for `results.aspx` from `http://www.wrox.com` – we're not going to reproduce it here as it is over five pages long!

3. Alter the `navbar.ascx` navigation bar, so that it points to the new `results.aspx` page. Amend the code as follows:

```
...
<p>
    <asp:HyperLink id="lnkGames" runat="server"
     NavigateUrl="Default.aspx">Upcoming Games
      </asp:HyperLink>
</p>
<p>
    <asp:HyperLink id="lnkResults" runat="server"
    NavigateUrl="results.aspx">Results
      </asp:HyperLink>
</p>
<p>
    <asp:HyperLink id="lnkChat" runat="server"
    NavigateUrl="Chat.aspx">Chat
      </asp:HyperLink>
</p>
...
```

4. Now open the Wrox United application and browse to the results page, shown in Figure 16-17:

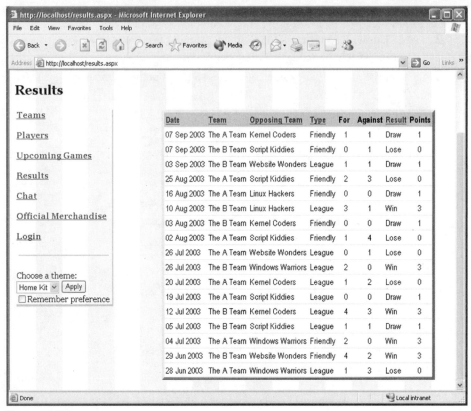

Figure 16-17

5. You can now see a complete list of the results of the games played. If you click on the column heading, it will sort the results by the appropriate column.

How It Works

We're only really going to look at the data-reading routine in the `TeamResults` function. We create a seemingly massive variable querystring that takes an enormous SQL statement. The SQL statement isn't as scary as it looks:

```
Dim queryString As String = "SELECT [Games].[Date], [Games].[WroxGoals],
    [Games].[OpponentGoals], [Teams].[TeamName], [Opponents].[OpponentName],
    [GameTypes].[GameType], [Games].[GameID] FROM [Games], [Teams], [Opponents],
    [GameTypes] WHERE (((Games].[WroxTeam] = [Teams].[TeamID]) AND
    ([Games].[OpposingTeam] = [Opponents].[OpponentID]) AND ([Games].[GameType] =
    [GameTypes].[GameTypeID]) AND ([Games].[Date] < now())) ORDER BY " & SortExp
    &  SortDir
```

Basically the SQL statement gets the date, opponent goals, team-name, opponent name, type of game and game identifier from the Games table. However, as this information is spread across the Games, Teams, Opponents, and GamesType tables, we have to perform joins to the Games table to extract this information. If you're not familiar with SQL don't worry, you don't need to be. You just need to understand that this query (a slightly modified version) will form the heart of our Web Service, as this is exactly the information we need to extract. The only difference is that we want to extract only one result as opposed to a whole set of results.

The rest of the code in this function then just creates a Command object and supplies the QueryString variable as the CommandText and runs the ExecuteReader method and returns the dataset as a DataReader object:

```
Dim dbCommand As System.Data.IDbCommand = New System.Data.OleDb.OleDbCommand
dbCommand.CommandText = queryString
dbCommand.Connection = dbConnection

dbConnection.Open
Dim dataReader As System.Data.IDataReader =
   dbCommand.ExecuteReader(System.Data.CommandBehavior.CloseConnection)
Return dataReader
End Function
```

This is exactly what we'll be doing – so let's not waste any more time just talking about it!

Try It Out Creating the Web Service

1. Go to Web Matrix and create a new latestscore.asmx XML Web Service.

2. Add the following code into the All window, making sure it replaces all of the default code created by Web Matrix:

```
<%@ WebService language="VB" class="LatestScore" %>

Imports System
Imports System.Web.Services
Imports System.Xml.Serialization
Imports System.Data
Imports System.Data.OleDb
Imports System.Configuration
Imports Microsoft.VisualBasic.ControlChars
'Inherit the WebService class that provides all the built-in features
'that are needed to create a Web Service.
Public Class LatestScore
    Inherits System.Web.Services.WebService

<WebMethod()> _
Public Function LatestScore(ByVal Team As String) As String
   Return GetLatestScore(Team)
End Function
Private Function GetLatestScore(ByVal Team As String) As String
 'Declare the database access objects
 Dim LibraryDr As OleDbDataReader
 Dim LibraryConn As OleDbConnection
```

```
    Dim LibraryCmd As OleDbCommand


    'Declare the connection string that grants access to the database
    Dim Conn As String =ConfigurationSettings.AppSettings("ConnectionString")


    'Declare the SQL that will be executed.
    Dim SQL As String = "SELECT
[Games].[WroxGoals],[Games].[OpponentGoals],[Opponents].[OpponentName],[Games].
[Date] FROM [Games], [Teams], [Opponents] WHERE (([Games].[WroxTeam] =
[Teams].[TeamID]) AND ([Games].[OpposingTeam] = [Opponents].[OpponentID]) AND
([Teams].[TeamName] =  " & quote & Team & quote &")) ORDER BY [Games].[Date] DESC"
    Dim MaxDate,LatestScore, WroxGoals, OpponentGoals, TeamName, OpponentName As
String


    'Open the connection to the database.
    LibraryConn = New OleDbConnection(Conn)
    LibraryCmd = New OleDbCommand(SQL, LibraryConn)
    LibraryConn.Open()
    LibraryDr = LibraryCmd.ExecuteReader(CommandBehavior.CloseConnection)

    if LibraryDr.Read()
       MaxDate = CStr(LibraryDr("Date"))
       WroxGoals = CStr(LibraryDr("WroxGoals"))
       OpponentGoals = CStr(LibraryDr("OpponentGoals"))
       OpponentName = CStr(LibraryDr("OpponentName"))
       LatestScore = MaxDate & " - " & Team & " " & WroxGoals & " " &
OpponentName & " " & OpponentGoals
    else
    'A row was not returned; this book does not exist.
    latestscore = "The team cannot be found in the database"
    End If

    LibraryDr.Close()

    Return LatestScore
End Function


End Class
```

3. You can now test the Web Service to see if it is working correctly. Go to http://localhost/latestscore.asmx and browse the LatestScore link that appears, as shown in Figure 16-18. You should be asked for a single parameter – the team. This can be either The A team or The B Team:

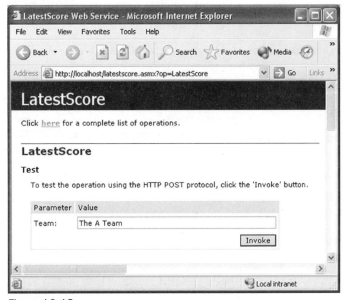

Figure 16-18

4. When you invoke this service, you should see the result shown in Figure 16-19:

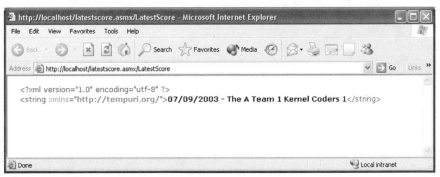

Figure 16-19

5. You'll get the score from the A Team vs Kernel Coders match which was played on the seventh of September. Go back to the `results.aspx` page and sort the columns by date. At the foot of the screen, you'll see that indeed this is the most recent match played (Figure 16-20):

Figure 16-20

Go back and check the Web Service for the B team and you'll see the result against the Script Kiddies, which is a 0-1 loss.

How It Works

Our Web Service has a single Web method that calls the `GetLatestScore` function and supplies it with a single parameter: the team name:

```
<WebMethod()> Public Function LatestScore(ByVal Team As String) As String
    Return GetLatestScore(Team)
End Function
```

The `GetLatestScore` function does all the hard work. We start by initializing three objects that will return the data from the database. These are the `OleDbDataReader`, `OleDbConnection`, and `OleDbCommand` objects:

```
Dim LibraryDr As OleDbDataReader
 Dim LibraryConn As OleDbConnection
 Dim LibraryCmd As OleDbCommand
```

Next we create a connection string to the database, using the `AppSettings` from our `Web.Config` file:

```
Dim Conn As String =ConfigurationSettings.AppSettings("ConnectionString")
```

The following line should also be familiar – it's where we create the querystring that will be used to extract our results from the database:

```
Dim SQL As String = "SELECT
[Games].[WroxGoals],[Games].[OpponentGoals],[Opponents].[OpponentName],[Games].
[Date] FROM [Games], [Teams], [Opponents] WHERE (([Games].[WroxTeam] =
[Teams].[TeamID]) AND ([Games].[OpposingTeam] = [Opponents].[OpponentID]) AND
([Teams].[TeamName] =  " & quote & Team & quote &")) ORDER BY [Games].[Date] DESC"
```

What's different here is that we have added a clause that orders the columns returned by the final date. SQL provides its own parameters for returning maximum values, but in our case, it's easier to *cheat*, by just sorting the data ourselves into the desired order and then taking the last value only. This variable contains a query that gets the Goals, Opponent's Goals, Opponent Team's name, and game date from the database, so it's a little bit simpler than the one used in `results.aspx`.

We create a condition so that only teams that match the team name supplied in the `Team` variable are returned. So if we have supplied the A Team, then it will only return the A team's results. In fact, we don't even need to return our own team name, as we already have been supplied that by the user, when they entered the team parameter to the Web Service.

Once we've created the query, we need to create a set of variables to store each of the different items of information in. Notice that they are all created as strings, although they don't have to be; it's just as we want to concatenate the information into one big string, it's easier to do it this way:

```
Dim MaxDate, LatestScore, WroxGoals, OpponentGoals, TeamName, OpponentName As
String
```

We open a connection to the database, and supply our SQL query to the `Command` object and run it against the database:

```
LibraryConn = New OleDbConnection(Conn)
LibraryCmd = New OleDbCommand(SQL, LibraryConn)
LibraryConn.Open()
LibraryDr = LibraryCmd.ExecuteReader(CommandBehavior.CloseConnection)
```

Now we're going to *cheat* here to keep the code short. As mentioned in `results.aspx`, we return a dataset. Now in the last example, we performed a check for a single row of data. If we're returning a dataset, then more than a single row is returned. However, to avoid having to create an array of information, most of it unwanted, we read each row into the variables, and then overwrite each row:

```
if LibraryDr.Read()
   MaxDate = CStr(LibraryDr("Date"))
   WroxGoals = CStr(LibraryDr("WroxGoals"))
   OpponentGoals = CStr(LibraryDr("OpponentGoals"))
   OpponentName = CStr(LibraryDr("OpponentName"))
```

So the first row will read the dates, goals, and name information into our four variables. However, as pointed out earlier, we sorted the information in the SQL query. We sorted our information in ascending order, by date, and restricted it to the results of only one team. Thus, we know that the last line of information in the dataset must be the most recent line. Plenty of information is read into the variables, but it is overwritten. Only the most recent set of information is kept. Because DataReaders move through datasets sequentially, and we have already sorted the dataset into ordered data, we know that only information from the last row – the one with the most recent date – is stored.

We concatenate this into the `LatestScore` variable:

```
        LatestScore = MaxDate & " - " & Team & " " & WroxGoals & " " & OpponentName &
   " " & OpponentGoals
```

We perform a check to make sure that the DataReader isn't empty. It would be empty only if someone supplied a team name that wasn't found in the database. Just in case this is true, the `LatestScore` variable is supplied with an appropriate message instead:

```
else
'A row was not returned; this book does not exist.
LatestScore = "The team cannot be found in the database"
End If
```

Last, we close the DataReader and return the contents of the function to the Web method:

```
LibraryDr.Close()

Return LatestScore
```

It's now a straightforward task to create a proxy client using the same method from our ISBN example and change the class so that it queries the `LatestScore` Web method instead. We're not going to supply the code here to do that, but instead leave that as an exercise for the reader to complete, as the code changes needed are minimal and Web Matrix can do most of the work for you.

We have a Web Service that takes a team name and returns as a string, the date and latest score for that given team name. That information is widely available to be used in anybody's application now, and not just ours. But how would someone else go about discovering this information so as to be able to use it?

Web Service Discovery

As you begin to build Web Service-integrated applications, it will become increasingly important to locate services that provide the functions you need, or alternatively post your own Web Services so that others can make use of them. UDDI is a Microsoft-backed initiative that allows you to do this.

Whenever an industry initiative gains the support of several large industry players, it will usually become mainstream. For this reason, UDDI is positioned to dominate the Web Service discovery field in the future. The UDDI service (accessible from http://uddi.microsoft.com or http://www.ibm.com/services/uddi/) lets businesses register themselves and list their existing Web Services at no charge.

Anyone can browse and search the UDDI database for a service that may suit their needs. UDDI provides information such as contact details (address, phone number, email address, Web site), business details (DUNS number and industry sector), and a discovery URL for each service. WSDL is a key component of the UDDI project.

Using http://uddi.microsoft.com/, you can search for businesses that provide Web Services, select the WSDL appropriately, and build your proxies (Figure 16-21):

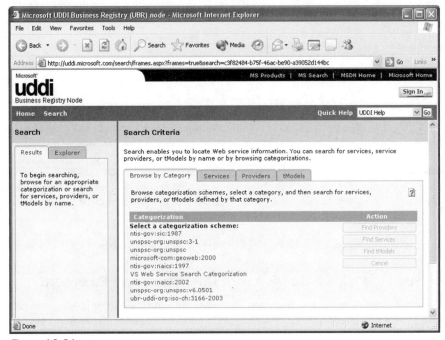

Figure 16-21

Securing a Web Service

Whether your Web Service is made available on a subscription basis or is completely free to the public, it is important to consider security. The reasons for securing Web Services can range from simple usage logging to strict access control. If your Web Service provides a very useful feature (of course it will!), it's helpful to keep track of who's using it. While you can log the usage of a Web Service that provides privileged information, more stringent security measures should be taken to make sure that the use of your Web Service is consistent with your purposes.

There are many options for securing Web applications and services. The following are the most common techniques, and will be discussed over the sections that follow:

❑ **Username-password**: This is used to provide custom database access control. This is an authentication service.

❑ **Secure Sockets Layer**: SSL is used to ensure that the data passing across the Web is encrypted. However, it does not protect the Web Services access itself.

❑ **IP address restriction**: This is used to specify the valid IP addresses that can access the service. However, you need a user's authentication even if the IP is the same.

❑ **Web Services Enhancements**: A toolkit from Microsoft that adds a whole new set of specifications for making your Web Services secure.

Please remember that these methods are not mutually exclusive, and can be combined to provide a higher level of security.

Username-Password Combination or Registration Keys

By requiring either a username and password pair or a registration key code as an input parameter, you can provide a way to track which consumers are using your Web Service. A simple database table or XML file containing each username-password pair or registration key code is all that's required to provide this kind of security. Considering that no authentication of the consumer takes place in this scenario, it is very simple for the client to share the username and password (or registration key) with others. However, when the data provided by the Web Service is not sensitive or proprietary in nature, this security method provides us with a quick and effective option.

Let's examine how you might apply this type of security to the ISBN Web Service.

Try It Out Securing a Web Service with Username and Password

You will be using the `security.mdb` database (provided with the code for this book and can be downloaded from www.wrox.com). This contains a very simple `Users` table consisting of usernames and passwords. Ensure this database is in the same path as the `isbn.asmx` file created earlier. Our security will only attempt to match details from the user with an entry in the Security table.

1. Reopen the ISBN Web Service (`isbn.asmx`) in Web Matrix, and make the following modifications to the `BookDetail` Web method:

```
<WebMethod ()> _
Public Function BookDetail(ByVal Isbn As String, ByVal strUsername As String, _
     ByVal strPassword As String) As String

    Dim SecurityDr As OleDbDataReader
    Dim SecurityConn As OleDbConnection
    Dim SecurityCmd As OleDbCommand
    Dim Conn As String = "Provider=Microsoft.Jet.OLEDB.4.0;Data Source="
        Conn += Server.MapPath("Security.mdb") & ";"
    Dim SQL As String = "select Username from Users where username = '"
        SQL += strUsername & "' and password = '" & strPassword & "'"
    SecurityConn = New OleDbConnection(Conn)
    SecurityCmd = New OleDbCommand(SQL, SecurityConn)
    SecurityConn.Open()
    SecurityDr = SecurityCmd.ExecuteReader(CommandBehavior.CloseConnection)

    If SecurityDr.Read() Then
      SecurityDr.Close()
      Return GetBookDetails(Isbn)
    Else
      SecurityDr.Close()
```

```
        Return "Login to library failed."
      End If

0   End Function
    ...
```

2. Save the result as `ISBNSecurity.asmx`. Notice that no changes have been made to `GetBookDetails`, as the core functionality of retrieving the book title from the database hasn't changed. The goal in this scenario is to provide a gatekeeper that prevents access to the internal logic if the consumer's username and password pair is not found in the database.

3. Browse to the `ISBNsecurity.asmx` Web Service to test this newly applied security. You will now see two extra textboxes: one for `strUserName` and one for `strPassword`, as shown in Figure 16-22:

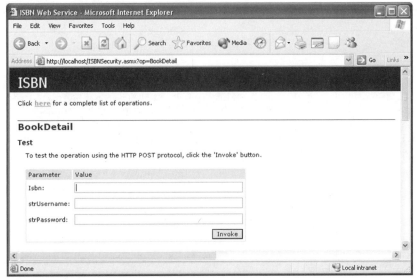

Figure 16-22

4. If you put in a number without specifying the correct security details, you will get the response shown in Figure 16-23:

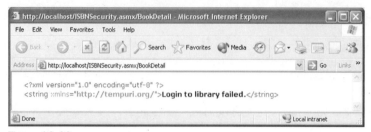

Figure 16-23

The only entry in our security database has the username `librarian` and the password `secret`. This is the only user that is permitted to access our Web Service; however, you can add more registered users by modifying the `Security` table.

How It Works

We have used nearly the same logic validating the login as previously used in `GetBookDetails` to look up a book. By adding this logic to the Web-callable `BookDetail` function, we completely prevent access to the internal `GetBookDetails` function if the login fails. First we create a connection to the security database and run the SQL command that retrieves the username if the user name and password supplied to the Web Service match any of those in the database.

```
Dim Conn As String = "Provider=Microsoft.Jet.OLEDB.4.0;Data Source="
      Conn += Server.MapPath("Security.mdb") & ";"
    Dim SQL As String = "select Username from Users where username = '"
      SQL += strUsername & "' and password = '" & strPassword & "'"
    SecurityConn = New OleDbConnection(Conn)
    SecurityCmd = New OleDbCommand(SQL, SecurityConn)
    SecurityConn.Open()
    SecurityDr = SecurityCmd.ExecuteReader(CommandBehavior.CloseConnection)
```

Now, if anything is returned, we run the `BookDetails` function and return the answer to the Web method:

```
If SecurityDr.Read() Then
      SecurityDr.Close()
      Return GetBookDetails(Isbn)
```

However, upon failure to login correctly, we return a simple string:

```
    Else
    SecurityDr.Close()
    Return "Login to library failed."
```

If the username and password combination is successfully located in the database, the result of the `GetBookDetails` function is returned just as before.

Secure Sockets Layer

The most common method of securing information on the Web is the *Secure Sockets Layer* (*SSL*). When you make an online purchase, you'll typically see a lock or key icon displayed in the browser's status bar to let you know you're communicating safely. Information passed between the browser and the Web site travels in an encrypted form. In the case of Web Services, applying SSL ensures that the data traveling between the consumer and the endpoint is encrypted, and thus, difficult to intercept.

SSL has no effect on the integrity of the data provided by your Web Service. When a value is returned to the consumer, it remains the same regardless of the encryption used in its transportation. The only downside is that it affects the overall performance of your site, as more processing is required. You can get more information about verifying your identity for use with SSL from a Certificate Authority like Verisign (www.verisign.com). We discuss SSL in more detail in the next chapter.

IP Address Restriction

Maintaining an IP address list of all registered users can help control the use of a Web Service. This approach presents a number of potential issues, the greatest being the never-ending maintenance of IP address ranges for each client. IP address restriction can take place at both hardware and software levels. A hardware application of this security typically involves firewall restrictions to specific IP addresses. Restricting IP access using software security often involves keeping a database table of clients and another with associated IP addresses.

Each time a Web Service is accessed, you can get the requester's IP address (using the HTTP headers) and confirm that it exists in the security tables. If a match is located, the Web Service executes normally. Another option for software-based IP-address security is at the Web server level. Most Web server software permits any number of IP addresses to be restricted or enabled. Within IIS, it's as simple as selecting the properties of a given site and changing the IP restrictions. Since maintaining IP addresses of clients can be terribly cumbersome, as well as overly restrictive (if a consumer's IP address changes frequently), this option is generally not recommended.

Web Services Enhancements

The *Web Services Enhancements* (*WSE*) toolkit is a set of classes that allow developers to build Web Services using specifications made from the *Global XML Architecture* (*GXA*) specs. The GXA specs are a set of specifications that cover security, Web Service discovery, routing and attachments that were developed jointly by Microsoft and IBM with the aim of building a framework by which all Web Services would be developed in the future. The largest part of the WSE is the WS Security specification, and this contains classes that can enable you to use authorization and authentication (both discussed in the next chapter) with your Web Services, as well as being able to sign and verify services and details for their encryption.

> The WSE toolkit can be downloaded from **http://msdn.microsoft.com/webservices/** for free. Further discussion of this is beyond the scope of this book.

Other Web Services Considerations

Web Services are bringing about a major paradigm shift, not seen since the early days of the Internet. Because of this, it's important to recognize that these new conveniences have their own set of advantages and disadvantages. We won't talk about all the ways to avoid the pitfalls (which would require a book in itself), but will consider some of key issues.

Network Connectivity

A few years ago, the idea of calling a remote function and retrieving a value from it seemed unlikely. Now that we have Web Services, this newfound ability to use or purchase a given function from any organization on the Web causes us to think about the issue of Internet connectivity.

It's important to realize, that just as your company's Internet connection must be reliable, so should your Web Service provider's connection. Furthermore, if a Web Service requires any additional Internet resources, their service vendor's network must also be stable. There are many potential failure points in this arrangement. Often, this can be compounded if a Web Service provider hesitates, or refuses, to disclose who *their* providers are, since they don't want you going directly to them!

Asynchronous Method Calls

Since SOAP can be transported using SMTP (the email protocol), we can write Web Services that make use of asynchronous method calls. Asynchronous communication is a sort of disconnected, two way interaction that doesn't require an immediate response. Most programming deals with synchronous communication, where you call a function and wait for it to complete and return a value:

```
Distance_To_Rome = DistanceBetween("Los Angeles", "Rome", "meters")
```

In a situation like this, our application will not continue until the `DistanceBetween` function completes its logic and returns a value, which is placed in `Distance_To_Rome`. While this suits our needs most of the time, it is not always appropriate, especially when dealing with Web programming.

Batch processing, slowing down of applications, and anticipated disconnections are three situations where we should consider the possible advantages of asynchronous communication. The great news is that your Web Service need not be tailored specifically for synchronous or asynchronous communication; this is the proxy's duty.

The following Visual Basic code snippet illustrates how you might implement asynchronous function calls, using events:

```
...
DistanceBetween("Los Angeles", "Rome", "meters")
...
Private Sub DistanceBetween_CalculationComplete(ByVal Distance as Integer)
   Distance_To_Rome = Distance
End Sub
...
```

If the application contains code such as this, we will issue a request to `DistanceBetween` to calculate the distance between two cities, and then move on with our code. When the `DistanceBetween` object completes its calculation, it fires the `CalculationComplete` event, which allows us to handle the returned value without making the rest of the application wait.

Because we can call a remote function without the need for immediate response (without breaking an application), our applications can support longer time intervals and handle poorer network conditions, such as dial-up situations.

In the case of SMTP, the SOAP request is packaged in an email format and delivered to a mailbox on the server, just as if it was an e-mail composed and addressed to another individual. The specification for SOAP over SMTP defines a process of retrieving this message from the mail server, executing the function required, and mailing the SOAP results to the consumer, again using SMTP.

Service Hijacking (or Piggybacking)

Once your Web Service is available to the public, you may attract a client who is particularly interested in the service you provide. They're so interested, in fact, that they consider wrapping your powerful Web Service inside one of their own and representing it as their own product. Without security safeguards in place (and legal documents as well), a client may repackage your Web Service as if it were their own function, and there's no way for you to detect that this is being done (though you may become suspicious by examining your usage log when your client who occasionally uses your Web Service suddenly shows an enormous increase in activity). Given the level of abstraction that Web Services provide, it would also be nearly impossible for any customers of your unethical client to know who really owns the functionality.

Some organizations use a combination of usage logging and per-use charges. In my opinion, a cleverer way to avoid piggybacking is by using false data tests. Within your Web Service, you could create an undocumented function that creates a result that only *your* logic could produce. You would then be able to determine whether this code is really yours and the client is piggybacking the Web Service, or if the client is truly using its own logic.

An example of implementing a false data test would be a Web Service that provides book information for a given ISBN. As in the ISBN Web Service, we may return some arbitrary details if a certain ISBN is provided and is not associated with a real book. If the ISBN ABCDEFGHIJ were entered, special codes or copyright information could be sent as the resulting book title. You could then test this on the piggybacking company suspected of stealing your Web Service. Since this hidden functionality would not be published, it would provide a great way to prove that a company was reselling your Web Service's logic without your legal approval.

Provider Solvency

Since the Web Service model is a viable solution, you're probably eager to add its functionality to your core information systems and mission-critical applications. As Web Services become more and more interdependent, it becomes increasingly necessary to research the companies from whom you consume Web Services. You'll want to make sure these providers have what it takes to remain in business. UDDI goes a long way towards helping you with this research by providing company information for each registered Web Service provider (including their DUNS number).

In the business world, nothing seems to impact and force sweeping changes more than insolvency, and if you find yourself in the unfortunate circumstance of lost functionality due to a bankrupt Web Service provider, you'll realize how painful the hurried search for a new vendor can be (with little room to bargain with your ex-service's competitors). Although the initial work can be a bit tedious, it is important to know, as far as you can, whether a potential Web Service vendor will still be in business five years from now.

The Interdependency Scenario

The basis for all these and other Web Service considerations is the issue of interdependency. It's possible that you wake up a given morning, start an application that has worked for years, and find that the Web Service that it relies on is no longer available.

To some extent, thanks to the UDDI search capabilities, you can investigate and assess potential providers, but at the end of the day a degree of faith needs to be put into the services of each provider you choose to consume.

Summary

In this chapter, you've seen that a Web Service exposes its functions as a service that other applications can use. We began by discussing what a Web Service is and how it is used. We recapped XML and HTTP and their uses within the Web Services architecture. We then delved into the process of building Web Services, and creating and compiling a Web Service proxy. You learned how to use Web Services in an application by incorporating a defined namespace and making use of its methods. Afterwards, we saw how to discover what Web Services we have available to consume, and finally, considered some of the ways to make a Web Service secure.

As .NET makes programmatic interfaces over the Web more commonplace, you'll gradually be able to see applications sharing and building upon the contributions made by the community of Web Service providers. Web Services will provide a powerful means of seamlessly assembling applications that can span multiple platforms and languages. For the user, a transition is on the horizon from the browser to the more specific applications that make use of Web Services. For the developer, ASP.NET Web Services will make the Internet a programmer's toolbox, with a greater assortment of tools than ever before.

Exercises

1. Explain the role of the Simple Object Access Protocol (SOAP) in Web Services.

2. What is the purpose of the WSDL?

3. How would you locate a Web Service that provides the functions you require?

4. Create a Web Service with a class name of `circles`, that calculates the area of a circle, the circumference of a circle and the volume of a sphere. (Area = $(Pi)r^2$; Circumference = $2(Pi)r$; Volume of a sphere = $4/3(Pi)r^3$.)

5. Create a Web Service that connects to the Northwind database and returns employee's addresses based on their last names.

6. Create an ASP.NET page containing a drop-down listbox in which a user can select names of Northwind employees to return their addresses.

7. Secure the Northwind employee Addresses Web Service so that no unauthorized users have access to it.

ASP.NET Security

As soon as you start making information available on the Web, you've got to stop and ask yourself "Who do I want to show this to?" The chances are, unless you actively do something to protect your site's resources, they'll be available to anyone who cares to look for them. Unlike corporate intranets the Web is a public forum, so many people out there could be interested in what your ASP.NET pages have to offer. You need to take considered action to prevent your pages and Web services being used and consumed by people who should not have access to them.

Fortunately, there are many ways of controlling who's looking at your information. However, security doesn't stop with access policies; it's equally important that the applications you write are secured. It's no good having a secure authentication procedure if your homepage has a list of the users' passwords on it, or if a password entered by a user is stored in a non-encrypted form by the ASP.NET page.

Security is both about the strict enforcement of such access policies and about common sense. If you were asked to create a secure application, you might face situations where the users and administrators themselves don't update their passwords or choose passwords that are easy to crack, don't patch their servers with the latest Windows updates, or don't use firewalls to protect their systems. How can you effectively deal with this? The message here is: be aware of the situation your application is likely to be deployed in, the kind of people who are likely to access it, and the kind of system it is likely to be maintained on. A secure system requires careful planning and you have to be certain of these issues when storing confidential and valuable information within the application.

This chapter covers the most common and effective ways of creating secure applications. In addition we will also cover some guidelines and best practices. However, our usage of Web Matrix will restrict what we *can* demonstrate. Specifically, this chapter will cover:

- ❏ What is security?
- ❏ Forms authentication
- ❏ Forms database authentication and authentication against our case study
- ❏ Authorization
- ❏ SSL and encryption

What Is Security?

First of all let's discuss what security actually is.

> **Security is a process that protects private property from the general public, and permits access based only upon being able to verify that each individual's identity is in accord with the access permissions granted to him or her.**

For example, you protect the possessions in your home by fitting a lock to your front door. You will be able to decide who has access to your property, and who does not, provided you only give the key to approved people. Further, you could fit a different lock to the door of your study, and place a second set of *access permissions* with regard to who could enter that area.

The ASP.NET Security Model

When you are implementing a security solution the first thing you need to consider is what type of security will be most appropriate for your site. This will depend on the type of resources that you're exposing to users (whether your data is sensitive, or you just want to keep a track of who's viewing what) and the nature of the users that visit your site.

Many sites traditionally feature three levels of *user security*:

❑ **Anonymous Users**: Anyone visiting the site

❑ **Registered Users**: Users who have logged into the site with a user name and password

❑ **Administrators**: Users who have logged into the site with an administrative username and password

Having levels of user security on your site can be a very powerful tool. It allows you to grant people access to your site without giving them *carte blanche* to go anywhere they like on it.

Preventing *anonymous* access to key areas of your site is one of the simplest ways to reduce the likelihood of people viewing information that they are not authorized to view. By restricting access to just a select set of *Registered* users and *Administrators*, you can drastically cut down on the number of people that can view specific, confidential areas of your site. However some sites, such as www.usatoday.com, are happy to allow anonymous access, as it is the nature of their business to let people pop in and read the newspaper without having to give details about who they are.

You should choose a level of security that is appropriate for your site, and perhaps combine the three to create a complete solution. For example, www.amazon.com allows you *anonymous* access to browse its products, but requires you to become a *registered* user to place order or request account information.

We're not interested just in general security though, but also how security measures are applied in the .NET Framework. In ASP.NET, the process of securing an application is split into two separate (but related) stages:

❑ **Authentication**: The process of checking whether users are who they claim to be. The process of authentication involves requesting details (such as a user name and password and maybe even a zip code or mother's maiden name) from a user. These details are then checked against a relevant authority, such as a database or a Windows domain server.

❑ **Authorization**: The process of granting a user (or a group of users) the permission to use a resource, or denying them access to a resource or a group of resources.

Primarily, this chapter will cover *authentication*. We will also cover authorization and look at a simple *tiered* approach to building Web sites, so as to allow normal users to see one level of the site, and an administrator to see another. We'll add a simple authentication and authorization system to the WroxUnited application later in the chapter.

Lastly, we'll look very briefly at an issue that affects both of these processes – *encryption*. Encryption is the practice of using mathematical formulae to scramble information and make it unreadable to anyone who might intercept it. There are several types of encryption, all of which require the use of shared secret information between the Web site and the intended recipient. This information is known as a key. As discussed in earlier chapters, the HTTP protocol sends information as pure text, so if someone was able to intercept an HTTP request or response that hadn't been encrypted, they'd be able to read the details contained within, from usernames and passwords to credit card details and account numbers.

 In ASP.NET, encryption is typically implemented through the use of the *Secure Sockets Layer* (*SSL*), which is used to encrypt the information that you are passing back and forth and protect it from eavesdroppers. However, the task of building secure Web sites can be a lengthy one, and as it requires the IIS Web server we're not going to cover it in detail. We recommend that anyone setting out to build a secure Web site refer to other more detailed texts on encryption, because its complexities are beyond the scope of this book.

Authentication

There are several methods of authenticating whether visitors to your site have permission to access the information that they are requesting. There are four types of authentication:

❑ **Forms-based authentication**: A powerful and flexible means of taking control of the presentation of your security features to the user. We'll discuss how you can use this to authenticate user details stored both in `web.config` and in a database.

❑ **Basic authentication**: A simple method of verifying users, mostly used for customization options rather than restricting access.

❑ **Integrated Windows authentication**: A very simple, quick, and easy means of authenticating users, but can only be used with Internet Explorer browsers higher than version 5.0.

❑ **Passport authentication**: Microsoft also has its own separate and centralized authentication service. It provides a single login for all registered member sites of http://www.passport.com and is in use on sites such http://www.ebay.com. To implement it on your server you would require the Passport SDK to be downloaded first.

Unless you are using IIS, you will only have access to forms-based authentication. This isn't an issue to worry though. As demonstrated in the first chapter, Web Matrix isn't a Web server that is intended for deployment over networks. By default, you can view pages on the Web Matrix server via only the machine that is actually running the server. Web Matrix's limited security options are not a problem because no one outside has access to the machine anyway.

Also, basic and integrated Window authentication have serious limitations with regard to the way they present themselves to your users and the kind of information you can use with them (all your users need accounts in the Windows user account database). Thus, we will concentrate on talking only about forms based authentication.

Implementing Forms-Based Authentication

Forms-based authentication uses cookies. When a user logs into your ASP.NET application using forms-based authentication, ASP.NET issues an authentication cookie that will be sent back and forth between the server and client during the ensuing Web requests. If the authentication cookie is *persistent* then a copy will be stored on the user's hard drive and whenever they visit your ASP.NET application again, they can be pre-authenticated based on it until the cookie expires. If the authentication cookie type is *nonpersistent*, then the authentication cookie will be destroyed at the end of each browser session. In this case when they visit your ASP.NET application again, you can't pre-authenticate them and they will have to provide their credentials all over again.

You can use persistent and non-persistent cookies very flexibly. On most sites, such as Amazon.com, whenever you log in, beneath the password textbox there will be a link labelled Remember my password. If you check this box when you log into the site it will place a persistent cookie on your local computer and will be able to pre-authenticate you on your subsequent visits to the site. If you don't check it, then a nonpersistent cookie is used and you'll have to login each time you visit.

You'll be pleased to hear that forms-based authentication is also easy to implement. All you have to do is create a configuration file (web.config), a login page to accept the credentials from the user and verify them, and a default page where you'll display the content you wish to restrict. Let's look at how to do it.

In the following example, we'll create a form that accepts two pieces of information from the user via two ASP.NET textbox server controls – the first will be the username and the second their password. For good measure we'll also include some validation controls to make sure that the boxes are not left blank. An additional validation control will display any messages there may be from the server-side code. Finally, we'll add a button server control to allow us to submit the form using the Login_Click event.

We'll send this to a form that will display the username of the currently logged in user, the type of authentication that we've used, and an option for them to logout.

Try It Out Forms-Based Authentication

1.	Create a folder called Ch17 in Web Matrix, under the path C:\BegASPNET11\ and select the Web.Config option as shown in Figure 17-1:

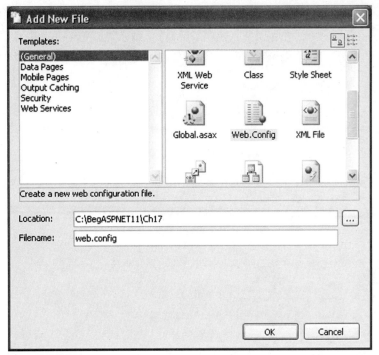

Figure 17-1

2. Click on OK, and completely overwrite the automatically generated code that appears in the web.config file with the following code:

```
<configuration>
  <system.web>
    <authentication mode="Forms">
      <forms name=".WroxDemo" loginUrl="login.aspx"
       protection="All" timeout="60" />
    </authentication>
    <machineKey validationKey="AutoGenerate" decryptionKey="AutoGenerate"
     validation="SHA1"/>
    <authorization>
      <deny users="?" />
    </authorization>
  </system.web>
</configuration>
```

3. Close the file, making sure that you save the changes to the file.

In the authentication mode="Forms"*, Forms is case-sensitive.*

4. Next create a file called `login.aspx` file `C:\BegASPNET11\Ch17 folder` and insert the following code in the All window:

```
<%@ Import Namespace="System.Web.Security " %>
<html>
<head>
<script language="VB" runat=server>
 Sub Login_Click(Src As Object, E As EventArgs)
    If txtEmail.Text = "Wrox" And txtPwd.Text = "MyPass" Then
     FormsAuthentication.RedirectFromLoginPage(txtEmail.Text,false)
    Else
     lblLoginMsg.Text = "Use Wrox as user name and password as " & _
                     "MyPass. Please try again"
    End If
 End Sub
</script>
</head>
<body>
<form runat="server">
<h1>Using Form based Authentication<BR>with Pre-Defined Credentials</h1><hr>
Users Name:<br />
<asp:textbox id="txtEmail" runat=server /> 
<FONT SIZE=2 COLOR="RED">*</FONT>

<br />Password:<br />

<asp:textbox TextMode="Password" id="txtPwd" runat=server />
  <FONT SIZE=2 COLOR="RED">*</FONT>
<br />

<asp:Label
 id="lblLoginMsg"
 ForeColor="Red"
 Font-Name="Verdana"
 Font-Size="10"
 runat=server />
<b />

<asp:button
 id="btnLogin"
 Text="Login"
 OnClick="Login_Click"
 runat=Server />
</form>
</body>
</html>
```

We've hardcoded our login details within this file. We've set the username to Wrox and the password to MyPass. This is not recommended practice, and is shown just for the sake of this example.

5. Save the file and close it.

6. Lastly, create another new file called `default.aspx`. Add the following code into the All window of this file:

```vb
<%@ Import Namespace="System.Web.Security " %>
<html>
<head>
<script language="vb" runat=server>
 Sub Page_Load(Src As Object, E As EventArgs)
  lblUser.Text = "<B>Your user name is:</B> " & User.Identity.Name
  lblType.Text = "<B>Your Authentication type is:</B> " & _
  User.Identity.AuthenticationType
 End Sub
 Sub Logout_Click(Src As Object, E As EventArgs)
  FormsAuthentication.SignOut()
  Server.Transfer("login.aspx")
 End Sub
</script>
</head>
<body>
 <form runat="server">
 <asp:label id="lblUser" runat=server/><br />
 <asp:label id="lblType" runat=server/><br />
 <asp:button text="Logout" OnClick="Logout_Click" runat=server/>
 </form>
</body>
</html>
```

7. When you request `default.aspx` from the browser, you should automatically be redirected to the login page, as shown in Figure 17-2:

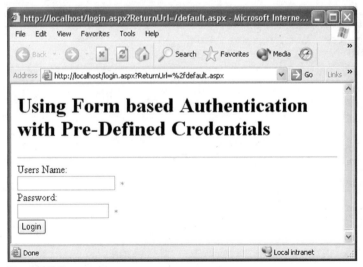

Figure 17-2

8. If you enter the login credentials incorrectly, you will receive the (rather insecure) error as shown in Figure 17-3:

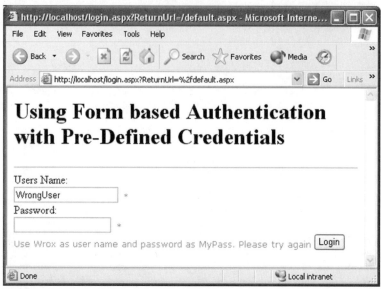

Figure 17-3

9. If you login correctly (taking care to enter the user name and password in the correct case) you will be granted access to the restricted page as shown in Figure 17-4:

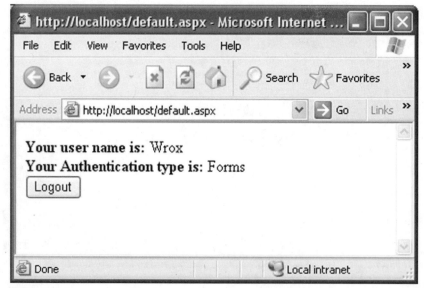

Figure 17-4

How It Works

When the browser requests the `default.aspx` file, the Web server first checks to see if we've logged in. Since we haven't, it serves us with `login.aspx` page instead and passes the authentication request to the ASP.NET runtime. This reads the `web.config` file and discovers that we're using forms-based authentication. The runtime will then look for the authentication cookie named in the `web.config` file (in the `name` element of the `<forms>` tag):

```
<authentication mode="Forms">
  <forms name=".WroxDemo" loginUrl="login.aspx"
  protection="All" timeout="60" />
</authentication>
```

In this file, we're using the `<forms>` tag to set the forms authentication properties. The following table describes the possible attributes for the `<forms>` tag:

Attribute	Description
Name	Name of the authentication cookie. If you are hosting more than one ASP.NET application from your Web server, make sure you give different names to each of the authentication cookies that you're using.
LoginUrl	The login page to which unauthenticated users should be redirected. This `loginUrl` can be on the same server, or a different one. If the `loginUrl` is on a different server then both servers should use the same `decryptionKey` parameter in the `machineKey` tag.
Protection	This method is used to protect the authentication cookie. The `<protection>` tag has four possible values (`All`, `Encryption`, `Validation`, `None`). Validation is the process of checking that the value decoded using the user key matches the value when decoded using the server's key – we look at it later in the chapter.
	When you set the value as `All`, both the validation and encryption will be performed against the authentication cookie to protect it. For the validation and decryption, the values specified in the `validationKey` and `decryptionKey` of the `machineKey` tag will be used. The `All` value is the default, and suggested, value for this parameter.
	When you set the value as `None`, the cookie will be transferred between the client and the server as plain text and you can turn off the encryption and validation with the `machineKey` tag.
	When you set the value as `Encryption`, the cookie will be decrypted as per the value specified in the `decryptionKey` of the `machineKey` tag and the content of the cookie will not be validated.

Table continued on following page

Attribute	Description
	When you set the value as `Validation`, the cookie will be validated, when received from the client, as per the value specified in the `validationKey` of the `machineKey` tag and the content of the cookie will not be encrypted and decrypted.
`Timeout`	The timeout value for the cookie to expire. The default value is 30 minutes.
`slidingExpiration`	This can be set to true or false, and is by default set to false. If it is set to true, then it indicates that the value in the timeout is to be renewed, whenever another request is made that accesses the cookie.

Next, the `machineKey` tag configures the encryption, decryption, and validation level for the authentication cookies. These values can be set for the machine-level, site-level, and application-level. The value can't be set for the sub-directory-level. The `machineKey` tag supports three attributes. Don't worry if these attributes don't make much sense now; we will talk about encryption later in the chapter.

Attribute	Description
`validationKey`	Specifies the validation key to be used when validating the authentication cookie data. The possible values for this element are either `AutoGenerate` or a manually assigned key.
	The minimum and maximum length of the key should be 40 characters (20 bytes) and 128 characters (64 bytes). `AutoGenerate` is the default.
`decryptionKey`	Specifies the encryption key to be used when validating the authentication cookie.
	Permitted values are the same as for `validationKey`.
`validation`	Specifies the type of encryption used for the data validation. The possible values are `SHA1`, `MD5`, and `3DES`.
	`SHA1` and `MD5` are hashing algorithms, and `3DES` is an algorithm used to encrypt and decrypt data.

The `<authorization>` tag is used to enable or disable access to an application. It can contain the following tags, which in turn have their own attributes:

Tag	Description
Deny	This can take three attributes: USER – the user name can be set to a particular user name or * (meaning all) or ? (meaning anonymous users) ROLE – this describes a particular role such as an administrator VERB – this can be set to a particular type of request such as HTTP GET or HTTP POST.
Allow	This can take three attributes: USER – the user name can be set to a particular user name or * (meaning all) or ? (meaning anonymous users) ROLE – this describes a particular role such as an administrator VERB – this can be set to a particular type of request such as HTTP GET or HTTP POST.

The `<authorization>` tag can be used to deny or allow access to particular users or particular groups of users or particular types of request, within the section of the file. An authentication cookie is only issued if it meets the requirements of this section.

If an authentication cookie is present, the ASP.NET runtime checks the `protection` attribute of the `<forms>` element and takes appropriate action based on its value. The `protection` attribute's settings of validation, encryption or none, are connected to the `<machineKey>` settings. So if the `protection` attribute is set to "encryption" ASP.NET will check the `web.config` `<machineKey>` for the encryption setting. Validation forms a first level of protection and then encryption can form a second and extra level of protection if needed.

If the cookie is valid, the requested page will be served back to the client. If the authentication cookie is not present, or invalid, then, the runtime will transfer the browser to the login page.

We specified the following in the `web.config` file:

```
<authorization>
<deny users="?">
</authorization>
```

This means that anonymous users are redirected to the login page. See Figure 17-2.

As you can see, the page URL holds a `QueryString` called **ReturnUrl** with a reference to the previous page (`default.aspx`) that we requested from the Web server. That's how the `RedirectFromLoginPage` method of the `FormsAuthentication` class knows where to transfer the browser back to once the user is successfully logged in. When you click the login button without entering the username and password, the validation controls display their error messages (refer back to *Chapter 14* for more information on this topic).

Login.aspx

Let's look at the logic in the `<script>` block in the `login.aspx` file.

Firstly we compare the `txtEmail` textbox value with the hardcoded value `Wrox`, and the `txtPwd` textbox value with the hardcoded value `MyPass`:

```VB
<script language="VB" runat=server>
 Sub Login_Click(Src As Object, E As EventArgs)

  If txtEmail.Text = "Wrox" And txtPwd.Text = "MyPass" Then
```

If the values match, we call the `RedirectFromLoginPage` method of the `FormsAuthentication` class. This method takes two parameters. The first is the username and the second is whether it is a persistent cookie or not. As this is set to `false`, our cookie will be nonpersistent:

```VB
    FormsAuthentication.RedirectFromLoginPage(txtEmail.Text, false)
```

If the login details don't match our values, we display a message via the `lblLoginMsg` label to the user telling them to use `Wrox` as the username and `MyPass` as the password:

```VB
  Else
   lblLoginMsg.Text = "Use Wrox as user name and password as " & _
                      "MyPass. Please try again"
  End If
 End Sub
</script>
```

Default.aspx

Figure 17-5 shows our `default.aspx` page:

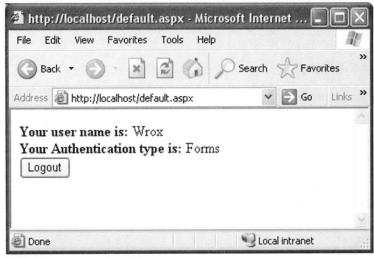

Figure 17-5

When using forms-based authentication, the authentication via login is only necessary when somebody who hasn't been identified tries to access the protected resource. The code just displays the user name and authentication type:

```vb
<script language="vb" runat=server>
 Sub Page_Load(Src As Object, E As EventArgs)
  lblUser.Text = "<B>Your user name is:</B> " & User.Identity.Name
  lblType.Text = "<B>Your Authentication type is:</B> " & _
  User.Identity.AuthenticationType
 End Sub
```

Then we add a `Logout` button to log the user out and redirect them back to the login page:

```vb
 Sub Logout_Click(Src As Object, E As EventArgs)
  FormsAuthentication.SignOut()
  Server.Transfer("login.aspx")
 End Sub
</script>
```

When we click this button the `SignOut()` method of the `FormsAuthentication` class is called. This will remove the authentication cookie from the client regardless of the persistence of the cookie. The user is then transferred back to the login page.

Forms-Based Authentication Using a Database

From what you've seen of forms-based authentication so far, it should be obvious that it is a very flexible and secure approach to authenticating users. However, the previous example had a major weakness – authentication took place against values hardcoded into the ASPX file. While this is OK for demonstration purposes (where there are only a few users), it is no good at all for production environments.

We'll fix this weakness in the following authentication example.

Try It Out   Authenticating Against a Database

For this example you'll need to download the `WroxDBAuth.mdb` database that's available with this book's code samples on www.wrox.com.

1. Create a new folder called `DB` in `C:\BegASPNET11\Ch17` and place the `WroxDBAuth.mdb` database in it.

2. Create a `web.config` file containing the following information and place it in the `Ch17` folder, overwriting the previous one:

```
<configuration>
  <system.web>
    <authentication mode="Forms">
      <forms name=".WroxDemo2" loginUrl="login.aspx"
      protection="All" timeout="20" />
    </authentication>
    <authorization>
      <deny users="?" />
    </authorization>
  </system.web>
</configuration>
```

3. Now, modify the `login.aspx` file used in the previous example from the All window as follows and then save it:

```
<%@ Page Language="VB" %>
<%@ Import Namespace="System.Web.Security " %>
<%@ Import Namespace="System.Data.OleDB" %>
<script language="VB" runat=server>
Sub Login_Click(Src As Object, E As EventArgs)
Dim strConn as string ="PROVIDER=Microsoft.Jet.OLEDB.4.0;DATA SOURCE=" &
server.mappath("DB/WroxDBAuth.mdb") & ";"
    Dim Conn as New OLEDBConnection(strConn)
    Conn.Open()
    Dim strSQL as string = "SELECT Pwd FROM Tbl_MA_Users WHERE Email = '" &
txtEmail.Text & "'"
    Dim Cmd as New OLEDBCommand(strSQL,Conn)
        'Create a datareader, connection object
    Dim Dr as OLEDBDataReader =
Cmd.ExecuteReader(System.Data.CommandBehavior.CloseConnection)
        'Get the first row and check the password.
    If Dr.Read()
      If Dr("Pwd").ToString = txtPwd.text Then
```

```
            FormsAuthentication.RedirectFromLoginPage(txtEmail.Text, false)
        Else
          lblLoginMsg.text = "Invalid password."
        End If
      Else
        lblLoginMsg.text = "Login name not found."
      End If
      Dr.Close
End Sub
</script>
```

. . .

4. Don't do anything to the `default.aspx` page from the previous example; it doesn't need changing at all for this one. Call up the `default.aspx` page in your browser and enter the login credentials as shown in Figure 17-6:

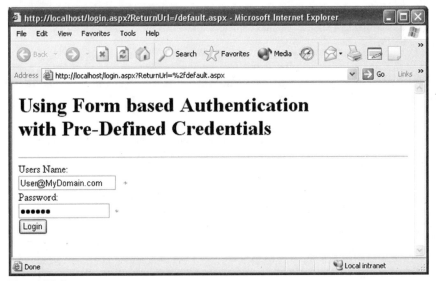

Figure 17-6

> The login details from the database are Username = `User@MyDomain.com` and Password = `MyPass` or Username = `NewUser@MyDomain.com` and Password = `MyPass`. Either will work.

5. If you've entered the details correctly, you'll be shown the `default.aspx` page as depicted in Figure 17-7:

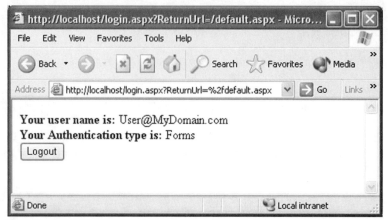

Figure 17-7

6. If you make a mistake, you'll be shown the `login.aspx` page again as in Figure 17-8, with an error message highlighted in red:

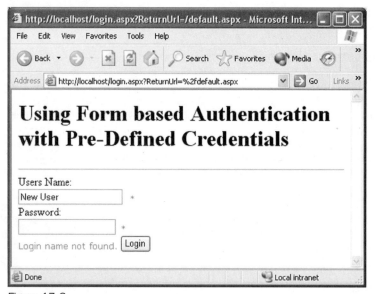

Figure 17-8

How It Works

The `login.aspx` page is the only one that has changed substantially from the previous example.

First of all, we include the `"System.Web.Security"` and `"System.Data.OLEDB"` namespaces for Security and Microsoft Access data access respectively:

```
<%@ Import Namespace="System.Web.Security" %>
<%@ Import Namespace="System.Data.OLEDB" %>
```

Then in the `Login_Click` event, we build a connection string for the Access database and declare an `OLEDBConnection` object to connect to the Access database and open the connection:

```
Dim strConn as string ="PROVIDER=Microsoft.Jet.OLEDB.4.0;DATA SOURCE=" & _
server.mappath("DB/WroxDBAuth.mdb") & ";"
Dim Conn as New OLEDBConnection(strConn)
Conn.Open()
```

Then we build a dynamic SQL statement into the `strSQL` variable, before creating an `OLEDBCommand` object by passing the dynamic SQL statement and the `OLEDBConnection` object to its constructor:

```
Dim strSQL as string = "SELECT Pwd FROM Tbl_MA_Users WHERE Email = '" & _
txtEmail.Text & "'"
Dim Cmd as New OLEDBCommand(strSQL,Conn)
```

Next, we create an `OLEDBDataReader` object and initialize it with the executed result of the `OLEDBCommand` object. We specify the `CommandBehavior` as `CloseConnection`. This makes sure that when we close the `OLEDBDataReader` object, the associated database connection will be closed.

Now we read the first record from the `OLEDBDataReader` object and compare the username and password with those entered by the user. If there are no rows in the `OLEDBDataReader` object, then the e-mail address entered by the user doesn't exist in the database (if it did, it would have been selected). As there can only be one unique e-mail address per entry, our database query can only return one row at maximum. If no rows are returned, we display the error message Login name not found. in the label control. If, instead, the password doesn't match, we display the error message Invalid password in the label control. If they both match we then transfer the user to the page that they originally requested:

```
'Get the first row and check the password.
If Dr.Read()
  If Dr("Pwd").ToString = txtPwd.text Then
    FormsAuthentication.RedirectFromLoginPage(txtEmail.Text, false)
  Else
    lblLoginMsg.text = "Invalid password."
  End If
Else
  lblLoginMsg.text = "Login name not found."
End If
```

After looking at some simple authentication pages, we're now nearly ready to see how we can integrate an authentication process into an existing application, namely the WroxUnited application, and see how it can be used to affect the functionality on offer to the user. Before we do this though, let's look at the associated process of authorization.

Authorization

You might just be wondering now, "it's possible to deny users access to all files on my Web site via the deny section, or allow individual users access, but if I want to allow users access to only *parts* of my Web site, what then?"

For example, what if you wanted to allow access to your site in general, but you have an admin section that you want to keep private to everybody except the administrators? It is possible to use web.config to provide an answer once again, by introducing some simple *authorization*. It was mentioned earlier that authorization is the process of checking whether a particular user should be granted or denied permission to a particular resource. This means by default, authentication must have already been performed when we first come to authorize a user. If you think about it, this is logical, as we have to confirm who a user is *before* we can check what things they are allowed to see.

In previous examples, you were actually using authorization to provide access to the applications, but rather than doing any checking, you were just letting all users though, and granting them all authorization. However, just about all security systems will need to be more sophisticated than this. You'll probably only want to let some users have authorization to areas and deny others.

So let's see how our web.config file can be changed to allow access to only the User@MyDomain.com, and deny the other account NewUser@MyDomain.com.

Try It Out Authorization for User@MyDomain.com

1. Go to Web Matrix, open the web.config file, and change the following code:

```
<configuration>
  <system.web>
    <authentication mode="Forms">
      <forms name=".WroxDemo" loginUrl="login.aspx"
      protection="All" timeout="60" />
    </authentication>
    <machineKey validationKey="AutoGenerate" decryptionKey="AutoGenerate"
     validation="SHA1"/>
    <authorization>
      <deny users="?" />
      <deny users="NewUser@MyDomain.com " />
      <allow users="User@MyDomain.com" />
    </authorization>
  </system.web>
</configuration>
```

2. Go back and run default.aspx again and enter the details for NewUser@MyDomain.com. This time, it directs you straight back to the login page. However, if you supply the details for User@MyDomain.com, it works just fine.

How It Works

In the `web.config` file, we've simply stuck in two extra lines:

```
<deny users="NewUser@MyDomain.com " />
<allow users="User@MyDomain.com" />
```

The first denies access to our `NewUser` account, while the second allows access to our `User` account. The line preceding these extra lines makes sure that no anonymous users are allowed access:

```
<deny users="?" />
```

We can use authorization to allow or deny specific users access to our application.

You might even wish to go further than this and allow say all users access to one section of your site, and deny them access and force them to login to say an admin area. First, create a separate subfolder underneath your main application; for example, if you had all your examples in `C:\BegASPNET11`, you could create a folder `C:\BegASPNET11\admin`. Then, to allow preferential or selective access, you can split the `web.config` file into two separate sections. If you look at the previous example, you can see that we have denied access to all users:

```
<configuration>
 <system.web>
   <authentication mode="Forms">
     <forms name=".WroxDemo" loginUrl="login.aspx"
     protection="All" timeout="60" />
   </authentication>
   <machineKey validationKey="AutoGenerate" decryptionKey="AutoGenerate"
    validation="SHA1"/>
   <authorization>
     <deny users="?" />
   </authorization>
 </system.web>
</configuration>
```

However, to enable access to the main site and deny access only to the files contained within the `admin` folder, you could change the file as follows:

```
<configuration>
 <system.web>
   <authentication mode="Forms">
     <forms name=".WroxDemo" loginUrl="login.aspx"
     protection="All" timeout="60" />
   </authentication>
   <machineKey validationKey="AutoGenerate" decryptionKey="AutoGenerate"
    validation="SHA1"/>
   <authorization>
     <allow users="?" />
   </authorization>
 </system.web>
 <location path="admin">
   <system.web>
     <authorization>
```

```
            <deny users="?" />
        </authorization>
      </system.web>
  </location>
</configuration>
```

First we've changed the authorization tags in the main part to allow access to the main site, and then added a new section under the `<location>` tag. The `<location>` tag has a `path` attribute, which is set to the name of the folder to be denied access to. Then we have a new set of `<system.web>` tags. This is a vital feature. The `<location>` tag can only be set outside the `<system.web>` section, but inside the configuration tags. It contains a `<system.web>` section that only applies to that one folder. Inside the new `<system.web>` section is a set of `<authorization>` tags and a deny attribute, that takes precedence in the `admin` folder, over the previously specified ones.

It was mentioned in *Chapter 15* that the `web.config` settings take priority over `machine.config` settings. Here the principle is the same – the settings for the individual folder in the location tag take precedence over the settings for the main site.

With these settings, we can now deny or allow users access to only specific parts of our site. Let's see a practical demonstration in the next example, where we add authentication to the WroxUnited application.

Adding Authentication to the WroxUnited Application

We'll add a password login system to the WroxUnited application, which we created over the course of *Chapters 10* to *13*. This will enable a user to log in to the application. It will then detect whether a user is an administrator or not and if so, display an extra panel in the user control navigation bar which will allow administrators to see special links that are hidden from users.

However, the WroxUnited application isn't a members-only club, it's something that all people should have access to. Therefore, we only want to block access to the administration section.

We can achieve this by adding forms-based authentication to the `web.config` file, and then by adding a login page as in our previous examples, but only making access to the login page via the main navigation bar. We'll use the same forms authentication process as in the previous example and just show how it neatly dovetails with the existing application functionality. We'll then add a login panel to the NAVBAR control and some code behind to generate the panel contents. We'll also add a logout button.

Try It Out Adding a Login Page to WroxUnited

1. Create a new `web.config` file and add the following code over the the auto-generated code and save the file in the `WroxUnited` folder:

```
<configuration>
    <system.web>
      <authentication mode="Forms">
        <forms name=".WroxUnited"
                          loginUrl="admin\login.aspx"
                          protection="Validation"
                          timeout="999999" />
      </authentication>
      <authorization>
         <allow users="*" />
      </authorization>
    </system.web>
  <location path="admin">
    <system.web>
        <authorization>
          <allow users="*"/>
          <deny users="*" />
        </authorization>
    </system.web>
  </location>
</configuration>
```

2. Next create an `admin` folder and download `playeradmin.aspx`, `teamadmin.aspx`, and `gamesadmin.aspx` into the folder.

3. Now, in the `admin` folder, create a login form called `login.aspx` with two text boxes called `UserName` and `UserPass`, a button called `LoginBtn`, and a label called `Msg`:

```
<html>
<head>
    <link id="css" href='..\<%= Session("SelectedCss")%>' type="text/css"
rel="stylesheet" />
</head>
<body>
    <form runat="server">
        <WROXUNITED:HEADER id="HeaderControl" runat="server"></WROXUNITED:HEADER>
        <h2>Login Page
        </h2>
        <table width="800">
            <tbody>
                <tr>
                    <td style="VERTICAL-ALIGN: top; WIDTH: 165px">
                        <WROXUNITED:NAVBAR id="NavBar" runat="server">
                        </WROXUNITED:NAVBAR>
                    </td>
                    <td style="VERTICAL-ALIGN: top">
                        <table>
                            <tbody>
                                <tr>
```

```
                                  <td>
                                      Username:</td>
                                  <td>
                                      <asp:TextBox id="UserName" runat="server">
                                      </asp:TextBox>
                                  </td>
                              </tr>
                              <tr>
                                  <td>
                                      Password:</td>
                                  <td>
                                      <asp:TextBox id="UserPass" runat="server"
                                       TextMode="Password"></asp:TextBox>
                                  </td>
                              </tr>
                          </tbody>
                      </table>
                      <asp:button id="LoginBtn" onclick="LoginBtn_Click"
                                  runat="server" text="Login"></asp:button>
                      <p>
                          <asp:Label id="Msg" runat="server" forecolor="red">
                          </asp:Label>
                      </p>
                  </td>
              </tr>
          </tbody>
      </table>
    </form>
</body>
</html>
```

4. Add the following code in the Web Matrix **Code** window:

```
Sub LoginBtn_Click(Sender As Object, E As EventArgs)

    Dim PlayersDB as System.Data.iDataReader
    PlayersDB = Players()
    While PlayersDB.Read()

        Dim PlayerLogin as String = PlayersDB("SiteLogin")
        Dim PlayerPassword as String = PlayersDB("SitePassword")
        Dim AdminLevel as String = PlayersDB("AdminLevel")

        If (UserName.Text = PlayerLogin And UserPass.Text = PlayerPassword) Then

            Dim UserNameCookie as New HttpCookie("UserNameCookie")
            UserNameCookie.Value = UserName.Text
            Response.Cookies.Add(UserNameCookie)

            Dim UserLevelCookie as New HttpCookie("UserLevelCookie")
            UserLevelCookie.Value = AdminLevel
            Response.Cookies.Add(UserLevelCookie)

            FormsAuthentication.RedirectFromLoginPage(UserName.Text, true)
```

```
      Else
        Msg.Text = "Invalid Credentials: Please try again"
      End If

  End While

  PlayersDB.Close()

End Sub

Function Players() As System.Data.IDataReader
  Dim connectionString As String =
ConfigurationSettings.AppSettings ("ConnectionString")
  Dim dbConnection As System.Data.IDbConnection = New
System.Data.OleDb. OleDb Connection(connectionString)
  Dim queryString As String = "SELECT [Players].[SiteLogin],
 [Players]. [SitePassword],[Players].[AdminLevel] FROM [Players]"

  Dim dbCommand As System.Data.IDbCommand = New
System.Data.OleDb.OleDbCommand
  dbCommand.CommandText = queryString
  dbCommand.Connection = dbConnection

  dbConnection.Open
  Dim dataReader As System.Data.IDataReader =
dbCommand.ExecuteReader (System.Data.CommandBehavior.CloseConnection)

  Return dataReader
End Function
```

5. In the All window, add the two registration tags to the top of the code after the `<@Page>` tag:

```
<%@ Register TagPrefix="WroxUnited" TagName="Header" Src="..\header.ascx"%>
<%@ Register TagPrefix="WroxUnited" TagName="Navbar" Src="..\navbar.ascx"%>
```

6. Next, add the login details to the navigation bar. Open `navbar.ascx` and add the following code to the existing code in the HTML window:

```
    <p>
        <asp:HyperLink id="lnkMerchandise" runat="server"
NavigateUrl="Merchandise.aspx">Official Merchandise</asp:HyperLink>
    </p>
    <asp:panel id="pnlLogin" runat="server" visible="true">
    <p>
        <asp:HyperLink id="lnkLogin" runat="server"
NavigateUrl="\admin\login.aspx">Login</asp:HyperLink>
    </p>
    </asp:panel>
    <hr width="95%" />
    <br />
    <p>
        Choose a theme:<br />
        <asp:DropDownList id="ddlTheme" runat="server">
            <asp:ListItem Value="WroxUnited.css" Selected="True">Home Kit
            </asp:ListItem>
```

```
            <asp:ListItem Value="WroxUnited2.css">Away Kit</asp:ListItem>
        </asp:DropDownList>
        <asp:Button id="btnApplyTheme" onclick="btnApplyTheme_Click"
runat="server"
        Text="Apply">
        </asp:Button>
        <br />
        <asp:CheckBox id="chkRememberStylePref" runat="server" Text="Remember
        preference">
        </asp:CheckBox>
    </p>
    <asp:panel id="pnlEdit" runat="server" visible="false">
        <hr width="95%" />
        <br />
        <p>
            Login Details:
            <asp:Label id="lblStatus" runat="Server"></asp:Label>
        </p>
        <asp:Button id="btnLogout" onclick="btn_Logout" runat="server"
Text="Logout"></asp:Button>
    </asp:panel>
</div>
```

7. Now, add both the following sub procedures to the **Code** window of `navbar.ascx` in Web
Matrix:

```
Sub Page_Load()
If (Request.IsAuthenticated = true) Then
  pnlEdit.Visible = true
  pnlLogin.Visible = false
  lblStatus.Text = "<br>You are logged in as: " & _
     Request.Cookies("UserNameCookie").Value
  if Request.Cookies("UserLevelCookie").Value = "admin" and _

right$(Request.ServerVariables("APPL_PHYSICAL_PATH"),11)="WroxUnited\"then
        lblStatus.Text &= "<br><br><a href='\admin\playeradmin.aspx'>Player _
        Admin Page</a><br>"
        lblStatus.Text &= "<br><a href='\admin\teamadmin.aspx'>Team Admin _
        Page</a><br>"
        lblStatus.Text &= "<br><a href='\admin\gamesadmin.aspx'>Games Admin _
        Page</a><br>"
Else if Request.Cookies("UserLevelCookie").Value = "admin" and _
        right$(Request.ServerVariables("APPL_PHYSICAL_PATH") ,6)="admin\" then _
        lblStatus.Text &= "<br><br><a href='playeradmin.aspx'>Player Admin _
        Page</a><br>"
        lblStatus.Text &= "<br><a href='teamadmin.aspx'>Team Admin _
        Page</a><br>"
        lblStatus.Text &= "<br><a href='gamesadmin.aspx'>Games Admin _
        Page</a><br>"
        End If
End If
End Sub
```

```
Sub btn_Logout(sender As Object, e As EventArgs)
```

```
      FormsAuthentication.Signout
      pnlLogin.Visible= true
      pnlEdit.Visible=false
      if right$(Request.ServerVariables("PATH_INFO") ,10)="admin.aspx" then
       Response.Redirect("..\default.aspx")
      else
       Response.Redirect("default.aspx")
      end if
End Sub
```

8. Open up the browser, view `default.aspx`, and go to the login page via the new link as shown in Figure 17-9:

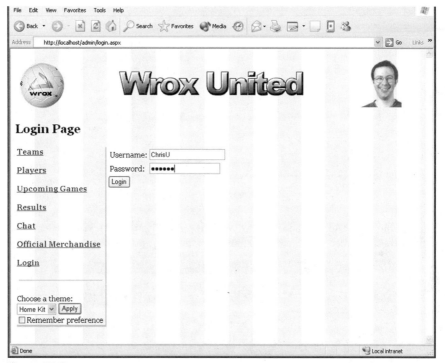

Figure 17-9

9. Login with the username ChrisU and the password **secret** and scroll down to see the login details panel on the navigation bar as shown in Figure 17-10:

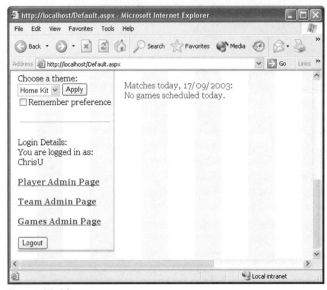

Figure 17-10

10. Click on the Player Admin Page link. As you can see in Figure 17-11, you have access to the administration screen and can make changes by adding and deleting new players:

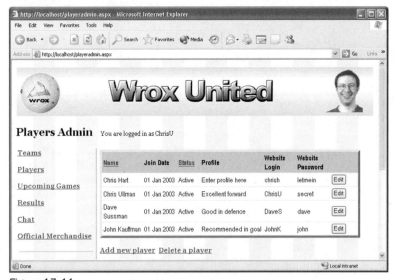

Figure 17-11

11. Now click on the logout button at the bottom of the login details panel. You're redirected back to the login page. This time enter the details **DaveS** and the password **dave**, and scroll down once logged in to arrive at the view depicted in Figure 17-12:

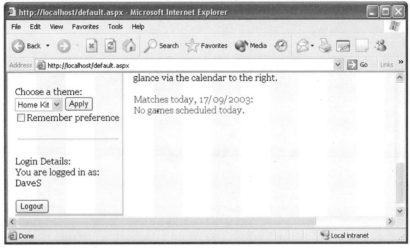

Figure 17-12

This time you can't see any links, just the user details. You should be unable to use the admin links. However, entering the URL would still take you to the relevant page; we haven't shut that door!

How It Works

The login system is able to offer a two-tiered view of the site because our code is able to detect from the user details, who the user is, authorize them, and then offer a different view of the Web site. If you go to WroxUnited database and check the `Players` table, you should find that:

SiteLogin	SitePassword	AdminLevel
ChrisU	Secret	Admin
DaveS	Dave	User

Let's go back to the code we created. The `web.config` file is almost identical to the one in the *Selective Access* section. We use forms-based authentication and allow access to the main site using the `<allow user="?">` tag, but we redirect access to the `login.aspx` page for the entire contents of the admin folder. We deny authorization to any anonymous user, using the `?`:

```
<authentication mode="Forms">
  <forms name=".WroxUnited"
         loginUrl="admin\login.aspx"
         protection="Validation"
         timeout="999999" />
```

```
                    </authentication>
                    <authorization>
                      <allow users="*" />
                    </authorization>

            </system.web>
        <location path="admin">
          <system.web>
                    <authorization>
                      <allow users="*"/>
                       <deny users="*" />
                    </authorization>
            </system.web>
        </location>
```

The `web.config` file handles most of the security.

Login.aspx

The login page is where the authentication against the `WroxUnited.mdb` takes place. The HTML is of no interest to us; it's the code-behind where the work is done. We have one sub procedure and one function. The sub procedure is activated when the user clicks on the Login button. We start by creating an instance of a data reader called `playersDb`, and then read in information from it by calling the `iDataReader` function:

```
Sub LoginBtn_Click(Sender As Object, E As EventArgs)

  Dim PlayersDB as System.Data.iDataReader
  PlayersDB = Players()
  While PlayersDB.Read()
```

The three pieces of information we are interested in are the `SiteLogin`, the `SitePassword`, and the `AdminLevel`. We create three variables to store each of the items in as they are read back from the WroxUnited database:

```
        Dim PlayerLogin as String = PlayersDB("SiteLogin")
        Dim PlayerPassword as String = PlayersDB("SitePassword")
        Dim AdminLevel as String = PlayersDB("AdminLevel")
```

Next we check if the username and password match a record in the database:

```
        If (UserName.Text = PlayerLogin And UserPass.Text = PlayerPassord) Then
```

If they do, we create two cookies. The first cookie stores the corresponding user name in a cookie called `UserNameCookie`, with no expiry date specified:

```
          Dim UserNameCookie as New HttpCookie("UserNameCookie")
          UserNameCookie.Value = UserName.Text
          Response.Cookies.Add(UserNameCookie)
```

The second cookie stores the corresponding admin level in a cookie called `UserLevelCookie`, also with no expiry date specified:

```
Dim UserLevelCookie as New HttpCookie("UserLevelCookie")
UserLevelCookie.Value = AdminLevel
Response.Cookies.Add(UserLevelCookie)
```

We then authenticate the login and redirect the user back to the original URL they requested:

```
FormsAuthentication.RedirectFromLoginPage(UserName.Text, true)
```

However, if we don't have any matches for the `UserName` and `Password` in the `Players` table anywhere in the WroxUnited database, we display an appropriate message, refusing them entry and urging them to try again:

```
Else
   Msg.Text = "Invalid Credentials: Please try again"
End If

End While
```

We finish the procedure by closing the `Players` table.

During this subprocedure, we call the `iDataReader` function. This function creates an instance of a `DataReader` object and populates it with the results of the following SQL query:

```
Dim queryString As String = "SELECT [Players].[SiteLogin],
[Players].[SitePassword], [Players].[AdminLevel] FROM [Players]"
```

This SQL query returns the site login, password, and admin level for every player in the `Players` table. This is the information with which we checked the contents of the `textname` and `password` textboxes in the `Login_Click` procedure.

Basically the `login.aspx` page checks a user's entry credentials and either allows them to move on to the default page or stops them at the login page depending on whether they enter valid details. If they do enter valid details, then the user name and admin level are stored in two cookies for use in the next section of the code.

Navbar.ascx

In the navigation bar, we created an extra `<asp:panel>` that contained a button and a label control. By default, the panel was made invisible:

```
<asp:panel id="pnlEdit" runat="server" visible="false">
```

This is because we wanted to enable it only once someone had correctly logged in. Behind the `<asp:panel>` are procedures. The first is a `Page_Load` procedure, which is executed whenever the navigation bar is loaded. When the bar is loaded, we check to see if the user has been authenticated:

```
Sub Page_Load()
If (Request.IsAuthenticated = true) Then
```

If they have been authenticated, the panel is made visible and the login link is made invisible:

```
        pnlEdit.Visible = true
    pnlLogin.Visible = false
```

The *only* time the panel shouldn't be visible is at the login page. To get to the main application, someone must have logged in correctly. Also we set the contents of the label control here. First we display the name of the contents of our `UserNameCookie`:

```
        lblStatus.Text = "<br>You are logged in as: " & Request .Cookies ("User
NameCookie") .Value
```

Then we check if the user is an administrator or not, by checking the contents of the `UserLevelCookie`. If the user is an administrator, we display three extra links to the admin control in our login panel. However we have a small problem here. These files are already in the `admin` folder. So we stick a `\admin` in front of our ASPX page name. However, if we are in the `admin` folder already, then this will stick an extra admin in front of our `admin` folder: for example, `admin\admin`. This would cause a file not found error. So we have to check to see our location in the application as well:

```
    if Request.Cookies("UserLevelCookie").Value = "admin" and

right$(Request.ServerVariables("APPL_PHYSICAL_PATH"),11)="WroxUnited\"then
            lblStatus.Text &= "<br><br><a href='\admin\playeradmin.aspx'>Player
            Admin Page</a><br>"
            lblStatus.Text &= "<br><a href='\admin\teamadmin.aspx'>Team Admin
            Page</a><br>"
            lblStatus.Text &= "<br><a href='\admin\gamesadmin.aspx'>Games Admin
            Page</a><br>"

        Else if Request.Cookies("UserLevelCookie").Value = "admin" and
        right$(Request.ServerVariables("APPL_PHYSICAL_PATH") ,6)="admin\" then
            lblStatus.Text &= "<br><br><a href='playeradmin.aspx'>Player Admin
            Page</a><br>"
            lblStatus.Text &= "<br><a href='teamadmin.aspx'>Team Admin
            Page</a><br>"
            lblStatus.Text &= "<br><a href='gamesadmin.aspx'>Games Admin
            Page</a><br>"

        End If
    End If
```

We use a pruned version of the server variable's `APPL_PHYSICAL_PATH` to determine whether we are in the `WroxUnited` folder or the `admin` folder. If it's `WroxUnited`, we need to add an `admin` folder to our ASPX admin page link. If we are already in the `admin` folder, we can create a link straight to our ASPX admin page. We just create three links and add them to the label control's text property to dump them straight to the screen.

The second procedure just handles the logout process. This is triggered when the logout button is pressed, and it simply uses the `FormsAuthentication.SignOut` method to automatically revoke authentication. We make the login panel invisible and the login link visible on the navigation bar. Then as we no longer want the user to be logged in, we dump them unceremoniously back at the login page:

```
Sub btn_Logout(sender As Object, e As EventArgs)
      FormsAuthentication.Signout
      pnlLogin.Visible= true
      pnlEdit.Visible=false
      if right$(Request.ServerVariables("PATH_INFO") ,10)="admin.aspx" then
       Response.Redirect("..\default.aspx")
      else
       Response.Redirect("default.aspx")
      end if
End Sub
```

There is one little caveat here as well; if we are in the admin section, the URL back to the home page is once again slightly different (it has an extra admin folder in). So we use the PATH_INFO server variable to determine whether or not we are on an admin page. If we *are* on such a page, we jump up one in the hierarchy; if we are *not*, we can go straight back to the home page. And there you have it, we have used authentication to create a very simple twotiered approach to our WroxUnited application.

Let's now quickly consider *encryption* of data on the Web and how it works with authentication.

Encryption using SSL

Over the past few years there's been an explosion in the amount of business conducted over the Internet. This business, known as *e-commerce*, comprises such things as online banking, online brokerage accounts, and Internet shopping. Today you can book plane tickets, make hotel reservations, rent a car, transfer money, and buy clothes using your PC.

Unfortunately this convenience comes at a price. Simply entering your credit card number on the Internet leaves you wide open to fraud as your information can be intercepted and read on route. This is because when information is transmitted between the client and server via the HTTP protocol, it is sent as normal text that could be viewed by anyone who was trying to *listen in* on the transactions you make.

You can use encryption to code the message, In encryption, the sender of the message uses a secret key to scramble (or encrypt) the message and the receiver needs the same key to be able to unscramble and understand. However, this method, known as secret-key encryption, has a drawback. The sender and receiver must agree on the secret key without anyone else discovering it. Anyone who intercepts the key in transit can decipher and read the encrypted messages.

In more recent times, secret-key encryption has been replaced with a method called public-key encryption. This method gives each user a pair of keys: a public key and a private key. Each person's public key is made available to public but the private key is kept under wraps. It works along these lines: If a user named Vervain wanted to send an encrypted message to another user named Rheingold, he can look up Rheingold's public key in a directory, and use it to encrypt the message before sending it. Rheingold can then use his own private key to decrypt the message and read it. This means that it's possible for anybody to send an encrypted message to Rheingold using the public key, but only Rheingold can use the private key to decrypt and read the message.

In ASP.NET, SSL is used to encrypt information that you send over to the server (not just your credit card number, the entire message) with a public key system. The server then receives this information, decrypts it, and proceeds with the transaction without the fear that your personal information has fallen into the wrong hands.

To do this, the SSL protocol uses hashing keys to encrypt the message, as well as authenticating servers before data is exchanged by the higher-level application. It maintains the security and integrity of the transmission channel by using encryption, authentication, and message authentication codes. SSL uses sophisticated hashing algorithms like MD5 and SHA1, which are very tough to break.

You can enable SSL in forms-based authentication very simply by using the `requireSSL` attribute. This was introduced in ASP.NET 1.1. By default, it is set to false, but if changed to true in `web.config`, it sets a secure property in ASP.NET, and the browser connected to it will return a cookie only if it is using SSL.

Try It Out   Enabling SSL

Note that you cannot create an SSL link with Web Matrix (it can only be done in ASP.NET with IIS, and this is beyond the scope of the book) but you can prevent your normal user from logging in by altering the `requireSSL` attribute, which is what we'll do now.

1.   Go to `web.config` created in the forms authentication databases example, and add the attribute as follows:

```
<configuration>
  <system.web>
    <authentication mode="Forms">
      <forms name=".WroxDemo2" loginUrl="login.aspx"
        protection="All" timeout="20"
        requireSSL="true" />
    </authentication>
    <authorization>
      <deny users="?" />
    </authorization>
  </system.web>
</configuration>
```

2.   Now go back to `default.aspx` and try to login now via http://localhost/default.aspx and supply the correct credentials. You'll find that instead of letting you in, it dumps you back to the login screen.

How It Works

This example code won't allow us access to our main `default.aspx` page in any circumstances, because we are using a straight http:// link, which, as we've just stressed, sends requests and receives responses in pure text. We would have to enable a secure http link to do this, but it isn't possible to enable a secure link with Web Matrix, as Web Matrix isn't intended to be deployed in a production setting.

To identify a secure link, the URL would have to be prefixed with https://, and Internet Explorer would have a small lock icon in the bottom right hand corner as shown in Figure 17-13:

Figure 17-13

Typically, you would supply such details as a password and login, over a secure https:// link. You can see that enabling SSL via the `requireSSL` attribute forces users to use the secure link. When you connect to a secure Web server using SSL, the server sends a certificate to you. This certificate could be created by one of many *Certificate Authorities (CA)*; common ones include:

❑   **Verisign**: http://www.verisign.com

❑   **Belsign**: http://www.belsign.be

❑   **Xcert**: http://www.xcert.com

These businesses provide a validation service performing a yearly validation to check if the business is a legitimate functioning one. So when you log on, you can be confident that a CA on your behalf has checked the business. Once the browser receives the certificate, it extracts a public key, which can be used to encrypt or decrypt information. To create a secure link using SSL, you would need to be using IIS.

We don't really need to go any further into this complicated process, but it gives you a feel for how standard secure transactions are conducted on the Internet. Further discussion of SSL is beyond the scope of this book, but you could find out more about if from a CA such as www.verisign.com, from whom you can also buy an SSL certificate to prove your server's identity.

Summary

In this chapter we've covered a few of the most important aspects of basic ASP.NET security.

We looked at how we can secure our applications flexibly using the more complex method of forms-based security that allows us to build our own user interfaces, and how we can improve upon the basic ideas of this approach by storing the user's details in a database. We then looked at how the associated process of authorization could be used to restrict access to specific areas of the site, or to specific users. We created a login panel for the Web site, with a simple two-tier system for normal users and for administrators. Lastly we touched upon the idea of encryption and finally we talked about the basic premises upon which SSL works.

With security we complete our tour of ASP.NET. We've covered a lot of subjects within this book, and hope that you've enjoyed it. If you're wondering what to do next, go back and learn each of the subjects the chapters focused on in more detail. Each chapter forms a stepping-stone from which you can go on to build sections of your own applications. Application building is something that can only be learned from experience. You can go back and add extra sections to the application presented in this book. We provide some extra pages on the Web site. Try adding those to the application. You can then customize it and play around with the code. See what effects you can have by tweaking it.

Next you can try building your own applications from scratch. It can be quite daunting at first, but you've already covered all of the main areas, so you've no need to worry. Base your own applications on the framework presented here, and don't be afraid to experiment. ASP.NET is a powerful tool and takes time to master. It's also something you can develop an individual approach for. We've presented a recommended way to do it, but within this framework there is plenty of room for you to create your own approach. Most of all, have fun. Happy developing!

Exercises

1. What is the difference between authorization and authentication?

2. Create an application that uses forms-based authentication that requires a user name, password, and a zip code before you can go to the main login page. Hardcode the username, password, and the zip code. Call it `zipcodelogin.aspx`.

3. Upgrade the application from exercise 2 to use the `WroxAuth.mdb` used in this chapter.

4. Create an account for a user named `John@MyDomain.com`, but deny him access in `web.config`. What happens when you try to log in as him? Can you think of a way of displaying a message to accompany this?

5. Create a new page called `newpage.aspx` on the example, and use `web.config` to ensure that only John has access to it. *HINT: Create a subfolder for this page.*

Exercise Answers

Chapter 2

This chapter discusses the structure of an ASP.NET page and the way that it functions in relation to the .NET Framework.

Exercise 1

State what the .NET Framework provides for programmers.

Solution

The .NET Framework offers the following:

- ❑ It provides a single tool for creating Windows-based applications and Web-based applications.

- ❑ It allows programmers to work with objects; this simplifies application development.

- ❑ It reduces the number of lines of code required to achieve a task.

- ❑ It allows different languages to work together within a single application.

- ❑ It incorporates tools to automatically accommodate devices beyond the desktop, including PDAs, mobile phones and wrist PCs.

Exercise 2

Which encompasses more code, a class or a namespace?

Solution

A namespace is made of one or more classes, so the namespace is larger.

Exercise 3

The ASP.NET module of code adds on to which part of Windows?

Solution

The ASP.NET module of code adds on to the *Internet Information Server (IIS)*.

Exercise 4

What special modifications must be made to the browser on the client-side in order to view an ASP.NET page?

Solution

None – a browser (by definition) displays HTML, and ASP sends out pure HTML. No special tags, software or plugins are required on the browser.

Exercise 5

Why does an ASP.NET page get compiled twice?

Solution

The first time, to the Intermediate Language, compiles as much as possible but without reference to the specific capabilities of a server. The second time, to the Common Language Runtime, is to further compile the code to take advantages of the actual server that will host the page.

Exercise 6

Why does the first display of an ASP.NET page take several seconds but subsequent views appear in only milliseconds?

Solution

Because the first time the page is requested it must be compiled to the CLR.

Exercise 7

What two attributes should always be included in all ASP.Net Web controls?

Solution

Always include the `runat="server"` and an `ID="MyControlName"` in all ASP.Net Web controls.

Chapter 3

This chapter considers the use of variables for holding data in Visual Basic .NET.

Exercise 1

Explain the difference between `<form>` and `<form runat="server">` and describe how each one is handled.

Solution

The HTML `<form>` tag provides space for user input. The input is sent back to the server without specific instructions for how to handle the input. The ASP.NET tag `<form runat="server">` will send the information back to an IIS .NET server that is able to automatically handle many basic functions of the user's input.

Exercise 2

What is a variable and how is it related to data types in VB.NET?

Solution

A variable is a place to temporarily hold information that can be used in the code. All variables in VB.NET must be declared as a type, a designation that identifies the kind of information the variable holds.

Exercise 3

Use string, numeric, and date variables to create an ASPX file that displays your name, age, and date of birth.

Solution

See file `57076_ch03_ans03.aspx`, available with the code download:

```
<%@ Page Language="VB" Debug="true" %>
<script runat="server">

    Sub Page_Load
        If IsPostBack
        Dim strName as String
        Dim bytAge as Byte
        Dim datDOB as Date

        strName = txtname.text
        bytAge = txtAge.text
        datDOB = txtDOB.text

        lblOut.text = "Your Name is " & strName
        lblOut.text += "<br>Your Age is " & bytAge
```

```
            lblOut.text += "<br>Your Birthdate was " & datDOB

          End If
      End Sub
</script>
<html>
    <head>
    </head>
    <body>
        <form runat="server">
        Please enter your Name: <asp:TextBox runat="server" ID="txtName"/><br/>
        Please enter your Age: <asp:TextBox runat="server" ID="txtAge"/><br/>
        Please enter your Date of Birth: <asp:TextBox runat="server" ID="txtDOB"/>
                                  <br/>
        <asp:Button runat="server" Text="Submit"/><br/>
        <asp:Label runat="server" ID="lblOut"/><br/>
        </form>
    </body>
</html>
```

Exercise 4

Arrange the following into groups of *Numeric, Textual,* and *Miscellaneous* data types. Rank the numeric according to the size number it can hold. Give an example of a value and use for each.

Integer, Char, Byte, Short, Boolean, String,

Long, Single, Double, Date, Decimal

Solution

The data types can be grouped in the following manner:

❑ **Numeric** (in order of increasing size):

1. Byte is good for people's ages or school grade levels.

2. Integer is good for quantity of goods sold if the amount does not go over 2 billion and does not have decimals.

3. Short is good for quantities of goods sold that need decimals, but do not go over 32,000.

4. Long could hold the distance to stars in kilometers.

5. Decimal could hold the value of an exchange rate to several dozen decimal places.

6. Single could hold the exact amount of load on a structural beam (including the decimal value).

7. Double could hold a representation of the ? to hundreds of decimal places.

- **Text** (small to large):
    1. Char could hold the value for a single Chinese character that represents a person's family name.
    2. String could hold a person's family name in a western language.
- **Miscellaneous**:
    1. Boolean could hold a True if a box in a form has been filled in.
    2. Date can hold a person's date of birth or the date when an order is shipped.

Exercise 5

Create an array containing your five favorite singers. Then concatenate the elements of your array into one string, and, after the opening sentence "My 5 favorite singers are:", display them in a clear way using the `<asp:label>` control.

Solution

See file `57076_ch03_ans05.aspx`, available with the code download:

```
<%@ Page Language="VB" Debug="true" %>
<script runat="server">

    Sub Page_Load
        If IsPostBack
        Dim strSingers(5)as String

        strSingers(0) = txtSinger0.text
        strSingers(1) = txtSinger1.text
        strSingers(2) = txtSinger2.text
        strSingers(3) = txtSinger3.text
        strSingers(4) = txtSinger4.text

        lblOut.text = "Your names of your favorite singers are:"
        lblOut.text += "<br>" & strSingers(0)
        lblOut.text += "<br>" & strSingers(1)
        lblOut.text += "<br>" & strSingers(2)
        lblOut.text += "<br>" & strSingers(3)
        lblOut.text += "<br>" & strSingers(4)

        End If
    End Sub

</script>
<html>
    <head>
    </head>
    <body>
        <form runat="server">
        Please enter the names of your your five favorite singers<br>
        <asp:TextBox runat="server" ID="txtSinger0"/>
        <asp:TextBox runat="server" ID="txtSinger1"/><br/>
```

```
            <asp:TextBox runat="server" ID="txtSinger2"/>
            <asp:TextBox runat="server" ID="txtSinger3"/><br/>
            <asp:TextBox runat="server" ID="txtSinger4"/><br/>
            <asp:Button runat="server" Text="Submit"/><br/>
            <asp:Label runat="server" ID="lblOut"/><br/>
        </form>
    </body>
</html>
```

Exercise 6

Describe a situation in which you would use each of the following and state why that choice is the best:

Solution

❏ **Arrays**: We need to store words of a document while looking for certain patterns in the wording. We need a very high speed but will not do resorting or additions in the middle of the index.

❏ **Arraylists**: Creating a list items in an order. At the beginning of the order we are not sure how many kinds of items there will be. Speed is less of an issue, but we need the flexibility of adding any number of items.

❏ **Hashes**: At an international sporting event, storing countries names and codes, then reading the names by looking up their codes. Hashtables are best because they avoid the use of a numbering index system, we can use the country codes directly for the indexing.

❏ **Sorted lists**: We want to display a glossary of abbreviations. The display will need to be on the page sometimes ascending and sometimes descending alphabetically. The sorted list allows us to avoid a numeric index (we can use the abbreviations) and to quickly read the list in order.

Chapter 4

This chapter looks at the key building blocks of VB.NET in the context of an ASP.NET page.

Exercise 1

For each of the following Boolean expressions, say for what integer values of A each of them will evaluate to True and when they will evaluate to False:

Solution

You can test your answers using the page named 57076_ch04_ans01.aspx in the download files.

1. NOT A=0

True for all integers except 0.

Without the NOT, the answer would be only zero. When we add the NOT, it reverses to be all numbers except zero.

2. `A > 0 OR A < 5`

True for all integers.

The left side alone would be true for all integers greater than zero (only zero and negative integers would be false). The right side includes all integers that are less than five, including zero and negative integers. With the OR clause an integer has to be within one of the two expressions in order for the whole expression to be true. When we combine these two sets of answers we get all integers. (The integers 1 to 4 are included by both expressions)

3. `NOT A > 0 OR A < 5`

True for integers 5 and below. Integers 6 and above will evaluate to false.

The issue here is precedence between the NOT and OR. The NOT is only applied to the expression on the left of the OR. Think of this problem as `(NOT A > 0) OR (A < 5)`. On the left we have true for any numbers that are not greater then zero, so true is for zero and negative numbers. On the right we have true for any number that is less then five. With the two sides of the OR combined, we have true for all negative numbers and zero and positive numbers up to 5. Numbers greater than and including 6 are true for neither side and thus resolve to false.

4. `A > 1 AND A < 5 OR A > 7 AND A < 10`

True for 2,3,4, 8, and 9 only.

Like the last problem, the issue is to establish the precedence of the operators. Think of this as `(A > 1 AND A < 5) OR (A > 7 AND A < 10)`. On the left of the OR we can see that only integers 2,3, and 4 would fit both criteria. On the right side of the OR the situation is similar; only 8 and 9 meet both criteria. When you consider the OR you have to combine those two answer sets.

5. `A < 10 OR A > 12 AND NOT A > 20`

True for all integers 9 and below (including zero and negatives) and for 13 through 20 inclusive. False for 10, 11, 12, and all integers above (and inclusive of) 21.

Think of this problem with some parentheses. The OR is the last to be evaluated, so our parentheses are `(A < 10) OR (A > 12 AND NOT A > 20)`. First look at the right side of the OR. Integers must meet both tests when there is an AND clause so that would be 13 through 20 are true. Now look at the left side of the OR. Any number less then 10 will be true. The final answer is the combination of those two answer sets.

Exercise 2

Suggest a loop structure that would be appropriate for each of the following scenarios and justify your choice:

Solution

1. Displaying a set of items from a shopping list stored in an array

This depends on whether we know the array is full or not. We can get the value of the upper bound of an array, but it is harder to know if all of the members have values. In most cases we would use a Do...While.

2.   Displaying a calendar for the current month

We can know how many days are in a month, so we know how many loops we will have to perform before we start looping. Therefore we can use the `For... Next`.

3.   Looking through an array to find the location of a specific entry

Assuming that we do not know the number of members when we start the loop it is best to use `Do... While`. If we can find out the number of members before the loop starts, we can use a `For... Next`.

4.   Drawing a chess board using an HTML table

Before we start the loop, we know a chess board is 8 by 8 squares, so we can use a `For... Next`.

Exercise 3

Write a page that generates a few random numbers between two integers provided by the user in text boxes.

Solution

See file `57076_ch04_ans03.aspx`, available with the code download:

```
<%@ Page Language="VB" Debug="true"%>
<script runat="server">

Sub Page_Load
  If IsPostBack
    lblOut.text = ""
    Dim intOutputCounter as integer
    For intOutputCounter = 1 to 10
        lblOut.text += "<br>" & int((1+txtHigh.text - txtLow.text) * rnd + txtLow.
                                      text)
    Next intOutputCOunter
  End If
End Sub

</script>
<html>
    <head>
    </head>
    <body>
        <form runat="server">
    <asp:TextBox runat="server" ID="txtLow"/>
    <asp:TextBox runat="server" ID="txtHigh"/><br/>
    <asp:Button runat="server" Text="Submit"/><br/>
    <asp:Label runat="server" ID="lblOut"/><br/>
        </form>
    </body>
</html>
```

Chapter 5

This chapter covers how the modularization and reusable code in ASP.NET works.

Exercise 1

Choose between using a sub and a function for each of the following scenarios, and justify your choice:

Solution

1. Calculate the due date of a book being checked out of a library.

Function because we will execute some code and return a value (the due date).

2. Find out on which day of the week (Monday, Tuesday, etc.) falls a certain date in the future.

Function because we will execute some code and return a value (the day of the week).

3. Display in a label a string determined by the marketing department and stored in a text file.

Procedure because we will only execute some code. There is no need to return a value.

Exercise 2

List where and when values are held when a variable is used as a parameter passed `ByVal`. Do the same for `ByRef`.

Solution

`ByVal` holds the value in the original place *and* in the procedure (or function). So while the procedure is running, two copies of the value exist, of which *one* may be modified in the procedure. The copy in the procedure will be destroyed at the end of the procedure.

`ByRef` holds the value in only one place. Thus changes made to the value during the procedure (or function) will take effect on the sole copy and thus be useable by both the procedure and the calling code. Although the end of the procedure will stop using the value, it will remain intact in the calling code.

Exercise 3

Write an ASP.NET page with a procedure or function that generates a set of random integers. Build an ASP.NET page that allows you to enter the lower and upper bounds, and generate a set of random numbers within that range.

Solution

Recall from *Chapter 4* the following formula:

RandomNumber = int((1 + *upperbound* − *lowerbound*) * rnd) + *lowerbound*

The ASP.NET page (file `57076_ch05_ans03.aspx`) would be written as follows:

```
<%@ Page Language="VB" Debug="true" %>
<script runat="server">

    Sub Page_Load
        If IsPostBack
          If IsNumeric(txtLower.text) AND IsNumeric(txtUpper.text) AND
                                        IsNumeric(txtQty.text)
            Call RowOfNumbers
          Else
            lblOut.text = "<hr>Please enter three numbers"
          End If    'data exists
        End If   'postback
        Call CleanUI
    End Sub



    '''''''''''''''''''''''''''''''''''''''''''''''''''''''''''''
    ' Clean up Input Boxes
    ' version 1.0
    ' 01 Jan 2004
    '
    '''''''''''''''''''''''''''''''''''''''''''''''''''''''''''''
    Sub CleanUI
        txtLower.text = ""
        txtUpper.text = ""
        txtQty.text = ""
    End Sub

    '''''''''''''''''''''''''''''''''''''''''''''''''''''''''''''
    ' Generate a Random Number
    ' version 1.0
    ' 01 Jan 2004
    '
    '''''''''''''''''''''''''''''''''''''''''''''''''''''''''''''
    Function GenerateRandomNumber(intLower as integer, intUpper as integer)
    Return int((1 + intUpper - intLower) * rnd) + intLower
    End FUnction


    '''''''''''''''''''''''''''''''''''''''''''''''''''''''''''''


    '''''''''''''''''''''''''''''''''''''''''''''''''''''''''''''
    ' Concatenate a row of numbers
    ' version 1.0
    ' 01 Jan 2004
    '
    '''''''''''''''''''''''''''''''''''''''''''''''''''''''''''''
    Sub RowOfNumbers
        lblOut.text = "<hr>Random numbers between " & txtLower.text
        lblOut.text += " and " &  txtUpper.text & " inclusive"
        lblOut.text += " (Quantity of " & txtQty.text & "):<br>"
        Dim intQty as integer
```

```
       For intQty = 1 to CInt(txtQty.text)
          lblOut.text += cStr(GenerateRandomNumber(txtLower.text,txtUpper.text))
          lblOut.text += "   "
       Next intQty
    End Sub

    ''''''''''''''''''''''''''''''''''''''''''''''''''''''''''''''

</script>
<html>
    <head>
    </head>
    <body>
    <form runat="server">
        Highest number: <asp:TextBox runat="server" ID="txtLower"/><br/>
        Lowest Number: <asp:TextBox runat="server" ID="txtUpper"/><br/>
        Quantity of Numbers: <asp:TextBox runat="server" ID="txtQty"/><br/>
        <asp:Button runat="server" Text="Submit"/><br/>
        <asp:Label runat="server" ID="lblOut"/><br/>
    </form>
    </body>
</html>
```

Chapter 6

This chapter discusses how ASP.NET revolves around an event-driven model, and how things occur in strict order and ways in which the ASP.NET page can react to user intervention. The solution files for some of the exercises are too long to be included here – these have been put up for download on the Wrox Web site.

Exercise 1

Explain why event-driven programming is such a good way of programming for the Web.

Solution

First, on the Web (more than in a desktop client) it is difficult to predict the actions and order of actions by the user. Writing our code to react to those actions that occur improves the user experience and the reliability of achieving our results.

Second, as Web sites become more complex with the input of more programmers, it is important to code with a design that makes maintenance easier, such as event-driven programming.

Exercise 2

Run the following HTML code in your browser (remember to save the page with an .htm suffix). Translate it into a set of ASP.NET server controls.

```
<html>
<head>
  <title>HTML Breakfast form</title>
</head>
<body>
  <form>
    <h4>Please enter your name:</h4>
    <input type=text/>
    <h4>What would you like for breakfast?</h4>
      <input type=checkbox name="cereal"> Cereal
      <input type=checkbox name="eggs"> Eggs
      <input type=checkbox name="pancakes"> Pancakes
    <h4>Feed me:</h4>
      <input type=radio name="when" value="now">  Now
      <input type=radio name="when" value="later">  Later
    <h4>Click 'submit' to process<h4>
    <input type="submit" value="Submit"/>
  </form>
</body>
</html>
```

Solution

HTML solution is in the `57076_ch06_ans02Breakfast.html` file available for download.

ASPX solution is in the file named `57076_ch06_ans02Breakfast.aspx`:

```
<%@ Page Language="VB" Debug="true" %>
<html>
<head>
    <title>ASPX Breakfast form</title>
</head>
<body>
    <form runat="server">
        <form>
            <h4>Please enter your name:
            </h4>
            <asp:TextBox id="txtName" runat="server"></asp:TextBox>
            <h4>What would you like for breakfast?
            </h4>
            <asp:CheckBoxList id="chkEntree" runat="server">
              <asp:listitem id="EntreeCereal" runat="server" value="Cereal" />
              <asp:listitem id="EntreeEggs" runat="server" value="Eggs" />
              <asp:listitem id="EntreePancakes" runat="server" value="Pancakes" />
            </asp:CheckBoxList>
            <h4>Feed me:
            </h4>
            <asp:RadioButtonList id="RadioButtonList1" runat="server">
              <asp:listitem id="TimeNow" runat="server" value="Now" />
              <asp:listitem id="TimeLater" runat="server" value="Later" />
            </asp:RadioButtonList>
            <h4>Click 'submit' to process
                <h4>
                    <input type="submit" value="Submit" />
```

```
                </h4>
              </h4>
           </form>
       </form>
  </body>
</html>
```

Exercise 3

Add a `Page_Load` event handler to the ASPX code you've just created in *Exercise 2*, to confirm the selections made in the following format:

Thank you very much _____

You have chosen _____ for breakfast, I will prepare it for you _____.

Solution

Solution in file named `57076_ch06_ans03Breakfast.aspx`

Exercise 4

Create a very basic virtual telephone using an ASPX file that displays a textbox and a button named Call. Configure your ASPX file so that when you type a telephone number into your textbox and press Call, you are presented with:

❑   A message confirming the number you are calling

❑   A Disconnect button, which when pressed, returns to your opening page, leaving you ready to type another number

Solution

Three solutions of increasing complexity are given here. We've presented the first `.aspx` file:

❑   Solution is in the file named `57076_ch06_ans04TS1.aspx`.

```
<%@ Page Language="VB" %>
<script runat="server">

    Sub cmdConnect_Click(sender As Object, e As EventArgs)
        lblStatus.Text = "Connected to" & txtTelNumber.Text
        lblStatus.Font.Italic=false
        cmdConnect.enabled=false
        cmdDisconnect.enabled = true
        End Sub

        Sub cmdDisconnect_Click(sender As Object, e As EventArgs)
        txtTelNumber.Text = ""
        lblStatus.Text = "no connection"
        lblStatus.Font.Italic=true
        cmdDisconnect.enabled = false
```

```
            cmdConnect.enabled = true
            End Sub

</script>
<html>
<head>
</head>
<body>
    <form runat="server">
        Please enter the number to dial:
        <asp:TextBox id="txtTelNumber" runat="server"></asp:TextBox>
        <br />
        <asp:Button id="cmdConnect" onclick="cmdConnect_Click" runat="server" Text
                ="Connect" BackColor="#C0FFC0" Width="101"></asp:Button>
        <asp:Label id="lblstatus" runat="server"></asp:Label>
        <asp:Button id="cmdDisconnect" onclick="cmdDisconnect_Click" runat="server"
                Text="Disconnect" BackColor="#FFC0C0" enabled=false></asp:Button>
    </form>
</body>
</html>
```

❏   Solution is in file named 57076_ch06_ans04TS2. aspx.

❏   Solution is in file named 57076_ch06_ans04TS3. aspx.

Exercise 5

Using the SELECT CASE or a collection, associate three particular telephone numbers with three names, so that when you press the Call button, your confirmation message contains the name of the person you are calling rather than just the telephone number.

Solution

Solution is in file named 57076_ch06_ans05Telephone.aspx.

Chapter 7

This chapter introduces concepts such as properties, methods, constructors, collections, and overloading, making use of plentiful examples relating to real-world objects.

Exercise 1

Our examples modelled some simple characteristics of real-world objects, such as animals. Think about other real-world objects that when turned into classes would be useful in programming.

Solution

You've probably used one of these objects without thinking about it. What happens when you go to the supermarket? You put items in a shopping basket. How many of those online sites have a shopping basket? Yep, pretty much all of them. In fact, the shopping basket is one thing where the concept maps really well from the real world into the virtual one.

Creating a shopping basket in .NET is actually a little more complex than you'd think, as it has to contain multiple items. You don't know in advance how many items people are going to put into it, so you can't have properties for each item. What you need is some sort of collection that expands as items are added. There are several collections supplied in the `System.Collections` namespace. It's worth experimenting with them.

Exercise 2

In the `Animal` class, the `Walk()` method accepts an argument of type `Integer`. Expand the `Walk()` method to use this `Integer` as the speed of walking. Think about how you'd store that speed and what you'd do with it.

Solution

Storing the speed internally in the class can be achieved by declaring a private variable, and modifying the `Walk()` method:

```
Private _Speed As Integer
Public Function Walk(Direction As Integer) As String
  _Speed = Direction
  If Direction >0 Then
    Return _Name & _
      ": you are now walking forwards at a speed of " & _Speed
  Else
    Return _Name & _
      ": you are now walking backwards at a speed of " & _Speed
  End If
End Function
```

You might also consider providing a property to access or set the speed.

Other options include adding methods to speed up and slow down the speed. For example:

```
Public Sub SpeedUp(SpeedUpBy As Integer)
  _Speed += SpeedUpBy
End Sub
Public Sub SlowDow(SlowDownBy As Integer)
  _Speed -= SlowDownBy
End Sub
```

Although these aren't very complex, they show the interaction between methods and properties.

Exercise 3

Taking the results from *Exercise 2*, think about how you'd add validation to the speed, to ensure it didn't exceed some set limits.

Solution

The interaction between methods and properties can be seen very clearly when we need to validate values. Consider the addition of speed to our `Person` class, which can be set via three methods: `Walk`, `SpeedUp`, and `SlowDown`. If we wanted to ensure that the speed never exceeded the range 100 to 100, where would we do this? In each method that accesses the `_Speed` variable? No, we don't want to have lots of repeated code. Remember how we said encapsulation is one of the key points of classes – we should encapsulate the speed as a property and do the checking there:

```
Public Property Speed As Integer
  Get
    Return _Speed
  End Get
  Set (ByVal Value As Integer)
    If Value < -100 Then
      _Speed = -100
    Else
      _Speed = Value
    End If
    If Value > 100 Then
      _Speed = 100
    Else
      _Speed = Value
    End If
  End Set
End Property
```

Now all accesses to the `_Speed` variable should be replaced with the property name:

```
Public Function Walk(Direction As Integer) As String
  Speed = Direction
```

If you don't want to expose the speed as a public property, make it private:

```
Private Property Speed As Integer
```

You still get the advantages of encapsulation, but without exposing the property.

Exercise 4

Describe the main differences between class inheritance and interface. When would you use one over the other?

Solution

The main difference between inheritance and class interfaces is that interfaces don't implement any functionality. They only define what the class must implement – not how it is done. Inheritance on the other hand provides a way to supply implementation to classes that inherit from a base class.

It's important to understand this difference and to think about where you'd use one method over another. Interfaces are good if you are defining the structure of a class for others to implement – perhaps in a team environment where you are writing common routines and require certain features to be present on the objects that will use those routines. Inheritable classes are good when you have to supply functionality to multiple child classes. The ASP.NET server controls are a perfect example, where much of the implementation is provided in the base `WebControl` class. An interface wouldn't be any use because each control would then have to implement the same functionality.

Exercise 5

Create a class called `PieceOfString` with a single read / write property (of type `Integer`) called `Length`. Create an instance of the class and set the `Length` to `16`. Now you can answer that age old question "How long is a piece of string?"

Solution

OK, OK, so it's not a real exercise. But I thought it was funny.

Chapter 8

This chapter looks at the use of the `Connection` and `Command` objects for opening data sources and retrieving information into `DataSets`.

Exercise 1

In this chapter we created a page that showed only the products for a selected category. Try and think of ways to enhance this to show products for either a selected category or all categories.

Solution

There are several possible solutions to this. The simplest is to employ another button to just fetch all of the products. However, this isn't the best approach because it can easily confuse the user. The best approach is to have the drop-down list show a selection allowing all categories. Two things need to happen to implement this. Firstly you need to add the all categories selection to the list, and secondly you need to customize the data fetching so that it fetches all rows.

The first part is simple, as we can simply add a new item to the list after we add the categories from the database. We can't add it to the list first because when we bind data to the list our manually added item would get overwritten. Our code now becomes:

```
Sub Page_Load(Sender As Object, E As EventArgs)

    If Not Page.IsPostback Then
        lstCategory.DataSource = GetCategories()
        lstCategory.DataValueField = "CategoryID"
        lstCategory.DataTextField = "CategoryName"
        lstCategory.DataBind()
        lstCategory.Items.Add(New ListItem("<all categories>", -1))
    End If

End Sub
```

This works by adding a new ListItem to the DropDownList. Every item in the list is a ListItem, contained within an Items collection. So we create a new ListItem (the arguments are the text and the value), and add it to the collection. This then appears at the end of the list.

Now that all selection is in the list we need to process it, and this can be done in the GetProducts function. We are automatically building a SQL string, with the placeholder and parameters, but these aren't required if we are showing all products. Since we've added the all option with a value of 1 (which isn't a real CategoryID) we can use that to change our SQL string. So, our code now becomes:

```
Function GetProducts(ByVal categoryID As Integer) As System.Data.DataSet
    Dim connectionString As String = "Provider=Microsoft.Jet.OLEDB.4.0; " & _
        "Ole DB Services=-4; Data Source=C:\BegASPNET11\data\Northwind.mdb"
    Dim dbConnection As System.Data.IDbConnection = _
            New System.Data.OleDb.OleDbConnection(connectionString)
    Dim queryString As String
    If CategoryId = -1 Then
      queryString = "SELECT [Products].[ProductName], " & _
        "[Products].[QuantityPerUnit], [Products].[UnitPrice], " & _
        "[Products].[UnitsInStock] FROM [Products]"
    Else
      queryString = "SELECT [Products].[ProductName], " & _
        "[Products].[QuantityPerUnit], [Products].[UnitPrice], " & _
        "[Products].[UnitsInStock] FROM [Products] " & _
        "WHERE ([Products].[CategoryID] = @CategoryID)"
    End If
    Dim dbCommand As System.Data.IDbCommand = _
            New System.Data.OleDb.OleDbCommand
    dbCommand.CommandText = queryString
    dbCommand.Connection = dbConnection
    If CategoryID <> -1 Then
        Dim dbParam_categoryID As System.Data.IDataParameter = _
                New System.Data.OleDb.OleDbParameter
        dbParam_categoryID.ParameterName = "@CategoryID"
        dbParam_categoryID.Value = categoryID
        dbParam_categoryID.DbType = System.Data.DbType.Int32
        dbCommand.Parameters.Add(dbParam_categoryID)
    End If

    Dim dataAdapter As System.Data.IDbDataAdapter = _
            New System.Data.OleDb.OleDbDataAdapter
    dataAdapter.SelectCommand = dbCommand
```

```
    Dim dataSet As System.Data.DataSet = New System.Data.DataSet
    dataAdapter.Fill(dataSet)

    Return dataSet
End Function
```

Here we simply create a different SQL string if we are showing products for all categories, and if the `CategoryID` is not 1, then a category has been selected so we add the `Parameter`.

Exercise 2

In *Exercise 1* we encountered the problem of wanting to bind data from a database to a `DropDownList` as well as manually adding an entry, where adding the manual entry could only be done at the end of the list. There are two ways to solve this problem – one using techniques shown in this chapter, and one using techniques not yet covered. Try and code the solution using the known technique, but see if you can think of a way to solve it with code we haven't shown.

Solution

The first solution to this problem is not to use data binding, but simply to manually add all of the data. We could do this by not using a DataSet and using a DataReader instead, looping through all of the records. This would allow us to add our all category first, and then all of the data. For example, assuming our `GetCategories` function returns a DataReader, we could do this:

```
Sub Page_Load(Sender As Object, E As EventArgs)

    If Not Page.IsPostback Then
        lstCategory.Items.Add(New ListItem("<all categories>", -1))

        Dim dr As System.Data.IDataReader = GetCategories()

        While dr.Read
            lstCategory.Items.Add(New ListItem(dr("CategoryName"), _
                                               dr("CategoryID")))
        End While
    End If

End Sub
```

Here we simply add all of the items from the data reader in the same manner as for the all item.

The other solution to this would be to add the all item to the first row of the data in the DataSet and then use the existing data binding. This is harder to do and we are not going to cover a solution here as it uses techniques that we'll cover in the next chapter. However, if you'd like to investigate before we cover it, then you need to discover what a DataSet contains. It contains a collection of `DataTable` objects, each of which contains a collection of `DataRow` objects. It's worth reading up on these to give yourself a head start!

Chapter 9

This chapter looks at the way information in DataTables and DataSets can be manipulated, and the results stored back to the data source from which they came.

Exercise 1

Load a DataSet with the Shippers table from Northwind and add the following data into it:

❑   Company Name: FastShippers

❑   Phone: (503) 555-9384

Solution

This isn't too hard as you've seen all of this code before, and can easily be done in the Page_Load event of an ASP.NET page:

```
Dim connectionString As String
Dim strSQL          As String
Dim data            As New DataSet()
Dim dbConnection    As OleDbConnection
Dim dataAdapter     As OleDbDataAdapter
Dim commandBuilder  As OleDbCommandBuilder


' set the connection and query details
connectionString = "Provider=Microsoft.Jet.OLEDB.4.0; " & _
                   "Data Source=C:\BegASPNET11\data\Northwind.mdb"
strSQL = "SELECT * FROM Shippers"

' open the connection and set the command
dbConnection = New OledbConnection(connectionString)
dataAdapter = New OledbDataAdapter(strSQL, dbConnection)

' fill the dataset with the data
dataAdapter.Fill(data, "Shippers")

' add a new row to the table
Dim table  As DataTable
Dim newRow As DataRow

table = data.Tables("Employees")
newRow = table.NewRow()
newRow("CompanyName") = "FastShippers"
newRow("Phone") = "(503) 555-9384"
table.Rows.Add(newRow)
```

Exercise 2

Using the CommandBuilder object, create an InsertCommand to insert this new data.

Solution

This simply requires the creation of an `OleDbCommandBuilder` object and the use of the `GetInsertCommand()` method, and send the changes back to the database:

```
' create the other commands
commandBuilder = New OleDbCommandBuilder(dataAdapter)
dataAdapter.InsertCommand = commandBuilder.GetInsertCommand()

' update the database
dataAdapter.Update(data, "Shippers")
```

Notice that we don't have to specify the other commands, as in this case we are only adding a row of data. If we had changed or deleted a row, those changes would not be reflected in the database, as we haven't specified the `UpdateCommand` or `DeleteCommand`.

Exercise 3

Using direct SQL commands, change the phone number of `FastShippers` to (503) 555-0000.

Solution

```
Dim connectionString As String = "Provider=Microsoft.Jet.OLEDB.4.0; " & _
  "Data Source=C:\BegASPNET11\data\Northwind.mdb"
Dim dbConnection As New OleDbConnection(connectionString)
dbConnection.Open()

Dim commandString As String = "UPDATE Shippers " & _
                              "SET Phone = @Phone " & _
                              "WHERE CompanyName = 'FastShippers'"

Dim dbCommand As New OleDbCommand(commandString, dbConnection)

Dim firstNameParam As New OleDbParameter("@Phone", OleDbType.VarChar, 24)
firstNameParam.Value = "(503) 555-0000"
dbCommand.Parameters.Add(firstNameParam)

dbCommand.ExecuteNonQuery()

dbConnection.Close()
```

This is much the same as examples you've seen previously, except that in those we added a row. In this case we use the SQL `UPDATE` command to set the `Phone` column to the value of the supplied parameter.

Exercise 4

Using the Web Matrix data templates, create an Editable DataGrid. Have a look at the code and see how many familiar techniques you see.

Solution

This uses many advanced features of the DataGrid, but the ADO.NET code is similar to that you've been working with. Take the `DataGrid_Update()` method for example, which caters for new and updated data. It either builds a SQL `INSERT` or `UPDATE` statement, uses `Parameters` to set the values, and then uses the `ExecuteNonQuery()` method of the DataAdapter to send the changes back to the database.

The `DataGrid_Delete()` method does a similar thing, constructing a SQL `DELETE` statement.

The `AddNew_Click()` method uses an interesting technique – it adds a new row to a table, but doesn't update the database. Instead it sets a flag indicating that a new row is being added. This means that the user can modify the data in the new row, or even cancel the addition before sending the changes to the database.

Chapter 10

This chapter explains how ASP.NET server controls derive their properties and methods from the various classes and objects that make up the .NET Framework. This chapter is where you see the Wrox United application taking shape.

Exercise 1

Consider a use for an HTML tag with `runat="server"` in the Wrox United application in place of one of the existing Web controls and explain why the HTML control is able to achieve the same result as the Web control.

Solution

You can make this change in several places in `Default.aspx` – for example, the `asp:Hyperlink` controls could be replaced with HTML anchor tags with a `runat="server"` attribute. You could also change the panel which displays match details and replace it with a `div` tag:

```
<div id="pnlFixtureDetails" runat="server" visible="false">
  <asp:Repeater id="MatchesByDateList" runat="server">
    <headertemplate>
      <span style="width:110px;height:25px">Date: </span>
      <span style="width:135px;height:25px">
        <%# EventCalendar.SelectedDate.ToShortDateString %>
      </span>
      <br />
    </headertemplate>
    <itemtemplate>
      <span style="width:110px">Wrox Team</span>
      <span style="width:135px"><%# Container.DataItem("TeamName") %></span>
      <br />
      <span style="width:110px">Opposing Team</span>
      <span style="width:135px"><%# Container.DataItem("OpponentName") %></span>
      <br />
      <span style="width:110px">Venue</span>
      <span style="width:135px">
```

```
            <%# venue(Container.DataItem("OpponentLocation"),
                Container.DataItem("Location")) %>
        </span>
        <br />
      </itemtemplate>
      <separatortemplate>
        <hr color="#b0c4de" width="200" />
      </separatortemplate>
    </asp:Repeater>
  </div>
```

This works because only the `Visible` property of the `Panel` control is being used in this exercise. This property is available to all server controls, including HTML controls. A `<div>` is a direct dropin replacement for a `Panel` in this case.

Exercise 2

Add another event handler to the `Teams.aspx` page that reacts to the selecting of the name of a player, and takes the reader to the `Players.aspx` page.

Solution

Add the following event-handling code to `Players.aspx`:

```
Sub PlayersList_ItemCommand(sender As Object, e As RepeaterCommandEventArgs)

  if e.commandname.equals("ShowPlayers") Then
    Response.Redirect("Players.aspx")
  End If

End Sub
```

Change the HTML as follows:

```
<asp:Repeater id="PlayersList" runat="server"
              OnItemCommand="PlayersList_ItemCommand">
  <ItemTemplate>
    <asp:linkbutton text='<%# Container.DataItem("PlayerName") %>'
                    style="color:darkred" runat="server" width="120"
                    CommandName="ShowPlayers" />
       <asp:Label text='<%# Container.DataItem("PositionName") %>'
                            id="playerposition" runat="server" />
    <br />
  </ItemTemplate>
  <headerTemplate>
    Players in: <%= selectedTeam %>
    <hr color="#b0c4de" width="250px" />
  </headerTemplate>
  <footerTemplate>
    <hr color="#b0c4de" width="250px" />
  </footerTemplate>
</asp:Repeater>
```

Exercise 3

Amend the code in `Default.aspx` so that if the user selects a date using the calendar for which there are no matches, nothing is displayed in the panel.

Solution

There are two ways you can achieve this result. The first of these is to modify the `EventCalendar_SelectionChanged` event handler as follows:

```
Sub EventCalendar_SelectionChanged(sender As Object, e As EventArgs)
    If Not DateList(EventCalendar.SelectedDate) is Nothing then
        pnlFixtureDetails.Visible = True
        MatchesByDateList.DataSource = _
          GamesByDate(EventCalendar.SelectedDate.ToShortDateString)
        MatchesByDateList.DataBind()
    Else
        pnlFixtureDetails.Visible = False
    End If

End Sub
```

Alternatively, you can change how non-match days are rendered in the calendar:

```
Sub EventCalendar_DayRender(sender As Object, e As DayRenderEventArgs)

    If Not DateList(e.day.date) is Nothing then

        e.cell.style.add("font-weight", "bold")
        e.cell.style.add("font-size", "larger")
        e.cell.style.add("border", "3 dotted darkred")
        e.cell.style.add("background", "#f0f0f0")
        e.day.isselectable = true

    Else
        e.cell.style.add("font-weight", "lighter")
        e.cell.style.add("color", "DimGray")
        e.day.isselectable = false

    End If

End Sub
```

Using the `isselectable` property, we can control whether or not a date is selectable. Setting this to `false` means that non-match days are not rendered as hyperlinks, and hence will not cause the panel to be displayed. The code in the subsequent chapters uses this property to achieve this result.

Exercise 4

Have a go at customizing `Players.aspx` to change the field that displays the name of the player into a hyperlink that, when clicked, will reveal a panel lower down the page that lists the team or teams that the selected player is a member of. You will find that the `Fields` editor of the `MxDataGrid` is very useful for this (select the `Fields` property builder when in **Design** view). You need to ensure that the clicking of the player name is handled correctly. You also need to add another method to extract team information (you may find that the `DataReader` function that returned the list of teams from the `Teams.aspx` page is useful here).

Solution

First, we need to change the `BoundField` into a `ButtonField`:

```
<Fields>
  <wmx:BoundField Visible="False" DataField="PlayerID"></wmx:BoundField>
  <wmx:ButtonField DataTextField="PlayerName"
    HeaderText="Name" CommandName="ShowPlayer"></wmx:ButtonField>
  <wmx:BoundField DataField="Profile" HeaderText="Profile"></wmx:BoundField>
  <wmx:BoundField DataField="JoinDate" HeaderText="Join Date"
    DataFormatString="{0:d}"></wmx:BoundField>
</Fields>
```

Notice we set a `CommandName` property on the field as well. We'll need this so as to intercept and handle commands. Let's now add a repeater that will show the teams for a particular player:

```
<p>
  <asp:Repeater id="TeamList" runat="server" Visible="False">
    <ItemTemplate>
      <asp:Label text='<%# Container.DataItem("TeamName") %>' style="color:darkred"
        runat="server" width="120" />    
      <asp:Label text='<%# Container.DataItem("PositionName") %>'
        id="playerposition" runat="server" />
      <br />
    </ItemTemplate>
    <headerTemplate>
      <%= selectedPlayer %>'s Teams:
      <hr color="#b0c4de" width="250px" />
    </headerTemplate>
    <footerTemplate>
      <hr color="#b0c4de" width="250px" />
    </footerTemplate>
  </asp:Repeater>
</p>
```

This should look very familiar – it's almost identical to the repeater from the `Team` page.

We also need to tell the `DataGrid` that we're going to be writing an `ItemCommand` event handler for it:

```
<wmx:MxDataGrid id="MxDataGrid1" runat="server"
   BorderStyle="None"
   BorderWidth="1px"
   DataKeyField="PlayerID"
   CellPadding="3"
   BackColor="White"
   AllowPaging="True"
   DataMember="Players"
   AllowSorting="True"
   BorderColor="#CCCCCC"
   DataSourceControlID="AccessDataSourceControl1"
   AutoGenerateFields="False"
   OnItemCommand="MxDataGrid1_ItemCommand">
```

Now, in **Code** view, we need to change the whole page script. Here it is:

```
Private selectedPlayer As String

Sub Page_Load
  Page.DataBind()
End Sub
Sub MxDataGrid1_ItemCommand(sender As Object, e As MxDataGridCommandEventArgs)

  if e.commandname.equals("ShowPlayer") Then
    ' Display details for selected player
    selectedPlayer = CType(e.CommandSource, LinkButton).Text

    Dim SelectedPlayerID As Integer = _
      Integer.Parse(CType(e.Item.Controls(0),TableCell).Text)

    TeamList.DataSource = GetTeamsByPlayer(SelectedPlayerID)
    TeamList.DataBind()
    TeamList.Visible = True
  Else
    TeamList.Visible = False
  End If

End Sub

' Function to look up the team or teams that the selected player is a member of
' Returns a DataReader that can be used for data binding
Function GetTeamsByPlayer(ByVal playerID As Integer) As System.Data.IDataReader
  Dim connectionString As String = _
    ConfigurationSettings.AppSettings("ConnectionString")
  Dim dbConnection As System.Data.IDbConnection = _
    New System.Data.OleDb.OleDbConnection(connectionString)

  Dim queryString As String = "SELECT [Players].[PlayerName], " & _
    "[Positions].[PositionName], [Teams].[TeamName] " & _
    "FROM [Players], [Positions], [PlayerTeam], [Teams] " & _
    "WHERE ((([PlayerTeam].[PlayerID] = [Players].[PlayerID])" & _
      "AND ([PlayerTeam].[Position] = [Positions].[PositionID])" & _
      "AND ([PlayerTeam].[TeamID] = [Teams].[TeamID]) " & _
      "AND ([Players].[PlayerID] = @PlayerID))"
```

```
    Dim dbCommand As System.Data.IDbCommand = New System.Data.OleDb.OleDbCommand
    dbCommand.CommandText = queryString
    dbCommand.Connection = dbConnection

    Dim dbParam_teamID As System.Data.IDataParameter = _
      New System.Data.OleDb.OleDbParameter
    dbParam_teamID.ParameterName = "@PlayerID"
    dbParam_teamID.Value = playerID
    dbParam_teamID.DbType = System.Data.DbType.Int32
    dbCommand.Parameters.Add(dbParam_teamID)

    dbConnection.Open
    Dim dataReader As System.Data.IDataReader = _
       dbCommand.ExecuteReader(System.Data.CommandBehavior.CloseConnection)

    Return dataReader
  End Function
```

The `GetTeamsByPlayer()` method is a very simple alteration of `GetPlayersByTeam()` from the `Teams` page. The only really tricky part on this page is that we need to obtain the player's ID number for the player the user clicked. In the `Teams` page, that was easy – we packaged up each team's ID as the `CommandArgument` for the `LinkButton` in the teams datalist. But datagrids won't let us do that, so we need to find another solution. Remember the fields we set up on the `players` datagrid? On the left hand side there was an invisible column that contained the player ID. This is how we get at it:

```
    Dim SelectedPlayerID As Integer = _
       Integer.Parse(CType(e.Item.Controls(0),TableCell).Text)
```

Chapter 11

This chapter deals with tracking users across pages, and looks at the objects that ASP.NET uses to enable this.

Exercise 1

Add some text, **Current Topic**, and a label control to the `Chat.aspx` page above the main chat box, which contains the text of the current topic (stored in the `Application` object). Add some default topic text to the `Global.asax` file, and also another box and a button to the page, allowing you to change the current topic.

Solution

You should start this exercise by adding the text and label control to the top of the page. This is a simple addition which you can do either in Design view, HTML view, or even All view.

- ❑ In Design view, type some text directly below the subheading that says Current Topic:, then drag a label control onto the page; set its ID to be `lblCurrentTopic`.

- ❑ Alternatively, enter the following code below the sub-heading:

```
<h2>Online Chat
</h2>
Current topic:   <asp:Label id="lblCurrentTopic" runat="server"></asp:Label>
<br />
...
```

In `Global.asax`, you need to enter some code that will store the details of a default topic when the application is first started:

```
Sub Application_Start(Sender As Object, E As EventArgs)
    Application("ChatLog") = "Hello, and welcome to the Wrox United Chat page!"
    Application("CurrentTopic") = "General free-for-all chat!"
End Sub
```

Back in `Chat.aspx`, add the following line to the `Page_Load` event handler:

```
Sub Page_Load
    txtChatBox.Text = Application("ChatLog")
    lblCurrentTopic.Text = Application("CurrentTopic")
End Sub
```

You can run the page at this stage, and the default topic, General free-for-all chat! will be displayed at the top of the page.

To make this exercise interactive, you need to add a couple more controls and another event handler. Below the two buttons, you should add another row to your table.

- ❑ In the first cell, enter some text to tell the user what to do (for example, Enter a new topic).

- ❑ In the next cell, drag a `TextBox` control, `txtTopic`, into the cell.

- ❑ Add another row. In the first cell, enter a non-breaking space. In the second, add a button control, `btnUpdateTopic`. Double-click this button to wire up an event handler for the click event.

Alternatively, enter the following code:

```
    <asp:Button id="btnPost" onclick="btnPost_Click" runat="server"
        Text="Post message"></asp:Button>
    <asp:Button id="btnClearLog" onclick="btnClearLog_Click" runat="server"
        Text="Clear log"></asp:Button>
    <hr />
  </td>
</tr>
```

```
<tr>
  <td width="150">
    Enter a new topic:
  </td>
  <td>
    <asp:TextBox id="txtTopic" runat="server" MaxLength="100" width="402px">
    </asp:TextBox>
  </td>
</tr>
<tr>
  <td>
     
  </td>
  <td>
    <asp:Button id="btnUpdateTopic" onclick="btnUpdateTopic_Click" runat="server"
      text="Update Topic"></asp:Button>
  </td>
</tr>
```

Finally, you need to add some code to update the contents of the Application object when the button is clicked:

```
Sub btnUpdateTopic_Click(sender As Object, e As EventArgs)

  Application("CurrentTopic") = txtTopic.Text
  lblCurrentTopic.Text = Application("CurrentTopic")
  txtTopic.Text = ""
End Sub
```

If all goes well, you'll see a page like Figure A-1:

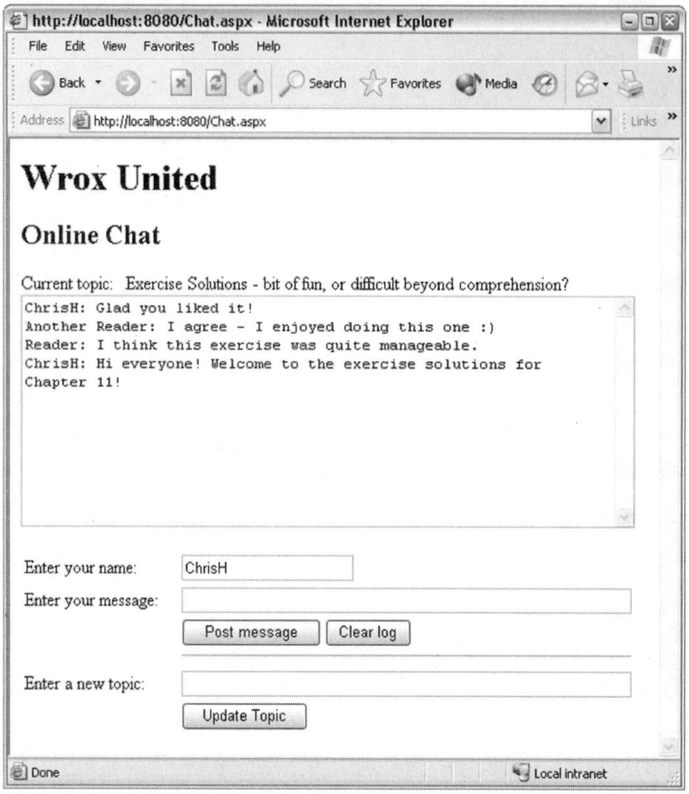

Figure A-1

Exercise 2

Add the session initialization code from the Stylesheet example to your `Global.asax` file.

Solution

You'll recall that, during the CSS example, the following code was included in the `Page_Load()` method:

```
If Session("SelectedCss") is Nothing Then
  If Request.Cookies("PreferredCss") is Nothing Then
    Session("SelectedCss") = "WroxUnited.css"

  Else
    Session("SelectedCss") = Request.Cookies("PreferredCss").Value

  End If
End If
```

This code can be shortened considerably by adding the following statement to `Global.asax`:

```
Sub Session_Start(Sender As Object, E As EventArgs)
  Dim basketTable as new System.Collections.Hashtable()
  Session("Basket") = basketTable
  ' From the exercise solutions to Chapter 11:
  Session("SelectedCss") = "WroxUnited.css"
End Sub
```

The code in `Page_Load` can now be changed to the following:

```
If Not Request.Cookies("PreferredCss") Is Nothing Then
  Session("SelectedCss") = Request.Cookies("PreferredCss").Value
End If
```

Exercise 3

Add a link to the `Merchandise.aspx` page from the front page of the site, and then apply the stylesheet used in the `Default.aspx` page to all the other pages in the site. You will need to add the `<link ... >` tag to the `<head ... >` section of each page, and you will need to ensure that the session initialization code is correctly configured in the `Global.asax` file from the previous exercise.

Solution

Adding the link to the `Default.aspx` page is quite simple – just add the following code to the list of links:

```
<p>
  <asp:HyperLink id="lnkMerchandise" runat="server" NavigateUrl="Merchandise.aspx">
    Merchandise</asp:HyperLink>
</p>
```

This will update the front page of the site as shown in Figure A-2:

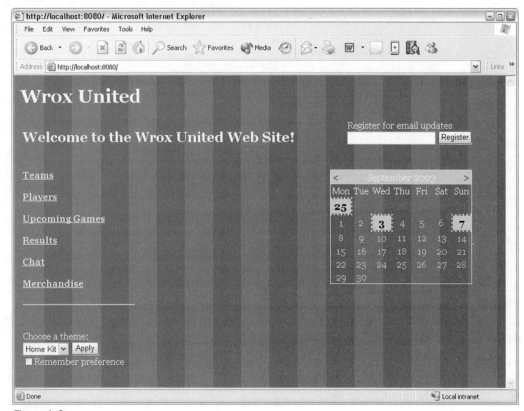

Figure A-2

Now you can add the `css` link to each of the other pages in the site:

```
<head>
  <link id="css" href='<%= Session("SelectedCss") %>'
    type="text/css" rel="stylesheet" />
</head>
```

Having said this, it's not quite as simple as it looks – take a look at the output of `Teams.aspx` when using the **Away** scheme, and you'll notice that the red links remain red – this is because the color was hardcoded when the page was created. You need to remove the color information from the tag:

```
<asp:linkbutton text='<%# Container.DataItem("TeamName") %>'
  CommandArgument='<%# Container.DataItem("TeamID") %>' id="TeamNameLink"
  style="color:darkred" runat="server" CommandName="ShowTeam" />
```

Once you delete the `style="color.darkred"` attribute, the links will inherit the styling defined for all hyperlinks.

`Players.aspx`, shown in Figure A-3 has some additional styling that will need to be amended:

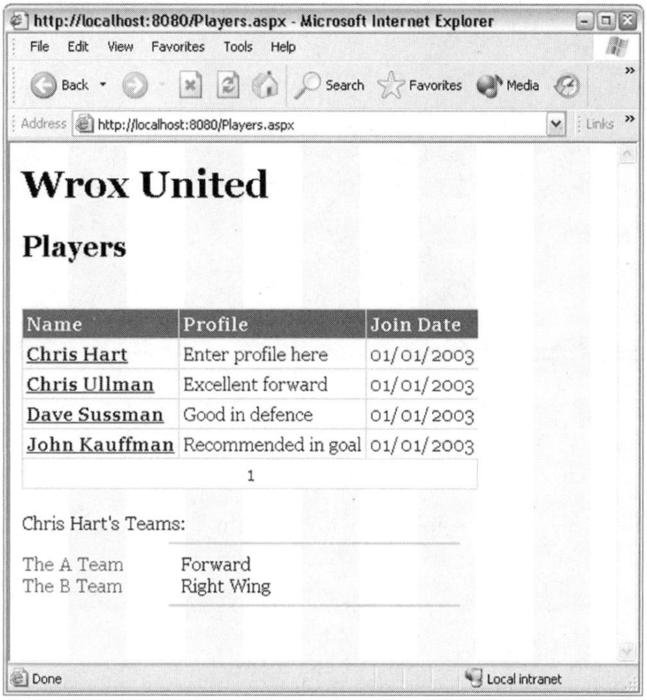

Figure A-3

You'll notice that the font color is blue, and the header bar is also blue – the theme for the site is red, white, and black, so this needs altering slightly. First, delete all the hardcoded styles from the control – you may find that the Properties pane is the most useful tool for this.

Next, you can add some custom styling. Here is some CSS code you can add to `WroxUnited.css`:

```
.datatablebody {
  background-color:"#ffffff";
  color:black;
  font-size:smaller;
}

.datatablebody td{
  padding:3;
}

.datatablehead {
  background-color:"#c0c0c0";
  color:black;
  font-weight:bold;
}

.datatablehead td{
  padding:3;
}
```

Once these styles are added, you can apply them to the control:

```
<ItemStyle cssclass="datatablebody"></ItemStyle>
<HeaderStyle font-bold="True" cssclass="datatablehead"></HeaderStyle>
```

This would produce Figure A-4 when the page is viewed:

Figure A-4

Chapter 12

This chapter covers the concepts of user controls and code-behind. The first three exercises for this chapter don't really have any new code to them, since it's really just a case of repeating and practicing adding user controls to pages and switching to using code-behind.

Exercise 1

Add the header control and navigation bar control to each page in the site. Remember to add the following code at the top of each page:

```
<%@ Register TagPrefix="WroxUnited" TagName="Header" Src="Header.ascx" %>
<%@ Register TagPrefix="WroxUnited" TagName="NavBar" Src="NavBar.ascx" %>
```

Exercise 2

Move the VB.NET code for each page (visible in the Code view in Web Matrix) into an associated code-behind file, making sure each control has a corresponding declaration in the code-behind file.

Exercise 3

Move the VB.NET code from the `navbar.ascx` control (which contains an event-handler) into an associated `.ascx.vb` code-behind file, following exactly the same technique as you used for the other pages on the site.

Exercise 4

Create a user control for the `Merchandise.aspx` page that enables you to easily add new items to the list. You will need to copy a row of the table from `Merchandise.aspx` into a new ASCX user control file. Make the properties on the image and button controls generic, and then add some public properties to programmatically set the values on each Web control in the user control. Here's some code to get you started.

Firstly, here's some code (currently in `Merchandise.aspx`) that could be placed in the control:

```
<tr>
  <td>
    <asp:Image id="imgCap" runat="server" Height="100px"
      ImageUrl="images/shirt.gif" Width="100px"></asp:Image>
  </td>
  <td>
    The Wrox United shirt, available in one size only</td>
  <td>
    <asp:Button id="btnBuyShirt" onclick="AddItemToBasket" runat="server"
      Width="100px" CommandArgument="Shirt" Text="Buy a shirt!"></asp:Button>
  </td>
</tr>
```

If you change the `ImageUrl` of the image, the `Text` of the button, and the `CommandArgument` to empty strings `""`, then you can set those in the `Page_Load` event. Consider the preceding example – the word `"Shirt"` features in all three of these attributes, so you could add a property like the following to store the name of the item (in this case, shirt), then use this value to construct the appropriate values for these attributes:

```
Private _itemName as string = ""

Public Property ItemName As String
  Get
    Return _itemName
  End Get
  Set(ByVal Value As String)
    _itemName = Value
  End Set
End Property
```

Here's an example of using this property to update another private variable:

```
If _imageName = "" Then _imageName = _itemName & ".jpg"
```

This could be used, for example, to provide a default image name.

You would also need to move the `AddItemToBasket()` sub to the control because the buttons now reside within this control. Since the name of the session is globally available, it's possible to set or update session values from the control just as easily as from a page.

You will need three properties in all. The first, `ItemName` is shown in the previous snippet. You can include an optional `ImageName` property, to override the default value (in case you want to use a `.gif`, for example). Finally, you need to store the text that describes the item in a `Text` property, and include the value stored in this property in the page using the following syntax:

```
<td><%=Text%></td>
```

All that remains then is to add the item to the page:

```
<WroxUnited:Product id="Shirt" runat="server"
   ItemName="Shirt"
   ImageName="shirt.gif"
   Text="The Wrox United shirt, available in one size only"/>
```

Solution

Firstly, the HTML of the `Product.ascx` user control:

```
<tr>
  <td>
    <asp:Image id="image1" Width="120px" ImageUrl="<%=imageLink%>"
      Height="120px" runat="server"></asp:Image>
  </td>
  <td>
    <%=Text%></td>
  <td>
    <asp:Button id="button1" onclick="AddItemToBasket" Width="100px" runat="server"
      Text="<%=buttonText%>"
      CommandArgument="<%=ItemName%>"></asp:Button>
  </td>
</tr>
```

Next is the code of the `Product.ascx` user control:

```
Private _imageName as string = ""

Public Property ImageName As String
  Get
    Return _imageName
  End Get
  Set(ByVal Value As String)
    _imageName = Value
  End Set
End Property


Private _text as string = ""

Public Property Text As String
  Get
    Return _text
  End Get
  Set(ByVal Value As String)
    _text = Value
  End Set
End Property

Sub Page_Load

  If _imageName = "" Then _imageName = _itemName & ".jpg"

  Dim imageLink  as String = "images/" & _imageName
  Dim buttonText as String = "Buy the " & _itemName & "!"

  Image1.ImageUrl = imageLink
  Button1.Text    = buttonText

End Sub
sub AddItemToBasket(sender as object, e as eventargs)

  Dim basketTable as System.Collections.Hashtable = Session("Basket")
```

```
      If basketTable(_itemName) Is Nothing
         basketTable(_itemName) = 0
      End If

      Dim itemCount as Integer = basketTable(_itemName)
      basketTable(_itemName) = itemCount + 1

   End Sub
```

In `Merchandise.aspx`:

```
<%@ Register TagPrefix="WroxUnited" TagName="Product" Src="Product.ascx" %>
   ...
<table width="600">
  <WroxUnited:Product id="Shirt" runat="server"
    ItemName="Shirt"
    ImageName="shirt.gif"
    Text="The Wrox United shirt, available in one size only"/>
  <WroxUnited:Product id="Hat" runat="Server"
    ItemName="Hat"
    ImageName="hat.jpg"
    Text="The official Wrox United hat!"/>
  <WroxUnited:Product id="Mascot" runat="Server"
    ItemName="Mascot"
    ImageName="mascot1.jpg"
    Text="The Wrox United cuddy mascot - a must-have for the younger supporters!"/>
  <WroxUnited:Product id="Plate" runat="server"
    ItemName="Plate"
    ImageName="team_s_b.gif"
    Text="This is a strange square collector's plate of the team!"/>
</table>
```

Exercise 5

Move the new code in `Product.ascx` into a code-behind file.

Chapter 13

This chapter covers how to compile a .NET assembly and use it from within our ASP.NET page. It also discussed the encapsulation of business logic into a reusable component. These exercises are separate from the Wrox United application, but you will find that concepts learned in this chapter will come in very handy when completing these exercises.

To help you, we've included a tiny Access database in the code download for this chapter called `Travel.mdb`. It's a small database that contains a list of locations, temperatures, and weather conditions. We've also included some images that correspond to various different weather conditions.

A common solution discusses *Exercises 1 and 2*.

Exercise 1

Build a data access component that connects to the `Travel.mdb` access database and retrieves data filtered by location, about the weather at that location. You may find the following SQL useful:

```
SELECT [Locations].[LocationName], [Locations].[CurrentTemperature],
  [WeatherTypes].[WeatherType]
FROM [Locations], [WeatherTypes]
WHERE (([WeatherTypes].[WeatherTypeID] = [Locations].[CurrentWeather])
AND ([Locations].[LocationName] = @LocationName))
```

If you use the Web Matrix **SELECT** Data Wizard, you can create a method called `GetWeatherByCity()` that takes the `LocationName` as a parameter, and returns a DataReader.

Exercise 2

Add another method to this data access component called `GetCities()` that selects all the `LocationNames` from the database and returns a DataReader.

Solution

Once you have created the two methods using the data wizards in Web Matrix, all that remains is to ensure that everything is in place ready for compilation. Note that we've used a namespace of `BegASPNET` and a class named `TravelData` – these will come in useful for the rest of the exercise solutions. This file is called `DataAccessCode.vb` in the code download:

```vb
' DataAccessCode.vb
'

Imports System

Namespace BegASPNET

  Public Class TravelData
    Public Sub New()

    End Sub


  Function GetWeatherByCity(ByVal locationName As String) As _
      System.Data.IDataReader
    Dim connectionString As String = "Provider=Microsoft.Jet.OLEDB.4.0;" & _
      "Ole DB Services=-4;" & _
      "Data Source=C:\BegASPNET11\Chapter13\Exercises\travel.mdb"
    Dim dbConnection As System.Data.IDbConnection = _
      New System.Data.OleDb.OleDbConnection(connectionString)

    Dim queryString As String = _
      "SELECT [Locations].[LocationName], [Locations].[CurrentTemperature], " & _
      " [WeatherTypes].[WeatherType] FROM [Locations], [WeatherTypes] " & _
      "WHERE (([WeatherTypes].[WeatherTypeID] = [Locations].[CurrentWeather]) " & _
      "AND ([Locations].[LocationName] = @LocationName))"
```

```
          Dim dbCommand As System.Data.IDbCommand = New System.Data.OleDb.OleDbCommand
          dbCommand.CommandText = queryString
          dbCommand.Connection = dbConnection

          Dim dbParam_locationName As System.Data.IDataParameter = _
            New System.Data.OleDb.OleDbParameter
          dbParam_locationName.ParameterName = "@LocationName"
          dbParam_locationName.Value = locationName
          dbParam_locationName.DbType = System.Data.DbType.String
          dbCommand.Parameters.Add(dbParam_locationName)

          dbConnection.Open
          Dim dataReader As System.Data.IDataReader = _
            dbCommand.ExecuteReader(System.Data.CommandBehavior.CloseConnection)

        Return dataReader
      End Function

      Function GetCities() As System.Data.IDataReader
          Dim connectionString As String = "Provider=Microsoft.Jet.OLEDB.4.0;" & _
            "Ole DB Services=-4;" & _
            "Data Source=C:\BegASPNET11\Chapter13\Exercises\travel.mdb"
          Dim dbConnection As System.Data.IDbConnection = _
            New System.Data.OleDb.OleDbConnection(connectionString)

          Dim queryString As String = "SELECT [Locations].[LocationName] " & _
            "FROM [Locations]"
          Dim dbCommand As System.Data.IDbCommand = New System.Data.OleDb.OleDbCommand
          dbCommand.CommandText = queryString
          dbCommand.Connection = dbConnection

          dbConnection.Open
          Dim dataReader As System.Data.IDataReader = _
            dbCommand.ExecuteReader(System.Data.CommandBehavior.CloseConnection)

        Return dataReader
      End Function

    End Class
End Namespace
```

We'll show you how to compile this file along with the two server controls once we've shown you some solution code for the next two exercises.

Exercise 3

Create a simple custom control that has one property, a temperature property that takes a temperature in Celsius and renders a string of text that displays the temperature in both Celsius and Fahrenheit:

*Fahrenheit temperature = Celsius temperature * (9/5) + 32*

The control should render a `<span>` tag that has a `style=color:<color>` attribute that can be used to change the color of the text for different temperature ranges. If the temperature is below 0 degrees Celsius, you should make the text blue, above 30 degrees it should be red, and all others should be orange.

Solution

The code for this control isn't too different from the code we used in the chapter. In the following code, you'll see that there are two properties in this control, one simple one for Celcius, one to convert that value into Fahrenheit. The Render method then spits out a `<span ... >` control when the control is rendered. Notice that we've used a string formatter to render the control exactly as we intended (adding a degrees symbol after each temperature value. This file is called `TemperatureControl.vb` in the code download:

```vb
Imports System
Imports System.Web
Imports System.Web.UI

Namespace BegASPNET

  Public Class TemperatureControl
    Inherits Control

    Private _tempInCelcius As Single

    Public Property TempInCelcius() As Single
      Get
        Return _tempInCelcius
      End Get
      Set(ByVal Value As Single)
        _tempInCelcius = Value
      End Set
    End Property

    Public Property TempInFahrenheit() As Single
      Get
        Return _tempInCelcius * (9.0 / 5.0) + 32.0
      End Get
      Set(ByVal Value As Single)
        _tempInCelcius = (Value - 32.0) * (5.0 / 9.0)
      End Set
    End Property
    Protected Overrides Sub Render(ByVal writer As System.Web.UI.HtmlTextWriter)
      Dim color As String

      If _tempInCelcius <= 0.0 Then
```

```
      color = "blue"
    ElseIf _tempInCelcius >= 30.0 Then
      color = "red"
    Else
      color = "orange"
    End If

    writer.Write("<span style='color:")
    writer.Write(color)
    writer.Write("'>")

    writer.Write("{0:##0.#}&deg;C ({1:##0.#}&deg;F)", _
      TempInCelcius, TempInFahrenheit)

    writer.Write("</span>")
  End Sub

End Class
End Namespace
```

Exercise 4

Create another control that takes the code built in the first two examples to produce a composite control that displays temperature data stored in the database for a specific city. Your control should render the following output:

❑   The name of the city

❑   The temperature at the specified city (use an instance of the control created in the previous example)

❑   An image control <ASP:Image ...> that displays one of a series of images (available in the code download for this chapter) that represents the style of weather currently being experienced at the specified city, for example, an image of a cloud if the weather is overcast.

Solution

This control only has one property, the name of the city to display. The tricky bit is to get it to render the output we're after. In the code listed below, you'll see that the output will be rendered in an HTML table. Notice also that it's very simple to nest the first control within this control. This file is called CityWeatherControl.vb in the code download:

```
Imports System
Imports System.Web
Imports System.Web.UI
Imports System.Web.UI.WebControls
Imports System.Web.UI.HtmlControls
Imports System.Data

Namespace BegASPNET

  Public Class CityWeatherControl
    Inherits Control

    Private _cityNameLabel As New Label()
    Private _temperatureControl As New TemperatureControl()
    Private _weatherImage As New Image()
    Private _travelData As New TravelData()

    Private _city As String

    Public Property City() As String
      Get
        Return _city
      End Get
      Set(ByVal Value As String)
        _city = Value
      End Set
    End Property

    Protected Overrides Sub CreateChildControls()

      Controls.Clear()

      Dim cityData As IDataReader = _travelData.GetWeatherByCity(City)

      Try
        If (cityData.Read()) Then

          Dim currentTemperature As Single = CSng(cityData("CurrentTemperature"))
          Dim weatherType As String = CStr(cityData("WeatherType"))

          _cityNameLabel.Text = City
          _temperatureControl.TempInCelcius = currentTemperature
          _weatherImage.AlternateText = weatherType
          _weatherImage.ImageUrl = weatherType & ".gif"

          Dim layoutTable As New Table()

          Dim topRow As New TableRow()
          Dim bottomRow As New TableRow()

          Dim cell1 As New TableCell()
          cell1.Controls.Add(_cityNameLabel)

          Dim cell2 As New TableCell()
```

```
           cell2.Controls.Add(_weatherImage)
           cell2.RowSpan = 2

           topRow.Cells.Add(cell1)
           topRow.Cells.Add(cell2)

           Dim cell3 As New TableCell()
           cell3.Controls.Add(_temperatureControl)

           bottomRow.Cells.Add(cell3)

           layoutTable.Rows.Add(topRow)
           layoutTable.Rows.Add(bottomRow)

           Controls.Add(layoutTable)

       Else

           Dim errorLiteral As New Literal()
           errorLiteral.Text = "No data available for city " & City

           Controls.Add(errorLiteral)

       End If

     Finally
       cityData.Close()
       cityData.Dispose()
     End Try

     ChildControlsCreated = True

   End Sub

 End Class
End Namespace
```

These three components now need to be compiled. In the download for these solutions, you'll find that there's a file called Compile.bat that contains the following code:

```
CD C:\BegASPNET11\Chapter13\Exercises
md bin

vbc /t:library /r:System.dll,System.Data.dll,System.Web.dll /out:bin/TravelSite.dll
  DataAccessCode.vb TemperatureControl.vb CityWeatherControl.vb
pause
```

This code will compile all three components into one assembly called TravelSite.dll. They are all based in the same namespace, so this is a fairly logical thing to do in real-life applications.

Exercise 5

Finally, add the following to an ASP.NET page:

❏ Add a drop-down listbox and databind that to the data reader returned by the `GetCities()` method in the data access component. Enable auto-postback for this control so that a postback occurs whenever the selection changes.

❏ Add a copy of the weather control created in the previous exercise to the page, and pass in the name of the currently selected city to the control to display the weather for that city.

Solution

All that remains is to add the `CITYWEATHERCONTROL` to a Web page. In this page, we've used a drop-down box for selecting a city, which posts back to the server automatically to refresh the page. This page is called `travel.aspx`:

```
<%@ Page Language="VB" %>
<%@ Register TagPrefix="TravelControl" Namespace="BegASPNET" Assembly="TravelSite"
%>
<%@ Import Namespace="BegASPNET" %>
<script runat="server">

  Sub Page_Load

    If Not Page.IsPostback
      Dim data as New TravelData()
      Dim reader as System.Data.IDataReader = data.GetCities()
      ddlLocations.DataSource = reader
      ddlLocations.DataValueField = "LocationName"
      ddlLocations.DataTextField = "LocationName"
      ddlLocations.DataBind()
    End If

    CityWeather.City = ddlLocations.SelectedItem.ToString()

  End Sub

</script>
<html>
<head>
</head>
<body>
  <form runat="server">
    <asp:DropDownList id="ddlLocations" runat="server" AutoPostBack="True">
    </asp:DropDownList>
    <br />
    <TRAVELCONTROL:CITYWEATHERCONTROL id="CityWeather" runat="server" />
  </form>
</body>
</html>
```

As long as you have the images in the same directory as the ASPX page, you should be able to see the results of your efforts as shown in Figure A-5:

Figure A-5

Chapter 14

This chapter explains the steps you can take to minimize errors and how to recover when things go wrong.

Exercise 1

How are parser errors different from compilation errors? Is there any difference between the ways they are displayed by ASP.NET?

Solution

When a page has errors that are caught during compilation by a .NET Framework *compiler* (remember that ASP.NET pages are compiled), ASP.NET generates a syntax error report with information about the error, and sends this information to the browser. When an error occurs while a page is being executed, this is a *parser error*. The difference is that ASP.NET sends a Stack Trace containing information about the error to the browser. This Stack Trace contains information about what was going on when the error occurred.

Exercise 2

Here are three portions of code – what is wrong with each section, and what type of error does it contain? How would you fix it?

❑   Section A:

```
<html>
  <head>
    <title>Syntax Error Example </title>
  </head>
  <body>
    <form method="post" action="syntaxerror.aspx" runat="server">
    <asp:TextBox id="txtQuantity" runat="Server />
    </form>
  </body>
</html>
```

❑   Section B:

```
<script language="vb" runat="server">
Sub Page_Load()
Dim intCounter, intLoop as Integer
intCounter=0
intLoop=0
do while intCounter<10
 intLoop = intLoop +1
End While
End Sub
</script>
```

❑   Section C:

```
<script language="vb" runat="server">
Sub Page_Load()
Dim a As String
Dim b As Integer
Dim c As String
a = "Hello"
b = "World"
c = a + b
End Sub
</script>
```

Solution

The sections, the errors they would generate, and a possible solution have been provided as follows:

❑   In section A, see the following line:

```
<asp:TextBox id="txtQuantity" runat="Server />
```

It is missing a closing quotation mark after `Server`.

❑   Section B is an infinite loop. We check the contents of `intCounter` to see if it has reached `10`, but increment the variable called `intLoop`:

```
do while intCounter<10
  intLoop = intLoop +1
End While
```

To correct this, change `intLoop` to `intCounter` (you could do it the other way round as well).

❑   In section C, b is declared as an integer, yet a string value is read into it:

```
Dim b As Integer
...
b = "World"
```

b should be declared as a string.

Exercise 3

Create a form with four textboxes and a submit button. Make one textbox take a user name, another take an email, another take a phone number, and the last take the user's gender. Use validation controls to make sure no there are no blank entries, that you can only enter numbers into the phone field, and that you can only enter a number between 1 and 140 in the age field. Also, but not necessarily with validation controls, make sure that the gender textbox only accepts male or female and that the email address contains a @. In what ways could this form be improved further?

Solution

The code should read as follows:

```
<form method="post" action="usingvalidationcontrol.aspx" runat="server">

<asp:Label text="Name" runat="server" />
<asp:TextBox id="txtUserName" runat="server" />
<asp:RequiredFieldValidator ControlToValidate="txtUserName" runat="server"
        ErrorMessage="Please enter a value in the Name Field">
</asp:RequiredFieldValidator>


<asp:Label text="Email" runat="server" />
<asp:TextBox id="txtEmail" runat="server" />
<asp:RequiredFieldValidator ControlToValidate="txtEmail" runat="server"
        ErrorMessage="Please enter a value in the Email Field">
</asp:RequiredFieldValidator>
<asp:RegularExpressionValidator   ControlToValidate="txtEmail"
    ValidationExpression="^\w+[\w-\.]*\@"
    ErrorMessage="This isn't a valid email address!"
    runat="server" />

<asp:Label text="Age" runat="server" />
<asp:TextBox id="txtPhone" runat="server" />
<asp:RequiredFieldValidator ControlToValidate="txtPhone" runat="server"
        ErrorMessage="Please enter a value in the Phone Field">
</asp:RequiredFieldValidator>
<asp:CompareValidator id="numbervalidatior"
    ControlToValidate="txtPhone"
    Type="Integer"
    Operator="DataTypeCheck"
    ErrorMessage="You must enter a number!"
    runat="server" />

<asp:Label text="Age" runat="server" />
<asp:TextBox id="txtAge" runat="server" />
<asp:RequiredFieldValidator ControlToValidate="txtAge" runat="server"
        ErrorMessage="Please enter a value in the Age Field">
</asp:RequiredFieldValidator>
<asp:RangeValidator id="Range1"
        ControlToValidate="txtAge"
        MinimumValue="1"
        MaximumValue="140"
        Type="Integer"
        EnableClientScript="false"
        Text="The value must be between 1 and 140!"
        runat="server"/>

<br />
<asp:Button id="btnComplete_Order" Text="Submit Form"
                        onclick="Submit Form" runat="server"/><br>
<asp:Label id="lblOrderConfirm" runat="server"/>
</form>
```

There are many ways that this could be improved, but here are a couple of ways:

- ❏ The email address could be checked to see that it took `text@text.text` format, or you could even check to see if it was a valid email. There are plenty of pre-written regular expressions for email validation. You can download some from http://www.regexplib.com.

- ❏ You could use an authentication tool such as *Passport* to check such details and not worry about the user having to input them. You should be aware when creating forms that there isn't a set of hard and fast rules, just that some ways of doing things will be more sensible than others.

Exercise 4

Write a `try...catch` error handler that will handle errors specifically for a divide-by-zero handler (as we did for invalid casts).

Hint: We haven't mentioned the specific class involved; you can find a list of class using the class browser.

Solution

There are many ways of doing this, as long as you include a `DivideByZeroException`. Here is a suggested method, complete with example divide-by-zero error:

```VB
<script language="VB" runat="server" >
  Sub StructuredErrorHandling ()
  Try
    Dim a as integer
    Dim b as integer
    Dim c as integer
    a=1
    b=0
    c=a/b
    'Handler for DivideByZero Exception
  Catch excep As DivideByZeroException
    Response.Write ("Error Occurred"& "<br>" & excep.ToString & "<br>")
    'Catch block using when clause and generic exception handler
  Catch When Err.Number <> 0
    Response.Write ("Divide By Zero error occurred" & "<br>")
  Finally
    Response.Write ("The Page Execution is completed" & "<br>")
  End Try
  End sub
</script>
```

Exercise 5

Create a custom error page for an HTTP 403 error **access is forbidden** and get it working for this chapter's code folder.

Solution

The following section should go in `web.config` in the `ch14` folder:

```
<configuration>
  <system.web>
    <customErrors defaultRedirect="userError.aspx" mode="On">
    <error statusCode="403" redirect="PageForbidden.aspx" />
  </customErrors>
  </system.web>
</configuration>
```

The page `Forbidden.aspx` can just say something like:

```
<html>
<head>
</head>
<body>
  <h1> You are not allowed access to this page.</h1>
</body>
</html>
```

Chapter 15

This chapter explains how ASP.NET applications can be managed from a series of XML configuration files.

Exercise 1

If you didn't know the particular setting of an element in the `config` file where would you look to find them?

Solution

In the `machine.config` file itself, which has examples of how to use many of the commonly used settings.

Exercise 2

Create a *friendly* custom error page for a file not found error and set the relevant `config` file so that it appears whenever a 404-error message is generated.

Solution

The following section should go in `web.config` in the `ch14` folder:

```
<configuration>
  <system.web>
    <customErrors defaultRedirect="userError.aspx" mode="On">
    <error statusCode="404" redirect="PageNotFound.aspx" />
   </customErrors>
  </system.web>
</configuration>
```

The page `PageNotFound.aspx` can just say something like:

```
<html>
<head>
</head>
<body>
  <h1> Sorry but this page cannot be found on our Web server.</h1>
</body>
</html>
```

Exercise 3

Create a page with two label controls that both display the time and create an output cache that lasts for 30 minutes and caches just one of the controls.

Solution

When fragment caching, you cache only in the ASCX file, so create an ASPX page that isn't cached that contains two user controls:

```
<%@ Page Language="VB" %>
<%@ Register TagPrefix="l1" TagName="mylabel1" Src="label1.ascx" %>
<%@ Register TagPrefix="l2" TagName="mylabel2" Src="label2.ascx" %>
<script runat = "server">
Function ServerTime() As String
  ServerTime = System.DateTime.Now.ToLongTimeString()
End Function
</script>
<l1:mylabel1 text="ServerTime()" runat="server"/>
<l2:mylabel1 text="ServerTime()" runat="server"/>
```

Then create two ASCXs, and only cache one of them. Consider `Label1.ascx`:

```
<%@ OutputCache Duration="1800" VaryByParam="none" %>
<asp:label id="mylabel1" text="ServerTime()" runat="server"/>
```

`Label2.ascx`:

```
<asp:label id="mylabel2" text="ServerTime()" runat="server"/>
```

Exercise 4

Create a cache that stores the following information "MyFavouriteColour = Orange", and expires it if it hasn't been updated for three minutes.

Solution

The following should serve the purpose:

```
Cache.Insert("MyFavoriteColor", "orange", null, DateTime.Now.AddMinutes(3),
NoSlidingExpiration)
```

Exercise 5

Create a cache that will expire whenever the contents of one of three files – XMLDoc1.xml, XMLDoc2.xml, and XMLDoc3.xml – change. Note they can all contain the following code:

```
<?xml version="1.0"?>
<address>
 <name>Rheingold Cabriole</name>
 <address>673 Chellingworth Place, Morningtown </address>
 <phone>333-444-555</phone>
 <email> Rheingold.Cabriole@fabemails.com</email>
</address>
```

Solution

```
Dim XMLFileDataSet As New DataSet
XMLFileDataSet.ReadXML("C:\BegASPNet11\ch15\address.xml")
Dim filedependency1 As New CacheDependency("C:\BegASPNet11\ch15\xmldoc1.xml")
Dim filedependency2 As New CacheDependency("C:\BegASPNet11\ch15\xmldoc2.xml")
Dim filedependency3 As New CacheDependency("C:\BegASPNet11\ch15\xmldoc3.xml")
Cache.Insert("address",XMLFileDataSet, filedependency1)
Cache.Insert("address",XMLFileDataSet, filedependency2)
Cache.Insert("address",XMLFileDataSet, filedependency3)
```

Chapter 16

This chapter teaches you how to expose functionality from your Web site to others as a Web Service.

Exercise 1

Explain the role of the *Simple Object Access Protocol (SOAP)* in Web Services.

Solution

SOAP is the protocol with which functions are called remotely in Web Services.

Exercise 2

What is the purpose of the WSDL?

Solution

The WSDL is an XML file that specifies the parameters that are used in the Web Services. By means of the WSDL file, consumers know what parameters to send to the Web Service and what values they will receive.

Exercise 3

How would you locate a Web Service that provides the functions you require?

Solution

To locate a Web Service, the UDDI service is used. Businesses register their Web Services on the UDDI database which then be searched for a service that may suit our needs.

Exercise 4

Create a Web Service; with a class name of `circles`, that calculates the area of a circle, the circumference of a circle, and the volume of a sphere.

$Area = (Pi)r^2$; $Circumference = 2(Pi)r$; $Volume\ of\ a\ sphere = 4/3(Pi)r^3$.

Solution

```
<%@ WebService Language="VB" Class="Circles"%>Imports System.Web.Services
Public Class Circles

  <WebMethod()> Public Function Areaofcircle(radius As Decimal) As Decimal
    Return radius*radius*3.142
  End Function

  <WebMethod()> Public Function CircumferenceofCircle(radius As Decimal) As Decimal
    Return 2 * 3.142 * radius
  End Function
```

```
  <WebMethod()> Public Function VolumeofSphere(radius As Decimal) As Decimal
    Return (4 / 3) * 3.142 * radius * radius * radius
  End Function

End Class
```

Exercise 5

Create a Web Service that connects to the Northwind database and returns employee's addresses based on their last names.

Solution

```
<%@ WebService Language="vb" Class="Addresses" %>
Imports System.Web.Services
Imports System.Data
Imports System.Data.OleDb
Public Class Addresses
    Inherits System.Web.Services.WebService

<WebMethod()> _
Public Function NorthwindAddresses(ByVal strLastName As String) As String
  Return GetAddress(strLastName)
End Function

Private Function GetAddress(ByVal strLastName As String) As String
  Dim objDataReader As OleDbDataReader
  Dim objConnection As OleDbConnection
  Dim objCommand As OleDbCommand
  Dim strConn As String = "Provider=Microsoft.Jet.OLEDB.4.0;Data Source=C:\BegASP
NET\ch18\Northwind.mdb;"
Dim strSQL As String = "SELECT Address  FROM Employees
WHERE lastName = '" & strlastName & "'"
  Dim strAddress As String

  objConnection = New OleDbConnection(strConn)
  objCommand = New OleDbCommand(strSQL, objConnection)
  objConnection.Open()

  objDataReader = objCommand.ExecuteReader(CommandBehavior.CloseConnection)

  If objDataReader.Read() Then
    strAddress = objDataReader(0)
  Else
    strAddress = "Address not found in the database"
  End If
  objDataReader.Close()

  Return strAddress
End Function

End Class
```

Exercise 6

Create an ASP.NET page containing a drop-down listbox in which a user can select names of Northwind employees to return their addresses.

Solution

```
<%@ Page Language="vb" Debug="true"%>
<%@ Import namespace="AddressService" %>

<script language="vb" runat="server">
Private Sub RetrieveAddress(ByVal sender As System.Object, ByVal e As System.Event
Args)
  Dim adr As New AddressService.Addresses()
  lblAddress.Text = adr.NorthwindAddresses(Request.Form("list"))
End Sub
</script>

<html>
  <body>
    <form runat="server">
      <asp:dropdownlist id="list" runat="server">
      <asp:listitem>Davolio</asp:listitem>
      <asp:listitem>Fuller</asp:listitem>
      <asp:listitem>Leverling</asp:listitem>
      <asp:listitem>Peacock</asp:listitem>
      <asp:listitem>Buchanan</asp:listitem>
      <asp:listitem>Suyama</asp:listitem>
      <asp:listitem>King</asp:listitem>
      <asp:listitem>Callahan</asp:listitem>
      <asp:listitem>Dodsworth</asp:listitem>
      </asp:dropdownlist>
      <asp:Button id="Button1" runat="server" Text="Submit" OnClick="Retrieve
Address"></asp:Button><br />
      <asp:Label id="lblAddress" runat="server" />
    </form>
  </body>
</html>
```

Exercise 7

Secure the Northwind employee Web Service addresses so that no unauthorized users have access to it.

Solution

```
Imports System.Data
Imports System.Data.OleDb

Public Class Addresses
    Inherits System.Web.Services.WebService

<WebMethod()> _Public Function NorthwindAddresses(ByVal strLastName As String, By
Val strUsername As String, ByVal strPassword As String) As String
```

```
  Dim objSecurityDR As OleDbDataReader
  Dim objSecurityConn As OleDbConnection
  Dim objSecurityCmd As OleDbCommand

  Dim strConn As String = "Provider=Microsoft.Jet.OLEDB.4.0;Data Source="
     strConn += Server.MapPath("Security.mdb") & ";"
 Dim strSQL As String = "select Username from Users where username = '"
     strSQL += strUsername & "' and password = '" & strPassword & "'"

  objSecurityConn = New OleDbConnection(strConn)
  objSecurityCmd = New OleDbCommand(strSQL, objSecurityConn)
  objSecurityConn.Open()

  objSecurityDR = objSecurityCmd.ExecuteReader(CommandBehavior.CloseConnection)
  If objSecurityDR.Read() Then
    objSecurityDR.Close()
    Return GetAddress(strLastName)
  Else
    objSecurityDR.Close()
    Return "Login to Northwind Employees Directory failed."
  End If
End Function

Private Function GetAddress(ByVal strLastName As String) As String
  Dim objDataReader As OleDbDataReader
  Dim objConnection As OleDbConnection
  Dim objCommand As OleDbCommand
  Dim strConn As String = "Provider=Microsoft.Jet.OLEDB.4.0;Data Source=C:\BegASP
NET\ch16\Northwind.mdb;"
  Dim strSQL As String = "SELECT Address FROM Employees WHERE lastName = '" & str
lastName & "'"
  Dim strAddress As String
  objConnection = New OleDbConnection(strConn)
  objCommand = New OleDbCommand(strSQL, objConnection)
  objConnection.Open()

  objDataReader = _
    objCommand.ExecuteReader(CommandBehavior.CloseConnection)

  If objDataReader.Read() Then
    strAddress = objDataReader(0)
  Else
    strAddress = "Address not found in the database"
  End If
  objDataReader.Close()

  Return strAddress
End Function

End Class
```

Chapter 17

This chapter gives a quick overview of some of the simple precautions that you can take using forms authentication and authorization to safeguard your ASP.NET pages.

Exercise 1

What is the difference between authentication and authorization?

Solution

Authentication is the process to check to see if a user is who they say they are, while authorization is checking whether a particular user has access to see a particular resource.

Exercise 2

Create an application that uses forms-based authentication that requires a user name, password, and a zip code before you can go to the main login page. Hardcode the username, password, and the zip code. Call it `zipcodelogin.aspx`.

Solution

The `web.config` file should be as follows:

```
<configuration>
  <system.web>
    <authentication mode="Forms">
      <forms name=".WroxDemo" loginUrl="login.aspx"
      protection="All" timeout="60" />
    </authentication>
    <machineKey validationKey="AutoGenerate" decryptionKey="AutoGenerate"
     validation="SHA1"/>
    <authorization>
      <deny users="?" />
    </authorization>
  </system.web>
</configuration>
```

The `zipcodelogin.aspx` file should be as follows:

```
<%@ Import Namespace="System.Web.Security " %>
<html>
<head>
<script language="VB" runat=server>
 Sub Login_Click(Src As Object, E As EventArgs)
   If txtEmail.Text = "Wrox" And txtPwd.Text = "MyPass" And txtZipCode.Text = "123
45" Then
     FormsAuthentication.RedirectFromLoginPage(txtEmail.Text,false)
   Else
     lblLoginMsg.Text = "Use user name, password and zip as " & _
                        "Wrox, MyPass and 12345 . Please try again"
```

```
    End If
  End Sub
</script>
</head>
<body>
<form runat="server">
<h1>Using Form based Authentication<BR>with Pre-Defined Credentials</h1><hr>
Users Name:<br />
<asp:textbox id="txtEmail" runat=server /> 
<FONT SIZE=2 COLOR="RED">*</FONT>

<br />Password:<br />

<asp:textbox TextMode="Password" id="txtPwd" runat=server />
  <FONT SIZE=2 COLOR="RED">*</FONT>
<br />

<asp:textbox id="txtZipCode" runat=server />
  <FONT SIZE=2 COLOR="RED">*</FONT>
<br />

<asp:Label  id="lblLoginMsg" ForeColor="Red" Font-Name="Verdana"  Font-Size="10"
 runat=server />
<b />

<asp:button  id="btnLogin" Text="Login" OnClick="Login_Click" runat=Server />
</form>
</body>
</html>
```

Exercise 3

Upgrade the application from *Exercise 2* to use the `WroxAuth.mdb` used in this chapter.

Solution

First add an extra field to the database file for zipcode, and add 12345 for each record in it. Then change the `login.aspx` file as follows:

```
<%@ Page Language="VB" %>
<%@ Import Namespace="System.Web.Security " %>
<%@ Import Namespace="System.Data.OleDB" %>
<script language="VB" runat=server>
Sub Login_Click(Src As Object, E As EventArgs)
Dim strConn as string ="PROVIDER=Microsoft.Jet.OLEDB.4.0;DATA SOURCE=" & server.
mappath("DB/WroxDBAuth.mdb") & ";"
    Dim Conn as New OLEDBConnection(strConn)
    Conn.Open()
    Dim strSQL as string = "SELECT Pwd FROM Tbl_MA_Users WHERE Email = '" & txt
Email.Text & "'"  & "ZipCode = '" & txtZipCode.Text & "'"
    Dim Cmd as New OLEDBCommand(strSQL,Conn)
        'Create a datareader, connection object
    Dim Dr as OLEDBDataReader = Cmd.ExecuteReader(System.Data.CommandBehavior.Close
```

```
Connection)
        'Get the first row and check the password.
     If Dr.Read()
       If Dr("Pwd").ToString = txtPwd.text Then
           FormsAuthentication.RedirectFromLoginPage(txtEmail.Text, false)
       Else
          lblLoginMsg.text = "Invalid password."
       End If
     Else
        lblLoginMsg.text = "Login name not found."
     End If
     Dr.Close
  End Sub
  </script>
```

Exercise 4

Create an account for a user named John@MyDomain.com, but deny him access in web.config. What happens when you try to log in as him? Can you think of a way of displaying a message to accompany this?

Solution

It just bounces you back to the login page without an error message. You could put the login process within an exception and if it returns to the login page then you could handle the exception and display an error.

Exercise 5

Create a new page called newpage.aspx on the example, and use web.config to ensure that only John has access to it.

Create a subfolder for this page.

Solution

Place newpage.aspx in the admin folder and then change web.config as follows:

```
<configuration>
  <system.web>
    <authentication mode="Forms">
      <forms name=".WroxDemo" loginUrl="login.aspx"
      protection="All" timeout="60" />
    </authentication>
    <machineKey validationKey="AutoGenerate" decryptionKey="AutoGenerate"
     validation="SHA1"/>
    <authorization>
      <allow users="?" />
    </authorization>
  </system.web>
  <location path="admin">
    <system.web>
```

```
        <authorization>
          <deny users="?" />
        <deny users="?" />
        <allow users="John@MyDomain.com" />
        </authorization>
      </system.web>
   </location>
</configuration>
```

Web Matrix Quick Start

To write ASP.NET pages, you can choose from several software tools. They range from very simple and cheap (Notepad) up through powerful and expensive (Visual Studio.NET). In this book, we use a tool called *Web Matrix*, because it is easy to learn, powerful enough for a beginner, and most importantly, free. If you haven't used Web Matrix before, this appendix will lead you through the basics in about an hour. We assume that you have downloaded and installed the software as described in *Chapter 1*.

This appendix will cover:

❑   ASP.NET Web Matrix and its uses

❑   Starting Web Matrix

❑   The screen

❑   Entering code

❑   Saving and viewing pages

❑   Reusing code

❑   Class browser

What Is Web Matrix?

Web Matrix is a *development environment*. This basically means it helps you to write new software (in this case, the ASP.NET pages). Web Matrix helps application development by providing:

❏   A group of tools that reduce the amount of typing needed to create a page.

❏   Several ways to view your pages during development.

❏   *Workspace*, a small Windows Explorer-like interface that lets you view the pages in your site.

❏   Automatic color-coding within your code to identify keywords, comments, and other kinds of code.

❏   A simple server that can compile and display pages in the same way as the more complex IIS or .NET Framework.

In short, Web Matrix is a great tool that can support almost everything we do in this book.

Web Matrix is developed and distributed under a different model from most development tools. It is *Open Source*, which means that anybody can see and improve the code that makes the tool. There is no charge for getting or using ASP.NET Web Matrix. Many add-ins and changes for this product are expected in the next few years.

For this book, we selected ASP.NET Web Matrix as our editor for the following reasons:

❏   It is free, a factor for many students starting in ASP.NET.

❏   It is small and simple, making it easy to download and install.

❏   Its interface is very similar to Visual Studio.NET so upgrading the path is easy.

Although the best things in life are free, that is not necessarily the case with development tools. There are some serious limitations to ASP.NET Web Matrix, particularly if you have used a more advanced tool such as Visual Studio or Visual Studio.NET:

❏   There is no *intellisense*, a Visual Studio tool that uses pop ups to help in function and statement completion.

❏   There is no F1 quick help.

❏   Web Matrix does not have collaborative tools to help teams of programmers.

❏   The basic coding model is not code-behind (which we encouraged you to use in the later part of the book). Web Matrix generates inline code.

❏   You do not get line-by-line error checking like in Visual Studio.NET (a big help if you are prone to typing and syntax mistakes).

❏   Web Matrix does not have an inbuilt debugger, watch windows, or immediate windows, all of which are useful troubleshooting tools available in Visual Studio.

❏   As you develop more complex pages, you will have to manually compile assemblies using the DOS command line. Some of these features may be implemented in future versions as people create different add-ins.

Overall, ASP.NET Web Matrix is a fine choice for a beginner, and when you want to work faster and on larger projects you can upgrade to Visual Studio.NET.

Starting ASP.NET Web Matrix

First download and install ASP.NET Web Matrix as described in *Chapter 1*. If it is already running then exit the software. Before starting ASP.NET Web Matrix, create your `BegASPNET11` folder as described in *Chapter 1*. Within that folder, create a `MatrixPractice` folder. Now start ASP.NET Web Matrix. After it loads, you get a wizard to create a new document. For now, change the location to the nascent `MatrixPractice` folder and then change the filename to `FirstPage`. You do not need to type an extension.

Keep all other options the same, especially the selection of Templates: (General), and in the top right graphical selector keep the choice of an ASP.NET page. Click OK to create the page. Note that in the center area you have a window with the title `FirstPage.aspx`. Double-click on the title bar to maximize the window.

The Screen

Let's start with a quick tour of the areas on the screen. The Web Matrix screen looks similar to Figure B-1:

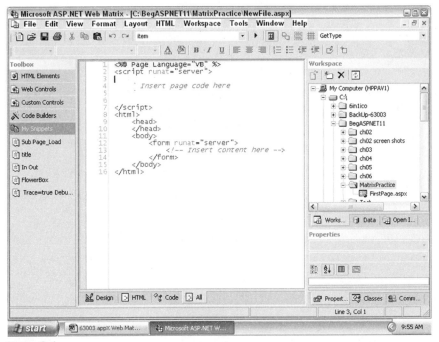

Figure B-1

The screen has six broad regions. First is the Menu, as shown in Figure B-2. This has the standard File, Edit, Window, and Help options as well as some choices discussed later in this appendix.

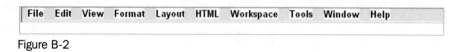

Figure B-2

There are one or more toolbars below the Menu as shown in Figure B-3. Again, many of these tools are familiar to you from other Windows applications. We will cover several of the new ones in this tutorial.

Figure B-3

To the left is a Toolbox with five subsections (as seen in Figure B-4, which shows an expanded view of the Web Controls toolbox): HTML Elements, Web Controls, Custom Controls, Code Builders, and My Snippets. Click on the title to expand a group of options.

Figure B-4

The center of the screen is the *Page Space*, where you type the code for the page. Later we will discuss the four tabs at the bottom that change the view between Design, HTML, Code, and All as shown in Figure B-5:

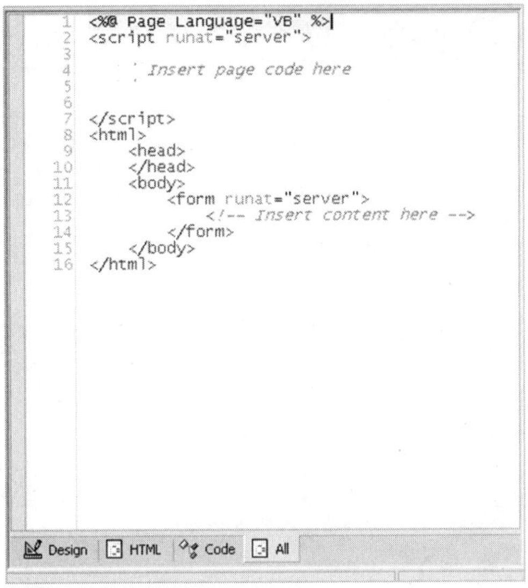

```
1   <%@ Page Language="VB" %>
2   <script runat="server">
3
4       ' Insert page code here
5
6
7   </script>
8   <html>
9       <head>
10      </head>
11      <body>
12          <form runat="server">
13              <!-- Insert content here -->
14          </form>
15      </body>
16  </html>
```

Design   HTML   Code   All

Figure B-5

The Workspace is similar to Windows Explorer. You should see all currently connected drives, local and networked. This area of the screen can switch to display available database connections as shown in Figure B-6:

Figure B-6

The Properties space at the bottom-right can display one of three sets of information: properties, the class browser, or a connection to the ASP.NET Web Matrix community. When you first open your page, the Properties box will be empty, as shown in Figure B-7:

Figure B-7

When you have controls on your Web pages, you will be able to select a control and view its properties, as shown in Figure B-8:

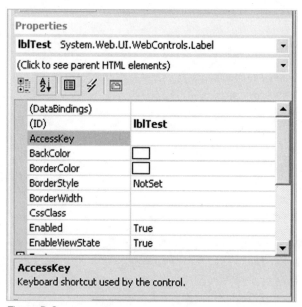

Figure B-8

Each area can be resized. In addition, the toolbar can be removed completely by hitting F2. Now that you know your way around the screen, let's begin to use Web Matrix to create ASP.NET Web pages.

How to Enter Code

You can add code to an ASP.NET page in four ways:

❑ Web Matrix automatically generates some code on your page. You have already observed this technique when you created your FirstPage.aspx (Figure B-1). The automatic code includes a page designator (in yellow), <script>, and <form> tags, and dividers for the HTML, head, and body of your page.

❑ You can type code directly into the page space at the center of the screen. Notice the four tabs at the bottom of the page space. If you click on All, you will see the page presented in the same way as if you were working in Notepad.

❑ You can add code using the Toolbox on the left side. Position your insertion bar on the page, open a group in the Toolbox, and double-click an option. Under Web Controls there are ASP.NET enabled controls, and under HTML Elements there are various tags.

❑ You can select a control and make changes in the Properties table. Code will be written or rewritten automatically to the page.

Try It Out   Code Entry

In this exercise, we will try adding code to our page by each of the four possible ways:

1. Check that FirstPage.aspx is open and maximized, and choose the All view. Observe that ASP.NET Web Matrix has already entered some standard code. That is the first method of code entry.

2. Position your insertion bar just after the <body> tag, and type a simple line of text to practice the second code entry method:

```
<body>
    Text for the page
        <form runat="server">
```

3. Now position your insertion bar in the <form> tag. You can keep the green comments or delete them – it doesn't matter. In the Toolbox, expand the Web Controls and double-click on TextBox. The code for the text box is inserted in the page, demonstrating the third code entry method.

4. At the bottom of the page space, click on the Design tab. Select the new text box by giving it a single click. When selected, there are eight gray handles around the object. The Properties section at the lower right corner of the screen shows the table of properties for the text box. (You may want to drag up the top of this area to see more of the table). Scroll down to the Width property, and in the right column type the number 50 and press Enter. Note the change in text box size. Switch back to the All view and observe the change to the TextBox tag in the form. That shows a fourth way to enter code, using the Properties box.

We have just demonstrated all four ways to enter text: automatically, by typing, by clicking a control in the Toolbox, and by changing a value in the Properties table.

Saving and Viewing Pages

Pages are saved in the same way as in all Windows applications, by going to File | Save | Save As. Always save files before attempting to view them in your browser. A common mistake is to make changes to a page and view it without saving. The changes are not visible and you can easily get frustrated. Also be sure that if you save a page with a new name (like `MyPage2`), when you switch to the browser it will show `MyPage2`.

A list of pages is visible in the explorer-like Workspace in the right central area of the screen. This area requires manual refreshes using the tool provided. Select a folder (not a file) prior to clicking the refresh.

As with all document windows within application windows, you can maximize or minimize your page window. Multiple pages can be open at once and they can be tiled or cascaded using the Window menu. Most programmers adjust the sizes of areas to suit the amount of screen they want to devote to code and to the various tools.

You can work on pages in one of two modes, depending on whether you want Web Matrix to revise your code to conform to XHTML standards. These revisions will not affect the appearance of the page in the browser; it just changes the indenting, tabs, returns, and the use of closing tags.

❑ Design Mode will have code layout revised to meet the XHTML standards.

❑ Preview Mode leaves your spacing, indents, tabs, and returns as is.

The Web Matrix mode can be set using Tools | Preferences | Web Editing | General. If you select Preview Mode, the formatting will never change. If you pick Design Mode, the code will be reformatted. Within Design Mode, you can start your pages in either the Design view (which means they will be automatically reformatted to XHTML before being displayed to you) or you can set the pages to open by default in Source (code) view. The word *design* is used two ways. Design *mode* reformats code layout to meet XHTML standards. Design *view* is a way to look at a page. In either case your change to the mode only takes effect the next time you open a page; it does not apply to currently open page windows.

> **If you don't want reformatting then use Preview Mode. If you use the Design view, select a default of Preview and don't switch to Design view manually. If you do want your code to be in XHTML format and you want the design tools, then use Design Mode.**

You have six options for viewing your work in the page screen. Four are available in Design Mode and two different ones in Preview Mode. In Design Mode you will find:

❑ Design view that shows the page similar to how it will appear in a browser. In this view , you can use various layout tools, such as absolute position. A page shown in Design view will *always* be reformatted to XHTML.

❑ All view that shows all of the code on the page.

❑ HTML view that shows only the non-script part of the page, which usually means the HTML tags.

❑ Code view that shows only the script part of the page.

Preview Mode supports two other types of views:

❑ Preview view is similar to Design view in that it shows approximately what the page will look like in a browser. The Toolbox is not available, but you can type in text.

❑ Source view displays all of the code. The toolbox is available.

None of these view options will display the result of executing code. For example, if you set the text of a label in the code of the Page_Load() event procedure to Bingo, you would still see the default label text in all the preceding views.

To run scripts, you must actually serve the page through IIS+ASP.NET or a substitute. Web Matrix includes a substitute (similar to the classic ASP Personal Web Server). To run a page, first save it (Ctrl-S) then strike F5 or select View I Start. Web Matrix will provide a Start Web Application dialog box for which you can accept the default port as shown in Figure B-9. We recommend that you change the application directory to the root of your project, C:\BegASPNET11. Now you can serve pages from anywhere in your Web application.

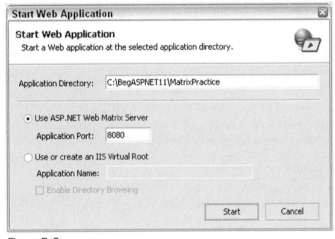

Figure B-9

Your computer will start a server process and display your page. Its scripts will be processed. You will see a pop-up notice stating that the service has started, along with an icon in the tray as shown in Figure B-10. Once the server is running, you can view other pages without restarting the server.

Figure B-10

Try It Out   Formatting Modes, Views, and Serving Pages

In this exercise, we will look at a simple page in various views and in a browser. In each case we will pay attention to our capabilities to work on the page.

1. Start Web Matrix but don't create a new file. Choose **Design Mode | Source** setting by going to **Tools | Preferences | Web Editing | General**. Note that in **Design Mode**, your code will be reformatted to XHTML whenever you view a page in **Design** view.

2. In the `MatrixPractice` folder create a file named `Exercise-Views.aspx`. Double-click the title bar to maximize the page. Confirm that you are in the **All** view. You can leave the green comments or delete them.

3. Staying in **All** view, use your snippets to add a title. Then type `View Exercises` in the `<body>` section. Position your insertion bar within the `<form>` tag and use the toolbar to add a label within the form. Add an attribute for `ID="lblTest"`. Change to the **Design** view, select `lblTest`, and change its `Text` property (in the property box) to **Default Text**. Save the file. You have now added code to your page in several ways, and the section of interest in the **All** view should look as follows:

```
<body>
    View Exercises
    <form runat="server">
        <asp:Label id="lblTest" runat="server">Default Text</asp:Label>
    </form>
</body>
```

4. Now let's experiment with the feature that reformats to XHTML. In the **All** view, change the style in which the tags are typed as follows. Start by removing the spaces to the left of the `<asp:label...>` tag. Then change the label to the single tag form. Your label tag should look like the following:

```
<form runat="server">
    <asp:Label id="lblTest" runat="server"/>
</form>
```

5. Switch to the **Design** view and back to **All** view. Note that whenever you switch to the **Design** view, the formatting of your code is changed to conform to XHTML standards.

6. Close the page. Change your preference to **Preview Mode** and reopen the page. There are now two different views available: **Preview** and **Source**. Note that in **Preview Mode** there is no reformatting to XHTML. Also, in **Preview Mode** you lose the toolbox and most of the icons on the toolbars.

7. Close the page and change your preference back to **Design Mode | Source** and reopen the page. Staying in **All** view, type the following between the `<script>` tags. Pay careful attention to the punctuation. This script code (as you will learn when you read the early chapters of the text) changes the text in `lblText` when a server serves the page:

```
<script runat="server">
    Sub Page_Load
        lblTest.text="New Text"
    End Sub
</script>
```

8. Switch to HTML view; you will only see the non-script part of the page. Switch to Code and you will see just the code. Switch to the Design view. Note that even though we have the new line of code in the script, the label's text does not change. Scripts are only executed (carried out) when the page is actually served by a server; in Design and Preview views it is only being displayed within ASP.NET Web Matrix.

9. With the page open in any mode and any view, click F5 to start the ASP.NET Web Matrix server and see the page in your browser. Accept the port, but change the Application Directory to `C:\BegASPNET11`. It can take up to two minutes for the server to start and prepare the page. Note that when you view the page in your browser, the server is actually serving it and thus the script is run and the text of the label changes.

Reusing Code

You will probably find yourself using the same small section of code on many pages. You can write it once, save it in Web Matrix, and then drag and drop it into subsequent pages. Once it is written, select the code and drag it into the toolbox category named My Snippets. After this, you can right-click and rename the snippet. To insert a snippet into a new page, merely position the insertion bar and double-click on the snippet's name in the toolbox. Select the text with your mouse cursor in the left edge of the lines so that you are selecting whole lines. Selecting partial lines leads to formatting inconsistencies when you later paste the code.

Try It Out Saving and Using Snippets

In this exercise, you will create a snippet to put a title in your pages.

1. Open Web Matrix. In the Workspace, select `C:\BegASPNET11\MatrixPractice`. Right-click and choose Add New File. In the top left corner, ensure that Templates: (General) is selected, and on the right side, the ASP.NET Page icon is selected. Confirm that the location is `C:\BegASPNET11\MatrixPractice`, and enter the file name as `SnippetSource.aspx`. The page should open in the page space, and double-click on its title bar to maximize the page. Change to the All view using the tab at the bottom.

2. Add a title as follows:

```
<html>
<head>
  <title>Example</title>
</head>
<body>
```

3. Select the title line and then drag it to the My Snippets section of the Toolbox. Right-click on the new snippet in the toolbox and rename it `Title`.

4. Now that our model of code is saved, we can customize the actual title in this page, as follows:

```
<head>
  <title>Snippet Source Example</title>
</head>
```

5. Now let's use the snippet in a new page. Create a new page named `SnippetTarget.aspx` following the same actions as in Step 1 of this exercise. Position the insertion bar after the head tag and then double-click on the Title snippet in the **Toolbox**. Finish the job by adding the text `Snippet Target` to the `<title>` of `SnippetTarget.aspx`.

Class Browser

In Visual Studio.NET you automatically get a display of various options as you type (intellisense). But in Web Matrix you have to find the names of those properties and their values on your own. The process is somewhat cumbersome and non-intuitive. After a few months of writing pages, the lack of intellisense may be the number one reason you pay the money for Visual Studio.NET.

The names of properties and their values are held in the *class browser*. It shares screen space with the **Properties** window in the lower right of the Web Matrix screen. Click on the **Classes** tab, and then you will probably want to make the window wider and higher while you use it. F2 toggles the **Toolbox** on and off to make more room. In the class browser, you will see a list of the names of classes, many of which will be completely foreign to your experience. Let's run through an example that shows how to use the tool.

Some of these examples use vocabulary and theory covered in the book, so if you've just started reading, you may have to follow the steps without a complete understanding of the terminology.

The technique to use the class browser consists of five steps:

1. In the **Properties** window, switch to the **Class** tab.

2. Expand a class until you see the object of interest, and then double-click on the object to open its description in the central screen.

3. In the central screen, expand the members of the object until you see the item of interest.

4. Double-click on that item to see a description.

5. Click on the hyperlink to read further documentation.

Note that when you open a class browser page, it is a sister to your ASP.NET pages in the center of the screen. You can switch between the windows with Ctrl-F6 or by going to **Windows** and then selecting your page. You can also tile the ASP.NET page and the class browser page.

Class Browser Property Look-Up

In this exercise, we will use the class browser to find out if we can set a checkbox's text to a certain alignment.

1. Create a page named `ExerciseClassBrowser1.aspx` in your `MatrixPractice` folder. Add an `asp:checkbox` (from the **Toolbox Web Controls**). Be sure you use **CheckBox**, and not **CheckBoxList**. Now you need to find out if you can align the text.

2. Open the class browser by selecting the **Class** tab at the lower right. Recall that all `<asp: >` controls are part of the ASP.NET Web controls class. Find that class in the list (near the top) and expand it by clicking on the + sign. In the list you see your `<asp:CheckBox>`. Double-click on it to open information on the control in the central part of the screen. On the left is a tree that gives you options to view the properties, methods, and other members of the **CheckBox**. If you expand **Properties**, you see a **TextAlign** option property available:

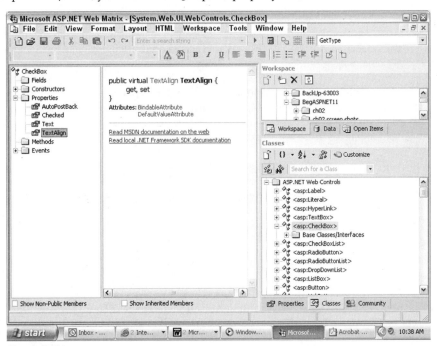

Figure B-11

3. To know the syntax and possible values, double-click on `TextAlign` property in the left side of the page (Figure B-11) and you get some details in the center panel. These details are not of much use so click on the link to read MSDN documentation on the Web.

4. The Web page gives many details that are of little use to you. However, if you scroll down you can see an example that shows the proper syntax. Near the top of the page is a section on property values with a link that takes you to a table of values, including `Left` and `Right`.

5. Now that you know that the `asp:Checkbox` control supports alignment of text and have learnt the acceptable values, add the following to your page. Remember to use Ctrl-F6 to switch between the ASPX page and the class browser information page. Take a look at the Design view or Preview View in the tab at the bottom of the page space. Change the `textalign` value to `right` to see the difference:

```
<form runat="server">
  <asp:CheckBox id="CheckBox1"
     runat="server"
     textalign="right">
  </asp:CheckBox>
</form>
```

What to Study Next

Web Matrix is introduced in detail through a free online book in PDF format. You can access the book by going to Help | Help Topics, and then scrolling down to Finding Answers and clicking the link to the book. There is also a guided tour of ASP.NET Web Matrix available on the same page. Additional resources are listed in the Web Community option tab below the Properties area.

ASP.NET Web Matrix offers many layout options that we did not cover here because they are not germane to the coding focus of this book. It is well worth your time to learn about absolute position, alignment, snap-to-grid and making controls the same size. All of these options are only available in the Design view when the page is in Design Mode (they rely on XHTML).

Another important feature is the find and replace facility under the Edit menu. Find... is invaluable when trying to locate where on a page a given variable is used. Likewise, you can save a lot of time by using Replace... when you have to change a variable name. This also prevents mistakes while retyping manually. Many times you will be working on pages on a remote site and transferring the pages using FTP. ASP.NET Web Matrix workspace supports FTP connections to look like a local drive.

Summary

ASP.NET Web Matrix is a free tool for developing ASP.NET Web pages. However, ASP.NET Web Matrix has limitations, including lack of tools that speed page development and ones that reduce the numbers of errors. ASP.NET Web Matrix also lacks troubleshooting and debugging tools. The logical upgrade path is Visual Studio.NET

The ASP.NET Web Matrix environment includes panes displaying tools, properties of objects, an explorer-like view of your site, and a central area called the page space, where you type. The Toolbox actually has five or more toolboxes overlaid.

You can enter code by typing, by double-clicking a tool icon, or by pasting a saved snippet of code. The characters of your page will automatically color-code according to their purpose. Code is edited and saved in essentially the same way as when you work with Word.

You can work in one of two modes. The **Design** mode will reformat your code to meet the XHTML standards. Although the reformatting does not affect functionality, it changes tabs and enters, and may add certain closing tags. The other mode, **Preview**, does not change your code but does limit the tools ASP.NET Web Matrix makes available. You can view the page space using one of five options, ranging from just the code, to just the user interface, to a preview of the entire page.

By clicking **F5** you can start the ASP.NET Web Matrix Web server to enable you to view a page without actually serving it on a dedicated server. Once the Web server is started, Web Matrix allows you to create, serve, and browse a page all on one machine.

Code that you write and expect to reuse on other pages can be saved to the **My Snippets** toolbar. A double click on a saved snippet makes a copy into the current page at the location of the insertion bar.

Web Matrix includes a class browser that provides the members of almost all objects. The class browser can be difficult for programmers new to .NET, but as your knowledge increases, the class browser can prove to be very useful.

The Wrox United Database

Starting from *Chapter 10* in this book, we worked through examples that were based around a fictitious soccer league team called Wrox United. These examples relied on a database for match and team information. In this appendix, we'll look at:

❑ How the Wrox United database is structured

❑ Downloading the database from the Wrox Web site and preparing it for use

The Database Design

As we've seen in the examples in *Chapters 10* to *13*, the Wrox United database has several different tables that store data about teams, players, matches, and much more. Let's take a look at a diagram of the database. The Figure C-1 was produced in the **Relationships** view in Microsoft:

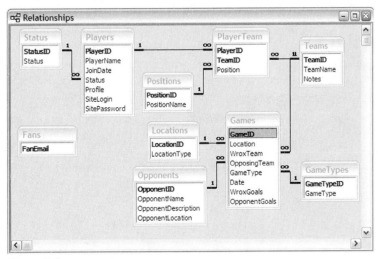

Figure C-1

Let's look at each of the different tables in turn, and see what columns they contain.

Players

This table holds the details for each of the players in the club. These players can be members of one or more teams, and can play in different positions. The `Players` table holds the core information for each player, and contains foreign key information to link to the `Status` table, which means that each player can be flagged as active, injured, or retired. This is a one-to-many relationship, where each player can be one of many possible status types.

Column	Type	Description
PlayerID	Integer/AutoNumber Primary Key, Unique	Unique identifier for each row in the database, generated automatically by the database whenever a new row is inserted.
PlayerName	String/Text, 50 characters	The name of a player.
JoinDate	DateTime	The date that the player joined the club.
Status	Integer/Number Foreign Key (to the StatusID column on the Status table)	A link to the Status table, used for specifying whether a player is active, injured, or retired.
Profile	String/Text, 255 characters	A brief description of the player.
SiteLogin	String/Text, 20 characters	A login name used to access restricted parts of the site.
SitePassword	String/Text, 20 characters	A password used to access restricted parts of the site.

Primary key-foreign key one-to-many relationships are a core part of relational database design, and enable us to minimize repetition in the data in the database. It also aids consistency, and avoids several different variations on the same data being stored.

For example, without this relationship, we could include a Status column in the Players table to store text describing the active status of a player. This is a fine solution if you have tight control over the data that's inserted into the database, but if you allow users to enter custom strings of text for the values in this column, you could end up describing a player as being injured using the text "injured", "Injured", "sick", or "ill" instead of simply selecting the Injured status from the Status table.

Status

The Status table stores the availability and status information that each player can select from. The available status types in the samples provided in the code download are Active, Injured, or Retired. However, you can enter whichever types you like in your database.

Column	Type	Description
StatusID	Integer/AutoNumber Primary Key, Unique	Unique identifier for each row in the database, generated automatically by the database whenever a new row is inserted.
Status	String/Text, 50 characters	Description of the status (injured, active, retired). Each player in the Players team has to select one of these values.

Teams

The Teams table stores information about each team in the Wrox United club. The name of the team and any associated notes can be stored here.

Column	Type	Description
TeamID	Integer/AutoNumber Primary Key, Unique	Unique identifier for each row in the database, generated automatically by the database whenever a new row is inserted.
TeamName	String/Text, 50 characters	The name of the team.
Notes	String/Memo	Description of the team, plus any additional information that may be useful. This field is long enough to hold several thousand characters of data.

PlayerTeams

This is a join table between the Players table and the Teams table. One player can be in many teams, and each team consists of many players. In this situation, we have a many-to-many relationship, and thus need to include a join table between these two tables to store information about both sides. In this way, the PlayerTeams table now stores many *unique* combinations of players and teams (hence if you were one of the players, you could only join Team A *once*, but you could *also* join Team B).

The other item of interest in this table is the `Position` column, which is a foreign key link to the `Positions` table. This enables you to specify, for each player, which position they play in a given team.

Column	Type	Description
PlayerID	Integer/Number Part of Primary Key	Link to the ID of the Player.
TeamID	Integer/Number Part of Primary Key	Link to the ID of the Team. Used together with the `PlayerID` column, the Primary Key constraint specifies that each combination of `PlayerID` and `TeamID` must be unique.
Position	Integer/Number Foreign Key (to the `PositionID` column on the `Position` table)	Used to specify, for each combination of Player and Team, the position the player plays in on that team.

Positions

This table stores details of the available positions that a player can assume in a particular team.

Column	Type	Description
PositionID	Integer/AutoNumber Primary Key, Unique	Unique identifier for each row in the database, generated automatically by the database whenever a new row is inserted.
PositionName	String/Text, 50 characters	Name of a position (left wing, defence, and so on).

Games

The `Games` table stores information about each match, including who is playing the match, where the match will take place, what type of match it is, when the match is scheduled, and the score, when known. A lot of the columns in this table are foreign keys to other tables, reusing data and centralizing information where possible.

Column	Type	Description
GameID	Integer/AutoNumber Primary Key, Unique	Unique identifier for each row in the database, generated automatically by the database whenever a new row is inserted.
Location	Integer/Number Foreign Key (to the LocationID column on the Locations table)	Used to choose a location for the game, from the list defined in the Locations table (for example, home or away).
WroxTeam	Integer/Number Foreign Key (to the TeamID column on the Teams table)	Link to the Teams table to select which Wrox team is participating in the game.
OpposingTeam	Integer/Number Foreign Key (to the OpponentID column on the Opponents table)	Link to the Opponents table to select which opposing team is participating in the game.
GameType	Integer/Number Foreign Key (to the GameTypeID column on GameTypes table)	Link to the GameTypes table to select the type of game (for example, a friendly or league match).
Date	DateTime	The date of the match.
WroxGoals	Integer/Number	The number of goals scored by the Wrox team.
OpponentGoals	Integer/Number	The number of goals scored by the opposing team.

GameTypes

This table is used to store the different types of games – for example, friendly or league.

Column	Type	Description
GameTypeID	Integer/AutoNumber Primary Key, Unique	Unique identifier for each row in the database, generated automatically by the database whenever a new row is inserted.
GameType	String/Text, 50 characters	The type of a match, for example, friendly or league.

Locations

This table stores types of location for a game – for example, home or away.

Column	Type	Description
GameTypeID	Integer/AutoNumber Primary Key, Unique	Unique identifier for each row in the database, generated automatically by the database whenever a new row is inserted.
GameType	String/Text, 50 characters	The type of a match, for example, friendly or league.

Opponents

The Opponents table stores details of the other teams in the league, and details of where they are based.

Column	Type	Description
OpponentID	Integer/AutoNumber Primary Key, Unique	Unique identifier for each row in the database, generated automatically by the database whenever a new row is inserted.
OpponentName	String/Text, 50 characters	The name of the opponent.
OpponentDescription	String/Memo	A description of the opponent that could be used, for example, to describe their strengths and weaknesses.
OpponentLocation	String/Text, 50 characters	The name of the home location of the opponent.

Fans

This table is completely standalone compared to the other tables. It only has one column and is used for storing email addresses of fans. You could expand this table to store more details about each of the fans registered in the database. Since email addresses are unique to an individual (in most cases), we can make this column the primary key for the table without the need for an additional key column.

Column	Type	Description
FanEmail	String/Text, 255 characters Primary Key, Unique	The email address for a fan. Since email addresses are individual, this field can be given a unique constraint and assigned as a primary key for the table.

Installing the Database

The quickest and simplest way to obtain a copy of this database is to download and install the appropriate database from the code download section of this book on http://www.wrox.com/. Access and MSDE are quite different in structure, so the process for installing each of them is also different. Let's look at how to install the Access version of the database first.

Installing the Access Database

Access is a simple database storage format. It's not designed for heavy usage, or for storing large amounts of data, but for small database projects it's very easy to use and distribute.

All you need to do to install this database is obtain a copy of `WroxUnited.mdb` from the code download for this book, and save it in the appropriate folder on your hard drive. As long as the path to the `.mdb` file is specified correctly in your connection string, you will be able to read data from the database.

There is, however, one adjustment you will need to make if you want to make changes to the database programmatically. Once you have downloaded the database, you need to right-click on the database file and select Properties to get the dialog shown in Figure C-2:

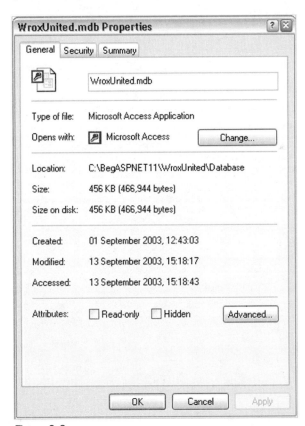

Figure C-2

Ensure that the Read-only checkbox is unchecked, and you will be able to make modifications to the contents of the database.

Installing the MSDE Database

MSDE databases are more tricky to install than Access databases, but since they are based on the more powerful SQL Server database engine, they are much more powerful and scalable.

MSDE databases are registered with the MSDE database server. The main database data file has a file extension of .mdf, and it has a corresponding log file with an extension of .ldf. To install the database, you need to have copies of the WroxUnited.mdf and WroxUnited_log.ldf files from the code download section.

> You must have a copy of MSDE / SQL Server installed before you can install the WroxUnited MSDE version of the database. SQL Server is the full-scale product, available to purchase, or as part of some MSDN subscription options. MSDE is a free download from Microsoft, and is exactly the same product, but with a more restrictive license. For more information, you should consult the Microsoft Web site (http://www.microsoft.com). Alternatively, you can download MSDE from http://www.asp.net/msde/default.aspx?tabindex=0&tabid=1

The easiest and most reliable way to install a new MSDE database from these two files is as follows:

1. Open up Web Matrix and switch to the Data view in the pane at the top right. In here, click the Add Database Connection button as shown in Figure C-3:

Figure C-3

2. In the window that appears, create a new MSDE database as shown in Figure C-4:

Add New Project
Projects:
Data
SQL
Access Database
SQL Server/MSDE Database
Create a new SQL database project.
OK
Cancel

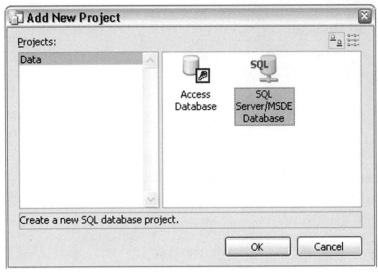

Figure C-4

3. A dialog will pop up asking for the name of the database. Click the Create a new database link at the bottom of the dialog as shown in Figure C-5:

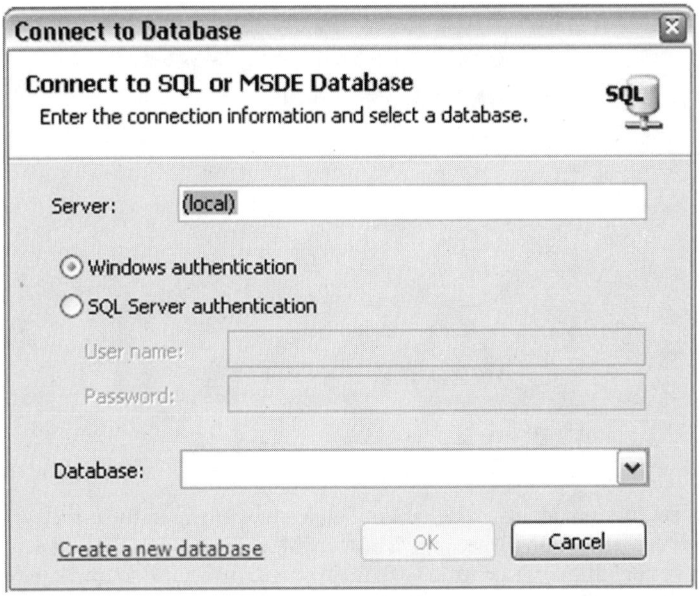

Connect to Database
Connect to SQL or MSDE Database
Enter the connection information and select a database.
SQL
Server:
(local)
Windows authentication
SQL Server authentication
User name:
Password:
Database:
Create a new database
OK
Cancel

Figure C-5

4. Finally, when prompted, enter WroxUnited as the name for the new database and click OK as shown in Figure C-6:

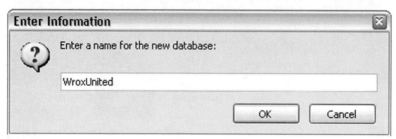

Enter Information

? Enter a name for the new database:

WroxUnited

OK   Cancel

Figure C-6

5. You will now see the new empty database appear in the Data pane as in Figure C-7:

Type keywords to search online help ▾

Data

⊞ WroxUnited.mdb on C:\BegASPNE
⊞ (local).WroxUnited

Workspace   Data

Figure C-7

6. This is where the fun begins; close down Web Matrix. Now, on the bottom right of your screen, in your system tray, you will see a SQL Server/MSDE icon with a green arrow next to it (you may have to click the round button with an arrow in it, to unhide the SQL Server icon). Right-click this icon and select MSSQLServer – Stop as shown in Figure C-8:

Figure C-8

7. Once the service has stopped, open an Explorer window, and navigate to C:\Program Files\Microsoft SQL Server\MSSQL\Data

This location may be slightly different on your system. If, for example, you are running a named instance of SQL Server, you will need to navigate to the MSSQL$InstanceName directory.

8. In this folder, you will need to replace the two WroxUnited files (`WroxUnited.mdf` and `WroxUnited_log.ldf`) with the files available in the code download as shown in Figure C-9:

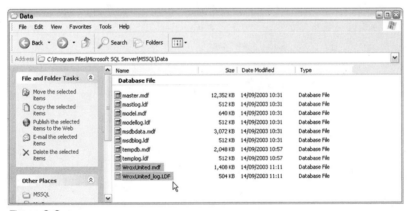

Figure C-9

9. Once you have done this, restart your SQL Server (again, by right-clicking on the icon in the System Tray), and then reopen Web Matrix. Note that it may take a couple of moments for your SQL Server to restart completely (hover your mouse over the icon in the System Tray for the exact status of the service – once it says Running \\MachineName MSSQLServer, you know that the service has fully restarted.

10. Expand the (local).WroxUnited node in the Data pane in Web Matrix, and you will see that the tables should have been imported successfully as shown in Figure C-10:

Figure C-10

Web Application Development Using Visual Studio .NET

This appendix is a brief overview of the key elements of Visual Studio .NET that you can use to create Web applications. You should work through the examples in *Chapters 10-13* to understand the sample application demonstrated in this appendix, and to understand the programming concepts we'll be using.

Visual Studio .NET is a huge tool. In the same way that you can start using Microsoft Word as a beginner one day, and still be learning about its many different features several years later, Visual Studio .NET has many thousands of wizards and tools available if you know where to look. This appendix concentrates on the core features that you'll use as a Visual Studio .NET Web developer.

Visual Studio .NET comes in many different packages. The lowest end, designed for developers on a budget, is the language-specific edition (Visual Basic .NET Standard or Visual C# Standard). Those with MSDN subscriptions or larger wallets may use Visual Studio .NET Professional or Visual Studio .NET Enterprise Architect. Each edition has a different subset of features available. The language editions are not only language-specific, but also have the following main restrictions:

❑   No option to create class library or server control projects.

❑   No option to modify the structure of SQL databases (create or edit tables in the Data Explorer). However, you can still view information in the database.

There are ways around each of these limitations – you can add classes to other projects (as we will do in this appendix) for adding compiled data access components or server controls to your Web applications. You can even modify the structure of SQL Server databases in Visual Studio .NET by using the SQL window and executing SQL commands directly against the database. However, a better idea is to edit databases using Web Matrix – it's a free tool, and you can edit existing databases or even create new databases using the Web Matrix Data pane.

> **In this appendix, all of the exercises will assume that you only have Visual Basic .NET Standard Edition. This will ensure that you can try out these exercises for yourself on any of the Visual Studio .NET family of products.**

In this appendix, we'll recreate some of the functionality built across *Chapters 10-13* of this book, concentrating on how to achieve similar results using the Visual Studio .NET environment and associated tools. We'll look at:

- ❑ Creating a Web application project, and the files that are created by default
- ❑ Visual Studio .NET's Solution and Project based architecture
- ❑ The main features of the environment that you'll need to be familiar with
- ❑ Adding HTML and Web controls to pages and adding some interactivity
- ❑ Creating custom user controls and adding them to pages
- ❑ Moving data access code into a separate class file (a technique that can be duplicated for any custom server controls you may need to write)

We won't be discussing how any of the code in this appendix works, because this is covered in depth in the earlier chapters.

Creating a Web Application Project

Open up Visual Studio .NET and create a new ASP.NET Web Application by clicking on either the New Project button on the Start page, or by selecting File | New Project from the main menu as shown in Figure D-1:

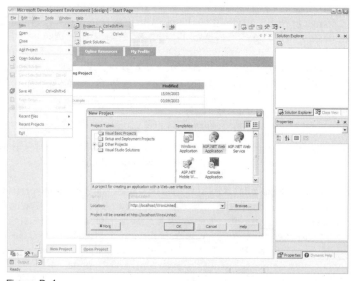

Figure D-1

Name the new project `WroxUnited` and click **OK**. Wait a few moments for Visual Studio .NET to create the new project and you will end up with the screen as shown in Figure D-2:

Figure D-2

Features of the Visual Studio .NET Environment

❑ **Solution Explorer**: Contains the root solution and any sub-projects represented in a heirarchical (tree) arrangement. Because we created just a project, a root solution was created automatically. This is where you can double-click files to open them, right-click to rename them, or select different views on the same file.

❑ **Toolbox**: Contains all the controls you'll need to use to create Web pages – simply drag and drop, or double-click, to add each control

❑ **Server Explorer** (not shown): Clicking the tab for the server explorer opens up another heirarchical tree representation of the server – you can use this to create connections to databases and view data held in these databases.

❑ **File Selector Tabs**: Contains a corresponding tab for each open file – simply click to make the selected file visible.

❑ **Properties Pane**: Contents change dynamically to reflect the properties available to the currently selected object. These properties change dynamically. In the screenshot shown in Figure D-2, the properties for the Web page itself are visible. Try clicking on items in the server explorer to view properties on each item in there. Later on, you'll see how to view properties on controls and edit them in this pane.

❑ **HTML / Design View**: Switch between the Design Surface or HTML view of a Web page, similar to the behavior seen in Web Matrix. Code view can be displayed by right-clicking on a page in server explorer and clicking View Code.

❑ **Design Surface**: In Design view, you can drag and drop controls from the toolbox onto the page. By default, elements are placed using absolute positioning (wherever you place them, they stay, and have x and y coordinates to place them on a page). Normally, we use Flow view (like in Web Matrix by default) to add controls to the top left of a page and work downwards, then use tables to arrange elements.

Visual Studio .NET Solutions and Projects

When you develop Web applications in Visual Studio .NET you need to move conceptually, from creating individual files to creating Web projects. You can create many different *projects*, and combine them into a *solution*. A solution is a collection of related projects. For example, you may have a solution that contains four projects. One project could be a Web application that is accessed by general visitors to a site. Another project could be a Web application that has user or role level access restrictions (an administration site that updates the application created in the first project). The third project could be a Web Service that exposes some of the functionality from the central Web server, and the fourth project could be a setup project that can be used to install all of the other applications onto a Web server.

If you create a new project, without first creating a blank solution, a solution file will be created at the same time, and stored in a central location. By default, solution files for Web applications are created in the `\My Documents\Visual Studio Projects\` folder. Hence you will find a folder within this location called `WroxUnited` that contains `WroxUnited.sln` and `WroxUnited.suo`. An `.sln` file is the solution file, and contains information about which projects exist within the solution. An `.suo` stores user preferences associated with the solution, including information on which files were open in the editor when you last opened the solution.

In contrast, all ASP.NET code associated with a project (and each individual project file) will be created within your Web root by default (`c:\Inetpub\wwwroot\`). If you look at the `C:\Inetpub\wwwroot\WroxUnited` folder on your system, you'll see (among other files) `WroxUnited.vbproj`. This is the project file for the Web application.

One Visual Studio .NET solution can consist of one or many projects. The solution file itself (the `.sln`) is a simple text file that describes which projects exist in the solution, and information about how they are compiled. Creating a new project without first creating a solution means that a new solution file will be created. However, you may prefer to first create a new blank solution so that you can then add new projects to that central solution (for example, having a solution called "BigWebSite", consisting of several projects including "SitePages" and "Administration Site" projects).

A project can be a member of more than one solution – the solution is simply a handy way of collecting together related projects so that the appropriate projects are all loaded when you open a solution in Visual Studio.

Files in a Web Application Project

By default, Visual Studio .NET will create many files whenever a new Web application is created including the following:

❑ A `Default.aspx` Web page (or Web form, as Visual Studio .NET refers to it)

❑ A relatively empty `web.config` file containing basic site configuration options

❏ A relatively empty `Global.asax` file containing event handler placeholders to which you can later add code

❏ A `Styles.css` template stylesheet that you can use, if you choose, to instantly add some style to your pages

❏ An `AssemblyInfo.vb` file that you'll rarely (if ever) need to amend in order to customize how your applications work

You will also notice that the Solution Explorer contains a References tab that contains the names of various DLL files that are referenced whenever Visual Studio .NET compiles your code. Visual Studio .NET only uses the code-behind method of creating Web applications, so although you can't see it by default, `Default.aspx` has an associated code-behind file called `Default.aspx.vb`.

Working with Web Pages

In the Solution Explorer, right-click on `WebForm1.aspx` and rename it to `Default.aspx`. Then, click on the design surface and look at the Properties pane. Find the entry for **pageLayout** and change it to **Flow Layout** as shown in Figure D-3:

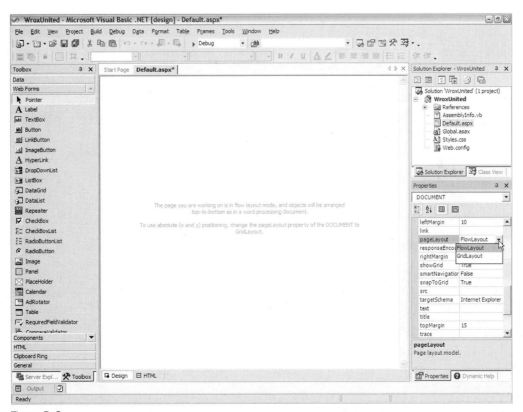

Figure D-3

Now let's add some basic content. In the toolbar just above the main pane is a drop-down box, much like in Web Matrix, where you can select a text style. Select Heading 1 from this menu as shown in Figure D-4:

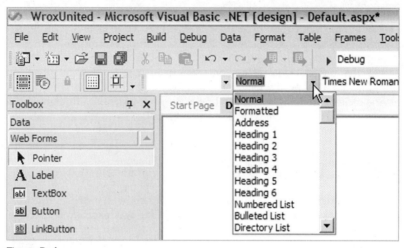

Figure D-4

Type in Wrox United as the header and press *Enter*. We'll be replacing this later with a user control, but for now, it helps to have a placeholder heading to identify the page.

Next, place your cursor directly below this heading, then select the Table menu and select Insert | Table to add a table that we can use to arrange the items on the page that appear below the heading as shown in Figure D-5:

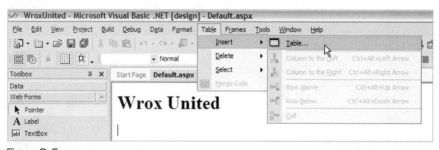

Figure D-5

Add a table that has 1 row, 2 columns, and is 800 pixels wide as shown in Figure D-6:

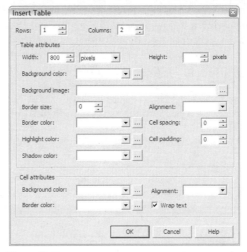

Figure D-6

Click inside the first cell and set its width to 580px in the Properties pane, then enter some Heading 2 style text that says Welcome to the Wrox United Web Site! as shown in Figure D-7:

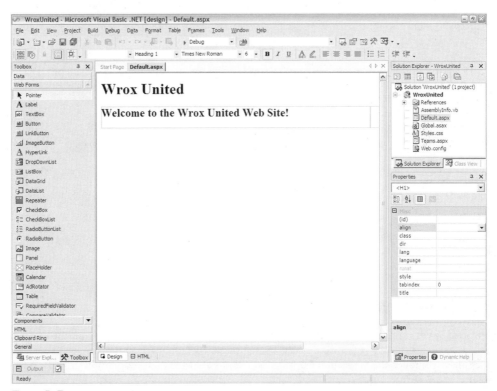

Figure D-7

Next, click to place the cursor in the second cell. From the Toolbox, ensure that the Web Forms controls are visible (click on the Web Forms bar if they aren't and they'll pop into view). Double-click a Label control in the toolbox, then a TextBox, followed by a Button, and finally a RegularExpressionValidator (you may have to scroll down to see this control using the down arrow at the bottom right of the active control toolbox).

For each of these controls, name them `lblRegister`, `txtEmailAddress`, `btnRegister`, and `validEmail` respectively. Set their text properties as shown in Figure D-8:

Figure D-8

Make sure you set the ControlToValidate property of the `RegularExpressionValidator` control to the textbox control (`txtEmailAddress`).

Compiling and Running Pages

This process is very simple to initiate – just click the Start button (the "Play" button on the main toolbar) to run the page. Whereas Web Matrix simply ran the page, allocating a port if necessary, Visual Studio .NET actually compiles the pages in the application, and you'll see this compilation process in action as shown in Figure D-9:

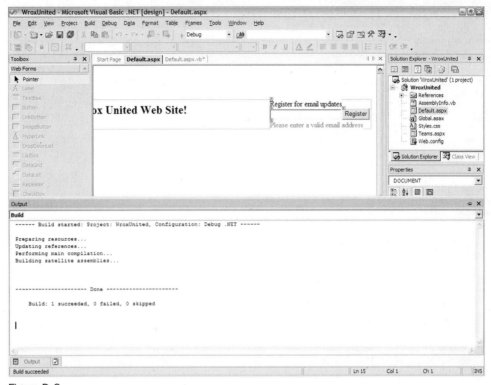

Figure D-9

The Output tab will pop up whenever you compile and run your applications. If any errors occur, you'll see them in here, and in the Tasks tab as well (located next to the Output tab at the bottom of the screen). We'll see this in action later on.

Once the page has loaded, you will find that, without entering any code, you can see the validation control in action as shown in Figure D-10:

Figure D-10

Adding Code to the Code-Behind Class

It's time to add some code to the page. The simplest way to display the code-behind file for this page is to double-click the `Button` control as shown in Figure D-11:

Figure D-11

Notice that just as in Web Matrix, a `Click` event handler method signature has been generated automatically in response to double-clicking the button.

Features of Code View

Notice that there are horizontal lines separating each method in the code – this is a Visual Basic .NET language feature that is designed to make the code view of a VB.NET page more familiar to VB6 programmers, who had this feature for years (it isn't used by default in C# projects).

Also notice the + and – signs next to each method. If you click on these, you'll see them expand and contract the code contained within them – this makes it much easier to navigate through big code blocks.

Notice the gray box labelled **Web Forms Designer Generated Code** – this contains code that is created for you behind the scenes to relate the controls on the page to the code-behind file (as we saw in *Chapter 12*). This appears in a gray box because the code within it is in a region. You can add custom regions to your code files by adding the following lines at the top and bottom of the section you want to add to a region:

```
#Region "My Region"
...
' Code to be contained in region goes here
...
#End Region
```

Once you add these statements, you can expand and contract the code contained between these two tags using the + and – boxes next to the #Region line.

Adding Code to Methods

If you refer back to the version of Default.aspx in *Chapter 11*, you may recall adding code that reacts to a user clicking the Register button on the page. Take the body of the btnRegister_Click method from the *Chapter 11* version of Default.aspx and paste it in to VS.NET. Add the highlighted lines to the sub, either by copying and pasting or typing (we'll discuss what happens when you type in code in just a moment):

```
Sub btnRegister_Click(sender As Object, e As EventArgs)
    Dim FanEmail as String = txtEmailAddress.Text

    'Check whether the email address is already registered
    'If not, we need to register it by calling the AddNewFanEmail() method
    If CheckFanEmailAddresses(FanEmail) = false Then
      AddNewFanEmail(FanEmail)
     End If

    ' Email has been registered, so update the display and attempt to a cookie
    txtEmailAddress.Visible = False
    lblRegister.Text = "You have successfully registered for email updates"
    btnRegister.visible = False

    Dim EmailRegisterCookie as New HttpCookie("EmailRegister")
    EmailRegisterCookie.Value = FanEmail
    EmailRegisterCookie.Expires = now.AddSeconds(20)
    Response.Cookies.Add(EmailRegisterCookie)

    End Sub
```

Notice that we haven't defined two important data-access functions yet, and these have been underlined for us using blue squiggly lines. Also, the code has been highlighted appropriately for us as shown in Figure D-12:

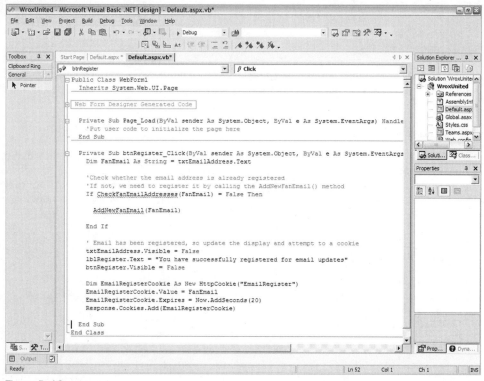

Figure D-12

We need to add the code that accesses the database in order to add a new user to the database, depending on whether their email address has already been added to the database or not. However, unlike Web Matrix, there aren't any useful data wizards on the left – unfortunately, we have to add the code by hand, but don't worry, because Visual Studio .NET has a useful feature known as *IntelliSense* that makes it all very easy. This will be discussed shortly.

Let's look at the two methods we need to add.

> **In this example, we will connect to the SQL Server version of the Wrox United database, created in the previous appendix. For installation instructions and more details, please refer to Appendix C.**

Let's amend the code slightly from the way it is presented in the chapters (because we will be using the SQL Server version of the database in this appendix), we will need to add the following code. For the `CheckFanEmailAddresses` function:

```
Function CheckFanEmailAddresses(ByVal fanEmail As String) As Boolean
   Dim connectionString As String =
ConfigurationSettings.AppSettings("ConnectionString")

   Dim dbConnection As System.Data.IDbConnection = New
System.Data.SqlClient.SqlConnection(connectionString)
   Dim queryString As String = "SELECT COUNT([Fans].[FanEmail]) FROM [Fans] WHERE
([Fans].[FanEmail] = @FanEmail)"
   Dim dbCommand As System.Data.IDbCommand = New

System.Data.SqlClient.SqlCommand
   dbCommand.CommandText = queryString
   dbCommand.Connection = dbConnection
   Dim dbParam_fanEmail As System.Data.IDataParameter = New System.Data.SqlClient
.SqlParameter
   dbParam_fanEmail.ParameterName = "@FanEmail"
   dbParam_fanEmail.Value = fanEmail
   dbParam_fanEmail.DbType = System.Data.DbType.String
   dbCommand.Parameters.Add(dbParam_fanEmail)

   Dim Result As integer = 0
   dbConnection.Open
   Try
     Result = dbCommand.ExecuteScalar
   Finally
     dbConnection.Close
   End Try

   If Result > 0 then
     Return true
   else Return false

   End If
End Function
```

And for the `AddNewFanEmail` function:

```
Function AddNewFanEmail(ByVal fanEmail As String) As Integer
   Dim connectionString As String =
ConfigurationSettings.AppSettings("ConnectionString")
   Dim dbConnection As System.Data.IDbConnection = New System.Data.SqlClient.Sql
Connection(connectionString)

   Dim queryString As String = "INSERT INTO [Fans] ([FanEmail]) VALUES (@FanEmail)"
   Dim dbCommand As System.Data.IDbCommand = New System.Data.SqlClient.SqlCommand
   dbCommand.CommandText = queryString
   dbCommand.Connection = dbConnection
   Dim dbParam_fanEmail As System.Data.IDataParameter = New System.Data.SqlClient
.SqlParameter
   dbParam_fanEmail.ParameterName = "@FanEmail"
   dbParam_fanEmail.Value = fanEmail
   dbParam_fanEmail.DbType = System.Data.DbType.String
   dbCommand.Parameters.Add(dbParam_fanEmail)
```

787

```
    Dim rowsAffected As Integer = 0
    dbConnection.Open
    Try
      rowsAffected = dbCommand.ExecuteNonQuery
    Finally
      dbConnection.Close
    End Try
     Return rowsAffected
  End Function
```

Just try typing in the first line of one of the methods, and you'll see that Visual Studio .NET will try to help you as shown in Figure D-13:

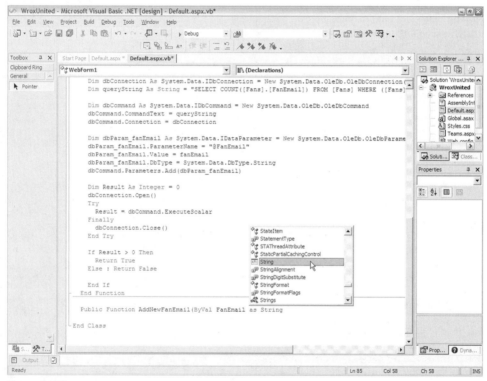

Figure D-13

Complete writing the first line, press *Return* and the End Function statement is added for us. You'll find that these kind of features save you a lot of time! Continue to add the code for these two methods and see what happens as you type – IntelliSense will pop up with helpful suggestions with each line you add. To accept a suggestion, either click on the appropriate suggestion from the list, scroll through the list using up or down, and press *Tab* or *Enter* when the appropriate statement is highlighted.

There's one thing left to do before the page can run – we need a connection string! Open the web.config that is created by default (double-click on it from the server explorer) and add the following code to the top:

```
<?xml version="1.0" encoding="utf-8" ?>
<configuration>
  <appSettings>
    <add key="ConnectionString"
      value="server='(local)'; trusted_connection=true; integrated security=SSPI;
            database='WroxUnited'" />
  </appSettings>
  <system.web>
...
```

You should see the screen as shown in Figure D-14:

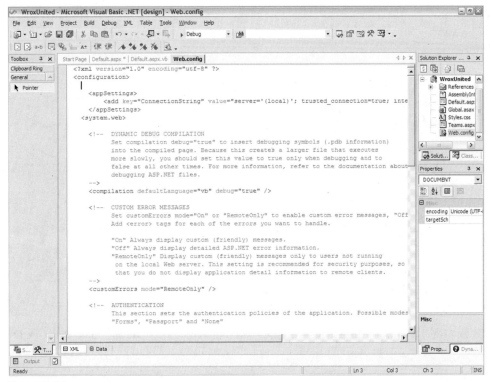

Figure D-14

You can now run the page again, enter an email address, and add it to the database as shown in Figure D-15:

Figure D-15

When you click the button, the display will change accordingly as shown in Figure D-16:

Figure D-16

Notice that invalid email addresses will cause the validation control to fire as shown in Figure D-17:

Figure D-17

Styling Controls and Pages in Visual Studio.NET

You can look at the HTML source for the page by clicking the HTML tab at the bottom of the main design area. In here, you'll see the HTML representation of all of the controls on the page, mixed in with the default HTML code for the page. Let's add a stylesheet to the application to give it a more familiar look and feel. Right click on the `WroxUnited` project (the entry just below the main root Solution 'WroxUnited' node in the tree), and select **Add | Add New Item** from the context menu as shown in Figure D-18:

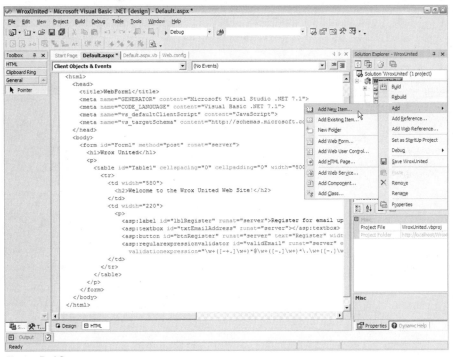

Figure D-18

In the popup dialog that appears, scroll down the types of files until you find a `.css` type, and enter `WroxUnited` as the name for the `.css` file as shown in Figure D-19:

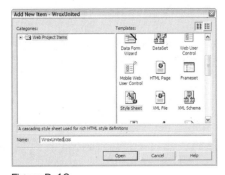

Figure D-19

Note there's a Styles.css stylesheet that's created by default with every new Web project. If you look at this file, you'll see a wide range of styles that you can use out of the box for new Web applications. Since you already have all the styling needed for the current version of the Wrox United application, you can remove this file from the project. If you right-click on this file, you can either select Exclude From Project or Delete. Exclude From Project will remove the entry in the solution file for this file, but will leave the physical file on your file system. Delete will permanently delete the file.

Back in the editor, you will see the newly-created stylesheet displayed in code form. To the left is the CSS tree – select the Body style node and click the Build Style... button directly above this panel as shown in Figure D-20:

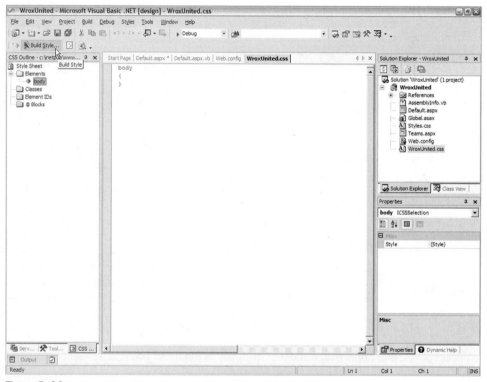

Figure D-20

The style builder dialog will pop up, and this is what you can use to apply a wide range of styling attributes to the body element as shown in Figure D-21:

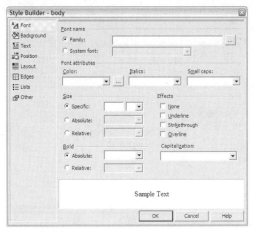

Figure D-21

You may recall that the CSS we used for the body element in *Chapter 11* was as follows:

```
BODY {
  background-image:url(images/background.gif);
  color:"#000000";
  font-family: georgia;
}
```

Let's build the style using the dialog. Set the Color to be black, then you could either enter the name Georgia in the Family box as shown in Figure D-22:

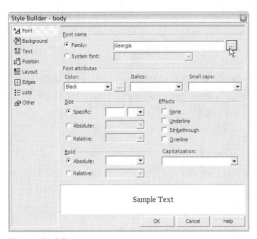

Figure D-22

Or click the ... button to launch the Font Picker as shown in Figure D-23:

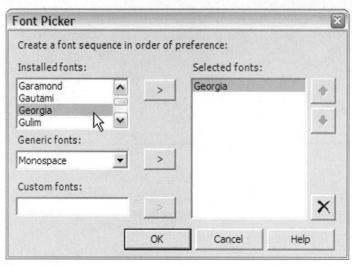

Figure D-23

To select a background image, you first need to exit this dialog, so click OK. Now in the Solution Explorer, right-click on the WroxUnited project and select Add Folder, name it Images. Highlight the folder, right-click and select Add Existing Item. Select `background.gif` from the Images folder of the Wrox United application built in *Chapters 10-13* of the book (it's a very small `gif` file that, when repeated, applies a set of pale vertical stripes to the page, a bit like a soccer shirt!) as shown in Figure D-24:

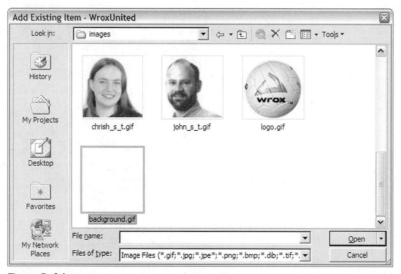

Figure D-24

You should now have the following in the Solution Explorer:

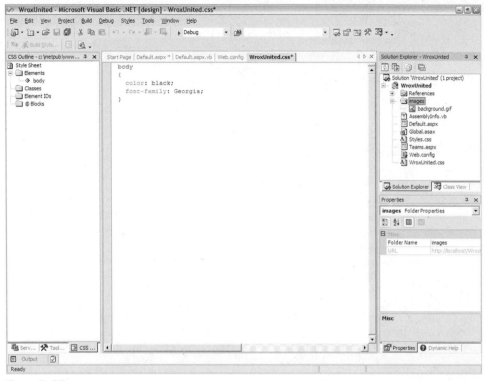

Figure D-25

Back in **Style Builder** for the `body` tag, select the **Background** icon on the left, then click the ... button next to the background image box to select the image as shown in Figure D-26:

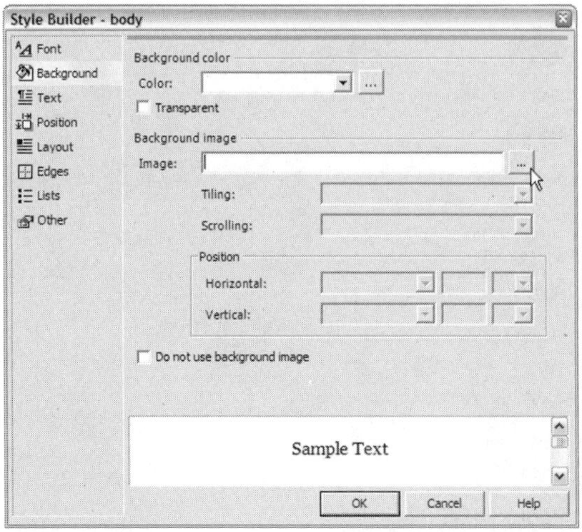

Figure D-26

Select the image from the dialog as shown in Figure D-27:

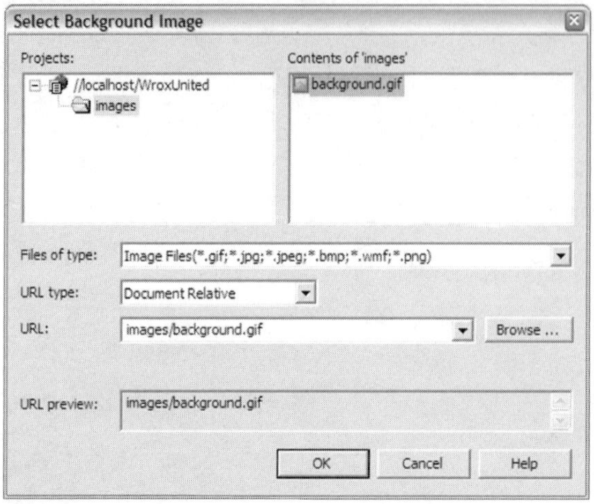

Figure D-27

Click **OK** twice to exit the Style Builder and the style will be built successfully. You can either build the rest of the styles in this manner, or you can copy in the rest of the stylesheet from the code from the rest of the book. For now, let's just add the code for the a tag. The original code for this was as follows:

```
a {
   color:"#8b0000";
   font-weight:bold;
}
```

To add this tag, right-click on the **Elements** node in the **CSS Browser** and select **Add Style Rule**. Select the A tag and click **OK** as shown in Figure D-28:

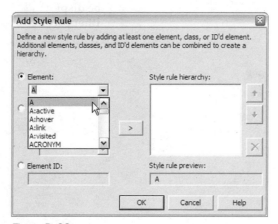

Figure D-28

As shown in Figure D-29 if you attempt to type in the style in Code view, you'll now have the benefit of IntelliSense:

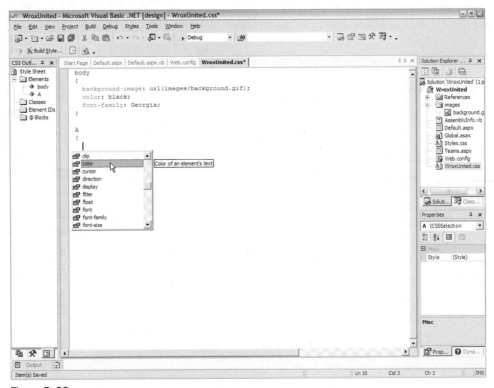

Figure D-29

> **If ever IntelliSense disappears, you can have it to be displayed by pressing Ctrl-Space. To accept an IntelliSense suggestion, either press Tab or Enter.**

Working in HTML View

Once you have built the basic stylesheet, you need to add it to the page. In the `<head>` section of the page (shown in HTML source view), add the `<link ... >` tag as shown below:

```
<meta name="vs_targetSchema"
      content="http://schemas.microsoft.com/intellisense/ie5">
<link rel="stylesheet" id="css" type="text/css" href="WroxUnited.css" />
</head>
```

You could change the href to point to a Session object, like we did in Chapter 11, but we'll not be implementing that in this example.

797

While you're in HTML view, change the `<title>` element of the page as shown below:

```
<title>Welcome to Wrox United</title>
```

This will ensure that the title bar of the page will have some more useful text in it for visitors to the site.

Switching back to Design view, you'll see the stylesheet has been applied as shown in Figure D-30:

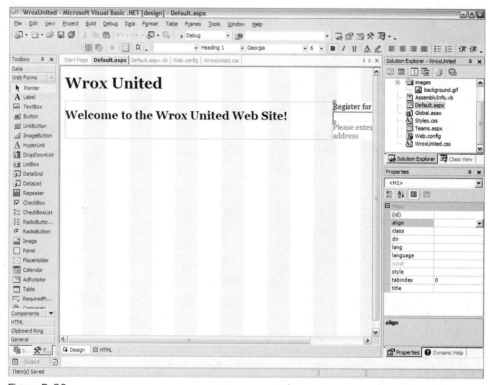

Figure D-30

Creating User Controls

It's time to replace the temporary header text in the page with a header control. Adding a user control is again performed via the Solution Explorer. As shown in Figure D-31, right-click on the WroxUnited project and select Add | Add Web User Control...

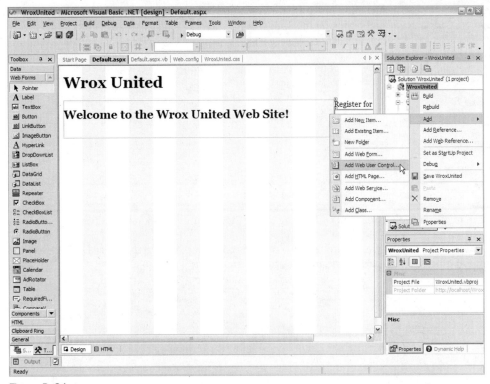

Figure D-31

Call this control `Header.ascx` as shown in Figure D-32:

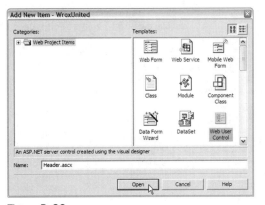

Figure D-32

The code used in the earlier chapters to create this control can be entered in HTML view, but first, add the images that we'll need. Right-click on the images folder and add the following files:

- ❑　`headbg.gif`
- ❑　`logo.gif`
- ❑　`teamlogo.gif`
- ❑　`chrish_s_t.gif`
- ❑　`chrisu_s_t.gif`
- ❑　`dave_s_t.gif`
- ❑　`john_s_t.gif`

You can make multiple selections by holding down Ctrl when you click on each file.

Add a table that is 100% wide, with one row and one column.as shown in Figure D-33. Delete the standard values for the spacing and border attributes:

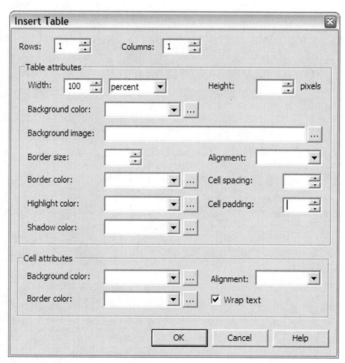

Figure D-33

For the row in this table, switch to HTML view and add a Style attribute. As you type, IntelliSense will offer the Style Builder to you, so click on the Build Style button as seen in Figure D-34:

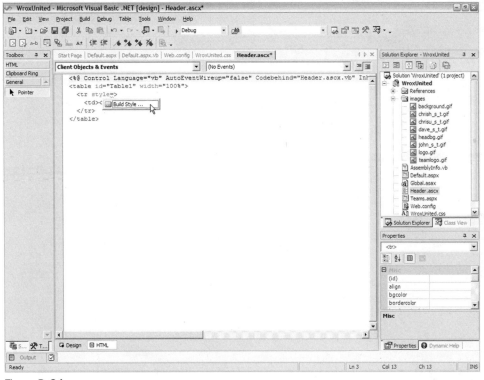

Figure D-34

In the style builder, select the `headbg.gif` image to use as the background for this row as shown in Figure D-35:

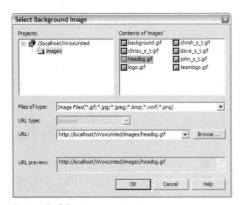

Figure D-35

Once this style has been added, you can add the inner table. You don't need to be in **Design** view for this – you can add a table in just the same way from HTML view. Position your cursor between the `<td>` and the `</td>` and use the **Table | Insert | Table...** command from the main menu as shown in Figure D-36:

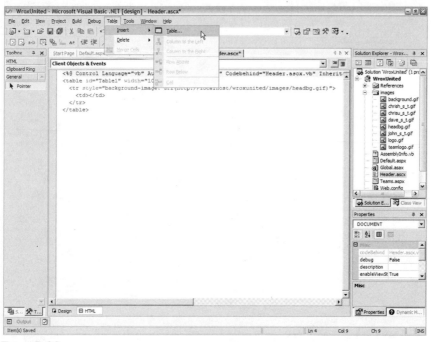

Figure D-36

As shown in Figure D-37, add a table that is 800 pixels wide with one row and three columns. Again, delete the standard values for the spacing and border attributes:

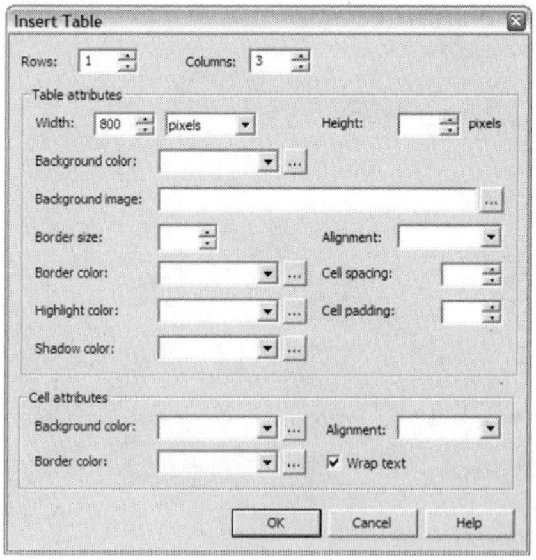

Figure D-37

Formatting Blocks of Code

I often find that Visual Studio .NET can be a bit messy at times – after adding this table, you can see that the code generated on my system was hardly tidy. In my default preferences (you can specify your own preferences via Tools | Options from the main menu) I specified that I wanted all tags to be in lowercase when editing HTML code, and I wanted to use two spaces indentation for all lines of code, yet the editor added the following code as seen in Figure D-38:

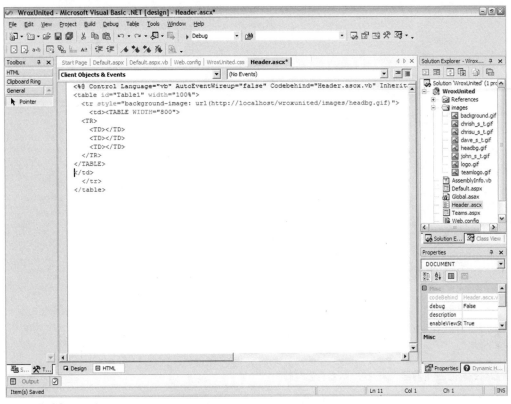

Figure D-38

The solution to this problem is to select all the code and use the **Edit | Advanced | Format Document** menu option. After running this, my code was spaced out a bit better, and my preferred capitalization rules were followed as seen in Figure D-39:

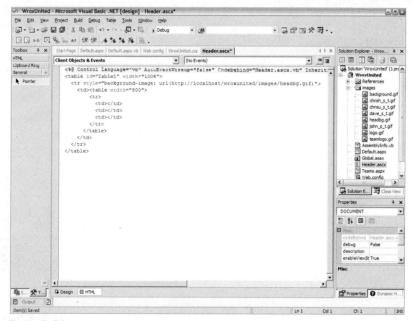

Figure D-39

You will find that the results of this will vary according to the default preferences you have on your system, but once you have set up the defaults as you like them, you'll find that this feature can be very handy!

Developing the User Control

In this table, set the row and cell attributes as shown in the code below. Leave the last cell empty for the moment:

```
<tr style="VERTICAL-ALIGN: middle">
  <td style="TEXT-ALIGN: left" width="200">
    <a href="default.aspx"><img src="images/logo.gif" border="0" /></a>
  </td>
  <td style="TEXT-ALIGN: center" width="400">
    <img src="images/teamlogo.gif" />
  </td>
  <td style="TEXT-ALIGN: right" width="200">

  </td>
</tr>
```

If you switch back to Design view, you'll see that the page is starting to take shape as seen in Figure D-40:

Figure D-40

Recall from the chapters that the header control had an `AdRotator` control that displayed different pictures of authors each time the page was requested. It's now time to add the `AdRotator` to the page. Either drag and drop this control into the right-most cell, or click to position your cursor in this cell and double-click the `AdRotator` control to add it to the page as shown in Figure D-41:

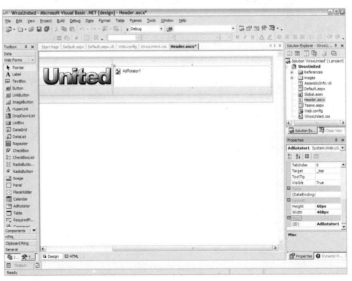

Figure D-41

By default, the control is created with standard width and height attributes. To fit our images, you should change these attributes in the `Properties` pane so that the width is 100 pixels and the height is 95 pixels. To select the source for the `AdRotator` control, you need to first create the XML source file.

Creating an XML File

Right click on the `WroxUnited` project and create a new file. In the dialog that appears, create a new xml file and call it `Faces.xml` as shown in Figure D-42:

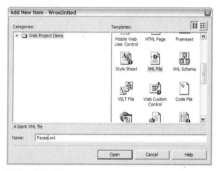

Figure D-42

In the newly created file, enter the code that we used previously:

```
<Advertisements>

  <Ad>
    <ImageUrl>images/chrish_s_t.gif</ImageUrl>
    <NavigateUrl>players.aspx</NavigateUrl>
    <AlternateText>Player: Chris Hart</AlternateText>
    <Impressions>80</Impressions>
    <Keyword>ChrisH</Keyword>
  </Ad>

  <Ad>
    <ImageUrl>images/chrisu_s_t.gif</ImageUrl>
    <NavigateUrl>players.aspx</NavigateUrl>
    <AlternateText>Player: Chris Ullman</AlternateText>
    <Impressions>80</Impressions>
    <Keyword>ChrisU</Keyword>
  </Ad>

  <Ad>
    <ImageUrl>images/dave_s_t.gif</ImageUrl>
    <NavigateUrl>players.aspx</NavigateUrl>
    <AlternateText>Player: Dave Sussman</AlternateText>
    <Impressions>80</Impressions>
    <Keyword>Dave</Keyword>
  </Ad>
```

```
<Ad>
  <ImageUrl>images/john_s_t.gif</ImageUrl>
  <NavigateUrl>players.aspx</NavigateUrl>
  <AlternateText>Player: John Kauffman</AlternateText>
  <Impressions>80</Impressions>
  <Keyword>John</Keyword>
</Ad>

</Advertisements>
```

Save the file, and that's all you need to do to create an XML file. Notice that with each element, Visual Studio .NET assists you by adding closing tags to all tags that you add.

Back in the `header.ascx` file, head to the **Properties** for the advertisement file again. Select the `AdvertisementFile` attribute and click on the ... button that appears. In the popup dialog shown in Figure D-43, select the `Faces.xml` file and click **OK**:

Figure D-43

The header needs one last thing before it's finished, and that's the custom text. In **HTML** view, add the following code to the bottom of the control (below the last `</table>` statement):

```
<h2><%= PageTitle %></h2>
```

Finally, right-click on `Header.ascx` and select **View Code**. You are now in the code-behind page for the header control. Add the following line of code directly above the `Page_Load` sub, as shown in Figure D-44:

```
Public PageTitle As String = ""
```

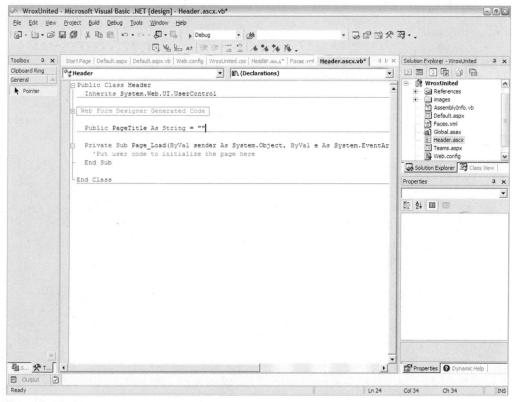

Figure D-44

That's the control finished. Time to add it to the page!

Adding a User Control to a Page

In **Design** view for `Default.aspx`, click and drag `Header.ascx` from the **Solution Explorer** onto the page, right before the main header, as shown in Figure D-45:

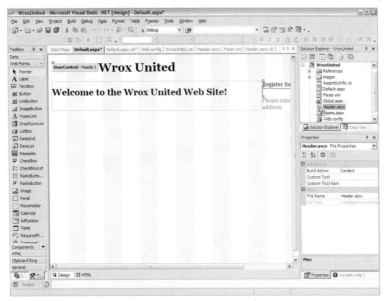

Figure D-45

You'll notice that this will add the control and the reference to the control to the HTML of the page. Also, notice that the control appears as a gray box, with no design-time appearance (Web Matrix, you will recall, provided a sample of the appearance of each user control as it was added to a page).

The newly added control is added with a default `TagName` of `Header` and `TagPrefix` of `UC1`. You can change this prefix to `WroxUnited` if you prefer, by editing the HTML of the page. Since we need to tidy up this page in any case, let's do that now. Amend the highlighted lines of code (notice that you need to remove the `<h1>` tag and the default header text):

```
<%@ Register TagPrefix="WroxUnited" TagName="Header" Src="Header.ascx" %>
<%@ Page Language="vb" AutoEventWireup="false" Codebehind="Default.aspx.vb"
    debug="true" Inherits="WroxUnited.WebForm1"%>
...
  <body>
    <form id="Form1" method="post" runat="server">
      <WroxUnited:header id="Header1" runat="server">
      </WroxUnited:header>
      <table id="Table1" cellspacing="0" cellpadding="0" width="800" border="0">
...
```

The `PageTitle` attribute isn't used on this page, but it exists for use on other pages where the email update registration box doesn't appear.

Running the page now will produce a more familiar appearance, as shown in Figure D-46:

Figure D-46

Adding Custom Classes

Right, back in the code it's time to look at adding a data access component. as shown in Figure D-47:

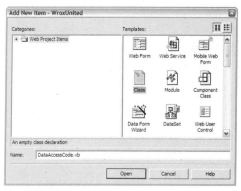

Figure D-47

In the code, add some `Imports` statements at the top of the code:

```
Imports System
Imports System.Data
Imports System.Collections
Imports System.Configuration
```

Now cut and paste over the data access methods from the code-behind page. Figure D-48 shows the code so far. Again, notice that the + and – icons on the left can be clicked to expand or contract blocks of code to make it easier to see which methods exist in the code:

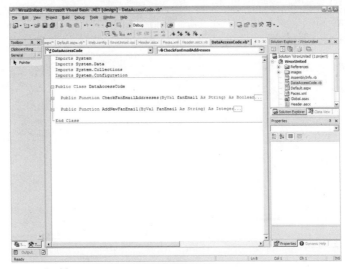

Figure D-48

Back in the code-behind for `Default.aspx`, we've managed to break the code by removing the two data access methods. The blue squiggly underlines in Figure D-49 indicate method calls that VS.NET can no longer find:

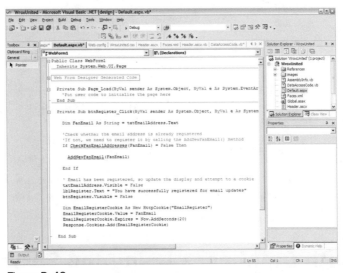

Figure D-49

Add the following line of code directly above the `Page_Load` method:

```
public Data as New DataAccessCode()
```

Then prefix each underlined method with "Data.". The code should now be able to locate the methods in question. Notice that as you do this, IntelliSense locates the list of available methods in this class and gives you hints about what their signatures look like, as shown in Figure D-50:

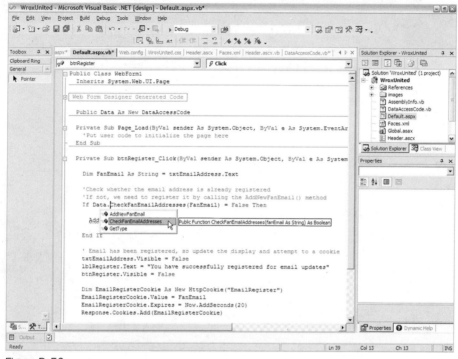

Figure D-50

Complete adding each method call with the Data object prefix, and you will be able to run the page, which should look and feel the same as before.

You can duplicate this methodology to create custom server controls in exactly the same way.

> *Professional and higher editions of Visual Studio .NET allow you to create entire custom class library projects and custom server control projects, but this functionality isn't available in the Standard language-specific editions.*

Working with Databases Using the Server Explorer

If you click the Server Explorer tab (at the bottom of the Toolbox), you can start to look at the database connectivity functionality of Visual Studio .NET. By default, this will look at little empty. Click on the Connect to Database button to add a new connection, as shown in Figure D-51:

Figure D-51

In the dialog that appears, select your SQL Server database server and select the WroxUnited database from the list, as shown in Figure D-52:

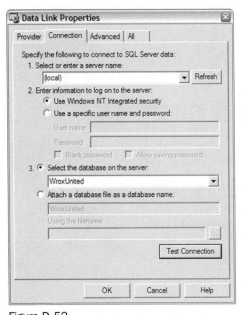

Figure D-52

In the Server Explorer, you will now see the newly added database connection in the list. Expand this connection, and double-click the Games table to view the contents of the table, as shown in Figure D-53:

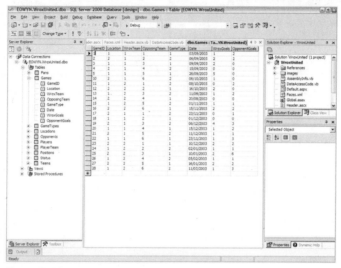

Figure D-53

In Standard edition, you can edit the data contained in the table, but cannot edit the structure of an existing table or create a new table. However, you can enter SQL view (Figure D-54), and if you know how to write SQL, you can enter any valid SQL statement, including CREATE TABLE, DROP TABLE, or even CREATE DATABASE statements:

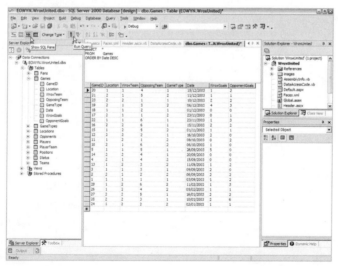

Figure D-54

If you are using Professional or higher editions of Visual Studio .NET, you can simply right-click on a table and create a new table, or alter the design of a table using the context menu. You can also create stored procedures and views in this way.

Debugging in Visual Studio .NET

One of the most powerful and indispensable features of Visual Studio .NET is its ability to debug code and fix errors. First, we'll look at break points and stepping through code line-by-line at run-time to fix runtime errors or exceptions, then we'll look at fixing errors at compile time.

> **Note that you can only debug if the compilation mode of your solution is set to Debug (see the drop-down box next to the Run button on the main toolbar). Once you finish debugging and are ready to deploy your site, set this to Release – you'll notice a significant performance boost on higher-traffic sites because debug code is much more processor intensive. If you're not debugging, turn it off!**

Using Breakpoints

In `Default.aspx.vb` (the code-behind for the Web page), click in the margin next to one of the lines of code, for example, the first line of code in the event-handler for the clicking of the button on the page shown in Figure D-55:

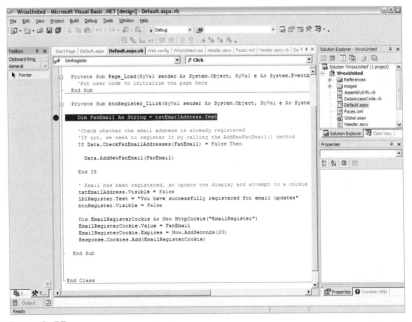

Figure D-55

Now run the page – notice that when you click the button on the page, you switch back to this view automatically:

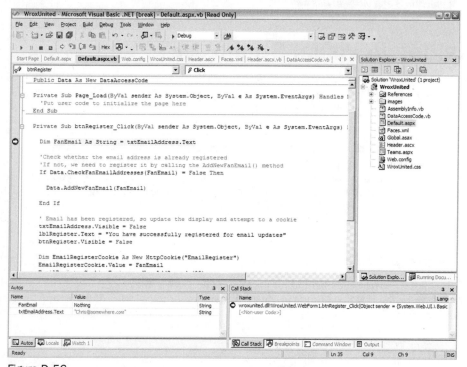

Figure D-56

In the window at the bottom left of Figure D-56, you can see the value entered into the textbox when the button was clicked. You can watch the values of controls on the page using this window. You can step through this code line by line to see what happens when each line of code is run by pressing **F11**. When you reach a method call, you can either press **F11** to jump into the code where that method is defined and watch as the code in that method is executed line by line (*Step Into*), or you can press **F10** to *Step Over* this method and continue with the next line of code in the current code block.

Pressing the Start button again will continue execution of the page, taking you back to the browser window, as if no interruption had occurred. This feature is particularly useful when fixing broken code. All you have to do is add a break point before the piece of code that is broken and step into the code, watching to see where the code breaks. This will often give you a clear idea as to why the code is not running as expected.

Fixing Design-Time Errors

You will often find that errors at design time will prevent a page from compiling correctly. For example, if you forgot to prefix one of the methods on the page with the `Data.` object reference, you would see an error message when you tried to run the page, as shown in Figure D-57:

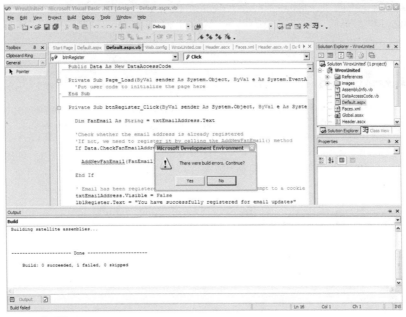

Figure D-57

In this situation, if you click **No**, you will see an entry in the Task list giving you a hint as to why the code would not compile as shown in Figure D-58:

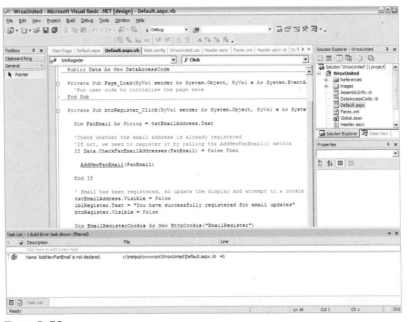

Figure D-58

It's now fairly obvious that the compiler can't deduce where the `AddNewFanEmail` method is declared, but once you add the `Data.` prefix, it'll soon find what it's looking for.

Suggested Exercises and Further Reading

After completing this appendix, you will probably feel a bit more confident with creating Web applications in Visual Studio .NET. The best way to increase your confidence further is to try out adding more controls and pages yourself. You may want to try to implement the whole of the Wrox United application in Visual Studio .NET – this would give you experience of working with many different controls in the Visual Studio .NET environment, as well as programming with many different ASP.NET techniques.

Visual Studio .NET is a large product, so if you really want to learn more about this tool, visit http://msdn.microsoft.com/vstudio/using/.

Installing and Configuring IIS

When using IIS, you need to install it before you install ASP.NET. The installation processes for IIS on Windows 2000 Professional, Windows XP Professional, or Windows Server 2003 don't differ significantly. The main difference is that Windows 2000 installs IIS 5.0, while Windows XP installs IIS 5.1, and Windows Server 2003 installs IIS 6.0. The options for installing are exactly the same; the only thing that might differ is the look of the dialog boxes.

> **You cannot install IIS on Windows XP Home Edition, and therefore cannot run ASP.NET on it. It will only work on Windows XP Professional.**

Before you install it though, it's worth noting that you might not have to do much in this initial stage, as it's possible you're already running IIS. We'll describe a process for checking whether this is the case as part of the installation process. Note that to install anything (not just ASP.NET, but *literally anything*) on Windows 2000, XP, and 2003 you need to be logged in as a user with administrative rights. If you're uncertain of how to do this, please consult your Windows documentation. Right, let's get started!

Try It Out Locating and Installing IIS on Your Web Server Machine

1. Go to the control panel (Start | Settings | Control Panel) and select the Add/Remove Programs icon. The dialog will appear, displaying a list of your currently installed programs as shown in Figure E-1:

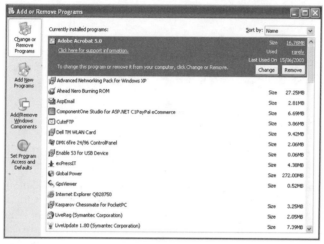

Figure E-1

2. Select the Add/Remove Windows Components icon on the left side of the dialog to get to the screen that allows you to install new windows components:

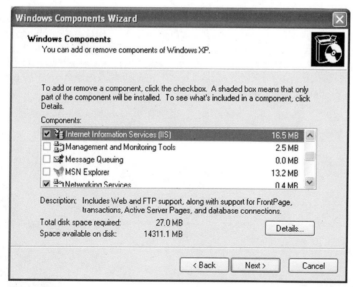

Figure E-2

3. Locate the Internet Information Services (IIS) entry in the dialog, and note the checkbox that appears to its left. Unless you installed Windows 2000 or XP via a custom install and specifically requested IIS, it's most likely that the checkbox will be unchecked (as shown in Figure E-2).

4. If the checkbox is *cleared*, then check the checkbox and click on Next to load Internet Information Services. You might be prompted to place your Windows 2000 or XP installation disk into your CD-ROM drive. It will take a few minutes to complete. Then go to Step 5.

OR

If the checkbox is *checked*, you won't need to install the IIS component – it's already present on your machine. Go to the *Working With IIS* section instead.

5. Click on the Details button – this will take you to the dialog shown in Figure E-3. There are a few options here for the installation of various optional bits of functionality. For example, if the World Wide Web Server option is checked then your IIS installation will be able to serve and manage Web pages and applications. If you're planning to use FrontPage 2000 or Visual Studio.NET to write your Web page code, then you'll need to ensure that the FrontPage 2000 Server Extensions checkbox is checked. The Internet Information Services Snap-In is also very helpful, as you'll see later in the chapter, so ensure that this is checked too; the other options (although checked here) aren't necessary for this book:

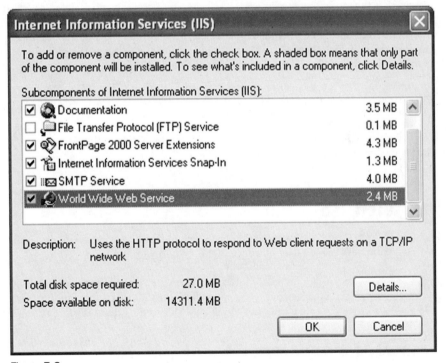

Figure E-3

How It Works

IIS starts up automatically as soon as its installation is complete, and thereafter whenever you boot up Windows. Thus you don't need to run any startup programs, or click on any short cuts.

IIS installs most of its components on your hard drive, under the `\WinNT\system32\inetsrv` directory; however, we are more interested in the `\InetPub` directory that is also created at this time. This directory contains subdirectories that will provide the home for the Web page files that we create.

If you expand the `InetPub` directory, you'll find that it contains several subdirectories:

- ❑   `\iissamples\homepage` contains some example classic ASP pages.

- ❑   `\iissamples\sdk` contains a set of subdirectories that hold classic ASP pages which demonstrate the various classic ASP objects and components.

- ❑   `\scripts` is an empty directory, where ASP.NET programs can be stored.

- ❑   `\webpub` is also empty. This is a 'special' virtual directory, used for publishing files via the Publish wizard. Note that this directory only exists if you are using Windows 2000 Professional Edition.

- ❑   `\wwwroot` is the top of the tree for your Web site. This should be your default Web directory. It also contains a number of subdirectories that contain various bits and pieces of IIS. This directory is generally used to contain subdirectories that hold the pages that make up our Web site – although, in fact, there's no reason why you can't store your pages elsewhere. The relationship between physical and virtual directories is discussed later in this chapter.

- ❑   `\ftproot`, `\mailroot` and `\nntproot` should form the top of the tree for any sites that use FTP, mail or news services, if installed.

- ❑   In some versions of Windows, you will find a `\AdminScripts` folder that contains various script files for performing some common 'housekeeping' tasks on the Web server, allowing you to stop and start services.

Working with IIS

Having installed IIS Web server software, you'll need some means of administering its contents and settings. In this section, let's see the user interface that is provided by IIS.

In fact, some versions of IIS provide two user interfaces, the *Microsoft Management Console (MMC)* and the *Personal Web Server (PWS)* interface (which is just included for those people familiar with PWS from Windows 98 and looking to migrate to IIS). Let's look at MMC, as the other interface is now obsolete.

The Microsoft Management Console (MMC)

The best part of MMC is that it provides a central interface for administrating all sorts of services that are installed on your machine. We can use it to administer IIS. In fact, when we use it to administer other services, the interface looks roughly the same. The MMC is provided as part of the Windows 2000 operating system – in fact, the MMC also comes with older Windows server operating systems.

The MMC itself is just a shell – on its own, it doesn't do much at all. If you want to use it to administer a service, you have to add a *snap in* for that service. The good news is that IIS has its own snapin. Whenever you need to administer IIS, you can simply call up the Internet Services Manager MMC console by selecting Start | Control Panel | Administrative Tools | Internet Services Manager:

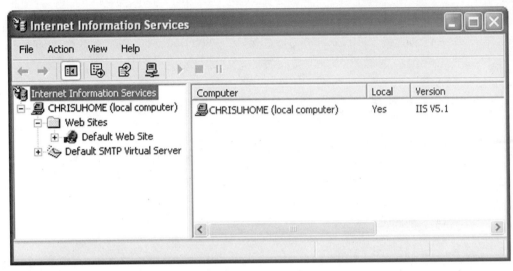

Figure E-4

Having opened the IIS snap in within the MMC, you can perform all of your Web management tasks from this window as seen in Figure E-4. The properties of the Web site are accessible via the Default Web Site node. We'll be using the MMC more a little later in the chapter.

Testing Your Installation

The next thing to do is test the Web server to see if it is working correctly, and serving pages, as it should be. We've already noted that the Web services should start as soon as IIS has been installed, and will restart every time you start your machine. In this section, we'll try that out.

In order to test the Web server, we'll start up a browser and try to view some Web pages that you know are already placed on the Web server. In order to do that, we'll need to type a URL (Uniform Resource Locator) into the browser's Address box, as we often do when browsing on the Internet. The URL is an http://... Web page address indicates which Web server to connect to, and the page to view.

What URL do you use in order to browse to your Web server? If your Web server and Web browser are connected by a local area network, or if you're using a single machine for the Web server and the browser, then it should be enough to specify the name of the Web server machine in the URL.

Identifying Your Web Server's Name

By default, IIS will take the name of your Web server from the name of the computer. You can change this in the machine's network settings. If you haven't set one, then Windows will generate one automatically – note that this automatic name won't be terribly friendly; probably something along the lines of P77RTQ7881. To find the name of your own Web server machine, select Start | Settings | Network and Dial-up Connections or Start | Settings | Control Panel | System (depending on which operating system you are using – if it isn't in one, try the other) and from the Advanced menu select Network Identification. This tab will display your machine name under the description Full computer name as shown in Figure E-5:

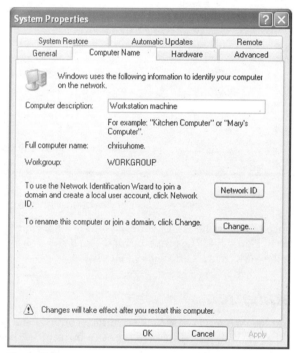

Figure E-5

My machine has the name chrisuhome, and (as you can see here and in Figure E-4) my Web server has adopted the same name. On a computer within a domain, for example a WROX_UK domain, it would be like WROX_UK/chrisuhome. However, this doesn't alter operation for ASP.NET. Browsing to pages on this machine across a local area network (or, indeed, from the same machine), I can use a URL that begins http://chrisuhome/

There are a couple of alternatives if you're using the same machine as both Web server and browser. Try http://127.0.0.1/.... Here, 127.0.0.1 is a default that causes requests to be sent to a Web server on the local machine. Alternatively, try http://localhost/...where localhost is an alias for the 127.0.0.1 address. You may need to check the LAN settings (in your browser's options) to ensure that local browsing is not through a proxy server (a separate machine that filters all incoming and outgoing Web traffic employed at most workplaces, but not something that affects you if you are working from home).

> Throughout the book, in any examples that require you to specify a Web server name, the server name will be shown as **localhost**, implicitly assuming that your Web server and browser are being run on the same machine. If they reside on different machines, then you simply need to substitute the computer name of the appropriate Web server machine.

Managing Directories on Your Web Server

Before installing ASP.NET, you need to make one last pit stop in IIS. This is because when you run your ASP.NET pages, you need to understand where to place your pages, and how to make sure you have the permission to access them. As this is governed by IIS, let's look at it now.

These days, many browsers are sufficiently advanced that you can use them to locate and examine files and pages that exist on your computer's hard disk. For example, you can start up your browser, type in the physical location of a Web page (or other file) such as `C:\My Documents\mywebpage.html`, and the browser will display it. However, this isn't real Web publishing at all.

First, Web pages are transported using HTTP protocol. Note that the http:// at the beginning of a URL indicates that the request is being sent by HTTP. Requesting C:\My Documents\mywebpage.html in your browser doesn't use HTTP, and this means that the file is not delivered and handled in the way a Web page should be. No server processing is done in this case. HTTP is discussed in *Chapter 2*.

Second, consider the addressing situation. The C:\My Documents\mywebpage.html string tells that the page exists in the \My Documents directory of the C: drive of the hard disk of the machine on which the browser is running. In a network situation, with two or more computers, this simply doesn't give enough information about the Web server.

However, when a user browses (via HTTP) to a Web page on some Web server, the Web server will need to work out where the file for that page is located on the server's hard disk. In fact, there's an important relationship between the information given in the URL, and the physical location (within the Web server's file system) of the file that contains the source for the page.

Virtual Directories

So how does the relationship between the information given in the URL, and physical location work? It works by creating a second directory structure on the Web server machine, which reflects the structure of your Web site. It sounds complicated, but it doesn't have to be. In fact, in this book it's going to be very simple.

The first directory structure is what you see when you open Windows Explorer on the Web server – these directories are known as *physical directories*. For example, the `C:\My Documents` folder is a physical directory.

The second directory structure is the one that reflects the structure of the Web site. This consists of a hierarchy of *virtual directories*. We use the Web server to create virtual directories, and to set the relationship between the virtual directories and the real (physical) directories.

When you try to visualize a virtual directory, it's probably best not to think of it as a directory at all. Instead, just think of it as a nickname or alias for a physical directory that exists on the Web server machine. The idea is that, when a user browses to a Web page that is contained in a physical directory on the server, they don't use the name of the physical directory to get there, instead, they use the physical directory's nickname.

To see how this might be useful, consider a Web site that publishes news about different sporting events. In order to organize his Web files carefully, the Webmaster has built a physical directory structure on his hard disk, which looks like Figure E-6:

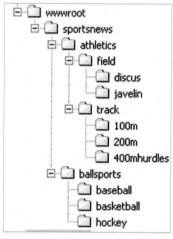

Figure E-6

Now, suppose you visit this Web site to get the latest news on the javelin event in the Olympics. If the URL for this Web page were based on the physical directory structure, the URL for this page would be something like this:

http://www.oursportsite.com/sportsnews/athletics/field/javelin/default.asp

That's okay for the Webmaster, who understands his directory structure; however it's a fairly unmemorable Web address! So, to make it easier for the user, the Webmaster can assign a virtual directory name or alias to this directory – it acts just like a nickname for the directory. Here, let's suppose we've assigned the virtual name `javelinnews` to the `C:\inetpub\...\javelin\` directory. Now, the URL for the latest javelin news is:

http://www.oursportsite.com/javelinnews/default.asp

By creating virtual directory names for all the directories (such as baseballnews, 100mnews, 200mnews, and so on) it's easy for the user to type in the URL and go directly to the page they want:

http://www.oursportsite.com/baseballnews/default.asp

http://www.oursportsite.com/100mnews/default.asp

http://www.oursportsite.com/200mnews/default.asp

Not only does this save the user from long, unwieldy URLs – it also serves as a good security measure, because it hides the physical directory structure from all the Web site visitors. This is good practice, otherwise hackers might be able to work out and access your files if they knew what the directory structure looked like. Moreover, it allows the Webmaster's Web site structure to remain independent of the directory structure on the hard drive – so he can move files on his disk between different physical folders, drives, or even servers, without having to change the structure of his Web pages. There is a performance overhead to think about as well, as IIS has to expend effort translating the physical path. It can be a pretty costly performancewise to have too many virtual directories.

Let's have a crack at setting up our own virtual directories and permissions (please note that these permissions are set automatically if you use the FrontPage editor to create a new site – so don't use FrontPage to set up this site for you unless you know what you're doing).

Try It Out   Creating a Virtual Directory and Setting Up Permissions

Let's take a quick look now at how you can create your own virtual directory. We'll use this directory to store the examples that we'll be creating in this book. We don't want to over complicate this example by creating lots of directories, so we'll demonstrate by creating a single physical directory on the Web server's hard disk, and using the IIS admin tool to create a virtual directory and make the relationship between the two:

1.   Start Windows Explorer and create a new physical directory named BegASPNET11, in the root directory of your hard drive. For example, C:\BegASPNET11 as shown in Figure E-7:

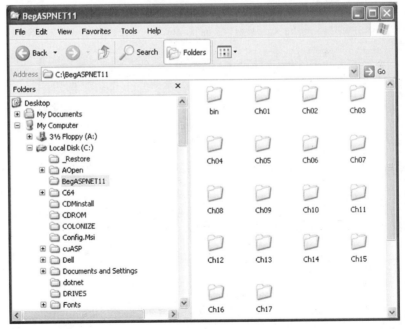

Figure E-7

2. Next, start up the IIS admin tool (using the MMC, as described earlier). Right-click on **Default Web Site**, and from the menu that appears select **New | Virtual Directory**. This starts the **Virtual Directory Creation Wizard**, which handles the creation of virtual directories for you and the setting up of permissions as well. You'll see the splash screen first as shown in Figure E-8. Click on **Next**:

Figure E-8

3. Type BegASPNET11 in the Alias text box as shown in Figure E-9; then click **Next**:

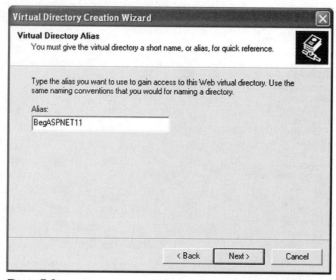

Figure E-9

4. As shown in Figure E-10, click on the Browse... button and select the directory C:\BegASPNET11 that you created in Step 1. Then click Next:

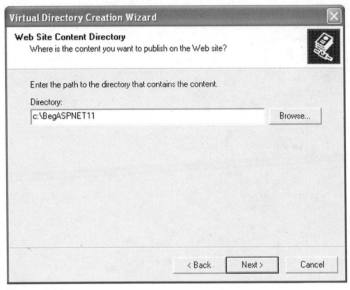

Figure E-10

5. Make sure that the Read and Run scripts checkboxes are checked, and that the Execute checkbox is empty. Click on Next as shown in Figure E-11, and in the subsequent page click on Finish:

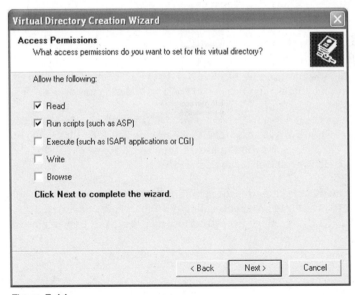

Figure E-11

6. The BegASPNET11 virtual directory will appear on the tree in the IIS admin window as shown in Figure E-12:

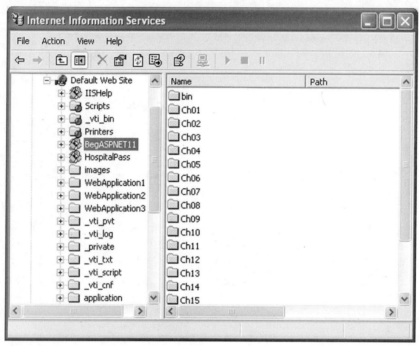

Figure E-12

How It Works

You've just created a physical directory called BegASPNET11, this directory has been used throughout the book to store our code examples. The download files from www.wrox.com are also designed to follow this structure. Within this directory we recommend that you create a subdirectory for each of the chapters in order to keep things tidy (this needn't be a virtual directory – just a physical one.)

You've also created a virtual directory called **BegASPNET11** as an alias for the physical BegASPNET11 directory. If while creating *Chapter 1* examples you place the ASP.NET files in the physical C:\BegASPNET11\ch01 directory, you can use the browser to access pages stored in this folder. You'll need to use the URL http://my_server_name/BegASPNET11/ch01/

Also you should note that the URL uses the alias /**BegASPNET11**; IIS knows that this stands for the directory path C:\BegASPNET11. When executing ASP.NET pages, you can reduce the amount of typing you need to do in the URL, by using virtual directory names in your URL in place of the physical directory names.

We also set the permissions read and run – these must be set or the IIS security features will prevent you from running any ASP.NET pages. The Execute checkbox is left unselected as allowing others to run applications on your own machine is a sure way of getting viruses or getting hacked. We'll take a closer look at permissions now, as they are very important. If you don't assign them correctly you may find that you're unable to run any ASP.NET pages at all worse still, anybody can access your machine, and alter (even delete) your files via the Web.

Permissions

As you've just seen, we can assign permissions to a new directory as you create it, by using the options offered in the Virtual Directory Wizard. Alternatively, you can set permissions at any time, from the IIS admin tool in the MMC. To do this, right click on the BegASPNET11 virtual directory in the IIS admin tool, and select Properties. You'll get the dialog shown in Figure E-13:

Figure E-13

It's quite a complicated dialog, and it contains a lot of options – not all of which we wish to go into now.

Access Permissions

The four checkboxes on the left (see Figure E-13) govern the types of access for the given directory and dictate the permissions allowed on the files contained within that directory. Let's have a look at what each of these options means:

❏ **Script source access**: This permission enables users to access the source code of an ASP.NET page. It's only possible to allow this permission if the Read or Write permission has already been assigned. But we generally don't want our users to be able to view our ASP.NET source code, so we would usually leave this checkbox unchecked for any directory that contains ASP.NET pages. By default, all directories created during setup have Script Source Access permission disabled. You should leave this as is.

❏ **Read**: This permission enables browsers to read or download files stored in a home directory or a virtual directory. If the browser requests a file from a directory that doesn't have the Read permission enabled, then the Web server will simply return an error message. Note that when the folder has Read permission turned off, HTML files within the folder cannot be read; however, ASP.NET code within the folder can still be run. Generally, directories containing information that you want to publish (such as HTML files, for example) should have the Read permission enabled, as we did in our earlier example.

❏ **Write**: If the write permission on a virtual directory is enabled, then users will be able to create or modify files within the directory, and change the properties of these files. This is not normally turned on, for reasons of security and we don't recommend you alter it.

❏ **Directory browsing**: If you want to allow people to view the contents of the directory (that is, to see a list of all the files that are contained in that directory), then you can allow this by checking the Directory Browsing option.

If someone tries to browse the contents of a directory that has Directory Browsing enabled but Read disabled, then they may receive the message seen in Figure E-14:

Figure E-14

> For security reasons, we'd recommend disabling this option unless your users specifically need it – such as when transferring files using FTP (file transfer protocol), from your Web site.

Execute Permissions

There's a dropdown list box near the foot of the Properties dialog, labeled Execute permissions – this specifies what level of program execution is permitted on pages contained in this directory. There are three possible values here – None, Scripts only, or Scripts and Executables:

❑ Setting Execute permissions to None means that users can only access static files, such as image files and HTML files. Any script-based files of other executables contained in this directory are inaccessible to users. If you tried to run an ASP.NET page, from a folder with the permission set to None, you would get the following – note the Execute Access Forbidden message in the page shown in Figure E-15:

Figure E-15

❑ Setting Execute permissions to Scripts Only means that users can also access any script-based pages, such as ASP.NET pages. So if the user requests an ASP.NET page that's contained in this directory, the Web server will allow the ASP.NET code to be executed, and the resulting HTML to be sent to the browser.

❑ Setting Execute permissions to Scripts and Executables means that users can execute any type of file type that's contained in the directory. It's generally a good idea to avoid using this setting, in order to prohibit users from executing potentially damaging applications on your Web server.

833

For any directory containing ASP.NET files that you're publishing, the appropriate setting for the Execute permissions is Scripts Only. There is one last bit about directory that needs pointing out though for users of Windows 2000.

Configuring Directory Security in Windows 2000

If you're running Windows 2000 Professional or Server, you might have one extra bit of configuration to do. In ASP.NET all ASPX pages run under a special user account named ASPNET. For security reasons this account has restricted permissions by default; ordinarily, this isn't a problem. The database samples in this chapter use Access. When updating data in a database Access creates a separate file (with a `.ldb` suffix), which holds the locking information. These are the details that stores who is updating records, and the locking file is created and removed on demand.

The security problem encountered is that we are running pages under the ASPNET account, which doesn't have write permissions in the samples directory. Consequently, any ASP.NET pages that update a sample Access `.mdb` database will fail. Setting the write permission is simple – just follow these steps:

1. In Windows Explorer, select the BegASPNET11 directory, where the samples are located.

2. Using the right mouse button, select the Properties menu option, and from the Properties dialog that appears, select the Security tab as shown in Figure E-16:

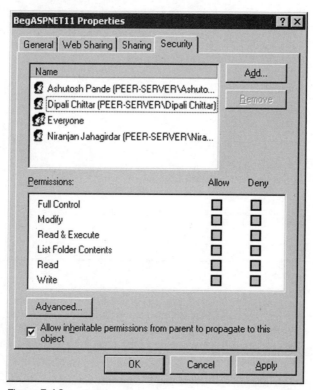

Figure E-16

3. Click the Add button to display the Select Users or Groups dialog. In the blank space enter ASP.NET and click the Check Names button. This checks the name you've entered and adds the machine name to it.

4. Click the OK button to return to the Properties dialog, and you'll see that the ASPNET user is now shown in the list of users as in Figure E-17. In the Permissions area, at the bottom of this screen, select the Write permission and tick it. This gives the ASPNET user write permission to the BegASPNET11 directory tree.

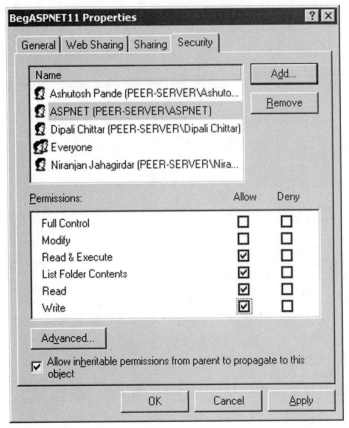

Figure E-17

5. Click the OK button to save the changes, and to close the dialog.

The security issue arises only if you need write access to a directory, in the same manner as required by our examples (which use Access). Most production Web sites wouldn't use Access as their database store, since Access isn't designed for a high number of users. In these cases SQL Server would be a more likely choice. The .NET SDK documentation has examples of connection strings for SQL Server.

Browsing to a Page on Your Web Server

Now you know the name of your Web server, and that Web services are running; you can test the installation by viewing some classic ASP pages hosted on your Web server by browsing to them with your Web browser. Let's test out this theory by viewing our default home page, which is http://localhost and should appear something like Figure E-18 (this was taken on Windows XP Professional, so it might appear a little differently, if you don't see it):

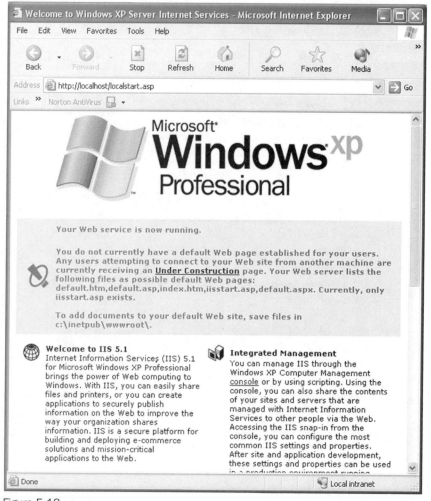

Figure E-18

If you see the screen as shown in Figure E-18, it means the install has worked and you can jump back to *Chapter 1* and the section on creating your first ASP.NET page.

What Do You Do if This Doesn't Work?

If you don't get this page, then take a look at the following steps as we try to resolve the problem. If it's not working correctly, then most likely you'll be greeted with the screen similar to Figure E-19:

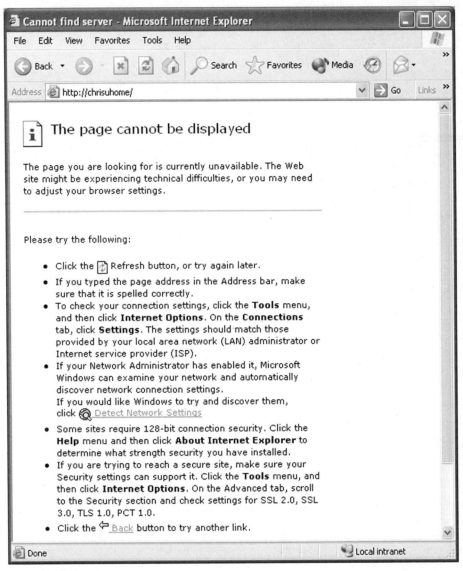

Figure E-19

If you get this page then it can mean a lot of things; however, one of the most likely problems is that your Web services under IIS are not switched on. To switch on Web Services, you'll first need to start the IIS admin snap in that we described earlier in the chapter (select Start | Run, type MMC and hit OK; then select Open from the MMC's Console menu and locate the iis.msc file from the dialog. Alternatively, just use the shortcut that you created there).

Now, click on the + of the root node in the left pane of the snap in, to reveal the Default sites. Then right click on Default Web Site, and select Start as shown in Figure E-20:

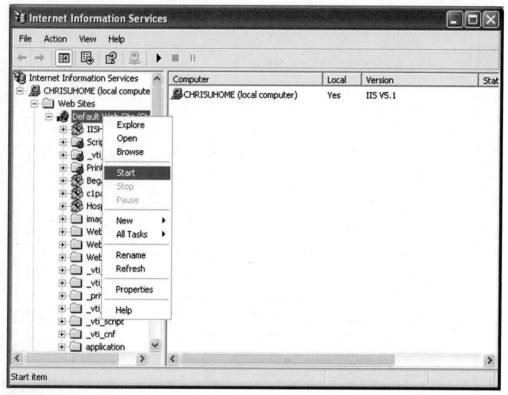

Figure E-20

If it's still not working then here are a few more suggestions, which are based on particular aspects of your PC's setup. If you're running on a network and using a proxy server (a piece of software that manages connections from inside a firewall to the outside world – don't worry if you don't have one, they're mainly used by big businesses), there's a possibility that this can prevent your browser from accessing your Web server. Most browsers will give you an opportunity to bypass the proxy server.

❑ If you're using Internet Explorer, you need to go to View | Internet Options (IE4) or Tools | Internet Options (IE5/IE6) and select the Connections tab. In IE5/IE6 press the LAN Settings button and select Bypass the proxy server for local addresses. In IE6, this section forms part of the Connections dialog and can be accessed by pressing the LAN settings dialog as shown in Figure E-21:

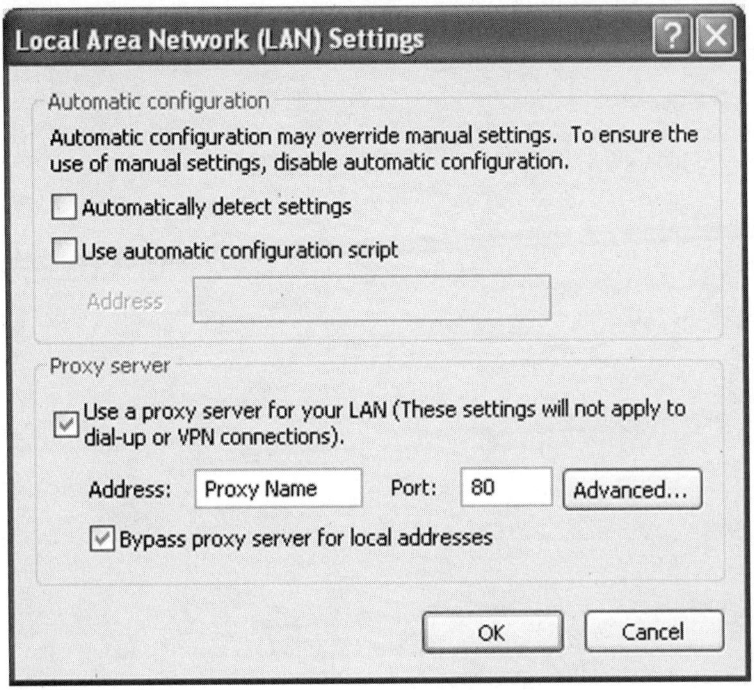

Figure E-21

❑ If you're using Netscape Navigator (either version 4.*x* or 6.*x*) and you are having problems then you need to turn off all proxies and make sure you are accessing the Internet directly. To do this, select Edit | Preferences; in the resulting dialog select Advanced | Proxies from the Category box on the left. Then on the right, select the Direct Connection to Internet option, and hit OK. Although you won't be browsing online to the Internet, it'll allow Netscape Navigator to recognize all variations of accessing local ASP.NET pages – such as http://127.0.0.1, http://localhost, and so on.

If you get the message as displayed in Figure E-22, it means the install has succeeded but you have some old install files on your machine:

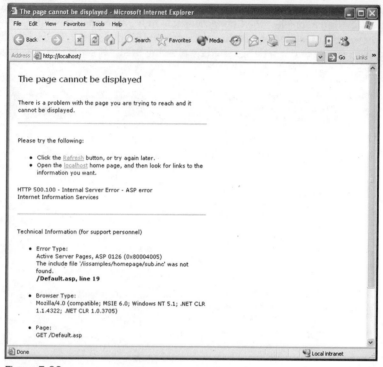

Figure E-22

This happens if you have an old installation of Visual Studio for example. To get rid of this, simply go to C:\inetpub\wwwroot, delete the default.asp file, and then run http://localhost. What is happening is that IIS will use default.asp as the home page, and not IIS's home page localstart.asp. If there is no default.asp then IIS will automatically use localstart.asp. Alternatively if you have customized default.asp, just go to http://localhost/localstart.asp to see that IIS has in fact installed correctly. So, you can jump back to *Chapter 1* and build an ASP.NET page and all the examples will work just fine.

Lastly, if your Web server is running on your home machine with a modem, and you get an error message informing you that your Web page is offline, this could in fact be a misperception on the part of the Web server. This can be corrected by changing the way that your browser looks for pages. To do this, select View | Internet Options (IE4) or Tools | Internet Options (IE5/IE6), choose the Connections tab and select Never dial a connection.

Of course, you might encounter problems that aren't covered here. In this case, the chances are that they would be related to your own particular system setup. We can't possibly cover all the different possible configurations here; but if you can't track down the problem, you may find some help at one of the Web sites and newsgroups listed in *Chapter 15*.

Index

A Guide to the Index

The index is arranged heirarchically, in alphabetical order, with symbols preceding the letter A. Many second level entries and some third level entries also occur as first level entries. This is to ensure that the users will find the information they require however they choose to search for it. Additionally, a full list of major examples is included under the Try It Out main entry of the index.

A